Writers and their Background

ALEXANDER POPE

Also in this series

S.T.COLERIDGE edited by R.L.BRETT

Alexander Pope

The study of literature is not a 'pure' discipline for the simple reason that works of literature are affected by the climate of opinion in which they are produced. Writers, like other men, are concerned with the politics, the philosophy, the religion, the arts, and the general thought of their own times. Some writers, indeed, have made their own distinguished contributions to these areas of human interest, while the literary achievement of others can be fully appreciated only by a knowledge of them.

The present series has been planned with the purpose of presenting such writers in their intellectual, social and artistic context, and with the belief that this will make their work more easily understood and enjoyed. Each volume contains a Reader's Guide to the writings of the author concerned, a Bibliography, and a Chronological Table which sets out the dates of the author's life and publications alongside the chief events of historical, intellectual and literary importance in his lifetime.

The editor, Peter Dixon, writes in his preface: 'For a man suffering under great physical handicaps, and excluded by reason of his religious faith from permanent residence in London, the diversity of Pope's interests and contacts is remarkable. Among his close friends he numbered not only the most important literary figures of the day but also distinguished politicians and churchmen, lawyers and doctors, painters and architects. His manifold interests and concerns, and the hopes, anxieties and passionate convictions to which they gave rise, are the very stuff of his poetry. The later satires, in particular, are so urgently engaged with the moral, political and cultural life of his time that, as with any great satirist, it becomes impossible to separate the "background" of events and attitudes in the public realm from the foreground of the writer's own action and involvement.'

Alexander Pope: Drawing from the studio of Sir Godfrey Kneller

Writers and their Background

ALEXANDER POPE

EDITED BY PETER DIXON

OHIO UNIVERSITY PRESS · 1972

© G. BELL & SONS LTD. 1972
PRINTED BY OFFSET AND BOUND IN THE
UNITED STATES OF AMERICA
FOR OHIO UNIVERSITY PRESS, ATHENS, OHIO
BY CUSHING–MALLOY, INC., ANN ARBOR, MICHIGAN.

LC 72-85534
ISBN 8214-0114-9

Contents

List of Illustrations

The Contributors

JOHN M. ADEN
Professor of English, Vanderbilt University

NORMAN CALLAN
Professor of English, Queen Mary College, University of London

HOWARD ERSKINE-HILL
Lecturer in English, University of Cambridge

DONALD FRASER
Lecturer in English Studies, University of Strathclyde

A. R. HUMPHREYS
Professor of English, University of Leicester

DUNCAN ISLES
Lecturer in English, Birkbeck College, University of London

PAT ROGERS
Lecturer in English, King's College, University of London

G. S. ROUSSEAU
Professor of English, University of California

JAMES SAMBROOK
Senior Lecturer in English, University of Southampton

To the Memory
of
Geoffrey Tillotson

Blest with a Taste *exact, yet unconfin'd;*
A Knowledge *both of* Books *and* Humankind;
Gen'rous Converse; *a* Soul *exempt from* Pride;
And Love to Praise, *with* Reason *on his Side.*

General Editor's Preface

THE STUDY of literature is not a 'pure' discipline since works of literature are affected by the climate of opinion in which they are produced. Writers, like other men, are concerned with the politics, the philosophy, the religion, the arts, and the general thought of their own times. Some literary figures, indeed, have made their own distinguished contributions to these areas of human interest, while the achievement of others can be fully appreciated only by a knowledge of them.

The Series to which this volume is an important contribution has been planned with the purpose of presenting major authors in their intellectual, social, and artistic contexts, and with the conviction that this will make their work more easily understood and enjoyed. Each volume contains a chapter which provides a reader's guide to the writings of the author concerned, a Bibliography, and Chronological Tables setting out the main dates of the author's life and publications alongside the chief events of contemporary importance.

Over the last few decades the work of scholars and critics alike has thrown a new light on Pope. Behind Pope the satirist we are beginning to discern the figure of a poet whose vision of the good life held up an ideal by which not only Augustan society, but our own, may be judged. This vision embraced not only literature, but the other arts, and brought within its compass religion, politics, morals and manners, in a comprehensive view of human life. Mr Peter Dixon of Westfield College, in the University of London, has brought together a team of scholars, many of whom have themselves contributed to this revaluation of Pope, and together they have produced a volume which does justice to the genius of Pope by placing him in the context not only of Augustan England but of that classical and Christian tradition he fought to preserve.

R. L. BRETT

Editor's Preface

For a man suffering under great physical handicaps, and excluded by reason of his religious faith from permanent residence in London, the diversity of Pope's interests and contacts is remarkable. Among his close friends he numbered not only the most important literary figures of the day but also distinguished politicians and churchmen, lawyers and doctors, painters and architects. His manifold interests and concerns, and the hopes, anxieties and passionate convictions to which they gave rise, are the very stuff of his poetry. The later satires, in particular, are so urgently engaged with the moral, political and cultural life of his time that, as with any great satirist, it becomes impossible to separate the 'background' of events and attitudes in the public realm from the foreground of the writer's own action and involvement. Pope's work has, too, a 'background' of another kind—a literary tradition dominated by the classics of Greece and Rome, extending through the Renaissance, and embodied, most immediately and influentially for Pope, in John Dryden. As an adolescent, Pope undertook without hesitation the arduous (but also delightful) discipline of accommodating his poetic talent to this tradition, so that when the time came he would be ready to embark on his own reinterpretation of the great traditional themes —as, for example, friendship, fame, the use of riches—in the light of his personal experience.

These considerations suggest that there is a rightness and inevitability about Pope's inclusion in the 'Writers and their Background' series; indeed he himself might well have considered his inclusion perfectly proper. For he was among the first to advocate the study of the context of an author's work, even going so far as to insist that such study is a necessary foundation for an informed critical judgment:

> You *then whose Judgment the right Course wou'd steer,*
> *Know well each A N C I E N T's proper* Character,
> *His* Fable, Subject, Scope *in ev'ry Page,*

> Religion, Country, Genius *of his* Age:
> *Without all these at once before your Eyes,*
> Cavil *you may, but never* Criticize.

Pope does not imply that an examination of the 'Genius' of a writer's age is a substitute for an assessment of his work. Such an examination is only ancillary to judgment, but it is an aid of considerable value, for it may prevent our criticisms from degenerating into mere cavils, and may help to steady our response and ensure a fullness and generosity of understanding and enjoyment.

All modern readers of Pope would agree that he is a poet who stands in some need of elucidation and commentary. His satires are notoriously allusive. Almost all his poetry is subtle and complex. He is, in short, a difficult poet. No-one was more keenly aware of this than the late Geoffrey Tillotson; at the same time no-one has done more to help readers through the difficulties, clearing away misconceptions about Pope's poetry and, with discernment and sympathy, calling our attention to its virtues and felicities. Many of the contributors to the present volume knew him as a colleague and friend; all of us, as readers of Pope, are in his debt. We join in offering this book as a memorial to a fine scholar and critic.

Not the least of Geoffrey Tillotson's achievements was his work for the *Twickenham Edition of the Poems of Alexander Pope*, an edition which has played a decisive part in the establishment of Pope's reputation; we have used its text in all quotations from his published poems. Three other definitive texts have similarly been used throughout: George Sherburn's edition of Pope's *Correspondence*, James M. Osborn's edition of Joseph Spence's invaluable *Anecdotes*, and Donald Bond's edition of the *Spectator* (5 vols, Oxford 1965). In citing dates, for example of Pope's letters, we have taken the year to begin on January 1st and not (as was customary in the 'Old Style' calendar) on March 25th. In the footnotes, as in the Bibliography, the place of publication is London, unless otherwise stated.

It is a pleasure to record here my gratitude to Mr Richard Barber for all his kind assistance. He has been a constant source of encouragement and friendly guidance, and has substantially lightened the work of both editor and contributors.   PETER DIXON

The main events of Pope's life*	The main events of Pope's lifetime	
	Literary and Intellectual	*Historical*
1688 Pope born (21 May), Lombard Street, London	Bunyan dies	'The Glorious Revolution': William of Orange lands at Torbay. James II flees to France
1689	Richardson born Locke's first *Letter concerning Toleration*	Coronation of William III and Queen Mary Act of Toleration
1690	Locke's *Essay concerning Human Understanding* and *Two Treatises of Government*	Battle of the Boyne
1694	Voltaire born	Queen Mary dies Bank of England founded
1696 School in a seminary at Twyford, Hants		
1697 Brief periods of schooling in London	Hogarth born Dryden's translation of Virgil pubd	
1698 *Family moves to Binfield, in Windsor Forest	William Warburton born	
1700	Dryden dies James Thomson born Dryden's *Fables* Congreve's *Way of the World*	
1701	Steele's *Christian Hero*	James II dies abroad Act of Settlement establishes Protestant Succession War of the Spanish Succession
1702	William King's *De Origine Mali* (trans by Edmund Law, 1731)	William III dies Accession of Queen Anne

* Approximate dates are indicated by an asterisk. Only the most important of Pope's many friendships have been entered, under the date when they began.

1703	*Short residence in London, to learn French and Italian		
1704	Friendship with Sir William Trumbull	John Locke dies Swift's *Tale of a Tub* Defoe's *Review* (to 1713) Newton's *Optics*	Battle of Blenheim Godolphin Lord Treasurer
1705	*Meets Wycherley, Walsh, and other London *literati*		
1707		Farquhar dies Fielding born Farquhar's *Beaux' Stratagem*	Union with Scotland ratified
1709	*Pastorals* pubd	Samuel Johnson born *The Tatler* (to 1711)	Henry Sacheverell prosecuted by Whigs for 'anti-Revolution' sermon
1710	Friendship with John Caryll	George Berkeley's *Principles of Human Knowledge* *The Examiner* (Tory journal; to 1714)	Trial and vindication of Sacheverell Fall of Whigs Triumph of Tories under Harley (later Lord Oxford)
1711	*Essay on Criticism* *Friendship with Martha and Teresa Blount, Gay, Addison, Steele	David Hume born Shaftesbury's *Characteristics* *The Spectator* (to 1712; 2nd series 1714)	Charter granted to South Sea Company
1712	'Messiah' pubd (in *The Spectator*) *The Rape of the Lock* (2-canto version) Beginnings of Scriblerus Club (Swift and Arbuthnot, joined by Gay, Parnell, Pope, and Lord Oxford) *Friendship with Bolingbroke	Arbuthnot's *Art of Political Lying* and *History of John Bull*	
1713	*Windsor Forest* Pope studies painting under Charles Jervas (to 1714) At work on trans of *Iliad*	Sterne born Swift appointed Dean of St Patrick's Addison's *Cato* *The Guardian*	Peace of Utrecht Struggle for power within Tory party between Harley and Bolingbroke

1714	*The Rape of the Lock* (enlarged) Scriblerus Club dissolves	Swift leaves for Dublin Mandeville's *Fable of the Bees*	Queen Anne dies Accession of George I Whigs in power
1715	*The Temple of Fame* *Iliad*, vol I *Friendship with Lady Mary Wortley Montagu	Campbell's *Vitruvius Britannicus*, vol I; beginning of Palladianism	Impeachment of Lord Oxford and Bolingbroke: Oxford imprisoned for high treason; Bolingbroke flees to France. Jacobite rebellion Louis XIV dies
1716	Pope's family moves to Chiswick *Iliad*, II *Friendship with Lord Burlington	Wycherley dies Gray born Gay's *Trivia*	Septennial Act
1717	*Three Hours after Marriage* (by Pope, Gay and Arbuthnot) performed at Drury Lane *Iliad*, III Pope's *Works* pubd (including 'Eloisa to Abelard' and 'Elegy to the Memory of an Unfortunate Lady') *Poems on Several Occasions*, ed by Pope Pope's father dies *Friendship with Francis Atterbury and Lord Bathurst	Benjamin Hoadly's sermon, *The Nature of the Kingdom or Church of Christ*, sparks off Bangorian controversy	
1718	*Iliad*, IV	Thomas Parnell dies	
1719	Pope and his mother move to Twickenham	Addison dies Burlington returns from Italian tour with William Kent Defoe's *Robinson Crusoe*	Jacobite uprising in Scotland Peerage Bill
1720	*Iliad*, V and VI Friendship with William Fortescue		South Sea Bubble
1721	Pope's edn of Parnell's *Poems*, with prefatory verse 'Epistle to Lord Oxford' Pope begins work on edn of Shakespeare	Smollett born Prior dies	Walpole Lord Treasurer

1722	Pope at work on translation of *Odyssey*, with Broome and Fenton	Defoe's *Moll Flanders*	Marlborough dies Atterbury charged with complicity in Jacobite plot
1723	Pope's edn of *Works* of John Sheffield, Duke of Buckinghamshire, suppressed by Gvt on suspicion of Jacobite tendencies Pope appears as witness in Atterbury's trial (House of Lords)	Sir Godfrey Kneller dies	Bolingbroke pardoned; returns briefly to England Atterbury exiled
1724		Swift's *Drapier's Letters* Defoe's *Roxana*	Lord Oxford dies
1725	Pope's edn of Shakespeare (6 vols) *Odyssey*, vols I–III	Francis Hutcheson's *Inquiry into the Original of our Ideas of Beauty and Virtue*	
1726	*Odyssey*, IV–V Swift, in London, a frequent visitor at Twickenham Friendship with Joseph Spence	Vanbrugh dies Swift's *Gulliver's Travels* *The Craftsman*, official Opposition journal, launched by Bolingbroke *et al.* (to 1736) Thomson's *Winter* Theobald's *Shakespeare Restored* rebukes Pope's edn	
1727	Pope–Swift *Miscellanies*, I–II *Pope and Lady Mary Wortley Montagu estranged	Sir Isaac Newton dies; first English trans of his *Principia* pubd Gay's *Fables*, 1st series (2nd, 1737)	George I dies Accession of George II
1728	Pope–Swift *Miscellanies*, III, including *Peri Bathous*; the hostility of the 'dunces' is aroused *The Dunciad . . . In Three Books* (Theobald as hero); their hostility is confirmed	Gay's *Beggar's Opera* Young's *Love of Fame* (pbd piecemeal 1725–8) William Law's *Serious Call to a Devout and Holy Life*	

1729	*The Dunciad Variorum* (with prolegomena, notes, etc)	Congreve dies Steele dies Swift's *Modest Proposal*	
1730		Cibber succeeds Eusden as poet laureate Thomson's *Seasons* *The Grub-Street Journal* (to 1737)	
1731	*Epistle to Burlington* (*Moral Essay* IV)	Defoe dies	
1732	Pope–Swift *Miscellanies*, IV (so-called 'third volume')	Atterbury and Gay die	'Patriot' Opposition to Walpole takes shape
1733	*Epistle to Bathurst* (*Moral Essay* III) Pope's first Imitation of Horace, *Satire II i: To Fortescue* *Essay on Man*, epistles I–III Pope's mother dies *The Impertinent* (version of Donne's Satire IV) Pope moves towards the Opposition party	Bolingbroke's *Dissertation upon Parties* (essays in *Craftsman*, completed 1734) Swift's *On poetry, a Rhapsody*	Walpole's Excise Bill proposed—and withdrawn
1734	*Epistle to Cobham* (*Moral Essay* I) *Essay on Man*, epistle IV *Satire II ii: To Bethel* *Sober Advice from Horace* (*Satire I ii*)		
1735	*Epistle to Arbuthnot* *Epistle to a Lady* (*Moral Essay* II) *Works*, vol II (including version of Donne's Satire II) Curll's edn of Pope's letters	Arbuthnot dies Bolingbroke retires to France Thomson's *Liberty*, I–III Hogarth's *Rake's Progress*	
1736	Friendship with Ralph Allen	Fielding's *Pasquin* Joseph Butler's *Analogy of Religion* Thomson's *Liberty*, IV–V Laws against witchcraft repealed	

1737	*Epistle II ii* ('Dear Col'nel. . . .') Pope's authorized edn of his letters *Epistle II i: To Augustus* Crousaz begins attacks on *Essay on Man*	Fielding's *Historical Register* and other dramatic satires Richard Glover's *Leonidas* John and Charles Wesley's *Psalms and Hymns*	Queen Caroline dies Playhouse Licensing Act Prince of Wales heads Opposition
1738	*Epistle I vi: To Murray Epistle I i: To Bolingbroke 1738 (Epilogue to the Satires)*, Dialogues I and II *The Universal Prayer* Bolingbroke visits Pope Warburton begins defence *Essay on Man*	Johnson's *London* Swift's *Genteel Conversation*	
1739	'Epistle I vii' (pbd in new edn of *Works*) Friendship with Warburton	Hume's *Treatise of Human Nature* (completed 1740)	War with Spain; capture of Porto Bello
1740	Pope refurbishes his grotto	Cibber's *Apology for his Life* Richardson's *Pamela* (completed 1742)	War of Austrian Succession Wyndham (leader of Tory Opposition) dies
1741	Pope publishes *Memoirs of Scriblerus* (collaborative work, dating in part from Scriblerian days) Warburton helps Pope prepare definitive edn of his works		Cartagena expedition
1742	*The New Dunciad* (i.e. Book IV)	Fielding's *Joseph Andrews* Young's *Night Thoughts*, I–III (completed 1743–5) Handel's *Messiah*	Walpole resigns
1743	*The Dunciad in Four Books*, with Cibber as hero Pope frequently visits Bolingbroke at Battersea Pope's health failing		Battle of Dettingen Carteret in power
1744	Pope dies at Twickenham (30 May)	Johnson's *Life of Savage* Akenside's *Pleasures of Imagination*	Carteret resigns Rise of the Pelhams

1: On Reading Pope

G. S. ROUSSEAU

What requisitions of a verity
Prompted the wit and rage between his teeth
One cannot say. Around a crooked tree
A moral climbs whose name should be a wreath.

Allen Tate, 'Mr Pope', *Mr Pope & other Poems*

WE LIVE in an age of multidimensional disorder—disorder that is evident in every walk of life and by no means confined to governments, courts, or great affairs. Intellectuals and other men who live 'by their minds'—to echo the late Bertrand Russell—experience this welter and have as much difficulty and anxiety in mustering an energy necessary to cope with it as soldiers and ministers of state had in previous ages.

What can an 'ancient poet' who was a member of at least three minorities: a Catholic, a cripple, and—not least of all—a poet teach such a disordered age? A poet who wrote in a medium (the heroic couplet) now rarely used by poets and misunderstood by many readers, and whose person, if summed up today, would hardly appear heroic to the 'Jet-Set' or the millions of television watchers all over the world. If, as Aeschylus' chorus chants in the *Oresteia*, 'Suffering teaches', then Alexander Pope is eminently qualified to continue instructing future ages of mankind, however disordered. For he endured much more than physical agony (he used to complain that he never enjoyed three days of consecutive health throughout 'this long Disease, my life'[1]); his mental anguish, moreover, was not altogether different from that of Coleridge in the Romantic Age, Baudelaire during the Second Republic, D. H.

[1] *Epistle to Arbuthnot*, 132.

Lawrence in the Edwardian Age, and Brecht in our own time. He would have understood perfectly well the insane dialogues of Vladimir and Estragon in *Waiting for Godot* and grasped with ease our Beckettian sense in the seventies—that 'we cannot go on'. If his own age now seems 'orderly' or 'neat', this is a figment of our historical imagination caused by the passing of time and Pope would have known it had not been so in actuality. The first half of the eighteenth century may have displayed different confusions from ours and may have apologized for them more obliquely, but the England of his lifetime (1688–1744) was far from being a halcyon calm, or, as George Saintsbury called it. 'The Peace of the Augustans'. Pope's struggle in making peace with his own epoch and in combatting personal adversity of a physical as well as meta-physical nature, embodies one of the most dramatic stories in western civilization. His struggle is in many ways our struggle—but it also represents the conflicts for fifty-six years of a deformed cripple, almost a dwarf (having shrunk to a height of four feet six inches), who was barred by a 'crazy constitution'[1] from the normal activities of most men—marriage, travel, recognition for merit by his government, and religious tolerance as a member of a Catholic minority in the heyday of Protestant power.

Despite all his anguish and suffering, Pope was a great poet; great not only among his contemporaries, but among poets of all times and all nations. Readers of English poetry posit that his verse has not the visionary depths of Blake's, the richly symbolic texture of Coleridge's, or the filmy dreamlike substance of Keats'. They also acknowledge that it lacks the religious breadth of Milton's panorama, Shakespeare's un-equalled versatility, or Chaucer's unforgettable characters. To point out differences and note limitations is a very different matter, however, from Robert Graves' imputation of 'technical incompetency'.[2] Nothing in fact, could be farther from the truth: Pope stands unequalled in his poetic craft. But technique alone does not assure a poet immortality or a resting place in Westminster Abbey. Pope succeeded, as all great bards must, by the compatible marriage of form and content, and by the discovery of a voice of his own and a pulsating heart that beats

[1] Pope to Caryll, 19 October 1729, *Corr.* III 61.
[2] *The Crowning Privilege*, 1955, 34.

like no one else's. His life also illustrates, almost better than any other English poet's, that poetry must precede all else among a great poet's priorities—this despite any exigencies whatsoever of his time. He was as much a product of his age as a sponsor of it; but it is far more significant that he assumed—again, like Wordsworth or Coleridge—the heavy burden of also becoming its spokesman:

> *Yes, the last Pen for Freedom let me draw,*
> *When Truth stands trembling on the edge of Law:*
> *Here, Last of* Britons! *let your Names be read;*
> *Are none, none living? let me praise the Dead,*
> *And for that Cause which made your Fathers shine,*
> *Fall, by the Votes of their degen'rate Line!*

(*Epilogue to the Satires*, II, 248-53)

Freedom and the law were only two of the 'causes' Pope championed; yet he did so from a firm belief that they constituted a pillar in the perennial edifice of civilization. Time has proved him right. His mighty themes—virtue, vice, corruption, pride, genuine versus perfunctory art, freedom, the law, to mention a few—are now the perpetual talk of social and natural scientists as well as of poets and critics. Pope is a great poet because he sang universal songs (and sang them all with great poise and subtlety) that have appealed and will appeal to men in all ages. The passage of time, however vast, will never blunt the universal allure of such masterpieces as *An Essay on Man, The Dunciad,* or *The Rape of the Lock.* When Dr Johnson wrote in his *Life of Pope* (1781), 'New sentiments and new images others may produce, but to attempt any further improvement of versification will be dangerous,'[1] he was primarily thinking of Pope's achievement in the couplet form, but he inferred in his next paragraph that the poet had scaled the same Olympian heights as other titans such as Chaucer, Milton, Dryden: 'After all this it is surely superfluous to answer the question that has once been asked, Whether Pope was a poet? otherwise than by asking in return, If Pope be not a poet, where is poetry to be found?'

It is found in great splendour in his collected works, in an *oeuvre* that extends many thousands of couplets written in a span of five decades.

[1] *Lives of the English Poets,* ed G. B. Hill, Oxford 1905, III, 251.

As Dr Leavis has noted[1] it is poetry of 'poise and subtle variety', but it is also poetry that impresses readers by its range and variety of subjects. Pope's development, unlike Keats', was monumental; the poet writing the *Pastorals* (1709) or *An Essay on Criticism* (1711) is a very different poet from the one whose sensibility presided over *An Essay on Man* (1733–34) and *An Epistle to Dr. Arbuthnot* (1735), or again, whose visionary imagination reflected *The New Dunciad* (1742). All were, to be sure, the work of one man but that man changed pyramidally from year to year, and so did his thinking. He grew, like his creatures in *An Essay on Man* 'plac'd on this isthmus of a middle state', into 'a being darkly wise, and rudely great' (II, 3–4). Yet, he was still a man with all the frailty implied therein. Hardly any poet has been more maligned than Pope for his frailties, and even fewer have suffered (as did he) a dichotomy of the man and his works. But his efforts in poetry did not terminate in a Sisyphean futility; for his renown, like Horace's, is indelibly cast in bronze, *monumentum aere perennius*, and it is accurate to state, as I have elsewhere, that no other poet except Shakespeare ever reaped such rich returns from his literary medium. As for his message to subsequently troubled worlds, perhaps Allen Tate, the American poet, has said the last word in the lines that could have been an epitaph. 'Around a crooked tree / A moral climbs whose name should be a wreath.'

I

Our guide will, indeed, take us the shortest way, will save us many a wearisome and perilous wandering, and warn us of many a mock road that had formerly led himself to the brink of chasms and precipices, or at best in an idle circle to the spot from whence we started. But he cannot carry us on his shoulders: we must strain our own sinews, as he has strained his; and make firm footing on the smooth rock for ourselves, by the blood of toil from our own feet.

(Coleridge, *The Friend*, in *The Collected Coleridge*, ed K. Coburn, I 55.)

A reader of English literature, desirous of traversing the entire length of Pope's poetic route will find himself at the foot of a bifurcated path—

[1] *Revaluation*, 1936, 72.

one fork of the road uncharted, with no means of knowing how to bypass the wasteful and tricky twists and turns; the other, as Coleridge's speaker intimates, clearly marked, through the aid of a guide, to avoid its many pitfalls.

Imagine that the charted road consists of five ascending levels, the highest signifying readers who have familiarized themselves with virtually every aspect of Pope's life and works, while the first or lowest requires the reader to disburden himself of two myths about the poetry and life of Pope: namely, that his verses are rational and emotionless (in his words—although he was not describing himself—'Correctly cold'[1]), and the erroneous notion that in his personal life he was a wicked satirist whose chief preoccupation lay in 'stinging' friends as well as enemies, described by some of his contemporaries as 'the wicked wasp of Twickenham'.

Both allegations are untrue, although it has taken much time and effort to make this pronouncement. Beginning students have somewhere encountered the generalization that Pope was a 'neoclassical' poet writing in an age that frowned upon intense feelings expressed in poetry, that extolled decorum, artificiality, and polite manners which were to be reflected in a poet's content and manner.[2] And yet, the poetry of Pope gives the lie to all these abstract statements: his verse does not accentuate the Ancients any more than Milton's did in the seventeenth

---

[1] *Essay on Criticism*, 240.

[2] This notion has been taught for decades in English and American universities but has recently come under fire from many different quarters. It was endowed with credibility by James Sutherland's widely read book *A Preface to Eighteenth-Century Poetry* (Oxford 1948), aspects of which were corrected by D. J. Greene in an important article, 'Logical Structure in Eighteenth-Century Poetry,' *PQ* XXXI (1952) 315–36 and which he has since been correcting. The most significant recent book dealing with these issues is Greene's *Age of Exuberance: Backgrounds to Eighteenth-Century English Literature*, New York 1970. For a corrective to Sutherland's recent volume in the Oxford History of English Literature series (*The Late Seventeenth Century*, 1969), the period in which Pope was growing up and inheriting from his teachers and advisers values and beliefs about literature, see G. S. Rousseau, *E-CS* II, 1969, 454–63.

century or Arnold's would in the nineteenth. Intense emotion is achieved not only in *Eloisa to Abelard* (1717) and numerous passages of his twenty-five thousand line translation of Homer's *Iliad* but also—and this is the more essential point—throughout his so-called satirical works, *An Essay on Man, Imitations of Horace, The Dunciad.* Finally, the widespread but inaccurate notion that the early eighteenth century was an age of decorum, artificial refinement, and polite manners will no longer hold water and it is unprofitable as well as historically incorrect to view Pope's poetry within a context that itself never existed. The logical fallacy of critics who do so is not difficult to grasp: (1) the early eighteenth century in England was an epoch of polite refinement; (2) Pope was the major poet of this age (1700–50); (3) therefore, Pope must be a poet who writes about this refinement and reflects it everywhere in his works. QED.

Nothing could be farther from the truth, as several of the chapters in this volume demonstrate, nor should we willingly accept the other myth about Pope's personality. No reader should form a hardened view of Pope-the-man from one or two preconceptions he has gathered from uninformed sources. Charges made against his physical deformity, Catholicism, and alleged meanness were sustained throughout his own lifetime and transmitted to the Victorians, who added further charges rendering him the most despicable poet in the entire history of English literature. J. V. Guerinot, the author of the most recent study of *Pamphlet Attacks on Alexander Pope, 1711–1744: A Descriptive Bibliography* (1969) asks (xxix), 'Could one think of another figure in English literature the standard critical and biographical studies of whom would repeat, however unconsciously, the rumours and defamations of his avowed enemies?' The answer is an emphatic no. As Guerinot's volume shows, Pope was condemned in his own lifetime chiefly for his deformity,[1] religion, and general stance as a satirist, castigations that

[1] He suffered from Pott's Disease, which caused him to shrink almost to dwarfish size, as well as from kyphoscoliotic tuberculosis, cardiac disorder, crippling arthritis, and chronic genital infections. See Marjorie Nicolson and G. S. Rousseau, "A Medical Case History of Alexander Pope," in *This Long Disease, My Life: Alexander Pope and the Sciences,* Princeton 1968, 7–82.

were expanded in the next century to a point of inanity. The Edwardians, no less than their predecessors, perpetuated the myth of Pope's
meanness, and when one of their spokesmen, Lytton Strachey, represents him as a monkey pouring down boiling oil on his victims,[1] how
much more this tells us about Bloomsbury than the poet of Twickenham! What began during Pope's lifetime as an attack by Grub Street
and a small coterie—Lady Mary Wortley Montagu, Lord Hervey,
Gildon, Dennis, Cibber—was enlarged during the nineteenth century
to the size of a national myth about one of England's greatest poets,
with the result that a critic as astute as Matthew Arnold had difficulty
keeping the man apart from his works and finally denounced him as 'a
classic of our prose'.[2] Only in the mid-twentieth century, after biographers like 'George Paston' (E. M. Symonds) and Edith Sitwell had
written highly biased accounts, did biographers—such as George Sherburn[3]—take up the gauntlet to write an objective account. Scholarship
is still working toward that end, but a new reader of Pope should be
apprised that almost all the biographies on the library shelf about the
poet are prejudiced in one way or another. The reader, like Descartes,
must turn back the dials to zero and start afresh. If he also brings to the
task of reading Pope anew a degree of Humean scepticism, it may
enable him to appreciate Pope's poetry and to comprehend that the
literary person who so shocked nineteenth-century editors like Elwin
was not Pope himself.

On the other hand, it would be an error to go too far in the opposite
direction. Biased accounts require corrective action but scholars sometimes err by counteracting inordinately. Pope was certainly not the vile
worm Grub Street said he was, or the conniving villain described by
contemporary novelists such as Richardson,[4] or Strachey's squalid
monkey; but neither was he merely another distinguished poet such as
his predecessor Dryden. Aspects of his life are unusual when meas-

---

[1] *Pope. The Leslie Stephen Lecture for 1925*, Cambridge 1925, 2.

[2] 'The Study of Poetry', *Essays in Criticism, Second Series,* in *Works*,
1903, IV 31.

[3] See *The Early Career of Alexander Pope*, Oxford 1934.

[4] See John Carroll, 'Richardson on Pope and Swift,' *University of
Toronto Quarterly*, XXXIII, 1963, 19–29.

ured by any yardstick and these must be taken into account in an allegedly objective survey of his life. He *was* deformed, Catholic, and not infrequently dishonest as evidenced by—to cite only two instances —his financial treatment of Fenton and Broome, assistants who helped him translate Homer's *Odyssey*, and the circumstances attending the publication of his letters in 1737. Moreover, although he remained unmarried, his attachment to two women in particular, Lady Mary Wortley Montagu and Martha Blount, created an atmosphere of illicit romance to no less a degree than the onslaught of personal attacks in *The Dunciad* (1728), *Imitations of Horace* (1733–38) and *New Dunciad* (1742) begot him enemies. His personal code of ethics was misunderstood by most men and unappreciated by all except a handful of friends (including Swift, Arbuthnot, Ralph Allen, and Lords Burlington, Bathurst and Cobham). To many of his contemporaries he appeared sickly in mind and body, an unfortunate recluse who seemed to spend unhappy days with a sickly mother and whose only palpable pleasure was derived from lampooning both friend and foe. Such, of course, was not the case. As Professor Maynard Mack has recently written:

> To be a great satirist, a man must have, literally and figuratively, a place to stand, an angle of vision. For Pope . . . the garden and the grotto supplied this. They supplied a rallying point for his personal values and a focus for his conception of himself—as master of a poet's 'kingdom,' a counter-order to a court and ministry that set no store by poets, a community bound by ties quite other than those uniting the 'pensioners' of St. Stephen, as he sardonically calls the members of Walpole's parliament.[1]

Pope's symbolic kingdom at Twickenham entailed far more creativity than immobility and, as the student who delves deeper into this chapter will learn, the garden and grotto were 'rallying points', in Mack's phrase, from which to remind the outside world of 'Courts and great Affairs'[2] that elsewhere—actually not very far up the sinuous Thames—another kind of kingdom existed built out of the shadowy

[1] *The Garden and the City*, 1969, 232, the first book in my estimate that offers a convincing account of Pope's personality and life style.
[2] *Epistle to Arbuthnot* 267.

substances of the imagination and the empire of dreams. If Pope's contemporaries misunderstood the symbolic significance the garden and the grotto held for the poet, we must not, two centuries later, overly censure their estimates of the poet's life and the reclusive world into which he appeared to have retired, because time, as Johnson intimated,[1] enhances impartiality. And yet, Dr Johnson himself as well as other early biographers—Owen Ruffhead, John Nichols, Thomas Tyers, Gilbert Wakefield—understood very little about Pope's *modus vivendi*. One unfortunate aspect of Pope's reputation in the last two centuries is that so many biographers and critics have converted into fact nebulous and fanciful legends depicting a monstrous existence and then interpreted his poetry as the product of such a man. These critics popularized the myth that his ideas—especially the philosophical ideas expressed in *An Essay on Man*—were a reflection of the odious sensibility that had conjured them, and with the lapse of time the man and his works became inseparable, both ungainly and forbidding.[2]

Another aspect worth mentioning is a reverence (idolatry may be too presumptuous) for Pope which, though minuscule in comparison with the following enjoyed, for example, by Shakespeare, does form a somewhat steady stream in the riptides of the last two centuries' literature. We expect occasional idolatry from his editors, biographers, and explicators and are surprised when it appears elsewhere, especially in remote and unexpected corners, such as William Whewell, an outstanding master of Trinity College, Cambridge and a distinguished scientist in his own right, who was struck by Pope's poetry on first reading him as a young man. He defended his achievement in corres-

[1] *Rambler* No. 60.

[2] Nowhere is this development more clearly visible than in Pope's reputation in countries other than England. During the eighteenth and nineteenth centuries his ideas were distorted in America, France, Italy, and Germany and beliefs that were originally uttered as neutral philosophic precepts were contorted into politically biased systems espousing the *status quo* and in general a reactionary theory of government. See Agnes Marie Sibley, *Alexander Pope's Prestige in America, 1725–1835*, New York 1949, and Leon Howard, 'The American Revolt Against Pope,' *SP* XLIX, 1952, 48–65; E. Audra, *L'influence française dans l'oeuvre de Pope*, Paris 1931; G. Lenta, *Pope in Italia*, Florence 1931.

pondence extending over many years with contemporaries torn between allegiances to Wordsworth and Coleridge and who could not have cared less about Pope's status:

> I do *not*, then, make Pope my idol. I should *not* rejoice to see his style restored. I do *not* perceive in him, or learn from him, the love of nature. I do not even insist upon his being called a poet. It is sufficient for me, who would not break the king's peace for a definition, that I receive from his writings pleasure *greater* and of a *different kind* from that which I should receive from similar writings in prose.[1]

Perhaps Whewell's comparison of the pleasure he derived from Pope's poetry with that of another's prose perplexes some of us, but in view of the metamorphosis that poetry underwent, this type of comparison loses its significance. By the turn of the nineteenth century lyric poetry (especially Wordsworth's variety) was deemed princess of the 'poetic kinds', a form in which Pope rarely dabbled. Notwithstanding this development, men like Whewell continued to read and enjoy Pope and occasionally discovered heroic attributes in his life style. Under the surface, Byron's admiration of Pope was attributable to a belief that he had achieved a greatness in verse shared only by two or three other English poets, as G. Wilson Knight and others have shown.[2] Another 'revolutionary', Julian Bell (1908–1937), the brilliant son of Clive Bell and nephew of Virginia Woolf who tragically died fighting in the Spanish Civil War, selected Pope from all English poets as the subject of a critical dissertation: such choice is noteworthy because Bell was, in the words of his most recent biographer, Peter Stansky,[3] 'a charming, intelligent and discontented young man' in the early 1930s, and

[1] Letter dated 30 August 1817 to Hugh James Rose, printed in *The Life and Correspondence of William Whewell*, ed Mrs Stair Douglas, 1881, 30.
[2] G. Wilson Knight, *Laureate of Peace: On the Genius of Alexander Pope*, London and New York 1954, ch. v; J. L. Mahoney, 'Byron's Admiration of Pope: A Romantic Paradox, '*Discourse* V, 1962, 309–15. See also Oscar Maurer, 'Pope and the Victorians,' *Studies in English 1944*, Austin, Texas 1945, 211–38.
[3] Peter Stansky and William Abrahams, *Journey to the Frontier*, Boston 1966, 88.

because he was a poet, not a scholar, whose interest in Pope, unlike Byron's concern, seems to have centred on the poetry itself. 'It has the qualities of great poetry,' he wrote on 8 December 1934 in the *New Statesman & Nation* (872), 'produced not by a genius for taking infinite pains—only charlatans and bores take infinite pains—but by a tried and practised genius.' Later scholars would, perchance, have disagreed with Bell's estimate but only the most obtuse among them would not perk up at his choice. Bred in Cambridge and Bloomsbury and exposed to the best minds of the Edwardian age, this young revolutionary disregarded literary figures then universally fashionable (the French symbolist poets, Proust, the whole imaginative literature of Germany)—and sought to discover his own sensibilities in the works of a 'tried and practised genius'.

Part of the dilemma of Whewell, Byron, and Bell, names not usually associated with Pope's, still lingers although in somewhat different form. These men had little in common but they all perceived something infinitely great about Strachey's 'fiendishly clever and spiteful monkey'. Today, when painstaking scholarship has revealed the symbolic dimensions of Pope's mode of life and the unequalled skill of his craftsmanship—'no other poet except Shakespeare ever reaped such rich returns from his literary medium'[1]—an inexplicable greatness, so succinctly expressed in *An Essay on Criticism* as 'a Grace beyond the Reach of Art' (155), draws sensitive readers to his verse. Perhaps the next few sections will shed some light on these graces.

II

Thus far the emphasis has been on Pope's life but by now the student will wish to explore the poems themselves. He ought to read the major poems—*The Rape of the Lock, An Essay on Man, An Epistle to Dr. Arbuthnot*, for example—but he will gain a clearer sense of Pope's poetic development if he reads the bulk of his poetry chronologically. He will then catch a glimpse of the monumental changes that occurred in

[1] G. S. Rousseau, intro. to *The Rape of the Lock*, New Jersey 1969, 4.

Pope's form, subject matter and tone. He will notice a long eleven-year gap between 1717 and 1728, during which period Pope was engaged in translating Homer's *Iliad* and *Odyssey*, the two masterpieces by a poet who was 'universally allow'd to have had the greatest Invention of any Writer whatever'.[1] Pope's translations, especially *The Iliad*, are 'original poems'—in fact his *Iliad* has been called the most distinguished long poem of the Augustan Age,[2] but more will be said about these translations later. At present it is important that the reader gain a sense of Pope's overall literary production and if possible read as well some of the lesser known poems, especially his various imitations of English poets (all written during 1700–1717), *Ode for Musick: On St. Cecilia's Day* (1713),[3] *The Temple of Fame* (1715), *The Universal Prayer* (1738), 'Ode on Solitude' (1717), and 'Verses on a Grotto by the River Thames at Twickenham' (1741). These, together with the great poems, clearly demonstrate how Pope began his poetic career as an imitator of other poets, later turned to the writing of witty satires and lampoons (*The Rape of the Lock*, *The Dunciad* of 1728), and finally, during the early 1730s when such poems as *An Essay on Man* and *Moral Essays* were taking shape, 'stoop'd to Truth, and moraliz'd his song' (*To Arbuthnot* 341). He abandoned poetry that was purely descriptive, devoid of lofty ideas and philosophical themes, and directed his efforts instead to poetry that blended a refinement of style and witty statement with a substratum of precepts concerned with universal morality and ethics. Such had been the tradition of Spenser and Milton, and now Pope, a poet who viewed his main task in life as the effecting of a daily routine such that he could live to the full the life of a poet, sought to join their rank, claiming that he, like them, veered from lesser lyrics 'not for Fame, but Virtue's better end.' This growth of a poet's imagination has been admirably studied by R. K. Root in *The Poetical Career of Alexander Pope* (Princeton 1938), focusing on Pope's early development, but most penetratingly by Maynard Mack in his Alexander Lectures delivered

1 Preface to *Iliad*: Twickenham VII 3.
2 See Johnson, *Lives of the Poets,* edn cit. III 236–40. See also E. M. W. Tillyard, 'Pope's Iliad', in *The English Epic and Its Background*, Oxford 1954, 498–509.
3 Dates of publication, not composition.

in 1963 at the University of Toronto which have already been cited: *The Garden and the City*.[1]

It is not exactly correct, however, to split Pope's development into two neat halves with the year 1730 or 1731 as the median. Pope, by his own admission in correspondence with his early literary advisers and later in *An Epistle to Dr. Arbuthnot* and in oral statements made to his faithful recorder Joseph Spence, had intended ultimately to 'moralize his song', to attempt to write poetry in the grand style of epic and the greater ode, but not until he believed he had mastered sufficiently well the art of couplets, his medium and genre. He accordingly began—as the reader who follows this guide will observe—by composing imitations and parodies, eventually progressed to pastorals (not a particularly difficult form to perfect but one that allowed the poet to exercise his invention), and later moved on to satires. Then came, I believe, the most consequential decision of his life: the translation of Homer's epics. As is well known, he had been translating Homeric lines and Ovidian fragments from his childhood, almost as soon as he had learned Greek and Latin. But this project, made appealing by the publishers, was another matter: Pope knew it would impede the stride of his poetic development; but he also judged correctly that it would prove most rewarding in the future. Surprisingly, his biographers—for example Sherburn's *Early Career* which discusses this period (1715–1726)—have not thus far emphasized the monumental effect of this undertaking on Pope's later career. Maynard Mack alone has focused his attention on this episode in recent years. Pope's translations, he informs us in a passage explaining what we ought always to have known, 'remind us that the place occupied by Homer, by the translating of Homer, and by epic poetry generally in Pope's career and in the sensibility of the eighteenth century is something of which we have yet to take adequate account in our biography, our literary history, and our criticism.'[2]

[1] For Pope's development see also Bonamy Dobrée, *Alexander Pope*, 1951; John Butt, 'Pope: the Man and the Poet,' in *Of Books and Humankind*, ed J. Butt, 1964; Rachel Trickett, *The Honest Muse: A Study in Augustan Verse*, Oxford 1967, 156–223.

[2] Twickenham VII lxx–lxxi, and for the next sentence *ibid*, ccxlix. Reuben Brower's chapter, 'True Heroic Poetry', in *Alexander Pope:*

Later in the same work, Mack goes even further. 'Without Pope's work on Homer, one feels, Timon's Villa, Cotta's "lone Chartreux", Selkirk's "Nepenthe of a Court", the back-handed praise of George Augustus, and many another of Pope's outsized creations could not have been what they are.' The point to be gathered is not that Pope was a neo-classicist fervidly hoping to restore prestige to Homer but that the Grecian bard's compositions acted as a grindstone to whet his imagination. He had, after all, first caught 'the itch of poetry'—as he told Broome in 1715 and Spence at a much later date[1]—while reading the *Iliad*, in Ogilby's translation, as a boy of eight, and to the very end of his life spoke of its poet with unmatched rapture. What we are therefore just beginning to learn is that Pope regarded his Homeric experiences as essential to the totality of his poetic career and that he conceived of his translation, especially the *Iliad*, as an 'original' poem, a type of Augustan epic, a looking glass through which a civilization—its manners, achievements, and frustrations—could be viewed. Nowhere to my knowledge is this stated more lucidly than in the introduction to the Twickenham Edition of his translations, a collaborative effort by Professors Mack, Callan, Fagles, Frost, and Knight.[2] Here the student will discover some of the reasons supporting Mack's argument about 'the place occupied by Homer' in Pope's writing career and will better comprehend how this experience of more than a decade's duration influenced his middle and late works.

We are now at the threshold of the latter phase of his development (1730–1743), the period that bridges *An Essay on Man* and *The Dunciad in Four Books*, followed shortly thereafter by his death on 30 May 1744. One thing is clear: many of the tendencies displayed in the poems of this mature period are readily found in earlier works—in

The Poetry of Allusion, Oxford 1959, is an admirable exposé of Pope's heroic mode and of the way 'he gives us the felt impression of a whole scene or of the Homeric style rather than accurate reproduction of the original text' (114), but Pope's impressionistic translations are not there viewed within the context of his entire poetic career.

[1] Pope to Broome, 16 June [1715], *Corr.* I 297; Spence §§ 29–30.
[2] The significance of this booklength introduction to other studies about Pope is discussed by G. S. Rousseau, *R E S* n.s. XX, 1969, 94–101.

poems written before the translation of Homer. The modulation of voices had been evident in such poems as *The Rape of the Lock* and the first *Dunciad* which were well shaped structures with a beginning, middle, and end, containing Pope's many moods, even though they may not have been perfect organic wholes.[1] But after his Homeric experience Pope was well armed with new poetic ammunition: greater facility than ever in composing couplets, a more subtle mode of allusion to the literary past and present, and—perhaps most significant—a new sensibility of a compulsive tension, arising from a conflict between an aloofness from worldly woes as a resident at Twickenham, and an artistic impulse to change for the better the ways of the world, giving his literary endeavours added impetus. This sentence could serve as a brief summary of Mack's *The Garden and the City*. One could also add that the whole of Pope's mature poetry is a metaphor for the horror of social and political reality, and for the impossibility of even a 'pure poet', like Pope, remaining untarnished. Pope continually engages in his late poetry in imagined dialogues with 'friends'—Arbuthnot, Fortescue, Bethel. And the astonishing aspect of these dialogues, especially the *Imitations of Horace*, is that Pope, despite the grotesque nature of all political life (even that from which he is excluded), is able to keep his persona intact.

Professor Mack also shows us the ebb and flow of Pope's development in the later years of his career; he, moreover, shatters a lingering notion that the twilight was unrelated to the dawn of his career. There had been continuity. It is indeed said that Pope acquired new interests, especially in politics, and cultivated new tastes, particularly in gardening and architecture. Yet, these interests and tastes were not altogether new; they had been a part of his sensibility for many years, the former noticeable when he was a 'town wit during his youth', the latter two

[1] William K. Wimsatt has recently demonstrated that Pope's later poems are no immutable organic wholes: see his essay 'Some Questions about a Metaphor' in *Organic Form: the Life of an Idea*, ed. G. S. Rousseau, 1972, 62–81. Others have noted this as well: Frank Brady, 'The History and Structure of Pope's *To a Lady*,' *S E L* IX, 1969, 439–62, and Greene's article cited on page 5 above, with particular reference to *An Essay on Man*.

obvious virtually as soon as he and his mother moved in 1719 to the small 'villa' at Twickenham. It is unfortunate that, except for Mack's recent volume, there is no source to which students may be directed for a reliable account of this development, notably its continuities. Sherburn's *Early Career* stops too soon and Brower's *Alexander Pope* is exclusively concerned with modes of allusion. Moreover, there is as yet no authoritative biography of Pope's whole life, though this task is now being undertaken by Professor Mack. Despite these lacunae in modern scholarship, an attempt must be made to understand Pope's career, and, to echo Matthew Arnold's remark about Sophocles, to view it steadily and whole. Its understanding is further enhanced by familiarization with the cultural milieu of the age; by studying Pope's relation with Swift (how much of his attraction was admiration of superior intellectual acumen?), Grub Street, and his aristocratic friends; and by reading, as a prolegomenon to its comprehension, such works as Austin Warren's *Alexander Pope as Critic and Humanist* (Princeton 1929), Maynard Mack's introduction to the Twickenham Edition of *An Essay on Man* (1950), James Hillhouse's *Grub-Street Journal* (Durham, North Carolina 1928), and two essays by Reuben Brower: 'An Allusion to Europe' (chapter i of his *Alexander Pope*), and 'Dryden and the "Invention" of Pope', in the *McKillop Festschrift*, 211–33.

III

The reader will now wish to grapple with aspects of Pope's poetic art. He has read both major poems and minor works, and has a mental sketch of the poet's lives: the one mythical, the other actual; in addition has acquired chronological knowledge of Pope's development which allows him to discuss Pope as a poet of three dimensions—a beginning, a middle, and an end. In fact, the poet had willed it so.

Viewing Pope's art atomically may prove a good approach to its study; that is by building from elements within couplets (especially what might be called rhetoric in the literal sense) to whole couplets and from couplets to verse paragraphs as if building a molecular structure atom by atom. The stringing together of these 'verse paragraphs'

(Pope's own term) in a particular poem is a large part of his total structure. There are, of course, other types of figurative structures, but we need only concern ourselves for the present with isolating under the microscope his wit, satiric postures, nature, invention and imitation of models, system of ethics. To achieve this depends on our ability to analyse their various components and to detect their relative actions and interactions: (1) rhetoric and metre (2) diction and imagery (3) allusion (4) verse paragraphs and (5) larger structures.

Before beginning this quasi-scientific approach it may be appropriate to pinpoint various stumbling blocks students should avoid in order to save time and effort. Critics of the eighteenth century are a kind of obstacle, as will be abundantly demonstrated in the forthcoming volume on Pope (edited by Dr John Barnard) in the Critical Heritage Series—a volume of critical commentaries voiced during and shortly after Pope's lifetime. Therefore we peruse Joseph Warton's *Essay* (1756–1782), Percival Stockdale's *Enquiry* (1778), Gilbert Wakefield's *Observations on Pope* (1796), and even Samuel Johnson's often brilliant 'Life of Pope', without discovering much information about Pope's couplet art. John Dennis' *Remarks on Mr. Pope's 'Rape of the Lock'* (1728) is an exception—his analyses seem to have overlooked nothing in Pope's art, not even an innuendo. The objective in these works naturally varies and all are an admixture of forms intermingling what we today would call biography, social background, and literary criticism. But we will have to look elsewhere to locate sources dealing with an anatomy of Pope's poetic craft.

Rhetoric, or 'the figures of witt' as Puttenham phrased it in his *Arte of English Poesie* (1589), is the stuff of Pope's poetry. 'It was our family priest', he remarked to Spence in 1743, 'who taught me the figures, accidence, and first part of the grammar.'[1] W. K. Wimsatt comments that in the poet's later years 'the figures were assumed by Pope under the general head of "correctness",' and that he 'seems to have been able to take them for granted'.[2] Pope's rhetorical sinews are so deeply ingrained in the whole tissue of his verse that he could afford to forget he had

[1] Spence § 17.
[2] 'Rhetoric and Poems: Alexander Pope', *English Institute Essays for 1948*, New York 1949, 193.

learned formal rhetoric and even mock the subject, as he did in Chapters X and XI of *Peri Bathous*, a comic treatment of 'Tropes and Figures'. In order to set his rhetoric in perspective a knowledge of the growth of the English couplet is necessary; and for this purpose the following two articles are required reading: George Williamson's 'The Rhetorical Pattern of Neo-classical Wit', (*MP* XXXIII, 1935, 55–81) concerning couplet theory from Puttenham in 1589 to Edward Bysshe in 1702; and Ruth C. Wallerstein's 'The Development of the Rhetoric and Metre of the Heroic Couplet, Especially in 1625–1645', (*PMLA* L, 1935, 166–209). Equipped with this background, the student will better understand the status of the English couplet at the time Pope tried his hand at this form and the precedents that were available to him. Let us now turn to Pope's innovations, especially his improvements upon Dryden. These have been discussed in various quarters but most eloquently by Elder Olson in 'Rhetoric and the Appreciation of Pope', (*MP* XXXVII, 1939, 13–35), who explains how Pope's use of rhetorical figures actually determines the quality and tone of his highly personal wit, and by W. K. Wimsatt in another piece entitled 'One Relation of Rhyme to Reason: Alexander Pope', (*MLQ* V, 1944, 323–338) which compares Pope's rhymes with Chaucer's.[1] Wimsatt lists the figures found in Pope's verse and offers many examples of each. The student of Pope's work needs to understand why Pope felt that rhetorical perfection was so necessary an element in his poems. But the effort involved in such understanding will prove worth while because the reader will learn that Pope was an astute and high calibred wordsmith.

Metre, not unlike rhetoric, also should claim attention. Pope's medium is usually the iambic pentameter rhymed couplet; yet within this metrical unit (and occasionally in others—triplets, trochaic pentameters, some iambic tetrameters in the short, minor poems) he deftly

[1] See also Wimsatt, p. 17 n. 2 above. Pope's rhymes, especially as they reflect his 'sense', have recently received further attention in I. Ehrenpreis, 'The Style of Sound: The Literary Value of Pope's Versification', in *Augustan Milieu*, 232–46. See also Rebecca Parkin, *The Poetic Workmanship of Alexander Pope*, Minneapolis 1955; and Patricia Meyer Spacks, *An Argument of Images: the Poetry of Alexander Pope*, Cambridge, Mass. 1971.

uses internal pauses and breathings, *caesuras*, for emphasis. These and other metrical techniques have been studied by Jacob H. Adler in *The Reach of Art: A Study in the Prosody of Pope* (Gainesville, Florida 1964), a work demonstrating that despite Pope's flouting of prosodical rules his actual practice shows considerable obeisance to eighteenth-century theory. In a more recent study J. P. W. Rogers scrutinizes Pope's grammar and concludes that 'the nature of his syntax—unambiguous, transparent, compact—was an essential pre-condition of his criticism of the world: for satire, in describing how things stand in relation to one another, demands a language which likewise connects and locates'.[1]

Diction and imagery are more controversial topics and there has been little agreement among critics. Since Pope's time critics have recognized that his poetic diction greatly differed from that of his predecessors, especially Oldham, Rochester and Dryden. More recently, a continuing debate has been brewing about the effects of Pope's diction on his 'poetry of statement', a phrase coined by Mark Van Doren. Geoffrey Tillotson has examined Pope's diction in relation to that of his predecessors and contemporaries,[2] and more recently Max Bluestone, Aubrey Williams, F. W. Bateson, and Maynard Mack have debated Pope's use of metaphor without reaching an acceptable conclusion, except that few critics will ever again read him as a poet of statement. Listed chronologically, their positions spanned a decade: Maynard Mack, '"Wit and Poetry and Pope": Some Observations on his Imagery,' in *Pope and his Contemporaries*, 20–40; two articles by Max Bluestone, 'The Suppressed Metaphor in Pope', *E in C* VIII, 1958, 347–54 and 'Pun and Metaphor and Pope', *E in C* IX, 1959, 440–3; Aubrey Williams, 'Submerged Metaphor in Pope', *E in C* IX, 1959, 197–201, and Bateson's attack on all three positions (*E in C* IX, 1959, 437–9). Pope's imagery in individual poems has been examined,[3] at

---

[1] 'Pope and the Syntax of Satire', in *Literary English Since Shakespeare*, ed George Watson, 1970, 236–65.

[2] 'Eighteenth-Century Poetic Diction', *Essays and Studies by Members of the English Association, 1939* XXV, 1940, 59–80, and *Augustan Studies*, 1961.

[3] For example, the five main images—animal-filth-disease-persecution-virtuous man – of *An Epistle to Arbuthnot*. See Elias F. Mengel Jr.,

times with 'a microscopic eye', and his syntax explored in two important works, again by the late Geoffrey Tillotson: *On the Poetry of Pope* (2nd edn, Oxford 1950),[1] especially chapter 3 on versification, and 'The Methods of Description in Eighteenth- and Nineteenth-Century Poetry', in the *McKillop Festschrift*, 235–238. Elsewhere, Tillotson notes that all the Augustans 'saw as an oxymoron, a cross-hatching, a contradiction in terms . . . To say what they saw inevitably required the couplet' (*Augustan Poetic Diction*, 1964, 15). This may overstate and simplify the case, but it does convey the important point that poets choose forms because something basic to the form coincides with their own view of life. Pope chose the antithetical style of heroic couplets because it permitted him to assert equivalences *as well as* antinomies. Either was insufficient. He wanted to express both.

Allusion, as Reuben Brower has expounded in *The Poetry of Allusion*, is a special province of Pope's poetry, used by him in a unique way for hitherto unknown poetic effects. Most poets are (of course) allusive—Chaucer, Milton, Yeats, T. S. Eliot—but Pope was an innovator. His allusions contribute to a modulation of his tone, especially inflation or deflation, serve to enhance a witty and often parodic context for a particular social world being dissected, and—more conspicuously—place his poetry within the grand context of European literature from Homer and Virgil to Milton and Dryden. No reader will fail to detect the prominent effect of these allusions. The novice need only compare a lyrical ballad by Wordsworth or a sonnet by Keats with the opening lines of *The Rape of the Lock* to note the difference:

> For Dryden and for Pope allusion, especially in ironic contexts, is a resource equivalent to symbolic metaphor and elaborate imagery in other poets. Through allusion, often in combination with subdued metaphors and exquisite images, Pope gets his purchase on larger meanings and evokes the finer resonances by

---

'Patterns of Imagery in Pope's *Arbuthnot*', *PMLA* LXIX, 1954, 189–97; rptd in *E A*.

[1] This book, first published 1938, opened up new possibilities in Pope criticism.

which poetry (in Johnson's phrase) 'penetrates the recesses of the mind'.[1]

Pope's 'purchase on larger meanings' greatly outweighed Dryden's because his advantage was twofold: wit from the context as well as from the allusion itself. This has been ably explained by Earl Wasserman in 'The Limits of Allusion in *The Rape of the Lock*', *JEGP* LXV, 1966, 425–444.

The next phase leads us to the study of larger units, the first of which is the verse paragraph. George Sherburn, in a pioneering article published almost three decades ago,[2] pointed out from an examination of Pope's manuscripts that his procedure in composing poetry seemed to encompass four steps: (1) the composition of initial prose notes, (2) turning the prose into verse paragraphs, (3) arranging the prose notes and verse paragraphs into an effective structure and (4) perfecting the couplets. Pope, an incorrigible reviser who rarely hurried into print,[3] probably worked on several poems at the same time, correcting, rearranging, and rewriting. His verse paragraphs do not enjoy the logical structure of a critical prose treatise, but when completed they happily partake of a felt coherence and sense of shape not usually achieved by poets. Nowhere, in my reading of Pope, have I found these verse paragraphs more splendidly arranged internally or clearly strung together than in the first two epistles of *An Essay on Man*:

> *The bliss of Man (could Pride that blessing find)*
> *Is not to act or think beyond mankind;*
> *No pow'rs of body or of soul to share,*
> *But what his nature and his state can bear.*
> *Why has not Man a microscopic eye?*
> *For this plain reason, Man is not a Fly.*
> *Say what the use, were finer optics giv'n,*
> *T'inspect a mite, not comprehend the heav'n?*

[1] Brower, *Alexander Pope*, viii.

[2] 'Pope at Work,' in *Essays on the Eighteenth Century presented to David Nichol Smith*, Oxford 1945, 49–64.

[3] 'My *Essay on Criticism* was writ in 1709 and published in 1711, which is as little time as ever I let anything of mine lay by me': Spence § 98.

> *Or touch, if tremblingly alive all o'er,*
> *To smart and agonize at ev'ry pore?*
> *Or quick effluvia darting thro' the brain,*
> *Die of a rose in aromatic pain?*
> *If nature thunder'd in his op'ning ears,*
> *And stunn'd him with the music of the spheres,*
> *How would he wish that Heav'n had left him still*
> *The whisp'ring Zephyr, and the purling rill?*
> *Who finds not Providence all good and wise,*
> *Alike in what it gives, and what denies?*   (I, 189–206)

Many such verse paragraphs must be read before the student can acquire a feeling for Pope's execution of the structural unit lying between individual couplets on the one hand, and an entire poem on the other. For the poet the verse paragraph corresponded somewhat to a theme in musical composition and it was his idiosyncratic but nonetheless consummate sense of poetic phrasing in verse paragraphs that added movement and sweep to his larger poetic structures.[1]

At this point the study takes the reader to the poems themselves. All Pope's poetry (with a very few exceptions) is satirical and it is accurate to describe his works as satires; but *satire* is an all-encompassing descriptive term revealing little about the structural principles upon which a poem is composed. To help us to grasp Pope's mods of satire there is Maynard Mack's essay 'The Muse of Satire,' *Yale Review* XLI, 1951, 80–92, describing the three voices of Pope's speaker or persona: the voice of the ethical man of high thoughts and deeds, the *naïf* or *ingénu*, and that of the public defender whose posture and angle of vision are almost always heroic. As Mack notes, 'though the construction in Pope's satires is by no means always so schematic [as in *Satire II i, To Fortescue*], it seems almost invariably to invoke the three voices of the *naïf*, the *vir bonus* [good man], and the hero'. Pope's satires, especially those arranged on formal principles,[2] achieve structural decorum

[1] More must be learned about Pope's methods of composition before we can theorise further about his verse paragraphs. Hopefully much will be learned from Maynard Mack's editing of Pope's extant MSS. See below, Part VI.

[2] For an historical exposition of the theory and practice of the verse

by the poet's attention to the rhetorical cast and mould of his art form, as several full-length studies have shown: Thomas Maresca, *Pope's Horatian Poems* (Ohio State University Press, 1966); Peter Dixon, *The World of Pope's Satires* (1968); John M. Aden, *Something like Horace: Studies in the Art and Allusion of Pope's Horatian Satires* (Vanderbilt University Press, 1969); and especially Howard D. Weinbrot, *The Formal Strain: Studies in Augustan Imitation and Satire* (Chicago, 1969). In addition to rhetoric, Pope's satires are unified by devices ranging from the *adversarius,* or interlocutor, to conversational raillery and the pose of unprecedented sincerity in a *tête-à-tête*, and, not least of all, to the older two-part structure of praise and blame.[1] The poetic strategy in each poem naturally varies, and we see Pope doing different things in such a satire as *The Rape of the Lock*, in which the mock-epic machinery lends the work a different tone from any other Popean satire, and, much later, in satiric epistles like *Arbuthnot* and *Bathurst*. Throughout these works Pope's range of satiric devices is impressive; Professor Weinbrot has stated the case admirably and tersely in *The Formal Strain* (164): 'The Muse of Satire wears many masks.'

In his effort to unravel Pope's art and to experience the pleasure of comprehending a didactic poem like *An Essay on Man*, the reader ought by now to attempt an understanding in depth of the poet's individual works. Of Pope's poems, *The Rape of the Lock* has received, of late, inordinate attention, perhaps because—in addition to its admitted excellence among his satires—it is the poet's work most often taught in colleges and universities all over the world. There are currently no less than three paperback casebooks entirely devoted to the poem—the Macmillan Casebook edited by John Dixon Hunt (1968), a slender volume in the Merrill Literary Casebook Series edited by David

---

epistle before Pope, see Jay Arnold Levine, *S P* LIX, 1962, 658–84, who concludes that Pope's 'full adherence to the rhetorical mode was not without precedence'.

[1] For these techniques see, respectively, Aden, *Something Like Horace* ch i; Dixon, *World of Pope's Satires,* ch ii; Weinbrot's excellent analysis of Pope's 'satiric spectrum', *The Formal Strain*, 129–64; and, for praise and blame, the first four chapters of Rachel Trickett, *The Honest Muse*.

Lougee and Robert McHenry (1969), and the Twentieth Century Interpretations volume edited by G. S. Rousseau (1969)—and several dozen important articles. Ever since its composition in 1711–1712 it has been a favourite among the poet's works. John Dennis, an important critic of the day, unwittingly contributed to its success and lustre of greatness when he attacked it in *Remarks on Mr. Pope's Rape of the Lock*. And later eighteenth-century poets and critics knowingly or unknowingly have continued a cult of its idolatry—Fielding, Dr. Johnson, Goldsmith, and many others. In more recent times the poem has come under the close scrutiny of several astute critics who have explained its mock-epic inflation and deflation, its allusions and their context, the sources of Pope's sylph machinery, his reasons for an expanded five-canto version, and the poet's gamut of images, metaphors, and rhetorical effects ranging from anaphora to zeugma. A few essays are especially deserving of mention and will greatly enhance the pleasure derived by assiduous readers who study their contents: Cleanth Brooks' explication of the poem's symbols—the 'rape' and its sexual overtones—in 'The Case of Miss Arabella Fermor', *The Well-Wrought Urn: Studies in the Structure of Poetry* (New York 1947); William Frost's demonstration of Homeric elements largely derived from the translating activity in which Pope was engaged while composing the poem: '*The Rape of the Lock* and Pope's Homer', *MLQ* VIII, 1947, 342–54; J. S. Cunningham's general explication of the poem in a small volume in the Studies in English Literature series (1961), and Geoffrey Tillotson's description of the circumstances of its composition in his introduction to the Twickenham Edition.[1]

An Essay on Man, Pope's optimistic philosophical poem, poses altogether different problems not the least of which is the search for a context that is historically sound and at the same time does not ravish the artistic meaning of the poem, especially its many elusive couplets. The circumstances of its composition, its dates of publication (1733–4) and

[1] Also recommended is Aubrey L. Williams' study of the glass and vessel imagery, 'The "Fall" of China and *The Rape of the Lock*,' *PQ* XLI, 1962, 412–25, suggesting that this image-constellation indicates the 'utter finality of the loss involved in the breaking of fine China, or of the frail bond of chastity' (418).

reception by Pope's contemporaries, are admirably dealt with by Maynard Mack (Twickenham III, i, xi–lxxx), and more recently by Marjorie Hope Nicolson and G. S. Rousseau, who have produced biographical evidence suggesting that 'the first three epistles of *An Essay on Man* were brought into publishable form under Bolingbroke's roof' in the spring of 1731.[1] As is well known, the poem immediately stirred a controversy on the Continent that raged for over a decade: its principal antagonist was a Swiss professor named J. P. de Crousaz, who attacked Pope on the grounds that his poem was religiously unorthodox, while William Warburton was its chief advocate; the main works were Crousaz's *Examen de l'Essai de M. Pope sur l'Homme* (Lausanne 1737) and, a year later, a *Commentaire sur la traduction en vers de M. l'Abbé du Resnel de l'Essai sur l'Homme* (Paris 1738), and Bishop Warburton's *A Vindication of Mr Pope's Essay on Man* (1739).[2] After Pope's death the poem found many champions, especially Voltaire who considered it the most sublime poem he had ever read, but also adversaries, not the least among them Dr Johnson (who judged it one of Pope's poorest works) and, more recently, John Sparrow in chapter 4 of his *Independent Essays* (1963). The Victorians and Edwardians contributed little towards its appreciation and only since the renascence of eighteenth-century studies after World War II, has there been a complete revaluation of the work. This reappraisal is virtually attributable to the singlehanded efforts of Professor Mack whose edition changed many preexisting notions about the poem and its history. Other scholars, taking their cue from Mack, followed suit, illustrating once again how influential one book can be on an entire generation of scholarship and on the tides of taste. Mack's Twickenham Edition challenged Johnson's superficial recapitulation:

> The *Essay on Man* was a work of great labour and long consideration, but certainly not the happiest of Pope's performances. The subject is perhaps not very proper for poetry, and the poet was not sufficiently master of his subject; metaphysical morality was to him a new study, he was proud of his acquisitions, and,

[1] *This Long Disease, My Life*, 40.
[2] The controversy is studied in detail by Audra in *L'influence francaise* . . .

supposing himself master of great secrets, was in haste to teach
what he had not learned.[1]

It also provided a context of literary and intellectual history for which
scholars had been searching for so long: Aquinas, Erasmus, Bacon,
Montaigne, Pascal, La Rochefoucauld, Charleton, the Cambridge
Platonists, Physico-Theologists and Deists, Shaftesbury, Hutcheson,
William King, to list the most important. A few other works, one pub-
lished before Mack's edition of 1950, are also of paramount interest.
First is Marjorie Nicolson's *Newton Demands the Muse* (Princeton 1946),
a pioneering study of the new astronomical imagery available to poets
like Pope after the publication of Newton's *Opticks* in 1704. In 1966
Miss Nicolson and I returned to this problem with specific reference to
Pope, and provided a background for the first two Epistles of the *Essay*
by demonstrating that Newtonian science was not only available to Pope
but that during his youth he attended lectures on the subject delivered
by William Whiston, Newton's successor at Cambridge University.[2]
Geoffrey Tillotson in *Pope and Human Nature* (Oxford 1958) explicated
the eighteenth-century concept with special reference to the *Essay*, and
B. A. Goldgar examined 'Pope's Theory of the Passions: The Background of Epistle II of the *Essay on Man*' in *PQ* XLI, 1962, 730–43.
The possibility of Lockean influence on the poem has been usefully
debated by Ernest Tuveson and Robert Marsh,[3] who jointly demonstrate that even if Pope had not actually read Locke's *Essay Concerning
Human Understanding*, the philosopher's epistemology was sufficiently
diffused to permeate the intellectual atmosphere in which Pope composed his poem. F. E. L. Priestley,[4] prompted by A. O. Lovejoy's *The
Great Chain of Being* (Cambridge, Mass. 1936) examined the concept of
'the Great Chain of Being' as a central idea and John Laird showed that
Pope, while doubtlessly influenced by Bolingbroke's philosophy, did

[1] *Lives of the Poets,* ed cit III 242–3.

[2] 'Pope and Astronomy', *This Long Disease* 131–239.

[3] In three separate articles: ELH, XXVI, 1959, 368–86; *PQ* XXXIX,
1960, 349–51; *PQ* XL, 1961, 262–9.

[4] 'Pope and the Great Chain of Being', *Essays in English Literature
from the Renaissance to the Victorian Age,* ed Millar MacLure and F. W.
Watt, Toronto 1964, 213–28.

not consistently follow it.[1] Most recently, an entire book which is unfortunately unavailable to me at the time of writing this section—Douglas H. White, *Pope and the Context of Controversy: The Manipulation of Ideas in 'An Essay on Man'* (Chicago 1970) is devoted to the poem.

The Dunciad, Pope's other long poem—his *Homer* will be treated later—poses still other problems. Critics continue to debate and to disagree whether or not it is more than a lampoon. Like all poems, especially long poems, the work is *sui generis*. But its history and growth, its accumulations and additions, its several published versions between 1728 and 1743 (each version manifesting a change of intellectual heart), render it extremely difficult to grasp and explicate this indictment of the perversions of learned discipline, itself an historical event. James Sutherland's monumental Twickenham Edition (1943; rev 3rd edn 1963) is a prerequisite even for those who cannot fully digest its immensely rich contents —and if only to see the formidable *Dunciad* on the page with all its dense apparatus, notes, and commentaries which is an experience—or phantasmagoria in eighteenth-century visual imagery. As this edition amply demonstrates, nothing in the poem's professed original, *A Tale of a Tub*, can compare with its own sprawling apparatus. Here the student will discover much he cares to know about the genesis of this satiric attack on Pope's contemporaries, his epoch, and indeed an entire civilization. The classic critical study of the work[2] is still Aubrey L. Williams' *Pope's 'Dunciad': A Study of its Meaning* (1955), which excels by keeping the poet apart from the poem and by demonstrating how deeply ingrained Pope thought the rule of Dulness was in an age that had debauched and inverted Miltonic values. Other explications enhancing our appreciation include Ian Jack's essay on

---

[1] *Philosophical Incursions into English Literature,* Cambridge 1946, 34–51.
[2] By this term is included all versions from the 1728 three-book poem to *The Dunciad in Four Books* pubd in 1743. In June 1728, about a month after *The Dunciad* first appeared, Pope wrote to Swift to announce that the poem would burlesque serious scholarship and be reprinted 'in all pomp . . . attended with *Proeme, Prolegomena, Testimonia Scriptorum, Index Authorum* and *Notes Variorum*' (*Corr.* II 503)—i.e. the *Dunciad Variorum* of 1729, (facs ed York 1968).

The Dunciad in *Augustan Satire* (Oxford 1952) chapter vii, Robert W.
Rogers' *The Major Satires of Alexander Pope* (Urbana 1955) and Thomas
R. Edwards' 'Light and Nature: A Reading of the *Dunciad*', *PQ*
XXXIX, 1960, 447–63—all concentrating on the satirist's intentions and
the imagery used to achieve his goals in portraying a culture on the
brink of permanent embalmment:

> *Lo! thy dread Empire, CHAOS! is restor'd;*
> *Light dies before thy uncreating word:*
> *Thy hand, great Anarch! lets the curtain fall;*
> *And Universal Darkness buries All.*
>
> (*Dunciad*, IV 653–6)

But the most sympathetic and enlightening piece of criticism I have seen
is Emrys Jones' Chatterton Lecture On An English Poet delivered on
13 November 1968 at the British Academy, simply entitled 'Pope and
Dullness'.[1] His opening remarks appropriately epitomize the status of
criticism in relation to Pope's last great poem:

> The strangeness of Pope's *Dunciad* is a quality that often gets lost
> from sight. During the last few decades criticism has worked so
> devotedly to assimilate the poem and make it more generally acces-
> sible, that, inevitably perhaps, we may now have reached the point
> of distorting it out of its original oddity. The *Dunciad* is both a
> work of art and something else: it is, or was, a historical event, a
> part of literary and social history, an episode in the life of Pope as
> well as in those of his enemies.

Assimilation of the poem has been enhanced, as I have already
indicated, by Professor Sutherland's edition; but no one has explored
it as an historical event—that is, investigated its impact on the future of
literature, the literally hundreds of imitations, attacks, and replies it
generated, and the reasons for its unprecedented popularity in its own
time, not so much as a satiric work of art but as a cultural force and
dynamic energy. This was explored least of all by Pope's contemporaries; Walter Harte's *An Essay on Satire, Particularly on the Dunciad*
(1730) illustrates the point. After 1728 a variety of literary works bearing titles ending with the suffix '*iad*' began to appear: *The Rapiad, The*

[1] *P B A 1968*, 1969, 232–63.

Popiad, The Moor-iad, The Female Dunciad.[1] If the composition of such works reached more or less the proportions of a national pastime among hacks, it also marked the inception of a new type of 'visual' satire, cast into the mould of a lampoon, imitating Pope's very original use of the space surrounding the text of the poem. Consequently, when Mr Jones examines Pope's overt purposes in the poem and concludes that they are manifold—and that these intentions had little, if anything, to do with the poem's extraordinary impact, he is doubtlessly right and is, at the same time, designating a new direction for criticism:[2]

> It seems altogether too simple to think of Pope as a defender of cultural standards confronting an army of midget barbarians. It might be nearer the truth to regard the *Dunciad* as having something of the quality of a *psychomachia*, to see Pope as dramatizing, or trying to reduce to order, his own feelings, which were possibly more divided and mixed than he was willing or able to acknowledge. (234)

The old notion of a unified sensibility in Pope's case is increasingly coming under fire. We are gradually learning that this poet, like other great poets, was torn in many directions, often unknowingly, and that this inner conflict was the driving force that impelled the several alterations of the *Dunciad*. The periodic changes of this work are a manifestation of an energetic impulse reflecting the intensity of allegiances tearing him with racking tension.

IV

The reader who has endured this tortuous road so far and wishes to continue will learn along the way that, although Pope was first and

[1] A good example is the anonymous *Scribleriad* (1742), Augustan Reprint Society, Los Angeles, 1967, ed A. J. Sambrook. Exploiting the unhappy and probably unlikely alliance between Cibber, Pope's newly enthroned dunce, and Lord Hervey, it is distinguished from numerous other similar lampoons by defending Pope. Unfortunately, no checklist of works inspired by *The Dunciad* has yet been compiled.

[2] A similar approach had already been taken by Tony Tanner ('Reason and the Grotesque: Pope's *Dunciad*', *Critical Quarterly* VII, 1965, 145–60—conveniently rptd in *E A 2*) whose focus is on the poem's energy and the radiation of different types of demonic forces.

foremost a poet, he had cultivated other interests ranging from drawing and architecture to gardening and the building of a grotto reputed to be the most picturesque in England. Suppose we begin with Pope's literary activities and then proceed to his other avocations.

Translation—or, imitation, as he might have called it—consumed most of his writing time when he was not composing 'original' poetry. During his youth he translated, paraphrased, and adapted Sappho, Statius, Tibullus, Martial, Boethius, Biblical psalms, Chaucer, Spenser and many others. But this activity was eclipsed by his attraction and dedication to Homeric poetry. A proper assessment of the significance and effect of Homer in Pope's life may be obtained by browsing through Spence's *Anecdotes*,[1] and Pope's correspondence during the years (1715–1720) when he was working most intensively on the *Iliad* and *Odyssey*; and then by reading J. P. Sullivan's representative selection of Pope's critical remarks on ancient authors, especially Homer.[2] In addition the student may find it helpful to consider the widespread reverence for Homer among Pope's contemporaries: in the magnificent gardens at Stowe belonging to Lord Cobham (a friend to whom Pope dedicated his first *Moral Essay*) is a statue of Homer, placed within the Temple of Ancient Virtue. The inscription proclaims him 'the first as well as best of Poets: Whose great and almost peculiar Excellence it was, that he made his Genius entirely subservient to the Cause of Virtue, and her Adherents; instructing Mankind, by the Help of Language universally known, in the godlike Arts of daring nobly, and suffering heroically'.[3] A sense of Pope's rapturous feeling for the ancient bard is conveyed in such works as Rudolf Sühnel's *Homer und die englische Humanität* (Tübingen 1958), Warren's *Alexander Pope as Critic and Humanist*, Douglas Knight's *Pope and the Heroic Tradition* (New Haven 1951), and most succinctly, and perhaps penetratingly, in Reuben Brower's masterful chapter, 'True Heroic Poetry', in his *Alexander Pope*. Matthew Arnold's now classic lectures *On Translating Homer* (1861), despite their shortcomings and inaccuracies, still afford an excellent insight into

[1] See especially §§192–210.
[2] 'Alexander Pope on Classics and Classicists', *Arion* V, 1966, 245–53.
[3] Anon, *A Description of the Gardens of . . . Lord Cobham*, 4th edn Northampton 1747, 15.

the kinds of problems Pope faced as a translator, as does a much briefer essay by Reuben Brower and W. H. Bond in their introduction to Pope's *Iliad* in the Macmillan Classics Series (New York, 1965). Practically all our modern translators of Homer—e.g. Richmond Lattimore, E. V. Rieu, Robert Graves, W. H. D. Rouse, Robert Fitzgerald—have written, at one time or another, about Pope's version[1], but a new study by H. A. Mason stands out for its critical incisiveness and for distinguishing precisely the differences and similarities of Homer's *Iliad* and Pope's.[2] The reception of Pope's Homer has never been gathered into a single volume; it is sufficient here to note that Gibbon's estimate of it as 'a portrait endowed with every merit'[3] has not been universally acclaimed—in fact Gibbon seemed to feel it necessary to qualify his own high praise, and added the words 'excepting that of likeness to its original'. Both translations have met with adversaries, the *Odyssey* more so than the *Iliad*, but most impartial readers, past and present—especially those equipped with a knowledge of eighteenth-century poetry—have rated them highly.

The Classics hold different meanings for different authors, and amongst the Classic authors the jump from Homer to Horace is broader than might first appear. But in the case of Pope this involvement with Homer and Horace reveals a far broader leap. While his Homeric imitation was undertaken in youth and middle age, his Horatian venture occurred late in life, when the poet in his most mature years elected to 'imitate' Horace.[4] The appeal of Horace to Pope, simply stated, is

[1] For a somewhat Empsonian discussion of one passage (*Iliad*, VIII, 553–563) in the hands of seven translators, including Pope, see G. S. Rousseau, 'Seven Types of Iliad', *English Miscellany* XVI, 1965, 143–67. Some important material is also found in M. M. Kelsall, 'What God, What Mortal? The *Æneid* and English Mock-Heroic', *Arion* XVIII, 1969, 359–79.

[2] *To Homer through Pope*, 1972.

[3] *Autobiography* (1907 edn) 27.

[4] Reuben Brower (*Alexander Pope*, 163) goes so far as to claim, 'the single fact that best expresses the difference between Dryden and Pope is the active presence of Horace as a writer and a symbolic figure in Pope's life and poetry'. In addition to Brower's chapter 'The Image of Horace,' much useful material is contained in G. K. Hunter, 'The

that the Roman offered him an opportunity to study man satirically. Whereas Homer symbolized for Pope a mythical and distant world to which he could retreat, Horace—in actuality a poet of retirement—seemed far more contemporary and 'relevant' to Pope's era. If Ovid's *Metamorphoses* gripped the young Pope's imagination and exquisitely revealed how a sylvan landscape inhabited by numinous deities undergoing mysterious Protean transformations could be embraced by a modern poet greatly concerned with the poetic continuity of his *oeuvre*, Horace's *Satires* and *Epistles* gripped him in another way. The Roman, like Pope, lived in an 'Augustan Age,' or at least an age that some men called 'Augustan' as an indication of its superior attainments. While Homer's universe appeared nonpolitical to Pope, Horace's, despite his attempted retreats to the Sabine farm, was just the converse. A long list of antithetical traits could be compiled to demonstrate how the two occupied completely different symbolic zones in Pope's mind. The point briefly to be made here is that his dabbling in Horace—like the Homeric involvement in the two previous decades—was another of his avocations: like gardening, 'Horace'—the real poet and the values he embraced—required cultivation and loving dedication. Pope's thoughtful dedication to the ideals of both poets was widely known among friends and enemies. His attachment was indeed intimate, his regard for them reverential, and he was constantly comparing himself with them in quasi-narcissistic dialogues:

> *There are, who to my Person pay their court,*
> *I cough like* Horace, *and tho' lean, am short,*
> Ammon*'s great Son one shoulder had too high,*
> *Such* Ovid*'s nose, and "Sir! you have an* Eye—"
> *Go on, obliging Creatures, make me see*
> *All that disgrac'd my Betters, met in me:*
> *Say for my comfort, languishing in bed,*
> *"Just so immortal* Maro *held his head:"*

"Romanticism" of Pope's Horace', *E in C* X, 1960, 390–404; Thomas R. Edwards, 'Heroic Folly: Pope's Satiric Identity,' *In Defense of Reading*, ed Reuben A. Brower and Richard Poirier (New York 1962) 191–205; and Maresca, *Pope's Horatian Poems*.

And when I die, be sure you let me know
Great Homer *dy'd three thousand years ago.*

(Epistle to Arbuthnot 115–24)

Much less pleasurable than his symbolic dedication to Homer and Horace was Pope's having been harnessed, as he called it in the Preface to his *Works of Shakespeare*, 'to the Dull Duty of an Editor'. How Pope actually fell into editing is unclear and may have been fortuitous. Whatever the real reasons, he edited the plays of Shakespeare with the help of Gay, Fenton, Dr William Cheselden, and some others, using a fairly extensive collection of early folios and quartos. But the tedium of the task was too much for him and—additionally—he seems to have had little interest in the scientific aspects of editing: emendation, explanation, and restoration of corrupt passages. This was, as James Sutherland writes, because 'Pope himself was the apotheosis of the common reader' and it resulted in an edition (first published in 1725) over which 'there lingers the easy grace of the amateur'.[1] His edition, which is not without some merit, prompted a scathing two-hundred page review by a Grub Street hack, Lewis Theobald, who titled it *Shakespeare Restored: or, a Specimen of the Many Errors, as well Committed, as Unamended, by Mr. Pope* (1726).[2] For this achievement Theobald two years later won himself the role of Pope's chief dunce in *The Dunciad*, which was to immortalize him far more than his criticism of Pope's edition of Shakespeare. Our concern, however, is for Pope, not Theobald, and we are concerned about his endeavours as an editor only in so far as they illuminate the poet. We know that Pope could not muster, either physically or mentally, the energy necessary to wade through learned tomes and perform the drudgery of editing.[3] We also know that his values caused

[1] 'The Dull Duty of an Editor', *RES* XXI, 1945, 202–15; rptd in *E A*. See also John Butt, *Pope's Taste in Shakespeare* (1936). Pope's Shakespeare, prepared for Jacob Tonson, a leading publisher, first appeared in 6 vols: in 1728 in 8, in 1731 and 1735 in 9, and in several other reissues before his death.

[2] See R. F. Jones, *Lewis Theobald* (1919).

[3] Ten years after publication, in 1736, Pope wrote that he undertook the Shakespeare Edition 'merely because he thought no body else would' (Twickenham V 191). Was he telling the truth? Had time dis-

him to place the finest 'spirit, taste, and sense' above textual and scientific exactitude. And we can now perceive why *The Dunciad*, his reply
to men with inferior values like Theobald's, is so much more than
another Brobdingnagian lampoon. What we have yet to recognize fully,
however, is that his experience of editing acted as a catalyst in his
appreciation of a life style and system of values which somehow always
eluded him despite his unswerving approval of such a way of life and
set of values. If his editorial failure taught Pope that his forte was
writing poetry, it also taught him to limit the domain of his aesthetic
ventures. Historical criticism lay outside his field of vision.

His prose, however little of it he wrote, demonstrates this fact even
more clearly. It is hardly worth while comparing him with such great
critics as Dryden or Coleridge, for nothing he composed in prose approaches the former's *Essay of Dramatic Poesy* or the latter's *Biographia
Literaria*. There is the brief preface to his *Works* of 1717, no critical
masterpiece, and the satiric *Peri Bathous: Of The Art of Sinking in
Poetry* (1728), a delightful, if somewhat shallow, work composed in the
heat of his editorial-*Dunciad* phase when verbal excoriation was his
daily menu.[1] Almost a quarter of a century earlier, in 1704, he had
written *A Discourse on Pastoral Poetry* to serve as a brief preface to his
own pastorals, a subject to which he returned in April 1713 in *Guardian*
no. 40. His criticism of epic appeared in various observations included
in the Homeric translations, his Preface to the *Iliad* (1715) conveying a
deep sense of the attachment he felt: it is probably Pope's most inspired
piece of prose. Perhaps of greater import than any except the last
mentioned work is the *Memoirs of the Extraordinary Life, Works, and*

---

coloured his true motives? In an important article, 'Pope's Shakespeare', *JEGP* LXIII, 1964, 191–203, Peter Dixon makes a case that
Pope's editorial preference was for Shakespeare the satirist. One
ponders the possibility that the satirical side of Shakespeare is what
prompted him in the first place and sustained him through the two-
year's experience.
[1] See the edition by Edna Leake Steeves (New York 1952), which
relates the treatise to Pope's rhetorical beliefs and provides a biographical context.

Discoveries of Martinus Scriblerus (first published in 1741 but written much earlier), which Pope edited and had a large hand in writing. This satire on Martinus Scriblerus, a fictional character whose name connotes a penchant for writing and who was supposedly born in Germany (where he inherited pedantic inclinations), was originally the idea of the 'Scriblerus Club'. Dr John Arbuthnot, John Gay, Jonathan Swift, Thomas Parnell, Robert Harley (the Earl of Oxford), and—not least of all—Pope were its members. After several sporadic meetings the Scriblerians decided to write a satire on scientific learning and drew on the professional medical knowledge of Arbuthnot, a high ranking physician. Pope and Swift, the best writers in the Club, were asked to edit and polish the lampoon, a prose work divided into seventeen brief chapters depicting the progress and education of this victim of cultural perversion. In 1950 Charles Kerby-Miller produced a scholarly and sumptuous edition of this work (Yale University Press; reprinted in 1966 by Russell and Russell, New York), containing an extensive introduction tracing the genesis of the work. Pope's other prose writings are conveniently collected in Norman Ault's *The Prose Works of Alexander Pope: Volume I. The Earlier Works, 1711–1720* (Oxford 1936).[1] Ault unfortunately died before the second volume could appear, but nothing included there would have changed our opinion of Pope as a prose writer. The first volume contains Pope's contributions to the *Spectator* and *Guardian*, about two dozen very succinct essays on fashionable topics ranging from city and country life to trivial but witty pieces 'On a Fan', 'On False Criticks,' and, perhaps most amusing of all, 'A Receit to make an Epick Poem'—a cookbook-type recipe which will indubitably enhance the writing skills of its readers.

Pope, unlike Dryden, had little interest in playwriting although he did collaborate with Gay and Arbuthnot in *Three Hours After Marriage* (1717), the only play written by the Scriblerus Triumvirate. It was

---

[1] Containing the best introduction to Pope's prose anywhere. There is now also a paperback edn in the Regents Critics Series: *Literary Criticism of Alexander Pope*, ed Bertrand Goldgar (University of Nebraska Press, 1965). This very useful volume reprints Pope's most important prose criticism, as well as *An Essay on Criticism* and excerpts from his correspondence.

acclaimed in its day,[1] especially by Grub Street, but Pope could not be induced to compose original plays. The poet's antipathy seems to have developed early in life: 'after I had got acquainted with the town,' he told Spence, speaking of London during his early twenties, 'I resolved never to write anything for the stage.'[2] Nor did he swerve from his course in later years. He continued to read new theatrical manuscripts for his friends, gave advice and consent to certain productions, composed—as is well known—prologues and epilogues, and scathingly lambasted actors and managers in his satires. But no artificial respiration—not even Malcolm Goldstein's attempt in his *Pope and the Augustan Stage* (Stanford 1958), can bring to life this fossilized chapter of his career.

Whereas Pope's involvement in prose and the theatre spelled failure, his participation in the arts, especially landscape gardening, architecture, and his grotto, brought him laurels of fame and success, as Dr Sambrook's chapter demonstrates. What is curious in the history of scholarship is the length of time that has elapsed before a meaningful context could be discovered for these activities. It is impossible here to rehearse his many gardening projects, ranging from the assistance he gave to Mrs Howard at Marble Hill and Lord Burlington at Chiswick, to his own mumblings in the letters about broccoli and pineapples, or, again, from his construction of new hothouses to a long and sustained crusade against those who promoted formal gardens without consulting 'the genius of the place'. All these tasks were performed well despite his 'crazy constitution'. And yet his critics, especially in the nineteenth century, made only garbled sense of these ventures. Part of the reason, as Maynard Mack has recently suggested, is that the Romantics misunderstood Pope altogether: 'he *is* a city poet, not simply in the obvious ways they saw, but in deeper ways they failed to see'.[3] Symbolically every garden has as its counterpart a city and every city—a garden. This

---

[1] See George Sherburn, 'The Fortunes and Misfortunes of *Three Hours after Marriage*', *MP* XXIV, 1926, 91–109, and a modern edn and introduction by Richard Morton and W. M. Peterson, Lake Erie College Studies: Painesville, Ohio, 1961.

[2] Spence § 34.

[3] *The Garden and the City*, 4.

was particularly true in Pope's mind and personality, which were permeated with a symbolic appreciation of the difference. At Binfield, then Chiswick, and finally at Twickenham he could celebrate the functions and festivities of the 'gentleman-gardener-farmer', as Professor Mack has called him. Gardening was thus a region of his mind to be tilled like the dewy soil; its plants, flowers, and exotic fruits, like the poet's poems, would illustrate the gardener's virtues and, more importantly, reveal the poet's visionary insight.[1]

Until very recently critics have concerned themselves only about Pope's actual gardening or his literal comments on gardens; but there is now available a vast literature on Pope's literal and psychological gardening. The best studies include such works as George Sherburn's ' "Timon's Villa" and Cannons', *Huntington Library Bulletin* VIII, 1935, 131–5, a study of Pope's relations, especially in landscape gardening, with Lord Burlington; A. Lynn Altenbernd, 'On Pope's "Horticultural Romanticism" ', *JEGP* LIV, 1955, 470–7, exploring Pope's theory of gardening as expressed in his *Moral Essays*, specifically in the *Epistle to Burlington*; the section on Pope and his friends (Kent, Burlington, Bathurst, Ralph Allen) in Edward Malins' *English Landscaping and Literature, 1660–1840* 1966, 26–48; and James M. Osborn's 'Alexander Pope: Apollo of the Arts', in *Papers of the Clark Library Seminars*, ed. T. Swedenberg (Los Angeles 1971), 1–24. Three important, indeed fascinating, essays by Maynard Mack, 'A Poet in His Landscape', 'The Shadowy Cave', and 'Secretum Iter', now constitute the first three chapters of *The Garden and the City*. Pope's activities as a gardener and architect cannot be viewed in isolation from those of his contemporaries, especially since his taste was influenced by them. He knew the work of

---

[1] An example is Pope's swan song to his great friend Swift, wherein he turns to the symbolic side of gardening to make his beckoning call. 'I am as much a better Gardiner, as I'm a worse Poet, than when you saw me: But gardening is near a-kin to Philosophy, for Tully says *Agricultura proxima sapientiae*. For God's sake, why should not you, (that are a step higher than a Philosopher, a Divine, yet have too much grace and wit than to be a Bishop) e'en give all you have to the Poor of Ireland (for whom you have already done every thing else) so quit the place, and live and die with me ?' (*Corr.* IV 6).

Horace Walpole, William Kent, Sir Godfrey Kneller, Charles Bridgeman, James Gibbs, Michael Rysbrack, and others, was also familiar
with the ideas in such treatises as his neighbour Batty Langley's *New
Principles of Gardening* (1728) and Stephen Switzer's *Ichnographia
Rustica* (1718)—indeed moved in social circles in which their taste was
noted.[1] Pope's involvement with architecture, which he told Martha
Blount he loved 'at his heart' (*Corr.* II, 17) has not as yet been fully
explored, nor is it perfectly clear how he related neo-Palladian style,
the rage of the time, to his own projects at Twickenham and elsewhere.
His activities in sculpture are treated in passing by Professor Mack in
The Garden and The City and will be discussed at greater length in a
forthcoming work by Morris Brownell, *Alexander Pope, Virtuoso: A
Poet and the Sister Arts*. Pope started painting as a youth, studied drawing
as a young man in London with Charles Jervas, a well-known drawing
master who was his close friend, and continued to sketch throughout
his middle years.[2] At home and on summer rambles, whether alone or
with aristocratic friends, he would draw sketches, in pencil usually but
also in watercolours, of romantic scenery and natural landscape. If
Pope had taken the Grand Tour and viewed sublime scenery—the
Alps—his sketches as well as his poetry may well have been different;
but he never left England and had to be contented with domestic
prospects. Once, on a summer trip in August 1734, he and Lord Peterborough set out in a dinghy down Southampton Water and picnicked at
Netley Abbey, a ruined Gothic monastery which seized Pope's imagination. 'The place is called Netley', he wrote to his confidante Martha
Blount, 'and is about 2 Leagues from this house [Lord Peterborough's]:
but you must go a good way about to it. I must go another day, &
finish my drawings, which I hope to show you soon.'[3] No trace of these
drawings or many others of Pope's has been found among the poet's

---

[1] For historical background see Selected Bibliography sect V c.
[2] See Norman Ault, 'Mr Alexander Pope: Painter', *New Light on Pope*,
1949, 68–100.
[3] This letter, 11 August [1734], was not available to George Sherburn
but has been printed and annotated by G. S. Rousseau, *PQ* XLV, 1966,
409–418.

remains,[1] an unhappy stroke of fortune, since their examination would certainly help us to understand better his aesthetic interests. Pope was something like Blake in this respect: poetry and painting were sister arts and he more than dabbled in both.[2] Pope's grotto has received so much attention in recent years that it deserves to be endowed with the name of a formal subject—grottology. The grotto underwent so many modifications—(Pope kept expanding and adding to it for two decades) and at the same time symbolized so many different things in his life that an attempt to summarize them in a few sentences is difficult. Perhaps three essays, deftly written, can perform that task better than any summary: Frederick Bracher's 'Pope's Grotto: the Maze of Fancy', *Huntington Library Quarterly* XII, 1949, 141–62, which recounts the tradition of the garden-grotto from the time of the Renaissance and shows how Pope turned his 'into a combination *nymphaeum*, rococo fairyland, and museum for virtuosi' (162); Benjamin Boyce's 'Mr. Pope, in Bath, Improves the Design of his Grotto', in the *McKillop Festschrift*, 143–53, describing Pope's annual changes and showing his attempts to transform the large grotto into a faithful representation of nature; and, finally, Maynard Mack's 'Shadowy Cave', in *The Garden and The City*, a study of the light and dark effects of the grotto, especially as they relate to his 'Verses on a Grotto'—'Pope's grotto', Mack concludes, 'as his imagination plays over it in the *Verses*, clearly defines itself as a point of proud resistance to the corrupt values associated by Juvenal's poem [Satire III] with modern Rome, and by his own poems with modern London and the Court of George II.'[3]

Nothing can vie, not even 'grottology', with Pope's own letters as a source for understanding his life. They fill five large volumes, or two thousand pages, in George Sherburn's monumental edition, extending

---

[1] 'Inventory of Pope's Goods taken after his Death', *N & Q*, 6th ser V, 1882, 363–5, containing *A Catalogue of the Goods at Twickenham*; rptd with annotations as Appendix B of Mack, *Garden and City*, 244–58.

[2] See Jean Hagstrum, *The Sister Arts*, Chicago 1958, ch viii, and W. K. Wimsatt's brilliant *Portraits of Alexander Pope*, New Haven 1965, which contains *en passant* much information about Pope's handling of the brush.

[3] 74–76.

from the first chatterings of youth to the muffled mutterings of old age. Like Keats', it is a great correspondence; not penetrating, perhaps, to the depth of that Romantic's 'negative capability' or descriptions of the 'egotistical sublime', but soaring to another kind of confessional truth about himself. The letters are witty and polished, elegant in their phrasing and their calligraphy (see plate 13). If they occasionally demonstrate conceit in the form of self-conscious dignity, they still portray Pope in a more perfect image of himself, to paraphrase his preface to the 1737 edition, than anything else he wrote. Compared with the correspondence of his contemporaries—Swift, Lady Mary, Horace Walpole, Lord Chesterfield, Samuel Richardson—his letters are more personable and revelatory of the life they describe. Precisely such comparison led George Sherburn to comment with cautious gravity in the introduction to his edition that 'in his own century no man did more to further the art of letter writing'—a rhapsodic generalization that might well be viewed with scepticism had it issued from the pen of another man; but Sherburn had hunted for, tracked down, read, edited, and annotated each and every one of Pope's letters and had read all other important eighteenth-century English correspondence as well. In contrast to this well calculated estimate is the ill-considered derogation of Elwin and Courthope: 'dry and frigid generalities'—derogation bred from misunderstanding and compounded by prejudice. If the Victorians had actually read Pope's letters, they would have discovered far greater emotion, passion, and feeling than the 'cool rationality' they expected to find. Here is Pope to Lady Mary:

> I fancy myself, in my romantic thoughts & distant admiration of you, not unlike the man in the Alchymist that has a passion for the Queen of the Faeries. I lye dreaming of you in Moonshiny Nights exactly in the posture of Endymion gaping for Cynthia in a Picture. And with just such a Surprise and rapture should I awake, if after your long revolutions were accomplishd, you should at last come rolling back again, smiling with all that gentleness and serenity (peculiar to the Moon and you) and gilding the same Mountains from which you first set out on your solemn, melancholy journey.   (*Corr.* I 439–40)

One year earlier, on 10 November 1716, he disclosed this sentiment to the same woman:

The more I examine my own mind, the more Romantick I find myself: Methinks it is a noble Spirit of Contradiction to fate and fortune, not to give up those that are snatched from us, but follow them with warmer Zeal, the farther they are removd from the sence of it. . . . I cannot be satisfied with strowing flowers over you, & barely honoring you as a thing lost; but must consider you as a glorious, tho' remote Being, & be sending Addresses and prayers after you. . . . Let them say I am Romantick, so is every one said to be that either admires a fine thing, or praises one.

(*Corr.* I 367)

Hardly 'dry and frigid generalities'! If anything, Pope tends in these musings, like Yeats much later, to want to show off his 'Romantick' side. He viewed letters, especially to women, as rhapsodies in which the tenderest emotions and deepest philosophical intimations could be expressed clandestinely.[1]

The history of the publication of Pope's correspondence is almost as intriguing as their contents. Briefly, the events are as follows. Edmund Curll, perhaps the most notoriously unethical publisher of the period, advertised in 1735 for documentary materials for a biography of Pope; Pope surreptitiously sent him a highly expurgated and incomplete set of his letters, copies of which he had kept over the years. When Curll published them as the authentic letters Pope claimed they were spurious and set out to rectify the gross injustice by publishing another version which he claimed were genuine. This summary of events, to be sure, omits the piquant details and does not explain that Pope throughout this episode revealed his most enigmatic personality and was virtually as dishonest as Curll—for he carefully edited the letters he printed, altering their phrases and (occasionally) the names of their recipients.[2] But it does set the stage for the drama surrounding the publication of

[1] But there are also intimate disclosures to men. 'This letter (like all mine) will be a Rhapsody': Pope to Swift, 28 November 1729, *Corr.* III 79.

[2] The complicated story is related in Maynard Mack, 'The First Printing of the Letters of Swift and Pope', *The Library* XIX, 1939, 465–85; Vinton Dearing, 'New Light on the First Printing of the Letters of Pope and Swift', *The Library* XXIII, 1943, 74–86; and Sherburn's introduction to *Corr.*

the letters of the foremost poet of his age.[1] Readers who are interested
in this drama can do no better than read Sherburn's introduction to the
Correspondence, as well as John Butt's essay, 'Pope Seen Through His
Letters', in *E-CEL*, 62-67, showing how these 1500 letters afford insight
into a most puzzling figure. Another approach is taken by Donald F.
Bond in 'The Importance of Pope's Letters', *MP* LVI, 1958, 55-9,
which establishes guidelines for successive editions and appraises the
efficacy of these documents for a study of Pope's era. An example of the
reliance of modern biographers on these letters is seen in the volume by
Nicolson and Rousseau, *This Long Disease, My Life*, a medical case
history of the poet's life which could not have come into being without
Sherburn's labours. Since 1956 many new letters have come to light and
have been published in various journals. They are listed, together with
their places of publication, in the *New CBEL*, vol. II (1971). No doubt,
additional letters will be discovered over the years, and we may be
confident that the revealing ones, as in Sherburn's collection, will cor-
roborate Pope's penchant for establishing friendship by 'talking on
paper'.

V

The student should now be sufficiently well versed in Popeana to
brave it on his own and seek answers to specialized questions. He may
be pondering such seemingly arcane questions as, what was Pope's
favourite colour, where are the manuscripts of his poems, what has
happened to his library? Did he like animals? Has anyone gathered a
truly definitive or merely a superficial bibliography of the many editions
of his works? He favoured red, especially in bookbinding, and few
objects pleased him so much as morocco bindings. His manuscripts
survive on several continents and more ought to be said about them.
Little is known about the contents of his library at Twickenham and no
catalogue has been discovered, nor is he known to have kept one. He
showed no affection for cats, but he adored dogs, especially the breed of
Great Dane, one of which in fact was to be found in his household

[1] Only 150 were published by Pope during his lifetime, about one-tenth
the number in Sherburn's collection.

continually, generation after generation, always bearing the name Bounce, and celebrated in his letters and poems. Several bibliographies have been gathered and offer a field day for those who enjoy detective work of an intricate nature.

Much more may be said about these and other similar matters, each of which singly gives a semblance of little importance, but when appraised collectively illuminates the portrait of an artist with a piercing vision of humankind. It would be an unforgivable omission, for example, for the guide not to explain as Norman Ault has,[1] why Pope was so fond of dogs and why the books in his library must have meant so much to him; a writer recounting Pope's life, moreover, would wish to comment on characteristic moments, such as the one in which he expressed a passing mood to his great friend Gay while composing in solitude at Twickenham early drafts of *An Essay on Man*:

> I am something like the Sun at this Season, withdrawing from the World, but meaning it mighty well, and resolving to shine whenever I can again. But I fear the Clouds of a long Winter will overcome me to such a degree, that any body will take a farthing candle for a better Guide, and more serviceable companion. My Friends may remember my brighter days, but will think (like the *Irishman*) that the *Moon* is a better thing when once I am gone. I don't say this with any allusion to my Poetical capacity as a Son of *Apollo*, but in my Companionable one, (if you'll suffer me to use a phrase of the Earl of *Clarendon*'s) For I shall see or be seen of few of you, this Winter. I am grown too faint to do any good, or to give any pleasure. I not only, as *Dryden* fairly says, *Feel my notes decay* as a Poet, but feel my Spirits flag as a Companion, and shall return again to where I first began, my Books. (*Corr.* III 135).

Pope was actually not so bookish as his adversary Lewis Theobald, nor as his neighbour Horace Walpole, who also lived in occasional seclusion at nearby Strawberry Hill, but he probably spent as much time in his library composing poetry as his neighbour spent in antiquarian researches. Present-day knowledge would be enhanced sizeably if the many books Pope owned, marked up, and read, suddenly were to come to light, but such a desideratum will probably remain unless, by a stroke

---

[1] 'Pope and his Dogs', *New Light on Pope*, 337–50.

of luck, a catalogue of these books is miraculously unearthed.[1] Austin Warren's *Alexander Pope as Critic and Humanist*, still deemed a landmark of Pope scholarship four decades after its publication, is all we have: his chapter, 'An Englishman's Reading in His Own Literature,' teaches us how extensively Pope read the 'Gothic' masters of his own tongue as well as the ancient classics—an important point that needed highlighting in the nineteen–twenties when the poet, whose image still lingered in the throes of Victorian opprobrium, was primarily viewed as an enemy of the 'spontaneous overflow of emotion' and a staunch defender of the ancients.

Unfortunately, the answers to these various questions and the amplification of points raised in mere passing cannot be amply treated here, but two areas deserve more than perfunctory comment: Pope's poetic manuscripts and the state of his bibliography today. If he were not such a compulsive reviser, his manuscripts would not command the unusual interest they hold for all students of poetic craftsmanship. Moreover, Pope's best poetry is a sufficiently large corpus in itself to merit, indeed necessitate, some guidance through the labyrinth of editions that appeared during and after his lifetime. R. H. Griffith's *Alexander Pope: A Bibliography* (2 vol, Austin, Texas 1922–1927; reissued London 1968) is the standard descriptive bibliography of Pope's writings from 1709 to 1751. Three additions to this important piece of scholarship, adding to its immense learning and correcting some of its details, will satisfy the demands of the most exacting students of descriptive bibliography.[2]

The survival of Pope's manuscripts is no less fascinating a chapter in history than the rest of his remains, whether his own or others' (e.g., the more than two hundred portraits studied by W. K. Wimsatt in

[1] At present one must cull the available information from Sherburn's index to *Corr.*, Osborn's index to Spence's *Anecdotes*, and Warren's study mentioned below. Allen Hazen's recent *Catalogue of Horace Walpole's Library*, 3 vol, New Haven 1969, is a perfect example of what the scholar dreams of having for Alexander Pope.

[2] See W. B. Todd, 'Concealed Pope Editions', *Book Collector* V, 1956, 48–52; D. F. Foxon, *ibid* 277–9; K. I. D. Maslen, 'New Editions of Pope's *Essay on Man* 1745–1748', *Publications of the Bibliographical Society of America* LXII, 1968, 177–88.

The Portraits of Alexander Pope); or, to turn to another area altogether, than the intriguing story of the publication of his letters in 1737, both the so-called 'pirated' and the allegedly 'authentic' edition. An almost complete list of these manuscripts was compiled and published by the late Professor John Butt in his Warton Lecture on English Poetry for 1954, printed in *PBA* XL, 23–39 (and reprinted in *EA*). Butt, in studying these manuscripts, scattered far and wide, listed the present locations of fifty-five autograph manuscripts and also suggested dates of composition for each. A gleaning of this important study will immediately reveal that no manuscripts of *The Rape of the Lock*, *Eloisa to Abelard*, the *Epilogue to the Satires*, for example, and several other important poems are known to survive; but this deficiency notwithstanding, Butt sensibly remarks 'how fortunate should we be if we could claim that even one poem had survived in the handwriting of Spenser or Donne or Dryden'. Pope readers everywhere must take heart at this encouragement. The actual reasons for the mysterious disappearance of certain manuscripts—all Pope's poems existed in his handwriting in the eighteenth century—and the survival of others are complicated, indeed too involved to be related in this chapter, but one brief example may serve to illustrate the often devious way in which individual manuscripts have travelled in a network not always controlled by scholars or collectors.

This regards the history of a unique copy of the first edition of *The Dunciad* containing Pope's own corrections, comments and additions in his handwriting. The history of this volume immediately following Pope's death in 1744 is unknown, but by 1777 Nathaniel Chauncy had inherited it together with other books and manuscripts from the enormous library of his brother, Dr Charles Chauncy, a wealthy London physician. In 1790 Nathaniel sold a large part of his inheritance, possibly including Pope's *Dunciad* manuscript;[1] whether or not he actually disposed of it in 1790, the book was not heard of again until 1889, at which time it curiously appeared together with the extensive collec-

---

[1] No record of its sale appears in the British Museum copy of the catalogue of the Chauncy Sale (Press Mark SCC 15.9 and 7004. cc. 10). See also the public announcement of the general contents of the sale in the *Gentleman's Magazine* LX, January 1790, 87.

tion of *orientalia* of William Nassau Lees, an Asiatic scholar. It turned up at Christie's on 30 July 1889 (Lees had died on 9 March) as lot 354 B, 'Autograph Manuscripts of Alexander Pope; From the Library of Dr Charles Chauncy', where it was sold with the manuscripts of *An Essay on Criticism, An Essay on Man,* and several of the *Moral Essays.* Its inclusion in the Nassau Lees sale does not imply that it was ever owned by Colonel Lees but merely that Christie's sold it with his estate. At this sale it was purchased for £16 by one Harvey,[1] a London dealer who had a shop at 4 St James's Street. Harvey, according to clients still alive who bought from him in the twenties and early thirties, was un unmarried Englishman, somewhat eccentric, who lived in North London. When, in the autumn of 1939, the possibility of a German air invasion of London was looming large, it may well have occurred to him to move the least expendable items in his shop, of which the precious *Dunciad* manuscript was one, to safer—and more remote—grounds. Did Harvey remove it to his Hampstead flat? That is the question, for Hampstead was not bombed whereas central London, including the St James's area, eventually was. Shortly after the Second War Harvey died and nothing more has been uncovered about the rare *Dunciad* volume. Might he have accidentally left it in St James's Street to be destroyed by the Germans? Was it sold with the rest of his collections? Was it hidden somewhere in North London and afterwards lost? Is it in the hands of one who is biding time in the hope that prices will further soar? Contrarily, is it buried deep in some collection, private or public, as were the Boswell papers until 1949, concealed without the owner's awareness of its identity? There are other enticing possibilities, not one of which has offered the slightest clue: all we know is that every trace of the manuscript disappeared after Harvey purchased it in 1889, and that today, almost a century later, it still has not come to light.

In the early sixties, when I first became interested in Pope's manuscripts, I wrote to John Butt about this mysterious copy of *The Dunciad,* asking him additionally about other strange disappearances of manuscripts formerly known to exist. We tossed the matter back and forth

[1] Manuscript records of Christie, Manson & Woods, Year 1889, 12.

for several years, until Butt concluded that the study of Pope's manu-scripts was still in its infancy. On 26 November 1964, shortly before his death in Edinburgh, Butt wrote to me:

> I do not think the question you ask about the disappearance of MSS has been asked before, nor for that matter has anyone en-quired why Pope MSS have survived. Some have survived be-cause in the first place Pope recognized their value as a record of rejected readings, and handed them for collation to Jonathan Richardson who preserved them. But Richardson also preserved for the same reason other MSS that have since 'disappeared,' notably the mysterious MS of *The Dunciad* known to Elwin and Courthope.[1] Others I suspect to have been preserved as 'keep-sakes' out of pure affection for the poet by his noble friends, in-cluding those MSS which now belong to the Duke of Devonshire and the Marquess of Bath. This offers a line of enquiry, i.e. whether the modern descendants of Pope's friends still happen to preserve other MSS.

Butt's suggested 'line of enquiry' has still not been undertaken, certainly not in America, nor in Britain among private collectors other than the noblemen mentioned in the appendix of his Warton Lecture. There are, moreover, other avenues of exploration regarding the his-tory of manuscripts prior to their recent sales: for example, what hap-pened to the Chauncy *Dunciad* between 1790 and 1889, when it strangely arrived at the Nassau Lees sale?[2] These and other perplexing questions remain, opening thereby a whole new area of Pope studies perhaps as enthralling as reconstruction of his 'villa' and garden at Twickenham or his grotto with a view of the Thames. A taste of the detective-like thrill of tracking down lost eighteenth-century manu-scripts is obtained by dipping into James L. Clifford's recent delight-ful book *From Puzzles to Portraits* (University of North Carolina Press, 1970), especially the chapter entitled 'Finding the Evidence'. Clifford, primarily a Johnson scholar, has scoured Great Britain for manuscripts pertaining to the Doctor; if such a systematic search were undertaken

---

[1] I.e., the same manuscript discussed in the above paragraph.
[2] A fuller account is given in my forthcoming article, 'The "Chauncy" MSS of *The Dunciad*, 1729–1939: A Tale of Two Centuries.'

for Pope there is no telling what might turn up—possibly even the lost Chauncy manuscript.

If such manuscripts were discovered, they would require editing, as do the existing manuscripts, and, after that, serious study. The Antean-like Maynard Mack has undertaken the Herculean labour of publishing all the known manuscripts of Pope, one of which has already appeared, his splendid Roxburghe Club Edition of *An Essay on Man: Reproduction of the Manuscripts in the Pierpont Morgan Library and the Houghton Library, with the Printed Text of the Original Edition* (Oxford 1962), printed on heavy paper and containing an introduction spelling out the value of such a far-flung—and expensive!—undertaking.[1] As Mack reasonably points out, only by careful scrutiny of the evolution of a poem will critics be able in Pope's case to arrive at a satisfactory understanding of the poet's meaning, both his craft and ideas. An example are the three opening verse paragraphs of *An Essay on Criticism* which underwent radical reshaping during the decade between 1708 and 1717, as R. M. Schmitz's study of the Bodleian manuscript, the only one known to survive, abundantly shows.[2] Pope rewrote the first verse paragraph several times, refined and sharpened the antithesis between 'Wit' and 'Judgment' in the second, and in the third inserted and then deleted three Latin quotations (two from Quintilian and one from Petronius); even more significant, he omitted the following passage on the grounds that its scientific allusions were either too stale and obscure, or too revolting for the common reader:

> *Many are spoil'd by that* pedantic *throng,*
> *Who with great pains teach youth to reason wrong.*
> Tutors, *like* Virtuoso's, *oft inclin'd*
> *By strange* transfusion *to improve the mind,*
> *Draw off the sense we have, to pour in* new;
> *Which, yet, with all their skill, they ne'er could do.*

Perhaps the transfusion of one animal's blood into another's was in

---

[1] A very few copies of this privately printed edn came on the market in 1962 at about £50.
[2] See *Pope's Essay on Criticism, 1709: A Study of the Bodleian Manuscript Text with Facsimiles, Transcripts, and Variants* (St. Louis 1962).

Pope's estimate a sufficiently grotesque image to be deleted from a poetic passage about learning in critics, and fools 'in search of *Wit*' (but, then, why did he originally compose and include the passage?). Whatever may have been Pope's real reasons for the change, the Bodleian manuscript alone can help us begin to discover them. Pope's extant manuscripts may not provide the answer to every mysterious passage or oblique allusion, but they do offer readers the surest clue to observation of the poet's mind in progress throughout what was usually a protracted time of composition.

I have intentionally wandered somewhat afield on the grounds that few subjects are as important for serious readers as Pope's manuscripts. An ancillary aid, secondary check lists, also requires mention, although much more abbreviated. For the first half of the century there is J. E. Tobin's *Alexander Pope: A List of Critical Studies Published from 1895 to 1944* (New York, 1945) and now a companion volume by Cecilia L. Lopez, *Alexander Pope: An Annotated Bibliography 1945–1967* (Gainesville, Florida 1970), thus omitting only the last five years, 1968–1972. The annual July issues of *Philological Quarterly* still publish a *catalogue raisonné* of all Pope scholarship for the previous year, and a new journal, *The Scriblerian*, published in Philadelphia and exclusively devoted to the Pope-Swift circle, publishes short comments and reviews on every item, whether a note or long essay, dealing with Pope.

VI

What remains but an estimate of Pope's achievement within the tradition of great English poetry and, more generally, all poetry? In poetic craftsmanship Pope's attainment is paramount, and one can justly conclude that he reaped from his medium all that it had to offer. But craft is not everything, as the Romantics and French symbolist poets knew and demonstrated in their critical writings. Poetry must be elevated to the realm of truth to have lasting influence. What, then, about Pope's far-reaching vision—his sense of man in all his moments of strength and frailty? And what conclusions can be drawn regarding Pope's vision of his immediate culture, its possibilities, its attainments and limitations, its role within the larger contours of history?

> *In vain, in vain,—the all-composing Hour*
> *Resistless falls: The Muse obeys the Pow'r.*
> *She comes! she comes! the sable Throne behold*
> *Of* Night *Primaeval, and of* Chaos *old!*
> *Before her,* Fancy's *gilded clouds decay,*
> *And all its varying Rain-bows die away.*
> Wit *shoots in vain its momentary fires,*
> *The meteor drops, and in a flash expires.*
> *As one by one, at dread Medea's strain,*
> *The sick'ning stars fade off th' ethereal plain;*
> *As Argus' eyes by Hermes' wand opprest,*
> *Clos'd one by one to everlasting rest;*
> *Thus at her felt approach, and secret might,*
> Art *after* Art *goes out, and all is Night.*
>
> (*Dunciad IV*, 627–40)

So ends *The Dunciad in Four Books*, Pope's last will and testament, his most apocalyptic vision and foreboding prognostication, but also— as the desperately sickened tone of these lines indicates—his harsh indictment of an entire epoch composed of supposedly enlightened 'Augustans' whom Pope aggregately called 'dullards' and 'dunces'— and hence his *Dunciad*. His tone of voice in this passage is resigned, no longer the ranting and rasping shrill curses and screams evident in *An Epistle to Dr. Arbuthnot* ('Sporus, that mere white Curd of Ass's milk') or *An Essay on Man* ('. . . drop into thyself, and be a fool!'). Such resignation, like the supine capitulation of Brecht or Hesse in their calmer moments, signifies Pope's calculated intention of leaving posterity with only *these* words, and in doing so he reveals himself every bit as prophetic as Blake or Yeats, for '*This is the way the world ends / Not with a bang but a whimper.*' All that remains for Pope until 'Universal Darkness buries All' is for 'Art after Art' to be obliterated: philosophy, metaphysics, mathematics, even the greater arts, not always thought to be such, religion and morality, until no '*human* Spark is left':

> *Lo! thy dread Empire, CHAOS! is restor'd;*
> *Light dies before thy uncreating word:*

> *Thy hand, great Anarch! lets the curtain fall;*
> *And Universal Darkness buries All.*
>
> > (*Dunciad IV*, 653–6)

This pair of couplets is Pope's last, and is as deliberate as the rest of his writing and poetic career. Their dark gloom and irredeemable finality mirror Pope's unflinchingly urgent sense that his culture in 1740 stood at the brink of the precipice. Nowhere else in his poetic *oeuvre* does he use the powerful word 'Anarch' except here[1] and its consequent uniqueness gathers tremendous attention and lends it a weighty gravity paralleled only by the melodramatic fall of 'the curtain' of civilization. Once such ravishment has befallen, 'Universal Darkness' pervades, covering the whole globe in Miltonic chaos where nothing is distinguishable.

The incredible aspect of Pope's epilegomenon in *The Dunciad* is not its dramatic bravura or chiselled couplets. Every reader of Pope knows that he was a master craftsman whose repertoire included these and many other startling poetic techniques. It is rather the complexity of his last phrase, 'great Anarch', which stuns and shows the pulse and rhythm of his thinking. For the last fifteen years of his life—and probably longer—Pope's imagination had dwelled perpetually on the subject of politics, as his mature poetry demonstrates, and we may be certain that his use here of a politically charged term, 'great Anarch', is highly significant. For Pope, the unrelenting enemy of culture, the indubitable abettor of chaos, is not merely anti-civilization—that would be tautology at best—but rather a complex constellation of political, cultural, and artistic figureheads who had permitted such miasma (to sustain one of Pope's dominant images throughout *The Dunciad*) to spread, and so much polluted verbal detritus to accumulate. Men of power—including Walpole, much of the Court of George II, the various Poets Laureate, and all 'Grub-Street'—represented the compo-

---

[1] Pope used the word 'anarchy' twice: in *Dunciad*, I, 14, 'She rul'd, in native Anarchy, the mind', and in *An Essay on Man*, III, 186, 'And Anarchy without confusion know'. See Edwin Abbott, *A Concordance to the Works of Alexander Pope*, London and New York 1875, which is incomplete and frequently inaccurate.

site 'enemy,' and it is to them as forcefully as to the remote future ages of man that Pope speaks in these final lines.

I am therefore amazed to discover learned students of the period chastising Pope for the narrowness of his vision because of a failure—so the argument goes—to speak out, loudly and unequivocally, against these weighty oppressors of culture. Such chastisers often postulate that Pope harshly reproved artistic mediocrity but never social or economic plutocracy. Two recent examples come to mind. At the last International Congress of Eighteenth-Century Studies held in Nancy during July 1971, Louis Kampf, a professor of modern literature at MIT whose knowledge of the Georgians, both their literature and culture, is not inconsiderable, presented a paper entitled 'The Humanistic Tradition in Eighteenth-Century England', part of the abstract of which follows:

> The historian of English literature ordinarily thinks of Swift and Pope as engaged in an heroic struggle to save civilization: the former attempts to bring order to chaos, the latter to save common sense from universal darkness. The scholars who have created this picture have done so by ignoring the thought of the Enlightenment and the historical conditions from which it emerged. Pope, Swift, and the other major literary figures in eighteenth-century England were fighting a rear-guard action against the Enlightenment. They opposed its political, philosophical and literary ideas; they attacked developments in science; they reviled—from an aristocratic stance—the bourgeoisie as a class; they ridiculed political democracy; and persecuted those writers who tried to write for the new and growing reading public.[1]

Nothing could be farther from the truth in Pope's case. And to criticize him for not living in France and espousing the philosophies of Voltaire, Diderot, and other *philosophes* is as patently ridiculous as condemning Bertrand Russell for not resettling in South Africa in order to engage in the fight against apartheid. While most of Kampf's argu-

---

[1] See 3ème *Congrès International des Lumières*, Nancy, France 1971, 'Résumés des Communications: Summaries,' 62–3. Parts of this address have now appeared in L. Kampf, 'The Humanist Tradition in Eighteenth-Century England—and Today,' *New Literary History* III, Autumn 1971, 157–70.

ments have recently been adequately refuted by literary historians, his tenuous notion that Pope in particular, among the Georgians, championed the aristocracy, 'from an aristocratic stance', requires some comment, if for no other reason than to demonstrate how such myths about this poet's political *Weltanschauung* have arisen and continue to arise. Such a notion is as obsolescent as it is untrue; as unfounded and historically suspicious as Jacob Viner's recent indictment of the Age of Pope, especially its two greatest satirists, Pope and Swift, for not using their 'sacred weapon'—satire—to extirpate the 'continuous and profound complacency among the English upper classes with respect to the economic structure of English society'.[1] One might as well accuse the papacy today of failing to champion the cause of sexual liberation among Roman Catholic nuns and priests: in theory such a deed is not so preposterous as first appears, but considered within the context of the history of the Catholic Church and of recent pastoral reform, the idea is ludicrous. Pope, to answer Kampf, simply did not know many of the ideas of the French *philosophes*; and even if he could have, he was so relentlessly concerned with, even obsessed by, the decline of artistic excellence and the decay of taste, so profoundly impressed by the admittedly egocentric notion that his own 'art' might ameliorate significantly this seemingly drastic situation, that he imposed upon himself, as if in quarantine, a strict isolation from all other social dilemmas. Such imposed discipline should not suggest he had not dwelled upon politics. He had. But another realm seemed more important, its rehabilitation more urgent. Pope, furthermore, to counter Viner's argument, did everything a frail dwarf wielding a virulent pen could do. The five volumes of Pope's published correspondence are *prima facie* evidence that he lost no opportunity to blast the aristocracy and dislodge them, even when courting them for favours (as was his wont), from their 'continuous and profound complacency'. Are not Pope's *Moral Essays* and *Imitations of Horace* literary bomb-shells intent upon toppling the aristocracy from its 'complacent' vantage? And even the deceptively aloof *Essay on Man*, especially its 'Epistle IV. Of the Nature and State of

---

[1] Jacob Viner, 'Satire and Economics in the Augustan Age of Satire,' in *Augustan Milieu*, 100.

Man, with respect to Happiness'—what are its most climactic moments
if not scathing attacks on the aristocratic segments of society, which
thrive on 'Vice' and exist to pervert and subvert 'Virtue':

> *Stuck o'er with titles and hung round with strings,*
> *That thou may'st be by kings, or whores of kings.*
> *Boast the pure blood of an illustrious race,*
> *In quiet flow from Lucrece to Lucrece;*
> *But by your father's worth if yours you rate,*
> *Count me those only who were good and great.*
> *Go! if your ancient, but ignoble blood*
> *Has crept thro' scoundrels ever since the flood,*
> *Go! and pretend your family is young;*
> *Nor own, your fathers have been fools so long.*
> *What can ennoble sots, or slaves, or cowards?*
> *Alas! not all the blood of all the HOWARDS.*

(IV, 205–16)

Henrietta Howard, Countess of Suffolk, was in fact the King's
whore, as Pope's blatantly crass line indicates, and here, as in numerous
other 'purple passages' in his greatest and most mature poetry, Pope uses
his 'sacred weapon' to damn, not mollify, the aristocracy, the Court,
the upper classes. This is the same Pope who had been commenting for
at least three decades on 'the Emptiness of the Court', who affirmed
again and again to his most intimate correspondents—Swift, Gay,
Bethel—that 'in England virtue dwells not with power' and sorely
complained about the lack of 'honest men' among noblemen and aristocrats, who damned Parliament as 'the devil's divan' and called the King's
poet and historiographer 'the two greatest liars in literature'.[1] Through-

---

[1] *Corr.* I 427; III 101; IV 423–424; IV 440. Dozens of similar sentiments
and phrases can be culled from Pope's correspondence. It is ironic,
moreover, that Pope's pronouncements against the Establishment,
especially the aristocracy, made so little impression on his contemporaries. But a close reading of his letters shows more evidence anti-
rather than pro-Establishment. Typical are the myths that arose during
his life and shortly after his death about his relation to Lord Bolingbroke. Thomas Birch, historian of the Royal Society, wrote to Philip
Yorke, the 2nd Earl of Hardwicke, on 5 October 1754: 'Pope's Excess

out 'this long Disease, my Life' Pope cultivated the Senecan friendship of certain aristocrats (like Bathurst, Burlington, Oxford and Peterborough), but he also reproved them and, upon occasion, even savaged them at the expense of incurring personal damage. He viewed the Court, its sun and satellites, King and ministers, as spreading disease throughout England and wrote to Swift on two different occasions, just in case the drift of his argument was overlooked, 'Courts I see not, Courtiers I know not, Kings I adore not, Queens I compliment not; so am never like to be in fashion, nor in dependence' (*Corr.* II 469; III 367). If he indulged the personal vanities of some noblemen, he mercilessly trounced the conceits and pretensions of others, rightfully boasting to one of the most influential noblemen of the day, Lord Carteret, that 'I take my self to be the only Scribler of my Time, of any degree of distinction, who never receiv'd any Places from the Establishment, any Pension from a Court, or any Presents from a Ministry.'[1] Nor was he deceiving himself about his stance as a public poet, as he often did with regard to aspects of his private life. He, unlike Gay, had no patronizing Duchess of Queensberry, and unlike Swift, no political party to please; and when he spoke out against the oppressor—the upper classes composed of 'sots, or slaves, or cowards' more often than any other group—his tone was not only acidulous and harsh but resolute and adamant in its sense of finality. 'Once more I tell you', he ranted to Allen almost at the end of his life, that 'I am sick of *this* World & the Great ones of it, tho they have been my intimate Acquaintance;' and to Bethel, the man after Swift to whom his sincerest disclosures were

---

of Admiration of Lord Bolingbroke is genuinely rallied; & a saying of his recorded, that his L[ordship] was a Superior Being, who did not originally belong to this System of ours; & when the last Comet appear'd, & came pretty near the Earth, Mr. Pope us'd to tell his acquaintance, that he should not be surprised, if in the Event it proved, that it was sent only to convey his L[ordship] home again.' See BM Add MSS 35,398 f 221.

[1] *Corr.* II 160, 16 February 1723. On 13 July 1723 Pope wrote to Gay, 'those we call Great Men . . . are really the most Little Creatures in the world' (*Corr.* II 181). The context of this passage is the aristocracy, especially Burlington House, where Gay was then residing.

uttered *tout-de-bon,* he abjured his own 'Englishness', noting that England is as 'profligate & poor' as the 'rest of Europe . . . where a few Kings have wealth, & a few Nobles the rest, to the Bloodshed or Slavery of the People' (*Corr.* IV 431, 396). This slavery constantly hovers as a theme in Pope's poetry and may have hovered as a *leit motif* in his mind; it resiliently parades throughout 'The Fourth Satire of Dr. John Donne, Versifyed', in which the Court is called 'Meer *Household* Trash', and thunders forth at the conclusion of his highly confessional *Epilogue to the Satires, Dialogue I,* where 'Nobles' and 'Slaves' are ironically juxtaposed in what must be regarded as Pope's final word on the subject:

> *See, all our Nobles begging to be Slaves!*
> *See, all our Fools aspiring to be Knaves!*   (164–5)

How prophetic was Pope in this inversion of 'Nobles' and 'Slaves'? Could he have foreseen that in a short while men across the English Channel would be destroying the Bastille, overthrowing the *Ancien Régime,* sending noblemen now 'begging to be Slaves' to the guillotine? Was he possibly voicing to Bethel in the letter cited above a Marxist sentiment, however procrustean, when dividing *tout le monde* into oppressors and oppressed, when rich and poor are preying on each other? Did he ever dream that he was uttering a profound truth of Georgian social and political history when he perfidiously asserted to Swift that 'in England virtue dwells not with power' and that among noblemen and aristocrats there exists a monumental dearth of 'honest men'?—men like the unusual 'Man of Ross'. Could the young Pope imaging in his *Pastorals* an idyllic bucolic world ever have dreamed that in his last years on earth he would abjure this *juvenilia* as nonsense, now viewing the entire world, garden and city, as a monolithic hot bed of corruption, ever have guessed that he would grow 'sick of *this* World & the Great ones of it'?

These and other similar questions are impossible to answer confidently—all we can do is speculate. But one thing is clear: however unaware Pope may have been of the veracity or prophetic nature of his disclosures, even when excoriating in his most fulgurant mood, he was most emphatically not a spokesman for the corrupt political machinery

—or so it seemed—tyrannically ruling his age. He may not have had 'the courage', as he once peacefully confessed to Swift, 'to be such a Satyrist as you'.[1] But he did take up the gauntlet, did have philosophical views about mankind and in almost every case these represent the diametric opposite of the ideas that have so mistakenly been attributed to him by scholars such as Kampf and Viner. If anything, his views are rarely rear-guard, and viewed within their proper context they more often than not challenge the magisterial authority of power: the Court, the Church, the landed gentry of Georgian England.

The student, having read 'On Reading Pope', will have his grumbles about these 'shored fragments', as T. S. Eliot may rightfully have dubbed them. They are fragments at best, without carefully worked out transitions and *sans* a primitive, let alone adequate, explanation of the reader's aesthetic response to the works of this great and now almost ancient poet. But they have attempted—and whether successfully or not is for the reader to judge—to provide an abundance of information in the manner of *Gradus ad Parnassum* and intentionally to discredit a number of wrong-headed preconceptions about Pope that the reader may bring to the reading of his poetry without actually having read a single poem: that *au fait* he liked to hobnob with the great and the mighty (even Envy had to own that), that all his poetry is nought but a catalogue of cool praise for kings and queens (and, perhaps, occasionally, for dukes and duchesses), that poetry in his conception ought to be 'cool and correct' but never emotionally charged or intellectually firebrand, and, finally—and this is the gravest misconception of all—that he was the voice of 'Reason' speaking to an age of rational men.

---

[1] *Corr.* III 366. The whole passage sheds light on Pope's view: 'You are sensible with what decency and justice I paid homage to the Royal Family, at the same time that I satirized false Courtiers, and Spies, &c. about 'em. I have not the courage however to be such a Satyrist as you, but I would be as much, or more, a Philosopher. You call your satires, Libels; I would rather call my satires, Epistles: They will consist more of morality than wit, and grow graver, which you will call duller.' However playful and ironic Pope is in this letter, there can be no doubt about the seriousness of his intention in distinguishing between his own works and Swift's, between 'satire' and 'philosophy'.

It was *au fond* an age of passion more than an age of reason and this sparrow, as he once referred to himself, who had revived the idea of the 'Ruling Passion' in his deepest philosophical poem, *An Essay on Man*, took it as a desideratum that passionate men should at least strive to be reasonable and preserve their common sense. Inwardly he knew they could not and thus his apodictic conclusion in *The Dunciad in Four Books*, which must have bewildered many readers in 1743, proclaiming universal darkness.

Light and darkness had been a perpetual theme of his poetry from *The Rape of the Lock* to the final *Dunciad*, and Pope would have enjoyed the Miltonic association and sense of continuity. Ultimately, though, he is gloomier than Milton in foreboding a worse end for man the imaginative creature. At one blot, all imagination dies. It is a brave vision, full of intellectual *frisson*, galvanic to those who ponder it in all its completeness, cut in the purest marble, portending doom but also beaming like Belinda with rays of sunshine: '*Belinda* smil'd, and all the World was gay.' A vision created, as Tate's poem 'Mr. Pope' suggests, half from wit and half from rage but from what source no one knows.

In closing I can think of no greater compliment to pay Pope than the homage paid him in this century by Pound and Eliot. When Eliot sent Pound an early version of *The Waste Land*, Pound excised the opening passage of 'The Fire Sermon (I)' written in imitation of *The Rape of the Lock*:

> *Admonished by the sun's inclining ray,*
> *And swift approaches of the thievish day,*
> *The white-armed Fresca blinks, and yawns, and gapes,*
> *Aroused from dreams of love and pleasant rapes.*
> *Electric summons of the busy bell*
> *Brings brisk Amanda to destroy the spell;*
> *With coarsened hand, and hard plebeian tread,*
> *Who draws the curtain round the lacquered bed,*
> *Depositing thereby a polished tray*
> *Of soothing chocolate, or stimulating tea.*
>
> *Leaving the bubbling beverage to cool,*
> *Fresca slips softly to the needful stool,*

> *Where the pathetic tale of Richardson*
> *Eases her labour till the deed is done.*
> *Then slipping back between the conscious sheets,*
> *Explores a page of Gibbon as she eats.*
> *Her hands caress the egg's well-rounded dome,*
> *She sinks in revery, till the letters come.*
> *Their scribbled contents at a glance devours,*
> *Then to reply devotes her practic'd powers. . . .*[1]

This is, to be sure, a pastiche, as Pound charged, but Eliot thought these lines, as Mrs Valerie Eliot has commented in her recent edition of the original manuscript, 'an excellent set of couplets'. Not so for Pound. 'For Pope has done this so well', he wrote to Eliot, 'that you cannot do it better; and if you mean this as a burlesque, you had better suppress it, for you cannot parody Pope unless you can write better verse than Pope—and you can't.'[2]

[1] *T. S. Eliot: The Waste Land*, ed Valerie Eliot, London and New York 1971, 23.
[2] *Ibid.* 127, quoting Eliot's intro to Ezra Pound, *Selected Poems*, 1928, xxi.

2: *Pope, God, and Man*

A. R. HUMPHREYS

THE AGE of Pope, it has been said, was less an age of reason, in any rigorous sense, than one of attempted clarity, 'of trying to define the limits of reason, of seeking a balance that must from now on replace the old impossible harmony'.[1] An extensive effort of elucidation went ahead, inspired both by the triumphs of science and by the enquiry into man's nature arising from the strains of the seventeenth century and from developing economic interests. The 'impossible harmony' of the Elizabethan world picture, based on classical and scholastic theories, yielded before a new (though also illusory) harmony, itself drawing much from classical and scholastic sources, yet re-interpreting these by the insights of new thought, and doing this while recognizing the powers and the limitations of reason, striving to temper man's pride in achievement with humility before God. The assumptions of Pope's age are, in fact, complicated, and the references in the following discussion to Hooker's *Of the Lawes of Ecclesiasticall Politie*[2] are meant to show that many Augustan tenets were already current in Elizabethan thought, however much modification they may have undergone.

The following attempt at explanation is oversimple; adequacy would demand nothing less than the two volumes Leslie Stephen required for his classic *History of English Thought in the Eighteenth Century*. What is offered here is a scheme of dominant conceptions, which might be endlessly qualified or controverted. If they sound little more than enlightened common sense, that is not due solely to the simplification

[1] Bonamy Dobrée, *English Literature in the Early Eighteenth Century, 1700–1740*, Oxford 1959, 16.
[2] Bks I–IV, 1594.

imposed: the Augustan outlook, reacting against the seventeenth century's extravagances and eccentricities, strongly preferred (and needed)
an accepted, often traditional, sense of things, which by definition cannot be original or radical. The topics raised are few but capacious—
ideas of God's creation, of man's place and faculties, and of social
relationships: in each case a few strokes must suggest the whole picture.
Fortunately these matters, and the very heart of their meanings, are
available in a great poet's work: Pope made a magnificent attempt to
define the world picture, and the social picture, of a whole culture in its
aspirations, policies, arts, and conduct, and to do this lucidly, critically,
dramatically, and profoundly.

First there need stating those leading agreements which lay behind
the age's resounding arguments. God, it was assumed, means man to be
thoughtful and sociable, unfanatical, mediating between extremes,
needing only clear moral vision to discern the truths divinely appointed
for reverent worship, the understanding of nature, and the government
of life, and to accept humbly the mysteries lying beyond those necessary
truths. Our current morass of agnostic, relativistic, or existentialist
bewilderments—a slough of despond, it often seems—was hardly suspected: Pope's generation inhabited 'a universe not only full and
various, but regular, created by a just and benevolent Deity whose
genial Providence governs all contingencies, comprehends every
catastrophe, from the bursting of a world to the fall of a sparrow. This
creation, as opposed to the one with which we are familiar, is characterized not only by Energy, but by Order.'[1]

It was common ground that 'the law that was to govern Adam was
the same that was to govern all his posterity, the law of reason'.[2] By
'reason' was meant not out-and-out rationalism but thoughtful consideration—'common sense', as Lady Mary Wortley Montagu defined it to
Pope, protesting that in perpetrating social evils 'Humane Nature [is]
not rational.'[3] This idea was no Augustan monopoly; for the Greeks,

---

[1] Martin Battestin, '*Tom Jones*: the Argument of Design', in *Augustan
Milieu*, 289–90.
[2] Locke, *Second Treatise of Government*, 1690, II. vi. 57.
[3] *The Complete Letters of Lady Mary Wortley Montague*, ed. Robert
Halsband, Oxford 1965–7, I 305.

reason is the universal heritage of humanity, however often neglected; for Christians, God has instilled it as an element of his own spirit into his favoured species, a species

> *who, not prone*
> *And Brute as other Creatures, but endu'd*
> *With Sanctitie of Reason, might erect*
> *His Stature, and upright with Front serene*
> *Govern the rest, self-knowing.*[1]

To be guided by reason is in all men's power. It is 'the candle of the Lord' (Psalm 20. 27) to the Cambridge Platonists (for whom, in Benjamin Whichcote's phrase, 'spiritual is most rational'—a rebuke to polemical frenzy). For Hooker the consensus of men's reason is 'the sentence of God himself'.[2] Spinoza, like the Stoics, holds that men have a uniform rational nature, as children of a common mother: Fénelon sees all men as constituted to think similarly: and Voltaire would maintain that thinking men hold similar principles and form one intellectual republic. Pope's *Essay on Man* may seem arrogant in asserting that only pride-crazed fools can deny a God who directs the best of possible worlds, yet behind the dogmatism there lie humility and reverence; reason is God's light to mankind to discover his goodness, and it leads right-minded men to the conclusions God intends.

The power of reaching these conclusions is given to all: despite its class structure the age genuflected towards moral and intellectual egalitarianism. Morally speaking,

> *Honour and shame from no Condition rise;*
> *Act well your part, there all the honour lies.*
> . . . .
> *Worth makes the man, and want of it, the fellow;*
> *The rest is all but leather or prunella.*
>
> (*Essay on Man*, IV 193–4, 203–4.)

Intellectually, men are qualified to understand their state, or to agree to take it on trust. We are equipped with adequate faculties to discover

[1] Milton, *Paradise Lost*, VII 506–10.
[2] Hooker, I. viii. 3.

evidence in the creation which will 'lead us to the knowledge of the Creator and the knowledge of our duty'.[1] Bolingbroke echoes Locke in the 'Fragments or Minutes of Essays' he sent to Pope, arguing that God has given us intellectual powers fitted to our condition and 'sufficient for all our real business in the world'.[2] That all-but-Arian theologian, Samuel Clarke, considered the divinely-ordained pattern of human duties evident to any man of ordinary capacity and unbiassed judgment: '*Virtue* and true *Goodness, Righteousness* and *Equity*', he held, are so excellent and praiseworthy in themselves that even the vicious must admire them.[3] Bolingbroke again sounds like an echo, insisting that the universal scheme offers itself for understanding and comprehension, regulated as it is by the unclouded logic of the divine mind—'Clearness, precision, and a true conformity to the nature of things, are the perfections of human, and much more of divine, laws'.[4]

The age was not monopolized by an élitist culture and the cosmic toryism of privilege. All men, it believed, can be rationally addressed; clear thought and language are all-important; morality, as classical and Christian traditions alike affirm, is integral to life and will gain the assent of any right-thinking man (a belief culminating in the sublime convictions of Godwin's *Political Justice*, 1793). This encouraging, if arguable, belief is not élitist. Dr Johnson was to appeal, in the *Life of Gray*, to 'the common sense of readers uncorrupted with literary prejudices'—readers, that is, who judge by their thoughtful experience of life—and it is in Johnson that one may best see how belief in a divinely-ordered hierarchical society can yet admit the strongest sense of individual worth. Pope's age draws on old traditions. It enlightens itself with that 'new Philosophy' which, unlike Donne's, did not call all in doubt; it felt (and Pope very much felt) reverence before the creation; and it looked upon men in general (and increasingly women in general, too) as partners in the march of mind.

[1] Locke, *Essay Concerning Human Understanding*, 1690, II. xxiii. 12.
[2] Bolingbroke, *Works*, 1754, III 374.
[3] Samuel Clarke, *A Discourse Concerning the Being and Attributes of God, the Obligations of Natural Religion, and the Truth and Certainty of the Christian Revelation*, 4th edn, 1716, part ii, 59.
[4] Bolingbroke, *Works*, IV 29.

The attempt to make all physical and metaphysical matters comprehensible has been called the first since Aristotle. Earlier generations, admittedly, had been amply instructed in moral, political, and theological duties; Church and State had seen to that, and at times there had been—as with Hooker—a sweet reasonableness in the explanations But Pope's work, in poems like the *Essay on Criticism, Essay on Man*, and *Epistles to Several Persons* (renamed *Moral Essays* by Warburton), resulted not only from a new individual genius but from a new general outlook, believing that not philosophers only (whether Aristotelians, Platonists, Epicureans, or Stoics), or instructed theologians and metaphysicians only, could discuss the nature of the universe. Few might understand Newtonian mathematics. But all could believe that Newton had shown one great, calculable principle to rule cosmic motion: the scientist, as Peter Shaw wrote of Robert Boyle, prefacing the latter's works (1725), 'shews us, that we inhabit a much wiser, and better regulated, a more active and instructive world, than is generally supposed'; moreover, 'since the late happy conjunction of mathematics and philosophy . . . a just theory of the celestial bodies is established, and the whole astronomical world levelled to our capacities'. This theme will be developed later.

The responsible, thinking man was, by definition, not fanatical or extremist. Sound judgment, he would have agreed, avoids 'either cloud of prejudice, or mist of passionate affection'.[1] Joseph Glanvill's *Vanity of Dogmatizing* (1661—a significant title) analyses on Baconian lines man's proneness to error, and pleads against dogmatic presumption. Locke opposed 'untractable Zealots in different and opposite Parties', moved as they were by unreasoning 'enthusiasm'.[2] The seventeenth century's extremism proved disastrous, and thinking of it Pope offered a vow of tolerance in *The Universal Prayer*:

> *Let not this weak, unknowing hand*
> *Presume Thy Bolts to throw,*
> *And deal Damnation round the land,*
> *On each I judge thy Foe.*

[1] Hooker, Preface, vii. 1.
[2] Locke, *Essay*, IV. xix. 11.

If decried as Laodicean, the sensible man would reply, with Whichcote, that extravagance in opinion is 'a kind of wildfire', indiscriminate and destructive, or with the statesman Halifax that men sailing the ship of state should not rock it by rushing from side to side.[1] Defoe, in *An Appeal to Honour and Justice* (1715), sees moderation as Britain's only safeguard: his adversary Swift, though to modern eyes an authoritarian Tory, repeatedly desires centrality as against extremes, and opens his *Sentiments of a Church-of-England Man* (written 1708) by asserting that no-one could support vehement religion or politics without offering violence to his integrity or understanding. Steele, Addison, Berkeley, and many others commend the middle road of comprehension: Pope, though (as will be seen later) imaginatively interested in aberrations from the norm, claims a middle position:

> *Papist or Protestant, or both between,*
> *Like good* Erasmus *in an honest Mean,*
> *In Moderation placing all my Glory,*
> *While Tories call me Whig, and Whigs a Tory.*

> (*Satire II i, To Fortescue*, 65–8)

Bolingbroke's *Idea of a Patriot King* (1738) proposes a monarchy above party (Whigs and Tories were currently contesting to make the monarchy serve their own ends); Fielding, in the first issue of *The True Patriot* (5 November, 1745), condemns factional strife as the real source of all the evils he sees afflicting the nation.

For communal understanding clear communications were essential, a seventeenth-century situation so exhaustively studied by recent scholarship as to call for only the briefest of treatments here. Bacon initiated the process of semantic rectification; the Royal Society sought, in Thomas Sprat's famous formulation, 'a close, naked, natural way of speaking; positive expressions; clear senses; a native easiness'.[2] Man was given reason, Locke observes, not to dispute fruitlessly but to discover sound propositions, and judgment requires ideas unconfused and

[1] George Savile, Marquis of Halifax, 'The Character of a Trimmer', *Miscellanies*, 1704, 88–9.
[2] Sprat, *History of the Royal Society*, 1667, II.xx.

clearly distinguished.[1] Wit, for Glanvill in his *Essay Concerning Preaching*,[2] is a quickness in the fancy to give things 'proper images', and Cowley, witty himself in the old fashion, still in his *Ode of Wit* commends the wit of clarity. Rymer forbids the poet to follow fancy, for its undisciplined inventions may be extravagant, and reason is to be his guide, a power common to all men, which will never divert him from what is natural.[3] Propriety of words and images is the ideal; they must, that is, truly and accurately illustrate the sense. Johnson selects as exemplary Pope's lines which compare ever-extending knowledge to Alpine heights rising beyond the foothills,[4] and a recent critic, Maynard Mack, has remarked how felicitous is imagery like 'the soul's calm sunshine', or

> *Self-love but serves the virtuous mind to wake,*
> *As the small pebble stirs the peaceful lake.*

> (*Essay on Man*, IV 168, 363–4)

Such things, immediately convincing in their illustrative quality, are triumphs of Augustan procedure.

Language, then, must avoid the obscurities which obstruct its purpose as the means of discourse, instruction, and social interchange.[5] Pope's own formulation is the best expression of the new ideals, particularly those of true wit (the masterly grasp of acknowledged truths) and true expression (the fresh definition of right meaning). The earlier seventeenth century's '*glaring Chaos* and *wild Heap* of *Wit*' is to yield to true style—

> Something, *whose Truth convinc'd at Sight we find,*
> *That gives us back the Image of our Mind:*

> . . . .

> [*For*] *true* Expression, *like th'unchanging* Sun,
> Clears, *and* improves *whate'er it shines upon,*
> *It* gilds *all Objects, but it* alters *none.*

[1] Locke, *Essay*, II.xi.2.

[2] 1678, 72.

[3] *The Critical Works of Thomas Rymer*, ed Curt A. Zimansky, New Haven and London 1956, 62.

[4] Pope, *Essay on Criticism*, 219–32.

[5] Locke, *Essay*, III.x. 10.

> *Expression is the* Dress *of* Thought, *and still*
> *Appears more* decent *as more* suitable . . . .
>
> (*Essay on Criticism*, 292, 299–300, 315–19)

Pope is saying not that literature merely relates, more wittily, what we already know, but that subjects need rendering for what in themselves they are (the work of God), not for what gymnastics the exhibitionist can perform upon them. Thus art shows reverence for creation, and Pope essentially agrees with Keats that poetry should 'startle and amaze' not with itself but with its subject; it should 'strike the Reader as a wording of his own highest thoughts, and appear almost a Remembrance'.[1]

The whole movement towards clarification and agreement inspires the very purpose of the *Essay on Man*, the prefixed 'Design' of which appeals to concord as against fractious aberrations. 'The science of Human Nature', it argues, 'is, like all other sciences, reduced to a *few clear points*: There are not *many certain truths* in this world'—so why contest uncertainties? Contests sharpen wits but harden hearts; so Pope will steer 'betwixt the extremes of doctrines seemingly opposite', will pass over 'terms utterly unintelligible', and will form 'a *temperate* yet not *inconsistent*, and a *short* yet not *imperfect* system of Ethics'. He does this, he tells Swift, 'in the Horatian way', 'to make mankind look upon this life with comfort and pleasure, and put morality in good humour' (*Corr.* III 81, 117). De Quincey was to call the *Essay on Man* a dry garden, *hortus siccus*. Yet it renders with intellectual, lyrical, and dramatic force an impressive consensus of ideas, cross-fertilizing old faith and new science, evolving from contentiousness into an agreed science of human nature, and explaining luminously the great things all men should know, and are capable of knowing. To say that Pope orders and formulates the familiar is not to prolong the conventional assumption that, as joint high priest with Dryden of Matthew Arnold's age of prose and reason, he merely dazzles with platitudes: his exposition is often passionate and profound, with a fervour of conception and definition which mark the

[1] Keats, letters of 3 and 27 February 1818. An effective definition of the concept of clarifying 'wit' will be found in E. N. Hooker's 'Pope on Wit', in R. F. Jones et al, *The Seventeenth Century*, Stanford 1951.

great, original, yet representative poet. Dr Johnson thought the *Essay on Man* intellectually shallow, yet wrote that its poetic power can 'enchain philosophy, suspend criticism, and oppress judgment by over-powering pleasure'. The modern reader, not requiring of the poem, as Johnson required, a revelation of truth, can add to Johnson's praise admiration for its depth of feeling and extraordinary scope.

Pope planned, but did not complete, a sequence of poems, the 'Opus Magnum', with the *Essay on Man* as the first instalment and ground-work—'what a scale is to a book of maps', he told Joseph Spence (§ 294). The whole scheme, displaying man's position in the divine order and in society, would be developed in other works; some of these, dealing with man as a member of society, were included in the *Epistles to Several Persons*, and fragments, dealing with man's intellectual nature, were incorporated in *The Dunciad*. One may regret that this audacious plan remained imperfect, yet it is not certain that a grand extension would have improved upon the *Essay on Man*'s vivid and challenging survey, or the *Epistles*' comic drama of the passions. As it is, Pope's purposes are amply demonstrated: he shows man's true path lying in the middle ground, between (for instance) Stoic severity and Epicurean indulgence, between Hobbes's and Mandeville's unillusioned materia-lism and Shaftesbury's and Hutcheson's optimistic benevolence; he takes opposing elements to combine in the human amalgam—Hobbesian egoism, Lockean confidence in social man, Stoic self-discipline to ensure happiness despite fortune's vagaries, anti-Stoic warmth of feeling to recognize that 'Passions are the elements of Life' (*Essay on Man*, I 170). Relishing the drama of opposites, he yet seeks to ally them in the collec-tive humanity of society:

> *These mix'd with art, and to due bounds confin'd,*
> *Make and maintain the balance of the mind.*
>
> (*Essay on Man*, II 119–20)

Johnson had no difficulty in deriding the wise air with which Pope offers his commonplaces. (He rejects also, understandably, Pope's jaunty dis-missal of life's tragedies.) Yet commonplaces are what, after all, man-kind in general lives by. Through experience they become common wisdom, and Johnson's own aphorisms are of no different kind, axioms proved on the pulses. Pope's work lives less by brilliant platitudes than by masterly expression of his moral sense of life and nature.

So much (or so little) for Augustan conceptions generally. What, next, were Augustan conceptions of God and his world? These were, in the main, traditional: God has designed the universe; man's intelligence must instruct him in his role of trust and duty, and his will must direct his obedience. In *Paradise Lost* Raphael counsels Adam to seek all such knowledge as is not impious, but not to aspire further:

> *But Knowledge is as food, and needs no less*
> *Her Temperance over Appetite, to know*
> *In measure what the mind may well contain,*
> *Oppresses else with Surfet, and soon turns*
> *Wisdom to Folly, as Nourishment to Winde.*[1]

From the evidence of nature man perceives the Great Designer, the Ordainer of Order: this confidence goes back to classical philosophers and mediaeval scholastics.[2] The great Chain of Being, connecting higher and lower orders throughout creation, was analogous to the chain of God's compulsive and attractive power, the 'faire cheyne of loue' binding fire, air, water, and earth 'In certeyne boundes',[3] derived ultimately from the golden chain by which Zeus sustains the universe (*Iliad*, VIII 19), and expounded to the Middle Ages by Boethius in *De Consolatione Philosophiae*. Cicero expatiates on the wonderful design of all things, and the body's perfect functioning for the purposes it serves. 'What Artificer but Nature', he asks, 'could so artfully have form'd the Senses?' 'Thus, if we every Way examine the Universe, it is apparent, from the greatest Reason, that the whole is admirably govern'd by a Divine Providence.'[4] In the universe, as Hooker noted, ancient philosophy perceived that 'Counsel is used, Reason followed, a Way observed; that is to say, constant Order and Law is kept', and he had himself

[1] Milton, *Paradise Lost*, VII 126–30.
[2] In his Cambridge inaugural lecture, *De Descriptione Temporum*, 1954, C. S. Lewis placed the line dividing mediaeval from modern in the early nineteenth century, not the sixteenth or seventeenth.
[3] Chaucer, *Knight's Tale*, 2987–93.
[4] Cicero, *The Nature of the Gods*, tr. Thomas Francklin (1739) 176, 169.

written the magnificent celebration of God-given rule which begins
'Now if nature should intermit her course', and ends 'See we not plainly
that obedience of creatures unto the law of nature is the stay of the
whole world?'[1] Nature's order had from of old confirmed belief in
nature's God. Bacon's essay *Of Atheism* sounded the theme of faith for-
tified by science, in the famous argument that by a smattering of philosophy the mind may be turned from God, to absorb itself in second
causes and go no further, but that 'when it beholdeth the chain of these
confederate and linked together, it must needs fly to Providence and
Deity'.

The theme of divine order and purpose is conveyed in the title of
John Ray's *The Wisdom of God manifested in the Works of the Creation*
(1691); Ray was an outstanding contributor to the biological sciences.
God's wisdom in the heavens and on earth is the recurrent theme of the
Boyle lectures, founded in 1691 by the will of Robert Boyle, propounder
of Boyle's Law, a scientist as devoted to theology as to chemistry.[2]
Aristotle had observed manifest design in the beauty of form and function evident in the natural world.[3] Boyle himself, in *The Christian Virtuoso* (1690), affirms that no intelligent man can deny a creator, evident
in the vastness, beauty, and regular motions of the heavenly bodies, and
the excellent structure of animals and plants, and he cites Galen's and
Pliny's admiration of anatomical structure in even the humblest of
creatures.

Belief in intelligent order and purpose naturally argued against mechanistic materialism. Thinking, probably, of Hobbes, Berkeley rejoiced
in his *Principles of Human Knowledge* (1710) that his idealism refutes
the outrageous philosophies which reduce everything to matter. 'The

[1] Hooker, I. ii. 3; I. iii. 2.
[2] E.g. Richard Bentley, *The Folly of Atheism and (what is now called)
Deism*, 1693: George Stanhope, *The Truth and Excellence of the Christian
Religion*, 1701–2; Samuel Clarke, *A Demonstration of the Being and Attributes of God*, 1705, and *A Discourse Concerning the Unchangeable Obligations of Natural Religion*, 1706; pubd together, with additions, 1716:
William Derham, *Physico-Theology*: or, *a Demonstration of the Being
and Attributes of God, from his Works of Creation*, 1713.
[3] Aristotle, *The Parts of Animals*, I.v. 645a.

absurdities of every wretched set of atheists' will, he believes, crumble before the faith that all exists in the divine mind, and that the constancy of natural law, far from betokening automatism, proves God's infinite beneficence. The materialism of Epicurus, Lucretius, and Hobbes finds its adherents, but a contrary chorus resounds also. 'If we attentively consider the constant regularity, order, and concatenation of natural things', Berkeley writes, 'the surprising magnificence, beauty, and perfection of the larger, and the exquisite contrivance of the smaller, parts of the creation, together with the exact harmony and correspondence of the whole, . . . and . . . attend to the meaning and import of the attributes One, Eternal, Infinitely Wise, Good, and Perfect, we shall clearly perceive that they belong to the aforesaid Spirit, who works in all, and by whom all things exist.'[1] God's purposes centre in man; man's origin is spiritual. Had Boyle lived to hear the opening lecture of the first Boyle series in 1692, Richard Bentley's *The Folly of Atheism*, he would have applauded its refutation of materialism, since it urged that man should believe himself divinely created, 'the offspring and image of the great King of Glory',[2] rather than, as materialists would hold, originated from the fertilizing influence of the sun upon the base matter of earth.

Satisfaction with God's design, as Boyle and Berkeley indicate, was both biological and astronomical. Age-old wonder at plant and animal structure was deepened by microscopy and by great advances in natural history. William Derham's Boyle lectures, *Physico-Theology* (1713), exult in the wonderful organization of the animal kingdom: 'what less than Infinite', Derham asks, 'could stock so vast a Globe with such a noble Set of Animals?' And Addison records with satisfaction that from antiquity enquirers had perceived in the anatomy of creatures the work of a thinking and all-wise Deity (*Spectator,* No. 543). The great Chain of Being seemed confirmed by natural history, each creature being perfectly designed for its particular place, as well as for its internal functioning. Locke reminded his readers that man's faculties fit his station; 'microscopical eyes' or quicker hearing would not suit the sphere to which he is allotted, for God has made us 'so as is best for us in our

[1] Berkeley, *Principles*, sect. cxlvi.
[2] Bentley, *Folly of Atheism*, 27.

present condition'[1] (compare *Essay on Man*, I 193–6). One must, then, rest content with the human lot:

> *What would this Man? Now upward will he soar,*
> *And little less than Angel, would be more;*
> *Now looking downwards, just as griev'd appears*
> *To want the strength of bulls, the fur of bears.*
>
> . . . .
>
> *The bliss of Man (could Pride that blessing find)*
> *Is not to act or think beyond mankind.*
>
> (Essay on Man, I 173–6, 189–90)

As for the astronomical satisfaction, the decades of Newton and his great contemporaries marked in effect the end of that bewilderment which prompted Donne to write, in his *First Anniversary*,

> *The Sun is lost, and th'earth, and no man's wit*
> *Can well direct him where to looke for it.*
>
> . . . .
>
> *'Tis all in peeces, all cohærence gone,*
> *All just supply, and all Relation.*

Astronomical wit now knew not only where to look for the celestial bodies but where they would be, and why they would be there, æons of years hence: coherence and relation were not only restored, they were incontrovertibly demonstrated. Solving problems that long had baffled the wisest, dealing not in logomachies but in observation and calculation, science had, as Thomson proclaimed in his poem *To the Memory of Sir Isaac Newton*, brought the heavens back to 'their first great simplicity' from such fantasies as Cartesian vortices:

> *O wisdom truly perfect! thus to call*
> *From a few causes such a scheme of things,*
> *Effects so various, beautiful, and great,*
> *An universe complete!*

The last *Spectator* (No. 635), by Henry Grove, showed Newton breaking forth, like a superior species, 'from amidst the Darkness that

---

[1] Locke, *Essay*, II. xxiii. 12–13.

involves human Understanding', enlightening not only fellow-scientists but mankind in general, both scientifically and religiously: 'The vast Machine we inhabit lies open to him . . . and while with the Transport of a Philosopher he beholds and admires the glorious Work, he is capable of paying at once a more devout and rational Homage to his Maker.'

The new movement shiningly renewed an old confidence. The evidence, or some of it, had been observed since the Chaldeans—indeed, prehistoric man—reckoned by the recurrence of celestial phenomena, or, for Christians, since, on creation's sixth day, God saw everything that he had made, and behold, it was very good. For the Stoics, cosmic order evinced divine order, and Cicero's *De Natura Deorum* was cited as a precedent by Newton, Barrow, Ray, Clarke, and others of a scientific turn. Likewise, Manilius's *Astronomica* describes how a divine and rational mind governs the heavenly spheres.[1] Yet in a real sense a new assurance had dawned for the Augustans:

> *Nature, and Nature's Laws lay hid in Night.*
> *God said,* Let Newton be! *and All was* Light.

Pope's astonishing epigram reflected the relief that old speculations, old assertions of trust, were now proven by objective demonstration. The spacious firmament on high, rescued from Ptolemaic complexity by Copernicus, Tycho Brahe, Kepler, and Galileo, had received its supreme rationalization from Newton; Bacon had exploded scholastic obscurantism; botanists and zoologists were confirming in an unprecedented way the marvels of biology. No wonder Clarke claimed with pride that modern astronomers, showing that even the comets moved predictably, had confirmed the exquisite regularity of celestial motion signalized by Cicero, and that if Galen, the second-century admirer of anatomical design, could revisit earth he would be amazed at 'the *Late Discoveries* in Anatomy and Physick, the Circulation of the Blood, [and] the exact Structure of the Heart and Brain'.[2] As Hooker had done, but with still more certainty, the Augustans saw 'the whole world and each part thereof so compacted, that as long as each thing performeth only

[1] First century AD; tr. Thomas Creech, 1697; see Bks I. vii, xii; II. i.
[2] Samuel Clarke, *Discourse* (1716 edn) i, 116ff.

that work which is natural to it, it thereby preserveth both other things and also itself'.[1] The conclusion was irresistible:

> *Nothing is foreign: Parts relate to whole;*
> *One all-extending, all-preserving Soul*
> *Connects each being, greatest with the least.*
>
> (*Essay on Man*, III 21–23)

Even before Newton rose to fame, Dryden in the *Essay of Dramatic Poesy* (1668) rejoiced that more discoveries had been made in optics, medicine, anatomy, and astronomy than in what he called 'all those doting and credulous ages from Aristotle to us'. If for the Stoics nature had been regular and rational, for non-Stoics it had often menaced with mysterious portents. That was now over: 'there is', Sprat announced, 'scarce any whisper remaining of such horrors: Every man is unshaken at those Tales, at which his Ancestors trembled: The cours of things goes quietly along, in its own true channel of Natural Causes and Effects'.[2] The inference was clear; science, clarifying and confirming faith,

> *Investigating sure the chain of things,*
> *With radiant finger points to Heaven again.*[3]

A copious literature of celebration erupted. In *Death's Vision* (1709) John Reynolds displayed the world of the new science to show God's greatness; in *The Ecstacy* (1720) John Hughes exulted about Newton; J. T. Desaguliers offered *The Newtonian System of the World* (1728) as the best model of government; Henry Brooke asked in *Universal Beauty*

> *why this Globe has its appointed place,*
> *And why not vagrant thro' the boundless Space?*[4]

and answered that all nature's excellences proceed from God's wisdom. Latitudinarian divines and the periodical essayists cheered their audiences with the same theme. Enthusiasm seems to have culminated in the 1720s and 1730s, when the outstanding contributions of Thomson and

---

[1] Hooker I. ix. I.
[2] Sprat, *History of the Royal Society*, III. xii.
[3] Thomson, *The Seasons*, 'Summer' 1549–50.
[4] 1735, I 265–6.

Pope raised the matter to high distinction. At a lower yet typical level, Henry Pemberton proposed in *The London Journal* of 26 April 1726, to publish a simple account of Newton's scheme, so that every normally cultured gentleman might form 'a comprehensive View of the Stupendous Frame of Nature . . . with the same Ease as he now acquires a Taste for the Magnificence of a Plan of Architecture, or the Elements of a beautiful Plantation'. Dilettantish though this sounds, one may respect its belief that any educated person might grasp salient intellectual and cultural concerns. Sprat had already congratulated the Royal Society on consisting mainly of 'Gentlemen, free and unconfin'd', rather than mere specialists or artificers.[1] To quote Coleridge's aphorism: 'in wonder all philosophy began; in wonder it ends; but the first wonder is the offspring of ignorance, the last is the parent of adoration.'

As well as creation's order and design, their correlatives of beauty and harmony nourished the imagination. To perceive this meant to react against any assumption that the 'real' world is a mathematical affair of extension and motion merely, and that the secondary, sensory, qualities which give life its experiential value are of an inferior order. The position to be rejected is defined thus by A. N. Whitehead: 'There is no light or colour as a fact in external nature. There is merely motion of material. . . . Nature is a dull affair, soundless, scentless, colourless; merely the hurrying of material, endlessly, meaninglessly. However you disguise it, this is the practical outcome of the characteristic scientific philosophy which closed the seventeenth century.'[2] Against this impoverishing doctrine, against Epicurean–Lucretian atomism, against Hobbesian mechanism, against the exclusion from his universe of the God who created its wonder and glory—against all these the poets, divines, and moralists revolted passionately. The universe was awe-inspiring for its divine mathematics, but soul-satisfying for its beauty and aptness. And the divine quality thus disclosed was, above all, supreme benevolence, 'the exuberant and overflowing Goodness of the Supreme Being' (*Spectator*, No. 519), thoughts of whom should induce 'a perpetual Cheerfulness' (*Spectator*, No. 93). Doubtless, as Defoe remarked in *The Storm* (chapter 1), 'the Christian begins just where the

[1] Sprat, *History of the Royal Society*, II. vii.
[2] Whitehead, *Science and the Modern World*, 1926, 76–7.

Philosopher ends', yet such contiguity implies coalition; 'no Christian', observed the deist Toland, 'says Reason and the Gospel are contrary to one another.'[1] They coincided in bringing good news.

To this enlightened mood, God was not the despot of wrath but the beneficent origin of

> *The mighty chain of beings, lessening down*
> *From infinite perfection to the brink*
> *Of dreary nothing, desolate abyss!*

Creation, through the plenitude of his creative will, abounded with all possible orders of existence; like Wordsworth's Nature-given joy 'in widest commonalty spread', goodness sprang without limitation from the

> *Source of Being! Universal Soul*
> *Of Heaven and Earth! Essential Presence. . . .*[2]

The chain (a classical idea) and plenitude (a scholastic one) were deeply satisfying beliefs, assuring the believer (this assurance rings richly and powerfully in Pope) of creation's profusion and consonancy together, its energy and order.

At once traditional and contemporary, orthodox and novel, the *Essay on Man* unites elements of classical thought and scholasticism, of classical and modern biological science (the divine art in natural creatures), of Stoicism and Deism (God proved not by Christian revelation but through nature), and of Shaftesburyan Platonic optimism (the ascending beauty and goodness of creation in the supreme work of divine inspiration). It accepts science's confirmation of a regular cosmos under immutable law, yet enriches and dramatises this by including the perpetually renewed creative dynamism of Aristotelian *physis* (Nature's principle of growth), of the opening of Genesis, of the great theodicy of the Book of Job (chapters 9, 26, and 38 to 41 particularly), and of the seventh book of *Paradise Lost*. It is, therefore, as much as any work of its time, scientific and religious together. Pope told Spence in 1734 that he had composed 'an address to our Saviour' as part of the *Essay* but

---

1 John Toland, *Christianity not Mysterious*, 1696, 23.
2 Thomson, *The Seasons*, 'Summer' 334–6; 'Spring' 556–7.

had omitted it on Berkeley's advice (Spence, § 305), perhaps because the *Essay* is concerned with God, but not with Christ; it is a religious but not a Christian work. Yet on the earliest surviving manuscript he wrote 'Thy will be done in Earth as it is in Heaven', a sign that its all-but-Leibnitzian optimism (though Pope denied knowledge of Leibnitz) is rooted in Christianity. The *Essay*'s first epistle ends in what sounds like deistic jauntiness; in fact, as the Twickenham edition makes clear, it is steeped in Platonic, Stoic, and Christian tradition so as to 'establish contact with the collective religious and moral past'.[1] 'Whatever IS, is RIGHT', far from being a Panglossian platitude, is natural religions' way of repeating 'Thy will be done': Pope's deism and Christianity are in close relationship, though the poem is not specifically Christian.

A tamer, yet characteristic, work, Richard Blackmore's *The Creation* (1712), opposes 'Bigots in Atheism' whose pride expounds the universe while disregarding its creator. It is not unimpressive, conveying as it does the wonder, beauty, and complexity of the world, in a spirit of reverent enthusiasm, and it elaborately vindicates the wisdom of God:

> *I would th'Eternal from his Works assert,*
> *And sing the Wonders of Creating Art.*[2]

Addison's paper ending with the noble ode, 'The Spacious Firmament on High', declares that the man of reverent mind perceives God not in theory only but in the depths of his feeling, so overwhelming is the evidence the world conveys (*Spectator*, No. 465). William Wollaston's *Religion of Nature Delineated* (1724) is deist in content (and so was censured by Swift) yet glows with an enthusiasm which allies it in spirit with the *Essay on Man*: Wollaston may be unorthodox, but he is not irreligious. God, he holds, reveals himself in Nature's every particle and motion, in the intricate structure and providential relationships of creatures, in the vastness of space and the lustre of the sun, and in 'the chorus of planets moving periodically, by uniform laws, in their several orbits'. Samuel Clarke maintains God's transcendent reality against Hobbes's materialism and Spinoza's submergence of God in nature, asserting that the supreme cause of all things is an intelligent being, and offering in

[1] Twickenham III i, lxxii.
[2] Blackmore, *The Creation*, I 12–13.

proof 'the excellent Variety, Order, Beauty, and Wonderful Contrivance and Fitness of all things'.[1] (As against all this, a Christian of a different persuasion like Pascal, whom the silence of the infinite spaces terrified, could maintain that only those already convinced of God will find him in nature; non-believers perceive nothing but 'obscurité et ténèbres', for nature cannot prove a God who is revealed only through Christ in the fallen world, a world where, to quote St Matthew, xi. 27, 'neither knoweth any man the Father, save the Son, and he to whomsoever the Son will reveal him.' From another point of view, few modern scientists would agree that nature offers comfort to the moral conscience.)

Yet if to Augustan optimism goodness were so manifest, in the constancy of natural law, the links of the chain of being, and the plenitude of creation, what about evil? If 'serene philosophy' occasioned faith and gladness, as Thomson asserted—

> *Effusive source of evidence and truth!*
> *A lustre shedding o'er the ennobled mind,*
> *Stronger than summer-noon—*

what about the precarious human condition—

> *this dark state*
> *In wayward passions lost and vain pursuits?*[2]

The Christian explanation, that man inhabits a world sinfully suffering 'the utter disturbance of that divine order'[3] is one which any even moderately orthodox Augustan would accept. Evil flouts God's design, a design which, allowing man alone of earthly creatures the freedom to choose,

> *gave [him] in this dark Estate*
> *To see the Good from Ill;*
> *And binding Nature fast in Fate,*
> *Left free the Human Will.*
>
> (*The Universal Prayer, 9–12*)

[1] *Discourse*, i 59–60.
[2] Thomson, *The Seasons*, 'Summer' 1732–4, 1800–1.
[3] Hooker I.vii.7.

But granted that, by traditional belief, the world has incurred the punishments of sin, what else might be said? For moral evil, man's pride continued to be the culprit, allied to excessive self-love. Of other evils there were two main divisions, evils of imperfection, and evils of suffering (or 'natural' evils). The former were thought to depend from the very chain of being and plenitude themselves; as William King maintained in *De Origine Mali* 'the World is as well as it could be made by infinite Power and Goodness',[1] but all creatures must fall short of God's perfection in proportion to their position on the chain, and so necessarily there are degrees of imperfection, of evil in that sense: for Pascal, 'the perfections of nature show that she is the image of God, her defects show that she is only his image'. Lack of some seeming desideratum, it was asserted, is no real evil; its absence may be necessary to the nature of the being lacking it—each creature is as well-endowed as its place allows.[2] Therefore,

> *Of Systems possible, if 'tis confest*
> *That Wisdom infinite must form the best,*
>
> . . . .
>
> *Respecting Man, whatever wrong we call,*
> *May, must be right, as relative to all.*
>
> (*Essay on Man*, I 43–4, 51–2)

Pope grounds this confidence on hypotheses, yet these—the 'if' and 'must'—do not really admit of doubt: doubt would be impiety.

As for 'natural' evil, that was considered a by-product of laws framed for the general good. Pain, King declared, may have a preservative value as a warning against the untoward; death, Clarke asserted, occurs because man is wisely not granted the inhuman gift of immortality.[3] (Swift's Struldbruggs prove how beneficent is this 'evil'.) Laws appointed for general efficacy cannot vary to benefit individuals; 'if a good man be passing an infirm building just in the article of falling, can it be expected that God should suspend the force of gravitation till he is gone by?'[4]

---

[1] 1702; tr. Edmund Law, *An Essay on the Origin of Evil*, 1731, 53.

[2] Clarke, *Discourse* i, 112.

[3] *Discourse*, i 112.

[4] William Wollaston, *The Religion of Nature Delineated*, 1724, 99.

> *Think we, like some weak Prince, th'Eternal Cause*
> *Prone for his fav'rites to reverse his laws?*
> *Shall burning Ætna, if a sage requires,*
> *Forget to thunder, and recall her fires?*
>
> (*Essay on Man*, IV 121–4)

Clearly not. Pope's discussion of this, mainly in the fourth epistle of the *Essay*, suffers from its aggressive tone, yet even that reveals how fully he accepts the wisdom of antiquity and of the Christian tradition on the subject. As far as he can, like his precursors and contemporaries, he explains evil rationally. Beyond that, his theodicy (and theirs) must trust the unknown, deeming, as Wordsworth's Wanderer was to do,

> *That the procession of our fate, howe'er*
> *Sad or disturbed, is ordered by a Being*
> *Of infinite benevolence and power;*
> *Whose everlasting purposes embrace*
> *All accidents, converting them to good.*[1]

How did the new philosophy of science relate to the old philosophy of moral life? One might, like Swift, deride the former as at best ridiculous and at worst totally misguided, indeed morally destructive. One might, less ruthlessly, admire the new enquiries yet still give preference to moral philosophy; the 408th *Spectator* (probably Pope's) holds that thought about human nature is the truest form of enquiry, since the understanding of right and wrong bears directly and centrally upon life, whereas the calculation of planetary motions is of secondary importance. The scientist may dazzle the mind but he fails to satisfy its deepest enquiries; Newton himself could not 'Explain his own beginning, or his end' (*Essay on Man*, II 38). So—'Trace Science then, with Modesty thy guide' (II 43).

Within that limitation, however, scientific triumphs could be extolled, in full confidence that physical gravitation and design (God's coordination of matter and motion, and his fitting of all things to their purposes) guarantee moral gravitation and design too, laws of appointed duties and relationships, those 'amazing Manifestations of Justice and

---

[1] Wordsworth, *The Excursion*, IV 13–17.

Goodness, which . . . appear to have run through the whole Series of God's Government of the *Moral* World'.[1] This confidence, too, was age-old; the Stoics had paralleled cosmic and moral order, as Cicero does in *De Natura Deorum*, Book 2, and Addison echoes them in *Cato*:

> *If there's a pow'r above us*
> *(And that there is all Nature cries aloud*
> *Through all her works) he must delight in virtue;*
> *And that which he delights in, must be happy.*[2]

Francis Hutcheson sought coherence in the sphere of moral conduct by analogy with 'some great Principles, or universal Forces, from which innumerable Effects do flow, [such as] Gravitation, in Sir Isaac Newton's Scheme'.[3] Science should neither withdraw man from God, nor make him vainglorious, nor distract him from moral contemplation; it should reveal how deeply God concerns himself in the moral as well as the physical universe. It offered its facts and its schema; moral philosophy found in it the confirmation of values.

What the universe, thus validated, affords to experience is order and uniformity, fullness and propriety, and the inspiration of beauty and grandeur. John Dennis, Pope's critic-adversary, founds the rules of art and poetry on universal order and rationality; nature he defines as the rule, order and harmony evident in the universe, qualities beautiful to mind and senses, arising from the perfect proportions and interactions of the creation.[4] Save in the world of man's sinful disorder there still rings clearly forth

> *the fair musick that all creatures made*
> *To their great Lord, whose love their motion sway'd*
> *In perfect Diapason.*[5]

Perpetually there is found recurring the tradition of a celestial dance (as in Sir John Davies's *Orchestra*, 1596) and of law with 'her seat [in] the

---

[1] Clarke, *Discourse*, ii, 143.

[2] Addison, *Cato*, V.i. 15–18.

[3] *Inquiry into the Original of our Ideas of Beauty and Virtue*, 1725, 31.

[4] *The Advancement and Reformation of Modern Poetry*, 1701, in *The Critical Works of John Dennis,* ed. E. N. Hooker, Baltimore 1939–43, I 202.

[5] Milton, *At a Solemn Musick*, 21–23.

bosom of God, her voice the harmony of the world'.[1] For Pope, the
world is like the scenery round his youthful home,

> *harmoniously confus'd:*
> *Where Order in Variety we see,*
> *And where, tho' all things differ, all agree.*
>
> (*Windsor Forest,* 14–16)

What counts for poetry, indeed for any imaginative interpretation of
the world, is the kind of Shaftesburyan vitalism which thinks of causes
not as mechanical but as seminal and originative.[2] Pope responds richly
to the sense not only of a marvellous universal order but of a full creative urge animating this order, with 'Wild Nature's vigor working at the
root' (*Essay on Man,* II 184):

> *Far as Creation's ample range extends,*
> *The scale of sensual, mental pow'rs ascends:*
> *Mark how it mounts, to Man's imperial race,*
> *From the green myriads in the peopled grass:*
>
> . . . .
>
> *See, thro' this air, this ocean, and this earth,*
> *All matter quick, and bursting into birth.*
> *Above, how high progressive life may go!*
> *Around, how wide! how deep extend below!*
>
> (*Essay on Man,* I 207–10, 233–6)

Creation revealed itself as ordered, dynamic, and beautiful. Science
could not only 'measure earth, weigh air, and state the tides' (*Essay on
Man,* II 20); in the Newtonian spectrum it also,

> *from the whitening undistinguished blaze,*
> *Collecting every ray into his kind,*
> *To the charmed eye educed the gorgeous train*
> *Of parent colours.*[3]

And Pope created his sylphs with their airy garments,

> *Dipt in the richest Tincture of the Skies,*
> *Where Light disports in ever-mingling Dies.*
>
> (*Rape of the Lock,* II 65–6)

[1] Hooker, I xvi. 8.
[2] A. S. P. Woodhouse, *The Poet and his Faith,* Toronto 1965, 130.
[3] Thomson, *To the memory of Sir Isaac Newton* 99–102.

Pope paid homage to Newton—no-one more memorably—yet knew that Newton's science, of cosmic mechanics or the nature of light, needed interpreting as experience. In many Augustan quarters the world presented itself as fresh vision, as exhilarating artefact; through sight particularly (the most prestigious Augustan sense) man recognized 'those admirable Works of God which every where surround us'.[1] And following Addison's lead in his 'Pleasures of the Imagination' papers (*Spectator*, Nos. 411–21) Akenside published his poem of that name in 1744, writing in the preface that it is the scenes the world presents, its 'most engaging prospects', which inspire the appreciation of divine benevolence.

If such is the nature of God in and through his creation, what of the nature of man? A little lower than the angels, crowned with glory and honour as the Psalmist saw him, yet fallen through sin, he offers a profound paradox. Behind Pope's striking expression of this (*Essay on Man*, II 3–18) lies a passage of Pascal, who deeply influenced him—'A profess'd Judge of all Things, and yet a feeble Worm of the Earth, the greatest Guardian and Depository of Truth, yet a meer Huddle of Uncertainty; the Glory and the Scandal of the Universe'.[2] Man knew himself, as in Sir John Davies's *Nosce Teipsum* (1599), to be 'a proud, and yet a wretched thing', redeemable if his pride were subdued in reverence, his wretchedness accepted as the deserved human lot and turned into content.

The sixteenth and seventeenth centuries abounded in psychological studies, homebred or translated:[3] the most influential were Hobbes's

[1] Derham, *Physico-Theology*, 112.

[2] *Thoughts on Religion*, trans. Basil Kennet, 3rd edn 1731, 162.

[3] The following list does not claim to be complete. Francis Bacon, *Essays*, 1597; John Davies, *Nosce Teipsum*, 1599; Thomas Wright, *The Passions of the Mind*, 1601: Robert Burton, *The Anatomy of Melancholy*, 1621; Edward Grimstone, *A Table of Humane Passions*, 1621, translated from Nicolas Coeffeteau, *Le Tableau des Passions Humaines*; Henry Cary, Earl of Monmouth, *The Use of Passions*, 1649, translated from J. F. Senault's *De l'Usage des Passions*, which was also translated by Walter Charleton, *The Natural History of the Passions*, 1674, and W. Ayloffe, *The Government of the Passions*, 1700; Thomas Hobbes, *Leviathan*, 1651; Timothy Nourse, *The Nature and Faculties of Man*, 1686; John Locke,

Leviathan, with its startling theme of egoism, and Locke's *Essay Concerning Human Understanding* and *Second Treatise of Government*, with their pleasing themes of sociability. Slightly less influential were Montaigne's essays, with their ruminating scepticism, La Rochefoucauld's sardonic maxims (Pope projected a contrasting set, 'in opposition to all Rochefoucaults Principles': *Corr.* II 333), and the benign readings of mankind by the Cambridge Platonists and Latitudinarian divines. And to this manifold interest must be added the encyclopedic commentary furnished by the Bible, classical philosophy, and Shakespeare.

To analyse human nature became a dominant Augustan concern. Is will the mainspring of action, or merely, as Hobbes thought, the last appetite in deliberating? Is it the virtuous restrainer of desire, or, as in Hume's view, only the slave of the passions, the means of attaining their ends?[1] Are the passions, Plato's unruly horses, to be extinguished? Or are they 'useful, and consistent with human Nature in its highest Perfection'?[2] These questions were anything but new; like earlier ages, the Augustans faced the question posed by Fulke Greville:

> *What meaneth Nature by these diverse Lawes?*
> *Passion and Reason, selfe-division cause.*

Stoicism was revived in the Restoration period, and several of the principal texts were translated.[3] Anti-Stoicism counter-attacked,

---

An Essay Concerning Human Understanding, 1690; T[homas] W[oodcock], *The Art of Knowing Oneself*, 1694, translated from Jacques Abbadie, *L'Art de se connoitre soi-meme*; Richard Steele, *The Christian Hero*, 1701.

[1] David Hume, *A Treatise of Human Nature*, 1739–40, II. iii.3.

[2] Timothy Nourse, *The Nature and Faculties of Man*, 1686, 105–6.

[3] The subject is well discussed in Steele. *The Christian Hero*, ed Rae Blanchard, Oxford 1932, xvii–xxv. The following are some of the main works: R[   ] G[   ], *A Discourse of Constancy*, 1654, and Nicholas Wanley, *War and Peace Reconciled; or, a Discourse of Constancy in Inconstant Times*, 1672, both trans. from Justus Lipsius, *De Constantia Libri Duo*, Antwerp 1584, earlier translated by J. Stradling, *Two Bookes of Constancie*, 1595; Charles Cotton, *The Morall Philosophy of the Stoicks*, 1664; 2nd edn 1667, translated from Guillaume du Vair, *La Philosophie Morale des Stoiques*, earlier translated by T[homas] J[ames], *The Moral*

recognizing passion's value, and condemning stoic pride: bravado about self-mastery, said Steele, is 'Bombast got into the very Soul', and whereas the Stoic, glorying in suicide, shows himself only proud or cowardly, the Christian bears his cross with humble courage.[1] If stoic discipline is virtuous, still more virtuous is the emotion of benevolence. And reason itself, God's light in man though it is, can, like stoic will, run to arrogance and impiety.

Passion also, of course, can corrupt; if following nature means following appetite, moral anarchy overrides moral law. Pope left unpublished those lines in his draft of *The Universal Prayer* which seemed to authorize profligacy:

> *Can Sins of Moments claim ye Rod*
> *of Everlasting Fires?*
> *Can those be Sins wth Natures God*
> *W^{ch} Natures selfe inspires?*

He took a modified stoic line—stoic insofar as rational guidance is essential, antistoic insofar as passion is recognized as primary. This position is not unlike Shaftesbury's, that man must be animated by passion yet master passion's importunity. 'Can anything be more desirable than to follow [Nature]?' Theocles asks Philocles in *The Moralists*, 'Or is it not by this freedom from our passions and low interests that we are recon-

---

Philosophy of the Stoicks, 1598; Roger L'Estrange, *Seneca's Morals, by Way of Abstract*, 1678; ten edns by 1711, earlier translated by Thomas Lodge, *The Workes of L. A. Seneca both Morall and Naturall* . . . , 1614; 2nd edn 1620; E. Walker, *Epicteti Enchiridion, made English in a poetical paraphrase*, 1692; seven edns by 1737; George Stanhope, *Epictetus his Morals*, 1694; five edns by 1741; Jeremy Collier, *The Emperor Marcus Antoninus his Conversation with Himself* . . . , 1701; three edns by 1726, earlier translated by Meric Casaubon, *Marcus Aurelius Antoninus . . . his Meditations*, 1634; five edns by 1692; George Stanhope, *Of Wisdom*, 1707; three edns by 1729, translated from Pierre Charron, *De la Sagesse*, Bordeaux 1601, earlier translated by Samson Lennard, *Of Wisedome*, 1608; seven edns by 1670; J[   ] W[   ], *The Porch and Academy Open'd; or, Epictetus's Manual newly turn'd into English Verse*, 1707.
[1] Steele, *The Christian Hero*, ed Blanchard, 63, 68.

ciled to the goodly order of the universe, that we harmonise with Nature, and live in friendship both with God and man?'[1] Yet Pope more
frankly than Shaftesbury recognizes wild Nature's vigour; he is much
less idealistic, much more seized with the dynamism of natural force,
concerned to render the drama of self-love and reason (*Essay on Man*,
II 53–110). Out of man's paradoxical nature he derives a series of tensions: God gives each man his character, yet each man must shape the
gift; reason is God's light, yet can betray; passion must activate, yet can
destroy; good and evil are absolutes, yet endlessly intermingle; 'nature'
demonstrates the good life, yet 'natural' desires blemish it. Neither these
perceptions nor the conclusion that man is a 'Chaos of Thought and
Passion, all confus'd' (*Essay on Man*, II 13) have novelty to recommend them, yet in Pope's work they are alive with dramatic feeling.
Man, created when the angels fell, the testing-ground of moral good and
evil, meant to display 'the noblest temper of the greatest and noblest
souls',[2] yet 'Still by himself abus'd, or disabus'd'—man seemed indeed
'The glory, jest, and riddle of the world' (*Essay on Man*, II 14, 18).

As gravitation rules the physical realm, ethical law, discerned by
conscience, must rule the moral one—'that Law, which is written in the
Heart [and] extendeth to all Nations'.[3] For the Augustans (to put it
roughly), conscience resides in the head or the heart. If in the head, it
perceives rationally how moral duties fit like data in geometry to produce the correct solution; there are actions, the deist Matthew Tindal
maintains, 'fitting' each circumstance, and just as physical causes produce physical results so too ''tis the Will of God, that Men shou'd observe, whatever the Nature of Things, and the Relation they have to
one another, make fit to be observ'd. . . . Thus we see how the reason
of things . . . teaches us our Duty in all cases.'[4]

Yet this 'intellectualist' persuasion lacked appeal; Bolingbroke, ac-
cusing it of 'dry, inward complacency', wished rather to address the

---

[1] Anthony Ashley Cooper, 3rd Earl of Shaftesbury, *Characteristics of
Men, Manners, Opinions, Times*, ed J. M. Robertson, 1900, II 148.
[2] William Law, *Serious Call to a Devout and Holy Life*, 1728, 482.
[3] John Maxwell, 'Dissertation on the Law of Nature,' in Richard
Cumberland, *A Treatise of the Laws of Nature*, 1727, Appendix II, 40.
[4] *Christianity as Old as the Creation*, 1730, 16.

feelings[1] and Fielding parodied it in Square, the hypocritical philosopher of *Tom Jones*. The alternative appeal, from the heart, offered adoration to God and affection to man. Men are righteous, John Maxwell declared, from other reasons than those which merely 'fit' their moral calculations, and shun sin from other reasons than that it is a public nuisance (and so 'unfitting').[2] Shaftesbury's strongest suit is his urging the 'beauty' of virtuous affections: Addison pleads the warm gratification of virtue, and cites Christ and Job on benevolent charity, though like Pope he counsels reasoned and steady generosity rather than reckless impulse (*Spectator*, No. 177).

The *Essay on Man*, inclusive in doctrine, accepts both these postulates. Recognizing the Chain of Being, and the functions ordained for each link, it holds also, however, with the deeper passion of Pope's real leaning, that intellectualist or stoic virtue is 'fix'd as in a frost' and that 'strength of mind is Exercise, not Rest' (*Essay on Man*, II 102, 104). Pope's ideal is the person well-tempered between intellect and sentiment, reason and feeling, yet in fact moved by generosity rather than cool calculation—people like Martha Blount in the *Epistle to a Lady*, or the Man of Ross in the *Epistle to Bathurst*, or Hugh Bethel, one of his longest-cherished friends, whom he praises to Swift in 1726 as 'too good and honest to live in the World' recommends, to Ralph Allen in 1744 as displaying every moral virtue (*Corr.* II 395; IV 494), and compliments directly in the *Essay on Man* (IV 126). Pope is no sentimental benevolist such as would later palpitate over good actions; his religion, sense of discipline, and intelligence preserve him from that. The best intentions unchecked by moral scruples can end disastrously, and he stands rather with Joseph Butler, who counsels good work, guided by Christian conscience, 'within the Bounds of Veracity and Justice'.[3] Pope's code, likewise, is considerate and careful benevolence:

> *Reflection, Reason, still the ties* improve,*   [*of society]
> *At once extend the int'rest, and the love;*
> *With choice we fix, with sympathy we burn;*

[1] Bolingbroke, *Works*, 1754, III 383.
[2] Maxwell 45.
[3] Butler, *Analogy of Religion*, 1736, 319.

> *Each Virtue in each Passion takes its turn;*
> *And still new needs, new helps, new habits rise,*
> *That graft benevolence on charities.*
>
> *(Essay on Man*, III 133–8)

Pope's sense of moral balance, as mentioned already, does not, like Stoicism, exclude the dramas of psychological variety. Goodness may lie 'in no extreme', yet an artist could find little pleasure in a centrality which cancelled all extremes in a sensible average. Pope's world, rather, like that of astronomy, is one in which God creates harmony from the co-existence, not the mutual cancellation, of competing and conflicting forces. Much depends for him on the role of the Ruling Passion. The idea that from birth each man has a particular bent goes back to antiquity; it appears in character-writers from Theophrastus onwards, in mediaeval 'humour' doctrines and Jonson's adaptation of these, and in Montaigne's theory of the 'forme sienne', the 'forme maistresse'. In each dramatic character, Dryden remarks, 'one virtue, vice, and passion ought to be shown . . . as predominant over all the rest'.[1] In drama this is accepted: in Pope's poems it provides the dynamics, the revelatory principle, of the human scene:

> *Search then the Ruling Passion: There, alone,*
> *The Wild are constant, and the Cunning known.*
>
> *(Epistle to Cobham*, 174–5)

Gravitation explains stellar eccentricities: the Ruling Passion decodes a character's oddest vagaries. And God implants these varying compulsions to provide the variety his universe needs:

> *A mightier Pow'r the strong direction sends,*
> *And sev'ral Men impels to sev'ral ends.*
> *Like varying winds, by other passions tost,*
> *This drives them constant to a certain coast.*
>
> *(Essay on Man*, II 165–8)

A similar doctrine was to control Adam Smith's *Wealth of Nations* (1776), where God's 'invisible hand' attunes together the innumerable com-

---

[1] 'The Grounds of Criticism in Tragedy', *Of Dramatic Poesy and other Critical Essays*, ed G. Watson, 1962, I 250.

peting interests of men, of whom few can see beyond their own ends yet all are interrelated in a providential whole. So, Pope believes, God disposes virtues and vices in order to

> *build on wants, and on defects of mind,*
> *The joy, the peace, the glory of Mankind.*
>
> . . . .
>
> *Wants, frailties, passions, closer still ally*
> *The common int'rest, or endear the tie.*
>
> (*Essay on Man*, II 247–8, 253–4)

This hardly differs from fatalism, of which indeed Pope was accused. If in fact man really is

> *Safe in the hand of one disposing Pow'r,*
> *Or in the natal, or the mortal hour,*
>
> (*Essay on Man*, I 287–8)

or if his weaknesses are the means to social good, he can only subside (gratefully?) into deterministic resignation. This belief is curiously at odds with Pope's satiric impulse, for if God, planning the interplay of individualisms, is a power

> *That counter-works each folly and caprice;*
> *That disappoints th'effect of ev'ry vice,*
>
> (*Essay on Man*, II 239–40)

is it not pointless, indeed impious, to chastise deviations? Pope the moralist lashing folly is at odds with Pope the believer trusting God's wisdom, and Pope the artist delighting in variety.

But that, no doubt, is another of life's paradoxes. The *Epistle to Cobham* explores the endless variations within each individual, and within humankind: the *Epistle to a Lady* treats the 'sweet vicissitude' of women and the ruling passions (love of pleasure and of sway) which systematize their mercurial instabilities. Pope's advocacy of centrality and balance pulls one way and his delight in idiosyncrasy, even when absurd, pulls another. He is equally fascinated, on the one hand, by the sweet temper and steady goodness of Martha Blount and, on the other, by the follies of Sappho, Silia, Narcissa, Philomedé, and Flavia, or by the whirling dangerousness of Atossa's 'eddy brain'.

Montaigne's essay 'Of the Inconsistency of our Actions' Pope thought the best he wrote (Spence § 318a). The subject fascinated him, and he would readily have endorsed the opening words of Isaac Watts's *Doctrine of the Passions* (c. 1725), that 'the Motions of the Heart of Man are infinitely various: The different Forms and Shapes in which our Passions appear, the sudden and secret Turns and Windings of them through the Heart, with the strange Mixtures and Complications of them in their continual Exercise, are innumerable and nameless.' There glow in Pope's lines both the vitality with which, anticipating Browning's Fra Lippo Lippi, he appreciates variety, 'the shapes of things, their colours, lights, and shades, Changes, surprises', and also the brilliance of his sensory and intellectual responses to that variety. Electricity seems to play upon all he writes; dramas of changeable states and passions flash before the mind; vivacities and volatilities dance before the attention, all in the interests of life's unpredictability:

> *All Manners take a tincture from our own,*
> *Or come discolour'd thro' our Passions shown.*
> *Or Fancy's beam enlarges, multiplies,*
> *Contracts, inverts, and gives ten thousand dyes.*
> *Our depths who fathoms, or our shallows finds,*
> *Quick whirls, and shifting eddies, of our minds?*
>
> (*Epistle to Cobham*, 25–30)

Much as Pope insists on eternal order, and rests deeply assured of it, what takes his eye is the shotsilk of change, the 'light and darkness in our chaos join'd' (*Essay on Man*, II 203).

In antiquity Heracleitus preached the interdependence of the One and the Many, unity created from the opposite tensions of dichotomies like night and day, good and evil, contrasting yet inseparable halves of a whole. Empedocles' doctrine that the world is activated by the endless struggle of love and strife, the former uniting, the latter dividing, is epitomized in Horace's *concordia discors* and Ovid's *discors concordia*.[1]

For Pope,

> *ALL subsists by elemental strife;*
> *And Passions are the elements of Life.*
>
> (*Essay on Man*, I 169–70)

[1] Horace, *Ep.* I.xii. 19 ; Ovid, *Metam.* I. 433.

As Sir John Denham wrote of nature,

> *Wisely she knew, the harmony of things*
> *As well as that of sounds, from discord springs.*[1]

Pope's phrase—'All Discord, Harmony, not understood'—means something slightly different, that discord is only apparent, harmony is the reality. Yet the difference is unimportant; in both formulations existence is dialectic, contraries cohere in a whole that includes and transcends them.

'As to the general design of Providence,' Pope told Spence, 'the two extremes of a vice serve like two opposite biases to keep up the balance of things. Avarice lays up (what would be hurtful); Prodigality scatters abroad (what may be useful in other hands). The middle [is] the point for virtue' (Spence § 297). This looks like Aristotle's doctrine of the Mean, but it is more dynamic. The wise man may avoid extremes, yet the wise Providence creates them, and having done so it achieves the Mean through their counteractions, as if a painter were to achieve a prevalent grey not by merging but by juxtaposing black and white. This idea of balance through contrasts lies behind the *Essay on Man* (II 185–216, 231–48) and the *Epistle to Bathurst* (161–228)—the story of miserly Cotta and his spendthrift son. It explains the exculpation, at first sight surprising, of the extravagant Timon, who by wasting his wealth scatters benefits around (*Epistle to Burlington*, 169–72). Happiness may lie 'in no extreme', in Martha Blount's equilibrium, or the decency of the man who

> *Attends the Duties of the Wise and Good,*
> *T'observe a Mean, be to himself a Friend,*
> *To follow Nature, and regard his End.*
>
> (*Windsor Forest*, 250–2)

But variety and energy are as integral to life as happiness: the harmony prescribed as man's inward ideal may be achieved by moderation, but the harmony prescribed over mankind as a whole Heaven achieves in quite different fashion, offsetting, not neutralizing, contrasting qualities in a total balance as an artist offsets light and shade (*Essay on Man*, II

[1] Denham, *Cooper's Hill* 203–4.

208–10), or as, directing different men to different ends (*Epistle to Bathurst*, 161), it interplays contrasted complementary energies, virtues, and vices, to maintain the world's 'order in variety'. 'Virtuous and vicious ev'ry Man must be' (*Essay on Man*, II 231); so, since the Fall must collective humanity. In the Empedoclean (and Lockean) political world, too,

> *jarring int'rests of themselves create*
> *Th'according music of a well-mix'd State.*
>
> (*Essay on Man*, III 293–4)

If, as for Sir Thomas Browne, 'Nature is the Art of God', human nature is that art directing the pattern of passions in the total drama God has devised, and the result is the world's endlessly varied tragi-comedy.

Of this total drama the intended upshot is happiness, 'our being's end and aim', not selfish hedonism but an active and grateful sense of fulfilment. For Aristotle, happiness, man's strongest desire, involves 'an activity of the soul in accordance with virtue or excellence'; for Cicero, 'those who achieve [virtue], guiding themselves by magnanimity and uprightness, are always happy'; for Hooker, likewise, all men desire a happy life, based on the unfettered exercise of righteousness.[1] 'Infinitely happy in himself from all Eternity', God so communicates his goodness as to show 'no other Design in creating Mankind than their Happiness',[2] the happiness not of every immediate pleasure but of virtue, happiness ordained to reward obedience to the divine will. The utmost possible happiness in life, moreover, is not a principle for mankind alone: all creatures, human and other, Shaftesbury declares, are meant to fulfil their purposes in the great scheme, and in that fulfilment to find their satisfaction.[3]

Utilitarianism became the time's characteristic doctrine. Its earliest formulation occurs apparently in Richard Cumberland's *De Legibus Naturae*;[4] Cumberland proclaims that the individual's surest happiness

---

[1] Aristotle, *Nic. Ethics* I.v; Cicero, *De Finibus* V. xxiv; 71; Hooker I. x 2.

[2] John Gay, intro. to King, *Origin of Evil*, 1731, xix.

[3] Shaftesbury, *Characteristics*, II 287.

[4] 1672; tr. John Maxwell as *A Treatise of the Laws of Nature*, 1727.

lies in doing good to others, society's surest happiness in affording collective goodness to its members. Happiness, Wollaston maintains, following Aristotle, 'is the end of society and laws,'[1] and must be maximized. The slogan Bentham was to popularize in the next century, 'the greatest happiness for the greatest numbers', occurs first in Hutcheson's *Inquiry into the Original of our Ideas of Beauty and Virtue*[2].

There is, then, no place for essential evil; God ensures 'always what is *Best* in the whole, and what tends most to the universal *Good*.'[3] Religion, thus confident, must be cheerful, 'rational and free', in spirit 'effusing gladness'.[4] So the *Essay on Man*, composed to put morality in good humour, dwells feelingly on the blessing shared by the virtuous mind which trusts divine benevolence obeys divine will, and knows that

> *What nothing earthly gives, or can destroy,*
> *The soul's calm sun-shine, and the heart-felt joy,*
> *Is Virtue's prize.*
>
> (IV 167–9)

The manifold recommendations of this ideal, from antiquity onwards, prompted Maren-Sofie Røstvig's admirable study.[5] Christianity, hitherto, had believed that man's intended end was salvation, through repentance for sin, and Christ's redemption of the world. The change was profound. The old faith was not, indeed, extinguished by the new, but until the Methodist revival it was eclipsed; little was heard of Christian dogma even in theological works. No earlier Christian century would have defined life's aim as 'Good, Pleasure, Ease, Content' (*Essay on Man*, IV 2), or have proclaimed,

> *Know, all the good that individuals find,*
> *Or God and Nature meant to mere Mankind;*
> *Reason's whole pleasure, all the joys of Sense,*
> *Lie in three words, Health, Peace, and Competence.*
>
> (*Essay on Man*, IV 77–80)

[1] Wollaston, *The Religion of Nature*, 178.
[2] 1725, II. iii. 8.
[3] Clarke, *Discourse* ii, 38.
[4] Thomson, *Liberty*, IV 561, 567.
[5] *The Happy Man: Studies in the Metamorphoses of a Classical Ideal*, 1954–8.

Such a definition is less Christian than Epicurean, the doctrine of the unruffled mind and noble content. It dominates the Horatian mood of much seventeenth- and eighteenth-century literature and, in the seventeenth century's later phase, inspired the desire 'to transform the Happy Man into a virtuous member of society rather than a self-centred recluse'.[1] Addison recommended readers moved by nature's beauties to 'moralize this natural Pleasure of the Soul . . . into a Christian Virtue' (*Spectator*, No. 393), and the effects of a similar desire, in Pope's case, are finely demonstrated in Maynard Mack's *The Garden and the City*: Pope found an Epicurean-Horatian bliss in his Twickenham retirement, yet from that vantage launched on the world of affairs the great moral satires of the 1730s and 1740s.

In so social an age the value of social virtue was strongly urged, and social doctrine shared the ethics of the New Testament, where Christ is the head of the body of believers, a head 'from whom the whole body fitly joined together and compacted by that which every joint supplieth . . . maketh increase of the body unto the edifying of itself in love' (Epistle to the Ephesians, iv. 16). Every man, Clarke writes, 'is bound by the Law of his Nature . . . [and] prompted by the Inclination of his uncorrupted Affections, to look upon himself as a part and member of that one universal body or community, which is made up of all Mankind; to think himself born to promote the publick good and Welfare of all his Fellow-creatures'.[2] Clarke was indeed Christian, and Pope too, though the way they express this fraternal idea is not specifically so: their 'universal body' is wider than the Christian church, and their aim of public welfare is a secular one. Still, they feel a religious conviction though they write in a secular manner: true happiness is found in serving God's design for humankind as, for Hooker, men are 'sociable parts united into one body' and live under a natural law 'which bindeth them each to serve unto others' good, and all to prefer the good of the whole before whatsoever their own particular'.[3] To believe that, and to follow the best lights of human nature—reverence, charity, good temper (*Sapiens sibi qui imperiosus*, Horace had affirmed—the wise man

---

[1] *Ibid.* II 56.
[2] Clarke, *Discourse* ii, 75.
[3] Hooker, I. iii. 5.

governs himself[1])—this is man's happy state. So, Steele proclaims in *The Christian Hero* (1701), God means men by natural society to enter sympathetically into the concerns of others, and the third *Guardian* deplores those 'Dry, Joyless, Dull Fellows' who refuse to 'make a Figure among Mankind upon Benevolent and Generous Principles'.

Life reveals, frequently, a self-love excluding social love: less frequently it reveals the reverse. Pope condemns the former; the latter he would admire as approaching saintliness (he honours the Bishop of Marseilles who attended his people during the plague in 1720: *Essay on Man*, IV 107–8), yet think unattainable by men in general. God has 'bade Self-love and Social be the same' (*Essay on Man*, III 318); for happiness they should coincide. If reasonable self-love is necessary for self-preservation, reasonable social love is necessary for humane existence. Cicero had said as much, had seen social feeling spreading out from family to society,[2] and had often been echoed, by Hooker, Locke, and Clarke among others. Bolingbroke's echo occurs in his 'Fragments or Minutes of Essays': 'we love ourselves, we love our families, we love the particular societies to which we belong, and our benevolence extends at last to the whole race of mankind'.[3] Wherever Pope derived the idea (the old belief that he merely versified Bolingbroke's propositions is now given up), he made fine poetry of it, with a potency that shows how much this secular extension of Christian charity meant to him:

> *Self-love thus push'd to social, to divine,*
> *Gives thee to make thy neighbour's blessing thine.*
> *Is this too little for the boundless heart?*
> *Extend it, let thy enemies have part:*
> *Grasp the whole worlds of Reason, Life, and Sense,*
> *In one close system of Benevolence:*
> *Happier as kinder, in whate'er degree,*
> *And height of Bliss but height of Charity.*
> *God loves from Whole to Parts: but human soul*
> *Must rise from Individual to the Whole.*
> *Self-love but serves the virtuous mind to wake,*

---

[1] Horace, *Satires* II. vii. 81.
[2] Cicero, *De Finibus* V. xxiii. 65, 67.
[3] Bolingbroke, *Works*, IV 11.

> *As the small pebble stirs the peaceful lake;*
> *The centre mov'd, a circle strait succeeds,*
> *Another still, and still another spreads,*
> *Friend, parent, neighbour, first it will embrace,*
> *His country next, and next all human race,*
> *Wide and more wide, th'o'erflowings of the mind*
> *Take ev'ry creature in, of ev'ry kind;*
> *Earth smiles around, with boundless bounty blest,*
> *And Heav'n beholds its image in his breast.*
>
> (*Essay on Man*, IV 353–72)

Virtue, then, is natural to man, and vice unnatural, even though virtue must resist 'natural' lusts and vice obeys them. This is the moral *concordia discors*, divine order beyond the paradoxes of phenomena. The analogies invoked from antiquity were recapitulated: the good man is an instrument in tune[1] (the traditional metaphor familiar from Herbert's *Deniall* and *The Temper*); virtue is health, harmony, beauty, truth, joy; vice is disease, discord, ugliness, falsehood, misery, disproportioned sin jarring against Nature's chime. Isaac Barrow's twenty-sixth sermon, 'Of the Love of our Neighbours', offers the familiar parallels: 'The practice of benignity, of courtesy, of clemency . . . [is] no less grateful and amiable to the mind than beauty to our eyes, harmony to our ears, fragrance to our smell, and sweetness to our palate; and to the same mental sense, malignity, cruelty, harshness, all kinds of uncharitable dealing, are very disgustful and loathsome.' Virtue brings inward security and peace, vice the torment of self-reproach—this is the message, too, of the first sermon of the influential Tillotson.

What, finally, did the doctrine of sociability mean in social and political order? Man, it had always been agreed, needs society, save for those eccentrics who seek salvation in seclusion; as Aristotle had said, 'No man would choose the possession of all goods in the world on the condition of solitariness, man being a social animal'.[2] What was new was less the kind of attention directed to this proposition than the

---

1 Benjamin Whichcote, 'The Venerable Nature, and Transcendent Benefit of Christian Religion', in E. T. Campagnac, *The Cambridge Platonists*, 1901, 46.

2 Aristotle, *Nic. Ethics*, IX. ix.

volume; reaction from seventeenth-century antagonisms inspired a crescendo of agreement that man must recognize his place in creation's design, his part in a scheme of mutual dependence and help.

> *God, in the nature of each being, founds*
> *Its proper bliss, and sets its proper bounds :*
> *But as he fram'd a Whole, the Whole to bless,*
> *On mutual Wants built mutual Happiness :*
> *So from the first eternal ORDER ran,*
> *And creature link'd to creature, man to man.*
>
> (*Essay on Man*, III 109–14)

For Hobbes, men submit of necessity to government; otherwise their natural aggressiveness would render life—in his famous phrase—'solitary, poor, nasty, brutish, and short'.[1] This sobering doctrine, predicated from Renaissance violences, most Augustans rejected in favour of Locke's encouraging account, that men combine under an agreed authority not to ward off reciprocal aggressiveness but to ensure that the necessary transactions of social life are impartially adjudicated: the mutual agreement for such an authority is the social contract defined by Hooker as men's 'growing unto composition and agreement amongst themselves [for] peace, tranquillity, and happy estate'.[2] Sceptics were few: Rochester was one, in the Hobbesian pessimism of his *Satyr against Mankind* (1679), Swift another (though quite Lockean in his sense of balanced constitutional powers), and Mandeville a third, in his study of human rapacity, *The Grumbling Hive* (1705, extended with commentary as *The Fable of the Bees*, 1714). Generally, Augustan doctrine confirmed Locke's heartening faith in mutual wants, mutual affections, mutual help, and mutual happiness. The good man, Shaftesbury declared, is the friend of mankind, and social affections, being natural, fulfil the individual's and society's idiosyncrasy.[3] Shaftesbury had edited Whichcote's sermons and doubtless found congenial the theme of benign religion and virtuous health—'Your Religion is the Mind's Health and good Temper, and it doth help to preserve the

---

[1] Hobbes, *Leviathan*, I xiii.

[2] Hooker, I. x. 4.

[3] Shaftesbury, *Characteristics*, II 41, 293–4.

Bodies Strength; As for instance, Sobriety, Gentleness, Temperance, Meekness, Modesty, Humility, . . . all these do spare and favour the Body; On the Contrary, Pride, Arrogance, Haughtiness, Presumption, Fierceness, Intemperance . . . these waste and spoil the Body.'[1] The qualities praised or dispraised, as agreeing or disagreeing with the precepts of religion, are those relevant to the good or ill of social as well as individual life. Hume, too, recommended social goodness as promoting physiological and psychological well-being—'the blood flows with a new tide; the heart is elevated; and the whole man acquires a vigour which he cannot command in his solitary and calm moments'; by instinct and judgment alike we know that generous qualities are the true expression of human nature.[2] Social virtue, then, is the individual and collective health which the divine order intends.

Similar health and harmony are intended in political dispositions. Locke's theory of the pre-political state of nature, followed by an agreed union for the preservation of life, liberty, and property, is closely versified in the *Essay on Man* (III 199–302). With great poetic vivacity Pope traces the process from patriarchy, with the community a loving and obedient family deducing the existence of a heavenly father from its experience of an earthly one, through the perversion of patriarchal authority into tyranny with its accompaniments of force, bigotry, and superstition, and finally to the emergence of balanced constitutional powers, neither anarchic nor tyrannic, the political version of 'the World's great harmony'. Within this order, and following God's will, man's labours and aspirations serve both himself and others, and his contributions to their good are reciprocated. As in Aristotle, politics means the working of the state to achieve its due end, the good life. Within the framework of just law man must exercise his spirit of brotherly love:

> *Man, like the gen'rous vine, supported lives;*
> *The strength he gains is from th'embrace he gives.*
> *On their own Axis as the Planets run,*
> *Yet make at once their circle round the Sun:*

1 Whichcote, 'The Work of Reason,' in Campagnac, 58.
2 Hume, *Treatise of Human Nature*, II.ii.4; III.iii.1.

> *So two consistent motions act the Soul;*
> *And one regards Itself, and one the Whole.*
>
> (*Essay on Man*, III 311–16)

This means, socially, honest effort for oneself and benevolence for others; politically, shunning the 'mad, ridiculous extremes' Swift castigated (in *Examiner*, No. 16, for instance, or the sermon he preached on the anniversary of Charles I's execution). It means the mutual adjustment of undespotic monarch, responsible aristocracy, and representative Commons, guarding the rights for the preservation which men had left the state of nature for that of law. In 1688, as Liberty proclaims in Thomson's poem, oppression had fled from Britain, from

> *my best established, last,*
> *And, more than Greece or Rome, my steady reign;*
> *The land where, king and people equal bound*
> *By guardian laws, my fullest blessings flow.*[1]

However Pope and Swift judged current politics (and their later satires verge on despair), however friends like Atterbury, Wyndham, and Bolingbroke spun in the whirligig of political fate, the constitutional basis was revered as right. An original, paradisal, patriarchal order, straight from the hand of God, had fallen into tyranny through the perversion of man's will, and now, by Locke's enlightened labours and the principles of 1688, had been redeemed in a new form, preserving the rights and liberties of Britain, and making her a model for the world:

> *Forc'd into virtue thus by Self-defence,*
> *Ev'n Kings learn'd justice and benevolence:*
> *Self-love forsook the path it first pursu'd,*
> *And found the private in the public good.*
>
> (*Essay on Man*, III 279–82)

The renewal of the patriarchal idea as constitutional monarchy, enlightened and just, governing yet consulting aristocracy and commonalty, so that it arouses 'admiration and love in every honest breast, confusion and terror to every guilty conscience', and so that 'the head and all the members are united by one common interest, and animated by

[1] Thomson, *Liberty*, I 316–19.

one common spirit'—this was the ideal promulgated in Bolingbroke's
Idea of a Patriot King (1738), and meant, no doubt, to edify George II
and allay party strife.[1] The political order it propounded accorded with
that providential harmony which the eye of rational faith saw as the
universal principle.

In the great scheme of Pope's poetry, then, a world of considerations
coalesced. Micro- and macrocosmic energy and order, shown by science to work with supremely intelligent power, and believed by faith
to reveal inexhaustible goodness; human psychology empowered by
God to discipline excesses to the intended 'fair weather within', yet,
through man's rebellion in a fallen world, breaking out into the freaks
and vagaries of tragi-comic mankind; this very rebellious variety of
temperament itself, like all the diversity of human activities, led by an
invisible hand intơ benign co-ordination; society designed as mutual
benevolences arising, by divine paradox, from men's very self-loves
themselves; and a political order forming 'Th' according music of a
well-mix'd State'—all this was a creed which did two seemingly con-
tradictory things for Pope. It enabled him to be passionately interested
in the many, in the kaleidoscope of individualisms, in the marvellous
characteristics of the world, and so to fill his work with vivid renderings
of life's infinite variety. At the same time he could, in a spirit both
classical and Christian, subsume all in the One, within which all phenomena function to a great and good end, not as meaningless entities in an
existentialist absurdity. Had he been entirely, or mainly, a philosopher,
his thought would have been general and theoretical: had he not been
a philosopher at all, he would have confined himself to the brilliant
recording of particulars. As it is, he is superbly alive to the world's
vitalities but also shows such ambitious scope of mind as to display,
masterfully and comprehensively, the 'mighty maze! but not without a
plan' (*Essay on Man*, I 6), to the contemplation of which he invites
Bolingbroke, and all his readers.

---

[1] *Letters on the Spirit of Patriotism and the Idea of a Patriot King*, ed A.
Hassall, Oxford 1926, 84, 93.

3: *Pope and the Social Scene*

PAT ROGERS

POPE WAS a parvenu and an outsider. His enemies liked to say so, and they were right in a deeper sense than they can have known. What particularly angered the dunces, it has been said, was the fact that Pope had 'made a fortune by literature and [was] thus free of the captivity they [were] enslaved to'.[1] There is a massive irony here, for Pope was peculiarly disadvantaged when he started out. He did not have it made for him. In retrospect, it is easy to suppose that great writers were bound to come through—that Alfred Tennyson was always Lord Tennyson, prosperous, secure and famous. It is a misleading assumption in general, and a wild distortion in the case of Pope. He inherited one disability, catholicism. And within a few years he had contracted another in the shape of Pott's disease, which left him a crippled dwarf. Either would have been enough to set him outside ordinary society: to limit his educational opportunities, to curtail his civic responsibilities, to blight his prospects. If we want to understand Pope's own social situation, we must give full weight to these two handicaps against which he pitted his will and his talent.

Of the two, his physical disability is the easier to allow for today. Much more strange to us is the slur involved in belonging to the Catholic faith. This was not just a matter of popular attitudes. It was an affair of the statute-book. After the heady innovations of James II, there was no likelihood that Williamite 'toleration' would extend to accepting papists as fully paid-up members of society. In Pope's lifetime Catholicism often connoted Jacobitism, which in turn spelt treason. There was

[1] J. V. Guerinot, *Pamphlet Attacks on Alexander Pope, 1711–1744*, 1969, xlii.

a succession of attempts on William's life, real or staged; in Anne's reign the war with Catholic France was stepped up, and the dynastic problem grew ever more acute. That the Hanoverian accession had not settled the issue in 1714 was shown by the rising of the Old Pretender the following autumn. It was not until the year after Pope's death that the second major rebellion took place, but in the interim a series of minor scares reduced England to a panicky alert, with show trials, informers and cipher-experts, intercepted letters and all the grubby paraphernalia of state intrigue.

This national insecurity bred anti-catholic measures, which seem extraordinarily petty, as well as repressive, to modern eyes. The year after Pope was born, a measure was introduced to expel Papists from London. By this act (1 Wm & M, c. 9) the justices of London and the home counties were empowered to arrest all such persons 'as are or are reputed to be Papists'. If the suspect then refused to take an oath of allegiance, he or she would be 'esteemed and adjudged a Popish Recusant Convict'. It was then forbidden for the individual to 'remaine continue or be within the said City or Cityes [London and Westminster] or Ten miles distance from the same'.[1] It was probably as a result of this act that Pope's father retired from his business as a linen merchant in Lombard Street. He moved first to Hammersmith, which, as Sherburn says, 'if not ten miles from Hyde Park Corner, was remote enough from the City to show his good intentions'.[2] Around 1700 the family moved to Binfield in Windsor Forest. It is customary to congratulate the poet on his good luck in missing urban squalor and enjoying his upbringing amid the rural delights of this sylvan refuge. But the young Pope must have felt in his inner self a strong contrary influence. A sense, that is, that he was being shifted gradually further and further from the centre of things: a consciousness of exclusion and exile. Pope's later drive for success may be seen as an attempt to recapture an inheritance denied him. All the wry jokes in his poems and letters count for little beside the brutally stark phrasing of the statute. Whig historians

[1] Statutes are quoted from *The Law and Working of the Constitution: Documents, 1660–1914*, ed. W. C. Costin and J. S. Watson, I, 2nd edn (1961); here 61–2.
[2] *Early Career of Alexander Pope* 36.

have described some 'precarious' toleration for the Catholics through non-enforcement of such laws;[1] but a Popish Recusant Convict needed no persecution complex to feel he was being driven out from society.

Other measures soon followed. By an act of 1700 (11 Wm III, c.4), Catholics were *inter alia* forbidden to 'keepe Schoole or take upon themselves the Education or Government or Boarding of Youth'. Pope's formal education, whether by private tutors or at a mysterious establishment near Hyde Park, was thus strictly illegal. He was to a considerable extent an autodidact: an early apostle of self-help, for religious rather than economic reasons. Further, the act laid down that Papists should be 'disabled and made incapable to inherit or take by Discent . . . any Lands Tenements or Hereditaments'.[2] By 1 Geo I, s. 2, c. 13, oaths were prescribed which effectively debarred Catholics from official posts, from the bar and other professions. In the same year, 1715, came a statute appointing commissioners 'to inquire of the estates of certain traitors', official double-talk for a scheme to compel Papists to register their estates as a prelude to jacking up the land-tax on this class. Pope's correspondence shows some anxiety on this score, for reasons his editor helps to explain: 'In anticipation of this device to increase tax on Catholics and possibly because of questionable title to the house and land at Binfield (for Catholics were not allowed to buy land, and the Popes had a sort of concealed ownership of the place at Binfield) the Popes had sold out and moved to Chiswick, there renting a new house.' (*Corr.* I 344 & n) Once again the law had forced the family to move on like the merest vagabonds. For one so immersed in filial piety as Pope, the psychic effect must have been incalculable. Finally, we should note 9 Geo I, c.18, by which taxes were yet further stepped up. 'If this Bill passes,' wrote Pope at the time, 'I shall lose a good part of my income. . . . I know I wish my country well and if it undoes me, it shall not make me wish it otherwise.' (*Corr.* II 173) The bill did pass. Later in life it seems that Pope had to vacate his house at Twickenham when the court moved to Hampton Court, and that in his final illness he

---

[1] W. E. H. Lecky, *A History of England in the Eighteenth Century*, 'Cabinet edn' (1892) I 352–3. Lecky's account of the 'perpetual insecurity' of Catholics in this period remains of great value.

[2] Costin and Watson, *Constitution*, 90–91.

was deterred from receiving medical attention in London by a royal proclamation occasioned by the first stirrings of the Forty-Five rebellion.[1]

This adds up to a long record of legal harassment. And it would not make things much better that a substantial minority of the population faced the same threats. It is true that the penal code was even harsher in Ireland. There, Catholics were excluded from positions of public trust although they made up three quarters of the population. Unregistered priests, if discovered, were to be branded on the cheek with a red-hot iron. But the state of affairs in England itself can be gauged from this anecdote related by Lecky: 'In 1729—in the reign of George II and under the ministry of Townshend and Walpole—a Franciscan friar, named Atkinson, died in Hurst Castle, in the seventy-fourth of his life and the thirtieth of his imprisonment, having been incarcerated in 1700 for performing the functions of a Catholic priest.'[2] It was not typical but it could still happen. Such medieval implacability was commoner in the statute-book than in day-to-day life, but that can hardly have consoled Pope and his fellow-sufferers.

Of course, Pope learnt to live with his disability—as with his 'own crazie health' (*Corr.* IV 299)—and even to laugh at it. Usually, however, there is an undertone of bitterness beneath the calm precision. As for instance in the lines on his father in *Epistle II ii*:

> But knottier Points we knew not half so well,
> Depriv'd us soon of our Paternal Cell;
> And certain Laws, by Suff'rers thought unjust,
> Deny'd all Posts of Profit or of Trust:
> Hopes after Hopes of pious Papists fail'd,
> While mighty WILLIAM's thundring Arm prevail'd.
> For Right Hereditary tax'd and fin'd,
> He stuck to Poverty with Peace of Mind;
> And me, the Muses help'd to undergo it;
> Convict a Papist He, and I a Poet.   (58–67)

The quasi-legal terminology ('posts of profit', 'fin'd', 'convict'—this

[1] Twickenham IV 168–9n.
[2] Lecky, *History of England*, I 356.

last the archaic form actually used in the Act) lends a quality of explicitness and reality to the complaint. We are dealing not with vague prejudices but with the letter of the law. Similarly there is an edge to Pope's voice when he writes in *To Bethel*:

> *Fortune not much of humbling me can boast;*
> *Tho' double-tax'd, how little have I lost?*

> *(Satire II ii 151–2)*

As a matter of fact, Pope always enjoyed guying measures of national security; he makes the Riot Act the occasion for a mildly comic gallantry (*Corr.* I 311). But the joke covers a wound. Pope needed to succeed as a poet, to make himself independent and financially stable, for purely personal reasons. But these factors were compounded by an urge to assert the power and value of his art in a society which offered him reduced citizenship. His poetry is a triumph of the spirit in an almost existentialist way. The community which blocked his chances is made the subject-matter of literature which will transcend that community. The style of a civilisation which made him a 'convict' and a pariah is turned with exquisite artistry into a satiric vehicle: its language of polite acceptance is converted into an idiom of oblique criticism and ironic qualification. Society imposed its pains and penalties on Pope, and Pope took his revenge as only a great imaginative writer can. He drew up his own penal code, and found in the fictive liberties of art the personal release that the repressions of life always threatened to deny him.

The England into which Pope was born was still predominantly rural. Indeed it was little better than scrubland over large tracts of the country. At the end of the seventeenth century, says Macaulay, 'many routes which now pass through an endless succession of orchards, hayfields, and beanfields, then ran through nothing but heath, swamp and warren'.[1] The fens had been drained, but much reclamation remained to be done. 'Huge, great and vast fens and marshes' survived even in southern England; in 1706 much of Romney Marsh was under water, and the defences had to be strengthened. As the Webbs record, 'In the

[1] T. B. Macaulay, *The History of England from the Accession of James II,* 1909 edn, I 241.

interior of England nearly every county had its hundreds or its thousands of acres of "moss" or swamp.' London itself was full of foul ditches, stagnant closes, obstructed sewers: its slums wore a half-rustic air, with pigs rooting among the offal from slaughter-houses.[1] Most of the primeval forest cover had disappeared, but timber still remained basic to the economy and woodland was much less scattered than today. Enclosure had begun, but save in a few counties it was little advanced. In Enfield Chase, just outside London, there was an area of twenty-five miles' circumference which was said to contain only three houses and scarcely any enclosed fields.

Moreover, the undeveloped state of the countryside was both cause and effect of poor transport facilities. Social life in the early eighteenth century was acutely affected by this circumstance, although the modern concept of 'communication', straddling geography and psychology, had not yet come into men's minds. Again Macaulay is to the point:

> The chief cause which made the fusion of the different elements of society so imperfect was the extreme difficulty which our ancestors found in passing from place to place. . . . Every improvement of the means of locomotion benefits mankind morally and intellectually as well as materially, and not only facilitates the interchange of the various productions of nature and art, but tends to remove national and provincial antipathies, and to bind together all the branches of the great human family. . . . On the best lines of communication the ruts were deep, the descents precipitous, and the way often such as it was hardly possible to distinguish, in the dusk, from the uninclosed heath and fen which lay on both sides.[2]

So the stories of travellers losing their way on the Great North Road; the almost farcical experiences of Celia Fiennes; the complaints of the pamphleteers, and the harsh words of travellers like Defoe; so the dreadful reputation of muddy Sussex, of Hockley in the Hole (literally), Baldock and a score of such places.

Pope cannot have missed any of this. He was a devotee of the

[1] Sidney and Beatrice Webb, *English Local Government* IV, 1922, 13, 16, 38, 88.
[2] Macaulay, *History of England*, I 242, 287–8.

'ramble' and spent much of his mature life in a sustained peregrination of the seats of the gentry, major and minor. His friends, such as Bathurst and the second Earl of Oxford, were equally incapable of staying still for long. Moreover, Pope was a great letter-writer, with a specially clear sense of what could and should be said in that medium. He was a crony of Ralph Allen, who did so much to improve the postal services. His health made riding difficult and brought home to him the dangers of the road. On one famous occasion he was catapulted into the River Crane, on his way back from a visit to Bolingbroke. As Gay told Swift, he was thrown out when the coach was overturned where a bridge had 'broken down', with the result that he was 'up to the knots of his perriwig in water'. (*Corr.* II 399) His hand was badly cut and at one time he feared that he would lose the use of two fingers of his right hand. Luckily, this did not prove to be so, and Pope contented himself with the reflection that the injury was 'a Fine paid for my life'. (*Corr.* II 405) Soon he was talking of travelling again, scarcely abashed.

Little of Pope's poetry is directly about travel. His satire of the Grand Tour in Book IV of *The Dunciad* is not diminished in effect by the fact that he did not and could not make such a journey himself. Nor, for that matter, did he ever see Rome, which hovers behind so many of his poems. He cannot have set eyes on uplands much grander than the Cotswolds or the Yorkshire Wolds. If we are indeed to set the poet in his landscape, to borrow a phrase from Maynard Mack, we shall think first of the mellow countryside of southern England. It is estates like John Knight's at Gosfield or Lord Harcourt's at Stanton Harcourt which fulfilled his needs best. His affinity with men like Bathurst was first of all a community of taste, not least in the matter of landscape planning. All his days, Pope was a poet of daylight and champaign; with Swift we think of the windy downs about Letcombe Bassett or the desolate landing-stage at Holyhead. For Swift, pastoral is a gaudy fiction, to be mocked by confronting its idealities with the sordid reality of city living. For Pope, idyll and georgic can still be lived out, approximately anyway, in the sylvan retirement of Cirencester:

To say a word in praise either of your Wood or You [Bathurst], would be alike impertinent each being, in its kind, the finest I know, & the most agreeable. I can only tell you very honestly,

(without a word of the high Timber of the one, or the high Qualities of the other) that I thought it the best company I ever knew, &
the best Place to enjoy it in. . . . Mr Gay is as zealously carry'd
to the Bower by the force of Imagination as ever Don Quixote
was to an Enchanted Castle. The Wood is to him the Cave of
Montesinos: He has already planted it with Myrtles, & peopled it
with Nymphs. The old Woman of the Pheasantry appears alredy
an Urganda; & there wants nothing but a Christal Rivulet to purl
thro the Shades, which might be large enough to allay Mr Lewis's
great Thirst after water.
                                                          (*Corr.* I 476–7)

The same desire to give an imaginative grace to the diurnal, to make
fancy irradiate the homely, appears in Pope's deep concern with his
garden, so well chronicled by Professor Mack, and discussed by James
Sambrook in the next chapter of this volume. And it shows, too, in
Windsor Forest, where the trees are at once concrete lumps of timber,
ready to 'bear *Britain*'s Thunder', to sustain her trade and strengthen
her fleet, and also features in the new 'Groves of Eden', pastoral
machinery *and* literal treetrunks.

As for Pope's consciousness of what might be called psychic space,
it is enough to quote the delicious poem he addressed to Teresa Blount,
'On her leaving the Town, after the Coronation'. The note is one of
half-comic elegy which he made his own:

> *Thus from the world fair* Zephalinda *flew,*
> *Saw others happy, and with sighs withdrew;*
> *Not that their pleasures caus'd her discontent,*
> *She sigh'd not that They stay'd, but that She went.*
>
> *She went, to plain-work, and to purling brooks,*
> *Old-fashion'd halls, dull aunts, and croaking rooks,*
> *She went from Op'ra, park, assembly, play,*
> *To morning walks, and pray'rs three hours a day;*
> *To pass her time 'twixt reading and Bohea,*
> *To muse, and spill her solitary Tea,*
> *Or o'er cold coffee trifle with the spoon,*
> *Count the slow clock, and dine exact at noon;*
> *Divert her eyes with pictures in the fire,*
> *Hum half a tune, tell stories to the squire;*

> *Up to her godly garret after sev'n,*
> *There starve and pray, for that's the way to heav'n.*
>
> (7–22)

The delicacy of touch is appropriate to the subject and the recipient. But it also enables Pope to convey much in little. The flat rhyme *spoon/ noon* beautifully suggests the monotony of the country round; the fact that through a transferred epithet even the tea-cup looks forlorn and bereft; the feckless stop-go enacted in the line 'Hum half a tune, tell stories to the squire'; finally the ten commonplace words creeping along to the dull conclusion—these are masterly strokes, rendering with deft economy the self-pity of the aimless girl. Pope goes on to describe the thoughts of Miss Blount as she pictures 'the fancy'd scene' of court gaiety. Once more his poetic workmanship is applied to dramatise a social situation—here, the exaggerated contrast between town liveliness and rural dumps. The theme was conventional; it is Pope's sense of poetic occasion—the neatness with which he chooses words, places rhymes, bends the metre—that brings these fashionable contrasts to life.[1]

A number of attempts have been made to tabulate the various classes in the social structure of eighteenth-century England. Unfortunately, neither the schemes of contemporaries such as Gregory King and Defoe, nor the taxonomies of later authorities, quite suit the case. Instead I have chosen to isolate four groups with whom Pope had significant dealings and whose social identity bears on his art. A representative figure is taken for each group in turn. The categories are, first, the peer and great landowner, exemplified by Lord Bathurst; second, the country gentlemen, here Hugh Bethel; third, the professional man, the instance being William Fortescue, advocate and later judge; fourth, women, as represented by Martha Blount. The last is not a status group familiar to modern sociology, though it may be none the worse for that. The truth is that in the eighteenth century there was one class structure for men, and another—parallel but independent—for

---

[1] For other aspects of the technique here, see my 'Pope and the Syntax of Satire', *Literary English since Shakespeare*, ed G. Watson, 1970, 29–50. And compare Pope's letter to Martha Blount, *Corr.* I 375.

their wives and daughters.[1] To separate women in this rough scheme is therefore not to perpetrate a sexual insult, but to follow the realities of the time. In each of these cases, I shall say something of the category at large; give a brief account of the individual selected, and of the course of their relations with Pope; and finally, examine a poem dedicated to the man or woman in question, with a view to assessing the 'social' implications that lie within the poetry.

At the top of the social scale, then, we find Allen Bathurst (1684–1775) first Baron and later first Earl Bathurst. He was not strictly an aristocrat by origin; his father was a knight, an MP and government servant, whilst his mother was the daughter of a baronet. The son was raised to the peerage in 1712, as one of the twelve Tory nominees elevated to the Lords in order to secure the passage of the Treaty of Utrecht. Another was George Granville, Baron Lansdowne, to whom is dedicated *Windsor Forest*—a poem celebrating the selfsame peace. Thus achieving a barony at the age of twenty-eight, Bathurst did not acquire an earldom for exactly sixty years more—which may be some kind of record. He was first elected member for Cirencester to the 1705 Parliament, which means that he spent some seventy years in public life. He survived Pope, a younger man, by four decades. This proves that he had stamina in plenty—a quality sometimes underrated, as when robustness is taken for coarseness. In some ways he was a kind of Tory version of Walpole. All this sounds unpromising material for recruitment to the select ranks of Pope's acquaintance. The case demands investigation.

It cannot be denied that Bathurst had his limitations. He was old-fashioned in many of his attitudes. The improvements he designed for his house at Cirencester were neither architecturally pure nor, it emerged in time, structurally sound. He was a rake of the eighteenth-century kind; more like Old Q than Lord Byron, with a sensuality that was bluff and direct rather than poetic and romantic. He was certainly no vulgarian—there is a clipped bitten-off sensibility struggling to express itself in his letters to Pope—but he was no aesthete either.

[1] On class-barriers for women, see Dorothy Marshall, *English People in the Eighteenth Century* 1957 268–9.

Along with women and (in a more lukewarm fashion) politics, land-scape-gardening was the great love of his life. But he pursued it with a measure of lordly insouciance, as though he might at any time find a more suitable occupation. In this respect, as in others, he contrasts markedly with another of Pope's friends, the Earl of Burlington. Burlington was prim and punctilious where Bathurst was casual and generous. More particularly, Burlington followed *his* passion, architecture, with the stiffness of an over-coached suitor; his buildings have some of the unbending pedantry that attaches to the singleminded amateur.

Bathurst entered the purple at a fortunate moment. In the 1720s, there were only 179 English peers, of whom a third were inactive for one reason or another. A measure to restrict the creation of new peerages had been defeated in 1719; but a conservative policy prevailed until the time of George III. This meant that early in the century the upper echelons of society were a closed corporation, with the strengths and defects of that situation.[1] Moreover, it was a good time to be a landowner on a large scale. After the collapse of the South Sea Company in 1720 there was a 'panic rush for less profitable but more secure investments in land', which meant that the social (as well as the investment) value of land went up.[2] The bigger owners consolidated their position at this juncture; Pope's latter-day friend, the Duchess of Marlborough, bought up a casualty of the Bubble in 1723, and 'thereafter hardly a year passed but what she bought an estate or two, until at her death [in 1744, less than six months after Pope's] she left some thirty in all'.[3]

In addition to this, careful planning could ensure the maintenance of family fortunes. 'The grand object of family policy,' it has been said, 'was to secure the continuance and enhance the wealth and position of the family, and to this end the succession to the property and the

[1] J. H. Plumb, *England in the Eighteenth Century*, Harmondsworth, 1950, 34; G. D. H. Cole and Raymond Postgate, *The Common People, 1746–1946*, 1966, 143.
[2] W. A. Speck, 'Conflict in Society,' *Britain after the Glorious Revolution*, ed G. Holmes, 1969, 147.
[3] A. L. Rowse, *The Early Churchills*, 2nd edn Harmondsworth 1969, 413.

marriage of the children, particularly the marriage of the heir or heiress were carefully regarded.'[1] So we have dynastic marriages such as those between Pope's friends the Harleys and the great Pelham-Holles line; elaborate conveyancing devices, and a series of ploys developed to strengthen the hold of one generation on its successors. These 'arrangements of immense complexity', as even Professor Habakkuk finds them, had far-reaching social consequences. Habakkuk has shown how

> the development of instruments for long-term mortgage enabled gentlemen both to survive the natural disasters of agrarian life or to undertake improvements that would otherwise have been beyond their means, and how the widespread use of stricter marriage settlements gave greater protection to estates from generation to generation; also, estates tended to grow in size and this in itself provided greater security from the follies of heirs and the disasters of time. . . . A stable gentry obviously encouraged social cohesion. . . .

On the whole this applies most forcibly to those who were already considerable landowners; they could employ the best lawyers, for one thing. Such men were in the most advantageous position to exploit mineral wealth, though they generally provided capital and encouragement rather than working the resources themselves. 'The mining of coal, the establishment of an ironworks or the quarrying of building stone were just as legitimate a part of estate exploitation as the letting of land to tenant-farmers.. . .'[2] This is shown by the Duke of Chandos, with whom Pope maintained an uneasy friendship, and who dabbled in many branches of industry. But equally the self-made Ralph Allen became a leading magnate in providing building-stone for public works in London.

Bathurst was more interested in silviculture than soap-boiling. All the same, he had his own strong dynastic sense, and indeed the planting

---

[1] G. E. Mingay, *English Landed Society in the Eighteenth Century*, 1963, 32.

[2] H. J. Habakkuk, 'England,' *The European Nobility in the Eighteenth Century*, ed. A. Goodwin, 1953, 2–6; J. H. Plumb, *Sir Robert Walpole: The Making of a Statesman*, 1956, 6–14; Plumb, *The Growth of Political Stability in England, 1675–1725*, 1967, 9–10; Mingay, 190.

of woods is an offering to posterity. Pope, of course, was alive to the fact. In 1722 he wrote to a friend of his desire to conduct a Mrs Digby round the park at Cirencester:

> How much I wish to be her Guide thro' that enchanted Forest, is not to be exprest: I look upon myself as the Magician appropriated to the place, without whom no mortal can penetrate into the Recesses of those sacred Shades. I could pass whole Days, in only describing to her the future, and as yet visionary Beauties, that are to rise in those Scenes: The Palace that is to be built, the Pavillions that are to glitter, the Colonnades that are to adorn them: Nay more, the meeting of the *Thames* and the *Severn*, which (when the noble Owner has finer Dreams than ordinary) are to be led into each other's Embraces thro' secret Caverns of not above twelve or fifteen Miles, till they rise and openly celebrate their Marriage in the midst of an immense Amphitheatre, which is to be the Admiration of Posterity a hundred Years hence. But till the destin'd time shall arrive that is to manifest these Wonders, Mrs. *Digby* must content herself with seeing what is at present no more than the finest wood in *England*. (*Corr.* II 115–16)

As has been pointed out, 'Posterity did not, in fact, have to wait a hundred years, and Bathurst died a mere fourteen before the 2¼-mile Sapperton Tunnel, with its crenellated Gothic and its sober classical openings, was dug under his property and the Thames and Severn Canal formally opened by King George III in person.'[1] And it is the literal truth that we can enjoy Cirencester today, as we can Cobham's Stowe and Oxford's Wimpole, more fully than could any contemporary. More striking yet, though, is the imaginative vigour of Pope's picture. He makes the development of inland navigation sound like an Elizabethan idyll, the marriage of Isis and Thames or something of the sort. The Augustans were the last writers who could compass such a union of fancy and reality.

To us, it may have a disconcertingly literary air. But then Georgian 'improvement' was highly bookish in inspiration. All Burlington's heroes were to be found in handsome folios; none of them survived on the face of the earth. Both architecture and landscape gardening were

[1] James Lees-Milne, *Earls of Creation*, 1962, 44. This work provides by far the best account of Bathurst.

'essentially historical and pictorial' in quality. Sentiment determined how fabric and timber should be arranged: if the first Great Architect could not be called in personally, at least his vice-gerent in moral and philosophical matters, the Earl of Shaftesbury, pointed the way.[1] And of course a house was more than a stately home or a showplace. In Habakkuk's words, 'With the family estate went the family house, the physical expression of the standing of the family and the tangible repository of its traditions.'[2] It was the focus of local life, the acme of patrician 'retirement', and a perpetual drain on its owner. But it could also be a plaything. Pope's own villa at Twickenham in a way could be regarded as a minuscule suburban country house and estate. Bathurst speaks of it with the sort of teasing affection one gives to small domestic pets. On one occasion he threatened, if Pope did not visit him, to 'send one of my wood-Carts & bring away your whole house & Gardens, & stick it in the midst of Oakly-wood where it will never be heard off any more, unless some of the Children find it out in Nutting-season & take possession of it thinking I have made it for them.' (*Corr.* III 134) Patent as the humour is, there *was* a sense in which the villa, the garden and the grotto might happily have been transported to Cirencester or Stowe, to be placed alongside the Gothic follies, Temples of Virtue and other mythopoeic *bric-à-brac*.

It was in this area, then, that the interests of Bathurst and Pope fell most closely into line. For the rest, we have some record of the peer as a speaker in the Lords: Samuel Johnson's stint as parliamentary reporter covered speeches on the inadequacies of the Gin Act, and on the somewhat technical subject of indemnifying evidence.[3] Bathurst was an inveterate tripper, and Pope frequently makes a joke of his inaccessibility. 'I had epistolized you sooner,' he writes on one occasion, 'but that knowing you were yet in your worldly pilgrimage . . . I did not know how to write *at* you; and even the post, all post haste as it is, cannot shoot you flying.' (*Corr.* IV 148) A worldly pilgrim Bathurst assuredly

[1] Lees-Milne 14–16.
[2] Habakkuk, 'England', 3.
[3] E. L. McAdam, *Dr. Johnson and the English Law*, Syracuse 1951, 26–6; Dorothy George, *London Life in the Eighteenth Century*, new edn, Harmondsworth 1966, 48.

was. 'In my late Peregrinations,' says Pope another time, 'I heard of you every where, where you *Had been*; where you *was*, no mortal cou'd tell.' (*Corr.* IV 192) As for worldliness, there are many references to Pope himself as 'one, who has out-lasted twenty, (or twenty thousand) of your Mistresses, in affection, attachment, & gratitude to you'. (*Corr.* IV 342) Sometimes Pope deals in a sort of comic insult: 'There was a Man in the Land of Twitnam, called Pope. He was a Servant of the Lord Bathurst of those days, a Patriarch of great Eminence, for getting children, at home & abroad. But his Care for his Family, and his Love for strange women, caused the said Lord to forget all his Friends of the Male-Sex; insomuch that he knew not, nor once rememberd, there was such a Man in the Land of Twitnam as aforesaid.' (*Corr.* II 292) And a more indirect version of this:

It is observd of Very Aged people, & such whose memories Long Life & much Business have worn away, that they better recollect Things long since past than those which are nearer. I therefore hope, My Lord you may have yet some glympse of remembrance, that there was at the latter End of Queen Anne's reign, a Poet of the name of Pope, to whom you sometimes afforded an hour of Conversation as well as reading (tho' indeed the former was the lesser Task of the two, for his Works were much longer than his Visits) you sometimes also, in those days, & evn to the middle or later end of the Reign of George 1st honor'd him with your Letters. . . . I also am sensible, that many Great & Noble Works, worthy a large Mind & Fortune, have employd your cares & time; such as Enclosing a Province with Walls of Stone, planting a whole Country with Clumps of Firs, digging Wells . . . as deep as to the Center, erecting Palaces, raising Mounts, undermining High ways, & making Communications by Bridges. Not to enumerate those many & Various Studies which possess your Lordships mind; in which it may suffice to say Every thing has place except Polemic Divinity, but chiefly & principally Natural Philosophy, & the Art of Medicine: Witness those Instructions, which Physicians, instead of giving, Receive from You, even while you are their Patient: They come, to feel your pulse, & prescribe you physick! presumptuous Men! they return with their own pulses examind, & their own Bodies purgd, vomited, or blooded.

Among all these Employments how can I expect to be rememberd?

(*Corr.* III 130)

The air of genial insolence, with calculated exaggerations ('Enclosing a Province'—Bathurst comically seen as a kind of Roman governor for a moment) and easygoing allusions, is immediately striking. I fancy Pope was much more at home with Bathurst than with Burlington. Sterne was to meet Bathurst when the latter was eighty-five; he called the baron 'a prodigy . . . A disposition to be pleased, and a power to please others beyond whatever I knew: added to which, a man of learning, courtesy and feeling.'[1] A man, in fact, whom Pope needed to patronise as little as to flatter with limp obsequiousness.

Pope came to know many of the great. For his Homer, as Leslie Stephen says, he 'received a kind of commission from the upper class to execute the translation. . . . Every person of quality . . . felt himself bound to promote so laudable an undertaking.' Perhaps, as Stephen contends, Pope became 'a little too proud' of his independence and his visits from the Prince of Wales.[2] But he had earned his place the hard way. An acquaintance which included Sheffield, Harcourt, Orrery, Egmont, Marchmont, the two Earls of Oxford, Peterborough and many others was a distinguished circle for the linen merchant's son to attain. This is disregarding non-aristocrats as eminent and as *comme il faut* as the retired Secretary of State, Sir William Trumbull. However, of all these men, it was Bolingbroke, Burlington and Bathurst who counted most; and Bathurst who perhaps excited Pope's deepest affection.

In the letters we detected a note of cocky and outspoken banter. My view is that some of this quality carries over to the splendid poem Pope dedicated *To Bathurst*. Recently there has been some tendency to read this work too solemnly. It is true that there are overtones of Biblical parable, as well as hints of major themes in classical myth.[3]

---

[1] Lees-Milne 55.

[2] Leslie Stephen, *English Literature and Society in the Eighteenth Century*, 1963 edn, 51, 65. Stephen remarks that the subscription list for the Homer seems 'almost a directory to the upper circle of the day'. This is a slight exaggeration. There were more aristocratic subscribers to Joseph Trapp's Virgil in 1718, though that attracted an even more overwhelmingly Tory and Oxonian clientele than Pope's translation. Bathurst subscribed to both works, Burlington and Fortescue to Pope's only.

[3] See E. R. Wasserman's reading of the poem, *Pope's 'Epistle to Bathurst'*, Baltimore 1960, especially 13–33.

But overall, the texture of the writing seems to me informed by a speed and a lightness of touch foreign to homiletic writing. The story of Sir Balaam at the climax is carried off with a curt, dismissive finality:

> *There (so the Dev'l ordain'd) one Christmas-tide*
> *My good old Lady catch'd a cold, and dy'd.* (383–4)

There is hardly time for the parenthesis; while 'catch'd' was already approaching a vulgarism. Pope mimics the language of the city ('a lucky Hit'; 'dull Cits'; 'chirping Pint'). And even in the more intense passages earlier, a slangy irreverence colours the diction—'gingling' (67), 'plaister'd' (92), 'a plum' (124). Hyperbole is everywhere, as in the servant's intervention:

> *A Statesman's slumbers how this speech would spoil!*
> *'Sir, Spain has sent a thousand jars of oil;*
> *Huge bales of British cloth blockade the door;*
> *A hundred oxen at your levee roar.'* (43–6)

The same qualities are apparent at the most morally fervent junctures of the poem. The fanciful invention of the letters is not far away when Pope writes in this accent:

> *Once, we confess, beneath the Patriot's cloak,*
> *From the crack'd bag the dropping Guinea spoke,*
> *And gingling down the back-stairs, told the crew,*
> *'Old Cato is as great a Rogue as you.'*
> *Blest paper-credit! last and best supply!*
> *That lends Corruption lighter wings to fly!*
> *Gold imp'd by thee, can compass hardest things,*
> *Can pocket States, can fetch or carry Kings;*
> *A single leaf shall waft an Army o'er,*
> *Or ship off Senates to a distant Shore;*
> *A leaf, like Sybil's, scatter to and fro,*
> *Our fates and fortunes, as the winds shall blow:*
> *Pregnant with thousands flits the Scrap unseen,*
> *And silent sells a King, or buys a Queen.* (65–78)

And then Pope turns directly to Bathurst, with a plain vocative—'What say you?' The picture is funny as much as sinister: the process of corruption is made all too easy (note *waft, flit, ship off*, all connoting the absence of effort). The point is not that Pope was not serious in the *Epistle to Bathurst*. He certainly was, though I suspect he cared less about the financial revolution than about, say, what it was to belong to the Catholic faith in a Protestant state. The issue is the level of the satire, or if you will the poetic temperature.

Professor Humphreys has said of the *Epistle to Burlington* that 'in lines of complex opulence the Earl is encouraged to enrich the beauty and bounty of his estates. . . .'[1] Quite so; the poem is addressed to a self-conscious aesthete, with scholarly tastes and earnest convictions. Though even here, in passing, the portrait of Timon incorporates in its presentation some of the subject's vulgarity—the Tritons *spew*, light *quirks* of music are heard, two cupids *squirt*, the painted saints *sprawl* like hoydens. With Bathurst it is different. Pope was addressing a worldly, sociable, cynical nobleman, who carried his stock of learning lightly and put on no false dignity with a man like Pope. So the poet can sometimes adopt a jaunty carriage—

> *What slaughter'd hecatombs, what floods of wine,*
> *Fill the capacious Squire, and deep Divine!*   (203–4)

Deep suggests (1) ironically, profound; (2) deep in his cups; (3) bottomless is capacity; (4) he knows which side his bread is buttered on; (5) with unplumbed depths of depravity. And sometimes, when he chooses to be more severe, he puts the metre into its sensible shoes and darkens the imagery:

> *Oh! that such bulky Bribes as all might see,*
> *Still, as of old, incumber'd Villainy!*
> *In vain may Heroes fight, and Patriots rave;*
> *If secret Gold saps on from knave to knave.*
> *Could France or Rome divert our brave designs,*
> *With all their brandies or with all their wines?*
> *What could they more than Knights and Squires confound,*
> *Or water all the Quorum ten miles round?*   (35–42)

In each case, however, there is a note of bold defiance absent from the poem to Burlington.

[1] A. R. Humphreys, *The Augustan World*, 1955, 5.

It is possible to explain this difference in several ways: there are, for one thing, dissimilarities in the actual subject-matter. Nevertheless, the important factor seems to me to lie elsewhere. The *Epistle to Burlington* is built on a poetic grammar of assent. The noble peroration of this poem diffuses a basic optimism. Burlington will carry out impressive public works. However badly he does it (the implication runs) the 'falling Arts' will be no worse off; and even a projector less gifted than the Earl might hope to improve on the roadmaking and church-building of the age. There are satiric overtones to the passage, but they by no means impugn the compliment to Burlington. *Windsor Forest* was not more confident in its yea-saying. But though Pope aligns the two lords ('Who plants like B A T H U R S T, or who builds like B O Y L E'), he underwrites Bathurst's attitudes to a greatly reduced extent. The point comes in *Epistle II ii* once more:

> *All vast Possessions (just the same the case*
> *Whether you call them Villa, Park, or Chase)*
> *Alas, my BATHURST! what will they avail?*
> *Join* Cotswold *Hills to* Saperton *'s fair Dale,*
> *Let rising Granaries and Temples here,*
> *There mingled Farms and Pyramids appear,*
> *Link Towns to Towns with Avenues of Oak,*
> *Enclose whole Downs in Walls, 'tis all a joke!*
> *Inexorable Death shall level all,*
> *And Trees, and Stones, and Farms, and Farmer fall.*   (254–63)

Burlington is to embark on a public works programme which will succeed insofar as it is judged by secular standards—in terms of immediate human benefit, or of patriotic glory, or of civic renown. Imaginatively Burlington is seen as a kind of magnified Chairman of the Town-Planning and Highway Engineering Department. Bathurst is judged by the harsher standards of private conduct. His failure is an infraction of the natural order of creation. Mortality is a challenge to Burlington. His inspiration will usher in an epoch when churches will stand for centuries, unlike the present rickety collection. Bathurst encounters mortality as a defeat, for his accomplishments are viewed *sub specie aeternitatis.*

I think Pope arranged matters so for a definite reason. He is less charitable towards Bathurst's achievements—as they are poetically conceived—because he shared the hopes and dreams of his friend, as he did not quite those of Burlington. Moreover, he felt a greater intimacy with Bathurst, which allowed him to portray a less comforting outcome for his efforts. It is notable that in *Liberty*, James Thomson (who knew neither peer well) distributes the honours more evenly:

> *Lo! numerous domes a Burlington confess—*
> *For kings and senates fit; the palace see!*
> *The temple breathing a religious awe;*
> *Even framed with elegance the plain retreat,*
> *The private dwelling. Certain in his aim,*
> *Taste, never idly working, saves expense.*
> *See! Sylvan scenes, where art alone pretends*
> *To dress her mistress and disclose her charms—*
> *Such as a Pope in miniature has shown,*
> *A Bathurst o'er the widening forest spreads,*
> *And such as form a Richmond, Chiswick, Stowe.* (V 690–700)

To return from this puffy rhetoric to the racy vigour and colloquial rhythms of the *Epistle to Bathurst* is to get an inkling of Pope's close and confidential relation to his friend. Thomson writes as a humble supplicant: Pope as virtually an equal, whose easy commerce with the nobility permits him freedom of speech.

The second category, that of the country gentleman, is represented by Hugh Bethel. The name of Bethel (1689–1748) is familiar only to students of Pope and a few local historians. He made no impact on national life. In this, however, he is altogether typical of his breed. Bethel happened to be a Whig; this was far from universal, but it was not uncommon. Not every knight of the shire was a Roger de Coverley or a Squire Western. Bethel was better educated than many of his class, although he seems not to have attended a university. He took a keen interest in the visual arts, and stood at the centre of a group of Yorkshire connoisseurs which included the talented amateur architect Colonel James Moyser. Partly owing to asthma, he was a frequent visitor to the

Continent, in particular Italy. This gave him a certain breadth to go with his plainer provincial virtues. It might be added that Bethel was a great-nephew of Slingsby Bethel, Dryden's 'Shimei', and that his brother—also Slingsby—was a City merchant. His home lay only a few miles from Burlington's country seat; he knew Bathurst well; and Martha Blount was also among his friends. In short, he completed a circle of intimacy, to some sectors of which—as the City—Pope stood in a marginal relation.[1] Like Bathurst, Bethel combined rural interests with a refined taste in polite learning. Unfortunately one letter from him only survives, and that has been mislaid since Elwin and Courthope printed it. The single example indicates that Bethel, if direct in utterance ('You are too thin and weak for an issue, and it would be very painfull to you. Lord Shel[burne], who has more flesh than you, was obliged to dry them up' (*Corr.* IV 511–2)) was thoroughly literate. Bethel was something of a valetudinarian, though this was combined with a measure of genuine invalidism. In this he contrasts sharply with Bathurst, who shrugged off illness after illness. The circumstances conditioned Pope's letters to Bethel, which broach the subject of health more often than any other topic.

If they were less well-placed than the great magnates, the prosperous gentry of Bethel's mould lost no ground in the early eighteenth century. Their political power was confirmed when they managed to get through Parliament an Act imposing property qualifications on members of the Commons in 1711. By this measure (9 Anne, c.5), MPs had to own real property worth 'the annual Value of Six hundred Pounds above Reprizes for every Knight of a Shire [county members] and the annual Value of Three Hundred Pounds above Reprizes for every Citizen Burgess or Baron of the Cinque Ports [borough members]. . . . '[2] The bill was introduced by Bolingbroke, but there is no doubt that it had the support of every shade of country opinion, from ardent Whig to vague Grumbletonian. This latter was a common breed, as Professor Plumb has remarked:

[1] I shall shortly publish an article on Bethel and his friends.
[2] Costin and Watson, *Constitution*, 117–18. For the circumstances, see Speck, 'Conflict in Society,' 136–7.

The small squires tended therefore to drift into the politics of re-sentment. Some called themselves old whig, others tory. They had their moments of hope in the reign of Queen Anne. At times they could win an election by sheer force of numbers, particularly in the county constituencies. They remained disgruntled, crochety, drawing consolation from the vituperation which the *Craftsman* [to which Pope may conceivably have contributed] poured on Walpole and his government. They developed a venomous hatred of place-holders, pensioners and the aristocratic world of London. They looked back with longing affection to the Stuarts, and some-times played the Jacobite. . . . [1]

Bethel was no Jacobite, and he was too balanced to dislike an aristocrat or a Londoner at sight. But then his brother became MP for the City of London, where even highflying Tories abjured such extreme 'politics of resentment'. Nevertheless Pope saw in Bethel an exemplar of old-fashioned 'virtue' (a term with strong political connotations at this period) and as a pillar of un-metropolitan sincerity: 'indeed for many years I have not chosen my companions for any of the qualities in fas-hion, but almost intirely for that which is the most out-of-fashion, sin-cerity' (*Corr.* II 501).

Besides, it was not at Westminster that this class came into its own. Sometimes the squires got together to push some measure through Par-liament, and there is a vestige of truth in Trevelyan's comment that Par-liament 'might be called the grand national Quarter Sessions'.[2] But the petty sessions and the ordinary quarter sessions were their real home-ground. It is important to remember that JPs carried out a great deal of administrative work, quite apart from their judicial functions.[3] Almost everything that could be termed welfare provision was in their hands. Until the growth of what the Webbs have cumbrously termed 'Statu-

1 Plumb, *Walpole*, 22.
2 G. M. Trevelyan, *Blenheim*, 1965, 112.
3 Cf. the following: 'By the eighteenth century the tradition had long been established that if anything wanted doing in the counties the jus-tices of the peace were the obvious people to entrust with the task': Marshall, *English People*, 120. The best modern treatment of the subject remains that of the Webbs, though there is a convenient survey in Esther Moir, *The Justice of the Peace*, Harmondsworth 1969, 77–101.

tory Authorities for Special Purposes', they ran sewerage, highways and the like. Indeed, when the turnpikes were first introduced, it was the county magistrates who administered their affairs. When specialised turnpike trusts were evolved, the bench remained prominent as private members of the board; but from the mid-eighteenth century, they were no longer managers in their own right. In addition to the JPs, there were a number of other local offices of varying prestige and power. The most coveted were those of Lord Lieutenant for each county. The least sought after was the post of Sheriff. 'It is an interesting sidelight that the only County office which was at once compulsory and expensive, that of the High Sheriff, was always imposed, unless occasionally a County personage deigned to accept it, on one of the minor gentry.'[1] It is eloquent testimony to Bethel's status, as comfortably less than a 'county personage', that he was threatened with the office in 1739. Pope wrote to express his concern on 'being told you were in danger of being Sheriff' (*Corr.* IV 206). It was not thus with baronets or even the old county families.

Many of Pope's rural friends were Catholics, such as the Carylls and the Englefields. This put them in a separate bracket. Others again were disguised literary men, such as Walsh, or successful entrepreneurs, such as Ralph Allen. Bethel, on the other hand, was authentic country stock; his ancestors survive today, in the same district and the same rank of unpretentious distinction. One can recognize his features in the collective portrait of the gentry supplied by Professor Mingay: 'Rational, unsentimental, and business-like, they were at the same time jealous of their status and anxious to maintain their 'port', fond of entertaining and not averse to some show and extravagance—and yet still careful to watch expenditure and keep minutely detailed accounts.'[2] Certainly Pope often writes to Bethel of bodily matters, and that includes not only health but gastronomic matters too. At first, in the 1720s, Pope tends to write in a moral vein ('I know your humanity, and allow me to say, I love and value you for it'—the agreeable impertinence of his dealings with Bathurst is gone, as 'allow me to say' indicates. (*Corr.* II 178)) But

[1] Webb and Webb, *Local Government*, IV 360; cf. Mingay 118.
[2] Mingay, 116. Relevant to this discussion are Mingay's comments on letter-writing, 137.

as the friendship proceeds, the relationship grows less stiff. The two men agree to exchange portraits; and indeed 'Mr Bethels Picture in a Gold Frame' hung in a place of honour in Pope's own room (the only portrait there) at Twickenham.[1] There is a gift of seeds, much in the manner of the present day. Once Pope sends Bethel a chicken for dinner. The poet likes to joke about the bracing Northern climate: he speaks of the 'bleaker Hills & Wolds of Yorkshire' dissipating an outbreak of fever. (*Corr.* IV 86) He recognizes, too, that Bethel's deepest involvement lay in the country life 'My Lord Burlington goes to Yorkshire. . . . I often wishd I could see you there, where I fancy you are most happy; for in Town you generally seem to think yourself not at home; & I would see my Friend quite at ease. . . . ' (*Corr.* IV 113) But Pope himself felt particularly unconstrained in this relationship: ''Tis only to you, and a few such plain honest men, I like to open myself with the same freedom, and as free from all disguises, not only of sentiment, but of style, as they themselves.' (*Corr.* III 519) Hence the suitability of Bethel for his role as the modern Ofellus in *Satire II ii*.

Pope had already celebrated his friend as 'blameless Bethel' in the *Essay on Man*. Now he portrays a blunt and shrewdly observant commentator, wholly bereft of Chesterfield's saving graces, but articulate and manly. In consonance with the aim of dropping rhetorical disguise, Pope adopts a direct, no-nonsense style. There are none of the large verbal gestures appropriate to Bathurst or Burlington; since the lesser gentry disdained lordly magnificence—the grand style of life—for a more cautious demeanour that one might almost call, anachronistically, bourgeois. Aptly, the vocabulary of this imitation is concrete, homely, even gross. It is replete with *objects*: 'a gilt Buffet', 'Plate to Plate', 'fish', 'plain Bread and milk', 'pheasant', 'hen', 'Carps and Mullets', 'small Turbots', 'a whole Hog', 'Rabbit', 'eggs, and herbs, and olives', and so on. These are drawn only from the first thirty-five lines. Later in the poem, to choose only the more notable instances, there occur oysters, crawfish, vinegar, cabbage, venison, sturgeon and ham-pie, bucks and much else. The characteristic note survives in Pope's rejoinder, after Bethel's own 'sermon' has ended:

[1] Maynard Mack, *The Garden and the City*, Toronto and London 1969, 255.

Content with little, I can piddle here
On Broccoli and mutton, round the year;
But ancient friends, (tho' poor, or out of play)
That touch my Bell, I cannot turn away.
'Tis true, no Turbots dignify my boards,
But gudgeons, flounders, what my Thames affords.
To Hounslow-heath I point, and Bansted-down,
Thence comes your mutton, and these chicks my own. . . . . (137–44)

At times the visceral emphasis grows almost nauseous; but wit and wordplay take off some of the oppressiveness:

. . . *The stomach (cram'd from ev'ry dish,*
A Tomb of boil'd, and roast, and flesh, and fish,
Where Bile, and wind, and phlegm, and acid jar,
And all the Man is one intestine war). . . . . (69–72)

Whatever Matthew Arnold may have thought of the earlier passage quoted, it is not entirely representative of the mature Pope. Yet this comic diminution through ironic self-display *is* frequent in the Horatian poems. Bethel, as a man of moderate means and a social equal, is a suitable recipient for this self-dramatising 'confession'.

As in the other cases studied here, it is clear that Pope knew exactly what he was doing in choosing Bethel as his addressee. It is not just the subject-matter, here food, which determines the character of the language or the texture of the verse. The tastes, acquirements and social standing of his friend come into it also. Bethel was practical, as Pope's choice of him as an executor makes evident. He was quite without the aristocratic breeding of Burlington, or the public importance of Bathurst. So we have a less elevated diction and a more intimate tone. Rhetorically, *Satire II ii* is as homely as its recipient. We have lost the wide historical sweep, the classical overtones and the epic implications of the *Epistle to Burlington*. Instead we are brought down to a domestic scale: 'five acres now of rented land' (line 136). In place of Rome, France, Spain, Asturian Mines, Chartreux, we have Hounslow and Banstead. The verse no longer echoes, as it did in the earlier poem, with Amphitrite, Nilus, Aldus, Milton, Laguerre, Versailles, Inigo Jones and Palladio. We are left with the glutton Oldfield, a tavern called the Bedford

Head, the cosily possessive 'my Thames'. Poetry mimics social pretension, and contracts its horns appropriately.[1]

The third example I wish to isolate is that of a professional man. The most obvious case to take might be that of a doctor. In the first place, Pope knew many members of the medical profession. There were intimate friends such as Arbuthnot; literary contacts such as Garth and Blackmore; advisers and practitioners, ranging from the eminent Cheselden to the quack Thompson, recommended perhaps by Bethel, whose treatment 'is said not to have delayed Pope's death.' (*Corr.* IV 499, 512) The full list would include George Cheyne; Richard Mead; his satiric butt John Woodward; William Oliver of Bath; Sir Hans Sloane, virtuoso and collector; Jeremiah Pierce; Simon Burton; and many more. Another quack to whom Pope possibly had recourse in his final despair was Joshua Ward, famous for his pills and effrontery. Second, the profession was at an interesting stage of development. It was not until the year after Pope's death that the surgeons were separated from the barbers, to whom they had been locked like Siamese twins for centuries. However, changes were already apparent in most branches of the profession; obstetrics was growing slightly less primitive, whilst William Hunter began surgical lectures in 1743. The influence of some major teachers on the Continent, where students had to go for a serious medical education, percolated gradually, with Herman Boerhaave of Leyden an especially important figure. One of Samuel Johnson's most impressive early works, indeed, is a biography of Boerhaave. Moreover, the noisy and abrasive quarrel with the apothecaries, which Garth turned into mock-heroic with *The Dispensary*, had spent its force by the end of Pope's life. Since Garth's poem was closely familiar to Pope, and in view of his own precarious health, one might have expected to see medical imagery suffuse his works—but this is not really the case.[2]

[1] For Pope's admiration of Bethel as 'the soul of friendship', and as a 'male bawd' who brought friends together, see Owen Ruffhead, *The Life of Alexander Pope*, 1769, 496.
[2] This paragraph is based on Lester S. King, *The Medical World of the Eighteenth Century*, Chicago 1958; and Sir D'Arcy Power, 'Medicine', *Johnson's England*, ed A. S. Turbeeville, Oxford 1933, II 265–86.

It is otherwise with the law, a profession which offers striking parallels to that of medicine. If the one had its quacks ('a pretender, basically ignorant, pretending to know when he did not. Also, he advertised. A variety of techniques was available, including . . . the carnival tactics of the mountebank'[1]) then the other had its demi-reps in the form of attorneys. Pope makes the connection explicit in his tribute to the Man of Ross:

> *Despairing Quacks with curses fled the place,*
> *And vile Attornies, now an useless race.*
>
> (*Epistle to Bathurst*, 273–4)

We must realise here that the attorney was regarded at this time as an inferior drudge, at best; a perjured rascal, at worst. Often he was the lackey of some Great Man; and Johnson was not distorting public attitudes when, in *London* (1738), he aligned 'the fell attorney' on the 'prowl' with street bullies. To see why this was so, we must look briefly at the structure of the profession.

In 1696 Gregory King had calculated that there were some ten thousand 'Persons in the Law', with an average income of £140.[2] The figure must include lesser clerks as well as scriveners, agents, and so on. Otherwise the total seems high, for as late as 1799 there were only just over 200 barristers, all based on London, plus a thousand London solicitors and attornies with twice that number in the provinces. The avocation of 'solicitor' in the modern sense had not properly evolved. Not only were attornies often ill-educated and disreputable, they were actually criminals in a number of cases. The appellation of '*Fleet* or *Wapping* solicitors' was applied to the dregs of the profession; and belatedly, attempts were made to remedy this blot on the law.

In 1725 the Legislature thought it necessary to provide that, if any person convicted of forgery or perjury or common barratry [vexatious litigation] practised as an attorney or solicitor, he should be transported for seven years; in 1739 that no attorney or solicitor who was in prison should be entitled to bring any action on behalf

[1] King 47.
[2] Dorothy George, *England in Transition*, new edn Harmondsworth 1953, 150.

of a client; and in 1760 that attornies or solicitors embezzling their client's money should not be able to take the benefit of the Act passed in that year for the relief of insolvent debtors.

Shocking as this picture may appear, it is amply confirmed by other contemporary evidence.

The solicitors for the parties in the famous *Highwaymen's Case* (1725), in which one highwayman brought a suit for an account against another highwayman, were imprisoned and fined £50 each. . . . One of the solicitors in this case, by name Wreathock, who had subsequently been transported for robbery on the highway, and who, on his return, had been readmitted as an attorney, was finally struck off the rolls.

Again, it was necessary for a court to rule that a turnkey of the King's Bench prison 'was not a fit person to be an articled clerk'; we also hear of persons who had stood in the pillory continuing to act unmolested. The Society of Gentlemen Practisers, founded some five years before Pope's death, did something to improve the situation: but it was a slow haul upwards. Nor was education for the bar without its faults. Since Elizabethan times, 'the study of English law [had] ceased to be part of a liberal education'. The subject became esoteric, technical, crabbed. And though men such as the great Sir William Blackstone believed that 'a competent knowledge of the laws of that society in which we live is the proper accomplishment of every gentleman and scholar', the expectation grew less and less realistic. To some extent the gap was filled by popular handbooks and abridgments, such as the numerous *vademecum* publications of Giles Jacob, 'scourge of Grammar' and 'blunderbuss of Law' (*Dunciad* 'B' III 149–50). Nevertheless, the picture is increasingly one of an arid specialization, a separation from humane studies and a provinciality of outlook. In Bentham's phrase, the law had not yet been taught to speak the language of the scholar and the gentleman.[1]

[1] Based on Sir William Holdsworth, *A History of English Law*, XIII, 1938, *passim*; quotations from 54, 58–9, 90, 96. Other information from Ronald Robson, *The Attorney in Eighteenth-Century England*, Cambridge 1959, 13, 23, 45. Robson points out (58) that Warburton began as an attorney.

It so happened that Pope was surrounded by the law all his days. His cousin married a judge, whilst his only close relative (apart from his parents) was a half-sister whose life was one long courtroom wrangle. Pope spent a good deal of time trying to sort out the affairs of Magdalen Rackett. Her husband died intestate; a trustee proved difficult; her annuities were not paid; one son ran into debts, one had proceedings of outlawry taken against him, and the other wanted to enter the law. This was a natural choice, insofar as household conversations can have revolved around little else: unfortunately, he was a nonjuror, which effectively prohibited his entry to the profession. The later years of this saga read like a parody of *Bleak House*, with Mrs Rackett hopelessly embroiled in Chancery. Pope consulted Fortescue, Murray and others in his efforts to help her; but her affairs truly required the services of a full-time legal department.

Added to this, Pope had his own battles to fight. In 1725 he was threatened by a 'monition' from Doctors Commons, the centre of ecclesiastical law. The point at issue was the erection of a monument to Sir Godfrey Kneller in Twickenham church; the widow's ambitious proposals involved removing the monument to Pope's own father. On this matter the poet consulted his friend Viscount Harcourt (1661–1727), a former Tory attorney-general and Lord Chancellor: 'My Lord, I am in Law, & in the worst Law, Spiritual Law.' (*Corr*. II 306). A year or two earlier Pope had been called before the House of Lords in the trial of Bishop Atterbury, who was accused of Jacobite conspiracy. His position had been made more difficult in advance 'by the disaffection implied in his edition of [the Duke of] Buckingham's *Works*', suppressed on ministerial authority a few months before.[1] At this juncture Pope must have felt more of an outcast than ever; the *London Journal* even reported that he 'is taken into Custody on Account of the Works of the late Duke of Buckingham'.[2] This rumour appears to have been false; but it must have had some plausibility.

In later years Pope's contacts with the lawcourts were slightly more pleasant, but still they were irritating enough. He twice had to enter

[1] *Corr*. II 306; Sherburn, *Early Career*, 228.
[2] *London Journal*, 2 February 1723—a reference the biographers seem to have overlooked.

Chancery suits regarding piracy of his works. On a third occasion he put in a bill against his perpetual antagonist, the bookseller Curll. The phrase '*Pope vs. Curll*' has been used in modern times as a description of a phase in literary history. It is also the exact legal reference for a suit adjudicated by Lord Chancellor Hardwicke in 1741. Satire, one observes, acts out fictively the conflicts that real life assigns to the courtroom or chambers. In this light it is interesting to observe that many dunces were connected with the law; one, Thomas Burnet, actually reached the bench. Concanen, as Pope observed, was 'surprizingly promoted to administer Justice and Law in Jamaica'.[1] Budgell, Gordon, Horneck, Jacob and Popple had a close personal involvement; Theobald and Aaron Hill were the sons of attorneys. Needless to say, all the dunces lived on the periphery of legal London: Defoe holds the record for Chancery suits (at least eight), quite apart from his familiarity with Newgate, the Queen's Bench court, the Fleet and other penal institutions. But there was a *Cibber vs. Cibber* suit, too, and innumerable Budgell proceedings (before he too landed in the debtor's gaol),[2] till one could easily see litigation as among the most characteristic duncely occupations.

Pope, then, had good cause to number lawyers among his friends. They could advise him on tangled family affairs; they could forward his own suits; and they could give him access to a leading haunt of Dulness. For criminal society proper, incidentally, Pope had another informant: Richard Savage, murderer, bohemian and poet, whose *Vagabond King* existence was so memorably portrayed by Johnson. At all events, Pope had at least three close friends in this province of life, disregarding the elderly aristocrat Harcourt. One of these men is relatively obscure: Nathaniel Pigott (d. 1737), Pope's own 'counsellor at Law', i.e. barrister. William Fortescue is much better known. And incomparably more eminent than either is William Murray, later Lord Mansfield (1705–93), among the greatest of all British jurists. Murray was later to become Chief Justice of the King's Bench and a man of great influence

---

1 Note to *The Dunciad* 'A' II 130.
2 Budgell's later life has been described as 'one long litigation'. He was a half-brother of Fortescue, curiously: Fortescue's mother married Budgell's father.

in public affairs at large. At the time Pope came to know him, he was a young Scottish advocate of obvious distinction, with a rising reputation as an orator. Before Pope died, he saw Murray enter Parliament, where he soon became known as an eloquent speaker, and obtain the office of Solicitor-General. Murray was the recipient of Pope's imitation of *Epistle I vi* as early as 1738. Pope showed himself as excellent talent-spotter. Unlike a number of middle-aged men, he was capable of appreciating the younger generation without making acolytes of them. Murray was to embody in his life the same concern with humane values, the same respect for stable society and the same 'creative' disposal of a learned heritage that mark Pope's own achievement.[1]

However, a closer and longer-lasting friendship was that with William Fortescue (1687–1749). Pope and he were much of an age. His legal talents, though they took him to the office in turn of baron of the Exchequer, judge of the Common Pleas and Master of the Rolls, were more modest than those of Murray; and Pope may have liked him none the less for that.[2] The two perhaps became acquainted around 1720, though Fortescue had previously figured in the distinguished list of subscribers to the *Iliad*. Fortescue handled investments for the poet; he chased up Mrs Rackett's business, he gave advice on copyright disputes, particularly those involving Curll; and he was originally to have acted as an executor along with Bethel—Pope later relieved him of this.[3] Pope seems to have felt that his own situation bore resemblances to Fortescue's. So he compares Fortescue's circuits as a barrister to his own travels: 'What an advantageous circumstance is it . . . to be a grave and reputable rambler?' (*Corr.* II 521) Or again, emphasising the link between satirist and public prosecutor which often informs Augustan criticism: 'God deliver you from Law, me from Rhime! and give us leisure to attend what is more important.' (*Corr.* III 486) More explicitly:

I for my part am willing to be old in Disposition, so far as to seek

[1] C. H. S. Fifoot, *Lord Mansfield*, Oxford 1936, 33 and *passim*; Holdsworth, *History of English Law*, XII 464–78.
[2] Edward Foss, *A Biographical Dictionary of the Judges of England*, 1870; Holdsworth, XII 245–6.
[3] *Corr.* IV 222; for the duration of the friendship, see IV 356.

Retreat & Peace: And You, as in the Character of a Judge, are also
Vir tristis & gravis. I am as content to quit the clamorous Part of a
Poet, Satire, as you could be to quit that of a Pleading Lawyer.
. . . More *Quiet* cannot be in any Law-Station [than that of Mas-
ter of the Rolls]; & *Quiet* is the Life of Innocence & Good
nature.   (*Corr.* IV 126)

On the whole the correspondence between the two men is brief,
businesslike and unexceptional. However, Fortescue must have had a
vein of humour. He may well have been introduced to the Pope circle
by John Gay, whose friend and fellow-Devonian he was. Fortescue is
said to have helped with the composition of one Scriblerian squib,
Stradling versus Stiles. He was also familiar with other habitués of the
circle, among them Bathurst and Martha Blount. It may be added that
Bathurst's son Henry became Lord Chancellor in 1771, thus further
cementing the legal connections of this group of men.

The imitation of *Satire II i* was published in 1733. Pope engaged in
genteel equivocation, but there is no serious room for doubt that the
'friend' representing Trebatius in the original was Fortescue. The poem
is interesting because of the density of legal allusion in its text. Here
Pope was enabled by the literary circumstances to develop a thread of
imagery that constantly flits through his later work. It should be noted,
for example, that the *Epistle to Arbuthnot* is described as 'a Sort of Bill of
Complaint', the technical term for a Chancery plaintiff's submission.
This fact is overlooked by all Pope's commentators: yet it provides a
key to the whole method of the *Epistle.* It is to be expected that a plaintiff in stating his case will be self-justificatory, sometimes denunciatory,
often allusive: he will seek to recollect material facts, and will adduce
evidence of his grievances. Pope speaks of a 'truer Information' regarding his case than has hitherto been available, so that the public can
'judge' the matter. When we come to the poem itself, we find within
sixty lines the following: *engross, apply to me, the Laws, the Mint, saving
Counsel, Term, libell'd, sues, Commission, Papers, judge* and many other
words with legal colouring more or less prominent. Throughout the
poem we find mention of templars, of giving a little senate laws, Japhet
in a jail, theft, libel and slander, 'Knight of the Post corrupt'. At the end
comes a tribute to 'the good Man', Pope's father:

> *No Courts he saw, no Suits would ever try,*
> *Nor dar'd an Oath, nor hazarded a Lye. . . .*   (396–7)

Virtue is directly opposed to the intricacies of the law.

In many other poems from this period, there are similar hints. A judge and a chancellor figure in the *Epistle to Cobham*, where a bequest is parodied ('I give and I devise . . . My lands and tenements to Ned,' 256–7). In the *Epistle to Bathurst*, two successive notes allude to Chancery suits involving rapacious villains of this piece, Hopkins and Crook. We also have the bankrupt pleading his cause at court, commissions and impeachments. The poem *To Murray* has judgments, 'Senate, Rolls and Hall', 'take the Counsel', among other references. *To Augustus* employs the rare and specialised phrase, 'Courtesy of England' (62), as well as law, justice and statutes. *To Bethel* ends with a striking collocation—mortgage, lawyer, Equity, Chancery. Still denser is the frequency in other poems. The *Epilogue to the Satires* uses *law* or its derivatives six times in a short space. Neither the vocabulary nor the allusions stray far from matters judicial and criminal: Jekyll, Jonathan Wild, Newgate, Judge Page and the Treasury Solicitor, Paxton, all figure. Most directly of all, the imitation of *Epistle II ii* has *law(s)* at least six times again. Its racy style is scattered with references to legal matters, often in a carefully mounted mimicry of the appropriate jargon: 'my Cause comes on', 'My Counsel sends to execute a Deed', 'There liv'd, *in primo Georgii* (they record) . . . ', and also

> *The Laws of God, as well as of the Land,*
> *Abhor, a Perpetuity should stand. . . .*   (246–7)

Cowper, Talbot and Murray make a glancing appearance; precise and explicit terms are employed, such as Exchequer [the court], Rolls, Sergeants, a *Property* (231: the italics give it the accents of a land-agent).

All these hints are brought together in the poem to Fortescue. What appears elsewhere as a casual motif is here made the structural and satiric centre-piece. The literal situation envisaged is that of Pope, mockingly self-belittled once more,

> *Tim'rous by Nature, of the Rich in awe,*
> *I come to Council learned in the Law.*   (7–8)

He asks for advice from his friend 'both sage and free' and 'as you use, without a Fee'. The interlocutor replies curtly, perhaps even gruffly, 'I'd write no more.' Shortly, he justifies this desperate remedy in equally abrupt terms:

> *You could not do a worse thing for your Life.*
> *Why, if the Nights seem tedious—take a Wife;*
> *Or rather truly, if your Point be Rest,*
> *Lettuce and Cowslip Wine;* Probatum est.   (15–18)

The stark rhythms and sharply imperative note go along with a certain pedantry (as in the third line, with *Or rather truly* and the prim subjunctive). The friend's self-satisfied conclusion, Q.E.D., is conveyed in the clipped finality of the Latin tag. None of the emollience and high-spirited colloquy of the *Epistle to Bathurst* here.

The friend retains this sharp-tongued air throughout (as in lines 42–4, 103–4). And Pope himself takes on a certain irritation: not the high-minded moral outrage of the *Epilogue*, but a captious, nervy quality:

> *Not write? but then I* think,
> *And for my Soul I cannot sleep a wink.*
> *I nod in Company, I wake at Night,*
> *Fools rush into my Head, and so I write.*   (11–14)

There are the familiar allusions (Judge Page, the Mint, thieves, with repetition of *the laws*). It is only at the end, however, that the drift becomes unmistakable:

> *This is my Plea, on this I rest my Cause—*
> *What saith my Council learned in the Laws?*
>   F. *Your Plea is good. But still I say, beware!*
> *Laws are explain'd by Men—so have a care.*
> *It stands on record that in* Richard's *Times*
> *A man was hang'd for very honest Rhymes.*
> *Consult the Statute:* quart. *I think it is,*
> Edwardi Sext. *or* prim. & quint. Eliz:
> *See* Libels, Satires—*here you have it—read.*
> P. Libels *and* Satires! *lawless Things indeed!*
> *But grave* Epistles, *bringing Vice to light,*

> *Such as a* King *might read, a* Bishop *write,*
> *Such as Sir* Robert *would approve—*
> F. *Indeed ?*
> *The Case is alter'd—you may then proceed.*
> *In such a Cause the Plaintiff will be hiss'd,*
> *My Lords the Judges laugh, and you're dismiss'd.* (141–56)

This conclusion is a masterpiece of controlled irony. Pope dramatises a collision of the law and good sense; the former is represented by a barbarous jargon and cumbrous precedents (beautifully emphasised by the strained rhyme *is/Eliz*), whilst the poet retorts with exaggerated deference. The joke at the end relies on the fact that Fortescue had been private secretary to Sir Robert Walpole, and remained a steady supporter of the prime minister. In many ways the poem is not wholly complimentary to Fortescue, any more than the earlier epistle was to Bathurst.[1] The overall note of jumpy petulance suggests not so much taking counsel's opinion as a cross-questioning; the dialogue proceeds in places more like a courtroom interrogation than easy conversation. Not just the diction and imagery, but the basic rhetorical mould, is conditioned by the legal setting.

This pervasive motif in the later poems could be related to a number of things: the fact, for example, that eighteenth-century culture was profoundly legalistic at its core.[2] This in turn may be connected with the desire of people at this time to discover continuities—and therefore precedents—after the constitutional upheavals of the previous age. The job of the law might almost be said to be papering over social cracks: at all events, the letter of the statute-book was held in peculiar reverence at a time when civil war was still a genuine alternative to peaceable and legitimate government. The early Hanoverians awaited the next rising or the next plot with the glum certainty with which California awaits her earthquake. More widely, however, I think that the forms of the law increasingly took on for Pope a symbolic meaning. They stood for the hocuspocus of the administrative machine, what today might be called the system. And in imagining the law so often as arbitrary, op-

---

[1] See the remarks of P. Dixon, *The World of Pope's Satires*, 1968, 32–3.
[2] Robson, *The Attorney*, 143, draws attention to this fact.

pressive or simply crass, Pope was adverting to something more than his own deprived role in society as a Catholic—though that assuredly came into it. He was striking against Whiggery, which is to say the politics of statutory reform, of money, of 'enlightenment' and of centralism. (Not of course that Walpole, say, aspired to or attained to all these things: I mean Whiggery as it historically evolved.) Like Burke, Pope believed in human and moral ties, in local associations and affections, in short in the old loose-knit Toryism—a politics that could not survive the growth of central banking, the rise of institutions like the East India Company, the floating of a huge national debt, the beginnings of industrialism. Beleaguered as he was by his religious faith, Pope must have sensed all his life that 'law makes long spokes of the short stakes of men'. He saw the judicial system, I think, increasingly as an agency of the new state machine; and lawyers as its handmaidens—deep as his personal affection for Fortescue was, their relationship lacked the social ease, the built-in intimacy, that his friendship with Bethel and Bathurst acquired. It is a classic encounter of conservative values and the new professional hierarchy.

Lastly we turn to women, an order only too symbolic. Here the obvious representative is Martha Blount (1690–1763), by far the most sustained of Pope's female friendships. For a moment he may have been more infatuated with Martha's elder sister Teresa; and just as transiently it was Lady Mary Wortley Montagu who stood at the centre of his affections. But these passions died: to say nothing of the fact that Lady Mary was too individual and too gifted to be representative of anything at any time. Acutely and gloriously feminine as she was in many respects, she would have been a remarkable person had she exhibited any or none of the usual sexual attributes. Her appeal does not depend on (though it includes) her womanliness. Finally, she happened to be a writer of talent, which made a big difference to a man as single-minded in his literary ambitions as Pope was.

Much more conventional, though far from dull, 'Patty' Blount exemplifies the attraction of Augustan femininity along with its tragedy. She came of an old Catholic family, and by the standards of the time she was well educated. Her personality is enigmatic. Capable of petty quarrels, she could excite lasting affection. Gossip early began to sprout around her relations with Pope, and it remains uncertain whether or not they were lovers. Fortunately this is not an essay on the Sexual Scene, and the point is of little moment: the Augustans were disposed to enjoy sex, but they unaccountably thought that it had less to do with the deepest areas of the human personality than had religion, say, or even filial duty. The result is that although women were respected, admired, teased, patronised and cajoled by men, as at all times, they were not intellectualised. We have annals of lust, long before *Fanny Hill* was written (by a son of Pope's friend William Cleland). But nobody thought they were a clue to the national psyche. Such a climate meant that women had in some ways more dignity and more consequence than today, although their rôle in the sociocultural scheme of things was sadly unimposing.[1]

The major disabilities of women, in fact, were more straightforward. They had minimal rights with regard to property and the like: hence Pope's long battles on behalf of his half-sister. They had few civic opportunities, and all professions were closed to them. If they married, they could exercise a respectable and indeed honoured function in the community; their social place was secure, or as secure as their husband's, and it does not seem to have occurred to them that this was a feebly vicarious hold on status. But a woman without a husband and children had limited chances of fulfilment, even in a rank which ensured her material comforts and unquestioned social privilege. There is an ominous truth behind Clarissa's words to Belinda in *The Rape of the Lock*:

> *But since, alas! frail Beauty must decay,*
> *Curl'd or uncurl'd, since Locks will turn to grey,*
> *Since painted, or not painted, all shall fade,*
> *And she who scorns a Man, must die a Maid;*
> *What then remains, but well our Pow'r to use,*
> *And keep good Humour still whate'er we lose?*

(V, 25–30)

Belinda frowned, upset by the general tenor of this speech. But even she, pretty, wilful, silly little Belinda, could recognise the kernel of

[1] For a representative Augustan view on the subjection of women, see *The Humourist* 3rd edn 1724, 100.

truth here: regardless of the tactics to be adopted, marriage was the only authentic choice of life. And the immeasurably more intelligent Martha Blount, self-willed and sprightly in wit, must have known that too. Now sexual independence as such was not the major worry, for that can always be exercised in defiance of the prevailing mores if only because sex can go on in private—if Pope or Martha engaged in physical love, we are quite in ignorance of it. But true personal independence, which comes of doing things *within* society instead of behind its back—this was what Pope, for all his civic restraints, effectively had, and Martha hadn't.

It is interesting to observe the terms in which the poet couches his delightful compliment to Martha at the end of the *Epistle to a Lady*. At first sight the tone might appear condescending, with its hint of roguishness and its gentle amusement. Yet we know from the preceding passage (lines 231–47) that Pope had a profound awareness of the pathos of the lonely old woman. And gradually we see that the prettiness of the writing betokens something other than superficial 'charm', and that examples drawn from the routine of polite society need not be routine in their imaginative implications:

> *Ah Friend! to dazzle let the Vain design,*
> *To raise the Thought and touch the Heart, be thine!*
> *That Charm shall grow, while what fatigues the Ring*
> *Flaunts and goes down, an unregarded thing.*
> *So when the Sun's broad beam has tir'd the sight,*
> *All mild ascends the Moon's more sober light,*
> *Serene in Virgin Modesty she shines,*
> *And unobserv'd the glaring Orb declines.*
>
> *Oh! blest with Temper, whose unclouded ray*
> *Can make to morrow chearful as to day;*
> *She, who can love a Sister's charms, or hear*
> *Sighs for a Daughter with unwounded ear;*
> *She, who ne'er answers till a Husband cools,*
> *Or, if she rules him, never shows she rules;*
> *Charms by accepting, by submitting sways,*
> *Yet has her humour most, when she obeys;*
> *Lets Fops or Fortune fly which way they will;*

> Disdains all loss of Tickets, or Codille;
> Spleen, Vapours, or Small-pox, above them all,
> And Mistress of herself, tho' China fall. (249–68)

This exquisite passage is proof that Pope does not need to make the hackles of his verse rise in ugly rancour to achieve moral seriousness. Put crudely, this is how to succeed in a man's world. The way to defeat a constricting but 'polite' code, as against draconian repression, is to simulate assent. The woman seems passive but needs courage, tenacity and will. In this case the moon's 'sober light' stands for constancy of purpose, an apparent gentleness, a quality of inviolacy. Of course to accommodate oneself to the norms of society in this way involves renunciation and loss. It also can represent a feat of self-mastery and thus of moral growth. Pope doesn't so much argue this as make the poetry show it, in its delicately charted growth of confidence, its air of settled calm.

That Pope responded intensely to the feminine world, *The Rape of the Lock* is enough to illustrate. Here we have a world of gossamer. Pope has deliberately feminised the epic, by replacing the martial hero with the vain coquette Belinda; and he has transformed the stern landscapes of Homer into a pretty-pretty boudoir atmosphere.

> Loose to the Wind their airy Garments flew,
> Thin glitt'ring Textures of the filmy Dew. . . . (II, 63–4)

With marvellous invention he ensures that the very language of the poem shall submit to the same process. The words have a tinsel-like ring. Moreover, there is a peculiar intimacy with the objects, a close-range sensuousness which involves both sight and touch. Only a writer who was acutely sensitive to the feelings of various materials, who had observed closely the visual effects produced by domestic objects, could have achieved this. At one point (III, 105 ff.) Pope has to describe the 'meal' usually consumed in epic. Of course, he reduces this to the sipping of coffee: and he contrives to give his language the same lacquered finish that the silverware displays. Again, the slightly barbarous heraldry of the playing cards is caught in the very diction of the ombre episode (III 37ff.: note *shining, velvet, sable, verdant, embroider'd, refulgent, dye,* and so on).

In short, the texture of the verse is exactly in consonance with the fundamental comic strategy of the poem. The *Rape* brings down Homer to a few inches of ivory: and the language enacts the same diminution, the same cosy familiarization, the same closeness to domestic furniture. Whether these things are of their nature 'feminine', I do not know; but they were certainly so regarded by the Augustans. So that this work, with a fashionable girl as its central character, is deliberately couched in an idiom of polished social converse. The *Epistle to a Lady* is addressed to a mature lady, although it includes much satire of less sensible women: accordingly, the verse keeps at a distance from the lofty port of *Bathurst*, the manly directness of *Bethel*, the querulous argufying of *Fortescue*. It exhibits instead a sympathetic humour, milder than that of the jokes in Pope's letters to Martha. It displays a range of moods from tenderness to scorn, from pathos to fulsome compliment; but throughout it conveys a special intimacy of tone.

Most of these qualities are seen in the correspondence, along with other attributes not present in the poem. For instance, Pope supplies Martha Blount with several evocative descriptions of romantic scenery in his letters, as of Stonor, Sherborne and the Bath region.[1] Occasionally Pope is moralistic ('This is an odd way of writing to a lady . . .' (*Corr.* I 319)), more often jocular. In the early years there is a kind of comic gallantry quite often. As time goes on, however, an undercurrent of sadness approaches the surface, and Pope applies himself more to 'the extreme Sensibility which I know is in [her] Nature' (*Corr.* IV 463). And the pictures of the social round are wearier in tone: 'But to be all day, first dressing one's body, then dragging it abroad, then stuffing the guts, then washing them with Tea, then wagging one's tongue, & so to bedd; is the life of an Animal, that may for all that I know have Reason in it . . . but wanted somebody to fetch it out.' (*Corr.* IV 211) Patty for her part is literate, rather less chatty than her correspondent, and innocent of self-conscious refinement. She was a woman of spirit and in her narrow circle she lived an estimable life. She made no false pretensions to intellectual attainments, unlike Queen Caroline; and if her scheme of living seems unambitious today, Pope's

1 *Corr.* I 429–30; II 236; IV 201–2. See also the letter of 11 August 1734, printed by G. S. Rousseau in *PQ* XLV, 1966, 409–18.

tribute in verse has vindicated her. It would outweigh much graver defects. To be the occasion of poetry so luminous—so assured that the recipient merits the compliment, and will accept it gracefully—so successful in adapting private communication to a public theme—this is a worthy memorial to any woman. For women in most societies have been content, rightly or wrongly, to be the private causes of public effects.

This has inevitably been a highly selective account of Pope's contacts. The arbitrariness is reduced by the fact that Augustan society was a sharply graded series of plateaux, and some historians have actually detected a deepening sense of caste in this age.[1] The categories selected here may have been the wrong ones; but the categories certainly existed. None the less, some omissions should be mentioned. A group of real importance in Pope's youth was formed by a number of literary men including Walsh, Wycherley and Garth. On the edge of this circle stood the man about town and *flaneur* represented by Henry Cromwell—this at a time when Pope liked to pose as a bit of a rake. Another interesting group were the clerics, including Atterbury, Walter Harte, Joseph Spence, William Broome and Abel Evans. A major figure here at the end of Pope's life was his literary executor, William Warburton. Another member is Stephen Hales, the only scientist Pope knew at all well. Such men, according to Professor Plumb, 'devoted themselves to everything but the administrative reform of the institution to which they belonged'.[2] But it is lucky that the country parson often had the time to function as research scholar, for Warburton, Broome and Spence all made significant contributions in their way to Pope's reputation. A thinner claim can be made for other occupations. Jervas was the only artist to have left his mark on Pope; Cobham was the lone soldier to have come at all close to the poet; whilst Samuel Buckley stood by himself as a kind of embryonic civil servant. Despite his parentage, Pope had few links with the City. He knew Alderman John Barber, a dubious character, less well than Swift, and his relations with Slingsby Bethel were far more formal than those

[1] Plumb, *Walpole*, 13; Moir, *Justice of the Peace*, 78.
[2] Plumb, *England*, 49.

with his brother Hugh. Pope's home at Twickenham was owned by a Turkey merchant called Vernon, but they managed landlord and tenant affairs in the best possible way—by never seeing each other from one year to the next. As for the hack writers and venal booksellers who crowd *The Dunciad*, they set quite a different problem. Pope rarely knew them personally, and though his satire has a 'social' component it is not one wholly explicable in class terms.[1]

Speaking of Pope, Leslie Stephen once wrote that 'the great author must have a people behind him; utter both what he really thinks and feels and what is thought and felt most profoundly by his contemporaries.' It was a bad instance to take. Pope did something unique. He made himself a highly respected position in the world through poetry accommodated to the social forms of the day. But, however polite and civilized the verse, Pope's vision was never softened into mild assent. Pope, it has been well said, was 'toughened by the forces of a society which could be harsh and violent';[2] his own situation as a Catholic brought that lesson home. And his friendships, even if they involved no questioning of the social structure in itself, provided the occasion for highly critical observations—on vainglory and gluttony, on feminine foibles and vexatious lawsuits. He was that most dangerous critic of society, who can ape its fashionable chat and fall in with its pointless conventions. He wrote of the social scene from within: but he was a fifth-columnist.

---

[1] Guerinot's comment (*Pamphlet Attacks*, xli) that 'the dunces, as a whole, belonged to the lower classes', is misleading. In origin a high proportion were middle-class; it was their writing which degraded them. See my *Grub Street*, 1972, 207–11.

[2] Stephen, *Literature and Society*, 129; Humphreys, *Augustan World*, 22.

4: Pope and the Visual Arts

JAMES SAMBROOK

AN ANONYMOUS biographer in 1744 wrote of Pope as a small boy
spending his leisure in 'Drawing, and such like improving and
rational Accomplishments'. There are scattered references between
1705 and 1712 to his painting and drawing, but his serious practical
study of the graphic arts appears to have begun about March 1713
when he started taking regular instruction from his friend the fashionable portrait-painter Charles Jervas.[1] During the year and a half under
Jervas—himself an industrious copier of Titian and Van Dyck—it seems
that Pope was engaged mostly in copying portraits and figure-paintings.
Spence enumerates 'a grave old Chaucer of his drawing from Occleve,
a Betterton, Lucius Verus (large profile), two Turkish heads, a Janizary
from the life, Antinous, St John praying, etc.', while Pope, in letters of
August 1713, reveals his industry (and impatience) with a list of his
'former performances' which he has now thrown away, including three
Dr Swifts, two Lady Bridgewaters, a Duchess of Montagu, a Virgin
Mary, the Queen of England, half a score (or half a dozen ?) Earls and
one Knight of the Garter; he depreciates his Crucifixion and a Madonna,
but concludes that his masterpieces have been one of Dr Swift and one
of Mr Betterton (Spence §108; *Corr.* I 187, 189). Of all these works only
the Betterton 'masterpiece' has survived (Plate 1). It is a competent
copy of Kneller's portrait, now in the National Portrait Gallery, though
Pope has changed the colour of Betterton's wig and given a more
saturnine cast to the mouth. The seventeen unspecified drawings found
in the garrets at Twickenham following his death have disappeared,

[1] N. Ault, *New Light on Pope*, 1949, 68–100; *Corr.* I 4, 115, 174–7, 187–9,
194; Twickenham VI 45–6.

and so has his red-chalk head of Wentworth after Van Dyck which was last seen in 1826.[1] Despite Warburton's assertion, it is doubtful whether Pope made the sepia drawing which was engraved as the well-known frontispiece to the *Essay on Man*.[2] The few surviving scraps of his ink drawing in the British Museum and the Bodleian have little aesthetic interest.[3]

Pope's serious activities as a painter seem to have been devoted wholly to portraiture; his own portrait was painted by other artists many times (perhaps more often than any other English writer) and the substantial collection of pictures that he accumulated at Twickenham consisted largely of portraits. The names of the artists have not been recorded (presumably Kneller and Jervas were among them) but the subjects of many are known, and these make it clear that the walls of Pope's house were, like his verse, a celebration of friendship.[4] The poet's admiration for the more distant great appeared in the series of marble busts in his library which included Homer (wrongly attributed by the poet to Bernini), Newton by Burlington's protégé Giovanni Battista Guelfi, and Spenser, Shakespeare, Milton and Dryden by the dreary classicist Peter Scheemakers (1691–1781).[5] He seems to have preferred these two second-rate practitioners to Rysbrack, who modelled Pope's head very much to the poet's dissatisfaction (*Corr.* III 100). The neo-classical ideal was present also on the staircase, which was adorned by three large *grisaille* panels (paintings in greyish monochrome) by Kneller after the most celebrated antique statues of Venus, Apollo and Hercules (Plate 2). Pope refers to this last statue in *The Temple of Fame*:

[1] *N & Q* 6th ser. V, 13 May 1882, 363; *Gentleman's Magazine* LXIV, April 1794, 315; *Walpole's Anecdotes of Painting with additions by the Rev. James Dallaway*, ed. R. N. Wornum, 1876, II 270 n.

[2] Benjamin Boyce, 'Baroque into Satire: Pope's Frontispiece for the *Essay of Man*,' *Criticism* IV, 196,; 14–27.

[3] BM Add MSS 4808, 4809; Bodleian MS Rawl. letters 90.

[4] 'Inventory of Pope's goods taken after his death,' in Maynard Mack, *The Garden and the City*, 244–58.

[5] Newton is now at Scone Palace, Perthshire, and the English poets at Hagley Hall, Worcs.; illustrated in G. W. Beard, 'Alexander Pope,' *Apollo* LVII, 1953, 4–6.

> *There great* Alcides *stooping with his Toil,*
> *Rests on his Club, and holds th'* Hesperian *Spoil.*   (81-2)[1]

Pope's house contained comparatively few landscape paintings—for English landscape was relatively insignificant beside portraiture—but he possessed work by both of the men he once described (Spence §109) as the best landscape painters in England, Peter Tillemans (1684-1734) and John Wootton (1678-1765). The piece by Wootton was 'a Ruen', presumably in the style of Gaspard Dughet (Gaspard Poussin) which Wootton introduced into England in the 1720s on his return from Rome. Obviously Pope could not afford to buy the work of the Continental masters, but it is perhaps noteworthy that his writings never mention Dughet and the greater names of Claude Lorrain and Salvator Rosa who were to be so influential upon the eighteenth century view of landscape.

References to painters in Pope's writings show that he shared the general preferences of his age which placed the Roman school first, the Venetian second and the Florentine and the rest nowhere. The six heavenly painters singled out for praise in the 'Epistle to Mr Jervas' (35-8) are Raphael, Correggio, Veronese, Titian, Annibale Carracci and his pupil Guido Reni. Modern opinion might not place Carracci—and certainly not Reni—so high, but throughout Pope's lifetime these two neo-classical practitioners of the grand style were usually counted amongst the greatest masters. Horace Walpole, for instance, declared in the Introduction to his *Aedes Walpolianae* (1747) that Annibale Carracci, Guido Reni and Raphael were the three perfect painters. Pope was again following contemporary taste when he spoke very highly (Spence §§596-7) of Carlo Maratta (1625-1713), who painted Madonnas in a serene sub-Raphaelesque style and was much studied and imitated by Jervas.

Pope's taste in painting and sculpture was occasionally consulted by his friends. On behalf of James Craggs's sister he supervised Guelfi's work between 1724 and 1727 upon the Craggs monument in Westminster Abbey (*Corr.* II 242, 246, 254, 456), and he was a member of the

---

[1] Twickenham II 250. See also Twickenham VI 212-13; James Lees-Milne, *Earls of Creation*, 1962, 32; Beard, 'Alexander Pope'.

committee of Burlington's associates who commissioned Scheemakers to carve the Shakespeare monument in the Abbey in 1741. This, like the Craggs composition, distantly derived from the Farnese Hercules with more civilized accessories replacing the classic hero's club. More revealing of his taste is the advice that Pope offered Ralph Allen in 1736 and 1740 on works of art to be copied in *grisaille* by Johann Vandiest for the adornment of Prior Park. As Pope wrote, 'A Man not only shews his Taste but his Virtue, in the Choice of such Ornaments' (*Corr.* IV 13), and the paintings chosen were highly moral subjects from Biblical and classical history. Thus the first classical subject was that well-known and highly popular example of stoical virtue *The Continence of Scipio*—after a sketch by Pietro da Cortona (1596–1669), a painter who combined erudite study of the antique with a high baroque boldness of style. Pope believed this drawing to be more expressive than the painting of the same subject by Sebastiano Ricci (1659–1734, much admired in the Burlington circle), and by the same criterion he recommended Nicolas Poussin's 'admirable piece for Expression' *The Death of Germanicus*, a solemn, stoically moralizing work whose composition and accessories were derived faithfully from the antique. This was a much-copied work, invariably praised for expression—that is, the painter's ability to render internal passions by their visible effects, 'to express the Motions of the Spirits, and the Affections or Passions whose Centre is the Heart: In a word, to *make the Soul visible*'.[1] Pope could have known this painting in the engraving of 1663 by Guillaume Chasteau (Plate 3), and through the work of two of his own close friends, the elder Jonathan Richardson, who painted a copy, and the younger, who wrote a detailed analysis of Poussin's painting in his *Account* (1722) of works of art in Italy.[2] For a Biblical moral subject Pope recommended *Joseph and his Brethren* by Eustache Le Sueur (1616–55) who was regarded in Pope's day as the pre-eminent painter of grace and was ranked along-

[1] *The Art of Painting: by C. A. du Fresnoy with Remarks, translated . . . by Mr. Dryden*, 2nd edn., 'corrected and enlarged' by Richard Graham, 1716, 33.
[2] Georges Wildenstein, 'Les Gravures de Poussin au 17ᵉ siècle,' *Gazette des Beaux Arts* XLVI, 1955, 256–7; Sir Anthony Blunt, *The Paintings of Nicholas Poussin, a critical catalogue*, 1966, 113–14.

side Poussin, only a little below Raphael, for his power to correct and 'raise' common nature into ideal forms.

In his *Theory of Painting* (1715) the elder Jonathan Richardson was merely restating the fundamental assumption of all High Renaissance art when he wrote: 'Common nature is no more fit for a picture than plain narration is for a poem: a painter must raise his ideas beyond what he sees, and form a model of perfection in his own mind which is not to be found in reality; but yet such a one as is probable, and rational.'[1] It was possible to raise nature for a moral end in portraiture and in landscape (as Salvator Rosa, Claude Lorrain and the Poussins had done),[2] but the greatest challenge and opportunity lay in history painting. So Pope wrote to Jervas in 1716: 'I long to see you a History Painter. You have already done enough for the Private, do something for the Publick; and be not confined, like the rest, to draw only such silly stories as our own faces tell of us' (*Corr.* I 377). Behind this wish lies the common assumption that the prerequisite of great art is the great subject—noble and instructive.

The notion of the sister-arts, and in particular the sister-hood of poetry and painting, had been rooted in men's minds from antiquity. The opening verses of that standard neo-classical treatise on the art of painting, C. A. de Fresnoy's *De Arte Graphica* (1668), contained both of the famous old slogans—'ut pictura poesis' (Horace, *Ars Poetica*, 361, though not intended by its author to be a precept), and the comment attributed by Plutarch to Simonides of Ceos that painting is mute poetry and poetry a speaking picture. The first treatise by any English poet on the graphic arts, Dryden's *A Parallel of Poetry and Painting* (1695) was prefixed to his prose translation of du Fresnoy and was of course well-known to Pope. The notion of parallelism between the graphic arts and poetry underlies such critical works by Pope's friends as the elder Jonathan Richardson's *The Theory of Painting* (1715), Addison's second Dialogue on Medals, and Spence's *Polymetis* (which was much influenced by Pope's conversation).[3] Richardson's *Explanatory Notes*

[1] *Works of Jonathan Richardson*, 1792, 73; cf. Bellori's *Lives*, 1672, tr. Dryden, 1695, *Essays of John Dryden*, ed. W. P. Ker, 1926, II 118.
[2] *Works of Richardson* 78, 79, 72.
[3] *Ibid.* 6, 65; Addison's *Works*, 1721, I 446; *Polymetis*, 1747, 36, 67.

and *Remarks on Milton's Paradise Lost* (1734), written with the collaboration of his son and Pope, refer to over fifty 'pictures' in Milton's poem, including 'prospects' and 'expressive' figure paintings.

It was to accompany an edition of Dryden's translation of du Fresnoy revised by Richard Graham and Jervas that Pope wrote his adulatory 'Epistle to Mr. Jervas' but his conventional observations on the sister-arts (13–20) serve to celebrate a personal friendship rather than to reveal true likenesses between the arts. The parallel between poetry and painting was commonly made on the basis of their common source of subject-matter, a shared mode of apprehension (the mind has an 'eye') and similar characteristics of style, such as design and 'colour' (an inexact term in literary criticism). It was perhaps with such criteria in mind that Pope in 1710 wrote of Crashaw and poets of his kind: 'their *Colouring* entertains the sight, but the *Lines* and *Life* of the Picture are not to be inspected too narrowly'. From his accompanying remarks it appears that '*Lines* and *Life*' are 'Design, Form, Fable' and 'exactness or consent of parts' while '*Colouring*' is 'pretty conceptions, fine metaphors, glittering expressions, and something of a neat cast of Verse' (*Corr.* I 109–10). Less explicitly, Pope commented in 1712 on the '*picturesque*' quality of a couplet in Ambrose Philips's famous Copenhagen ice-scene, comparing it with 'winterpieces' by Homer, Virgil, Horace, Milton and Congreve. At this date Pope's mind was running on verbal painting, for he was revising *Windsor Forest* and 'endeavouring to raise up round about me a painted scene of woods and forests' (*Corr.* I 166–8). Later, in his Preface and Notes to his translation of the *Iliad*, Pope repeatedly drew attention to Homer's ability as a word-painter (e.g. Twickenham VII 187, VIII 32), while the Index includes a sizable section headed 'Painting, Sculpture, &c.' where the reader is referred to passages that Pope considered picturesque or statuesque. If Pope noted that Homer's 'heroic scenes' were pictorial he made them even more so in translation, by halting action to elaborate a description and by adding colour epithets and indications of perspective not in the original.[1]

In his own verse Pope shows repeatedly that one art may 'reflect

[1] See Ault 91–5; Jean H. Hagstrum, *The Sister Arts*, Chicago 1958, 229–33.

images' to its sister-arts—the phrase occurs in the Epistles to Jervas and Addison. Several of his shorter poems describe real or imagined works of art (Twickenham VI 9, 45, 66, 156, 202, 211); *The Temple of Fame* is an extended description of imaginary architecture and sculpture; the *Epistle to a Lady* opens in an imaginary gallery whose portraits display unmistakeable motifs from High Renaissance and *seicento* art; the sylphs in *The Rape of the Lock* reminded one eighteenth-century critic of Correggio; pictorial or sculptural models lie behind such poetic creations as the personifications of the Thames in *Windsor Forest*, of Melancholy in *Eloisa to Abelard* and of Dulness surrounded by Guardian Virtues' in *The Dunciad*.[1] The celebrated landscape in *Windsor Forest* was praised as a piece of 'Painting in Poetry' from its very first appearance (cf. *The Guardian* No. 86, 19 June 1713), though modern critics have been unable to agree on what kind of painting has been put into poetry—Raphael's, Claude's and a water-colourist's have been suggested.[2] Though our irrepressible sense of the picturesque leads us to read in, for instance, the 'here' and 'there' of *Windsor Forest* pictorial concepts such as plane, depth and perspective, such concepts have no *formal* equivalents in poetry. Poetry and other arts often have common subject-matter, and Pope claims no more than that in his declaration that 'images reflect from art to art', but Lessing's objections to deeper analogies remain unanswerable.

Although the effort has been made, there is little profit in attempting to find stylistic parallels between Palladian architecture and Pope's verse,[3] but Pope's activities as a publicist of the English Palladian movement call for some comment. This movement had effectively begun in 1715 with the publication of *Vitruvius Britannicus*, Vol. I, by

[1] Hagstrum, 217-21, 236-7; R. W. Williams, 'Some Baroque Influences in Pope's *Dunciad*,' *British Journal of Aesthetics* IX, 1969, 186.

[2] E. W. Manwaring, *Italian Landscape in Eighteenth Century England*, New York 1925, 97; C. Hussey, *The Picturesque*, 1927, 30; Ault 88; D. R. Clark, 'Landscape Effects in Pope's Homer,' *JAAC* XXII, 1963-4, 25.

[3] B. Fehr, 'The Antagonism of Forms in the Eighteenth Century,' *English Studies* XVIII, 1936, 193; refuted by G. Giovanni, 'Method in the study of Literature in its relation to the other Fine Arts,' *JAAC* VIII, 1950, 194.

Colen Campbell, containing one hundred engravings of English buildings (existing or planned) whose designs were inspired by Roman
models, and of the first volume of an English translation of Palladio's
Four Books of Architecture (1570, based on a treatise by Vitruvius) with
plates especially redrawn by Giacomo Leoni. Burlington at once
became patron to both Campbell and Leoni and placed himself at the
head of a campaign to spread a new (or rather a revived-antique)
'correct' style of building to replace the baroque of Wren and Vanbrugh.
On his second Grand Tour in 1719 he examined the architecture of
ancient Rome and Palladio's work in northern Italy; particularly he
saw in the country houses built by Palladio near Vicenza how the villas
described by Horace and Martial might have contemporary counter-
parts. From this tour he returned with another devotee of Palladio,
William Kent. Burlington and his fellow Palladians were, of course,
fully aware that they were treading in the footsteps of Inigo Jones, and
both the volumes of 1715 mentioned above celebrated Jones quite as
much as they did Palladio.

Pope showed an early interest in architecture of a sort in *The Temple
of Fame*, written in 1711, but, despite some critics' efforts to see it as
Palladian (or, for that matter, Baroque), the Temple's architectural
design is a great deal less plausible than its allegory. It was a few years
later that Pope met Burlington, and by the end of 1716 he was a member
of what was fast becoming a kind of private academy at Burlington
House. Probably it was here that he imbibed his enthusiasm for Palladianism. In 1716 he visited George Clarke in Oxford and examined
Inigo Jones's drawings for the great unexecuted rebuilding of Whitehall
in the Palladian style.[1] Two of these drawings were widely influential
on taste when they were engraved for the second volume of *Vitruvius
Britannicus* (1717) and William Kent's *The Designs of Inigo Jones* (1727).
For his own building projects Pope read Palladio and engaged Palladians—Campbell in the summer of 1718 for a town house never built,

---

[1] *Corr.* I 376; this is one of Pope's 'edited' letters, but Sherburn accepts
its date, 29 November 1716, as likely. The drawings are now at Worces-
ter College, Oxford. See Avril Henry and Peter Dixon, 'Pope and the
Architects: A Note on the *Epistle to Burlington*,' *English Studies* LI,
1970, 437–41.

James Gibbs, a less doctrinaire Palladian but far more capable architect, for alterations soon afterwards to the house Pope leased in Twickenham, and Kent for a new portico of brick and stucco at Twickenham in 1732–33.[1] The Twickenham villa as it appears shortly after this addition was a comfortable, if undistinguished, little box or 'goose pie' of a house (see Twickenham X, opp. 272). Pope's library contained plaster busts of Palladio and Inigo Jones; he possessed a collection of engravings of Roman buildings which he studied carefully and annotated; he wrote too, in Latin, a treatise on 'the old buildings of Rome', based upon Graevius's writings on Roman antiquities, 1694–1725 (Twickenham II 230–31 note). Among the *Pope's Homer* MSS. in the British Museum are several small drawings in Pope's hand which may be connected with his own building projects. These include the ground plan of a small town house and garden,[2] plans of three floors of another building which may well be the central block of the Twickenham villa,[3] and rougher sketches of elevations[4] which do not appear to refer to those plans or to the Twickenham villa. For one of these elevations, see Plate 7—a chastely Palladian design featuring a Venetian door. About 1724 he proposed and sketched a portico, presumably in the Palladian style, to mask the Tudor building at Sherborne Castle, and about seven years later he offered William Forbes advice on the correct proportions of doors and windows (*Corr.* II 236–7; III 225).

Pope knew nothing of Palladio's work at first hand, and the few members of Burlington's circle who did discounted its exciting variety of texture and unusual combinations of colour, choosing rather to admire Palladio's regularity, restraint in ornament, mathematical proportions and scholarly use of the classical orders. They saw in his work the operation of a few simple, invariable, rational principles of structure and design—a system well suited to the spirit of Newton's age. Characteristically Pope reduced all the rules of architecture 'to three or four heads: the justness of the openings, bearings upon bearings, and the regularity of the pillars' (Spence § 559). The *Epistle to Burlington* (1731)

---

[1] *Corr.* I 516, 475 n; II 50; III 322, 328–9, 356, 359; Mack, 16–17.
[2] BM Add. MS 4809 ff. 66b, 67b.
[3] BM Add. MS 4808 f. 30b.
[4] BM Add. MS 4808 f. 200b; 4809f. 84b, 86b.

marked Pope's public emergence as advocate of the now widely accepted Palladian style—with the immediate result that the poet's figure was
added to a new version of Hogarth's satiric engraving *Burlington Gate*
(Twickenham III ii, frontispiece). The Epistle is in part a hymn to
Palladianism, placing Burlington in a kind of architectural apostolic
succession:

> *Erect new wonders, and the old repair,*
> *Jones and Palladio to themselves restore,*
> *And be whate'er Vitruvius was before.*   (192–4)

Burlington and Kent restored the great portico at St. Paul's Covent
Garden and repaired or rebuilt other works by Jones. The greatest of
the new wonders was Burlington's newly completed *villa suburbana*—a
combination of *salon* and art gallery—in the grounds of his Jacobean
house at Chiswick. With its exterior modelled (not very closely) on
Palladio's Villa Capra near Vicenza and its interior decorated by Kent,
using designs by Inigo Jones for several features, it was a temple of
Palladianism (Plate 4). Since the poet's first concern is with the moral
nature of house-builders and the quality of life embodied in Palladian
buildings. Pope's *Epistle* gives no exact directions on architectural
matters. Its ridicule of Timon's inconvenient, pretentious 'villa' and its
brief hit at Vanbrugh (the 'Guide' of l.20) are paralleled by Pope's
earlier mockery of that baroque masterpiece Blenheim Palace.[1] By
1731 the Palladian permeation was so complete that Pope had no need
to specify the 'noble rules' laid down by Burlington, but he recognized
that, by simplifying architecture to the study of a few 'correct' Renaissance and antique models, Burlington had filled the land with 'imitating
fools'. It is not clear, however, which imitators Pope had in mind—
apart from Thomas Ripley (l.18) who executed Campbell's design for
Walpole's Houghton, which was conceivably a model for Timon's
villa.[2]

   The *Epistle to Burlington* is the nearest thing we have to Pope's
'gardening poem' (Spence § 310); and it was partly due to Pope's

---

[1] *Corr.* I 431–2, closely paralleled by the epigram 'Upon the Duke of
Marlborough's House at Woodstock,' often attributed to Pope (see
Twickenham VI 412).
[2] Mack 122–3, 272–8.

practice and precept in both arts that men came to look upon gardening
as one of the sister-arts to poetry (cf. Thomson, *Liberty*, V, 1736, 683–
700). As with architecture (another sister-art according to Thomson)
stylistic parallels with poetry are hard to find,[1] but the practitioners of
the different sister-arts accept the same aesthetic principles. Thus early
eighteenth-century gardeners take their slogans from Horace's *Ars
Poetica*; and Stephen Switzer, in his gardening handbook *The Nobleman,
Gentleman and Gardener's Recreation* (1715), declares that the precepts
of Pope's *Essay on Criticism* are applicable to gardening.

Pope's tastes in painting, sculpture and architecture follow those of
his age and group, but in gardening claims have been made for him as
an originator of new taste. Philip Southcote and Horace Walpole, for
instance, made such claims,[2] but as amateur gardeners themselves they
may have been inclined, like Pope, to belittle the professionals, and
there are no indications in Pope's early statements on gardening and in
his own garden layout at Twickenham that he was in any way more
revolutionary than those established professionals Stephen Switzer and
Charles Bridgeman. Pope's later ideas (for example, those communi-
cated to Spence after 1728) seem to be contemporary with William
Kent's practice in the 1720s and 1730s.

Much of the theory underlying eighteenth-century landscape gardening is, of course, found in seventeenth-century texts well known to
Pope. In *The Elements of Architecture* (1624) Sir Henry Wotton had laid
down the rules of building from Vitruvius, Alberti and Palladio, and
then declared: 'as *Fabricks* should be *regular*, so gardens should be
irregular, or at least cast into a very wild *Regularity*'.[3] Bacon, in his
essay 'Of Gardens', allowed for the area farthest from the house to be
framed 'to a natural wildness', while for the part nearest to the house
the gardener should scorn the knots, figures and scrollwork of bedded
flowers and lay out instead a four acre lawn. Milton condemned

---

[1] I find unconvincing the comparison between Pope's Twickenham
garden and his couplet art in Mario Praz, *Mnemosyne*, 1970, 42–3.
[2] Spence §§ 603, 1121; I.W.U. Chase, *Horace Walpole, Gardenist*, Princeton and Oxford 1943, 28.
[3] *Reliquiae Wottonianae*, 2nd edn 1654, 269–70. Pope had read the *Elements*; see Spence, § 617.

'curious knots' too, and Spence, Horace Walpole and other garden theorists were fully alive to the significance of his Garden of Eden as a protest against formality.[1] Sir William Temple writing in 1685 'Upon the Gardens of Epicurus' had referred to 'the newest mode' of casting a garden 'all into grass plots and gravel walks', and had raised—but then dropped—the possibility of laying out English gardens in what he conceived to be the Chinese manner of 'sharawadgi' or pleasing wildness. Addison, in *Spectator* 414 (25 June 1712), revived Temple's allusion to Chinese gardening; earlier, in *Spectator* 37 (12 April 1711), he had described Leonora's garden as 'a kind of wilderness' with its woods, bowers, shady walks, grottos, rivulets and lake.

In *Guardian* 173 (29 Sept. 1713) Pope declared that 'the Taste of the Ancients in their Gardens' was for 'the amiable Simplicity of unadorned Nature', but there is no indication that the four acre garden of Alcinous which Pope then went on to describe from Homer was at all irregular in form. It was a 'natural' garden in Pope's view simply because it was well-ordered and fruitful and contained none of the artful topiary that was so prominent in Pliny's gardens and was so fashionable in seventeenth-century England, but which had been despised by both Bacon and Addison (*Spectator* 414). (However, in conversation with Spence years later, Pope recommends topiary on the large scale with his proposal for a Gothic cathedral or Roman temple in poplar trees—an imposition of art upon nature less bizarre only than his suggestion of carving a Welsh mountain into a statue (Spence § 619). Pope's much-quoted remark on regular gardens in the Preface to his translation of the *Iliad* (1715) is not a plea for landscape gardening but merely a statement that the beauties of wild nature are not those of art. The opening paragraph of *Spectator* 425 (8 July 1712) describes a garden:

> You descend at first by twelve Stone Steps into a large Square divided into four Grass-plots, in each of which is a Statue of white Marble. This is separated from a large Parterre by a low Wall, and from thence, thro' a Pair of Iron Gates, you are led into a long broad Walk of the finest Turf, set on each Side with tall Yews, and on either Hand border'd by a Canal, which on the Right divides the Walk from a Wilderness parted into Variety of

[1] Spence §1115; Chase 14–16.

Allies and Arbours, and on the Left from a kind of Amphitheatre, which is the Receptacle of a great Number of Oranges and Myrtles.

Norman Ault has shown that this essay is very probably by Pope (*Prose Works* xlix–li), and certainly there is nothing here inconsistent with *Guardian* 173, and nothing revolutionary in either. This ideal garden is in the style fashionable about the time of William III and Anne; varied examples of the type may still be seen at Canons Ashby in Northamptonshire (home of the Drydens), Westbury Court in Gloucestershire and Melbourne Hall in Derbyshire; Temple's five acre garden at Moor Park in Surrey, laid out between 1680 and 1699, is an unpretentious variant of this type (Plate 5).[1]

All those gardens, actual or ideal, were smallish, but the great practical achievement of seventeenth-century gardening was, of course, the very large-scale, grand, formal manner originated by the Mollets but associated pre-eminently with André le Nôtre, the French Royal Gardener who (it should not be forgotten) is highly praised in Pope's *Epistle to Burlington* (46 and note). In the great French garden long vistas, elaborate fountains, canals, great parterres and flights of steps are ordered upon rectilinear axes so that the garden reflects on a vast scale the structural solidity of the palace. The French gardeners devised the *patte d'oie* or goose-foot—the half-circle from which diverge five avenues carrying the eye outwards—while in the groves away from the main axes of their layouts they devised surprising little secret gardens decorated with statues and water-works.

Though the French grand manner of gardening was attempted in England at Hampton Court, Cannons and elsewhere, economy, not to speak of the problem posed by the growth of planted materials in highly formal layouts, eventually encouraged a less elaborate manner of large-scale gardening. Thus, shortly after her accession, Queen Anne ordered her Gardener, Henry Wise, to reduce by two-thirds the cost of keeping up the Royal gardens, and in 1704 the box *broderie* at Hampton Court was replaced by turf in what Switzer proudly called 'the plain

[1] C. Hussey, 'Templum Restauratum,' *Country Life* CVI, 29 Nov. 1949, 1578–81.

but noble English manner'.[1] There was virtue in economy. The purpose of Switzer's practical advice in *Ichnographia Rustica* is to unite utility and beauty in the garden. The starting point of Addison's gardening theory in *Spectator* 414 is in the frequent plantations that may turn as much to the profit as to the pleasure of the owner. John Evelyn's influential *Sylva* (1664) had taught that planting was a profitable investment and lordly pleasure as well as a patriotic duty; thus Bathurst created an enormous timber value in his landscaping at Cirencester Park, and, incidentally, provided a profitable field for investment by Pope and his other literary friends. Addison had suggested that a whole estate might be thrown into a kind of garden and from this Switzer developed his notion of 'Extensive or Rural and Forest Gardening' where the timber and pasture parkland is united with formal garden features such as basins and terraces to make a single design. An imaginary garden of this kind is portrayed in *Ichnographica Rustica*, 1718 (Plate 6) and an actual example in the 1742 edition of Switzer's book (see below, p. 161 and note 1).

Addison had praised the large seventeenth-century French and Italian gardens because their extent gave an exalted pleasure to the imagination, but English gardens were already being laid out to provide unconfined prospects—particularly if Vanbrugh had a hand in siting the house, as he did in 1713 at Duncombe Park, Yorkshire, or in 1715 at Claremont, Surrey.[2] The lack of formality and wide vistas of Rochester's garden at Petersham—close to Twickenham and very well known to Pope—were praised in 1718 by both Switzer and Samuel Molyneux, the latter in terms evidently derived from Addison's writings.[3] Pope on his travels in the early 1720s found well-established 'irregular' gardens disposed over varied slopes and commanding wide views (*Corr.* II 86, 236–9).

[1] *Ichnographia Rustica*, 1718, I 83.
[2] C. Hussey, *English Gardens and Landscapes, 1700–1750*, 1967, 140–6 (Pope ridiculed Duncombe Park's owner in *Imitations of Horace: Satire II ii* 178); L. Whistler, *The Imagination of Vanbrugh and his Fellow Artists*, 1954, 144–55.
[3] *Ichnographia Rustica*, I xxxviii; A. J. Sambrook, 'Pope's Neighbours: an early landscape garden at Richmond,' *JWCI* XXX, 1967, 444–6.

Pope's injunction in the *Epistle to Burlington* to consult the 'Genius of the Place' was already being obeyed by gardeners. Thus Bridgeman's plan for a garden to cover the gentle, even slope at Eastbury in Dorset is far more geometrically tight than his almost contemporary design (*c.* 1716) for the more abrupt contours at Claremont which enjoyed what Colen Campbell called a 'singularly Romantick' site, while the existence in 1718 of Wray Wood on its low hill and the curving line of the old village street in front dictated—or inspired—a certain informality in the garden layout at Castle Howard in Yorkshire.[1] Similarly, the retention of an old lane's oblique line gave the first asymmetrical bias to the garden at Stowe as it developed under Bridgeman's hand from 1713. In this garden, which survives, even under the later work of Kent and Capability Brown, as his masterpiece, Bridgeman gained his effects by the interplay of formal avenues, lakes, lawns and parterres, with irregular woodland walks and the use of the 'ha ha' or sunk fence (a French device first described in A.-J. Dezallier d'Argenville's *Theorie et Pratique du Jardinage*, 1709) to break the barrier between garden proper and park. The lakes are regular in shape, and Bridgeman seems to have resented Pope's suggestion that the 'floating' of the north lake over old parterres placed him among the revolutionary gardeners.[2]

[1] Whistler, *The Imagination of Vanbrugh*, chs. i, v, vi, vii; Hussey, *Gardens and Landscapes*, 38–9, 89–131; Switzer gives Wray Wood and the wood in Rochester's garden at Petersham as the earliest examples of the new, freer style of gardening, *Ichnographia Rustica* I, xxxviii.

[2] In the 1731 editions of the *Epistle to* Bridgman Pope wrote:

> The vast Parterres a thousand hands shall make,
> Lo! Bridgman *comes, and floats them with a Lake.* (73–4)

But in 1735 'Cobham' was substituted for 'Bridgman'. Warburton's note on the couplet is: 'This office, in the original plan of the poem, was given to another Man of TASTE; who not having the SENSE to see a compliment was intended him, convinced the poet it did not belong to him.' There is a further reference in a couplet once intended for inclusion in the *Epistle to Arbuthnot* but never printed by Pope:

> If Bridgeman, while his head contrives a maze,
> Knows not, good man, my satire from my praise.
>
> (*E–C*, III 263, n4)

For the historian, Bridgeman stands midway between Le Nôtre and Brown; so does Pope who, in the *Epistle to Burlington*, praises Le Nôtre and, as it happens, prophetically damns the vandalism that would be perpetrated by Brown. For 'Villario', 'Tir'd of the scene Parterres and Fountains yield/ . . . finds at last he better likes a field' (87–8). The tendentious term 'semi-formal' is applied to Bridgeman's work, but for Bridgeman and Pope Stowe and similar contemporary gardens were 'natural' according to the current definition of that infinitely accommodating term. Pope thought that Bathurst should have 'considered the genius of the place' and raised two or three artificial mounts at Richings 'because his situation is all a plain, and nothing can please without variety' (Spence § 609). All beauties were comprehended in variety (Spence § 604), and if variety of contour and cover were not provided by the original site then it should be supplied by man; so much is implied too in Pope's praise of two Gloucestershire gardens— Dodington and Rentcomb.[1]

The most detailed description that Pope has left of any garden is a highly laudatory account of Lord Digby's at Sherborne in Dorset (*Corr*. II 237–9) which in the early 1720s had reached a 'semi-formal' state, where a geometrical central vista of terraces, canal and regular groves remaining from Sir Walter Raleigh's layout in the Renaissance Italian style was flanked by irregularly contoured areas treated informally. (After Pope's death all was destroyed by Brown.) Pope found this garden beautiful because it was, by his criterion, 'very Irregular'. Its straight colonnade of limes was of 'standard' (that is unclipped) trees, while the yew topiary upon its terraces was restrained to simple pyramids. Six grass terraces at right angles to the side-walls of the garden descended to a level valley which contained a T-shaped canal and two regular groves of horse-chestnut between which was a large bowling-green. Beyond that four more grass terraces rose, one planted with vines, and two which were to be turned into a 'wilderness' with 'wild winding walks'. Beyond the end wall of the garden above the fourth terrace 'the natural Ground rises, & is crownd with several venerable Ruins' of a Norman castle. From the valley floor it was pos-

[1] *Corr*. II 514, 86; the first garden *is* Dodington, despite II 513 n4.

sible to take winding paths leading out of the rectilinear layout. One of these followed an uncanalized piece of water into part of the woodland which closely bounded both side-walls of the garden; embellished by nature and art, it continued under hanging ivy, past a cascade and a rustic stone seat flanked by urns, over a sham-ruin bridge, and up and round through the trees to emerge near the ruined Norman castle. Pope (disconcertingly anticipating the tidy-mindedness of the present-day Department of the Environment) suggested that this ruin would be improved if 'mixd with Greens and Parterres', the open courts, 'thrown into Circles and Octagons of Grass or flowers', and seats provided 'to enjoy those views, which are more romantick than Imagination can form them'.

Pope's other suggested improvement at Sherborne was for 'a little Temple built on a neighboring round Hill that is seen from all points of the Garden & is extremely pretty. It would finish some Walks, & particularly be a fine Termination to the River to be seen from the Entrance into that Deep Scene I have described by the Cascade where it would appear as in the clouds, between the tops of some very lofty Trees that form an Arch before it, with a great Slope downward to the end of the said river.' Here he has recognized the possibility of imitating in gardens the effects of landscape painting (cf. Spence §§ 603, 606–14). Others had seen this too; Addison had said 'a man might make a pretty landskip of his own possessions' (*Spectator* 414), and, more significantly because more practically, Vanbrugh had pleaded and plotted as early as 1709 for the retention in Blenheim Park of the remains of Woodstock Manor, which, suitably planted about 'wou'd make One of the Most Agreeable Objects that the best of Landskip Painters can invent'.[1] The most notable early garden laid out in this painterly manner was Rousham in Oxfordshire where Bridgeman in the 1720s laid out the main lines for Kent's famous work in the 1730s.[2] In 1728 Pope found it 'the prettiest place for water-falls, jetts, ponds inclosed with beautiful scenes of green and hanging wood'.[3] In Pope's case the parallel between

---

[1] David Green, *Blenheim Palace*, 1951, 92–7, 303–4.

[2] Hussey, *Gardens and Landscapes*, 147–53.

[3] *Corr.* II 513, where 'scenes' has the sense of painted stage hangings: cf. 'Back fly the scenes', *Epistle II i, To Augustus*, 315.

gardening and landscape-painting may have implied no more than that gardeners would now strive not for geometrical symmetry but for the occult balance of a correctly composed picture. Unlike Horace Walpole, Pope never compares a garden landscape with the work of any named painter; nevertheless it is possible that the system of 'retiring and again assembling shades' (in Walpole's phrase)[1] that Pope worked out in his own garden may owe something to the contrast of deep and shallow spaces in a background that one finds in Titian and in Nicolas Poussin and other seventeenth-century painters.

Pope, like men in all ages, loved to 'seek some ruin's formidable shade' ('Epistle to Mr Jervas', 30) in order to mourn pleasurably over vanished grandeur, and his recognition of and desire to develop the picturesque qualities of the garden at Sherborne were quite as much sentimental as they were aesthetic. The murmuring waters, the commemorative urns, the temple in the clouds and the ruins were all designed to induce, by association, certain sensations—solemn or gay. For the gardeners of Pope's generation it was all-important to add a temporal significance to the spatial forms of a pictorial landscape composition; the ruins, grottos, statues, urns, inscriptions, views of church spires, obelisks, columns and temples all brought references to human life and feeling—ideas of classic art, of martial grandeur, of British 'liberty', of morality, of mortality, of Christian hope, and so on. Hence the English early Georgian garden (like the sixteenth-century Italian and the seventeenth-century French) still represents the architect's as much as the gardener's approach to external nature. As Pope reminded Burlington, attentiveness to nature was shown as much in rearing the Column, bending the Arch and sinking the Grot as in contouring, planting or inundating the ground. In Pope's view, and nearly everyone else's, the finest garden of the age was Stowe where associative monuments were thicker on the ground than in any other great garden.[2]

Pope saw Stowe through several stages of its growth and change

---

[1] Chase 28.

[2] Detailed descriptions in Pope's lifetime include: Gilbert West, *Stowe, a Poem*, 1732; Sarah Bridgeman, *Plans of Stowe*, 1739; Anon., *A Description of Stowe*, 1744. A convenient modern account is Hussey, *Gardens and Landscapes*, 89–113.

and was himself commemorated in the Temple of British Worthies there, but he is not known to have advised on or assisted in the layout of the garden. Though there are several contemporary tributes to Pope's influence on gardening it is by no means exactly clear where and how he helped his many gardening friends (who included the professionals Bridgeman and Kent, and such amateurs as Burlington, Bathurst, Digby, Cobham, Lyttelton and Peterborough). Gay's *Epistle to Lord Burlington*, written in 1715, states that Pope is eating fruit at Chiswick, but this is not to imply that Pope was helping Burlington to lay out either that garden or the one that was begun about 1722 to provide a setting for the Palladian villa, built 1725–29. The new garden, begun by Bridgeman and continued by Kent, as it took shape in the 1730s had a *grande allée* with subsidiary avenues in goosefoot form, closely clipped and focused on buildings. The canal was set off the main axis and very slightly serpentined by Kent; the wildernesses between the avenues contained winding paths; there were 'associative' buildings, obelisks and statues (Plate 9). According to Horace Walpole Pope was consulted in 1719 by Bridgeman over the layout of the Prince of Wales's grounds at Richmond Lodge, while Pope's correspondence shows that in 1723–24 he was involved, with Bridgeman and Bathurst, in designing a garden for Lady Suffolk's new house, Marble Hill at Twickenham (*Corr.* II 197, 240). A fourth suburban garden associated with Pope was Richings, or Riskins, Bathurst's Buckinghamshire estate.[1] By about 1740 this was 'semi-formal' in character. The main axis was down a straight canal 555 yards long, beyond which the view continued into the surrounding countryside across a ha ha. In the areas flanking this main axis paths in goose-foot or serpentine form were cut through groves which contained such features as 'a cave' (probably a freestanding grotto or hermitage)[2] and 'little arbours interwoven with lilacs, woodbines, syringas and laurels', and through 'Promiscuous Kitchen Quarters'. This last feature was in keeping with Switzer's advice, and may have owed something to Mr Spectator's garden which

[1] Engraved plan, Switzer, *Ichnographia Rustica*, 2nd edn, 1742, reproduced in P. Dixon, *The World of Pope's Satires*, 1968, opp. p. 73; description, W. H. Ward & K. S. Block, *A History of Iver*, 1933, 199–201.

[2] A. J. Sambrook, 'Additions to *OED*,' *N & Q*, CCXI, 1966, 209.

was 'a confusion of Kitchen and Parterre, Orchard and Flower Garden. . . . mixt and interwoven' (*Spectator* 477, 6 Sept. 1712).

Pope declared in 1725 that his ideal garden would combine the waters of Riskins with the woods of Oakley at Bathurst's other, larger estate at Cirencester Park. Thus both of Pope's ideal features were very large and by no means informal, for at Cirencester, between about 1715 and his death in 1775, Bathurst planted a series of forest parks stretching for five miles and cut by great, geometrically aligned avenues to create a grand and highly productive piece of 'extensive or forest gardening'.[1] Pope watched and commented on the planting from the beginning (and invested in it), and was allowed to direct the rebuilding of a banqueting house in the woods.[2] Begun in 1721 and enlarged in 1732, this was one of the first eighteenth-century castellated follies (Plate 8)—though Switzer had earlier recommended the erection of 'Lodges, Granges, etc.' in the form of 'some antiquated place'. Pope was also consulted over the design of a classical temple, the Hexagon (*Corr.* IV 25).

The Earl of Peterborough was celebrated as naturalist and gardener even before Pope was born (it was in his garden at Fulham in 1688 that the first tulip tree flowered in England[3]); in the 1730s Pope was his frequent visitor at Bevis Mount, near Southampton, and in 1736, after Peterborough's death, he engaged to finish laying out the garden there (*Corr.* IV 33–6). The chief feature of the garden, as described in 1753,[4] was the Mount, an ancient fortification, skirted by a woody labyrinth containing grottoes and alcoves, and crowned by 'a bowling green, or [English] parterre, adorned with fine Italian marble statues', on one side of which was a vineyard exposed to the south, and on the other a summerhouse with cellar beneath. The place-name 'Pope's Walk' survived here, as it did also at Richings. In 1726 Pope was giving advice on the gardens at Wimpole in Cambridgeshire (though Bridgeman was

---

[1] Lees-Milne 21–56; Hussey, *Gardens and Landscapes*, 78–83.
[2] *Corr.* II 207; *The Correspondence of Jonathan* Swift, ed. H. Williams, Oxford 1963–5, IV 199–200.
[3] M. Hadfield, *A History of British Gardening*, 1969, 137.
[4] Quoted in F. J. C. Hearnshaw, 'Bevis Mount,' *Papers and Proceedings of the Hampshire Field Club* V, 1904–6, 114–20.

chiefly responsible for these),[1] in 1734 at Tottenham Park, Wiltshire, and in 1739 at Cornbury, Oxfordshire (*Corr.* II 376–7; III 417; IV 189). Between 1737 and 1743 he seems to have had a considerable hand in laying out Ralph Allen's gardens at Prior Park near Bath.[2]

Pope's own gardening probably began near the end of 1718 when he rented the Twickenham villa with its small plot of land running down to the Thames. In November 1719 he rented two acres of ground over the road from his house, but he may already have had land there; certainly, before 1734 the garden across the road extended to five acres.[3] From the beginning he planted busily to form groves, arcades and 'wildernesses' (*Corr.* II 44, 263, 296, 328), and by 1726 most of the principal features had been created—a large mount from Kent's design, a bowling-green, an open temple made of shells and an amphitheatre either designed by Bridgeman or imitated from him.[4] Most important, the grotto had been dug by 1722 (*Corr.* II 125, 142). The verses 'To Mr Gay' (1720), referring to the 'gay parterre', 'chequer'd shade', 'morning bower' and 'ev'ning colonnade', suggest that Pope was already exploiting the east-west alignment of the garden to create variations of light and shade with their associated *Allegro* and *Penseroso* moods, but the main organizing feature of, and the most powerfully associative object in, the finished garden did not appear until 1735 when Pope raised the memorial obelisk to his mother.[5] I presume that, from the beginning, there was a kitchen-garden in the obvious place—south of the garden proper; Pope's broccoli—a rarity at that date—is mentioned in 1723. In the 1730s letters and verse refer to vines planted south of a wall within the garden, to fruit-trees, some of which may have formed the quin-

[1] Lees-Milne, 215

[2] *Corr.* IV 84, 206, 217, 362, 429, 444. Pope is said to have designed a little bridge there; see B. Boyce, *The Benevolent Man*, Cambridge, Mass., 1967, 114, plate 10c.

[3] See A. J. Sambrook, 'The Shape and Size of Pope's Garden,' *E–C S* 5, 1972, 450–5.

[4] Spence §§1060, 1062; *Corr.* II 86, 328, 376. Peter Willis, the biographer of Bridgeman, thinks it 'extremely likely' that Bridgeman was engaged by Pope at Twickenham; see 'A Poet's Gardener,' *The Listener* LXXII, 1964, 1007–9.

[5] *Corr.* III 453; Mack, Plate 11.

cunxes of the main garden, and to the melons and pineapples grown in his hot houses, or 'stoves'. Pope always writes as a practical gardener, whether the subject is vegetables, fruit or hedge-cutting (*Corr.* IV 377; III 451–2, 225). There is no evidence that he grew flowers, and *Dunciad* IV 403 shows that he despised florists.

The famous *Plan* published in 1745 by Pope's gardener John Searle shows the main features of the garden,[1] and in Plate 10 I have redrawn that plan to show (as the 1745 *Plan* does not) the correct overall shape of the garden and the correct alignment of these features. From the east front of the house a grass plot, or 'English parterre', sloped down towards the river between screens of trees and shrubs which masked or replaced garden walls mentioned in 1720 (*Corr.* II 59); in these screens were four niches containing, on stone terms, busts of Homer, Virgil, Marcus Aurelius and Cicero (Spence, § 620), and the screens ended at the water's edge each with a small stone pavilion. The basement storey of the house contained the grotto which was continued as a passage under the road and into the garden proper where it was aligned with a straight path of flints and pebbles (not cockle shells as Pope had intended: *Corr.* II 286) which led through a thicket or 'wilderness', under an arcade of interlaced, overhanging trees to an open temple made of shells. Kent's drawing (Plate 11) may be a design for the re-building of the Shell Temple in 1736 (*Corr.* III 512; IV 22); the stone niches shown flanking the temple do not appear on Searle's plan or in any description of the garden and there is obvious fantasy in the allegorical group on the left and the sacrificial dolphin in the foreground, but this is probably an accurate representation of the Temple itself (and of Pope, Kent and Bounce on the right). From the Shell Temple one could enjoy a surprising view looking back down the dark arcade and grotto to the brightness beyond, and 'see Sails on the River passing suddenly and vanishing as thro' a Perspective Glass' (*Corr.* II 296). Beside the Shell Temple was Kent's large mount—a very old-fashioned feature—composed of 'rude and indigested Materials; it is covered with Bushes and Trees of a wilder Growth, and more confused Order, rising as it were out of Clefts of Rocks, and Heaps of rugged and mossy Stones; among which a narrow intricate Path leads in an irregular

[1] Mack, Plate 21.

Spiral to the Top; where is placed a Forest Seat or Chair, that may
hold three or four Persons at once, overshaded with the Branches of a
spreading Tree.[1] The rude mount beside the smooth lawn and rococo
temple introduced the element of variety that the new race of gardeners
thought essential. As Shenstone would remark later: 'Are there not
broken rocks and rugged grounds to which we can hardly attribute
either beauty or grandeur, and yet when introduced near an extent of
lawn, impart a pleasure equal to more shapely scenes?'[2] From this
mount (and set off obliquely from the narrow vista back through the
grotto) the main prospect along the central axis of the garden ran due
west, at first between two regular groves, then across a broad bowling-
green, then narrowing between two small mounts covered with unclipped laurel, bay, holly and other evergreens, then broadening into a
shady glade planted regularly, narrowing again, widening slightly into
a lighter but smaller glade and finally narrowing to terminate upon the
obelisk to the poet's mother. Perspective and point of view were carefully controlled, and with them, mood. Pope declared 'You may distance
things by darkening them and by narrowing the plantation more and
more toward the end, in the same manner as they do in painting, and as
'tis executed in the little cypress walk to that obelisk' (Spence § 610),
and Horace Walpole spoke of 'the solemnity of the termination at the
cypresses that lead up to his mother's tomb'.[3] Throughout its length this
main vista was punctuated regularly by pairs of urns or statues that
would call to mind the order of the classical world. That such associations could be very complex is indicated by Maynard Mack's comment
on an ornament proposed by Pope for the Thames shore of his garden.[4]

North of the central axis was a 'wilderness' or closely planted thicket
which contained a diagonal path aligned upon the obelisk, various serpentine paths and, north of the Shell Temple, an Orangery (that is a
glade in which orange trees could be set out in tubs) from which

[1] Description by a visitor in 1747, quoted in Mack 241. Presumably
the mount was raised with spoil from digging the underground passage.
[2] 'Unconnected Thoughts on Gardening,' in *The Works in Verse and
Prose of William Shenstone*, 1764, II 126.
[3] Chase 28.
[4] Mack 37–40.

radiated a slightly asymmetrical goose-foot which provided a variety of cross-views into the central area. South of the central axis a thinner screen of trees and bushes and a wall hid the vineyard, the stoves (that is hothouses) and kitchen garden. A large object shown on Searle's plan south-east of the Shell Temple may have been the site of the 'Bridge-mannick' amphitheatre—perhaps similar to the ones that Bridgeman built of concentric turf ramps at Stowe, Eastbury and Claremont—but, since Searle does not name it and his plan does not have the hard out-line that such a feature would require, this may be a former amphi-theatre 'reverting to Nature', or some other shallow depression. The garden's bounds were concealed by dense thickets to create a secret, enclosed space within which the Bridgemannic principle of a relatively formal, straight central axis with flanking areas treated irregularly was applied in a somewhat freer way and upon a smaller scale than Bridge-man usually worked to. It was a serious work of art, the tranquil and graceful setting for an Horatian life-style, but it had too a certain toy-like quality (cf. *Corr.* II 328; and above, p. 114). 'Rococo', in the sense of an 'art of pleasure', is, of course, quite inadequate to describe Pope's poetry, but the term seems appropriate to the purpose and the style—a somewhat formalized asymmetry on a small scale—of his garden, while the grotto was undeniably rococo in the root sense, 'rocaille', which described the shells, pebbles and rocks out of which such elegant toys were made.

   Grottoes, providing a cool summer retreat, were essential features of both the Italian and French styles of gardening in the sixteenth and seventeenth centuries; among the designers of such works were Raphael, Vasari and Le Nôtre. From the outside grottoes usually looked like any other garden building, but their gloomy interiors of shell and tufa (a honeycombed, spongelike volcanic rock), dripping water, were intended to recreate the classical *nymphaeum*, a natural cave sacred to a nymph. Later grottoes sought to imitate Nature yet more closely and were commonly excavated in cliffs or hillsides, but Pope sensibly and conveniently made his grotto in the cellars of his house and along the underground passage to the garden. The seventeenth-century grotto contained elaborate water-works, and Pope too designed his restrained and beautiful variant of such devices by disposing Plates of Looking glass in the obscure Parts of the Roof and Sides of the Cave, where a sufficient Force of Light is wanting to discover the Deception, while the other Parts, the Rills, Fountains, Flints, Pebbles, &c. being duly illuminated, are so reflected by the various posited Mirrors, as, without exposing the Cause, every Object is multiplied, and its Position represented in a surprizing Diversity. Cast your Eyes upward, and you half Shudder to see Cataracts of Water precipitating over your Head, from impending Stones and Rocks, while saliant Spouts rise in rapid Streams at your Feet: Around, you are equally surprised with flowing Rivulets and rolling Waters, that rush over airey Precipices, and break amongst Heaps of ideal Flints and Spar. Thus, by a fine Taste and happy Management of Nature, you are presented with an undistinguishable Mixture of Realities and Imagery.[1]

Pope's grotto in its first completed state, by 1725, was a straight tunnel consisting of a light, open porch lined with smooth stones and a chamber lined with shells, rocks and 'Pieces of Looking-glass in angular forms' (both of these parts were in the basement storey of the house), and, beyond, the passage beneath the road, which was widened at the west or garden end into a dark little porch lined with shells, flints and iron ore and containing a spring whose waters were led back through the grotto 'in a perpetual Rill, that echoes thro' the Cavern day and night' (*Corr.* II 296–7). Even more than the garden the grotto was a retreat from the shows and bustle of the world; it provided refreshment to the spirit, but it was also, as Maynard Mack has shown, a symbol of poetic consciousness.[2]

In 1740 Pope extended the grotto by widening the portico fronting the Thames and incorporating three more rooms and a transverse passage so that the grotto occupied most of the cellarage beneath the central block of the house (see Plate 12). The perpetual, murmuring rill that gave the place the character of a *nymphaeum* was now led over 'three falls' (*Corr.* IV 267) to flow through one of the new rooms into a basin planted round with maidenhair, hartstongue and fern, while—to serve reason as well as fancy—the whole grotto was made

[1] Description of 1747, quoted in Mack 239.
[2] Mack 59–76.

something of a geological museum with correctly stratified rocks supplied by the Cornish geologist William Borlase, and exotic minerals from Europe, Africa and America given by other friends.[1] The portico fronting the Thames was faced with smooth, worked Bath stone, whereas the garden-porch was entered through a sham-ruined arch of rough, tufa-like limestone; within the grotto itself there was in a small compass enormous variety of texture, colour and exotic association—Cornish metallic ores, Vesuvian lava, West Indian coral, gold ore from Peru, Italian marble and much else, all played over by the moving light from the river outside, the trickle of water within, the mirrors and the alabaster lamp.

Pope repeatedly claimed that his grotto imitated Nature and owed little to Art. In the 'Verses on a Grotto' (1741) he wrote:

> *Thou who shalt stop, where Thames' translucent Wave*
> *Shines a broad Mirrour thro' the shadowy Cave,*
> *Where lingering Drops from Mineral Roofs distill,*
> *And pointed Crystals break the sparkling Rill,*
> *Unpolish'd Gemms no Ray on Pride bestow,*
> *And latent Metals innocently glow:*
> *Approach. Great NATURE studiously behold!*[2]

It was an ancient truism often repeated by Pope that 'all Art consists in the Imitation and Study of Nature'.[3] Switzer's notion of gardening was 'a well-balanced pursuit of Nature', and he sweepingly declared that if 'the beauties of Nature were not corrupted by Art, gardens would be much more valuable'.[4] Addison observed in *Spectator* 414 that as works of Art rise in value by their resemblance to Nature, so works of Nature are more pleasant the more they resemble those of Art. The beauty sought by Pope in his grotto and garden, and by Bridgeman and Switzer in their 'semi-formal' garden designs was defined by Francis Hutcheson

---

[1] Benjamin Boyce, 'Mr Pope, in Bath, improves the design of his Grotto,' *McKillop festschrift* 143–53; John Searle, 'An Account of the Materials which comprise the Grotto,' reprinted in Mack 259–62.

[2] Twickenham VI 382; cf. *Corr.* II 297; IV 228–9, 254, 261.

[3] *Guardian* 173; cf. Spence §560; *Essay on Criticism* 68ff.

[4] *Ichnographia Rustica*, 1718, I xvi–xx.

in 1725 as 'Uniformity amidst Variety' or, as a modern writer has elaborated this, 'Order amid Nature's infinite Variety, and Variety amid mankind's Order'.[1] The Order was itself 'natural' in any case, inasmuch as external nature, the whole phenomenal world, was God's art. Pope perfectly expresses that gardening ideal where man's Art follows Nature in his lines on the Genius of the Place which—shaping the natural contours—is itself a painter and designer:

> *Consult the Genius of the Place in all;*
> *That tells the Waters or to rise, or fall,*
> *Or helps th'ambitious Hill the heav'n to scale,*
> *Or scoops in circling theatres the Vale,*
> *Calls in the Country, catches opening glades,*
> *Joins willing woods, and varies shades from shades,*
> *Now breaks, or now directs, th'intending Lines;*
> *Paints as you plant, and, as you work, designs.*
>
> (*Epistle to Burlington*, 57–64)

The relationship between Art and Nature is felt in these formal yet relaxed couplets, so well-attuned to the speaking voice, but what is most striking in this famous, this canonical, passage is the sense of movement and growth it conveys. It reminds us that every eighteenth-century landscape garden grew, by the normal processes of 'external nature', into a finished work of art through years, even generations, after its conception.

The principle of following Nature was applicable as much in architecture as in the directly representational arts of painting and sculpture. Palladio wrote: 'Architecture therefore being, as all other Arts are, an Imitation of Nature, will never admit to any thing either repugnant to, or inconsistent with that Order and Harmony which Nature observes in all her works.'[2] To follow Nature in architecture is to imitate the rational order, the equilibrium, proportion, harmony and uniformity, which underlies the whole of empirical reality; it is to give physical shape to such time-honoured notions as those conveyed in the *Essay*

---

[1] Francis Hutcheson, *An Inquiry into the Original of our Ideas of Beauty and Virtue*, 1725, I. 2, iii; Hussey, *Gardens and Landscapes*, 38 n.

[2] *Palladio's Four Books of Architecture*, 1733–4, Bk I xx. This echoes Alberti, *De Re Edificatoria*, IX 5.

on Man. To follow Nature is also to imitate the ancients, as Pope had reminded the readers of the *Essay on Criticism*; Raphael, Alberti and Palladio revived the theories of Vitruvius, while Pope believed that his own taste for 'the amiable Simplicity of unadorned Nature' in gardens was 'the Taste of the Ancients' (*Guardian* 173).

Spence, who may well have derived this notion from Pope, linked the arts of gardening and painting in their fundamentals when he stated as the first of the 'general aims' of gardening 'to follow "beautiful Nature" (as Raphael, and not Caravaggio and the Dutch painters)' (Spence § 1069). It had long been understood that the painter's art was to 'raise Nature', and the poet's task, similarly, lay in 'mending and perfecting Nature where he describes a Reality' and 'adding greater Beauties than are put together in Nature, where he describes a Fiction'.[1] Implicit in most writings upon art in Pope's day was the Renaissance distinction between 'common nature' and some theoretical ideal of Nature as a prelapsarian condition or a system of ideal forms latent within empirical reality. The famous epitaph upon Raphael described him as victor over nature and Raphael himself had said 'Because real beauty is rare to find, I follow a certain idea that hovers before me (a conception of beauty), living in my mind.'[2] In this he spoke across the years direct to Pope's generation.

In the recreation of Nature's ideal forms the artist found beauty, but, as Hutcheson observed, 'The most moving Beauty's bear a Relation to our *moral Sense*' and 'we join the Contemplation of *moral Circumstances* and *Qualities*, along with natural *Objects* to increase their Beauty.'[3] So Horace had made the knowledge of morals essential to the good poet,[4] and critics from Alberti to Pope had agreed that history painting (which represented '*moral Actions, Passions and Characters*'[5]) was

---

[1] Addison, *Spectator* 418.
[2] Letter to Castiglione, quoted in Oskar Fischel, *Raphael*, trans. B. Rackham, repr. 1964, 216.
[3] *Of Beauty and Virtue*, II. 6. vii.
[4] *Ars Poetica* 309, 312–16.
[5] *Of Beauty and Virtue*, II 6, ix; Alberti's views are quoted in Anthony Blunt, *Artistic Theory in Italy, 1450–1600*, Oxford 1940, 11–12; cf. Pope's advice to Allen and Jervas (pp. 146–7 above, and references).

1. Copy in oils by Pope of Kneller's portrait of Betterton (see p. 143).

2. Grisaille by Kneller of the Farnese Hercules (see p. 144).

3. *Nicolas Poussin's The Death of Germanicus engraved by Chasteau (see p. 146).*

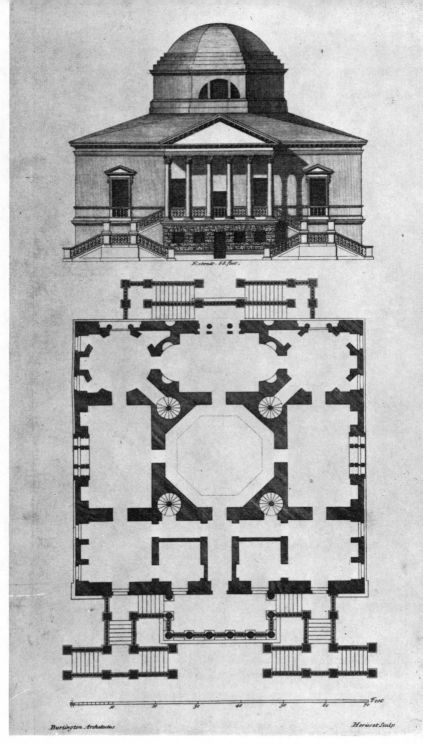

Extends. 68 feet.

Burlington Architectus   Herisset Sculp

4. *Elevation and plan of Chiswick House in William Kent's* Designs of Inigo Jones, *1727 (see p. 152).*

5. *Perspective drawing of Sir William Temple's garden at Moor Park, Surrey* (see p. 155).

6. *Plan for an ideal 'extensive garden' in Stephen Switzer's* Ichnographia Rustica *1718* (*see p. 156*).

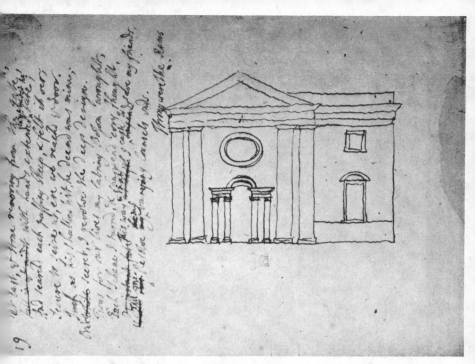

7. Drawing by Pope in his Homer MS. (see p. 150).

8. Banqueting house in Cirencester Park (see p. 162).

9. (overleaf) Rocque's plan of Chiswick Park, 1736 (see p. 161).

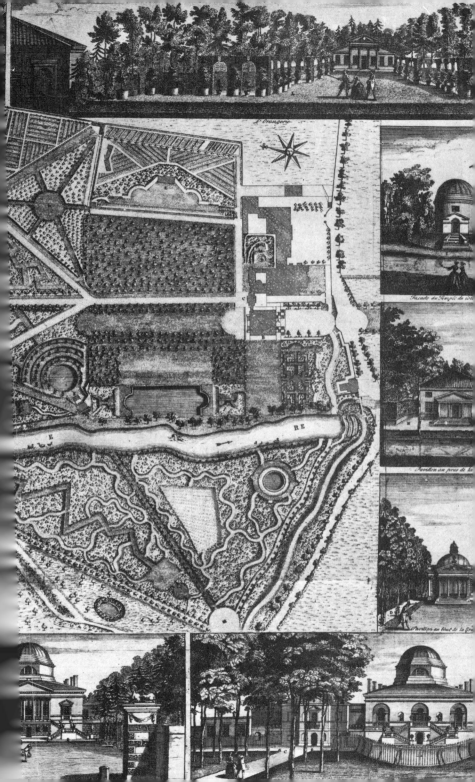

L'Orangerie

Fasade du Temple de ...

Pavillon au prés de la ...

Pavillon au bout de la Gra...

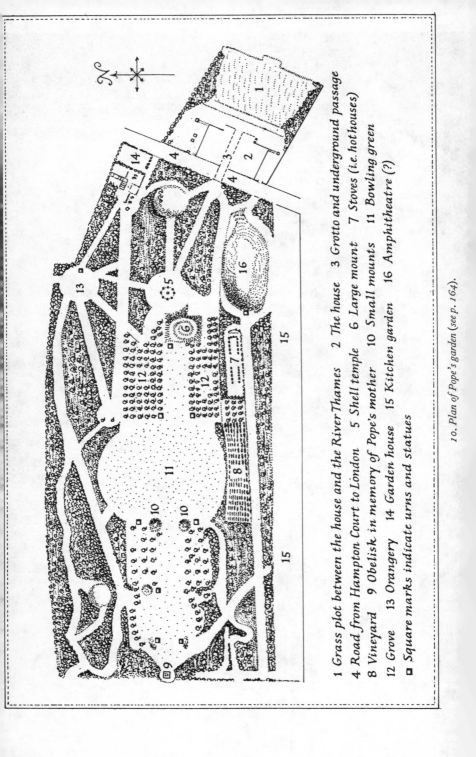

1 Grass plot between the house and the River Thames   2 The house   3 Grotto and underground passage
4 Road from Hampton Court to London   5 Shell temple   6 Large mount   7 Stoves (i.e. hothouses)
8 Vineyard   9 Obelisk in memory of Pope's mother   10 Small mounts   11 Bowling green
12 Grove   13 Orangery   14 Garden house   15 Kitchen garden   16 Amphitheatre (?)
▫ Square marks indicate urns and statues

10. Plan of Pope's garden (see p. 164).

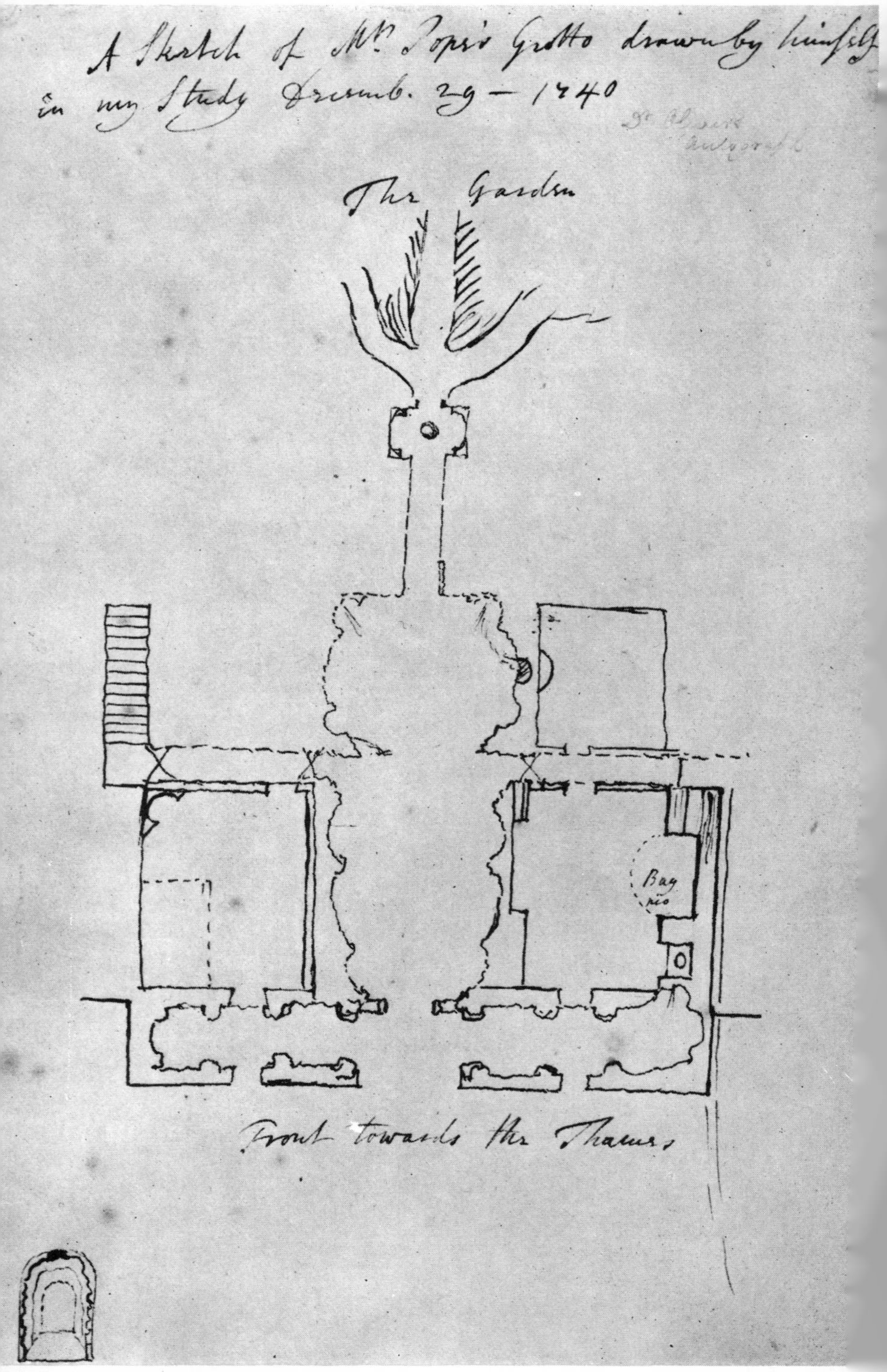

A Sketch of Mr. Pope's Grotto drawn by himself in my Study December 29 — 1740

The Garden

Bag no.

Front towards the Thames

12. Pope's plan of his grotto (see p. 167).

new Capacity of a Greek Translator, and I hope, by y^e assistance of
such sollicitours as Mr Caryll, to make Homer's works of more value
and benefit to me than ever they were to himself. What I have in
particular to desire further is, that you will send me y^e Subscript=
=ons by y^e first setting of y^e Parliam^t at which time it will be
necessary for me to know exactly what number we have secure
there being then to be printed a List of those who already have subscribed, or
shall too y^t time: upon y^e Credit & figure of which persons a great p^t of y^e
success with ye Town will inevitably depend.

I now think it pretty certain, that I shall be warmly Supported on all
sides in this undertaking.

As to ye Rape of ye Lock, I belive I have managed ye Dedication so nicely
y^t it can neither hurt ye Lady, nor ye Author. I writ it very lately, and
upon great deliberation; the young Lady approves of it, and ye best
advice in ye Kingdom, of ye men of sense, has been made use of in it

en to ye Treasurers. A Preface which salvd ye Lady's honour,
thout affixing her Name, was also prepard, but by herself
perseded in favour of y^e Dedication. Not but that, after all
ols will talk, and Fools will hear 'em.

13. *Extract from a letter from Pope to J. Caryll, 9 January 1714, about the* Iliad *translation and*
The Rape of the Lock *(see p. 40).*

AN
ESSAY
ON
CRITICISM.

IS hard to ſay, if greater want of
skill
Appear in writing or in judging
ill;
But, of the two, leſs dang'rous is th' offence
To tire our patience, than miſlead our ſenſe.
Some few in that, but numbers err in this,
Ten cenſure wrong for one who writes amiſs;

L 2   A fool

Plate I. *Vol. I, facing the general Title.*

15. The Works of Alexander Pope Esq., *ed. William Warburton, 1751; vol. I, frontispiece (see p. 303).*

16. The Dunciad, An Heroic Poem. In Three
Books, *1728; frontispiece (see p. 305).*

superior to all other kinds. A garden—even a grotto—might represent moral ideas. Pope's own most famous visual artefacts were the emblems of his noblest personal, social and political values. His grotto was haunted not only by uncorrupted modern patriots but by Numa and Evander,[1] and his garden, with its pious filial obelisk, urns inscribed from Virgil and Politian, and other associative objects, declared the moral qualities of its maker's heart and mind. These were—like the Art that raises and corrects Nature and declares the poet's power—'classical' in the richest sense.

[1] Mack, 60–76.

5: Pope and Politics: 'The Farce of State'

JOHN M. ADEN

PERHAPS NO writer of the eighteenth century came more gingerly to politics than Pope, who was by circumstance, temperament, and reflection distrustful of the political life into which he was yet drawn so memorably. The factors which eventually brought him in, though doubtless many and subtle, were ultimately, one suspects, four: Catholicism, Tory wit, patriotism, and Walpole.

The resulting history conforms pretty much to the decades of the poet's maturity: the period to 1710, in which he was commencing poet and creating that reputation in letters which would make him attractive to politics; the teens, in which he was courted by both parties, and in which, though he gave himself in Scriblerian fellowship to one, he yet studiously smiled on both alike; the twenties, in which he struggled to maintain a truce between the ministry and overtures of Walpole on the one hand and the beckonings of revived Scriblerianism and emerging opposition on the other; the thirties, in which he was forced as much as drawn into the Opposition, only to grow bitter at its self-disgrace; and that part of the forties granted him, in which he was thrown by that bitterness into the only consolation left him, the company, as he could grasp it, of the sage of Battersea, Lord Bolingbroke. It is a history of mingled remonstrance, coyness, and tears, but it produced the greatest political poetry of its, or perhaps any other, age.

However unwitting or unwilling, at any rate, Pope was politics' child first and last, born in the year of a Glorious Revolution, dying on the eve of an inglorious rebellion, and suffering between the slings and arrows of outrageous political fortune, both real and fancied. He grew up under the contests and dissensions of Whig and Tory rivalry, saw them culminate in the defeat and rout of his friends, endured (not always unappreciatively) the rise to power of the most gifted politician of his age, and came at last, under that Great One's despotism and corruption, into his opposition.

Pope was not yet a year old when an inept Catholic monarch was manoeuvred off the throne and a determined Protestant placed upon it in a revolution of far-reaching significance. Pope was a Catholic too, a circumstance no less political for him than it was for the nation and its once and future kings. Catholicism had provoked the revolution, as it had plagued, agitated, and disgraced English politics—and would continue to do so—from before the Popish Plot through the Forty-Five and after. The consequence was, for the Catholic constituency, traumatic, to say the least:

> . . . Roman catholics . . . by a series of enactments dating from Elizabeth's time to within the first quarter of the eighteenth century, were legally little better than pariahs. Their priests could be fined £200 and were liable to the penalties of high treason for saying Mass; their schoolmasters, not approved by the bishops, could be fined 40s. a day and their harbourers £10 a month; their laymen could have an oath denying even the spiritual authority of the pope tendered to them by any two J.P.s, and on refusal were liable to the penalties of recusancy, which included a fine of £20 a month for not attending church, inability to hold any office, keep arms in their houses, maintain suits at law, travel over five miles without a licence, or be an executor, guardian, doctor, or lawyer; by the legislation of Charles II's reign no Roman catholic could sit in parliament or on corporations, nor could he hold any civil, military, or naval office under the Crown; by an act of William III the nearest protestant kin could claim their lands from Roman catholic heirs; and by acts passed in George I's reign the landed property of Roman catholics was subjected to special disabilities, including a double land tax.[1]

[1] Basil Williams, *The Whig Supremacy, 1714–1760*, 2nd edn revised C. H. Stuart, Oxford 1962, 68–9. Sir George Clark, *The Later Stuarts, 1660–1714*, 2nd edn Oxford 1955, 153, remarks another Williamite act to the effect that no Roman Catholic could possess arms or own a horse worth more than £5. Cf. Pope's statement to Caryll after the death of Queen Anne: 'The greatest fear I have under the circumstances is the loss of my poor horse . . .' (*Corr.* I 241).

Such regulations not only precipitated the retirement of the poet's father in 1688 and dictated the character of the poet's education,[1] but influenced the steady residential flight of the family from the city to its environs.[2]

While, except for taxes, such codes were not always enforced, they were always, like a sword of Damocles, suspended over Catholic heads. Pope could jest about them—'The poor distressed Roman Catholicks, now un-hors'd and Un-charioted, cry out with the Psalmist: Some in Chariots, & some in Horses, but We will invocate the name of the Lord' (*Corr.* I 309)—but they continued to affect his life in troublesome and serious ways. In 1738 he wrote to Allen, 'I have a great inclination to pass a Month with you this Winter, but Any Court drives me away; it has been thrice my fate to be dispossest of my own House, when there was one at Hampton Court' (*Corr.* IV 134). Pope commemorates all this in *Epistle II ii* (1737):

> *Bred up at home, full early I begun*
> *To read in Greek, the Wrath of Peleus' Son.*
> *Besides, my Father taught me from a Lad,*
> *The better Art to know the good from bad:*
> *(And little sure imported to remove,*
> *To hunt for Truth in* Maudlin's *learned Grove.)*
> *But knottier Points we knew not half so well,*
> *Depriv'd us soon of our Paternal Cell;*
> *And certain Laws, by Suff'rers thought unjust,*
> *Deny'd all Posts of Profit or of Trust:*
> *Hopes after Hopes of pious Papists fail'd,*
> *While mighty W I L L I A M' S thundering Arm prevail'd.*
> *For Right Hereditary tax'd and fin'd,*
> *He stuck to Poverty with Peace of Mind;*
> *And me, the Muses help'd to undergo it;*
> *Convict a Papist He, and I a Poet.*[3]

---

[1] See Spence §§14ff.

[2] Sherburn, *Early Career*, 159, 215. See also *Corr.* I 336–7 and note; also 344–5.

[3] 52–67. Cf. the references to taxation and land-holding in *Satire II ii (To Bethel)*, 151–6. Pope had acknowledged these ignominies as early as 1713, in an adaptation of Donne's Second Satire.

Francis Beauchesne Thornton has said it well: ' . . . the penal laws straitened Pope his whole life long, both in mind and substance.'[1] They account, in ways easier to sense than to define, for his distrust of party and, at the same time, his instinctive sympathy for Toryism.

Before embracing that fellowship, however, Pope was too young, too removed, and too busy commencing poet to be overly caught up in these disabilities or with the politics in which they were suspended. Until that time his only close political acquaintance was Sir William Trumbull, retired Secretary of State, whose ministrations to the young poet were not, we may suppose, fundamentally political at all, but literary and rural. Still, Sir William was an old Tory, and only a little before had ministered to another promising youngster, Henry St. John, discoursing with him of arbitrary power, Roman political example, and patriotism.[2] In 1717, adapting some lines applied earlier to the Catholic Jacobite, Lord Caryll, Pope published an epitaph on Sir William suggesting that, at least by then, he recognized some political legacy from that source:

> *Honour unchang'd, a principle profest,*
> *Fix'd to one side, but mod'rate to the rest;*
> *An honest Courtier, yet a Patriot too,*
> *Just to his Prince, yet to his Country true. . . .*[3]

It may be that Pope wished to advertise himself as much as Trumbull in these lines, but if so it must be remembered that they antedate both the Hanoverian uneasiness and the climax of the Whig and Tory courtship that preceded it. As early as 1711, in short, Pope was voicing a moderate political sensibility and, what is just as interesting, anticipating a much later opposition and patriotic credo.[4]

---

[1] *Alexander Pope: Catholic Poet*, New York 1952, 5.
[2] See Jeffrey Hart, *Viscount Bolingbroke, Tory Humanist*, 1965, 25–6.
[3] Twickenham VI 169.
[4] It would not be correct to assume, as many have, that because Pope was non-partisan in this earliest period he was therefore non-political. From his earliest poetry on we have evidence of a decided political conscience, coloured essentially by the revolution, the Williamite régime, and the prospect of its renewal in Hanover. That it does not loom in the early record must not be taken to signify its absence.

By that earlier time, however, it had all begun. Pope had made the acquaintance of Addison and Steele, whose faint praise proved unequal to the recruiting undoubtedly intended, Addison's disclaimers notwithstanding. In the same year (1711) Pope met Gay, in the following Swift, Arbuthnot, and Parnell, and hard on the heels of these Harley, St. John, and Atterbury. In this company he found the kind of welcome his talents deserved and a political conscience more adaptable to his background. The Tory wits were willing, moreover, at least for the time, to accept him on terms of political immunity, happy enough, as far as politics was concerned, to have him of the faith if not on the firing line. Pope did, as it turns out, commit himself to the extent of commemorating the Peace of Utrecht in *Windsor Forest*, but that, he must have known, would not necessarily spell partisanship.[1]

Most of what little political animus informs the verse of Pope's early years appears after that, and takes, as often as not, a facetious turn. This is not true of course of the Prologue to *Cato* (though it is of the comment thereon), but it characterizes the Scriblerian addresses to Harley, the Barnivelt spoof, and the epigrams. The boldest in this vein is *The Court Ballad* (1717), a breezy lampoon on the ladies in waiting to Princess Caroline. In it Pope rallies the Townshend—Sunderland quarrel, the Prince of Wales's household in Leicester Square, the King's return from Hanover, *and* standing armies! He grows serious, however, in the 'Epistle to James Craggs', which, though not published until later, was written perhaps as early as 1718, in commemoration of Craggs's appointment as Secretary of State succeeding Addison. After describing the blamelessness of the unofficed Craggs, Pope goes on to say:

> *All this thou wert; and being this before,*
> *Know, Kings and Fortune cannot make thee more.*
> *Then scorn to gain a Friend by servile ways,*
> *Nor wish to lose a Foe these Virtues raise;*

[1] The Peace was Tory inspired, of course. Lord Lansdowne was principally responsible, and Pope dedicated the poem to him. Lansdowne was among an earlier, less generally purposeful, political acquaintanceship of Pope, including patrons of his pastoral promise like Halifax, Sheffield, Wharton, Dorchester, and Somers. See Spence II 616–17.

> *But candid, free, sincere, as you began,*
> *Proceed—a Minister, but still a Man;*
> *Be not (exalted to whate'er degree)*
> *Asham'd of any Friend, not ev'n of Me.*
> *The Patriot's plain, but untrod path pursue;*
> *If not, 'tis I must be asham'd of You.*[1]

As these contrasting moods suggest, Pope's political stance during this period is not easily fixed. That is perhaps as Pope intended it, for reasons almost certainly as prudential as philosophical, though also, it may be, because to some extent he enjoyed the courtship of his Whig and Tory suitors. Whatever the reasons, they provoke a variety of response on his part—now frivolous, now teasing, now annoyed or thoughtful—and it is not always easy to sort him. In the twenties, and even after, Swift would more than once bridle at such uncertainty.

The correspondence for these years is rich in testimony of Pope's hate and love alike of the political animal. As early as 1704 he registers resentment of the 'Violence of Party' (*Corr.* I 2) which he ridicules in the *Essay on Criticism* (456-9), but after the *Cato*, in 1713, he will profess amusement, if not flattery, at the political reaction to his part in that episode, clapping him, 'sore against his will', into a Whig (*Corr.* I 175). But after the pursuit of his allegiance commenced in earnest and as he drifted, however unpartisan and indocile, into the society of the Tories and out of that of the Whigs, he was rarely suffered to enjoy the pleasure, or the safety, of the game. What he no doubt wished might be a coquetry with both proved more often a lusty dodge-ball, with him between.

He is fretted on the one side by the imputations of Whiggism arising out of his contributions to the *Guardian*, and by the dour admonishments and exceptions of Addison, who, less than candidly no doubt, counsels

---

[1] See Twickenham VI 209-10 and note. One cannot be certain, but there are hints of political reference in the *Temple of Fame*, published 1715, but written, according to Pope, in 1711, perhaps even earlier, though revised between then and publication. See Twickenham II 236. The suspicious lines are, notably, 159-60, 173-4, 320-21, 406-11, 464, 513 *ad fin.*

him not to content himself 'with one half of the Nation . . . when [he] might command them all . . .';[1] and on the other by the charges in Button's and the Hanover Club 'That I was entered into a Cabal with Dean *Swift* and others to write against the *Whig-Interest* . . .' (*Corr.* I 229). On the death of the Queen he thanks God that he is 'below all accidents of state-changes by my circumstances, and above them by my philosophy', and he hopes that this sad event will 'put an end entirely to the divisions of Whig and Tory . . .' (*Corr.* I 241). Party spirit, he protests to Blount, is 'at best . . . the madness of many for the gain of a few' (*Corr.* I 247). It is not hard, in view of such contentiousness, to understand the reticence, and even equivocation of one in his position.

He takes the playful tack in his greetings, direct and indirect, to Gay on his return from Hanover in 1714—'Whether return'd a triumphant *Whig* or a desponding *Tory* . . .' (*Corr.* I 254). If, he says to Ford, Gay 'is afraid of corresponding with Tories, tell him I am a Whig, and he may write to me . . .' (*Corr.* I 259). But Swift brings him up sharply in a letter of 28 June 1715, in reply to Pope's complaints of his not writing:

> . . . you must give me leave to add . . . that you talk at your ease, being wholly unconcerned in publick events; for, if your friends the Whigs continue, you may hope for some favour; if the Torys return, you are at least sure of quiet. You know how well I lov'd both Lord Oxford and Bolingbroke, and how dear the Duke of Ormond is to me: do you imagine I can be easy while their enemies are endeavouring to take off their heads? *I nunc, & versus tecum meditare canoros*—Do you imagine I can be easy, when I think of the probable consequences of these proceedings, perhaps upon the very peace of the nation, but certainly of the minds of so many hundred thousand good subjects? Upon the whole, you may truly attribute my silence to the Eclipse, but it was that eclipse which happened on the first of August.   (*Corr.* I 301)

Pope had, as it turns out, already expressed (to Martha Blount) his anxiety over the fate of Bolingbroke and Oxford (*Corr.* I 293), but this

---

[1] *Corr.* I 196–7. Cf. Pope's letter, I 209 and the following from Spence (§146): '[Addison] used to talk much and often to me of moderation in parties, and used to blame his dear friend Steele for being too much of a party-man.'

rebuke from Swift must have jolted him out of any hopes of complacency he may yet have entertained. In July his mood is sobered, and nostalgic: '. . . *Old England* is no longer *Old England*, that region of hospitality, society, and good humour' (*Corr.* I 306). And he is stirred by the spectacle, in the same month, of Oxford impeached and imprisoned (*Corr.* I 307).

By late 1717, with the crisis over, Oxford acquitted, and Bolingbroke at least safe, the mood lightens again and the flirtation is resumed. Pope goes to Hampton Court, meets the Prince, 'with all his Ladies', and writes of them and of Stanhope (later Earl of Chesterfield) and Pulteney in terms both playful and ingratiating (*Corr.* I 427, 450–1). But with Atterbury he is again solemn and sermonic: 'Contemplative life is not only my scene, but it is my habit too. . . . In my politicks, I think no further than how to preserve the peace of my life, in any government under which I live. . . . I hope all churches and all governments are so far of God, as they are rightly understood, and rightly administered. . . . In a word, the things I have always wished to see are not a Roman Catholick, or a French Catholick, or a Spanish Catholick, but a true Catholick: and not a King of Whigs, or a King of Tories, but a King of England.' (*Corr.* I 454). Still resentful of 'political fur[y]' and annoyed at the estrangement in the Royal family, he writes to Caryll in January of 1718 that he hopes posterity will say of him at least, 'that in the 4ᵗʰ year of K. George, and in the days of the Bishop of Bangor, Pope writ and caused no disturbance but to Lintot.' (*Corr.* I 461–2)

Though he continued to resist entrapment in the twenties, Pope was much chastened by the events and influences of that decade, beginning, in its first year, with the South Sea fiasco. Pope himself had ventured modestly, and, it would seem, lost modestly; but he was shaken by the spectacle of mammonism and public greed. 'Indeed,' he wrote to Caryll after the fall, 'I think all the morals that were among us, are gone. . . . If ever a nation deserved to be punished by an immediate infliction from heaven, this deserves it . . .' (*Corr.* II 57). Even more unsettling, though, was the arrest and trial of Atterbury on charges of conspiracy (1722–3). Though Pope felt obliged to protest his own innocence and loyalty, he offered himself as a character witness for his friend: 'Indeed my Lord,' as he told Carteret, 'I love my Country, better than any Personal friend I have; but I love my Personal Friend so well, as not to abandon, or rail at him, tho' my whole Country fell upon him' (*Corr.* II 160). After Atterbury's speech in his own defence, Pope wrote to him: 'I am far prouder of that word you publickly spoke of me, than of any thing I have yet heard of my self in my whole life. Thanks be to God, that I a Private man, concerned in no Judicature, and employed in no Publick cause, have had the honour, in this great and shining incident . . . to enter, as it were, my Protest to your Innocence, and my Declaration of your Friendship' (*Corr.* II 169).

Happily, Atterbury's banishment found consolation, and its sobering effects consolidation, in the pardon, about the same time, of Bolingbroke, who returned to England briefly in mid year. 'Lord Bolingbroke is now return'd,' Pope chirps to Swift, '(as I hope) to take me, with all his other Hereditary Rights . . .' (*Corr.* II 184). His pleasure in the reunion must have been heightened by the absence of the old partisan severity and by Bolingbroke's willingness to 'take' him on terms no more compromising than those of philosophy and the Muse.[1] Bolingbroke had renounced Jacobitism in the *Letter to Sir William Windham* (composed 1717, published 1753), and he now writes Swift how philosophy and persecution have driven him 'out of Party' and 'cursed Company' (*Corr.* II 187–8).

Bolingbroke's return, and Swift's need to convey his 'Travels', roused the Dean out of a 'scurvy sleep' and brought him back into the correspondence and company of the Tory wits—all, that is, save Oxford, who died in 1724, a loss repaired, for Pope at least, by Bolingbroke's settling the next year at Dawley, hard by Twickenham. From there, deprived of parliament, Bolingbroke began the arduous and ultimately futile task of organizing the opposition to Walpole and Robinocracy.

Swift arrived in 1726, with *Gulliver*, itself an opening salvo. Pope and others read in manuscript his *History of the Four Last Years of the Queen*, but Pope would still write him after his return to Ireland in the old dismissive, bantering vein: 'Surely . . . you are now above all parties of

[1] Cf. Bolingbroke's letter to Pope, 18 February 1724 (*Corr.* II 218–22) and Pope's reply (*Corr.* II 226–9). Pope tries in vain to sell Swift this happy issue out of all their afflictions: *Corr.* II 321 and 332–3.

men, and it is time to be so . . .' (*Corr.* II 412) 'Don't fancy,' he adds, 'none but Tories are your friends; for at that rate I must be, at most, but half your friend . . .' (*Corr.* II 413) It was only a few weeks later that Bolingbroke, with the Pulteneys, launched *The Craftsman*, the official organ of the Opposition for the next ten years. In its pages, besides running attacks and cross fire, appeared the papers later to constitute Bolingbroke's *Remarks on the History of England* and *A Dissertation upon Parties*.

Those on the history of England (Nos. 218–55: 5 September 1730 to 22 May 1731) epitomize the platform Bolingbroke hoped to establish for the Opposition: the incompatibility of the 'spirit of liberty and the spirit of faction' and the 'ballance of the parts' of government in the preservation of constitutional liberties.[1] Among the virtues of Elizabeth, Bolingbroke's paragon of constitutional monarchs, are, the author is at pains to publish, her prudent economy, her preference for the standards of 'wisdom or courage' over that of 'money', her encouragement of commerce, and her policy of England first in foreign affairs.

The *Dissertation upon Parties* (originally Nos. 382–96: 27 October 1733 to 2 February 1734) is, in effect, a continuation of this history, focussing on the evils of party and the necessity of renouncing it. Party is traced from its emergence in the Exclusion Movement to its persistence beyond the Revolution intended, among other things, to repudiate it. The old Whig-Tory distinction is declared no longer meaningful, either historically or philosophically. In its place Bolingbroke identifies a threefold outgrowth of the challenge of constitutional government: those opposed to the present government but loyal to the constitution (the Opposition), those opposed to the government and constitution alike (Jacobites and republicans); and those attached to the government but subversive of the constitution (Walpole and company). The second group is declared now insignificant; the first and third are identified with country and court: constitutionalists and anti-constitutionalists. Among other perversions or unfulfilled promises of the Revolution, Bolingbroke cites the want of free elections and frequent parliaments, and of mixed and balanced government, the persistence of standing

---

[1] *The Works of the late Right Honourable Henry St. John, Lord Viscount Bolingbroke*, pub. David Mallet. 1754, I 292, 296.

armies, the increase of taxation and revenue officers, the growth of venality, corruption, and luxury, and the overthrow of traditional standards by the rise of a moneyed interest.

Meanwhile, Swift made a second, and last, visit in 1727, working with Pope on their miscellanies and building such bridges as he could toward his own rehabilitation. George I died in June, and Walpole, between Compton's inability and Caroline's loyalty, survived the succession. Gay did not fare as well, and his friends were embittered over his ill treatment by the new court. For that they had at least the satisfaction, next year, of the *Beggar's Opera* and the *Dunciad*.

Pope's tone in the early months of 1728 betrays his own resentment at the treatment of Gay (and of Swift as well),[1] but Walpole survives that too, though the poet declines publicly acknowledging the Minister's good offices until such time as he should be 'out of Power' (*Corr.* III 294). Swift meanwhile continues uneasy in this tolerance, which he acknowledges with a hint of equivocation worthy of Pope himself:

> I look upon my Lord Bolingbroke and us two, as a peculiar Triumvirate, who have nothing to expect, or to fear; and so far fittest to converse with one another: Only he and I are a little subject to schemes, and often upon very weak appearances, and this you have nothing to do with. I do profess without affectation, that your kind opinion of me as a Patriot . . . is what I do not deserve; because what I do is owing to perfect rage and resentment, and the mortifying sight of slavery, folly, and baseness about me, among which I am forc'd to live. And I will take my oath that you have more Virtue in an hour, than I in seven years; for you despise the follies, and hate the vices of mankind, without the least ill effect on your temper; and with regard to particular men, you are inclin'd always rather to think the better, whereas with me it is always directly contrary. I hope however, this is not in you from a superior principle of virtue, but from your situation, which hath made all parties and interests indifferent to you, who can be under no concern about high and low-church, Whig and Tory, or who is first Minister.   (*Corr.* II 497)

With the banning of Gay's *Polly* and the Duchess of Queensberry for promoting it under the very nose of the King, Pope is again distres-

---

[1] See letters to Swift, 28 January and 23 March 1728: *Corr.* II 469, 480.

sed with the court, though he continues on terms with its Minister, to whom he appeals the altercation with Lady Mary over 'The Capon's Tale'.[1] Meanwhile he stood firm before Swift's efforts to engage him: 'You know my maxim to keep clear of all offence, as I am clear of all interest in either party. . . . I have given some proofs in the course of my whole life, (from the time when I was in friendship of Lord Bolingbroke and Mr. Craggs even to this, when I am civilly treated by Sir R. Walpole) that I never thought myself so warm in any Party's cause as to deserve their money . . .' (III, 81). He had—for all the gibes at party hacks, party journals, and court, to say nothing of the dedication to the Dean—gone on record to the effect of partisan indifference in the *Dunciad*, albeit out of the mouth of Settle:

> *(Diff'rent our parties, but with equal grace*
> *The Goddess smiles on Whig and Tory race,*
> *'Tis the same rope at sev'ral ends they twist,*
> *To Dulness, Ridpath is as dear as Mist.)*
>
> ('A' text, III, 283–6)

Sir Robert, who would eventually bring to pass what Swift could not, had established his position by capitalizing the failure of another Tory venture, the South Sea Company. In the ministerial reshuffle following the crash in 1720 and the death of Stanhope in 1721, Walpole, who had been in opposition since 1717, and who was now deemed the most likely to rescue and 'skreen' the Bubble, was returned to the government as Chancellor of the Exchequer and First Lord of the Treasury.[2] The death, shortly thereafter, of Sunderland left him virtual possession of the ministry, a proprietorship he was to retain for the next twenty years.

The opposition to his régime, which first took shape under Pulteney

---

[1] See *Corr.* III 53, 59, 60. Pope's relation to Walpole remains one of the most elusive chapters of their history. There is no doubt that Walpole was as anxious to keep the peace as Pope. In 1724 he subscribed for ten sets of the *Odyssey*; in 1725 he apparently visited Pope at Twickenham (*Corr.* II 323), and Pope attended his 'Sunday Tables' and other company on a number of occasions (*Corr.* II 368, 441, 530; III 11–12, 53, 112, 139).
[2] For pertinent accounts of the Bubble see J. H. Plumb, *Sir Robert Walpole, I : The Making of a Statesman*, 1956, 293ff., and Isaac Kramnick, *Bolingbroke and his Circle*, Harvard 1968, 63–7.

and Bolingbroke in *The Craftsman*, eventually came to embrace an assortment of political 'outs': Jacobitical Tories under Shippen, Hanoverian Tories under Wyndham, and disaffected Whigs of one vintage or another. These last included Pulteney himself and Carteret, and later, after the failure of the Excise Bill (1733) and the dismissal of those not supporting it, Chesterfield, Bolton, Stair, Montrose, Marchmont, and Cobham. With Cobham came his Cubs, the 'Boy Patriots', George and Richard Grenville, Lyttleton, Cornbury, Polwarth, Pitt, and Murray. Still others, like Jekyll, Somerset, Bristol, Egmont, and Argyle, though not of the Opposition itself, proved susceptible of opposition behaviour from time to time.[1] To these of the political profession must be added the literary cohorts, the Tory wits, or, as Plumb styles them, the 'Twickenham set': Pope, Gay, Swift, Arbuthnot, and their friends and patrons, like the Duchesses of Queensberry and Marlborough and Lady Suffolk. These in turn are supported from the flanks by such dramatists, journalists, and poets as Thomson, Fielding, Mallet, Glover, and others.

But impressive in quality and number as the Opposition became, it never achieved cohesion or leadership, and never therefore real effectiveness. The constituency was too diverse, mutually suspicious, and plagued by self-seeking ever to accomplish the solidarity necessary to unseat or even seriously embarrass the ministry.[2] The failure of the Excise Bill, though it swelled their number, was not itself an Opposition victory, if even a victory at all in any but the pyrrhic sense.

Not even the acquisition of the Prince of Wales could do the trick. Frederick Louis had come to England in 1728, already cool toward his father, and it was not long before he and the Opposition found each other and entered into a compact of sorts against court and ministry. When, in 1737, the Opposition undertook to carry his long-standing clamour for allowance to parliament, and met with failure, the Prince retaliated by withdrawing his wife, *en travail*, from the royal roof. When, in turn, the King ordered him and his sympathizers out of Court, the Prince, like his father before him, set up his own court, whither resorted a hapless Opposition.

[1] Keith Feiling, *The Second Tory Party, 1714–1832*, 1959, 26.
[2] See Archibald Foord, *His Majesty's Opposition, 1714–1830*, 1964, ch. iv.

The acquisition of the Prince did serve to remove the stigma of Jacobitism, and afforded at least a flickering promise of rallying point and eventual victory, but Frederick possessed neither the character nor the talent required to consolidate the Opposition. Still, it was around him, in lieu of a better, that Bolingbroke and those who advocated a broadly-based administration planted their vain hopes and published their aspirations for English polity.

Bolingbroke's *Letter on the Spirit of Patriotism* (1736, published 1749) was itself an attempt to bid the Opposition awake, arise, or be forever fallen. It condemned Jacobitical Messianism and inaction, and the failure of the enlightened constituency to live up to its ideals. 'What passes among us for ambition,' Bolingbroke complained, 'is an odd mixture of avarice and vanity: the moderation we have seen practised is pusillanimity, and the philosophy that some men affect, is sloth.'[1] He admonished the Opposition that it must be as disciplined, ready, and industrious as the government if it ever hoped to prevail.

The Idea of a Patriot King (1738, published 1749), written with the Prince in mind, represents Bolingbroke's culminating thoughts on political redemption: a nation ruled by a virtuous prince, without recourse to party or faction, for the good of the people and the preservation of their liberties. Such a prince would oppose excess of power, regal or ministerial, make the people's cause his own, and reject party for 'broad bottom' government.[2]

Bolingbroke had already complained of foreign policy. By now Englishmen of every sort had come to resent the peace without honour that suffered the resurgence of French power and influence at the expense of English, and that tolerated Spanish seizure of English shipping and indignity to English seamen. Complaints on these and other scores began as early as the Treaty of Hanover in 1725, denounced, in the words of Lecky, 'as intended only to protect the German dominions of the King, as strengthening, by our alliance, the Power on the Continent we had most reason to fear, as placing us unnecessarily in hostility to

[1] Bolingbroke, *Works*, III 19.
[2] For analyses of Bolingbroke's political thought, see especially Hart and Kramnick.

the Emperor, who was the main obstacle to French ambition'.[1] National pride rankled further under the double humiliation of Porto Bello, during the blockade of which, disabled by Walpolian scruple, the fleet rotted until 1728; and the unopposed Spanish siege of Gibraltar in 1727. Matters were not improved in the thirties by Sir Robert's refusal to honour, in the War of Polish Succession, the British commitment to the Emperor under the Treaty of Vienna, as a result of which Fleury succeded in further consolidating French power and authority.

Not the least resentful of the peace policy was the King himself, who was intensely hostile to the French and whose appetite for military glory chafed mightily under Walpole's reluctance to engage. Finally, the death of Queen Caroline in 1737, the continued outrages of the *guarda-costas*, and the notoriety of Jenkins's testimony in 1738, proved too much for the policy and its maker. Walpole summoned a last desperate effort in the Convention of Pardo, but clamour, ministerial as well as popular, drove him at last, on October 19, 1739, to declare war.

The war went badly, and so did the domestic scene, with bread riots, resistance to impressment, and mounting discontent. In February 1741, motions were put in both houses for the Minister's removal, but the Opposition fell apart, and Shippen and Cornbury led their followers out. Still, elections went poorly, and when parliament met in December the ministry had only a bare majority. After a few weeks of wrangling, and following defeat on a minor question of electoral irregularity, Walpole resigned on February 2, 1742, accepting a peerage as Earl of Orford.

But if Robin was broken, so was the Opposition. Wyndham's death in 1740 had already dealt it a crushing blow. Then, when the promised hour came round at last, Pulteney temporized, followed Walpole into the peerage, and accepted a place in the cabinet without portfolio. By autumn the Opposition managed to secure at least the admission of Gower to the Privy Seal, Bathurst to a court place, Cobham to the rank of field marshal, and Murray to the office of Solicitor-General; but Pulteney declined to support the agitation for triennial parliaments, and Sandys and Barnard busied themselves defusing the inquisition into Sir Robert's administration.

[1] W. E. H. Lecky, *A History of England in the Eighteenth Century*, 'Cabinet edn' 1892, I 409.

For a year Carteret and the King were in Europe, the one conducting a complex diplomacy in the War of the Austrian Succession, the other snatching at last a moment of glory at Dettingen—neither of which pleased the Opposition, especially Pitt, or for that matter the cabinet itself. By his return in the autumn of 1743 Carteret was the object of determined hostility. Wilmington had died in July and was replaced, as prime minister, not by the Earl of Bath (Pulteney), but by Henry Pelham. Though the new ministry angled for Cobhamite support, Cobham remained faithful and voted against Hanoverian subsidy. It became more and more obvious that he must be appeased, and at last, in November 1744, Carteret was let out, Cobham in, and his 'boys' given minor offices and promises. The Opposition had been absorbed, and in a year the Pelhamites were firmly entrenched. Bolingbroke was a hermit at Battersea. Pope was dead.

The thirties had been the turning point for the poet, though they began quietly enough. In 1730 his relationship with Walpole and the court was perhaps the best it ever was. Towards its end Arbuthnot reported to Swift that Pope was 'now the great reigning poetical favourite' (*Corr.* III 151n), and the correspondence is full of his visits to Walpole and Court alike. Early in the year he was embarrassed by Swift's imputation to him, in the *Libel on the Reverend Dr. Delany*, of antipathy to court and ministry, though he would later (1733) acknowledge that to be 'the best panegyrick on myself, that either my own times or any other could have afforded, or will ever afford to me' (*Corr.* III 91). Meanwhile he must have taken comfort in No. 218 of *The Craftsman*, in which Bolingbroke describes the new spirit abroad in politics: 'A ferment, a spirit, call it which you please, is raised; but I bless God it is not the blind and furious spirit of party. . . . It is, I think, a revival of the true old English spirit which prevailed in the days of our fathers, and which must always be national, since it has no direction but to the national interest; *est jam una vox omnium*, and I hope we shall never have occasion to add, *magis odio firmata quam præsidio*.'[1]

Except for rumblings over the Timon portrait, 1731 and 1732

[1] Quoted in Walter Sichel, *Bolingbroke and his Times*, 1901-2, II 264.

remained low in pressure. In the first Pope continued busy with the *Essay on Man* and the *Epistle to Burlington*, the latter of which appeared in December. Walpole, it is true, fades from the correspondence, and is replaced by much of Dawley and Stowe, but there is nothing to indicate rupture. In 1732 Pope continued working on the *Essay* and frequenting Dawley, and though 'estranged from politicks' (*Corr.* III 276), in correspondence with one who waxed warm to sardonic on the subject, Lord Peterborough. There was, as Pope reported to him and to Gay, 'nothing stirring but poetry' (*Corr.* III 318). He could scarcely divine his prophetic power when he added, 'Indeed they say 'tis sometimes so just before an Earthquake' (*Corr.* III 312).

It was not long before it struck, and Pope was jolted by more than one shudder during the year. It began with the cooling of Court relations following the publication of *Satire II i (To Fortescue)* in February of 1733 and the declaration of war by Hervey and Lady Mary in *Verses Address'd to the Imitator of Horace* in March. It was to strike thrice more before the year was out: in the death of his mother in June, the dismissal of his friends following the failure of the Excise, and in Hervey's *Epistle from a Nobleman to a Doctor of Divinity* in November. Of all these trepidations, however, none was more politically decisive than the retaliation on his friends following the Excise. It is a curious footnote to this history that Whig misfortunes worked where Tory never could to bring Pope out into the open on politics.

Pope to be sure had fired the first shots. In the *Epistle to Bathurst* (January) he had scorned the gold that 'bribes a Senate' and the 'paper-credit' which 'Can pocket States, can fetch or carry Kings'; taken pot shots at Hervey, Wharton, Chartres, Cadogan, Lady Mary and spouse, Molly Skerrett and the Excise, and Peter Walter; and concluded with a ringing indictment of venality and politics. But he had fired a few rounds into patriotic venality too, and into 'Party-rage', and so might have expected to come off with some semblance of impartiality. It is not so with *Satire II i*. There he confined his sniping to such courtiers, ministers, royalty and measures as Walter, Chartres, Hervey, George and Caroline, Dartineuf, the brothers Fox, Lady Mary, Sir Robert, standing armies and the peace policy, while he awarded decoration to such as Shippen, Bolingbroke, and Peterborough. Pope cannot have been too surprised at the reaction; he must have been ready for a breach.

The *Essay on Man* takes a more philosophical but no less pointed address to the cause, especially in Epistle III, with its celebration of kingship founded in VIRTUE, its rejection of 'Th'enormous faith of many made for one', and its account of the rescue of true government by 'Poet or Patriot', teaching 'Pow'r's due use to People and to Kings' and 'Th'according music of a well-mix'd State'. It is apparent that Bolingbroke has done *his* work.

Donne proved as handy as Horace before the year was out, when Pope turned him to deadly advantage in *The Impertinent*, published anonymously in November. Donne's court and courtier are made over in the image of Pope's with daring skill. The passage in which the latter, like the interlocutors of the *Epilogue to the Satires*, unwittingly implicates his own domicile is damaging in Pope's best style:

> *Then as a licens'd Spy, whom nothing can*
> *Silence, or hurt, he libels the* Great Man;
> *Swears every* Place entail'd *for Years to come,*
> *In* sure Succession to the Day of Doom:
> *He names the* Price *for ev'ry* Office *paid,*
> *And says our* Wars thrive ill, *because* delay'd;
> *Nay hints, 'tis by Connivance of the Court,*
> *That* Spain *robs on, and* Dunkirk's *still a Port.*

(158–65)

The sniping continues in the *Epistle to Cobham, Satire II ii (To Bethel)*, and *Sober Advice* of 1734, the first with a tribute to the patriotic ruling passion of Cobham, the second with more on Sir Robert and Hervey.[1] In 1735 light to heavy fire is sustained in the *Epistle to Arbuthnot, To a Lady*, and volume II of the *Works*. But the year's losses were keen: Arbuthnot died in February, Bolingbroke left for France in May (to remain, save for a brief interval in 1738, for six years), and Peterborough died in October. Only the visit of the Prince earlier in the same month could be counted a bright spot, though there were Cornbury, Cobham,

[1] For a close analysis of the political allusion in *To Bethel* see John M. Aden, *Something Like Horace*, Nashville 1969, 27–46.

and others in whose company the poet could and did find consolation. The most depressing experience of the year was the illness and leave-taking of Peterborough, who, in one of his last interviews with Pope, 'declaimed with great Spirit against the Meanness of the present Great men & Ministers, & the decay of Public Spirit & Honour' (*Corr.* III 487–8). At last, in mid October, just before Peterborough's death, Swift was able to say, 'It pleaseth me to find that you begin to dislike things in spite of your philosophy; your Muse cannot forbear her hints to that purpose' (*Corr.* III 505).

The political aspect of the *Epistle to Arbuthnot* is familiar, though one would note again its tribute to neglected Gay, its devastating portrait of Hervey, and its stirring character of the poet himself:

> *Not Fortune's Worshipper, nor Fashion's Fool,*
> *Not Lucre's Madman, nor Ambition's Tool,*
> *Not proud, nor servile, be one Poet's praise*
> *That, if he pleas'd, he pleas'd by manly ways. . . .*   (334ff.)

To a Lady hits at Sappho again, has a go at Caroline, and praises Queensberry, but otherwise contents itself with one of the shrewdest poetic appraisals of womankind on record. In the *Works* appeared an updated version of Pope's imitation of Donne's Second Satire, in which Pope rakes his fire over Sappho, the Excise, standing armies, scolding Germans, court sycophants, and the inevitable Peter Walter.

The 'Great World sleeps,' he writes in August 1736, '& I am glad on't,' satisfied no doubt to work undistracted on the *Epistle to Augustus*. But the patriotic current still moves. In May appeared *Bounce to Fop, an Heroick Epistle*, in which Pope offered the Prince a whelp, which by December apparently had been accepted (*Corr.* IV 48). And he opened and closed the year with notices to Swift of 'a race sprung up of young Patriots' (*Corr.* IV 6), 'who look rather to the past age than the present, and therefore the future may have some hopes of them. If I love them, it is because they honour some of those whom I, and the world, have lost, or are losing. Two or three of them have distinguish'd themselves in Parliament, and you will own in a very uncommon manner, when I tell you it is by their asserting of Independency, and contempt of Corruption' (*Corr.* IV 51).

In 1737 the poet is much at Cornbury's, in London, but also rambling in the autumn to Southampton, Cirencester, and Bath, among other places, happy, as he tells Bethel on his return, 'to have escaped much of the disagreeable noise, & the impertinent chatter of this place, about the late Difference of the Courts' (*Corr.* IV 86). The Queen died in November, of which fact he took more charitable notice in a letter to Allen shortly thereafter than he would in the *Epilogue to the Satires* a few months later. Two other events of the year would not have escaped his notice: the launching of *Common Sense*, in which Lyttelton and Chesterfield took part, and the publication of Glover's *Leonidas*.

Pope himself published, in April and May, *Epistle II ii* ('Dear Col'nel . . .') and *Epistle II i* (*To Augustus*). In the first he invokes Cobham's name, Bathurst's and Murray's; describes his own childhood under catholic penalty (quoted earlier); glances at the court and takes sideswipes at the likes of Dodington. The *Epistle to Augustus* is rich in ridicule of the King, his age and his court; mindful of Swift's Irish patriotism; and audacious in its valedictory salute to George:

> *Oh! could I mount on the Mæonian wing,*
> *Your Arms, your Actions, your Repose to sing!*
> *What seas you travers'd! and what fields you fought!*
> *Your Country's Peace, how oft, how dearly bought!*
> *How barb'rous rage subsided at your word,*
> *And Nations wonder'd while they dropp'd the sword!*
> *How, when you nodded, o'er the land and deep,*
> *Peace stole her wing, and wrapt the world in sleep;*
> *Till Earth's extremes your mediation own,*
> *And Asia's Tyrants tremble at your Throne. . . .* (394–403)

One Thousand Seven Hundred and Thirty Eight (to borrow his style) was a climactic year for Pope and Opposition alike. It begins with his bid for Murray's political allegiance in *Epistle I vi*, followed in short order by the politically turned imitation of Swift in *Satire II vi*, the resonating address to Bolingbroke in *Epistle I i*, and the clarion dialogues of the *Epilogue to the Satires*.

By July Bolingbroke is back, to remain until April of 1739, and in

October Lyttelton, who is much in Pope's discourse, addresses to him an impassioned plea for Patriotic office:

> We are just returnd from My Lord Bathurst's where His R. H. [the Prince] gave and recievd much Satisfaction. I wish you had been of the Party, because I know He Wishes it, and because he can not be too often in your company. Don't complain of your being Useless to him; a Friend is never so, especially to a Prince. . . . Be therefore as much with him as you can. Animate him to Virtue, to the Virtue least known to Princes, though most necessary for them, Love of the Publick; and think that the Morals, the Liberty, the whole Happiness of this Country depends on your Success. . . . if you had any Spirit in you, you wou'd come to Bath, and let the Prince hear every day from the Man of this Age, who is the Greatest Dispenser of Fame, and will be best heard by Posterity, that if he wou'd Immortalize himself, the only way he can take, is to deserve a place by his conduct in *some writings*, where he will never be admitted only for his Rank.
>
> (*Corr.* IV 138–139)

Pope's reply affects demurrer, goes on to give a circumstantial account of a conference with Wyndham on the Opposition's resentment of the self-serving behaviour of Carteret and Pulteney and the strategy devised to cope with it, and concludes with a word for the Prince after all: 'Pray assure your Master of my Duty & Service: They tell me he has every body's Love already. I wish him Popular, but not Familiar, and the Glory of being beloved, not the Vanity of endeavouring it too much. I wish him at the Head of the Only Good Party in the Kingdome, that of Honest Men; I wish him Head of no other . . .' (*Corr.* IV 143–4).

The Royal family figures much in the poetry of this year, along with court and ministry, venality and corruption, the latter of which Murray is warned of and beckoned Cornbury's way instead. The Prince's poverty of purse is flaunted and the King's punks, foreign and domestic, deplored. The Royal and rival houses, punningly linked with those of parliament, receive notice in *Satire II vi* (line 144); the poem ends on a note of Liberty and, it may be, pre-Hanoverian nostalgia as well:

> *'Give me again my hollow Tree!*
> *'A Crust of Bread, and Liberty.'*[1]

[1] See Aden chs. 4, 5.

Epistle I i (To Bolingbroke) abounds in political mood and gesture, from patriotic fervour—

> *Sometimes a Patriot, active in debate,*
> *Mix with the World, and battle for the State,*
> *Free as young Lyttelton, her cause pursue,*
> *Still true to Virtue, and as warm as true:*   (27–30)

to Hanoverian sneer:

> *Slave to a Wife or Vassal to a Punk,*
> *A Switz, a High-dutch, or a Low-dutch Bear—*   (62–3)

Walpolian taunt:

> *Be this thy Screen, and this thy Wall of Brass;*
> *Compar'd to this, a Minister's an Ass;*   (95–6)

venal reproach:

> *'Get Place and Wealth, if possible, with Grace;*
> *'If not, by any means get Wealth and Place;'*   (103–4)

courtly scorn:

> *Adieu to Virtue if you're once a Slave:*
> *Send her to Court, you send her to her Grave;*   (118–9)

Sapphic salute ('Linnen worthy Lady Mary', 164), and Bolingbrokian tribute: 'Guide, Philosopher, and Friend'(177).

The first dialogue of the *Epilogue* adds Jekyll, Allen, Lyttelton, and the Prince to the catalogue of heroes; Gazetteer 'Osborne' (the journalist James Pitt), Dodington, Henry Fox, Selkirk, De La Warr to that of culprits; and rings again the changes on Sappho, Hervey, Caroline, George, and Peter Walter. The picture of the Court is crushing:

> *There, where no Passion, Pride, or Shame transport,*
> *Lull'd with the sweet* Nepenthe *of a Court;*
> *There, where no Father's, Brother's, Friend's Disgrace*
> *Once break their Rest, or stir them from their Place;*
> *But past the Sense of human Miseries,*
> *All Tears are wip'd for ever from all Eyes;*
> *No Cheek is known to blush, no Heart to throb,*
> *Save when they lose a Question, or a Job.*   (97–104)

The Triumph of Vice, with which the dialogue ends, needs no reprise, unless it be to note the inclusion of patriots in the general corruption. Dialogue II calls the roll of cast-off heroes past and present: Somers, Halifax, Shrewsbury, Carleton, Stanhope, Atterbury, Pulteney, Chesterfield, Argyle, Wyndham, and the Prince; to which it adds, in other praise, Cobham, Polwarth, Lyttelton, and St. John ('All-accomplish'd'). And there is the poet himself:

> *So proud, I am no Slave:*
> *So impudent, I own myself no Knave:*
> *So odd, my Country's Ruin makes me grave.*   (205–7)

Sir Robert is not slighted, being accorded the guarded respect he regularly receives at Pope's hands. Seen him I have, says the poet in the first dialogue:

> *but in his happier hour*
> *Of Social Pleasure, ill-exchang'd for Pow'r;*
> *Seen him, uncumber'd with the Venal tribe,*
> *Smile without Art, and win without a Bribe.*
> *Would he oblige me? let me only find,*
> *He does not think me what he thinks mankind.*
> *Come, come, at all I laugh He laughs, no doubt,*
> *The only diff'rence is, I dare laugh out.*   (29–36)

The second dialogue acknowledges his wit and amiability (133–5), but reminds the Great Man and his minions alike:

> *Sure, if I spare the Minister, no rules*
> *Of Honour bind me, not to maul his Tools*   (146–7),

which he proceeds to do, most heartily.

Though bereft of Bolingbroke in April, Pope continues in conversation, correspondence, and visitation with the patriots during 1739. The account he gives Swift in May will serve to sum up his political year:

You ask me how I am at Court? I keep my old Walk, and deviate from it to no Court. The Pr[ince] shews me a distinction beyond any Merit or Pretence on my part, & I have receiv'd a Present from him, of some Marble Heads of Poets, for my library, and

some Urnes for my Garden. The Ministerial Writers rail at me,
yet I have no quarrel with their Masters, nor think it of weight
enough to complain of them. I am very well with all the Courtiers,
I ever was, or would be acquainted with; at least they are Civil
to me. . . . The Duchess of Marlborow makes great Court to me,
but I am too Old for her, Mind & body. Yet I cultivate some
Young people's friendship, because they may be honest men. . . .
There is a Lord Cornbury, a Lord Polwarth, a Mr Murray, & one
or two more, with whom I would never fear to hold out against
all the Corruption of the world.   (*Corr.* IV 178)

In May, in volume II, part 2, of his works in octavo, appeared another
imitation in the manner of Swift, the forepart of *Epistle I vii*, wherein
he enters his plea for 'Constitution' and 'Independency'—to the dis-
cordancies of Georgian days subtly chording the harmonies of Queen
Anne.[1]

Pope's sense of the plight of patriotism is keenest in 1740. In February the elder Marchmont died and Polwarth succeeded to the title,
but lost thereby his place in the Commons, 'reduced', as Pope says, 'to
Philosophy, as Bolingbroke . . . before you . . .' (*Corr.* IV 228). In
June Wyndham died, and Pope writes Marchmont at length of this
doubling of their affliction. The letter is redolent with bitterness and
despair.[2] He writes in the same vein to Bolingbroke in September:

> . . . the loss of Sir Wm Windham must have been felt more
> deeply, as a particular, by You than by any other: and I see
> nothing so manly, nothing so edifying, as your not deserting the
> com: Cause of your Country at this juncture. . . . Your Resolu-
> tion to return . . . if She wants to be saved, & will or can be
> saved, is by far a more disinterested one than any of her Sons can
> pretend, & every one, who knows either her Condition or your
> Ability . . . must rest his chief hope upon it. Lord M[archmont]
> does so in the ultimate Resource. . . . unless You animate him to
> act by that hope [he] will drop all thought of action. . . . Lord
> Chesterfield despairs as much; but resolves to act. He & Lyttelton
> think alike & act the best part, that I believe ever was acted, in
> their conduct & Counsels to their Master [the Prince].
>   (*Corr.* IV 260–1)

1 See Aden 86–9, 103–4.
2 *Corr.* IV 248–51.

In October Pope writes to Marchmont, now 'retired' in Scotland, begging him to follow Bolingbroke's example of sacrifice for the cause.

The fragment *One Thousand Seven Hundred and Forty, A Poem*, apparently dating from sometime after Wyndham's death, gives 'ruined' but poignant testimony of Pope's despondency. Pulteney there 'foams a Patriot to subside a Peer', and but 'damns the market where he takes no gold'. Shippen knows only 'fire and sword', 'Good C[ornbury] hopes, and candidly sits still', while Gower, Cobham, and Bathurst 'pay thee [Britain] due regards/Unless the ladies bid them mind their cards'.

> *As for the rest, each winter up they run,*
> *And all are clear, that something must be done.*
> *Then urg'd by C[artere]t, or by C[artere]t stopt,*
> *Inflam'd by P[ulteney], or by P[ulteney] dropt*
> *They follow rev'rently each wond'rous wight,*
> *Amaz'd that one can read, that one can write:*
> *So geese to gander prone obedience keep,*
> *Hiss if he hiss, and if he slumber, sleep.*
> *Till having done whate'er was fit or fine,*
> *Utter'd a speech, and ask'd their friends to dine;*
> *Each hurries back to his paternal ground,*
> *Content but for five shillings in the pound,*
> *Yearly defeated, yearly hopes they give,*
> *And all agree, Sir Robert cannot live.*   (29–42)

Perhaps now Pope could appreciate Swift's old impatience with him.

The mention of Sir Robert leads to another of those ambivalent characters Pope is wont to apply to him, now, 'fated to appear,/Spite of thyself a glorious minister', with lines unfinished but clearly hinting at rescue—at making honest at least (as with Molly) the land he has whored before. This is followed by strokes at his brother and at 'Hervey and Hervey's school', until the patriot failure crowds in again:

> *The plague is on thee, Britain, and who tries*
> *To save thee in th'infectious office dies,*
> *The first firm P[ulteney] soon resign'd his breath,*
> *Brave S[carboro]w lov'd thee, and was ly'd to death.*
> *Good M[arch]m[on]t's fate tore P[olwar]th from thy side,*
> *And thy last sigh was heard when W[yndha]m died.*   (75–80)

The conclusion is plaintive Bolingbroke, of *The Idea of a Patriot King:*

> *Alas! on one alone our all relies,*
> *Let him be honest, and he must be wise,*
> *Let him no trifler from his [father's?] school,*
> *Nor like his [father's father?] still a [fool?]*
> *Be but a man! unministered, alone,*
> *And free at once the Senate and the Throne;*
> *Esteem the public love his best supply,*
> *A ● 's true glory his integrity;*
> *Rich with his [Britain?] in his [Britain?] strong,*
> *Affect no conquest, but endure no wrong,*
> *Whatever his religion or his blood,*
> *His public virtue makes his title good.*
> *Europe's just balance and our own may stand,*
> *And one man's honesty redeem the land.* (85 *ad fin.*)

The rest is all but anticlimax. Pope continues troubled over the situation in 1741, confessing to Allen in July that he is 'as dejected as possible, for I love my Country, & I love Mankind, and I see a dismal Scene Opening for our own & other Nations' (*Corr.* IV 351). He remains in frequent association with those patriots who are left, one of whom, Lyttelton, exhorts him again, towards the year's end, to action.

The consummation devoutly to be wished, Walpole's resignation, brought none of the promise it was so long deemed to hold. As it neared, Pope wrote the Duchess of Marlborough: 'I said nothing to your Grace of Patriots, & God forbid I should. If I did, I must do as they do, & Lye: for I have seen none of 'em, not even their Great Leader [Pulteney], nor once congratulated any one Friend or Foe, upon his Promotion, or New Reveal'd Religion, or Regeth ration [*sic*], call it what you will; or by the more distinct & intelligible Name, his new Place or Pension. I'm so sick of London, in her present State . . .' (*Corr.* IV 382).

Bolingbroke returned in April, to remain until mid June, on the business of his father's estate, during which time he and Pope, with their friends, were much together. Pope confides to Bethel that 'The Turn of affairs here has by no means made me think better of the situation of it,

than before . . .' (*Corr.* IV 396). Still, he expresses the hope to Warburton that '*Accidents* & *Occasions* may do what Virtue would not'
(*Corr.* IV 404), and in August he reports to Orrery that 'the Publick is
in Expectations of New Promotions of more of our Friends' (*Corr.* IV
413). But his 'Heart is [still] sick of This bad World' in December
(*Corr.* IV 429), and he passes the holidays with Murray, Marchmont,
Cornbury, '& some others' at Twickenham (*Corr.* IV 431).

None of these years is, of course, without its literary business (or
diversions, such as 'Grottofying'), and in March of 1742 appeared *The
New Dunciad*, the first edition of Book IV of the poem. Though still in
good part 'literary' in flavour, the new book takes ethical and political
directions hardly avoidable at this juncture. Its 'dread Chaos, and
eternal Night' are those, not of wit simply but of morality and politics:
'Of dull and *venal* a new World to mold' (15, my italics). It begins with
ominous notice of the Licensing Act of 1737, with its gagging of patriotic tragedy like Brooke's *Gustavus Vasa* and Thomson's *Edward and
Eleonora*, and satiric comedy (farce) like that of Fielding. As Mother
Dulness holds audience, among 'her sons, the Great' throng 'Courtiers
and Patriots' alike, and conspicuous in their midst are Hervey and
Walpole. It is Walpole whom Mother Dulness fancies may to her
following

> *add one Monarch more;*
> *And nobly conscious, Princes are but things*
> *Born for First Ministers, as Slaves for Kings,*
> *Tyrant supreme! shall three Estates command,*
> *And MAKE ONE MIGHTY DUNCIAD OF THE LAND!* (600–4)

At Mother Dulness's yawn, Nature nodded, and

> *Lost was the Nation's Sense, nor could be found,*
> *While the long solemn Unison went round:*
> *Wide, and more wide, it spread o'er all the realm;*
> *Ev'n Palinurus [Walpole] nodded at the Helm:*
> *The Vapour mild o'er each Committee crept;*
> *Unfinish'd Treaties in each Office slept;*
> *And Chiefless Armies doz'd out the Campaign;*
> *And Navies yawn'd for Orders on the Main.*   (611–18)

Truant to all this corruption and decay—translated now into terms of dulness—are such as Chesterfield, Wyndham, Talbot (Earl of Shrewsbury), Murray, Pulteney, and Atterbury.

In October of 1743 appeared *The Dunciad, In Four Books*,[1] and sometime during the year Pope sketched out a plan for what may have been intended as a patriotic epic on the subject of Brutus. Bolingbroke returned for two visits, between March and May, and again in October, when he stayed until after Pope's death the following May. Pope is much in his company, and in that of Marchmont, but his health is worsening, and that, as well as his business about his works, may account for the sparsity of political discourse in the letters. He is roused by the death, in July, of Spencer Compton (Earl of Wilmington) to declaim once more of political irresponsibility (*Corr.* IV 458), but on Hervey's death in August he can muster only a 'Requiescat in pace!' (*Corr.* IV 466), and of Swift's decline only, 'I am sorry to hear of the Dean. My Letter must end, or it will grow melancholy' (*Corr.* IV 483). In December he tells Allen, 'I have lived so much at Battersea, & to & fro, from thence to London, that I am seldome or never of late at Twitnam, nor I believe shall, while my Lord Bolingbroke stays in England. I have nothing to do but to remove from one warm Fireside to another, at this smaller distance, & from one Friends Side to another' (*Corr.* IV 486).

Jacobitical fright in early 1744 revived the interdict on Catholic presence in the capital and kept Pope from the medical attention that London alone could afford him. Before this he continued to shuttle from town to Battersea, after which, close to the end, Bolingbroke and others, Spence included, gathered about him at Twickenham. 'O great God! What is man?' sobbed Bolingbroke.[2] The end came on May 30, and with it, for the poet who resented it and who resisted it as long as he could, the 'Farce of State'.

---

[1] See Maynard Mack, *The Garden and the City*, 150ff. This work is indispensable to the study of Pope and politics.
[2] Spence §647.

6: Pope and the Financial Revolution

HOWARD ERSKINE-HILL

I

'*Much injur'd Bl[un]t! why bears he Britain's hate?*' In 1735 Pope added to this line of his *Epistle to Allen Lord Bathurst* (published 15 January 1733) the following note:

> Sir JOHN BLUNT, originally a scrivener, was one of the first projectors of the South-sea company, and afterwards one of the directors and chief Managers of the famous scheme in 1720. He was also one of those who suffer'd most severely by the bill of pains and penalties on the said directors. The fraudulent Conveyance he made of part of his Estate, to the value of fifty thousand pounds, to John Ward of Hackney being detected, thro' a Misunderstanding between these two Friends, he not only lost that great Sum, but had forfeited his Life, without a Pardon for the discovery. He was a Dissenter of a most religious deportment, and profess'd to be a great believer. Whether he did really credit the prophecy here mentioned is not certain, but it was constantly in this very style he declaimed against the corruption and luxury of the age, the partiality of Parliaments, and the misery of party-spirit. He was particularly eloquent against *Avarice* in great and noble persons, of which he had indeed liv'd to see many miserable examples. He died in the year 1732.[1]

Blunt is a strangely neglected figure in the economic history of Britain.[2]

---

[1] Twickenham III ii. 104 (note to l. 135). I have not been able to substantiate the third sentence, which Pope later omitted.

[2] Even *DNB* is silent about him, but the *G.E.C. Complete Baronetage*, 1902-9, has a short account, V 48-9. The primary sources for a life of Blunt are:

In 1720, however, his career had reached a peak of celebration and notoriety. Pope would have known about him then, if not before, from the public news. But the poet had other and better sources of information in some of his closest friends. James Craggs the younger, for example, knew Pope in 1715, became a minister in 1717, was deeply involved in the negotiation of the fatal agreement between the Stanhope-Sunderland administration and the South Sea Company, and was on terms of intimacy with Pope throughout South Sea year.[1] Again, the founding of the South Sea Company, to which Pope's note also alludes, was an essential part of Robert Harley's Tory strategy in the year 1711, and Swift was to a large degree in Harley's confidence. Indeed, when Swift was preparing his *History of the Four Last Years of the Queen*, between August 1712 and May 1713, he sought Blunt's assistance in regard to the handling of the National Debt by the previous administration. Blunt's memorandum on this subject may be seen incorporated in

---

(1). (Sir John Blunt) *A True State of the South Sea Scheme*, 1722 (rev. edn 1732): ignored in modern discussions of the South Sea Bubble. The attribution to Blunt, derived from Abel Boyer, *The Political State*. XXXVI, 235, is accepted by L. W. Hanson, *Contemporary Printed Sources for English and Irish Economic History, 1701–1750*, 1963, 3965 (p. 423).

(2). *The Secret History of the South-Sea Scheme*, in *A Collection of Several Pieces of Mr. John Toland*, 1726, I 404–47 'enlarged and corrected', but not written, by Toland (404). This anonymous tract gives relatively 'inside' knowledge of Blunt's activities in 1720. A letter from Toland to the director Sir Theodore Janssen (pp. 466–9; see also 469–75) stresses the same point as the work: the comparative innocence of the outer circle of South Sea directors. This suggests Janssen as author of *The Secret History*. Attribution to so respected and formidable a figure would, if plausible, lend the work further authority, though it must be remembered that Janssen had every reason for resentment against Blunt.

(3). *The Case of the South Sea Directors, No. 3* (*The Case of Sir John Blunt*), 1721.

(4). *The Particular and Inventory of Sir John Blunt* . . . , 1721.

(5). *The Will of Sir John Blunt*, Principal Probate Registry, Literary Dept., Somerset House.

The chief secondary works are John Carswell, *The South Sea Bubble*, 1960; and P. G. M. Dickson, *The Financial Revolution in England*, 1967.

[1] *Corr.* I 306; II 51, 53, 57.

Swift's text.[1] Sometime after June 1720 Swift revised his *History*, ackknowledging in a footnote his debt to 'Sir John Blunt', a Baronet since that date. He brought it to England in 1727, and Pope was reminded of its contents when, at his own house, he, Swift and Bolingbroke (the latter, with Blunt, one of the original directors of the South Sea Company) discussed the possibility of its publication.[2] In Swift and Bolingbroke Pope had two friends in an almost unique position to inform him, retrospectively if not at the time, of the character and projects of John Blunt during the years of the Tory administration.

These facts suggest two things. The first is that Pope's lines and note on Sir John Blunt in *To Bathurst* have some authority, carefully interpreted, as historical evidence. The second, and more important, is that more information about Blunt than could be given in the standard edition of *To Bathurst* may demonstrate the central importance of Pope's theme in the economic history of that time, and throw new light on the poem itself.[3] Such information enables us to trace a relationship between economic, social and political facts, and an art which responded to them, judged them, and in a sense harmonized them through that judgement.

II

John Blunt was born in 1665, the son of a Baptist shoemaker of Rochester.[4] On 5 March 1689 he became free of the Merchant Taylors' Company, in the City of London, by virtue of apprenticeship to Daniel Richards, a scrivener of Holborn.[5] Four months after the ending of his apprenticeship his first marriage took place; he became a Liveryman of the Merchant Taylors on 11 March 1691, and we know that between

[1] Swift, *The History of the Four Last Years of the Queen*, ed. Herbert Davis and Harold Williams, Oxford 1951, x–xi, 71–2.
[2] *Ibid.* xii; and for Bolingbroke's directorship, BM Add. MSS 25494 f.4.
[3] Twickenham III ii. 104. E. R. Wasserman, *Pope's 'Epistle to Bathurst'*, stresses the learned rather than the social and economic background of the poem.
[4] *G.E.C. Baronetage* V 48–9.
[5] Carswell 19.

1699 and 1702 he was living in the parish of St. Michael's Cornhill.[1] In 1693 and again in 1702 he wrote to the Treasury proposing a new method of keeping public accounts.[2] The first important step in his career, however, was taken, probably in 1703, when he became secretary of the Sword Blade Bank. Created in 1692 as a chartered stock company for the manufacture of the new grooved sword, this strange institution had, by the opening of Anne's reign, fallen into the hands of the men whom Defoe was to call the 'three capital sharpers of Britain', Elias Turner, Jacob Sawbridge, George Caswall—and of Blunt. Its charter was now used to hold land and issue stock in the purchase of forfeited Jacobite lands in Ireland. This operation, which involved the connivance of the government, was curious and significant. The Sword Blade did not pay cash for the land but issued stock. Neither was the stock issued for cash but for Army Debentures, vouchers for unsecured government debts for military expenditure, which had depreciated in value. The Sword Blade offered the original, nominal, value for these, the part of the Irish lands in the transaction seeming to offer convincing security. Army Debentures appreciated rapidly as a result, and the Sword Blade partners, who had previously invested in them at the lower price as private individuals, were able to sell at a handsome profit. The government was paid with its own obligations for assets (the Irish lands) which it could not profitably use, and was thus able to cancel a considerable public debt. It also extracted from the Sword Blade partners a loan in cash, which could have been the price of its readiness to deal with the upstart company. The transaction is likely to have been worthwhile for the partners chiefly because it made them major creditors to the government with all the business prestige which that involved. The Jacobite lands proved hard to get possession of, but the *idea of land* was the essential confidence-producing factor in the transaction. The whole operation was an exercise in credit. It indicates the nature of Blunt's future career, and we may remember that a scrivener at this time was essentially one involved in the paperwork of business transactions.

[1] *G.E.C. Baronetage* loc. cit.; City of London: Guildhall Library, Wardmote Inquest Book of Cornhill, MS 4069-2, f. 420v, 427v, 431v.
[2] *Calendar of Treasury Papers 1702–7* LXXX no. 4, 20–21.

The Sword Blade operation, clinched at a visit by Blunt to the Treasury on 1 June 1704, was an impudent attempt to challenge the Bank of England at its own game. It is in the rôle played by the Bank of England from 1694 onwards that we see the beginning of the Financial Revolution in Britain. Under the leadership of William III Britain was engaged in a continental war on a scale never previously known. No existing source of revenue or means of collection could meet the need for immediate and substantial funds. New sources had to be found, and of these the Bank of England was chief. In return for a charter incorporating them as a joint-stock bank, Gilbert Heathcote and his syndicate had, in 1694, lent the government a million and a half pounds in *Bank of England notes*, retaining for banking the cash put up by the shareholders. Immense financial prestige now accrued to the new institution. In 1697 the Bank offered the government a further loan by incorporating depreciated exchequer tallies in an issue of new stock—the model for the Sword Blade loan of 1703–4. The act of parliament which provided for this operation prolonged the Bank's charter until 1710 and strengthened its position against possible rivals. The Sword Blade, however, though hardly a serious rival in 1697, already had its own charter. It may be supposed that the Bank of England viewed the Sword Blade loan with anger, and in 1707, in return for a further loan, the government extended the Bank's charter until 1732 and passed legislation strengthening its monopoly still further.

Blunt and his partners in the Sword Blade were not the only people to regard the Bank of England with a jealous eye. It was recognized as a great political as well as financial power, and the landed gentry in particular saw in it a threat to their parliamentary influence. Swift was to put their case forcefully in his *History of the Four Last Years of the Queen*.

> By all I have read of the History of our own Country, it appears to me, That National Debts secured upon Parliamentary Funds of Interest, were things unknown in *England* before the last Revolution under the Prince of *Orange*. . . . it was the Business of such as were then in Power to cultivate a money'd Interest; because the Gentry of the Kingdom did not very much relish those New Notions in Government, to which the King . . . was thought to give too much way. . . . Thus, a new Estate and Property sprung

up in the hands of Mortgagees, to whom every House and Foot of Land in *England* paid a Rent Charge free of all Taxes. . . . So that the Gentlemen of Estates were in effect but Tenants to these New Landlords; many of whom were able in time to force the Election of Burroughs out of the Hands of those who had been the old Proprietors. . . .   (68–70)

When, in August 1710, Queen Anne dismissed Godolphin, the Whig Lord High Treasurer, Robert Harley assumed office to face, not only the Tory desire to check the power of the 'money'd Interest', but also the fact that under the continuing strain of the war the Godolphin-Bank of England financial system was beginning to break down. Harley's aim was twofold. Firstly he sought to bring the War of the Spanish Succession to an end. Secondly, since the need for immediate military expenditure was as great as ever, he had to find new financial backing. Heathcote and the Bank of England, heavily committed to Godolphin and Whig policy, assured themselves that Harley would never do it. They reckoned without the opportunism and sharpness of the Sword Blade.

It may seem surprising that Harley, the moderate Tory, and Blunt, the Baptist shoemaker's son and a man of the City if ever there was one, could contemplate alliance. The chief reason was expediency; each seemed the only one to offer what the other sought. But it was not quite so extraordinary as it looks. The Harleys, a parliamentarian family in the Civil War, took care to cultivate their connections with the dissenting interest. Edward Harley had represented Leominster, a stronghold of dissent, since 1698, and in the elections of 1710, following Harley's assumption of office, the family captured both the Leominster seats with the help of Blunt's Sword Blade partner Caswall, whose family were influential Baptists in the borough.

Blunt and Caswall now recommended that the creditors of the state should be incorporated, and the short-term public debt cancelled in return for a commensurate issue of stock.[1] The suggestion was unoriginal: it was an attempt to supplant the Bank of England in its own characteristic procedure. But there was a new political ingredient in the otherwise old recipe: the prospect of trade with Spanish America (in

[1] P. G. M. Dickson, *The Financial Revolution*, 64–5.

slaves among other commodities) on a successful termination of the war. Harley and his advisers evolved a concept which could dispel the crisis in public credit and provide the new Tory government with the necessary financial backing. This was the South Sea Company. From Harley's point of view it was most adroit. The opportunity of breaking into the carefully protected trade with the Spanish Indies was one of the chief commercial goals of the war. Since nobody, least of all the Whigs, could deny that the campaigns of Marlborough had been highly successful, it must have seemed probable that at the end of the war Britain would secure this trade. But when would the end be? Here Harley's political brilliance can be seen. It was precisely the Tories' desire to bring the long and expensive war to a speedy conclusion which divided them from the Whigs; with great skill Harley linked the saving of the public credit with the fulfilment of the Tory foreign policy. From Blunt's point of view, the proposal was equally satisfactory. The familiar Bank of England operation was given a new credibility by the prospect of South Sea trade. This was the confidence-creating element in the scheme. As in 1703 Blunt had a strong public assurance that tangible assets would be available—but as in 1703 they were not yet secured. Practice was teaching Blunt the dangerous lesson that a good prospect of material advantage is alone sufficient to raise public credit. But above all, Blunt had helped Harley to put the Bank of England's nose out of joint. They were out and he was in. He could not have hoped for more.

Harley was able to overcome his initial financial difficulties; Blunt and his Sword Blade partners helped make the new State Lottery a success, and in May 1711 the proposal for the South Sea Company was put to the Commons. The legislation was rapidly despatched and by September the Charter had been granted. On 10 September 1711 Blunt is first mentioned in the Minutes as a director,[1] and had in fact been responsible for the drawing up of the charter. While he partly relied on Bank of England precedent, it is probable that he so contrived things that the Company might be controlled by a relatively small group. Five directorships went to the Sword Blade partners: Blunt himself, his

[1] BM Add. MSS 25494 f.3.

nephew Charles Blunt, Caswall, Jacob Sawbridge and Benjamin Tud-
man. All were to be prominent in the notorious future of the Company.
It is an historical irony, unlikely, in later years, to have been lost on
Pope, that it was these men, above all Blunt himself, who were behind
the measure so enthusiastically celebrated by Swift in his *Examiner*
paper for 7 June 1711:

> The Publick Debts were so prodigiously encreased, by the Negli-
> gence and Corruption of those who had been Managers of the
> Revenue; that the late Ministers, like careless Men, who run out
> their Fortunes, were so far from any Thoughts of Payment; that
> they had not the Courage to state or compute them. . . . The late
> Chancellor of the *Exchequer* [Harley], suitable to his transcendant
> Genius for Publick Affairs, proposed a Fund to be Security for
> that immense Debt, which is now confirmed by a Law; and is
> likely to prove the greatest Restoration and Establishment of the
> Kingdom's Credit.[1]

III

By the year 1719 three things were clear to John Blunt. The first was
that the South Sea Company had triumphantly survived the fall of the
Tory administration and the accession of a new dynasty to the throne.
While, with a new Whig government, the Bank of England was back
in favour, no government could afford to ignore a possible source of
large-scale credit. The South Sea Company now enjoyed a kind of
parity with the Bank of England. The Prince of Wales was appointed
Governor, then the new King himself, and each invested in its stock.
The second recognition was that, for various reasons, notably the outbreak of a new war with Spain in 1718, the Company had almost completely failed as a trading venture. The third was the amazing apparent
success of the great Scottish economist John Law in bringing the whole
economy of France under the control of a revolutionary new system.
At the heart of Law's thinking was the conviction that contemporary
monetary practice, having evolved in piecemeal and pragmatic fashion

[1] Swift, *The Examiner and other Prose Pieces Written in 1710–11*, ed
Herbert Davis, Oxford 1940, 170.

might be brought under rational control for the greater benefit of society. Law rejected the assumption that money should be intrinsically valuable in favour of the concept of a systematic paper currency whose value should be determined by skilled financiers, recognized throughout the land, and guaranteed by the power of government. Provided the value of the currency were not arbitrarily fixed, but made to correspond to accessible wealth, such a system could be trusted to facilitate trade, release the latent resources of an economy, and increase general prosperity. Such were the ideas which Law put to the Regent, Philippe d'Orléans, soon after the death of Louis XIV. They were rejected; nevertheless Law advanced steadily towards control of the French economy. With his founding of the Banque Générale, his acquiring dominant interest in the Mississippi Company, and his taking over the French National Debt, he had gained, by August 1719, the total control of a major national economy which he had earlier been denied. If many in Britain regarded this with apprehension, Blunt reacted with emulous excitement. Another director of the South Sea Company (probably Sir Theodore Janssen) gives us a vivid picture of him at this time, under the name of Appius:

> . . . the progress of the Mississippi Company about that time having intoxicated, and turned the brains of most people, APPIUS'S mind was thereby wonderfully affected, and from his natural inclination to Projects, so inflamed, that he could brook no longer the narrow thoughts he had entertained before, of engaging for one or two branches of the public Funds only; but carried on his views for taking in at once all the national Debts, the Bank and East India Company included: often saying, 'That as Mr. LAW had taken his pattern from him, and improved upon what was done here the year before in relation to the Lottery of 1710, he would now improve upon what was done in France, and out-do Mr. Law.'[1]

The proposal which Blunt now attempted to put before the Sunderland-Stanhope administration seems to have been no less ambitious than the aims of Law. In the first instance, at least, he wished to manage the

---

[1] *The Secret History of the South Sea Scheme* (hereafter referred to as 'Secret History') 406–7.

whole of the National Debt through an amalgamation of the funds of the Bank of England, the East India Company and the South Sea Company.[1] This shows a staggering boldness of conception and (the Bank and East India Company must have thought) a staggering impudence. Yet in France Law was apparently demonstrating to the world that such schemes could succeed. It is certain, however, that though Blunt might have equalled Law, he could never have outdone him: this most important of Blunt's projects, like his earlier operations, is essentially imitative. Even so there was little chance of such a scheme being accepted without radical modification. Yet, paradoxically, it may have been a sounder scheme in its original form than as it emerged after negotiation with the politicians. The South Sea Company itself could hardly have been in a worse position to take over more public debt, having failed to acquire a solid basis of wealth through trade. But if the resources of all three companies had been amalgamated, the deficiencies of the South Sea might have been made good, and Blunt himself (as he doubtless intended) master-minded the operation. Blunt certainly realized the need for some confidence-creating element in his new scheme, and perhaps was still sensible enough to try for more than this. If we can trust his own retrospective account, he proposed that the Company be granted the Africa Trade, Nova Scotia, and the French part of St. Christopher's, as 'solid supports to the Stock'—a point usually forgotten in accounts of the South Sea Scheme.[2]

First reactions from the government were if anything hostile, but Blunt's eagerness to undertake a major conversion of public debt was too attractive to be ignored. Discussion took place, and the proposal for amalgamating the resources of the three companies was dropped. What emerged was that the South Sea Company would propose to take over the remainder of the National Debt (that not already being undertaken by other companies) and would convert it into stock as government creditors came forward to make the exchange. For the privilege of becoming the government's sole creditor for this debt, the Company would, in the event of a successful conversion, charge a favourable rate

[1] *Ibid.* 406–7; *The Parliamentary History of England* (hereafter referred to as '*Parliamentary History*') 1806–20 VII, 1811, 883; and Dickson 95.
[2] [Sir John Blunt,] *A True State of the South Sea Scheme*, 1722, 18, 20.

of interest, and would also offer a very large sum as a gift to be devoted to buying off such creditors as might be reluctant to convert their assets into South Sea stock. The value of the debt to be taken over has been calculated in round figures at £31 million; that of the reduced rate of interest at £400,000 a year; and the gift was to be £3 million.[1] This offer must have seemed a brilliant political prospect to the government. When it was put to the Commons, however, and James Craggs asked for unanimous acceptance, supporters of the Bank asked that other tenders should be considered. Competition between the Bank and the Company now entered a quite irresponsible phase, with the government equally irresponsibly attempting to extract from each even more favourable, and thus less realistic, terms. Blunt agreed to drop the proposal concerning the Africa Trade,[2] and to raise the amount of the gift. Perhaps all things seemed possible in the light of Law's achievement, and Blunt's urgent conviction that he could become a new Law unto Britain. In fact he was now proposing to raise credit, not as Law taught in correspondence to accessible wealth, but far beyond that point. It was to be an operation in pure credit, with no solid supports to the stock at all. Chancellor Aislaby, if his later account is to be trusted, was one who expressed misgivings:

> . . . we had a meeting, where the lords of the treasury, and those in the administration, were present, in order, as sir John Blunt says, to persuade the South Sea Company to advance their proposals, and to offer four millions certain [ie. the gift]; It was then, my lords, that I again expressed my fears of this undertaking, and declared, that I did not see how the South Sea Company could go through with it, if they were to give any more money for it, without the assistance and concurrence of the Bank, and much less, if the Bank opposed them; and upon this, I proposed . . . that the scheme should be divided between them and the Bank, which drew from Sir John Blunt this memorable saying, 'No, sir, we will never divide the child.'[3]

We can see from this Blunt's vehement sense of competition with the Bank, his 'high spirit' with opposition, and the pronounced biblical bias

[1] Carswell 104–6.
[2] *A True State* 19–20.
[3] *Parliamentary History* VII 884.

of his thought and expression. The allusion to Solomon's judgement concerning the disputed child reminded his listeners that he only was the true begetter of the Scheme, and that the wisdom of Solomon would not dispute his possession. It was with this high resolution that Blunt, having importuned the court of the Company to let him propose to the government what he thought fit, outdid the Bank's rival offer and clinched his deal by raising the figures of the gift to £7½ million.[1]

On 7 April 1720, when the South Sea Bill received the royal assent, the stock of the Company stood at 335. Clearly Blunt could only fulfil the obligations for which he had bargained so hard if there were to be an enormous appreciation in the value of the stock. Blunt saw this, and it was 'his avow'd Maxim, a thousand times repeated, *That advancing by all means of the price of the stock, was the only way to promote the good of the Company*'.[2] He set about it with great short-term skill. His means were money-subscriptions and loans. Stock was offered to the public at a certain price; there was about the Scheme an air of excited speculation, in every sense, and the stock was rapidly disposed of, appreciating in market value as a result. The inflow of cash from the subscription then made possible substantial loans from the Company to the public, which released funds for further speculation, and drove up the price of the stock still higher. Carswell describes Blunt's method concisely:

> Like Law, he had constructed a financial pump, each spurt of stock being accompanied by a draught of cash to suck it up again, leaving the level higher than before. As fast as stock issued . . . the money received for it was returned to the market to support the prices and take up fresh issues at the higher price. . . . Law's pump fed an open spray, which watered, and eventually drowned, the economy. Blunt's was meant to be a closed circuit.   (135,146)

Blunt carried out this manoeuvre, with variations, four times between March and September 1720, and on each of the first three occasions drove up the price of his stock higher than before.

There were several reasons for his spectacular success. The author of *The Secret History* (410) alleges that 'all ways and means, Bribery not

---

[1] *Secret History* 408–9. The detailed figures of these negotiations may be found in the best account: Dickson 93–101.

[2] *Secret History* 423.

excepted', had been used to get the South Sea Bill passed. This 'bribery' had consisted of the conveying of stock to persons whom the Company wished to oblige; when, as each party expected, the stock appreciated, it was sold back at the higher price. The only cash to change hands was the difference between the earlier and the later price. Among those obliged in this way were the Duke of Sunderland, Secretary Craggs and his father Postmaster Craggs, Chancellor Aislaby, and (through Secretary Craggs) two of George I's mistresses. There is the further *possibility* that the King and the Prince of Wales also received 'fictitious' stock.[1] In all but the last instance there was little secrecy about these transactions; it was in the personal interests of some of the mightiest men of the land that the stock should appreciate, and this was known. Where the leaders of the nation had shown their interest, many were eager to follow. In addition, Blunt imitated Law in courting the interest of the polite, not merely that of the mercantile world. In speech he went further: 'on all occasions he freely declared his opinion, without mincing the matter, that he was not for disposing of the Company's money to traders and such other fair dealers; but to those who frequented the Alley [Exchange Alley]; and to Ladies and young Gentlemen, who came from the other end of the town, with a spirit of gaming: for such, according to him, were the most likely to advance the price of the stock.'[2] Among these polite speculators was Alexander Pope who, having remarked to his friend Eckersall: '. . . tis Ignominious (in this Age of Hope and Golden Mountains) not to Venture', had purchased £500 worth of stock, on behalf of himself and Teresa Blount, in early March of South Sea Year.[3]

Three further factors contributed to the appreciation of the stock. The first was the reconciliation of the Walpole Whigs, out of power, with the ruling Stanhope-Sunderland group, opponents and proposers respectively of the Scheme. There was a simultaneous reconciliation between the King and the Prince of Wales. Both raised public confidence. The second was John Hungerford's parliamentary enquiry into

[1] Carswell 126. For a considered account of South Sea bribery, see Dickson 110-12.
[2] *Secret History* 446.
[3] *Corr.* II 33-4, 38.

the wave of new financial projects sweeping London in the spring of 1720. The enquiry resulted in the passing, in June, of the 'Bubble Act', which indiscriminately suppressed all joint stock companies not authorized by charter. This meant that there was more money available for speculation in the South Sea, though it may have contributed ultimately to failure of confidence in the Company. The third factor contributing to the appreciation of the stock was the ominous news from France. Law's system, set in motion with twice the intelligence of Blunt's, was getting out of control. Inflation was threatening the French economy, and Law vainly attempted to curb the mania for speculation which he had himself released. The immediate result of the great economist's failure for John Blunt was that the speculators' market shifted from Paris to London, thus increasing the demand for South Sea stock. Joseph Gage, the 'modest Gage' of Pope's *To Bathurst*, who had bid for the crown of Poland with his Mississippi fortune of £13,000,000, was now in London, speculating in Exchange Alley.[1]

In the early summer of 1720 Blunt was at the height of his triumph. More than half of the government creditors had subscribed their holdings into the Company towards the end of May, and the stock was still rising. Blunt might well have spoken of 'this Bold undertaking' which 'Providence had blessed with success, much beyond expectation . . .'.[2] It is possible that he felt sustained by a personal and religious destiny:

He visibly affected a prophetick stile, delivering his words with an emphasis and extraordinary vehemence: and used to put himself into a commanding posture, rebuking those that durst in the least oppose any thing he said, and endeavouring to inculcate, as if what he spoke was by impulse, uttering these and such like expressions: *Gentlemen, don't be dismayed: you must act with firmness, with resolution, with courage. I tell you, 'tis not a common matter you have before you. The greatest thing in the world is referred to you. All the money in Europe will centre amongst you. All the nations of the earth will bring you tribute.*[3]

On 9 June Blunt, 'but one in thirty one' in his own falsely modest phrase,

[1] *To Bathurst* 130–1: Twickenham III ii. 103; Carswell 143.
[2] *Secret History* 425.
[3] *Ibid.* 443.

was deservedly singled out from the other thirty directors to receive the honour of a Baronetcy, 'for his extraordinary services in raising public credit to a height not known before'.[1] His third money-subscription opened on 17 June, and £5,000,000 worth of stock was issued at the fantastic level of 1000. The subscribers, almost all nominated by chief members of the government and Company, included half the notables of the nation; practically nobody of influence and importance but now had some interest in the Company. And still Blunt and his inner ring of directors were besieged with requests for further subscriptions. It must have been at this time that, 'one day, at the treasury . . . when a relation of a great man, asking sir John for a subscription, the upstart knight, with a great deal of contempt, bid him go to his cousin Walpole, and desire him to sell his stock in the Bank, and by that means he might be supplied.'[2] Blunt seems now to have lost any caution he ever had in his treatment of his colleagues in the Company; he ordered a fourth loan, 'and the Cashiers lent upwards of three millions in one day, without acquainting the Committee of Treasury with it . . .'. The Committee complained constantly of 'irregularity and confusion' and Blunt's answer, while it acknowledges a truth in his handling of people, appears to have in it a touch of hysteria: *The more confusion the better; People must not know what they do, which will make them the more eager to come into our measures; the execution of the Scheme is our business; The Eyes of all Europe are upon us; Both houses of Parliament expect to have it done before their next meeting . . .'.[3] This reply refers to the second and final stage of the conversion of the outstanding national debt, which took place, at 800, on 14 July and 4 August 1720. With this in train, the Scheme was at last executed, and Blunt, who thought (or seemed to think) that 'he had the world in a string' retired to Tunbridge Wells for a holiday. 'In what splendid equipage APPIUS went to the Wells, what respect was paid him there, with what haughtiness he behaved himself in that place, and how he and his family, when they spoke of the Scheme, called it *our Scheme*, is not the subject of this discourse' writes the *Secret*

---

[1] *Secret History* 443; Carswell 157–8.

[2] *Parliamentary History* VII 801.

[3] *Secret History* 429.

History.[1] It was perhaps now that he declared 'that in any other nation but this, they would have given him a reward of 500000l. for the service he had done to his country'.[2] But Blunt cannot have had the complete confidence he took care to display. On 25 June, Blunt's son Henry had joined with Turner, Caswall and Sawbridge of the Sword Blade to form a new bank into which a great sum was immediately paid, presumably to insure against disaster.[3] From Tunbridge he wrote by every post instructing his brokers to sell parts of his South Sea stock, and we know that in June and July he began (though not on a great scale) to buy land.[4] On 13 July he had paid £20,400 for a manor in Essex; the next day part of the remaining debt was converted into stock at 800; four days later the price of the stock began to fall. Blunt must have expected it, though probably not a disaster of the dimensions which occurred. For effectively the South Sea Bubble had now burst.

IV

For a time Blunt and the Company fought the trend. A fourth money-subscription on stiff terms, and at the previous rate of 1000, was offered on 24 August. Once again it was exceeded, and among prospective buyers turned away were those on a list from the Court of Hanover, and the apparently still credulous Robert Walpole.[5] An incentive to stockholders in the form of a dividend was announced on 30 August: 30% for the current year, with a guaranteed 50% for the next twelve. This amazing offer, however proportionate to the expectations of a speculator who had bought stock at 1000, was not credible. It jogged

---

[1] For Blunt's conversion of debt into stock, in 1720, see Dickson 135; for his journey to Tunbridge, see *Secret History* 431.
[2] *Secret History* 436–7.
[3] Carswell 185.
[4] *Secret History* 431–2; *The Particular and Inventory of Sir John Blunt*, 1721, 23. See Dickson 146–7, on land purchase by Company directors.
[5] Carswell 177. On Walpole's unwise timing of his South Sea invest-ment, see J. H. Plumb, *Sir Robert Walpole: The Making of a Statesman*, 1956, 315–16, and Dickson 109.

people to their senses, and on 2 September the stock had sunk as low as 755. On 8 September a General Court was held, packed with friends of the directors, and encouraging speeches were made by the Duke of Portland, the elder Craggs, and John Hungerford, who exulted in 'such wonderful Things in so short a Time' and praised the Company for having reconciled 'all Parties in one common Interest, and thereby laid asleep, if not wholly extinguish'd, our Domestick Jars and Animosities', and for enriching the nation.[1] But already the loss sustained by courtiers, politicians, nobility, gentry, officers of the army and navy, merchants and businessmen, who had subscribed to stock at 1000, amounted to a national disaster. Foreign money now left London for newer bubbles at Amsterdam and Lisbon. Worst of all, despite the fourth money-subscription, the Company had nothing like enough cash to meet its obligations, nor was there any immediate hope of profit from its original purpose: trade.

To such a situation Blunt had nothing left to offer. The initiative was now with parliament. There were two important developments in the Commons. First, Robert Walpole moved adroitly forward to political power, as a traditional supporter of the Bank of England, but now reconciled to the increasingly embarrassed government. Only the Bank, it seemed, could help the situation now, and Walpole employed two plans involving the Bank, the 'Bank Contract' and the 'Engraftment Scheme', as potent weapons to achieve his political ends. Sunderland and Stanhope brought him into their ministry, and it was understood that the joint policy should be one of construction rather than recrimination. Such a policy was naturally welcome to the government and the Company, but it was arguably also best for the nation. On this nice point turns the whole question of Walpole's subsequent rôle as a 'screen' for a public cheat. For—and this was the second development in the Commons—it soon became clear that a powerful alliance of Whig, Tory and Jacobite back-benchers were strongly against drawing a veil over the misjudgements and suspected misdemeanours of the South Sea Scheme. Prominent among these were Shippen, the leader of the Jacobites, Sir William Wyndham, and Sir Joseph Jekyll, each of whom Pope

[1] Boyer, *Political State* XX 181-2.

was subsequently to praise respectively for bluntness, justice, and unswerving principle.[1] On 20 December Walpole and Jekyll clashed in the Commons, the former urging that to 'unravel what had been done, they should not only ruin the South Sea Company, but instead of alleviating, aggravate the present misfortunes', while the latter stood firm for 'public faith, equity and justice, which the South Sea Managers had notoriously violated', and implicitly denied that Walpole's 'Engraftment Scheme' could do so much to restore public credit as a full enquiry.[2] Both measures went forward, and on 11 January 1721 a Committee of Secrecy was set up with full powers to investigate the conduct of the Company.[3]

How guilty a man was Sir John Blunt? Was the South Sea Scheme a calculated cheat? Clearly Law's scheme was not, and Blunt's, conceived when Law's was rising to a peak of acknowledged success, was in avowed imitation of Law. If Law had sought to benefit the French economy as a whole, while Blunt had constructed a closed system to benefit only the Company and the government, subscribers who bought stock at a high rate did so of their own free will. Blunt certainly misled the public, but perhaps deluded himself too; he could hardly have foreseen from the beginning the disastrous fall in the stock, since this would clearly be equally disastrous for himself. It is unlikely that Blunt, ambitious and unscrupulous though he was, framed his Scheme as a public deception. As he was to write: 'there was no evil Design in the first preparing this Scheme.'[4] And he must have believed that, even without 'solid supports', the value of the stock could be raised and fixed high. But he seems to have been carried away by his own success in shortterm manipulation of the market, and perhaps hardly faced the consequences of what he was doing when he carried out the second stage of the conversion of public debt at 800. It is at this point that real duplicity appears, yet Blunt may still have half-believed that his own

---

[1] *Satire II i (To Fortescue)* 51–2; *Epilogue to the Satires*, Dialogue II 88–9, Dialogue I 38–41: Twickenham IV 9, 318, 300–1.

[2] *Parliamentary History* VII 690 (see 684–91 for a fuller picture of their difference of approach).

[3] *Commons Journals* XIX 399.

[4] *A True State of the South Sea Scheme* 56.

expertise and Providence might save the day. But after the failure of the dividend-offer, on 30 August, even half-belief was impossible. From then on he merely kept up a front. Apart from the Scheme itself, however, there were in the early months of 1721 other questions being asked, almost equally important, concerning irregularity in the conduct of the Company, the honesty with which the South Sea Bill had been procured, and the selling of 'fictitious' stock. These reflected on the integrity not only of Blunt and the directors, but also of the government, even perhaps the court, in a most serious way.

We should know little about these matters if it were not for Blunt himself. It is the final irony of Blunt's career that he now supported Jekyll's insistence that parliament should 'discover' the 'distemper' before attempting the cure, against the screening policies of Walpole. He put himself in the power of the Committee of Secrecy and, unlike the Company cashier, Robert Knight, who absconded rather than reveal all he knew, agreed to tell them the truth. Blunt must have realized that he could not hope to conceal the whole truth, that he was likely to be considered chief culprit in the national disaster, but that something might be salvaged from the wreck of his fortune and career through co-operation with the Committee. It is probable too that his religion and his liking for a righteous moral stance played a part in this decision. Having confessed his own offences, he could, with some integrity, help to expose those who had not yet confessed theirs. The turning-point of his resolution is preserved in the Committee of Secrecy's First Report:

> *Sir John Blunt* said . . . that after this examination on Friday the 27th of January last, Mr. Joye [the late Deputy-Governor of the Company] came to his lodgings, and asked him touching what had passed in his examination before your committee. That sir John Blunt told him, he had said nothing of the ministry: What! says Mr. Joye, nor of the ladies neither? To which sir John replied, that he had not.
>
> That on Saturday the 28th of January last, soon after sir John Blunt had been again examined by your committee at the South-Sea house, Mr. Joye came to him, and asked him what had passed; that sir John told him he was under an obligation of secrecy; that he loved him very well, and that the best way was to tell the whole truth: What, says Mr. Joye, of the ladies, and all? Yes (says sir

John) the examination is very strict, and nothing but the truth
will do [1]

There is a wry irony in the spectacle of these two gravely embarrassed
men holding out as long as possible before they revealed the illicit
gains of the King's mistresses—'the ladies'—and in the way expediency
and morality embrace in Blunt's final remark: '. . . nothing but the
truth will do'. Thus it was that the politicians were arraigned. Charles
Stanhope, defended by Walpole among others, was acquitted by a
mere three votes, though certainly guilty. In the next trial 'Walpole's
corner sat mute as fishes', and Aislaby was condemned. Sir George
Caswall went the same way. The mob lit bonfires in the streets as they
were taken to prison. Sunderland, the greatest of them all, was another
matter. Walpole exerted all his influence to procure an acquittal.
Sunderland took his stand on a flat denial of the charges, so that, as
Broderick, the Chairman of the Committee, wrote afterwards: 'the
question in truth, was neither more nor less than whether we should
give credit to that assertion, or sir John Blunt's oath.' Attempts to
falsify the oath were unconvincing, and the stronger appeal of the
defence was: 'If you come into this vote against lord Sunderland, the
ministry are blown up, and must . . . be succeeded by a tory one.'[2]
Such was the view of the prosecution. It is hardly surprising that many,
looking back on these events from the 1730s, felt them to have been
crucial in the subsequent development of the political situation. Between
1713 and 1732 there was no better chance of a new Tory government.
Sunderland was acquitted, probably wrongly, by 233 votes to 172. The
directors of the Company were treated with severity. Blunt was the
third richest of them, *The Inventory of Sir John Blunt* showing his estate
to have amounted to £183,349.10.8¾.[3] When his case came up, the
supporters of the Committee felt he should be rewarded for his disclosures. Jekyll spoke warmly for him, and moved that he be allowed
to keep £10,000, but the Walpoles and their supporters went out of

[1] *Parliamentary History* VII 720.
[2] *Ibid.* VII 756.
[3] *The Particular and Inventory of Sir John Blunt*; The Abstract of Sir
John Blunt 3.

their way to stress his guilt as 'the chief contriver and promoter of all
the mischief', his history as a fraudulent projector, and his personal
arrogance. In the end he was allowed £1000, which was subsequently
raised to £5000.[1]

Blunt gave his own account of these events in *A True State of the
South Sea Scheme* (1722). In it he made as restrained and plain a defence
of the directors as the case would allow. Unlike the *Secret History*, this
work neither praises nor blames individuals, nor does it follow the
example of the Committee of Secrecy in pointing to corruption in high
places. It blames envious competition on the Bank of England's part for
forcing the Company to undertake the conversion of public debt on
terms so risky that the directors had no alternative but to exploit 'the
general disposition of the People' and drive up the price of the stock in
response to an inordinate public demand for money-subscriptions (p. 20).
Second to the Bank of England, Blunt blamed 'THE DISTEMPER
OF THE TIMES, which captivated the Reason of Mankind in General,
not only in *England*, but in all the neighbouring Countries, who leaving
the usual Methods of Labour and Industry to gain Estates, were all
tainted with the fond Opinion of being rich at once; which caus'd many
Persons to engage much beyond their own Fortunes, not only in *South
Sea* Stock, but in every *pernicious Bubble*, that could be devis'd. And
here needs only an Appeal to every Man's own Conscience, and to
desire him to reflect on the Operations of his own Mind at that Time,
and what he did and saw, and knew to be done by others.' Blunt's
righteous tone finally breaks through the restraint as he recalls:

> HOW did Persons of all Ranks and Stations, lay aside all manner
> of distance, and almost Decency, to become the humble Suitors
> for Subscriptions: not only to the *Directors* of the *South Sea* Com-
> pany, but also to the *meanest* and *vilest* of *People*. . . . (41)

There is some truth in both these points. But the defence is evasive
since Blunt had, at the nation's peril, exceeded the Bank's competitive-
ness and deliberately exploited the distemper of the times. Perhaps
Blunt genuinely did not see his own irresponsibility. His will, made out
in his own now shaky hand on 13 February 1732, speaks of 'my Estate

---

[1] *Parliamentary History* VII 801-2; Carswell 258.

of above Two Hundred Thousand pounds which hath been most un-
justly taken from me by a cruel & unjust Act of parliament' and makes
provision for the eventuality of its being returned' . . . in Case it shall
at any time hereafter please God to inspire ye Nation with yt due sense
of Justice as to make any Restitution. . . .'[1] He lived out the remainder
of his life quietly, added £8000 to the sum parliament had left him, and
retired to Bath where he died, in January 1733, shortly after having
been fined by the Court of Chivalry for usurping the arms of the family
of Blount of Sodington.[2]

V

Literary reaction to South Sea Year and the events that led up to it was
traditional in outlook and metaphor. The sceptical common-sense which
held that wealth was never reliable except in coin or kind found expression in *A South Sea Ballad; or, Merry Remarks upon Exchange Alley
Bubbles. To a new Tune, call'd 'The Grand Elixir; or, the Philosopher's
Stone discover'd*'; the title of which may speak for itself.[3] Defoe, in his
prophetic *Anatomy of Exchange Alley* (1719) spoke of projectors ready
to 'Stock-jobb the Nation, Couzen the Parliament, ruffle the Bank, run
up and down the Stocks, and put the Dice upon the whole Town'. He
feared the occasion of a 'degenerated Government' and even the sub-
version of the dynasty 'for a half *per Cent*'; and the metaphors he uses
are of comets, distempers, plagues and 'the general Deluge' which
were to become the common terms in which men spoke of South Sea
Year.[4] Pope used the metaphor of the 'universal deluge' in a letter to
Atterbury; the latter, in a speech in the Lords, used that of the 'pesti-
lence'.[5] It was, however, Pope's friend George Berkeley, in his highly
significant *Essay Towards Preventing the Ruin of Great Britain* (1721),

[1] The Will of Sir John Blunt ff.5–6; Principal Probate Registry, Literary
Dept., Somerset House.
[2] *G.E.C. Baronetage* V 49.
[3] Boyer, *Political State* XX 177–9.
[4] [Daniel Defoe,] *The Anatomy of Exchange Alley: Or, a System of
Stock-Jobbing . . . By a Jobber*, 1719, 39, 62, 55, 40–42.
[5] *Corr.* II 54; *Parliamentary History*, VII 697

who connected the 'South-sea affair' with the fundamental Augustan fear that such civilization as had been achieved in Britain would decline into a new dark age. He saw the Bubble merely as the symptom of a deeper malaise, 'not the original evil', assumed a cyclical pattern of the rise and fall of civilizations, and concluded with the prospect of a people who

> degenerated, grew servile flatterers of men in power, adopted Epicurean notions, became venal, corrupt, injurious, which drew upon them the hatred of God and man, and occasioned their final ruin.[1]

All these attitudes and images are drawn together by Pope in the *Epistle to Bathurst.*

To Bathurst is on the whole about city wealth, as *To Burlington* had been about landed wealth. Further, Pope is here concerned with the new financial operations, with the Financial Revolution. Thus the couplet about wealth, which

> . . . *raises Armies in a Nation's aid,*
> *But bribes a Senate, and the Land's betray'd,*   (33–4)

seen against the developments we have been examining, reminds us that the most obvious recent instance in Britain when money had raised armies in a nation's aid was the founding of the Bank of England in 1694 to help finance William III's wars against France, which helped secure the nation of Holland; and that the most recent instance of money bribing a senate and betraying a land was undoubtedly Blunt's promotion of the South Sea Scheme. References to John Ward, papercredit, Gilbert Heathcote, Joseph Gage, South Sea Year, among many others, serve to keep the contemporary world of high finance in the focus of our attention; the allusions become more and more explicit until they climax in the apostrophe to Blunt:

> *Much injur'd Blunt! why bears he Britain's hate?*
> *A wizard told him in these words our fate:*
> '*At length Corruption, like a gen'ral flood,*
> '*(So long by watchful Ministers withstood)*

---

[1] *The Works of George Berkeley, Bishop of Cloyne,* ed. A. A. Luce and T. E. Jessop, 1948–57, VI 84–5.

> 'Shall deluge all; and *Av'rice* creeping on,
> 'Spread like a low-born mist, and blot the Sun;
> 'Statesman and Patriot ply alike the stocks,
> 'Peeress and Butler share alike the Box,
> '*And Judges* job, and *Bishops* bite the town,
> 'And mighty Dukes pack cards for half a crown.
> 'See Britain sunk in lucre's sordid charms,
> 'And France reveng'd of *ANNE's* and *EDWARD's* arms!'
> No mean Court-badge, great Scriv'ner! fir'd thy brain,
> Nor lordly Luxury, nor City Gain;
> No, 'twas thy righteous end, asham'd to see
> Senates degen'rate, Patriots disagree,
> And nobly wishing Party-rage to cease,
> To buy both sides, and give thy Country peace.   (135–52)

At the obvious level these lines attack Blunt through irony. He is presented as a hypocritical puritan (as in great measure he was) and Pope
deploys his irony by creating an account of South Sea Year such as
Blunt the puritan moralist might have given (and in one respect *did*
give). Pope's note assures us that the wizard's prophecy is in Blunt's
own vein; but without the *Secret History* and *A True State of the South
Sea Scheme* we should not know how remarkably closely it matches the
'prophetick stile' and apocalyptic tone of his utterances, or the self-
righteous contempt with which he told how 'Persons of all Ranks and
Stations' laid aside 'all manner of distance, and almost Decency', to get
stock. But Pope also inserts into the prophecy about Britain after the
Bubble the metaphor used by Defoe, by himself, and by many others,
for the Bubble Year: that of the deluge. Again, to those familiar with
Blunt's behaviour at the height of his apparent success (his acceptance
of a baronetcy, the 'splendid equipage' in which he travelled to Tunbridge, and the £500,000 from the nation which he declared to be his
just reward) the couplet beginning 'No mean Court-badge . . .' has an
especially sharp point. The phrase 'righteous end' is especially appropriate to the man who attributed his success to Providence, and who
seems to have felt himself guided by some kind of personal destiny.
And the last couplet, while certainly pointing to political corruption
since 1721, probably also alludes ironically to the reconciliation of the

Sunderland and the Walpole Whigs (proponents and opponents of the South Sea Scheme) in the spring of 1720, which, the following Autumn, John Hungerford had so publicly praised the Company for bringing about. On this reading, the opening phrase: 'Much injur'd Blunt!' ironically compliments his actual guilt and his self-righteous style.

And yet, as R. A. Brower observes, much of what Blunt 'foresees' is unironically true.[1] A consideration of Blunt's career reinforces this sense that there is ambiguity somewhere in the passage. It is not just that Pope had himself speculated in the Bubble and come off with 'half of what he imagined he had', but that Blunt had been in alliance with so many of his friends, and had helped further the schemes of those, such as Harley and Swift, whom Pope admired. An honest satire against Blunt could hardly avoid some sense of moral involvement, or at least paradox. And indeed history provided the paradox, for had not Blunt truly revealed public corruption to the Committee of Secrecy, and had not Jekyll, the politician of principle, urged that Blunt should be less severely penalised on this account? Had not Blunt's career revealed corruption as much as caused it? Had not his accusation of avarice in great and noble persons been fully justified, as Pope's note records? From this recognition springs the less obvious significance of the passage, the double irony by which Blunt really is 'Much injur'd' since, however guilty, he had been treated as a scapegoat for a widespread guilt which, in a few eminent cases, had been 'screened' and gone unpunished. Indeed, as Berkeley had written, the South Sea affair was not 'the original evil' but the sign of a deeper and more ominous distemper. Pope could now see the omen confirmed, since it was out of the South Sea affair that Walpole, who screened Sunderland and showed no mercy to Blunt, had laid the foundation for his long and (in Pope's view) shamelessly corrupt ministry. It is with this appropriateness that Pope puts into Blunt's mind the prophecy of what Berkeley had feared, and what Bolingbroke's *Craftsman* was now thundering against the government: the pervasive corruption of Walpole's administration, and the national decline which this meant. Thus the full force of the con-

[1] R. A. Brower, *Alexander Pope: The Poetry of Allusion*, Oxford, 1959, 254-5.

cluding lines of the 'prophecy' is by no means ironical in its judgement of Britain in the 1730s. Blunt is here credited with what Pope believed to be the truth.

The lines which lead up to and include the apostrophe to Sir John Blunt are not all that his career contributed to the *Epistle to Bathurst*. If the financial world of the city, Swift's 'money'd Interest', has been in Pope's sights for much of the poem, it is never so clearly focused upon as in the tale of Sir Balaam at the end. The setting and character-type identify themselves at once:

> *Where London's column, pointing at the skies*
> *Like a tall bully, lifts the head, and lyes;*
> *There dwelt a Citizen of sober fame,*
> *A plain good man, and Balaam was his name;*
> *Religious, punctual, frugal, and so forth;*
> *His word would pass for more than he was worth.*   (339–44)

This is one of Pope's composite portraits. His artfully ambiguous portraiture can, within a single poem, use an individual as a model in one portrait, and present him explicitly by his own name in another. This is the case with Sir John Cutler in the present epistle.[1] In certain portraits Pope wishes to keep alternative applications open because in the end they are not really alternatives at all but parts of the same truth; he wished his reader to think of Cutler for 'Old Cotta' but not so certainly as to exclude other and more contemporary applications. So it is with Sir Balaam. Clearly the tale does not refer to history in the specific way that the apostrophe to Blunt does, but stands as a piece of literature with more general human significance. Yet Pope could not afford to let his readers forget that he was dealing with their own society, possibly with individuals they knew themselves. Specific pointers are given, one of them to Thomas Pitt, sometime Governor of Fort St. George, Madras. Pitt 'made a great deal of money in underhand ways, was remarkably

---

[1] F. W. Bateson makes a convincing case that Pope had Sir John Cutler in mind for 'Old Cotta' (lines 179–98), but Cutler also appears under his own name in 315–34: Twickenham III ii. 108; see E. R. Wasserman on Pope's multiple allusion in such portraits, which seems to apply to Old Cotta and Sir Balaam: *Pope's 'Epistle to Bathurst'* 56–7.

pious, owned an estate in Cornwall, and bought and represented the
rotten borough of Old Sarum'. Furthermore he bought 'a Gem', the
Pitt diamond, when he was in India, and made an astronomical profit
by selling it, through the agency of John Law, to Philippe d'Orléans.[1]
Plainly Pope wanted his readers to think of Pitt, but then again of
others. For he gives us a London citizen, not an Indian *nabob*, and thus
the gem is pledged to Balaam in England, not in a far country. Other
details point not at Pitt, but at someone such as Blunt. Like Balaam Blunt
was a confirmed city-dweller; his house in Birchin Lane was hard by
Exchange Alley, where he might well be said to have been 'Constant at
. . . Change'.[2] 'His word would pass for more than he was worth' had
a sharp relevance to Blunt, whose whole career was based on the manipulation of credit, rather than solid industry or trade. Balaam having
made a fortune from the gem,

> *The Tempter saw his time; the work he ply'd;*
> *Stocks and Subscriptions pour on ev'ry side,*
> *'Till all the Daemon makes his full descent,*
> *In one abundant show'r of Cent. per Cent.,*
> *Sinks deep within him, and possesses whole,*
> *Then dubs Director, and secures his soul.*   (369-74)

Pitt had little concern with stock companies; trade and land were the
forms of wealth he sought. But 'Stocks and Subscriptions' were the very
stuff of Blunt's life. And the profusion with which they pour upon
Balaam (a new sinister Jove in a shower of—paper credit) suggests such
spectacular successes as the South Sea Company and the South Sea
Scheme when each was first launched. Pitt was never a director, but
Blunt was the chief director of the Company which drew from the
public the biggest shower of stocks and subscriptions Britain had yet
seen. Pitt was never knighted or ennobled, but Blunt became *Sir* John
and a baronet when the stocks and subscriptions which he had contrived
seemed to have raised public credit 'to a height not known before.'
Blunt had then bowed at court. Balaam's fall conforms to the lives

---

[1] Twickenham III ii. 121-2.
[2] *The Particular and Inventory of Sir John Blunt*; Sir John Blunt's Account
1; Carswell 16.

neither of Pitt nor Blunt, but is closer to Blunt's, for both Balaam and Blunt are unmasked as having betrayed the nation, are arraigned by parliament, and forsaken by the court. Many members of parliament felt that Blunt should forfeit his life, and Pope seems at one point to have expected this.[1] But if his life was not forfeit, his wealth certainly was, and Pope must have felt that the monarchy, which had been deeply involved in South Sea speculation, and which since 1721 had been closely tied to Walpole, was an indirect beneficiary of Blunt's downfall. These facts, I suggest, lie behind the conclusion of the tale:

> *Wife, son, and daughter, Satan, are thy own,*
> *His wealth, yet dearer, forfeit to the Crown:*
> *The Devil and the King divide the prize,*
> *And sad Sir Balaam curses God and dies.*　　　　(399–402)

Taken as a whole, this tale is of a man who abandons faith in providence in favour of chance and the world. What he *had* thought 'God's good Providence' he later regards as 'a lucky Hit', with all the associations of an 'atheistic' Epicurean theory of creation which this last phrase carried.[2] Blunt had attributed the height of his success to providence, yet the South Sea Scheme was really the most reckless gamble on his part. It has been observed that the tale of Sir Balaam unites in one man the avarice and profusion which are dominant themes of the contrasting portraits at the centre of the epistle. Blunt's life also shows these extremes, not only in his abandoning an earlier and simpler way of life when, at the height of his success, he travelled to Tunbridge in his new chariot, but because in the South Sea affair he recklessly staked his own and the nation's fortune on his success—and lost.

The composite portrait of Sir Balaam is probably based as much on Blunt as on Pitt. It comprehends the lives of both men, but is not confined to them in its final meaning. It would not be in place in the present essay to discuss Pope's supremely appropriate and expressive artistry in the tale of Sir Balaam. It is enough to note the great familiarity and

---

[1] See the third sentence of Pope's original note to l. 135 of *To Bathurst*, quoted at the beginning of this essay.

[2] See Howard Erskine-Hill, 'The Lucky Hit in Commerce and Creation', *N & Q* n.s. XIV, 1967, 407–8.

sureness of touch with which Pope deals with Balaam's world ('"Live
like yourself", was soon my Lady's word; And lo! two puddings
smoak'd upon the Board'), and the pervasive though slightly elusive
sense of sympathy, of Balaam never really having a chance in the ways
of his world, which is finally clinched by the epithet 'sad' in the last
line.[1]

The career of Sir John Blunt was almost entirely shaped by the
Financial Revolution. The arrangements for public credit between the
government and the City, established with the foundation of the Bank
of England, were the model for, and obstacle to, his ambition throughout his life. By comparison with the solid city men who helped found
the Bank (they included Sir Theodore Janssen, the probable author of
the *Secret History*) Blunt had small constructive importance in this
Revolution. Rather, he was the most notorious figure it threw up in
Pope's time; his importance is largely owing to the damage he did. A
close reading of *To Bathurst* does not suggest that Pope identified the
Financial Revolution with Blunt, but rather that to the poet Blunt
identified its dangers. Of all the city figures to whom Pope refers, the
most conspicuous, the most fit for his conservative argument, and the
man whom he was in a position to know most about, was Blunt. His
career displayed, besides a self-righteous style, that inability to con-
ceive, or unwillingness to regard, the good of the Commonweal, which
Swift, Bolingbroke and the Tories felt was the peculiar evil in the
notion of creating a new moneyed interest, in opposition to the landed
interest. To regard the good of the nation required a comprehensive
view of society. The ownership of land, the Tory argument contended,
obliged even the most selfish to confront the needs of others; the lives
of Blunt and Balaam, on the other hand, showed an increasingly narrow
concern with money, indeed with 'paper-credit', for its own sake. If
the poem espouses this view, it does not do so in a shallow or facile way.
Pope recognizes the abuses and follies peculiar to the landed interest;
we have seen in the apostrophe the ambiguity with which Blunt is

[1] This aspect is noticed by T. R. Edwards, Jr., *This Dark Estate: A
Reading of Pope*, Berkeley, 1963, 60–61, though he exaggerates when he
speaks of Balaam's 'amiable mindlessness'.

attacked and yet also in a sense defended; and in the tale Balaam's world seems to give him no defence against the devil. Pope has rounded out his political viewpoint with a fullness of human response to the historical facts. And where both these facts and their treatment are concerned, a consideration of Blunt's life in relation to the *Epistle to Bathurst* calls in question the dismissive view of the Twickenham editor: 'Pope's indignation with the wicked capitalists of the City of London is obviously second-hand and worked up . . . for the occasion . . . in this poem Pope too often gives the impression that he doesn't know what he is talking about.'[1] What should rather impress us is the resourcefulness and knowledge with which Pope, in a poem on the use of riches, confronted the relatively new and highly important economic developments of his age. And we should admire how Pope has assimilated material, which later poets would have rejected as unpoetic, into some of the most expressive poetry in the language.

[1] Twickenham III ii, xxxiv. It is fair to say that neither Bolingbroke nor Swift, despite their concern with the 'money'd Interest', ever produced so sustained and detailed a human exploration of the new business interests of the City as this *Epistle*.

7: Pope and the Classics

NORMAN CALLAN

OF THE four poets—Spenser, Milton, Dryden, Pope—who form the English classical pantheon, Pope is the most orthodox, at least in the matter of following in Virgil's footsteps. Spenser produced no georgic, nor did Milton; Dryden, of course, translated all Virgil's poems superbly, but the furthest he got in original 'Virgilian' composition was the aspiration to write an epic on the exploits of the Black Prince in Spain. Only Pope completely fulfils the Virgilian *cursus honorum* of pastoral, georgic, epic with the *Pastorals* (1709), *Windsor Forest* (1713) and the translation of Homer's *Iliad* (1715–1720).[1] The point is perhaps of some importance because it indicates Pope's absolute commitment to the classical tradition. The account of his early education, as given to his friend Spence and hinted at in the *Imitations of Horace*—

> Bred up at home, full early I begun
> To read in Greek, the Wrath of Peleus' Son,   (*Epistle* II ii 53–4)

would seem to be biographically dependable.[2] He was not an outstanding classical scholar like Milton, for whom Latin at any rate must have been almost as natural as English, but he had read voluminously, and, since he was very much a man of his age, the greater part of what he had read had been either Latin or Greek.

---

[1] The 'originality' of Pope's Homer will be touched on later. Pope had also made plans for an epic poem on Brutus (see Friedrich Brie, 'Pope's Brutus,' *Anglia*, LXIII, 1939, 144–85).

[2] 'Mr. Pope's first education was under a priest. . . . He set out with the design of teaching him Latin and Greek together.' 'When I had done with my priests I took to reading by myself. . . . In a few years I had dipped into a great number of the English, French, Italian, Latin, and Greek poets' (Spence §§ 14, 24).

The first half of the eighteenth century, that is to say Pope's lifetime, was not an age of great classical scholarship. Greek studies at Oxford and Cambridge were superficial (Greek was usually written without accents) and although Joshua Barnes's edition of Homer (1711) was a landmark in Homeric editing, little or no attempt was made to study the *Iliad* and the *Odyssey* in their historic content. The one great classical scholar of the age was Richard Bentley, whose text of Horace is still treated with respect, and it is significant that Bentley figures widely in Pope's satires as one of the pedant dunces whose

> *Pains, reading, study, are their just pretence,*
> *And all they want is spirit, taste, and sense.*
> *Comma's and points they set exactly right,*
> *And 'twere a sin to rob them of their Mite.*
> *Yet ne'r one sprig of Laurel grac'd these ribalds,*
> *From slashing* Bentley *down to piddling* Tibalds.[1]

But if the cultural attitude of the age towards careful scholarship was casual, or even derisive, there were certain advantages. Latin at any rate was more widely read than at any other time, and the major poets, notably Virgil and Horace, were reverenced for their achievement in establishing the poetic forms in which, as it seemed to the eighteenth century, all poetry must forever be cast. Moreover, perhaps largely as a result of this, the sense of historic remoteness which characterized the scholarship of the nineteenth century was absent. When the nineteenth-century scholars Lang, Leaf and Myers set out to translate the *Iliad* they chose a mediaeval diction as remote from their own age as possible. When Dryden tackled Virgil he sought to make him speak such English as he would have done had he lived in Dryden's age. Dryden, and Pope also, approached classical authors as if they had lived in an earlier time but not all that much earlier. They were aware of differences, of course, but they were differences of 'fashion', and in treating the classical poets *as* poets they assumed that their aims were the same as their own. This treatment of what is past as merely the antecedent of what is present is

[1] *An Epistle to Dr Arbuthnot*, 159–64. To be fair to Pope, part of his grievance against Bentley may have been the latter's egregious 'editing' of Milton (1732).

characteristic of the age as a whole. It can lead to distortion and even absurdity, but it can also produce the sense of immediacy which enables Pope to recognise and transpose the topical relevance of Horace's satire for the reign of George the second.

Born into such an age and being of a temperament which responded with great sensitivity to the cultural tone of his age, inevitably Pope developed as a classical poet. When conceiving a poem it was natural that it should be cast in terms of one of the classical kinds and in an idiom which evoked the manner of that particular kind. But his poetry is no mere historical accident: he took to imitating classical models because (he told Spence) 'I saw how defective my own things were and endeavoured to mend my manner by copying good strokes from others'.[1] Thus Pope from the outset is committed to the practice of 'imitation', and what began as an exercise developed as a habit of mind, though one with far wider implications than the 'copying' he speaks of to Spence.

Imitation is a word which nowadays has derogatory associations, suggesting plagiarism and lack of originality. For Pope's age, however, it had the meaning of a specific form of literary creation. Dryden, in his discussion of modes of translation, had cited it as a procedure 'where the Translator (if now he has not lost that name), assumes the liberty not only to vary from the Words and Sense, but to forsake them both as he sees occasion'.[2] This is one sense in which Pope accepts the term, and he defends the practice in the *Guardian* (no. 12):

> But over and above a just Painting of Nature, a learned Reader will find a new Beauty superadded in a happy Imitation of some famous Ancient, as it revives in his Mind the pleasure he took in his first reading such an author. Such Copyings as these give that kind of double Delight which we perceive when we look upon the Children of a beautiful Couple; where the Eye is not more charm'd by the Symmetry of the Parts, than the Mind by observing the Resemblance transmitted from Parents to their offspring, and the mingled features of the Father and the Mother.[3]

[1] Spence § 46.
[2] Preface to *Ovid's Epistles* (1680). It was in a later edition of this collection that Pope's *Sapho to Phaon* first appeared.
[3] *The Prose Works of Alexander Pope*, ed Norman Ault, 90–91.

But Pope's application of the practice is much wider than this: it goes back to Horace's advice in the *Ars Poetica*, which Pope echoes in the *Essay on Criticism*:

> *Be* Homer*'s Works your* Study, *and* Delight,
> *Read them by Day, and meditate by Night,*
> *Thence form your Judgment, thence your Maxims bring,*
> *And trace the Muses* upward *to their* Spring.[1]

These are Pope's instructions to the critic, but equally they describe his own practice as a poet. All Pope's major poems are linked in one way or another to classical prototypes, some more closely than others, and by studying the nature of some of these links one can learn a good deal about his poetry.

It is not surprising that one of Pope's first 'originals' should have been Ovid. By nineteenth-century classical standards Ovid is in the second rank of poets, but he has been the source-book of mythology for most English poets from Chaucer onwards, and, what is more important here, he has a style which is easily recognised, and, unlike the more subtle styles of Virgil or Horace, adaptable to English. Baldly described, this consists in an elaborate and sophisticated technique of antithesis applied to an imagined situation in which there is a conflict to be stated between the two extremes of passionate longing and passionate reproach. It is dramatically effective in that it presents with vivid intensity the dialectic of sexual passion, but it is unreal in that the reader is always aware of the intervening poet who is reducing a situation which is confused to one of analytical lucidity.

One of Pope's earliest published poems is his translation of the *Epistle of Sapho to Phaon* (the fifteenth letter of the *Heroides*). The sensitiveness with which he has caught the mood of Ovidian dialectic is evident from the opening couplet:

> *Say, lovely Youth, that dost my Heart command,*
> *Can* Phaon*'s Eyes forget his* Sapho*'s Hand?*

Here Ovid's typical antithesis between the laborious hand and the spontaneous eye is presented with expert concision, perhaps more slick

---

[1] 124–7. Cf. *Ars Poetica*, 268–9: 'vos exemplaria Graeca/nocturne versate manu, versate diurna.'

than the original. The heroic couplet also fits the Ovidian elegiac like a glove, and the whole piece is a skilful reproduction of both the content and the manner of the original in the form which Dryden has called 'Paraphrase, or Translation with Latitude, where the Author is kept in view by the Translator, so as never to be lost, but his Words are not so strictly followed as his Sense, and that too is admitted to be amplified, but not alter'd'.

In *Sapho to Phaon* Pope's relationship to his original is simply that of a translator whose business is to render his author justly. How complex this kind of relationship became will appear when we look at the translation of Homer's *Iliad*. First, however, it might be as well to touch on *Eloisa to Abelard*, another Ovidian heroic epistle, but this time with no direct connexion to a Latin original. The material for this poem Pope got from John Hughes's prose translation from the French of the imaginary letters of Abelard to Eloisa (1713): moreover the writing of fictitious heroic epistles from historical figures had been fashionable in English literature since Elizabeth's day. So he was already well furnished with materials and models. But the poem is essentially an original creation: it is, in fact, a perfect example of 'imitation' as described in the *Guardian* essay. In the first place Pope seizes on the right form for his purpose, one which evokes echoes of an earlier writer but into which he infuses an imaginative passion seldom present in Ovid's statuesque creations.[1] This form he implements in a manner and language which are perfectly Ovidian and yet entirely personal. His evocations of sympathetic landscape:

> methinks we wandring go
> *Thro' dreary wastes, and weep each other's woe;*
> *Where round some mould'ring tow'r pale ivy creeps,*
> *And low-brow'd rocks hang nodding o'er the deeps.*
> *Sudden you mount! you becken from the skies;*
> *Clouds interpose, waves roar, and winds arise.*
> *I shriek, start up, the same sad prospect find,*
> *And wake to all the griefs I left behind.*   (241–8)

---

[1] I think Ovid's 'Ariadne Theseo' (*Heroides* X) comes nearest to the spirit of *Eloisa to Abelard*, but I have found no direct echoes.

recall Ovid's but at the same time are in keeping with the Gothick manner of Pope's own day. His analysis of conflicting passions uses all the subtlety of Ovidian antithesis:

> *I waste the Matin lamp in sighs for thee,*
> *Thy image steals between my God and me,*
> *Thy voice I seem in ev'ry hymn to hear,*
> *With ev'ry bead I drop too soft a tear.*   (267–70)

but is full of religious innuendo which gives the situation complexity and immediacy. *Eloisa to Abelard* is a *tour de force*, but it is unique of its kind, for Pope has not only re-created the poetry of a past poet; in the process he has created a poem which is entirely contemporary and personal. Nothing could better illustrate the way Pope reacted to what he read, absorbed it, and used it for his own poetic purposes.

Pope's *Iliad* (Bentley is reputed to have said that you must not call it Homer) was a tremendous undertaking. As a project it was conceived about 1707, and completed in 1720, the volumes appearing at yearly intervals from 1715 onwards. The translation of the *Odyssey*, in which he had the help of collaborators, followed, and was completed in 1726. Thus Homer took up some twenty years of his working life, and nothing could illustrate more clearly his total commitment to what he regarded as the greatest of all poems by the greatest of all poets. Basically Pope's relation to his original is that of a translator (in Dryden's sense of 'paraphrase'). He worked conscientiously from the Greek text, and, as 'he did not abound in Greek' (Johnson's words), he sought the help of orthodox Greek scholars, especially his friend Thomas Parnell, who contributed an 'Essay on the Life, Writings and Learning of Homer' to the first volume. But Pope's *Iliad* is much more than this. In the first place he attaches to his rendering a mass of 'Observations' which take up more space than the translation itself.[1] These cover commentary on

---

[1] Pope's *Iliad* ran to six volumes, in itself a formidable task for the modern reader. Worse still, since the end of the eighteenth century the commentaries have been excluded from printed texts generally available, until Maynard Mack's magnificent Twickenham edition in 1967. In spite of these difficulties, no one can have an adequate understanding of Pope's poetry without some acquaintance with his *Iliad* as originally

Homeric 'antiquities' (drawn largely from the medieval Greek commentator Eustathius of Thessalonica), discussions of points of Homeric
Greek, and, above all, Pope's own comments on the interpretation of
Homer in the widest possible field of morals, presentation of character,
and the *ordonnance* of the poem as a whole. These last, together with
Pope's own 'Preface' are an essential part of the whole work, and when
taken into consideration justify the view of Pope's *Iliad* as an original
composition, in which he achieves what was for the age the summit of
literary creation, the epic poem.

There is another reason why the poem should be approached in this
light. Since the early nineteenth century our knowledge of the Homeric
poems and the age in which they came into being has increased enor-
mously. The genesis of the poems and the existence of a single author
have been called in question. With the increase of knowledge Homer
has come to be seen as more remote and perhaps more tragically profound. None of these problems of the modern scholar existed for Pope
(though Bentley had an inkling of them). Even the difference between
'primary' and 'secondary' epic was not recognized. For Pope, as for
Dryden, the *Iliad* and the *Odyssey* were poems on the same footing as
the *Aeneid*, and their authors were to be critically compared, often very
perceptively.[1] In the twentieth century, therefore, to read Pope's
Iliad as simply a version of the original is to court the Chesterfieldian
response that it is a poem about a bully and a whore. It must be seen as a
document in sensibility—both Pope's own sensibility and that of his age.
Nowhere is Pope's passionate belief in literature as the index of morals
to be seen more clearly (because free from irony) than in his Observations on Homer's characters. For instance in Book I, the quarrel between
Agamemnon and Achilles, his comment on the latter is:

> Here, where the Passion of Anger grows loud, it seems proper
> to prepare the Reader and prevent his Mistake in the Character of
> *Achilles*, which might shock him in several Particulars following.
> . . . [The poet] resolved to sing the Consequences of Anger: he

---

published. At least Pope's Preface must be read. Maynard Mack's
general introduction (Twickenham VII) is the best account and evaluation of the poem.
[1] See especially the comparisons in Pope's Preface.

consider'd what Virtues and Vices would most conduce to bring
his moral out of the Fable. . . . And thus we must take his *Achilles*, not as a meer heroick dispassion'd Character, but as one compounded of Courage and Anger. . . . These are the Lights and
Shades of his Character, which Homer has heighten'd and darken'd in Extreams. . . . When Characters thus mix'd are well
conducted, tho' they be not morally beautiful quite through, they
conduce more to the end, and are still poetically perfect. . . .

(*Observation xxiii, at line 155*)

If Pope's version is read without the comment it can easily be seen as a
neatly antithetical piece of Ovidisation which not only misrepresents
the directness of Homer but gives a false impression of the gravity of
Pope's attitude to his original.

Pope's use of the antithesis in his rendering, which can only briefly
be touched on here, is aimed always at making plain the implicit moral.
Thus Homer says 'Apollo . . . angry with the King, sent a dread plague
throughout the host, and the people were being destroyed'. Pope renders this:

> The King of Men his Rev'rend Priest defy'd,
> And, for the King's Offence, the People dy'd.   (I 13–14)

The greatness of Homer lies in the stark, unpointed simplicity. As for
Pope's version, perhaps we must not call it Homer, but it is Pope at his
most deeply committed. He did not recognize the existential tragedy of
Homer: he attempts always to give it a moral, even Christian slant,
which is why the work should be read in the light not of modern scholarship but of Pope's own age.

While Pope was still 'involved' with Homer he published three
other works which have classical affinities. These were the *Pastorals,
Windsor Forest* and *The Rape of the Lock*.

The *Pastorals* were written (Pope tells us) when he was sixteen, and
passed through the hands of several of his literary friends, during which
time they were probably much polished and revised. There are four
poems named after the four seasons. The models are primarily Virgil's
Eclogues, but the titles suggest Spenser's *Shepherd's Calendar*, and the
opening lines of 'Summer' echo Spenser's *January*, as Pope tells us in his
first note to the poem. Other 'originals' are Theocritus, Bion and Mos-

chus, but the poems are full of echoes from English pastoral poetry, including Dryden's translation of the *Eclogues*.

The pastoral poems are 'imitations'. Structurally most of them resemble Virgil, particularly in the use of the amoebean stanza form, and
their *dramatis personae* are, like Virgil's, shepherds whose manners are
'not too polite nor too rustic'. But, though the resemblances are apparent, there is not the same astonishing empathy as is to be found in
Eloisa to Abelard, where Pope seems possessed with the very spirit of
Ovid. In Virgil's *Eclogues*, despite the 'artificiality' of which many have
complained, there are always transcendental nuances which suggest
spiritual relationships between man and nature only possible for a poet
living in a pantheistic age. Though Pope (in 'Winter') imitates the apotheosis of Daphnis in Virgil's fifth eclogue there is nothing like the ecstasy of Virgil's,

> *ipsi laetitia voces ad sidera iactant*
> *intonsi montes: ipsae iam carmina rupes,*
> *ipsa sonant arbusta: deus, deus ille, Menalca . . .*[1]

which Milton catches so admirably at the end of *Lycidas*.

This quality in Virgil Pope replaces by delicate allusion and exquisite skill in depicting formalised landscape:

> *Here where the* Mountains *less'ning as they rise,*
> *Lose the low Vales, and steal into the Skies,*
> *While lab'ring Oxen, spent with Toil and Heat,*
> *In their loose Traces from the Field retreat;*
> *While curling Smokes from Village-Tops are seen,*
> *And the fleet Shades glide o'er the dusky Green.*

('Autumn', 59–64)

Passages such as this and the better known 'Where-e'er you walk' from
'Summer' are no bad substitute for Virgil's ethereal pantheism which no
one has ever been able to reproduce.[2]

[1] 62–4. E. V. Rieu (Penguin Classics) has the words, though not the
ecstasy: 'For very joy the shaggy mountains raise a clamour to the
stars; the rocks burst into song, and the plantations speak. "He is a god,"
they say; "Menalcas, he is a god."'

[2] The fifth of Pope's *Pastorals, The Messiah* 'Written in imitation of
Virgil's Pollio', was published separately. Discussion of it does not

It is for this kind of thing that one first reads *Windsor Forest* (1713). The inverted landscape reflected in the river:

> *Oft in her Glass the musing Shepherd spies*
> *The headlong Mountains and the downward Skies,*
> *The wat'ry Landskip of the pendant Woods,*
> *And absent Trees that tremble in the Floods;*
> *In the clear azure Gleam the Flocks are seen,*
> *And floating Forests paint the Waves with Green.*   (211–16)

is evidence of Pope's precise observation touched with a delicate fancy. But *Windsor Forest* is not a pastoral (in the technical sense anyway), it is Pope's contribution to the Georgic tradition and, like Virgil's poems, carries a considerable weight of patriotic implication.[1] The direct ancestor of the poem is Denham's *Cooper's Hill*, which is the first in the English tradition of what Johnson in his Life of Denham calls 'local poetry, of which the fundamental subject is some particular landscape to be poetically described, with the addition of such embellishments as may be supplied by historical reflexion or incidental meditation.' Structurally *Windsor Forest* resembles *Cooper's Hill* quite closely, with the 'Virgilian' myth of Lodona replacing Denham's stag hunt; but the effect of the two poems is literally an age apart. The attraction of Denham's poem lies in the nervous logical texture of the thought which is closer to the way of the Metaphysicals (the poem was written in 1642) than to Pope's more leisurely mental processes. Despite the title it contains little or no description of landscape: Windsor and St Paul's are used to symbolize points of conflict. The body of the poem is made up of abstract or near-abstract meditations on the nature of sovereign power. It has about it a certain air of political urgency which recalls some of Horace's political odes in Book III.

Windsor Forest, on the other hand, is Virgilian, and all the more

---

belong here, because, apart from the opening lines, which are a 'rejection' of Virgil's 'Messianic Eclogue', it draws its material from passages in *Isaiah*. These it develops periphrastically in the heroic diction which foreshadows Pope's *Iliad*.

[1] For a full and interesting discussion of the relation of *Windsor Forest* to the *Georgics*, see John Chalker, *The English Georgic*, 1970.

attractively so because most of the Virgilian elements are *suggestive* of the kind of things Virgil is doing in the *Georgics* rather than direct resemblances. The *Georgics* was a patriotic poem, written to glorify the yeoman tradition of the Republic, and at the same time the principate of Augustus as a return (or at least an approach) to the Golden Age. Pope's motivation is similar but not the same. *Windsor Forest* celebrates the Peace of Utrecht, the reign of Queen Anne and the fact that

> *Peace and Plenty tell, a STUART reigns.*

The implications are thus less profound though they are serious enough (*Windsor Forest* is no *jeu d'esprit*). Again, the *Georgics* is an heroic poem— that is to say Virgil is presenting a rural subject in heroic diction which elevates it to epic level because the theme (the greatness of Rome) *is of universal importance*. This is something many eighteenth-century imitators of the *Georgics* did not fully grasp. They regarded it as a brilliant trick (Virgil 'breaks the clods and tosses the dung about with an air of gracefulness'[1]) which they were always trying to emulate. Pope does not make this mistake. He creates his own heroic diction, which is Miltonic rather than Virgilian:

> *With slaught'ring Guns th'unweary'd Fowler roves,*
> *When Frosts have whiten'd all the naked Groves;*
> *Where Doves in Flocks the leafless Trees o'ershade,*
> *And lonely Woodcocks haunt the watry Glade.*
> *He lifts the Tube, and levels with his Eye;*
> *Strait a short Thunder breaks the frozen Sky.*   (125–30)

and in this he celebrates what is really the subject of the poem, the ordered landscape of the Thames valley and all it implies:

> *Here Hills and Vales, the Woodland and the Plain,*
> *Here Earth and Water seem to strive again,*
> *Not* Chaos-*like together crush'd and bruis'd,*
> *But as the World, harmoniously confus'd:*
> *Where Order in Variety we see,*
> *And where, tho' all things differ, all agree.*   (11–16)

---

[1] Addison, 'An Essay on Virgil's *Georgics*' (1697), in his *Miscellaneous Works*, ed A. C. Guthkelch, 1914, II 9.

The relationship to Virgil is thus a fragile, allusive one, which suggests rather than imitates—the only direct imitation is the myth of Lodona, which seems to me the one forced part of the poem, in the worst Lilian Gish manner—and is quite unlike his powerful evocation of Ovid in *Eloisa to Abelard*. Pope, it would seem, wisely recognizes the inimitability of Virgil, and this Georgic poem is both stronger and more delicate because he is content to suggest indirectly.

The Rape of the Lock and *The Dunciad*, Pope's two mock-epic poems, have an entirely different relation to classical originals from anything we have seen so far. In previous instances he has been concerned to widen the range of a poem by evoking likenesses of one kind or another to an earlier one. In these two he is using an original (the epic poem as a whole) as a contrast in order to limit his subject by pointing out social absurdity in the one case, and moral and literary vulgarity (which he calls 'Dulness') in the other. This is perhaps only a long way of saying that the two poems are parodies, but the term needs close definition. Most parodies mock their originals by exaggerating stylistic characteristics in a banal context. Lewis Carroll's 'Sitting on a Gate' for instance, derides the solemnities of Wordsworth, and A. E. Housman's 'Fragment of a Greek Tragedy' (perhaps rather shockingly) of Aeschylus. But this is not Pope's form of parody. To mock Homer or Virgil or Milton thus would be for him the ultimate blasphemy. When he presents Arabella Fermor's toilet in terms of Here adorning herself to beguile Zeus (*Iliad XIV*, 153ff.) he is literally comparing small things with great in order to stress the moral pettiness of his own age. It is a dangerous technique, but Pope carries it off, chiefly, I think because the details of both passages are aesthetically exquisite. All the same, Pope is uneasy about the morality of the episode in the *Iliad*.[1] Similarly in the *Dunciad* ('B', II 69ff.), when the degraded morality of Curll is presented in terms of excremental filth, Pope echoes episodes from the *Iliad* and the *Aeneid* in which the physical details are crudely disgusting, pointing this out in an ironical note, so that the effect is an obscene caricature of Curll, which in no way reflects on Homer or Virgil. It is by his inspired tact in choosing just the right episodes from his originals for

[1] See Pope's *Iliad* XIV 199ff., and his long Observation at this point.

parody that Pope achieves his satiric purpose, and this in turn points to his intimate knowledge of his originals. When he wrote the *Rape of the Lock* he was already contemplating translating Homer and had the *Iliad* at his fingertips. Even here, however, in the first version he forgets Homer's gods and goddesses, and it is only with the addition of the Sylphs and Gnomes in 1714 that the poem attains its perfectly proportioned artistic form. By the time the *Dunciad* begins to emerge Pope has finished with Homer, and structurally at least the poem depends more on the *Aeneid*. But both the *Rape of the Lock* and the *Dunciad* are clear evidence of Pope's total immersion in the great epic poems of the past. They are also a remarkable indication of how widely this epic poetry must have been known in Pope's day. True, the *Dunciad* has copious referential notes, but it is obvious that the success of the poem must have depended largely on the reader's recognition of the travesties from his own knowledge. Once again this is an argument for reading Pope's *Homer* not as a crib but as a poem of Pope's own day. Nowadays Pope's *Dunciad* at least claims priority over his *Iliad*, but a study of the latter can throw much light on Pope's later work.

The last of Pope's classical forebears is the Roman poet Horace. As it affects almost all his mature poetry this relationship is by far the most important. It is also less direct and harder to define than those which have been touched on so far. Since it is concerned almost exclusively with Horace's *Satires* and *Epistles*, and since these are not the most widely known of Horace's work, it would perhaps be as well to say a brief word about them first.

Horace's *Satires* (two books) and *Epistles* (two books) are hexameter poems treating topics ranging from comic descriptions of everyday existence to ethical discussions on how to live the good life. These topics have one point in common: they are all contemporary—that is to say they treat social life as it was lived and felt in Augustan Rome, and (almost always) their focal point is the poet himself, either his own experiences or his reflexions on how to live honestly in the corrupt society of his day. Many are autobiographical (e.g. the sixth satire of the first book), and some (e.g. the first satire of the second book, which Pope imitated) are defences against attacks on the writing of satire, for which Horace, in his early days as a satirist, had been frequently assailed.

Some of the first satires are full of references, usually pretty opprobrious, to Horace's contemporaries,[1] but as he becomes established in the circle of his patron Maecenas the personal references diminish, giving way to more general reflexions on social follies and corruptions.

So much for the subject-matter of Horace's satire: even more important, as regards Pope at any rate, is its tone and manner. Often this is called 'conversational'; but such a description must cover much more than an easy unpretentiousness of language and an apparently casual felicity in handling what is, in fact, a strictly demanding verse form. The central characteristic is the implied presence of an audience, usually one person, a friend, who plays sometimes an active part (for instance Horace's lawyer friend Trebatius, in *Satires* II i),[2] more often a passive but still positive one. The presence of this willing listener—for that he should be a listener rather than a reader is essential to the tone—who *can* intervene, even if he does not, is more evident in the *Epistles*, which are addressed to specified people, than in the *Satires*, but it is always there in the *Satires*, if sometimes only by implication. Thus, in *Satires* II ii, the auditory is implied as a group of friends who are invited (*discite*) to hear Ofellus's discourse on plain living.[3]

The effect of this shadowy but very present audience is to give a dramatic quality to what is often abstract ethical meditation. But it also implies the presence of the writer-speaker as a clearly defined personality. This, of course, is Horace himself, but it is Horace under varied

[1] 'Flute girls, drug quacks, beggars, actresses, buffoons' (*Satires* I ii 1). (In this and all following citations from Horace, text and translation are from the Loeb edition of Horace's *Satires, Epistles and Ars Poetica*, ed. H. R. Fairclough, rev. edn 1929.) Pope (*Sober Advice* (*from Horace*), 1–2) renders this line as follows:

> *The Tribe of Templars, Play'rs, Apothecaries,*
> *Pimps, Poets, Wits, Lord* Fanny's, *Lady* Mary's . . .

[2] Fortescue, in Pope's *Imitation*.

[3] Pope's *Imitation* expands as well as modernizes Horace:

> *What, and how great, the Virtue and the Art*
> *To live on little with a chearful Heart,*
> *(A Doctrine sage, but truly none of mine)*
> *Lets talk, my friends, but talk before we dine . . .*
> *Hear Bethel's Sermon. . . .* (1ff.)

disguises. The technique of the satiric *persona* he clearly describes in the tenth satire of the first book:

> *est brevitate opus, ut currat sententia neu se*
> *impediat verbis lassas onerantibus auris;*
> *et sermone opus est modo tristi, saepe iocoso,*
> *defendente vicem modo rhetoris atque poetae,*
> *interdum urbani, parcentis viribus atque*
> *exenuantis eas consulto.*[1]

Thus the speaker is Horace, but Horace imaginatively projected as wit, buffoon, patriot, moralist, a friend and host, and so on.

This immediately raises questions of the motivation of the satirist which cannot be gone into here. Doubtless the ostensible aim of satire is to expose vice or folly by mockery or direct condemnation. But in Horace's case it obviously affords a medium for self-dramatization in which he can (literally) express *himself*, while avoiding the reproof of being a cantankerous misanthrope. The psychological implications of this are probably far-reaching, but the point here is that the deployment of the *persona* gives a line not only on the satirist's technical virtuosity but on his basic motive for writing satire. In other words I am suggesting that Horace as a satirist is not primarily a moral philosopher but (in no bad sense) an exhibitionist; and this, in turn, seems to indicate the attractive bond between him and Pope.

Even from such a brief account of Horace's satire the reasons for the hold which it had on the eighteenth century, and especially on the outstanding poet of the age, will, I hope, be evident. The life of Augustan Rome and Augustan London was affluent, sophisticated and corrupt. Poetry (good and bad) was a widespread social activity, and could therefore be a moral force. The immediate audience for whom both poets wrote (Augustus, Maecenas and their circle of cultivated friends

---

[1] 'You need terseness that the thought may run on, and not become entangled in verbiage that weighs upon wearied ears. You need a style now grave, often gay, in keeping with the role, now of orator or poet, at times of the wit who holds his strength in check and husbands it with wisdom' (9–14). The original quotation was used by Pope as an epigraph to the 'Epistles to Several Persons' (*Works*, 1740).

in Horace's case, in Pope's a body of friends which formed a kind of supporters club, and included such notable people as Atterbury, Swift, Arbuthnot, Burlington and Bathurst), was cultured and influential. The intellectual temper of both ages was acquiescent rather than speculative, but at the same time philosophical, seeking to interpret, though not question, universal laws in terms of experience. The two cities, Rome and London, were noisy, brilliant and vulgar, a fact which lent itself to the fiction of fastidious withdrawal from the *profanum vulgus*. Thus Pope, imitating from the second epistle of Horace's second book:

> *'Oh but a Wit can study in the Streets,*
> *And raise his Mind above the Mob he meets.'*
> *Not quite so well however as one ought;*
> *A Hackney-Coach may chance to spoil a Thought,*
> *And then a nodding Beam, or Pig of Lead,*
> *God knows, may hurt the very ablest Head.*
> *Have you not seen at Guild-hall's narrow Pass,*
> *Two Aldermen dispute it with an Ass?*
> *And Peers give way, exalted as they are,*
> *Ev'n to their own S-r-v-nce in a Carr?*
> *Go, lofty Poet! and in such a Croud,*
> *Sing thy sonorous Verse—but not aloud.*[1]

The points of similarity, physical and metaphysical, in the life of the two cities are innumerable, and part of the appeal of Pope's *Imitations* lies in his skill in finding up-to-the-minute equivalences, whether of persons or ideas. But his affinity with Horace does not consist solely or even principally in this. When, in 1733, he was in the midst of the uproar created by his supposed slandering of his friend Chandos in the *Epistle to Burlington*, Bolingbroke pointed out to him how the first satire of Horace's second book would 'fit his [Pope's] case'. The poem is one of Horace's defences of himself as a satirist: Pope imitated it, and published it within

---

[1] 98–109. Horace (70–80): '"Yes, but the streets are clear, so that nothing need hinder you in conning verses." In hot haste rushes a contractor with mules and porters; a huge crane is hoisting now a stone and now a beam; mournful funerals jostle massive wagons; this way runs a mad dog: that way rushes a mud-bespattered sow. Now go, and thoughtfully con melodious verses.'

a few days. This was the first of the *Imitations of Horace*, and it is to be noted that Pope undertakes it because Horace's case fits his own, not merely in circumstantial details but because Horace's defence was of a kind that Pope could and would wish to make. Moreover it must be admitted that in giving his detractors 'an answer from Horace' he was in some measure using the Latin poet as a shield. Perhaps it was 'more dignified', as he claimed; but it cannot be escaped that in this and all the other *Imitations* he was dodging some of the odium for his attacks on contemporaries by being able to point to a classical 'original', just as he probably felt that he was toning down the acrimony of the *Dunciad* by presenting his butts as Homeric heroes. Another point may perhaps be noted in this connexion. In attacking the manners and morals of Roman society Horace had not pulled any punches: the second satire of the first book (Pope entitled his *Imitation Sober Advice (from Horace)*) is a masterpiece of scurrilous indecency. In this Pope seldom fell short of his model. But with him the animus is perhaps alleviated by a kind of inverted patriotism. By equating London with Rome, even on the worst possible terms, he was at least making a comparison with the greatest city the world had known.

It would be wrong, however, to seek for the nexus between the two poets solely in the *Imitations of Horace*. In the early *Essay on Criticism* the affinity is already to be seen, not only in the balanced tone and epigrammatic phrasing but in the way moral and literary ideals are linked with and illustrated by the experience of day-to-day life.

> *First follow NATURE, and your Judgment frame*
> *By her just Standard, which is still the same* . . . .
> Art *from that Fund each* just Supply *provides,*
> *Works* without Show, *and* without Pomp *presides*. . . .
>
> (68ff.)

Here the relationship between creative nature and art is presented in a metaphor from parliamentary finance. This is essentially the Horatian way—Do you think Virtue but words, and forests but firewood ?[1]—and

---

[1] *Epistle* I vi 31f. Pope has:
   Who Virtue and a Church alike disowns,
   Thinks that but words, and this but brick and stones. (65–6)

Pope has absorbed it perfectly even this early in his poetic career. After he had 'stoop'd to Truth, and moraliz'd his song' (about 1730) there is not one of his poems (except possibly the *Dunciad*) which has not at least some tincture of Horace, and mostly they are designed and expressed 'in the Horatian way'. Thus he tells Bolingbroke that the *Essay on Man* is to be 'a system of ethics in the Horatian way', and a reading of the first twenty lines shews it to be miraculously such. The *Moral Essays* (more properly called 'Epistles to Several Persons') are, in fact Horatian verse epistles, deploying all the Horatian skill in suggesting an auditor and a debate that has already been going on between the poet and his friend for some time. In the opening line of the first epistle (*To Cobham*),

> *Yes, you despise the man to Books confin'd* . . .

that 'yes' is a masterstroke of Horatian implication. In the *Moral Essays* too are to be found all Horace's skill in apt illustration, ranging from the personal reference to the extended moral fable, and the consummate flexibility in handling an exacting poetic form.

The *Moral Essays* are essentially Horatian poems, but the 'most Horatian thing' Pope ever wrote is the *Epistle to Dr Arbuthnot*, which was later called the *Prologue to the Satires*, and rightly finds its place among the *Imitations of Horace*. There is, strictly speaking, no Horatian 'original' for the *Epistle to Dr Arbuthnot*, but I think the starting point may have been the sixth satire of Horace's first book, which is almost entirely an autobiographical poem. If this is right it is worth reading the sixth satire to see how exactly Horace 'fits Pope's case', and also how Pope expands and develops what is little more than an autobiographical sketch into a complete *apologia pro vita sua*. Above all we can see Pope adapting the Horatian satiric *persona*. In the implied dialogue between Horace and Maecenas ('You will say . . .', 'What then shall we do . . . ?') the poetic 'ego' is both the poet expressing his deepest affections and the projected image of the poor boy who has made good. In the *Epistle to Dr Arbuthnot* the poet-speaker is much more fully dramatized. He is the urbane man, pestered by fools, and also let it be said, the venomously vituperative enemy of Sporus. But in this passage particularly the *persona* is also the poet championing virtue and attacking vice—to Virtue only, and her Friends a Friend.[1] Moreover, as we have seen elsewhere, there is alleviation of the bitterness, this time in the delicate self-mockery which is, perhaps, the greatest charm of the poem, and which detractors of the Sporus passage are apt to forget. The image projected is indeed a complex one.

To anyone reading the Horatian 'originals' alongside Pope's *Imitations* it must occur that Pope's poems are very 'unlike' Horace's. The impact of Horace comes from his pithy abruptness. Pope is expansive, discursive, full of evocative images—'Bare the mean Heart that lurks beneath a Starr' comes from Horace's 'strip off the skin with which each strutted, all bedecked, though foul within'[2]—and as a versifier he is amazingly fluent, the very antithesis of his original. In fact, risking blasphemy, I think Pope the better poet. But in the use of the *persona* to project the inner personality he and Horace are at one. Pope was always a poet of morals. In his earlier poetry (*Windsor Forest* and the *Essay on Criticism*) he implied standards of patriotism, morality, and, most of all, the identity of artistic and moral values. These standards persist throughout the whole of his poetic work, but it is not until he finds himself fully in the Horatian satiric *persona* that he attains his true freedom of expression. In this Horace and he go hand in hand in song.

In a necessarily restricted essay it is not easy to avoid suggesting that Pope's poetry cannot be appreciated without a comprehensive knowledge of Latin and Greek. Nothing could be further from the truth. As I have pointed out, Pope was not a classical scholar, and it is doubtful whether he would have been grateful for being called one. I suspect that he always read Latin (even Horace) with some difficulty and Greek (even Homeric Greek) with a good deal more. Ovid may have been the exception, and it may be that he learnt some of the art of antithesis from the *Heroides*. Johnson says of Pope's translation that 'Homer doubtless owes to his translator many Ovidian graces which are not exactly suited to his character.' But even this may be doubted. There were plenty of English poets writing antithetical couplets (Dryden not the least) for Pope to learn from. As for the other Ovidian devices which he

---

[1] *Satire II i (To Fortescue)*, 121.
[2] *Satire II i*, 108. Horace, 64–5.

uses—the periphrases and rhetorical questions—they are at least partly Miltonic, for Milton was a great admirer of Ovid, and *Paradise Lost* abounds in mannerisms acquired from him. Even the heroic diction, which Wordsworth and Coleridge so abominated, is derived from Virgil through Milton. A knowledge of Horace's *Satires* and *Epistles* is chiefly desirable to emphasize the parallels between Rome and London, not to 'explain' Pope's *Imitations*.

On the other hand Pope *had* read widely in Latin and Greek, and what he had read became embedded, in transmuted form, in his poetry. This was the way of thinking and writing in his age. But more important is the fact that Pope was a poet who saw life through literature— London, as it were, through Horatian Rome. As Reuben Brower has demonstrated, his poetry is a tissue of allusion. Naturally much of this allusion is to classical poets because they were *the* poets of his age. Even so the allusion is, quite as often as not, to an English translator—Dryden, or Sandys, or Creech. What matters in understanding Pope's poetry is not a precise knowledge of classical reference but a recognition that the classical element is there, and a knowledge of what it stood for with Pope.

The writer who sees life through the spectacles of books runs the risk of literary remoteness. What saves Pope from this is his passionate conviction that good literature and good life were synonymous; and that a corruption of literary standards meant a corruption of moral standards. These standards, both literary and moral, derive from the great writers of the classical epochs, and it is in this that a recognition of Pope's classical affinities is important.

8: *Pope and Criticism*

DUNCAN ISLES

NO HARD and fast lines can ever be drawn between literary theory, the principles of literary criticism, and creative literature. It is obvious that great literature is in itself a form of implied literary theory, in that it discovers, exploits, and passes on new literary possibilities, and necessitates the re-consideration or amendment of existing critical principles. Alexander Pope belongs to that select group of creators (including Sidney and Dryden before his time, and Johnson, Wordsworth, Coleridge, Shelley, Arnold, James, and T. S. Eliot in subsequent times) who have significantly extended and reinforced the theoretical elements implicit in their writing by their explicit published discussion of matters relating to criticism, and their analyses of the works of other writers. In terms of both implicit and overt criticism, Pope's ability and influence dwarf that of any other writer in his lifetime, with the possible exception of Addison.[1] The following discussion will survey the nature and particular emphases of Pope's literary criticism. This survey will be conducted in three main sections, the first dealing with the early critical discussion culminating in *An Essay on Criticism*, the second with the 1711–1729 period when Pope's activities as a literary theorist and practical critic were at their height, and the third with the critical considerations embodied in the great satires and imitations of the 1730s. The

[1] Although Pope is extremely concerned with, and sensitive to, the literary, cultural, moral, and philosophical problems of his own day, his critical principles are largely derived from his predecessors—notably Aristotle, Horace, Longinus, Boileau, Dryden, and Swift. With regard to his relationship with contemporary critics, particular attention should be paid to John Dennis: see his *Critical Works*, ed. E. N. Hooker, 2 vols., Baltimore 1939–43.

aspects of Pope's criticism which have been given particular attention here are its emphasis on strength and emotional impact (operating within a framework of controlled rationality) rather than subservience to any set of 'rules'; its generally enlightened treatment of the complex relationship between the various and to some extent competing factors influencing the creative writer; its mingling of overt and ironic modes of exposition; and, finally, its salutary tendency towards amalgamating purely literary considerations with wider and deeper social, cultural, and moral issues.

The publication of *An Essay on Criticism* in May 1711 was immediately preceded by Pope's 'great reading period' in Windsor Forest. His reading between about 1701 and 1709 had included 'all the best critics' as well as 'almost all the English, French, and Latin poets of any name, the minor poets, Homer and some other of the greater Greek poets in the original, and Tasso and Ariosto in translations' (Spence §44). From 1705 to 1709, the Twickenham editors suggest (I 202), his critical reading was consciously directed towards gathering material for *An Essay on Criticism*, the formal writing of which was probably under way by the latter year. His poetic experiments had begun in early childhood, and had included drama, translation, and an epic poem on Deucalion, culminating in the writing, publication, and favourable reception of the four *Pastorals* (begun c. 1704, published 1709). He was fortunate both in having a sensible and sympathetic mentor in William Walsh, who gave critical advice and corrected his poems, and in being permitted in his turn to advise, and to correct the poems of, William Wycherley. This dual involvement as pupil and adviser must have done a great deal to prevent Pope's critical ideas from hardening into abstract dogma, and to inculcate into his mind the concept of the critic as friendly constructive adviser rather than as grim impersonal legislator. Walsh's best-known advice to Pope was to cultivate correctness (Spence §73), but one feels that his converse emphasis on spirit, genius, and the avoidance of purely 'mechanical Rules' was even more influential:

> . . . a Man may correct his Verses till he takes away the true Spirit of them; especially if he submits to the correction of some who pass for great Critics, by mechanical Rules, and never enter into the true Design and Genius of an Author.　　　(*Corr.* I 21)

Pope's critical reading had led him to accept that Horace 'had . . . taught the Romans [the] rules of Poetry' (*Corr.* I 37). His own first major critical work, *A Discourse on Pastoral Poetry* (written c. 1704, circulated in manuscript among his friends, and published in 1717) shows that he had become familiar with classical principles, and could write *genre*-based criticism neatly, pragmatically, and sensibly. In his early correspondence, however, the critical emphasis seems to be more on the importance of one's direct response to a great writer's work and the over-riding necessity for life, vigour, and simplicity in poetry, rather than the importance of 'rules'. After a childhood attachment to Dryden, Spenser, and Waller (Spence §43), his most admired authors through-out the 1704–1711 period would appear to have been Homer, Virgil and Dryden. His basic poetic likes and dislikes are clearly implied in his ad-verse criticism of Crashaw, 'whose works may just deserve reading':

> All that regards Design, Form, Fable, (which is the Soul of Poetry) all that concerns exactness, or consent or parts, (which is the Body) will probably be wanting; only pretty conceptions, fine metaphors, glitt'ring expressions, and something of a neat cast of Verse, (which are properly the dress, gems, or loose ornaments of poetry) may be found in these verses. . . . These Authors [who write 'for diversion only'] shou'd be consider'd as *Versifiers* and *witty Men*, rather than as *Poets*.
>
> (*Corr.* I 109–10)

Later in the same discussion, when he criticizes authors who 'wou'd rather be admir'd than understood', Pope sees the 'ambition of sur-prising a reader' as 'the true natural cause of all Fustian, or Bombast in Poetry', recommends 'an easier and more unaffected expression', and places majesty above sweetness. In discussing Walsh's correction of his own poems, he sees life and force as more important than correctness and polish:

> . . . sometimes our First thoughts are the Best, as the first squeezing of the Grapes makes the finest and richest Wine.
>
> (*Corr.* I 19)

Similarly, in discussing his own correction of Wycherley's poems, his central concern is to achieve concentration, force and simplicity (*Corr.* I

16). The most impressive individual item within his early criticism, how-ever, is surely the analysis of Homer in a letter to Ralph Bridges, 5 April [1708] (*Corr.* I 44), where both his relative valuation of critics and creative writers and his emphasis on strength and simplicity are beauti-fully and forcefully expressed. He describes himself as 'one, who values the Authority of one true Poet above that of twenty Critics or Com-mentatours'. As for Homer, one of his 'distinguishing Excellencies' is 'that Rapture and Fire, which carries you away with him, with that wonderfull Force, that no man who has a true Poetical spirit is Master of himself, while he reads him.' To emphasize this aspect of Pope's criticism is not to say that he despised classical criticism or was indif-ferent to technical perfection; his own discussion of versification (*Corr.* I 57 and 106–108) exemplifies his respect for necessary 'rules'. The suggestion rather that he (like Johnson after him) regarded the evoca-tion of strength and emotional response as a first priority, to take precedence over elegance and refinement (though not morality) if need be. He was already aware that the culture of his day needed the support of a strong, persuasive literature in its struggle against 'the gentle Reign of Dulness' as manifested in both 'Country Fools' and the foolish, false 'Town-Wits' whose characteristic was to be 'pertly in the Wrong' (*Corr.* I 11). Pope's reaction to this cultural erosion, now and throughout his life, was to turn to the past; not primarily to the critics for 'rules', but to the great Greek, Roman, and English writers, in an attempt to emulate their strength in modern poetry.[1]

Even the degree of maturity, accomplishment, and critical know-ledge found in Pope's early criticism is hardly sufficient to prevent our surprise at the ambitiousness of *An Essay on Criticism*. The most striking initial impact of this project is perhaps his sheer audacity in attempting it—an audacity that was to be similarly manifested throughout his career in such works as the *Iliad* and *Odyssey* translations, the edition of

[1] Throughout the following discussion, the concept of emulation is used in the Longinian sense of receiving, 'a powerful illumination and inspira-tion . . . through submission to the ancient masters' (Wimsatt and Brooks, *Literary Criticism*, 1957, 100), and thence in one's own works 'imitating' their spirit rather than (or in addition to) their form and content.

Shakespeare, and *An Essay on Man*. In *An Essay on Criticism*, the young
Pope was committed not only to laying down the critical law to writers
much older and more experienced than himself, but also to emulating
(and to some extent competing with) the best of the many verse-
epistles written on critical topics from Horace's *Ars Poetica* onwards.
According to Reuben Brower, contemporary readers 'could relax and
enjoy Pope's marvellous "feat of words" as he led them through familiar
intellectual scenes. Their preparation for reading . . . "with the same
spirit that its author writ" was not doctrinal, not a matter of knowing
the right things, but literary and poetic. They were soaked in the essays
in verse of Dryden, Buckingham, Rochester, Roscommon, Sheffield,
and countless others; and above all they knew Horace from studying
and imitating him in school and from reading numerous translations and
imitations in English and French. The allusion to Horace in the *Essay on
Criticism* would have been obvious, especially to readers familiar with
Boileau's *L'Art poétique*.'[1] Despite Pope's inability to match Horace's
'large rhythmic flow of talk', Brower sees him as emerging with credit
from the comparison. Similarly, in relation to the most-admired critical
verse epistles in English, Addison's praise in *Spectator* 253 (20 December
1711)[2] leaves us in no doubt that Pope's challenge was considered to have
scored a notable triumph: 'I cannot conclude this Paper without taking
notice that we have three Poems in our Tongue, which are of the same
Nature, and each of them a Master-piece in its kind; the Essay on
Translated Verse, the Essay on the Art of Poetry, and the Essay upon
Criticism.' Addison's earlier remark in the same essay that, like Longinus, 'our *English* Author has . . . exemplified several of his Precepts in the very Precepts themselves' recognises Pope's outstanding
gift of embodying the positive poetic standards suggested by his
argument in the smoothness, vigour, excitement, and technical brilliance of his own poetry—not only in the onomatopoeic *tours de force* of
Part II, but in his constant demonstration of the 'true Wit' that is one of
his main criteria. Throughout *An Essay on Criticism*, too, his satiric skill
is self-evident, and his structural dexterity in creating a unity of argument behind the attractive Horatian façade of 'graceful Negligence'

[1] *Alexander Pope: The Poetry of Allusion*, Oxford 1959, 188–9.
[2] Ed. D. F. Bond, II 483–6.

is now generally recognized.[1] Another admirable aspect of his discussion is that he 'tried against severe odds to make a limited thing as general as possible'.[2] Thus, literary theory, poetic practice, critical practice, moral philosophy, and an over-riding concern for morality merge into one another—sometimes, admittedly, to the detriment of argumentative clarity.

An Essay on Criticism, then, is obviously successful in terms of poetic achievement and structure. With regard to Pope's critical arguments it must be emphasized that, however complete in itself *An Essay on Criticism* may be as a poem, in terms of critical discussion it is only the first major stage of a thirty-year debate. It by no means encapsulates all his literary theory, and is a constricting medium for detailed discussion by virtue of its elegant compactness and its commitment to both the exposition and reconciliation of the main (and sometimes mutually incompatible) aspects of contemporary theory and the enunciation of his own poetic criteria. It may be claimed in general that his discussion is at its best when he allows himself to speak out firmly in support of his own innate poetic convictions. These (as manifested in his own poetry) lay stress on emotional and intellectual power, reverence for certain classical and English authors, and direct emulation of these authors' qualities in modern writing. Conversely, he is at his worst when he distorts his own instincts in attempts to reconcile them with restrictive, exaggerated, or negative theories relating to the importance of 'rules', the obligation to accept all aspects of classical theory, and the use of classical writers' insights as substitutes for, rather than supplements to, personal experience.

The positive worth of Pope's discussion emerges with particular clarity in his treatment of the desired relationship between the good critic and the creative writer. His most specific explication of the critic's function, and its perversion in modern times, appears in the following passage:

> *The gen'rous Critick* fann'd *the* Poet's Fire,
> *And taught the World*, with Reason *to* Admire.

[1] See A. Fenner, 'The Unity of Pope's *Essay on Criticism*', *PQ* XXXIX, 1960, 435–46; rprd in EA.
[2] G. Tillotson, *Pope and Human Nature*, 68.

Then Criticism the Muse's Handmaid prov'd,
To dress her Charms, and make her more belov'd;
But following Wits from that Intention stray'd;
Who cou'd not win the Mistress, woo'd the Maid;
Against the Poets their own Arms they turn'd,
Sure to hate most the Men from whom they learn'd.

(100–7)

The harmony of logic, language, structure, and imagery which characterizes Pope's most successful arguments is particularly noticeable here, where four lines each are devoted to ancients and moderns, with a common linking image of domestic service. The opening couplet shows the critic in relation to both poet and audience, applying intellectual or spiritual stimulus (not restraint) to the poet's natural genius, and teaching the reading public how to respond sensitively yet judiciously to literature. The 'Handmaid' image reinforces and extends the concept of the critic's dual function. The critic is now the handmaid who (like Betty in *The Rape of the Lock*) uses her expertise—not necessarily shared by or divulged to her mistress—to adorn existing beauty and thereby increase its public attractiveness. Detailed interpretation of the image creates considerable problems. Is not natural—though flawed—beauty to be preferred to adornment, for example? Is the critic's main function to enhance existing beauties or to cover up unsightly defects? And is the critic to fulfil his function of adornment by teaching 'rules' to the poet (a procedure which does not fit the image), or by revising the poet's works himself, as Pope did for Wycherley? Whichever way we interpret the passage in detail, however, the general drift remains the same. The critic, it is implied, cannot create genius, but should give positive assistance and stimulus to the good writer, and should help to narrow the gap between poet and reader in two ways, by making the poet's work intrinsically more attractive, and by teaching the reader to judge sensitively and sensibly. In the corresponding portrayal of the bad modern critic, the degree of degeneration is beautifully conveyed by the shift of emphasis in the domestic service image; now, we are dealing not with the relationship between the servant and the employer, but with the ungentlemanly conduct of a rejected suitor who demeans himself by flirting with the maid. Subsequently, the bad critic is seen as mutineer, turning his weapons against those who both supplied them and taught their use, and (in 108–11) as apothecary turned quack-doctor, attacking his mentor and (presumably) killing his patients by misunderstanding and misapplying the genuine doctor's knowledge of 'Nature' in the shape of scientific principles. Thus, the bad critic is the false wit who comes to criticism through failure as a poet, learns his trade by reading and misunderstanding the ancient or modern poets, and proceeds to pervert the public taste and diminish the reputation of good writers.

Pope's positive view of the true critic's function is evident throughout the above passage. The emphasis is on the good writer's natural ability and the critic's power to encourage, assist, and adorn it by means of a harmonious and fruitful relationship. Critics learn their 'rules' from poets, and there is little or no emphasis on the critic's function as restrictive legislator, dictating 'rules' to the poet; in fact, the only '*Rules*' referred to are '*mistaken*' (110), and applied by bad critics.

Similarly, in a later description of the good critic, we are shown a firm, cultivated, and gentlemanly friend, rather than a stern abstract theorist whose function is to constrict the manifestations of a poet's talent within rigid limits:

> *But where's the Man, who Counsel* can *bestow,*
> *Still* pleas'd *to* teach, *and yet not* proud *to* know ?
> *Unbiass'd, or by* Favour *or by* Spite;
> *Not* dully prepossest, *nor* blindly right;
> *Tho' Learn'd, well-bred; and tho' well-bred, sincere;*
> *Modestly bold, and Humanly severe?*
> *Who to a* Friend *his Faults can freely show,*
> *And gladly praise the Merit of a Foe?*
> *Blest with a* Taste *exact, yet unconfin'd;*
> *A* Knowledge *both of* Books *and* Humankind;
> Gen'rous Converse; *a* Soul *exempt from* Pride;
> *And* Love to Praise, *with* Reason *on his Side?*   (631–42)

This portrayal of the good critic may be less dynamic than the consideration of the poet-critic relationship in lines 100–7, but this is more than made up for in the poem's following and concluding passage (643–744). Pope's survey of the great critics of the past and present is certainly the most passionate and forceful element in the *Essay*'s serious aspect. Despite his own general description of it in the contents-list (added in 1736) as a 'History *of* Criticism', it would seem fairer to see it as the presentation of a series of carefully-selected exemplars (five ancient, five modern) who between them embody all the qualities to be expected from the hypothetical ideal critic. Certainly, its very omissions (particularly that of Dryden), would have made Pope's survey far more inaccurate and discourteous than could reasonably be expected of him had his intention been to present an objective historical account. Aristotle is the bold intellectual explorer who studies Nature with Homer's guidance and codifies the 'nature' (that is, the natural inherent principles) of good writing for the benefit of others. With reference to Pope's difficulties in dealing with the question of 'laws' elsewhere in the poem, it should be noted here that Aristotle's exploration and subsequent mastery of Nature is achieved primarily through the use of his own intellect and observation (Homer being the guide, not the source of knowledge); that poets accept his legislation through respect for his apparent depth of knowledge rather than through servility; and that his 'laws' are not necessarily infallible, but are susceptible to extension or modification in the light of any further discoveries of principles from 'Nature'. After Aristotle, Horace is seen as the great creative writer, the emotional impact and critical implications of whose poetry are reinforced by his cool, bold critical assessments and his gracefully negligent but sensible re-statement of general principles. Dionysius is the archetypal 'Muse's Handmaid' whose sympathetic interpretation of Homer reveals new beauties to the reader. Quintilian, on the other hand, is the good teacher, who organizes existing principles into a clearly-defined critical system for the benefit of future critics. As a fitting climax, Longinus (to whom Pope devotes the passage's most enthusiastic and evocative language) exemplifies the restrained fire (emotional involvement controlled by intellectual justice) strengthened by creative power which enables him to embody his discoveries in the act of exposition. The suspicion that Pope is particularly attracted to the critical position of Longinus is given more substance in 1728, when he chooses to present his best prose satire of bad criticism (*Peri Bathous: Or . . . The Art of Sinking in Poetry*) as a parody of Longinus' *On the Sublime*, so that by ironic reversal Longinus' *Sublime* arguably becomes the epitome of good criticism.

Next, after the interlude of the Dark Ages, five moderns are presented. Pope apparently takes some trouble to select his five in such a way as to provide analogies with his ancients. Thus Erasmus, like Aristotle, is the powerful and fearless intellect who re-establishes order in the face of unruly barbarism. It is significant that, compared with Aristotle, Erasmus introduces religious and moral considerations to Pope's survey; his guide is presumably God the creator of Nature, rather than Homer its greatest simulator, and he revives morality and religion as well as literature. Vida's function, too, seems to be made deliberately analogous to that of Horace as the poet-critic. The correlation between the ancients and the remaining three moderns (Boileau, Buckingham, and Walsh) is less clear-cut. Boileau, rather strangely, is uncharacterized other than as a Horatian disciple acting as legislator to a servile nation. Buckingham seems to introduce a new dimension as the gentleman-critic who combines learning with moral goodness. Pope's former mentor Walsh offers some analogy with Dionysius, this time encouraging the young writer (Pope himself), rather than explicating the great. Finally, it is noticeable that among the moderns there is no Longinus figure, which might very well suggest that Pope had a candidate in mind for that role whom modesty forbade him to name. No matter how we interpret the detailed relationship between ancients and moderns, however, the same general emphases emerge. In the good critic, Pope demands intellectual vigour, boldness, strong emotional response to literature, creative power sufficient to enable the critic to exemplify as well as expound, and moral qualities sufficient to make him a good man. Despite Pope's acceptance of Aristotle's qualifications to preside over the wit of his contemporaries, the exact relationship between Aristotelian criticism and the modern writer is left open, while in the case of Boileau and the French, Pope's enthusiasm for exact obedience to a rigid code of laws is decidedly lukewarm.

We have seen that, when Pope is not committed to detailed examination of conflicting current doctrines, his criteria appear to be very much in line with his own poetic practice, and his emphases positive. On the other hand, his attempt to present a 'critical synthesis' as 'the

logical culmination of nearly a century's effort to harmonize the extremes and variables of critical thinking' (Twickenham I 209) sometimes
leads him into vagueness, exaggeration, and self-contradiction. In this
respect some attempt should be made to indicate the nature of Pope's
difficulties by brief reference to the critical opinions embodied in other
English critical verse-epistles. His most important predecessors were
Sir William Soames, whose translation of Boileau's *Art poétique*, was
revised by Dryden and published as *The Art of Poetry* in 1683; John
Sheffield, Earl Mulgrave, whose *Essay upon Poetry* appeared in 1682;
and Wentworth Dillon, Earl of Roscommon, author of *An Essay on
Translated Verse* (1684).[1] All these poems are pleasant to read, all make
good use of the heroic couplet, and all were extensively borrowed from
in *An Essay on Criticism* (as even the most cursory examination of the
Twickenham annotations will soon reveal); on the other hand, none
came remotely close to Pope's creative genius in embodying his principles in his own poetry. Pope's manuscript annotations in his own copy
of *The Art of Poetry* show both his care in studying the work and its
usefulness (in conjunction with Boileau's original) in formulating his
general criteria. His exhortations in *An Essay on Criticism* not to
write without genius, to know the nature of one's own special talent, to
aim for stylistic variety, correct versification, purity of language, and
unity of design, to write slowly and carefully, to behave morally, and to
submit one's work to competent judges are all found as headings in his
Art of Poetry notes, along with many others both positive and negative.
Pope's major departures from Boileau/Soames are, first, to identify
adherence to 'Nature' rather than to 'Reason' as the central guiding
principle; second, to refrain from detailed discussion of the 'rules'
associated with the style and content of the various recognized literary

---

[1] Texts of the *Essays* of Sheffield and Dillon will be found in *Critical
Essays of the Seventeenth Century* ed. J. E. Spingarn, II 286–96 and 297–
309, respectively. References below are to *page*-numbers in this edition.
I am indebted to J. A. Means for the opportunity of consulting—in his
'Pope's *Essay on Criticism*: A Study of the Technique', M. Phil. thesis,
Birkbeck College, 1968—xeroxes of the annotations in Pope's copy of
the Soames/Dryden *Art of Poetry* (now in the Huntington Library)
referred to below.

genres (such as pastoral, elegy, ode, comedy, tragedy, and epic); and, third, to pay far more attention to the Longinian elements of grandeur and *je ne sais quoi* in literature. Sheffield's *Essay upon Poetry* is considerably sprightlier than the *Art of Poetry* in every respect, being a lucid, attractive, rationalistic exposition of the art of poetry which emphasizes the reverence due to the great writers of the past (English as well as classical), but makes little appeal to any particular set of 'rules'. For Sheffield, the soul of writing is 'Genius', his evocative description of which was incorporated by Pope into his own description of 'Nature'.[1] 'True Wit', Learning, inspiration by Nature, and the embodiment of Fancy controlled by Judgment are also cited as central requirements. With regard to more technical criteria, Sheffield follows Boileau in presenting a survey of *genres*, in which unity, clarity, hard work, the illusion of ease, and the combination of heat and fury with smoothness are among the qualities recommended, whilst heaviness, incoherence and obscenity must be avoided. Homer, Virgil, Shakespeare, Fletcher, Denham, and Dryden are all recommended as models within the appropriate *genres*, and particular emphasis is laid on the English dramatists' skill in moving the passions ('the dull are forc'd to feel, the wise to weep', 292). On the whole, then, Sheffield's work must have been most congenial and helpful to Pope. In fact, Sheffield surpasses Pope in his consistency, in that he covers the fairly limited field of his poem (brief considerations of general principles and the *genres*) persuasively, coherently, and without self-contradiction. He therefore makes a useful index of Pope's self-inflicted difficulties in choosing to attempt the more specialized and controversial art of criticism. In this respect, Roscommon comes closest to Pope in choosing to examine the special problems of the translator, who, like the critic, is concerned with evaluating and interpreting the works of other writers. Roscommon is much akin to Pope in spirit, and comes nearest to rivalling him in poetic merit. He goes further than Pope in his emphasis on Longinian qualities, his insistence that the faults of Homer must be recognized, and his plea for greater use of Miltonic blank verse in English poetry. Like Pope, he wants poetic sound to echo sense; insists that the would-be

[1] Sheffield 286–7; cf. *An Essay on Criticism*, 68–79.

translator must know not only his own talent, strengths and weaknesses but also his own ruling passion; demands morality in literature; and (with regard to criticism) suggests the chief person with whom to compare a poet is himself. Roscommon's central poetic virtue (unlike Boileau's 'Reason', Sheffield's 'Genius', and Pope's 'Nature') is 'Majesty', which appears very close to the Longinian 'sublime'.

This brief examination of Pope's English predecessors should in itself give some indication of the extent to which it was possible for critics who could all be reasonably described as 'neo-classical' (that is, in revering the works of the 'ancients', recognizing the validity of classical criteria and *genres*, and desiring to see these criteria and *genres* applied to English literature) to diverge in their more detailed emphases. In general, Pope's selection of emphases says a great deal for his grasp of the practical realities of writing poetry, his common sense, and his powers of intelligent discrimination between conflicting ideas. The priority given to following 'Nature', in the sense of becoming intimately familiar with the general principles (emanating from the Creator) governing human nature and the entire universe surrounding it, is an emphasis both logical and rich. It becomes an increasingly desirable alternative to the more abstract 'Reason' in the light of Pope's own increasing awareness in his later writings of the complexities involved in following his own advice. Pope is equally intelligent and constructive in his use, definition, and correlation of the notoriously evasive and unsatisfactory terms currently used to describe the main human qualities involved in the creative and critical process, such as 'Judgment', the analytical and reasoning faculty; 'Fancy', the irrational imaginative faculty; 'Taste', the faculty of aesthetic discrimination, related in a variety of ways to Judgment and Fancy by various theorists; and 'Wit', the hardest of all to define, as it tended to be used as a term of approval for the expression of attractively lively intelligence and an antonym to 'dullness', and as such could be defined in any number of ways in relation to Judgment and Fancy. With regard to 'Wit' in particular, Pope's usage is both evocative and sensible. True Wit is the sum of the characteristics in the human mind that make intellectual, cultural, and (to a great extent) moral life possible. The constant Battle between creative Wit and destructive Dullness (the latter often manifesting itself as false Wit) is a constant theme throughout Pope's poetry. His definition of the literary manifestation of true Wit as:

> . . . Nature *to Advantage drest,*
> *What oft was* Thought, *but ne'er so well* Exprest,
> Something, *whose Truth convinc'd at Sight we find,*
> *That gives us back the Image of our Mind*   (297–300)

is a reasonable statement of a common approach. It reflects a valuable aspect of literary expression while falling far short of covering the importance and use of 'Wit' in Pope's own philosophy and writings. On the other hand, his controversial couplet, 'Some, to whom Heav'n in Wit has been profuse,/Want as much more, to turn it to its use' (80–81), comes appreciably closer to expressing the term's centrality in Pope's mind as representing a fusion of all the best elements of the human mind in the right proportions.

In Pope's treatment of the relationship between poet and critic, his use of his predecessors, and his selection and treatment of terminology, we have seen the operation of a strong, common-sense intelligence, augmented by a great creative writer's insight. His satirical exposure of critical shortcomings in Part II is beyond serious criticism, and manifests criteria that are self-evidently constructive, enlightened, and liberal, with particular emphasis on response to a poem's unity, life, and emotional impact. Most of his discussion of the good critic's conduct in Part III commands assent, although here his logic becomes somewhat impaired by his desire for the critic to be all things to all men; candid and diffident, outspoken and tactful, and a far cry from Pope's own habitual practice of pungent and most ungentlemanly censure of aspects of existence that do not meet with his approval. His most serious problems appear when he is dealing either with the nature and validity of 'rules', or with the relationship between 'regular' literature conforming to the 'rules' and 'irregular' literature where another set of principles has to be invoked. His uncertainty with regard to critical legislation appears to be reflected in his habit of exaggerating principles that he is unsure of. Thus, his exclusion of all but good creative writers as potential critics, his extreme interpretation of the limits of 'proud Man's pretending Wit' and the individual talent, and (conversely) his claim that *all* classical writers must be revered, display a most uncharacteristic rigidity that can most reasonably be attributed to over-compensation for lack of certainty. This kind of breakdown in Pope's logic appears at its worst when he is considering the relationship between following Nature by one's direct observation on the one hand and by reading the ancients, who may already have achieved the optimum degree of penetration, on the other. The definition of 'rules' as '*Nature Methodiz'd*' (89) is sensible, placing inherent literary principles on the same basis as scientific laws. The following account of 'how learn'd *Greece* her useful Rules indites' (92–99), however, is too illogical to be taken seriously, and fails to reveal the identity, status, and authority of the original Greek codifiers. Nor does it indicate why acceptance of these critics' 'rules' should be preferable to relying on one's own direct knowledge of Nature and one's direct response to great writers. Similar problems recur in Pope's fictitious account of Virgil (130–140). The claim that copying Nature and copying the 'Ancient *Rules*' (139) are identical is not justified by the evidence provided, and flies in the face of the whole concept of following Nature at first hand. Aristotle is introduced by sleight of hand (138), although no reason is given as to why Virgil should prefer Aristotelian principles to those of his own discovery. The confusion increases when Pope moves on to considering the '*nameless Graces*' in relation to the 'Rules' that he has just claimed to be equivalent to direct observation of natural principles (141–168). Here he makes the fatal mistake of confusing the act of scientific discovery (where the whole is never known, and knowledge can be increased, but valid laws are by definition universally applicable) with legislation, where man-made laws can be suspended at will. The description of the phenomenon of nameless graces itself, then, is convincing, but Pope's attempt to reconcile this with a more rigid system of 'rules' fails completely. In fact, his 'Pegasus' simile (150–1), if taken at its face value, would imply that the great writer (as a winged creature in the image) can not only 'deviate' from the 'common Track', but dispense with it entirely, thereby demonstrating that the creative insight of a great poet is perfectly capable of discovering its own principles—which may come much closer to Pope's own opinion than the case that he was dutifully attempting to make.

Pope's difficulties with regard to 'rules' must not, of course, be allowed to detract from the achievement of *An Essay on Criticism* as a whole. Poetically, he had produced by far the best verse-epistle on criticism in the English language. The main drift of his criticism was positive, directed towards the creation of powerful, emotionally moving literature, normally (but not exclusively) within the limits of good judgment, good taste, and the precedents created by the great writers of the past. In what can be considered his second period as a literary critic, from the publication of *An Essay on Criticism* to that of the *Dunciad Variorum* in 1729, Pope took every opportunity of continuing his critical debate with the reading public and re-affirming his central principles. This was by far his most prolific critical period, in both verse and prose. It was in this period that his own major work as a practical critic was accomplished, in his translation of *The Iliad* and edition of Shakespeare. It could hardly be claimed that any radically new principles emerged from this eighteen-year period of critical speculation, but new developments can certainly be detected in his presentation and technique of critical discussion. First, we have his increasing use of prose as a medium, culminating in the *Peri Bathous* and the fusion of prose and poetry in the *Dunciad Variorum*. Second, we see a pronounced increase in Pope's liking for stating his positive critical principles by savage parody and ridicule. Third, we see an increasing tendency towards fusion of literary, social, and moral criticism, so that shortcomings in one sphere act as a reliable index to shortcomings in another; the Dunces are morally degenerate, whilst the inhabitants of the Court world of *The Rape of the Lock* are culturally impoverished (the Baron's reading being limited to romances) as well as socially superficial.

Although, with the obvious exception of *The Dunciad*, Pope's major poetry of this period is not primarily directed towards critical discussion, his refusal to compartmentalise his areas of concern automatically ensures that a good deal of important criticism becomes incidentally incorporated. The most significant poem in this respect is *The Temple of Fame*, which particularly reinforces Pope's emphases on the importance of literature and the need for literary strength (even if achieved at the expense of correctness, elegance, or any of the other qualities popularly associated with the 'Augustans'). The power of music and poetry

is seen in the portrayal of Orpheus and Amphion on the West face of
the Temple (83–92) and '*Druids* and *Bards*' on the Gothic North (127).
Inside, the occupants of the six columns given pride of place in 'the
Centre of the hallow'd Quire' are Homer, Virgil, Pindar, Horace,
Aristotle, and Cicero. Homer's vivacity, boldness, fire, strength of expression, and occasional negligence are emphasized (182–95). Virgil, on
the other hand, is seen as careful, grave, sedate, humble, and a wor-
shipper of Homer (196–209). The classical references in *An Essay on
Criticism* are now amplified and extended by reference to Pindar
(praised for his bold, careless, irregular greatness and startling verisimi-
litude), Horace (who tempers Pindar's fire), Aristotle with his penetrating gaze into the secrets of Nature, and the graceful Cicero. Finally,
the young author himself describes the hardships of the literary life,
with its unpopularity and lack of security. *Windsor Forest* states Pope's
love of harmonious confusion, and 'Order in Variety', and endorses the
principle of emulation, with Pope inviting comparison between his own
poem and those of Milton and Virgil. Complimentary references are
made to Denham and Cowley (259–82), and Pope's literary patriotism
is strongly manifested in his advice to Granville (283–328).

   In the minor poems published between 1711 and 1727, Pope's critical debate is vigorously continued on both the serious and satiric levels.
His genius for criticism by lampoon, parody and satire is clearly manifested, as is his desire to relate literary criticism to the other arts and his
over-riding criterion of powerful, emotive expression, usually contained within a boundary of regularity. Comic verse can be used as a
means of literary commendation through raillery, as we see in his five-
poem sequence on *Gulliver's Travels*. His approval of raillery as a mode
of expression is evident in the *Epistle to Miss Blount, with the Works of
Voiture*. Here, Pope not only commends Voiture's letters, but takes the
occasion both to point out the serious qualities that underlie Voiture's
wit and to emulate Voiture's achievement in his own elegantly witty
discussion of serious comedy and farce. Voiture is praised for his charm,
gaiety, elegance, good-natured wit, and conversation, but also (on a
more serious level) for his learning, his truth to Nature, his strength in
animating his art by the force of his own personality, and (a favourite
topic of Pope's) his capacity for forming friendships. In Pope's generic

discussion, serious comedy is seen as creating both pleasure and moral instruction, within the limits of the unities of time and place, whereas farce is graceful, trifling, and irregular.

Despite Pope's fondness for affectionate raillery, however, the bulk of his critical poetry of this period takes the opposite approach by attacking bad writers, and their characteristic stupidity and weakness, without mercy. The *Epigram Occasion'd by Ozell's Translation of Boileau's Lutrin* condemns John Ozell's inverted critical standards as manifested in his treatment of the ancients, Boileau, and Wycherley, so that 'those were slandered most whom *Ozell* prais'd'. Similarly, Sir Richard Blackmore's impenetrable dullness and abuse of wit is savagely lampooned in *Verses to be Placed under the Picture of England's Arch-Poet*, whilst the flat insipidity of the pastoral-writers Ambrose Philips, Eustace Budgell, and Walter Carey is beautifully reflected in the trivialized name-dropping of *The Three Gentle Shepherds*. Philips' emptiness is again attacked in *Macer*, one of the three *Characters* of 1715. The literary parasite who fawns on authors but spurns them if a greater 'name' enters the room is contemptuously flattened in the second Character, the unidentified *Umbra*. The third, *Atticous*, is perhaps the most perceptive and subtly-drawn character-study in all Pope's works. Although primarily directed at Addison, its portrayal of the great writer whose literary worth is undermined by his narrow-minded spitefulness, self-conceit, and jealous treachery is a prime example of following Nature by creating a representative character who is still to be seen all around us.

With regard to literary theory, the most exciting miscellaneous poems of the period are probably *To Mr. Addison, Occasioned by his Dialogues on Medals*, and, in particular, the *Epistle to Mr. Jervas*. Both are concerned with relating other arts to literature. In *Addison*, the art of making medals is seen as a means of preserving the glories of the past. Dull antiquarians may misuse them by revering them only as antique objects (preferring patina to clarity), but the truly learned man will make them reveal their historical truth, and will pass this truth on to the world. In this poem, then, Pope succeeds in amalgamating and correlating, by both satire and positive statement, a great many of his most important moral, cultural, philosophical, and literary concerns. His constant fear of the damage done by Time in causing culture and civilization to degenerate is vividly conveyed in his picture of the ruins of Greece and Rome. The medal (and, by implication, poetry) acts both as a reminder and a medium of cultural continuity. Pope's cultural concerns merge into patriotism (as in *Windsor Forest*) in his plea that Britain might imitate Greece and Rome by making her own medals, whilst his desire to save British culture from ruin is further demonstrated in his attack on pedantic dullness, and commendation of good sense and true learning. *Jervas* is even more interesting in encapsulating Pope's central criteria whilst discussing the relationship between poetry and painting. The dominating quality referred to is energy, or 'flame'. '*Dryden*'s native fire' is commended. Pope significantly refers to his own 'regular . . . rage' (that is, his use of powerful expression within a framework of regularity), and his association with the painter Jervas is described in terms of 'mingling flame with flame' so that 'each from each contract new strength and light'. His brief comparative critique of Renaissance Italian painting contrasts '*Raphael*'s grace' with '*Guido*'s air', '*Caracci*'s strength' with '*Coreggio*'s softer line', and '*Paulo*'s free stroke' with the climactic '*Titian*'s warmth divine.' Finally, his attitudes towards balance, liveliness, spontaneity, and strength in the arts, and his views concerning the function of 'rules', are all strikingly summarized in his descriptions of his own 'numbers' as potentially 'strong [as the Muses]' charms, and gentle as their soul', and (particularly) of Jervas' art, where Pope comes close to providing a general creative aesthetic:

> *Soft without weakness, without glaring gay;*
> *Led by some rule, that guides, but not constrains;*
> *And finish'd more thro' happiness than pains!*

Pope's concern for the development and preservation of a distinctively British culture, and his prowess in demolishing dullness by satire are apparent in the group of poems written for or about the theatre at this time. His irony tends to be directed towards the audience as well as towards the shortcomings of particular plays or dramatists. The *Prologue Design'd for Mr. Durfy's last Play* looks back to Swift's *Tale of a Tub* and forward to *The Dunciad* in establishing its positives through ironic reversal. By appearing to praise a typical presumptuous 'Modern' who ignores the literature of the past, relies on his own ingenuity (like the Spider in *The Battle of the Books*), and writes purely for commercial gain, Pope endorses the principles of subduing pride and following the ancients. In the *Epilogue to Jane Shore*, irony is directed towards the audience in order to underline the moral function of serious comedy; if the spectator fails to respond correctly to the characters, this brings out his own moral failings. Similarly, the speaker of the *Prologue to the Three Hours After Marriage* leaves a fool's cap on the stage for anyone to take. The audience is again reminded that disapproval will simply indicate that the play's satire has found a target. Elsewhere in the Prologue, Pope condemns the irrationality of public taste, the hatred accorded to wits and men of sense by fools, and the bad dramatists' love of translating and incompetently borrowing foreign plots and misapplying French neoclassical rules. The implied contrast is therefore between good and bad imitation, with approval of native British plots treated in the light of emulation of the ancients as opposed to slavish submission to neo-classicism. This desire for vigorous native drama inspired but not dominated by the classics is powerfully and overtly stated in the serious *Prologue to Mr Addison's Tragedy of Cato*. Here, Pope gives the criteria for a *genre* of tragic writing which seems to exploit the best of all worlds. It is to evoke truly British feelings by an appeal to emotional as well as intellectual response, at the same time maintaining Aristotelian dignity and decorum by means of a careful selection of noble themes conveyed in a plot taken from classical history. Thus, in *Cato* itself, tears are demanded from the audience, but they are tears for fallen patriotism rather than for the fallen warrior, or the unfortunate lover in heroic drama. In the course of arguing on behalf of his persuasive blueprint, which neither *Cato* itself nor any subsequent eighteenth-century play came near to fulfilling, Pope condemns over-reliance on French and Italian influences, and rejects any appeal to the emotions of the audience on unworthy grounds. That the legitimacy of pathetic themes is, however, a thorny and subjective problem becomes apparent in Pope's own devastating Swiftian lampoon entitled *On a Lady who P-st at the Tragedy of Cato*, written in the same year as the official Prologue (1713). Here, he qualifies his official view by condemning an over-facile acceptance of emotional response as a good thing in itself and indirectly criticizing

Cato for supplying politically-biased emotional luxuriance by stealth. The ironic implication that loss of bladder-control is to be taken as the ultimate proof of direct appeal to the emotions is a sharp reminder that, however much Pope approved of emotional appeal, it had preferably to be achieved within a rational, moral framework.

In turning from Pope's poetry of the period 1711–27 to his critical prose, the same basic divisions into overtly serious and ironic modes, and the same central preoccupations, are apparent. With regard to prose, however, we have the additional category of practical criticism, where Pope is concerned with detailed analyses of major works. It is within this category that his best critical work falls, although to say this is not to detract from the magnificent ironic achievement of the *Peri Bathous*, or the interest of the earlier miscellaneous prose pieces.

With regard to Pope's ironic prose (culminating in the *Peri Bathous*), his early *Critical Specimen* lampoon of John Dennis in response to Dennis's attack on *An Essay on Criticism* is a good demonstration of his ability within this mode, even though the sparkle of his poetry is missing. The *Critical Specimen*, in the form of proposals for, and specimens from, a proposed biography of Dennis, is somewhat overdone, and consequently lame, but a useful attack is made on 'Modern' principles involving a refusal to study classical authors and an undue reverence for the sublime. Here again, it is seen that Pope is clear-sighted enough to recognise the limits of his own enthusiasm for powerful, emotionally-appealing literature, declining to accept it at the price of a break in the link between the present and the past. His first major satirical periodical publication is the paper in *Spectator* No. 457 (14 August 1712) advocating a new monthly review to be entitled *An Account of the Works of the Unlearned*. This proposal to produce a periodical specially for dunces and dullards in all fields (such as law and politics as well as literary scholarship and criticism) is, of course, an embryonic form of the *Peri Bathous* and *Dunciad*. Ironic endorsement of undesirable literary standards was further developed with regard to both theme and quality in two *Guardian* essays published in 1713. The first, on pastoral poetry (No. 40, 27 April) is an excellent piece of ironic exposure, demonstrating by false praise the weakness and crudity of Ambrose Philips' Spenserian pastorals in relation to Pope's own classicized, idealized work in the same *genre*. The second (No. 78, 10 June) is the 'Receit to Make an Epick Poem' later incorporated in the *Peri Bathous*. Here again, Pope used the *Tale of a Tub* device of allowing a hack writer to expose his own appalling lack of taste and sense by expounding his own criteria. The hack writer's ignorance, love of mediocrity, and excessive reliance on a code of mechanical rules are particularly singled out for attack, and destroyed with the most delightful wit. In 1714 a permanent vehicle for this kind of ironic narration was conceived in the shape of Martinus Scriblerus, Quixotic polymath and pedant, by the newly-formed and short-lived Scriblerus Club.[1] The first major work to be published under Martin's banner was Pope's culminating prose satire, *Peri Bathous: Or, Martinus Scriblerus his Treatise of the Art of Sinking in Poetry*, published in March 1728. The entire cast of 'Modern' thought is satirized through the views of its narrator. Martinus's perverted critical standards are devastated in his attempt to adapt Longinus' doctrines to the needs of modern mediocrity. With the brilliant use of false argument that was to become so predominant in his great satires of the 1730s, and with strong echoes of Swift's *Battle of the Books* and *Tale of a Tub*, Pope provides Martinus with the basic argument that, since mediocrity is literature's natural mode, and is so much more common than genius, the literary world's greatest need is for a system of rules to enable the mediocre to reach the poetic depths rather than soar to the heights. The ingenuity of Martinus' perversion of Longinus to this end is enlivened by Pope's selection of poetic examples illustrating every aspect of bathos and hence automatically classing as Dunces every author so quoted. Pope succeeds in making his narrator's language exemplify in itself the principles of half-educated, conceited, flashy, bombastic, and incoherent exposition of trivia that constitute his poetics. His style is made a marvellous blend of woodenness and false wit. It is prevented from alienat-

---

[1] The Club members were Pope, Swift, Arbuthnot, Parnell, and Gay, with occasional participation by Robert Harley, Earl of Oxford. Martin Scriblerus' *Memoirs*, which were to have been the keystone of the Club's proposed satirical attack on 'all the false tastes in learning' (Spence §135), remained unpublished until 1741, but the project gave direct or indirect rise to *Gulliver's Travels*, *Peri Bathous*, *The Dunciad*, and *The Beggar's Opera*. See *Memoirs of Scriblerus*, ed. C. Kerby-Miller.

ing the reader (as Swift was in serious danger of doing in similar circumstances in *A Tale of a Tub*) by the variety provided in the illustrations, and the scholarly excitement involved in following the close parody of Longinus in detail.

As a climax to Pope's satiric attacks on undesirable literary, cultural, and moral standards, *The Dunciad* appeared in May 1728, to be followed in April 1729 by *The Dunciad Variorum, with the Prolegomena of Scriblerus*. The *Variorum* in particular marks a fusion of both the aims and techniques of Pope's verse and prose satire throughout the past eighteen years. Thematically, all aspects of the world of witless, senseless, materialistic, uncultured Dulness come together and are given the strongest moral significance. The reign of Dulness herself threatens the total eclipse of all aspects of a vigorous, moral culture. As a satire, the work is brilliantly conceived both in structure and in detail. The mock-heroic mode, besides providing an extra dimension of enjoyment for learned readers as they watch the deliberate distortion of familiar epic devices, is a constant reminder of the best of the culture that is being destroyed, The appalling disparity between Pope's characters and those normally to be found within the epic framework, emphasizes still further the worthless degeneracy of Pope's opponents. The physical movements of the characters are deliberately stripped of all grace, beauty and dignity in order to emphasise the presence of moral ugliness, and excrement and filth are used to contaminate and degrade by association all that they touch. With regard to narrative technique, Pope now has two simultaneous narrative voices at his disposal; the disgusted representative of true cultural standards in the poem, and the team of dunces (Scriblerus, Theobald, and others) in the prolegomena and commentary. Pope uses his voices brilliantly, contrasting the clear ringing tones of the main narrator and the ludicrously dull, soporific, leaden pedantry of the 'learned' addenda.

If the *Dunciad*s are Pope's most sensational critical writing of this period, the serious prose criticism is perhaps the most acute and constructive detailed analysis of literary texts and theories, and the most impressive display of critical method, to be produced by any writer in the first half of the century. Among the early *Spectator* and *Guardian* papers, the essay on affectation (*Spectator* No. 404, 13 June 1712) re-states the

Essay on Criticism argument that each man has a particular 'Genius' which can be discerned by self-knowledge, or neglected through affectation. With regard to Pope's insistence upon strength of literary expression it is interesting to find his essay on reason and the passions (*Spectator* No. 408, 18 June 1712), accepting that passion is the primary motivating force, claiming that 'the greatest Geniuses have commonly the strongest Affections', and advocating the possession of strong passion controlled by 'the Reins of Reason and the Guidance of Judgment'. His *Guardian* essay on false critics (No. 12, 25 March 1713) is a particularly important résumé of ground covered in *An Essay on Criticism*. He considerably modifies and clarifies his view of the relationship between Nature, the works of the ancients, critics as lawgivers, and the modern creative writer. The process of learning criticism by studying and applying the 'rules' of other critics is viewed with strong distrust. In examining generally-accepted critical principles, he shows that the automatic demand for structural regularity is not applicable to all forms of poetry, to the extent 'that sometimes gentle Deviations, sometimes bold and even abrupt Digressions, where the Dignity of the Subject seems to give the Impulse, are Proofs of a noble Genius'. Similarly, the demand for 'ease' in writing is qualified by the argument that 'there are some Things which must be written with Strength, which nevertheless are easie'. Most important, in examining the opinion '*That all that is good is borrowed from the Ancients*' he argues that, given the uniformity of Nature, modern treatment of a great many topics is bound to resemble that of the ancients, but that a writer's main resource is direct observation of Nature, supplemented, rather than replaced, by specific imitation of classical writers:

> All that the most exquisite Judgment can perform is, out of that great Variety of Circumstances, wherein natural Objects may be considered, to select the most beautiful; and to place Images in such Views and Lights, as will affect the Fancy after the most delightful manner. But over and above a just Painting of Nature, a learned Reader will find a new Beauty superadded in a happy Imitation of some famous Ancient.

The poet's relationship with the past and with his contemporaries is further examined in the Preface to Pope's 1717 *Works*. The relationship of ancients to moderns is seen in a rather more servile light than in either *An Essay on Criticism* or the essay on false critics. The ancients are claimed to have penetrated as far into Nature as human common sense permits; the modern must therefore be content to imitate them, remembering at the same time to be a good man as well as a good writer. The alternative path to knowledge through direct observation of Nature is not stressed, but neither is dependence on any particular set of 'rules', so that the mode of communication between ancients and moderns tends to be seen as one of direct contact. The critic's role, therefore, does not appear to be central or indispensable to the poet's development. Modern critics, in fact, are a hindrance, being blamed for biased irrationality, expecting too much from writers, and failing to judge works as a whole, so that truthful judgment is hard to come by, and 'the life of a Wit is a warfare upon earth' (Twickenham I 6). With regard to both the treatment of bad writers and the attainment of self-knowledge, Pope adopts a more sympathetic stance than at any other time during this period. The bad author, according to him, deserves to be better treated than the bad critic, and self-knowledge can be attained only by trial and error. In those respects at least, then, Pope puts further emphasis on liberality in urging the reading public to be charitable and to leave the writer free to experiment.

There is no doubt about the liberality of Pope's central principles in the critical work done in connection with his translation of *The Iliad*. In his critical discussion 'he struck a . . . blow for light and insight', acknowledging 'the supremacy of imagination and . . . its indivisibility from judgement' (Twickenham VII xlvii). In the course of almost six years' scholarship and critical assessment, he was obviously obliged to exert continual discrimination in the selection of appropriate translations. In addition, his 'Observations' on each book show him struggling (usually very sensibly) to digest and make sense of previous Homeric criticism, and to comment on the work's development and beauties. At the end of his translation, too, he provides a copious series of indexes involving practically every conceivable aspect of the work (such as characters of gods, characters of heroes, speeches, and images), thereby providing the raw material for extremely detailed criticism. In so doing, he reminds us that, despite his insistence that we see literary works as a whole, he shares our consciousness that detailed analysis must precede informed generalization. Pope's own major critical statement, of course, comes in his Preface, published in 1715. Here, the opening sentence sets the tone of the whole piece: 'Homer is universally allow'd to have the greatest Invention of any Writer whatever', being the creator of rich, wild, irregular, natural beauty, impatient of restraint. The keynote of Pope's discussion, as in the *Epistle to Mr Jervas*, is strength: 'It is to the Strength of this amazing Invention we are to attribute that unequal'd Fire and Rapture, which is so forcible in *Homer*, that no Man of a true Poetical Spirit is Master of himself while he reads him'.[1] Here, then, is the sublime epitome of strong literature appealing to the emotions, and one can readily understand Pope's willingness to see Homer and Nature as the same when the works formulated such strong, dynamic liberal literary principles within him. Homer's fire, which 'can over-power Criticism, and make us admire even while we disapprove' is here seen as the supreme literary quality. It is possessed to some extent by Virgil (where it burns evenly, and generates light without much heat), by Lucan and Statius intermittently, by Milton through the 'Force of Art' rather than supreme genius, and by Shakespeare more or less accidentally; in its supreme form, however, it is to be found only in Homer himself. Throughout his subsequent, detailed examination of every aspect of Homer's art, Pope shows himself as the archetype of the critic as author and reader's sympathetic friend.

Pope's involvement in the subsequent *Odyssey* translation was not nearly so great. The Postscript, however, whilst not reaching the critical heights of his work on *The Iliad*, is an excellent comparative study of the two Homeric epics. Pope regrets *The Odyssey*'s comparative lack of 'fire', but finds compensation in such aspects as the clearly articulated moral, the regular plot, and the presence of much of *The Iliad*'s 'vivacity and fecundity of invention' (Twickenham X 385), strength of image and colour, well-drawn description, and harmoniously varied language.

Next to *The Iliad*, Pope's best and most extensive engagement in

---

[1] Twickenham VII 4; this passage is apparently derived from Pope's letter to Ralph Bridges, quoted above, p. 253.

detailed analysis is found in the critical element of his Shakespeare edition, published in March 1725.[1] Once again, his realization of the necessity for detailed observation of particulars as a prelude to sound generalization is shown in the provision of highly detailed indexes. His selection of 'some of the most shining passages' and of scenes 'where the beauty lay not in particulars, but in the whole' is indicated by a system of marginal commas and asterisks as 'a shorter and less ostentatious method of performing the better half of criticism (namely the pointing out an author's excellencies)'. The choice shows his sound, sensible taste, his critical independence in favouring currently unfashionable plays (such as *Antony and Cleopatra* and *Titus Andronicus*), and his own moral preoccupation with the themes of friendship, pride, and the ever-present danger of chaos and disorder. In the Preface, Shakespeare is seen as the purest known example of the poet of Nature, his works deriving from direct observation unimpeded by the 'strainers and channels' of the past that had influenced even Homer. He excels in natural and individual characterization, effortless power over the passions ('the heart swells and the tears burst out just at the proper places,' 162), in 'the coolness of reflection and reasoning' and in the appropriateness of his thought to the matter in hand. On the negative side, his genius is seen to suffer through his being a professional actor, obliged to pander to a debased audience by the use of vulgarity and sensationalism. It is regretted, too, that he did not benefit from Ben Jonson's revival of the principles of classical drama. Throughout his argument (and in direct contrast to *An Essay on Criticism* (Pope is paradoxically fortunate in that his lack of expertise in detailed logical discourse, and his relative unfamiliarity with Shakespeare's period, works to his advantage in enabling him to produce a bold, clear-cut image of his author which penetrates further

---

[1] The text of the *Preface* used here is from *The Literary Criticism of Alexander Pope*, ed. B. A. Goldgar. Pope's selection of outstanding Shakespearian passages is examined in J. Butt, *Pope's Taste in Shakespeare*, 1936; P. Dixon, 'Pope's Shakespeare', *JEGP* LXIII, 1964, 191–203; and J. M. Newton, 'Alive or Dead?. . .', *Cambridge Quarterly* III, No. 3 1968, 267–273. The difficulties inherent in Pope's claim that Aristotelian criteria are inapplicable to Shakespeare are analyzed in P. Ramsey, 'The Watch of Judgment', *Criticism and Aesthetics* 136–7.

towards the heart of his achievement than a more scholarly attempt might have done. Thus, his indifference to Shakespeare's indebtedness to his predecessors enables him to concentrate on the theme of original genius. His very influential theoretical observation that 'to judge therefore of Shakespeare by Aristotle's rules is like trying a man by the laws of one country who acted under those of another' (164) would have presented difficulties of inhibiting and mind-boggling complexity if he had paused to consider it in relation to the notion of general Nature and universally valid criteria. It is also noteworthy that his best criticism is concerned with writers (Homer and Shakespeare) to whom the criteria of humanly-formulated 'rules' are largely inapplicable. The Preface to Shakespeare in particular certainly substantiates our earlier impression that Pope's natural mode of response to the literature of the past was to perceive its worth through direct observation rather than through the filter of other critics' principles.

In the final phase of Pope's literary career, his concern with literary criticism manifests itself in at least four different ways. First, in his private conversation, as recorded by Joseph Spence, his interest in the art of poetry, and the evaluation of individual English writers, continues undiminished. Second, his implicit exposition of literary theory through his own creative practice could be said to reach its peak in the great satires of the 1730s, where the medium of the heroic couplet and the *genre* of literary imitation are developed and exploited as never before or since. Third, the fusion of moral and critical principles already noted in *The Dunciad* and elsewhere is further consolidated, particularly in the image of the good poet as good man, created in the narrative *persona* of the satires. This *persona* may be fundamentally Pope himself, but a Pope carefully edited to integrate with, and provide positives for, the moral and thematic concerns of his poetry. Fourth, the overt discussion of literary criticism in the poetry of this period follows on from (and culminates in) *The Dunciad* in its negative emphasis on the shortcomings of immoral dullness rather than on moral wit. The positives, of course, are implied by ironic reversal, by the qualities inherent in his poetry, by the nature of his narrative *persona*, and by the positives stated in his previous works. Thus, the criteria of thoughtful, graceful strength expounded in the earlier criticism provide a 'background' of standards in relation to which both the perversions of the Dunces and the virtue of Pope's own passionate involvement in 'moralized song' can be measured.

A vast amount of indispensable evidence relating to Pope's critical opinions is contained in his conversation throughout the 1730s (Spence, §§ 380–556 *et passim*). He continues to insist upon judging poems as a whole, making poetic language musical and onomatopoeic, and rejecting mediocrity (§§ 385, 396, 397, 407). Creative writing is seen to involve the four major elements, or 'tours', of design, language, versification, and descriptive 'expression' (§ 380). Long lists of those he considers to be the best English poets, dramatists, and prose writers of the past are provided (§§ 389–90, 408–505). He appears, however, to have taken a gloomy view of the literary *achievement* (though not necessarily potential) of his own lifetime (§ 485). His own critical balance and sensitivity are particularly well illustrated in his *critiques* of *Paradise Lost* (§§ 395, 459), where he analyzes Milton's power of modulating his poetic tone in response to the nature of his subject matter, and admires his achievement in making blank verse (normally unacceptable in English poetry) bearable by his sublimity. Finally, Martha Blount's report that she had 'often seen him weep in reading very tender and melancholy passages' (§ 409) records a concrete manifestation of the sensitive response that underlies all his criticism.

In his own poetry and prose of the period, Pope's mock-heroic and ironic attacks upon the dull world of the Dunces came to a magnificent head in the publication of *Memoirs of the Extraordinary Life, Works, and Discoveries of Martinus Scriblerus* in 1741 and the revised and extended four-book *Dunciad* in the following two years. As *Scriblerus* was the joint work of the Club, the exact nature of Pope's contribution outside his editorial labours cannot be known exactly, but the work as a whole is brilliantly successful in conveying all the negative qualities inherent in lack of judgment and sense (manifested, incidentally, just as much in distorted excess of reverence for the social habits and historical remains of the ancients as in a total failure to appreciate classical literature). In providing the most important single source of background material for the ongoings of Walter, Toby, and Tristram in Sterne's *Tristram Shandy*, Pope's decision to publish the work made a very far-reaching contribution to the development of English prose fiction. The four-book *Dunciad*, of course, achieves the same general impact, and has the same relationship to Pope's literary criticism, as the *Dunciad Variorum*, with a considerably increased degree of detail, depth and penetration. One need hardly labour either the comprehensiveness of the destruction of all culture portrayed in Book IV, or the increased effectiveness as literary satire achieved by substituting the brainless and self-important hack-of-all-work Colly Cibber as the central figure in place of the more specialised pedant Lewis Theobald. Here, the amalgamation of critical, cultural, and moral concerns in the negative aspect obviously reaches its height.

Throughout the 1730s, Pope's central preoccupation was with *An Essay on Man*, the *Moral Essays* (*Epistles to Several Persons*), and the Horatian imitations. With regard to literary criticism, the most interesting (though by no means the only) relevant issues involved in both *An Essay on Man* and the *Epistle to Cobham* are the complexities involved in any attempt to 'follow Nature', and Pope's consequential attempt to rationalize the complexities by means of the doctrine of the Ruling Passion. The former exposition adds considerable retrospective enrichment to the concept of 'following Nature' as advised in *An Essay on Criticism*. The failure of the latter provides an interesting comparison with Pope's earlier attempt—in parts of *An Essay on Criticism*—to fit the complexities and irrationalities of literary creation within a coherent framework of 'rules'. In *An Essay on Man*, human ability to understand Nature is seen as severely limited. Reason and instinct, remembrance and reflection, thought and the senses, are all intimately related. Even Newton (the exemplar of penetration into Nature, as were Homer, Aristotle, and Aquinas in *An Essay on Criticism*) cannot 'describe or fix one movement of his Mind' (Epistle II, 36), and Pope's mechanistic theory of the Ruling Passion does little to bring human complexity within the range of understanding. The opening couplet of the *Epistle to Cobham* emphasizes the barrenness of any attempt to bypass direct observation of Nature by recourse to second-hand accounts: 'Yes, you despise the man to Books confin'd,/Who from his study rails at human kind'. Stress is laid throughout on the importance of emotional and irrational factors involved in our coming to terms with the world about us, and we are constantly confronted with the near-impossibility of making any kind of objective assessment of human character. Here again, the proposed solution of recourse to the Ruling Passion comes nowhere near to imposing acceptable order upon the chaos that Pope has so convincingly portrayed.

An Epistle from Mr Pope to Dr Arbuthnot is of particular significance in bringing together with such unity of impact so many of Pope's critical concerns—the attack on Grub Street, the nature and function of satire, and Pope's defence of almost every aspect of his career. The *Character* of Atticus is given even greater force and subtlety by its juxtaposition with its new setting. Pope's analysis of false critics and criticism (151–172) is remarkable for its lucidity and symmetry. Again the emphasis is on the necessity for strength and life in criticism as in creative writing. Even the 'sober' critics who are not motivated by financial want, rage, or madness are condemned for their dull, plodding, parasitic dullness, their undue concentration on ludicrously unimportant *minutiae*, and their total lack of creative ability, 'spirit, taste, and sense'. Their mediocrity is implicity contrasted with Pope's graceful argument. Two bad critics, Bentley and Theobald, are singled out as exemplars, and are counterbalanced by two great creative writers, Milton and Shakespeare, who have suffered from their attentions, The good modern poet, exemplified by Pope himself, takes a tolerantly constructive approach to their attacks, smiling at their errors and submitting to their correction when it is justified.

Creative feebleness, and the relationship between morality and literature, come under further scrutiny in the *Epilogue to the Satires*, Dialogue I and Dialogue II. They embody what is perhaps eighteenth-century literature's most powerful argument in defence of the moral satirist's art, which draws the pen for freedom with complete integrity and impartiality, 'when Truth stands trembling on the edge of Law' (*Dialogue II* 249). The necessity for a combination of wit and morality is made clear not only by the implied immorality of writers who temper their criticism in order to please the powerful or to avoid giving offence, but also in the ironic false criticism that Pope is 'too *Moral* for a Wit' (Dialogue I 4).

Within the Horatian imitations themselves, the positive nature of Pope's provision of an 'art of imitation' by his own practice needs no comment or illustration. It must be remembered that specific critical statements made in the imitations may derive from Horace's original satire or epistle. To counter-balance this, however, we have Pope's skill in both selecting from and adding to the original argument, in such a way as to express his own ideas in a Horatian context. Pope's self-defence in *The First Satire of the Second Book of Horace, Imitated* (*To Mr Fortescue*) is of particular interest in its criticism of poetry which is either feeble, like Lord Fanny's; smoothly and emptily panegyric; bombastically heroic; or 'nobly wild, with *Budgell*'s Fire and Force', where strength and emotional appeal are employed outside the context of judgment upon ludicrously ignoble subjects. *The Second Epistle of the Second Book of Horace, Imitated* takes a similar approach to bad writing, and amplifies the critical discussion by attacks on the reading public's fickleness and the bad writer's motivation. The perversion of critical standards by dishonest flattery, pride, and complete lack of taste, is exemplified in the 'two Brother Sergeants' passage (127–138), and further condemned by the implied comparison with '*Milton*'s Genius' and '*Homer*'s Spirit' (136). In the discussion of the good poet's language (157–179), the creative process is seen as a severe discipline. Words which lack 'Force, or Light, or Weight, or Care' must be eliminated, bold and expressive old words revived, and new words sensibly coined, in order to achieve a poetic language 'serenely pure, and yet divinely strong'.

In this final period the two most important poems (with the exception of *The Dunciad*) relating to critical matters are the *Epistle to Burlington* and *The First Epistle of the Second Book of Horace, Imitated* (*To Augustus*). In both poems there is a fusion of literary criticism with other interests. In *To Burlington*, Pope is primarily concerned with taste as manifested in art, architecture, and landscape gardening. His method of using literary works as indices of character and moral worth is applied with particular effectiveness. Locke's rationality, Milton's sublimity, and modern literature of any kind, are conspicuously absent from Timon's library. The worlds of Don Quixote's Spain (160) and Gulliver's Brobdignag (104) bring out the foolish intransience of Timon's world, and the overblown magnificence of his villa in relation to his own puniness. Similarly, antiquarian books and 'rare monkish Manuscripts' (cunningly degraded and contaminated by proximity to Pembroke's ambiguously 'dirty' gods) are used as symbols of tasteless dullness in 'the Prodigal', Hearne, Mead, and Timon himself (6–10, 133–138). Numerous analogies are drawn or implied between painting, architecture, and literature. In Pope's summary of the principles of architecture (47–70), it is interesting to see strong similarities to *An Essay on Criticism*, though the aspect of 'Nature' stressed here is topographical rather than human. The definition of 'True Wit' in *An Essay on Criticism* is very much in the spirit of Pope's criteria of landscaping; the demands to 'consult the Genius of the Place in all', and to achieve unity through following 'Sense, of ev'ry Art the Soul', are familiar aspects of Pope's literary aesthetic. In *Burlington*, too, we are faced with the equally familiar problem of the relationship between Nature and the Rules— with the added complication, we may note, that in architecture Pope has no strong over-riding positive, no achieved embodiment of all that he considers best in architecture, to act as an exemplar analogous to Homer or Shakespeare in literature. He is apparently on safe ground when he commends the 'just' and 'noble rules' of Burlington's Palladianism, and scorns the ridiculous results of ignorant misapplication of the rules where pilastered façades have been built on to old property. The sterility of mechanically-applied regularity is equally strongly reflected in the absence of 'artful wildness' in Timon's garden. Pope's ultimate architectural aesthetic, therefore, appears to come very close to his central literary concerns, in being a pragmatic union of the neo-classical beauty of Palladian architecture, and the subtle beauty of irregular natural energy, harnessed rather more tightly than in literature within a framework of strict control. Initially, the 'deep Harvests' (175) evoke a wonderful sense of natural freedom and energy in both obliterating and enriching Timon's monstrosity, but in Pope's final advice to Burlington 'the dang'rous Flood' becomes 'obedient Rivers' and 'the roaring Main' the 'subject Sea', through the strict controlling powers of arches and walls.

Within the *Epistle to Augustus*, Pope's delicately-balanced blend of straightforward discussion and subtle false argument demonstrates his imitative genius and critical concern, whilst testing his readers' wit and critical response to their utmost limits. The range, compactness, and dazzling *legerdemain* of transition from topic to topic of Horace's original *Epistle* are in themselves more than sufficient to challenge any reader. Horace eulogises Augustus, pleads for his patronage of modern literature and gracefully apologizes for the poet's maladroit uncouthness in boring and pestering him, and so alienating his interest. The Romans' literary tastes and achievements are seen as being trapped in a vicious circle of false evaluation. The literate public has insufficient self-knowledge to know its own talents, so that everyone writes poetry, regardless of merit, and insufficient judgment to subscribe to rational aesthetic criteria, so that the public taste is fickle, and theatre audiences applaud performances for superficial splendour rather than true worth. Greek influence has enabled the potentially great Roman literature to overcome its original primitivism, but much remains to be done, and is worth doing. The development of modern literature, however, is severely handicapped by the misguided general assumption that only the literature of the past is worthy of admiration; that the writings of antiquity, in fact, are perfect, whilst contemporaries are *ipso facto* worthless, and can achieve only posthumous recognition. With regard to literature, then, Horace differentiates between great potential and poor performance in his own time, and between constructive and inhibiting reverence for the writers of the past. Pope takes over Horace's literary argument, brilliantly adapting it to, and illustrating it by, the literature of his own country. In addition, he expands and elaborates Horace's already elaborate structure, almost to the point of overloading, by turning eulogy of Augustus into an ironic attack on George II, which is almost treasonable in its savagery. Its main ironic mode is that of false argument. One is presented with the world of *Windsor Forest* on the surface (where the kingdom's achievements both emanate from, and reflect, the greatness of the ruling dynasty) and the world of *The Dunciad* lurking underneath (where George's consummately lethargic dullness in politics, war, and culture is both the source and the emblem of England's cultural degeneracy). Thus, the literary discussion is presented both for its own sake and as a satirical device to expose George's inadequacies. Our analysis of Pope's critical statements must therefore take into account his ulterior motives, together with the complication that his evaluation of past and present literature is being conducted within the framework of Horace's argument, rather than his own. By this time, too, Pope could rely on his readers having prior knowledge of the judgments expressed in his previous works. These combinations are particularly important in relation to his treatment of past English writers. Thus, when Pope exposes Shakespeare's and Jonson's materialism and indifference to posterity, Spenser's archaisms, Sidney's poor prosody, Milton's quibbling and use of prosaic verse, and Dryden's obscenity, he is presenting their shortcomings as evidence for the claim that English literature still has ample potential for development. This development will be lost if the reading public's slavish veneration for the past is allowed to obliterate its commitment to the present and its obligations towards the future. The undue emphasis that he is obliged to put on the shortcomings of his favourite authors is therefore a specialised extension of his critical activity, rather than a dramatic revaluation of his cultural position. This special pleading must be seen in the context of his earlier critical discussions, and by no means detracts from his insistence on the necessity to maintain contact with the past, and his sensitive appreciation of the strength and comprehensiveness of earlier writers, particularly Homer and Shakespeare. It must be admitted that his temporary desertion of the criterion that works must be seen as a whole is occasionally taken to dangerous lengths, particularly when he is obliged to use a series of perfectly sound appreciations of 'Shakespeare's Nature', 'Cowley's Wit', and so on (79–88) as examples of the reading public's hackneyed veneration of the past. For the most part, however, Pope's critical attitude in *Augustus* is positive and exciting. His passionate insistence that the battle for cultural survival must be fought in the present, for the benefit of the future. however good the literature of the past may have been, is his clearest public articulation of the criteria implied in his own creative work throughout his career. His portrayal of the complexities of his own literary world, where high poetic potential, public love of literature, low poetic performance, and irrational public reaction were so confusedly mingled, is the clearest of its time. In view of Pope's desire to see modern literature developing its potential, with the values of the past firmly, but not exclusively, in mind, it is perhaps significant that his most important and influential immediate critical disciple was not a poet, but a writer of prose fiction: Henry

Fielding's work combines respect for the classics with a desire for modern development in a manner highly reminiscent of Pope's suggestions. Finally, whatever the particular cultural area examined in any particular work, it is always noticeable that his demand for literary vigour and emotional appeal remains central. In the *Epistle to Augustus*, his definition of the 'Poet' as dramatist conveys this emphasis in its most memorable form:

> *Let me for once presume t'instruct the times,*
> *To know the Poet from the Man of Rymes :*
> *'Tis He, who gives my breast a thousand pains,*
> *Can make me feel each Passion that he feigns,*
> *Inrage, compose, with more than magic Art,*
> *With Pity, and with Terror, tear my heart.*   (340–5)

9: *Pope and the Idea of Fame*

DONALD FRASER

THE IDEA of fame has a long history in European literature and thought. 'Literary fame' means the immortality of written words and of the people, places and events which are recorded in them, and this proposition was often affirmed by classical and Renaissance writers. 'Love of fame' generally refers to men's craving for this immortality, or for recognition and approbation, and many other writers, especially those of a sceptical temperament, saw little of value in this desire, even when they admitted that it could stir men to worthy deeds. These are the major themes of fame, and although they may be approached from the 'literary' or the 'philosophical' standpoints, neither is really separable from the other. The whole topic commanded the continuing interest of both classical and Christian worlds. Poets were concerned about their ability and responsibility to commemorate (or castigate) men in 'lasting verses', the relationship between this and the poet's future reputation, and the ultimate question of whether fame has any substantial validity at all; Pope too, at the end of the Renaissance, found these questions a live issue.

The Temple of Fame (1715), a fairly free imitation of Chaucer's *Hous of Fame*, displays his early interest in the idea. In this poem Pope presents first a visionary survey of legendary heroes and literary masters, imaged as allegorical figures in and around the temple; next follows a series of judgments on contemporary seekers after fame, made under the rather arbitrary patronage of the goddess Fame, and then a virtuoso description of the house of Rumour. The style of the poem is an intriguing mixture of Pope's grand manner and contemporary satire, but his conclusion has a surprisingly personal tone. In a kind of epilogue, fame is treated not as the abstract idea of lasting renown, nor as the fictional figure who adjudicated over human endeavours, but as a subject of serious philosophical and ethical discussion. And the youthful poet himself appears to be offering this manifesto as his genuine personal opinion on this topic:

> *While thus I stood, intent to see and hear,*
> *One came, methought, and whisper'd in my Ear;*
> *What cou'd thus high thy rash Ambition raise?*
> *Art thou, fond Youth, a Candidate for Praise?*
>   *'Tis true, said I, not void of Hopes I came,*
> *For who so fond as youthful Bards of Fame?*
> *But few, alas! the casual Blessing boast,*
> *So hard to gain, so easy to be lost:*
> *How vain that second Life in others' Breath,*
> *Th'Estate which Wits inherit after Death!*
> *Ease, Health, and Life, for this they must resign,*
> *(Unsure the Tenure, but how vast the Fine!)*
> *The Great Man's Curse without the Gains endure,*
> *Be envy'd, wretched, and be flatter'd, poor;*
> *All luckless Wits their Enemies profest,*
> *And all successful, jealous Friends at best.*
> *Nor Fame I slight, nor for her Favours call;*
> *She comes unlook'd for, if she comes at all:*
> *But if the Purchase costs so dear a Price,*
> *As soothing Folly, or exalting Vice:*
> *Oh! if the Muse must flatter lawless Sway,*
> *And follow still where Fortune leads the way;*
> *Or if no Basis bear my rising Name,*
> *But the fall'n Ruins of Another's Fame:*
> *Then teach me, Heaven! to scorn the guilty Bays;*
> *Drive from my Breast that wretched Lust of Praise;*
> *Unblemish'd let me live, or die unknown,*
> *Oh grant an honest Fame, or grant me none!* (497–524)

Pope's response to the question is ambivalent without being vague; recognizing all its practical drawbacks, he would nevertheless accept an honestly-earned fame while still attempting to remain indifferent to its possession. Although this may seem like a 'personal viewpoint', its specific ingredients are mostly derived from established traditional views on the moral aspect of fame. For instance, the association of fame, 'the casual Blessing', with mere fortune, was well-known to Montaigne: '. . . what is more accidental than Reputation? . . . 'tis Chance that helps us to Glory'.[1] Pope could easily have met the worldly-wise sentiment that fame is 'So hard to gain, so easy to be lost', in Addison's *Spectator*, Nos. 255, 256 and 257 (22–25 December 1711), which set out to show 'that Fame is a thing difficult to be obtained, and easily lost'. He could have found in many sceptical writers the statement that 'Fame is but breath', and the witty turn of 'that second Life in others' Breath' (which so effectively devalues the hope of fame) depends on this aphorism, as well as on a memory of more confident allusions to fame as breath, such as Oldham's promise that a friend's virtues would make his name 'lasting as the Breath of Fame'.[2] In the *Essay on Man*, Pope began his critique of fame by re-using this idea: 'What's Fame? a fancy'd life in others breath' (IV 237).

Even the general attitude of Pope's conclusion to the *Temple of Fame*—disparagement of worthless fame linked uneasily with a reluctance to forgo it—has a long classical heritage.

> *Nor Fame I slight, nor for her Favours call;*
> *She comes unlook'd for, if she comes at all.*

This median position of indifference to fame had been advocated by Seneca; since fame *will* follow after virtuous actions, one should accept it, but without ever actively seeking or desiring it.[3] It would be a mistake to imagine that Pope adopted these conventional opinions without thought. In other public and private statements, he persistently laid claim to this stoic attitude. In a letter to Wycherley of 20 May 1709, he appropriated Falstaff's words on honour to his own view on fame: '*If i comes, it comes unlook'd for; and there's an End on't*' (*Corr.* I 60); in the

---

[1] Montaigne, *Essays*, Book II, ch. xvi, trans. Charles Cotton, 3rd edn 1700, II 476–7.
[2] John Oldham, 'To the Memory of my Dear Friend, Mr. Charles Morwent,' st. xlii, *Works*, 1722, II 308.
[3] Seneca, *Epistulae Morales*, lxxix. 13.

manuscript of the 'Preface' to the *Works* of 1717, his apology for pub-lishing included the same sentiment: 'As for fame, I shall be glad of any I can get, and not repine at any I miss'.[1]

The final couplet further illustrates Pope's reasonably consistent attitude, displaying a remarkable similarity to the last stanza of his earliest surviving poem, the 'Ode on Solitude.' It also shows once again how elements both traditional and individual combine in Pope's mani-festo, for the 'Ode' itself was composed of thoroughly conventional desires for a retired life and unnoticed death. Pope might have drawn some elements directly from Lord Roscommon's 'Ode on Solitude' or from George Granville's or Cowley's well-known translations of the chorus from Act II of Seneca's *Thyestes* for his final stanza:

> *Thus let me live, unseen, unknown;*
> *Thus unlamented let me dye;*
> *Steal from the world, and not a stone*
> *Tell where I lye.*

Here, with obvious determination, Pope is forswearing ambition, repu-tation, and the dubious fame of being remembered after death. He puts the same phrases into the mouths of the small group of modest folk in the *Temple of Fame* who aspire to no fame, begging the goddess only to grant them obscurity:

> *But safe in Desarts from th'Applause of Men,*
> *Would die unheard of, as we liv'd unseen.*   (360–61)

In this poem the goddess indignantly refuses their modest request, insisting on blazoning 'those Virtues which the Good would hide' (369), and this perhaps prompted Pope to the more realistic aspiration which ends the *Temple of Fame*:

> *Unblemish'd let me live, or die unknown,*
> *Oh grant an honest Fame, or grant me none!*

Whereas in the 'Ode on Solitude' he would be 'innocent' (15) *and* 'unknown', now these have become alternatives—'unblemish'd *or* un-known'. He would accept for himself, or even ask for ('grant'), the

---

[1] *Works of Alexander Pope Esq.*, ed William Warburton, 1751, I xi.

renown of well-doing, provided this could be achieved by 'honest' means.

So, while the materials on which Pope bases his 'philosophical' discussion of fame are commonplace, it is clear that he has tried to make these views his own. The repetition of these themes in his work is a sign that he has assimilated them so fundamentally that he could afterwards modify them. Their reappearance is a mark not of habit, but of interest and thoughtful concern, for fame is to Pope a debatable question, not a settled conclusion.

Pope's vivid sense of the unreliability of fame in this coda is natural, coming as it does after the confusions, 'All neither wholly false, nor wholly true' (457), of the house of Rumour. But the first part of his poem had proposed a much less melancholy view of fame. There Pope asserts that the fame of the ancient heroes and worthies whom he exhibits on the outer walls of the temple, and within it on elevated thrones and shrines, will *not* pass away. The images of light, of elevation, of incense and sweet sounds with which Pope surrounds them are all standard concomitants of fame in classical and Renaissance writing. After the legendary heroes 'To whom old Fables gave a lasting Name' (130), and the historical figures of rulers and philosophers, Pope's survey of the truly famous reaches its climax with his writers, 'the greatest Names in Learning of all Antiquity' (Pope's note to 178ff.). He stresses their primacy by their central position, exalted above the rest (as 'the Learned World' are also first to appear before the goddess' shrine, 298):

> But in the Centre of the hallow'd Quire
> Six pompous Columns o'er the rest aspire;
> Around the Shrine it self of Fame they stand,
> Hold the chief Honours, and the Fane command.   (178–81)

He then describes, with the additional infusion of religious imagery which adds further to their dignity, the figures of Homer, Virgil, Pindar, Horace, Aristotle and Cicero.

Besides their paramount position among the other occupants of the temple, these writers in person even surpass the fame which they have given in their writings to the subjects of their works. Swift stated this idea with sarcastic exaggeration: 'Whatever the Poets pretend, it is plain they give Immortality to none but themselves: It is *Homer* and *Virgil* we reverence and admire, not *Achilles* or *Aeneas*. . . .'[1] While Pope is not so open about it, his allegorical picture has similar implications, as a comparison with his source will show. In Chaucer's *Hous of Fame*, the pagan writers 'bear up' their subjects on their shoulders (Twickenham II 378–9), whereas in the *Temple of Fame* Pope elevates his writers above their subjects: 'The Columns on which they are rais'd are adorn'd with Sculptures, taken from the most striking Subjects of their Works' (178n). Their literary works serve as the foundation of their individual fame as authors; Pope's language insists on the 'Motion and Life' (192) in all this 'living Sculpture' (204), as if the subjects' liveliness were evidence for their makers' immortality, and as if authorial fame were ultimately supreme. Similarly, it is really the fame of authors which is discussed in Pope's coda, for he mentions particularly the kind of fame of which 'Bards', 'Wits', or 'the Muse' are inclined to be so fond.

In *Essay on Criticism* (1711) Pope had actually appended his own 'modest' aspirations as a poet to a passage which asserted, with few misgivings, the pre-eminent immortality of the ancient writers:

> *Still green with Bays each* ancient *Altar stands,*
> *Above the reach of* Sacrilegious *Hands.*
>
> . . . .
>
> *See, from each* Clime *the Learn'd their Incense bring;*
> *Hear, in* all Tongues *consenting* Paeans *ring!*
>
> . . . .
>
> *Hail* Bards Triumphant! *born in* happier Days;
> Immortal *Heirs of* Universal *Praise!*
> *Whose Honours with Increase of Ages* grow,
> *As Streams roll down,* enlarging *as they flow!*
> *Nations* unborn *your mighty Names shall sound,*
> *And Worlds applaud that must not yet be* found!
> *Oh may some Spark of* your *Cœlestial Fire*
> *The last, the meanest of your Sons inspire,*
> *(That on weak Wings, from far, pursues your Flights;*

---

[1] Swift, 'Thoughts on Various Subjects,' *A Tale of a Tub*, ed Herbert Davis, Oxford 1939, 242.

> Glows *while he* reads, *but* trembles *as he* writes)
> *To teach vain Wits a Science* little known,
> *T'*admire *Superior Sense, and* doubt *their own!*   (181ff.)

Although Pope may be a *humble* follower, his willingness to testify about his own personal ambition in the immediate context of the ancients' everlasting achievements suggests at least a wishful recognition that a modern might aspire to such poetic permanence.

The headpiece for *An Essay on Criticism* in the *Works* of 1717 embodies this suggestion with remarkable clarity (Plate 14). In a grove the laurelled busts of Homer and Virgil stand on two plinths, while in the background Pegasus, the immortal horse of the Muses, flies above Parnassus. Before the altars a gowned figure bows in homage; this can only be the youthful bard, Pope himself. At his back stands Fame, trumpet in hand, pointing him towards his great exemplars. The illustration symbolizes precisely Pope's homage to their abiding fame, *and* the motivation of renown which incites him to emulate them.

If Pope's ascetic choice of retirement before renown in the 'Ode on Solitude' now seems a little compromised by this ambition, and by his ambivalent conclusion to the *Temple of Fame*, it would appear to be completely negated by his imitation of 'Part of the Ninth Ode of the Fourth Book of Horace.' Although Pope never published this himself, its theme obviously was relevant to him as a 'moral poet' at the climax, in the late 1730s, of his career in public and personal poetry. Horace's ode, which J. B. Leishman has called 'the most impressive single treatment of the theme of poetic immortality in the whole of European poetry',[1] praises the enduring art of lyric poets, naming many of them as fit to follow Homer. In his imitation, Pope transfers the scene and cast to England, but still declares his assent to Horace's belief in poetic fame, attempting to give his verse, by exclamations, oracular repetitions and rather pompous grammar, th e heavy dignity of a heart-felt lament

> *Lest you should think that Verse shall die,*
> *Which sounds the Silver Thames along,*
> *Taught on the Wings of Truth, to fly*
> *Above the reach of vulgar Song;*

[1] J. B. Leishman, *Themes and Variations in Shakespeare's Sonnets*, 1961, 29.

> *Tho' daring Milton sits Sublime,*
> *In Spencer native Muses play;*
> *Nor yet shall Waller yield to time,*
> *Nor pensive Cowley's moral Lay.*
>
> *Sages and Chiefs long since had birth*
> *E're Caesar was, or Newton nam'd,*
> *These rais'd new Empires o'er the Earth,*
> *And Those new Heav'ns and Systems fram'd;*
>
> *Vain was the chief's and sage's pride*
> *They had no Poet and they dyd!*
> *In vain they schem'd, in vain they bled*
> *They had no Poet and are dead!*

Pope now follows Horace (rather than Seneca) in assuming that to die unwept and unknown is a deplorable fate, and that the natural desire of chiefs and sages is to be remembered in deathless verses. These lines strongly emphasize that the powers of immortal memory lie only with poets, and the first two stanzas plainly imply that Pope himself could fill the place of the poet whose absence he must lament. Now he presents himself, a poet who lives by the Thames, as a follower and successor to the great English poets. When Pope declared his allegiance to the ancients in *An Essay on Criticism*, it was in the context of their literary fame, and here there is the same convergence of themes. The lyric poets Waller and Cowley share some of the glory which Milton and Spenser derived from epic because their verses are equally lasting, and it is on this criterion that Pope hopes to align himself with them.

This poem is mainly concerned with the immortal fame which great poets can give, although the corollary—that the poet too will be famous—is implied. It was usually by innuendo that Pope claimed this noble office, and he was careful not to make conspicuous promises that men would live for ever in his verse; nevertheless, he did consider himself, according to the tradition, a poet capable of dispensing fame, and he sometimes concealed such claims in jocular treatments of the theme. For example, his 'thank-you' poem written 'On receiving from the Right Hon. the Lady Frances Shirley a Standish and Two Pens' (*c.*1739), under cover of a love-compliment presents the poet in his customary rôle as scourge of vice and celebrant of virtue, dispenser of praise and blame. Pope is in fact gently declining the lady's request that he should abandon the public arena and return to personal lyrics, but by replying in comic terms he ensures that his commitment to moral song is not too self-advertising. The comic element in the poem is only meant to deflect hostile attention from Pope's serious claim that he wishes to influence society by his deployment of fame and infamy.

The poem begins with a splendid mock-heroic vision, in the manner of a baroque mythological painting, of Athena presenting armour to a warrior:

> *Yes, I beheld th'Athenian Queen*
> *Descend in all her sober charms;*
> *'And take (she said, and smil'd serene)*
> *Take at this hand celestial arms:*
>
> *'Secure the radiant weapons wield;*
> *This golden lance shall guard Desert,*
> *And if a Vice dares keep the field,*
> *This steel shall stab it to the heart.'*
>
> *Aw'd, on my bended knees I fell,*
> *Receiv'd the weapons of the sky;*
> *And dipt them in the sable Well,*
> *The fount of Fame or Infamy.*

'The life of a Wit is a warfare upon earth' Pope had said in the 'Preface' to his *Works*. In this heroic metaphor the pen becomes the sword; the golden lance serves the function of eulogy, which is the usual reward of virtue (or 'Desert'), while the steel which is to destroy vice stands for Pope's satirical poetry. The recipient's immediate reaction to this gift is to dispense his judgments on moral issues, and his metaphoric terms for this are 'Fame or Infamy'. In other words, Pope views himself, in his guise of public commentator, as a poet whose duty is to give his subjects renown, or commit them to contempt. Praise and blame are to be made public.

The quasi-religious awe with which he receives 'the weapons of the sky', these 'celestial arms', is typical of the reverence which he always displayed for satire, that 'sacred Weapon . . . To all but Heav'n-

directed hands deny'd' (*Epilogue to the Satires:* Dialogue II 212, 214).
Pope sees himself as a warrior, 'arm'd for *Virtue* when I point the Pen'
(*Satire II i, To Fortescue,* 105), in the holy war against Vice on behalf of
Virtue. But lest we should accuse him of excessive self-importance
about his position as arbiter of fame and infamy, Pope makes the donor
(in the person of Flavia) respond with this commonsense deflation of
his epic periphrasis:

> '*What* well? *what* weapon? *(Flavia cries)*
> *A standish, steel and golden pen;*
> *It came from Bertrand's, not the skies;*
> *I gave it you to write again.* . . .'

This is a reminder that however sublime the poet's civic responsibility
may seem, by its very nature it must be performed in the ordinary
erring world which so demands his attention. In the rest of the poem,
Pope makes no real answer to Lady Frances' conclusion begging him
not to intervene further in the public sphere; he thus implies that once
he had 'stoop'd to Truth, and moraliz'd his song' he could never relin-
quish the sacred weapons.

Although poets are prone to think of fame as a future reward, it does
not refer exclusively to great renown achieved in the eyes of posterity.
Men seem also to have a strong desire for a good reputation among their
contemporaries, and Locke even maintained that this was the basis of
their obedience to the laws:

> He who imagines commendation and disgrace not to be strong
> motives to men to accommodate themselves to the opinions and
> rules of those with whom they converse, seems little skilled in the
> nature or history of mankind: the greatest part whereof we shall
> find to govern themselves chiefly, if not solely, by this *law of
> fashion*; and so they do that which keeps them in reputation with
> their company, little regard the laws of God, or the magistrate . . . .
> no man escapes the punishment of their censure and dislike, who
> offends against the fashion and opinion of the company he keeps,
> and would recommend himself to.[1]

[1] John Locke, *An Essay Concerning Human Understanding*, II. xxviii. 12,
ed. A. C. Fraser, Oxford 1894, I 497.

Pope bases the social utility of fame and infamy on this premiss. Thus, the infamy which satire confers on its victim is a kind of punishment, and it *may* even cause him to reform; if not, it can at least, by the power of example, stand as an awful warning to other men to shun such villainy.

In a letter addressed to Swift by Pope and Bolingbroke in 1732 Pope expounds this view of satire, which assumes that poetic infamy can be a good influence in society: 'I know nothing that moves strongly but Satire, and those who are asham'd of nothing else, are so of being ridiculous. I fancy if we three were together but for three years, some good might be done even upon this Age; or at least some punishment made effectual, toward the Example of posterity, between History, Philosophy, and Poetry, or the Devil's in it' (*Corr.* III 276). Pope's first hope is that ridicule (meaning the contempt of one's fellowmen) could do good 'even upon this Age' by persuading evil-doers to live morally. Then, lest this should seem too optimistic, he proposes that satiric infamy will 'at least' punish them even if it brings about no reformation. And such punishment might eventually be effectual in another direction, for the ugly sight of victims exposed to embarrassing contempt should work 'toward the Example of posterity', urging future generations to abstain from vice.

There are two character-sketches at the end of the *Essay on Man* which exemplify Pope's opinion that fame and infamy are ethically useful; at the same time, they raise the familiar question of the possession and worth of personal fame. Towards the end of Epistle IV, Pope gives a satirical catalogue of 'external goods', including fame, and proves 'That even these can make no Man happy without Virtue' ('Argument', Epistle IV). His definitive proof is made through an example of the type of man whose universal ambition brought him every possible external good, without making him happy:

> *If all, united, thy ambition call,*
> *From ancient story learn to scorn them all.*
> *There, in the rich, the honour'd, fam'd and great,*
> *See the false scale of Happiness complete!*   (IV 285–8)

The phrase 'ancient story' tells us what Pope intends; by its placing in the poem, his 'ancient story' will serve the rhetorical function of providing a notable example which *can* affect behaviour. It endorses Pope's high ideal, mentioned to Spence in 1743, of the purpose of reading: 'I should read . . . to make myself and others better. I would mark down: "on such an occasion the people concerned proceeded in such a manner; it was evidently wrong and had a very ill effect; a statesman therefore should avoid it in a like case." Such an one did good or got an honest reputation by such an action: I would mark it down in order to imitate it where I had an opportunity' (Spence § 578).

In furtherance of his first principle, Pope records the story for others to read, thus giving publicity to the notorious life and death of such a 'Hero'. The sombre Juvenalian tone, and the imperatives which command the reader's awed attention, highlight its ethical purpose of making men better.

> *In hearts of Kings, or arms of Queens who lay,*
> *How happy! those to ruin, these betray,*
> *Mark by what wretched steps their glory grows,*
> *From dirt and sea-weed as proud Venice rose;*
> *In each how guilt and greatness equal ran,*
> *And all that rais'd the Hero, sunk the Man.*
> *Now Europe's laurels on their brows behold,*
> *But stain'd with blood, or ill exchang'd for gold,*
> *Then see them broke with toils, or sunk in ease,*
> *Or infamous for plunder'd provinces.*
> *Oh wealth ill-fated! which no act of fame*
> *E'er taught to shine, or sanctify'd from shame!*
> *What greater bliss attends their close of life?*
> *Some greedy minion, or imperious wife,*
> *The trophy'd arches, story'd halls invade,*
> *And haunt their slumbers in the pompous shade.*
> *Alas! not dazzled with their noon-tide ray,*
> *Compute the morn and ev'ning to the day;*
> *The whole amount of that enormous fame,*
> *A Tale, that blends their glory with their shame!*
>   *Know then this truth (enough for Man to know)*
> *'Virtue alone is Happiness below.'*   (IV 289–310)

The poet has presented this history of universal greatness in order to discourage men from following it. Truly great men are to be emulated,

but this is an exemplum which operates by inversion, inviting our scorn
and expecting horrified aversion from its painful tale.

The didactic function of this story, as a symbolic portrait, is obvious;
if we can also recognize in it some features derived from a real person,
its power to confer infamy and to inculcate morality may be increased.
There seems little doubt that Pope thought primarily of the great Duke
of Marlborough in conceiving this portrait. Although only after 1734,
when Pope revised and expanded it (in manuscript), does the portrait
become so unmistakably one of Marlborough that it could not then be
published in its new form,[1] even the original version in Epistle IV suggested enough of the Duke's notorious qualities to enable malicious
readers to identify him. In a letter of 1731, Pope linked the character and
history of Marlborough with their exemplary function in the *Essay on
Man*: 'I have been busy in the Moral Book I told you of: many exemplary Facts & Characters fall into it daily, but which render it less fit
for the Present Age. The Fate of the Marlborough family is a Great one,
which the death of the Marquess of Blandford has renewd my Reflec-
tions on.'[2] The day of the Duke's funeral in 1722 had already given
Pope occasion to 'moralize . . . on the vanity of human Glory'[3] and
in the *Essay* too, the exemplum bears out this tragic note, blending with
the poem's stress on man's limitations—'His time a moment, and a point
his space' (I 72)—and the ultimate brevity of human achievements in
face of 'the lurking principle of death' (II 134). The frontispiece to the
Essay, which also emphasizes these themes, contains another possible
reflection on Marlborough, for the fallen statue is a sardonic allusion to
the great warrior's glorification in a series of contemporary tomb-
paintings.[4] The equivalent portrait in the poem is effectively a satirical
epitaph, setting out to contradict such extravagant praise as Addison
had awarded him in *The Campaign* (1705):

[1] See 'Character of Marlborough', Twickenham VI 358–9.
[2] To Hugh Bethel, 8 September 1731: *Corr*. III 227 and note. Blandford
was the first Duke's grandson.
[3] To Atterbury, 27 July [1722]: *Corr*. II 127.
[4] This idea is suggested and explored by Benjamin Boyce, 'Baroque
into Satire: Pope's Frontispiece for the "Essay on Man,"' *Criticism* IV,
1962, 14–27. The frontispiece is reproduced in Twickenham III i.

> *Unbounded courage and compassion join'd,*
> *Temp'ring each other in the victor's mind,*
> *Alternately proclaim him good and great,*
> *And make the Hero and the Man compleat.*   (219–22)

There is an extra couplet in the manuscript version which further underlines the exemplary function of the portrait even as it stands in the *Essay*. Pope asks:

> *Who now his fame or fortune shall prolong*
> *In vain his consort bribes for venal song.*   (27–8)

The poet made two significant comments on this, First, he apparently told Warburton that he had refused the Duchess of Marlborough's offer of 'a very considerable sum' to insert a good character of her husband (Spence, § 365). Then, writing in 1736 to the Earl of Orrery about Marlborough's 'meaner mixture with his great Qualities', he said: 'But I lament with you his negligence, in not procuring what real Merit he had, & what shining Virtues as a Public man, to be better transmitted to Posterity' (*Corr.* IV 36). Pope, who boasted that he could not flatter, was unwilling to assist in prolonging the great General's fame by celebrating him in a commissioned eulogy (although he does admit his greatness, the brightness of 'his Noontide ray'). Instead, having concluded that Marlborough is a figure of blame, whose story shows us what to avoid rather than what to emulate, Pope exploits his undoubted fame for an admonitory purpose. Thus the final couplet shows him 'damn'd to ever-lasting fame', a conclusively infamous example:

> *The whole amount of that enormous fame,*
> *A Tale, that blends their glory with their shame!*

It is also most important that this 'Tale' passes directly, with a 'Know then' that draws the inference, to the aphoristic moral which all the satirical instances have been tending towards:

> *Know then this truth (enough for Man to know)*
> *'Virtue alone is Happiness below.'*

After this direct statement of the 'moral', there is a change in direction, pointed out by Warburton in his note on line 311: 'Hitherto the poet

had proved, NEGATIVELY, that Happiness consists in Virtue, by shew-
ing it consisted not in any other thing. He now . . . proves the same
POSITIVELY, by an enumeration of its Qualities. . . .' As the shame
of Marlborough provided evidence on the negative side, the proof
positive of Pope's case is conversely strengthened by an adulatory
portrait of Bolingbroke, his guide, philosopher and friend. Sixty lines
in praise of the happiness which comes only from virtue and a submission to Providence lead the poet to this final address, which is at
once an exhortation to himself, a character-sketch that balances Marlborough's infamy, and the fulfilment of the invocation to St John which
opened the poem:

> *Come then, my Friend, my Genius, come along,*
> *Oh master of the poet, and the song!*
> *And while the Muse now stoops, or now ascends,*
> *To Man's low passions, or their glorious ends,*
> *Teach me, like thee, in various nature wise,*
> *To fall with dignity, with temper rise;*
> *Form'd by thy converse, happily to steer*
> *From grave to gay, from lively to severe;*
> *Correct with spirit, eloquent with ease,*
> *Intent to reason, or polite to please.*   (IV 373–82)

Bolingbroke's status as virtuous example is defined when Pope begs
him to 'Teach me, like thee . . .'; the portrait expresses what Bolingbroke is and what Pope would be. St John is both friend and genius, 'master of the poet, and the song' and Pope accordingly would emulate him
in life and in thought. As the philosopher was his 'Genius', or inspiration,
Pope would be moulded by his 'converse', and as Pope's 'Friend', St
John can teach him the wisdom of life in success and adversity. So
Bolingbroke's function in the poem is the reciprocal of Marlborough's;
two great men exemplify the positive and negative aspects of virtue.
The Duke stands for false greatness, all that must be scorned, while the
Viscount is the poet's mentor, inspiring the themes of the poem and sus-
taining them in his life. The artistic contrast is clear.

But Pope does not mean Bolingbroke's fame to be solely of the exemplary kind; with these notable compliments he also sets out to make him

as celebrated as his opposite was notorious. No matter that Pope has before attacked fame as an illusive vanity, and a breath (II 245–6, 267–70; IV 237–8). Now he is certain that Bolingbroke's qualities will ensure him fame, and the verse asserts this inevitability through several run-on lines, and with urgent questions and repetitions:

> *Oh! while along the stream of Time thy name*
> *Expanded flies, and gathers all its fame,*
> *Say, shall my little bark attendant sail,*
> *Pursue the triumph, and partake the gale?*
> *When statesmen, heroes, kings, in dust repose,*
> *Whose sons shall blush their fathers were thy foes,*
> *Shall then this verse to future age pretend*
> *Thou wert my guide, philosopher, and friend?*
> *That urg'd by thee, I turn'd the tuneful art*
> *From sounds to things, from fancy to the heart. . . .*
>
> (IV 383–92)

The image used for Bolingbroke's fame is a curious one. The stream of time usually carries all things away, but here his name is said to shoot along it with doubled speed to an assured triumph. Pope is alluding to fame as a wind here, for St John's 'name' seems to represent a sail which gathers in the 'gale'. Johnson gives two senses for 'expand': first, 'to spread; to lay open . . . as a sheet', and second, to 'dilate', or 'diffuse', quoting this passage in evidence.[1] Cowley's familiar piece on fame—'Some swell up their sleight sails with pop'ular fame'—and Steele's figure of the voyage of life with conscience as our ballast, and fame as our sail, may confirm this precise sense of the metaphor.[2] So fame here can be a wind much more secure than breath, which is an odd contradiction of the poet's earlier critique of fame.

This inconsistency is compounded by Pope's metaphoric claim to

---

[1] Johnson, *Dictionary*, 4th edn 1773, 'Expand', 1, 2. Pope uses the first sense in *Odyssey* XII 105–6:

> *O fly the dreadful sight! expand thy sails,*
> *Ply the strong oar, and catch the nimble gales.*

[2] Cowley, 'Of Agriculture,' *Essays, Plays and Sundry Verses*, ed. A. R. Waller, Cambridge 1906, 410; Steele, *The Christian Hero*, 1701, ch. iv.

association with Bolingbroke's fame; he hopes to follow the triumph and share the fame, but only as a humble attendant. The question form suggests his uncertain modesty, as does the formula 'urg'd by thee' which rhetorically implies the writer's humility before his patron and the public. But to 'pretend' can apply to a proclamation sent forward 'to future ages' as well as to a presumptuous profession, and it is not unlikely that Pope, at the end of 'that Poem, in which I am immortal for my Morality',[1] again failed to restrain himself from his usual hope of speaking to posterity. If the phrasing of that remark is basically jocular, we nevertheless know that Pope did take a very serious pride in being praised for his philosophical poetry. A month later he wrote again to Swift: 'I must first acknowledge the honour done me by Lord Orrery, whose praises are that precious ointment Solomon speaks of, which can be given only by men of Virtue: All other praise, whether from Poets or Peers, is contemptible alike: and I am old enough and experienced enough to know, that the only praises worth having, are those bestowed *by* Virtue *for* Virtue' (*Corr.* III 372).

Another of Pope's favourite themes is hinted at in this conclusion; he liked to hope that he would be personally remembered in future generations on account of his worthy and noble friendships. This declaration of genuine pride in being known for a friend and compeer of Bolingbroke (and of Swift) is not unlike the sentiment in his poetic address to Bolingbroke:

> You are indeed almost the only men I know, who either can write in this age, or whose writings will reach the next: Others are mere mortals. . . . If I can think that neither he nor you despise me, it is a greater honour to me by far, and will be thought so by posterity, than if all the House of Lords writ Commendatory Verses upon me, the Commons order'd me to print my Works, the Universities gave me publick thanks, and the King, Queen, and Prince crown'd me with Laurel. You are a very ignorant man; you don't know the figure his name and yours will make hereafter; I do, and will preserve all the memorials I can, that I was of your intimacy; *longo, sed proximus, intervallo*. . . .[2]

[1] To Swift, 20 April 1733: *Corr.* III 366.
[2] To Swift, 17 August 1736: *Corr.* IV 27–8. *Aeneid* V 320: 'But next by a long distance. . . .'

By the Latin phrase Pope means that he himself comes next, though far behind, and that is exactly the implication of the boat-metaphor. Pope hopes that fame will accrue to him because he is St John's 'friend'.

The idea that a great man's fame might be shared with a friend was amusingly applied in Pope's own case by the engraved frontispiece (Plate 15) to *The Works of Alexander Pope Esq. In Nine Volumes Complete. . . . Together with the Commentaries and Notes of Mr. Warburton* (1751). A bust of the editor William Warburton, on a medallion which matches Pope's in size, hangs like a pendant beneath the poet, while figures representing History (or Poetry?) and Fame herself, with laurels and a trumpet, sit in adoring attendance below. In his own relation to Bolingbroke, of course, Pope would not have made such an avowal of equality. His claim to follow is couched in conventionally modest terms, although it is never easy to catch Pope in one mind about his own worth or reputation.

As there are ambiguities in Pope's attitude towards his own fame and the future fame of his verses, so his motives in attributing fame and infamy are not straightforward. His frequent boast that his verses acted as a guardian of national virtue was sometimes compromised by the existence of private enmities and friendships. For instance, when dispensing infamy Pope was not always so high-minded as he appeared to be in demolishing Marlborough's reputation for the edification of posterity. Because the Duke was already dead, the poet had no occasion to pretend that he might be reformed; nor was there any point in offering to 'punish' him by satiric ridicule. This was, however, the basic purpose of much of Pope's satire, and he admitted as much in his imitation of Horace's *Satire* II i (To Fortescue). This is a defence of his satire, and the poet describes quite frankly his aims and methods in the genre; he exploits man's natural tendency to feel shame when he is exposed to ridicule and public contempt. But when he formulates his own response to personal attacks on himself, he reveals that for him the attribution of infamy may not be a disinterested act of public necessity, but one which in fact brings the poet a deeply aesthetic enjoyment:

> *Satire's my Weapon, but I'm too discreet*
> *To run a Muck, and tilt at all I meet;*

. . . .
But touch me, and no Minister so sore.
Who-e'er offends, at some unlucky Time
Slides into Verse, and hitches in a Rhyme,
Sacred to Ridicule! his whole Life long,
And the sad Burthen of some merry Song.   (69–70, 76–80)

These technical details of the poet's craft are Pope's own addition to
Horace, who had said more simply that his enemy would smart, and his
name be sung throughout the town. The ease of 'Slides' and 'hitches',
the witty antithesis of 'sad' and 'merry', and the confidence in the apostrophe to ridicule, all suggest the artist's almost detached delight—beyond
morality—in his creation, and in the poetic aptness with which names
are yoked perfectly in satiric rhymes. The artistic aptness, though, is
still a functional part of the satirist's *moral* purpose in casting ridicule
and ensuring lifelong infamy, because by incorporating the offender's
name neatly into the song's refrain the poet makes the ridicule more
memorable and thus more effective.

It is in the *Dunciad* that Pope's artful destruction of men's good repu-
tations is seen at its most skilful; his treatment of the dunces brought
them public shame, at the same time providing further evidence to posterity of the immorality of Pope's satiric art: 'Of the *Persons* it was
judg'd proper to give some account: for . . . it is only in this monument that they must expect to survive. . . .'[1] This returns us again to
the theme of Pope's own fame as a poet, to glance at one item in his
credo which he came to overlook. In the *Temple of Fame*'s idealistic
declaration on fame the young poet had guaranteed what he would not
do to gain it:

Or if no Basis bear my rising Name,
But the fall'n Ruins of Another's Fame:
Then teach me, Heaven! to scorn the guilty Bays;
Drive from my Breast that wretched Lust of Praise. . . .

                                                    (519–22)

Now perhaps Pope simply meant by this the kind of competitive emulation between poets which, when fed by envy, could so easily end in

[1] 'Advertisement', *Dunciad Variorum*, 1729: Twickenham V 8.

mere detraction. In the *Essay on Criticism* he had already condemned
the tendency of modern critics to seek fame at the expense of other
writers:

> Now *they who reach* Parnassus' *lofty Crown,*
> *Employ their Pains to spurn some others down;*
>
> . . . .
>
> *To what base Ends, and by what abject Ways,*
> *Are Mortals urg'd thro'* Sacred Lust of Praise*!*   (514ff)

But to forgo competitive emulation would be an impossibly restrictive
programme for any man of genius. Pope's praise of Britain in *Windsor
Forest* depends on asserting that the beauties of the landscape and of his
poem emulate *and* surpass the nations and landscape poems of their predecessors. His later fondness for the mode of imitation, and his desire to
be the first poet who was wholly 'correct', also imply a wish to excel
which could only be realized by comparisons with the work of others.
Even his ambition to succeed Milton and others presupposes *some* kind
of comparison.

But in the case of Pope's punitive satire, there is a direct contradiction of this credo, and the frontispiece (Plate 16) to the *Dunciad in three
Books* (1728) demonstrates how far Pope, perhaps unwittingly, had fallen short of his 1715 declaration. The owl, bearing a banner labelled
'The Dunciad', is standing on a pedestal of duncical books, all of which
are mentioned with contempt, by name, in this edition of the poem.
Now, since the word 'Basis' could denote the foundation of an altar, a
pedestal or pillar,[1] this illustration becomes an emblem of Pope's
achievement in literary satire; he is destroying the artistic reputation of
these writers, and at the same time raising a monument to his own satirical skill on the *basis* of their infamy. There could be no more graphic
statement of the dependence of satirist's fame on victim's infamy.

Pope's motives were equally diverse when he came to mention in
his poetry those he loved or admired. For instance, by himself engaging
to imitate Bolingbroke, Pope drew attention to the exemplary function
of fame in his portrait. But the other element of fame was also present
here, for in promising fame to Bolingbroke while he was still alive Pope

[1] See Dryden's *Aeneid* VI 260; Johnson, *Dictionary*, 'Basis', 4.

meant to publicly celebrate his mentor, rewarding his achievements with the fame he considered them to deserve. His portrait of the Man of Ross was created with a similar dual objective. First of all, it is clear that Pope publicized this good man's life-story for the definite purpose of example. John Kyrle had died in 1724 and seven years later Pope was trying to find from his publisher Jacob Tonson 'an Exact information' and 'any Particulars' about him, because 'I intend to make him an Example in a Poem of mine'. When preparing his *Epistle to Bathurst* for the press, Pope wrote again to Tonson, avowing 'my honest purpose of setting up his fame, as an example to greater and wealthyer men, how they ought to use their fortunes'.[1]

It should not be thought that Pope has mentioned fame idly here; two of his early manuscript versions of the portrait begin with a phrase which proves that he was preoccupied with the conventional images of fame when making the portrait. The question 'But all our praises why should Lords engross?' (249), which now begins the passage, originally read:

> *Yet all our Incense why should Lords engross?*
> *Rise, honest Muse! and sing the Man of Ross. . . .*[2]

'Incense' is a traditional metaphor for 'immortal fame', and the very word which Pope had used for celebrating modest private virtue in the *Temple of Fame*:

> *And live there Men who slight immortal Fame?*
> *Who then with Incense shall adore our Name?*
> *But Mortals! know, 'tis still our greatest Pride,*
> *To blaze those Virtues which the Good would hide.*
> *Rise! Muses, rise! add all your tuneful Breath,*
> *These must not sleep in Darkness and in Death.*   (366–71)

With the picture of John Kyrle, Pope, in his rôle as 'honest Muse', substantiates the prophecy that fame *will* be given to virtue.

So there is also a sheerly commemorative purpose in setting up the Man of Ross's fame. At the end of the portrait Pope stresses the man's

[1] 14 November 1731: *Corr.* III 244; 7 June 1732: *Corr.* III 290.
[2] E. R. Wasserman, *Pope's 'Epistle to Bathurst'*, Baltimore 1960, 64–5, 90–1.

modesty, comparing it to the elaborate obsequies and fine tomb of the miser Hopkins:

> *'And what? no monument, inscription, stone?*
> *His race, his form, his name almost unknown?'*
> *Who builds a Church to God, and not to Fame,*
> *Will never mark the marble with his Name:*
> *Go, search it there, where to be born and die,*
> *Of rich and poor makes all the history;*
> *Enough, that Virtue fill'd the space between;*
> *Prov'd, by the ends of being, to have been.* (283–90)

Pope's respect for Kyrle's self-effacement does not deter him from praising the man in public. He actually makes the fact that Kyrle's tomb had no inscription a reason for his own poetic praise, as well as an example of modesty to richer men: 'I was not sorry he had no monument, and will put that circumstance into a note, perhaps into the body of the poem itself (unless you entreat the contrary in your own favor, by your zeal to erect one). I would however, in this case, spare the censure upon his heir (so well as he deserves it), because I dare say, after seeing his picture, every body will turn that circumstance to his honour, and conclude the Man of Ross himself would not have any monument in memory of his own good deeds' (*Corr.* III 290–1). Pope's note in the poem explains this: 'The person here celebrated . . . whose true name was almost lost (partly by the title of the *Man of Ross* given him by way of eminence and partly by being buried without so much as an inscription) was called Mr. John Kyrle' (250 n). By this device he manages to commemorate and celebrate the man by name, without formally violating his desire to remain unknown.

With this portrait Pope also managed to elude the frequent accusation that he was always praising his friends, and that this invalidated his eulogies. In Dialogue II of the *Epilogue to the Satires* he proffered this portrait as evidence that he was willing to celebrate any man of proven virtue:

> *Yet think not Friendship only prompts my Lays;*
> *I follow* Virtue, *where she shines, I praise* . . .
> . . . .

> *I never (to my sorrow I declare)*
> *Din'd with the MAN of ROSS, or my LORD MAY'R.*
> . . . .
> *To find an honest man, I beat about,*
> *And love him, court him, praise him, in or out.*   (94ff.)

However, this could not entirely absolve him from the further charge
that it was too often aristocrats that he named in his verse; his main response to this insinuation was to show that at least they were currently
out of favour at court, and to reiterate, with varying degrees of subtlety,
that they *were* his friends, and merely happened to be noblemen:

> *Names, which I long have lov'd, nor lov'd in vain,*
> *Rank'd with their Friends, not number'd with their Train;*
> *And if yet higher the proud List should end,*
> *Still let me say! No Follower, but a Friend.*   (90–3)

This was the pose he adopted for his final address to Bolingbroke; he
had already tried it out in 1721 in what he claimed was 'the only Dedication I ever writ', the prefatory verses which introduced Parnell's posthumous *Poems on Several Occasions* (1722). With obvious concern for
his integrity, Pope called his 'Epistle to Robert, Earl of Oxford, Earl
Mortimer' 'this paper of honest Verses'[1] and justified the phrase by
carefully presenting Robert Harley, Earl of Oxford, as the friend of the
poet; the poem commemorates the friendship between Swift, Parnell,
Oxford, and (by implication) the poet himself. The final paragraph of
the original manuscript version which Pope sent to Harley made it very
plain that the poem was to celebrate him in the traditional way, even
though he might try to evade his proper glory by retirement:

> *In vain to Desarts thy Retreat is made;*
> *Fame, and the Muse, pursue thee to the Shade.*
> *'Tis theirs, the Brave man's latest steps to trace,*
> *Re-judge his Acts, and dignify Disgrace. . . .*[2]

When the poem was published, 'Fame' had dropped out, and solely 'The
Muse attends thee to the silent Shade' (28), but this does not negate the
purpose and effect of the poem, which is to see historical justice execu-

---

[1] To the Earl of Oxford, 21 October 1721; *Corr.* II 90.
[2] See Geoffrey Tillotson, 'Pope's "Epistle to Harley": An Introduction
and Analysis,' *Pope and his Contemporaries*, 66n.

ted. 'The Muse shares the purpose of history—reflecting and distinguishing, giving praise to the truly great and blame to the vicious.'[1]

The prominence which is given to 'the Muse', who typically conceals and reveals at once the poet himself, is a reminder that it is Pope who fearlessly dignifies Harley's later years by his faithful attendance as a friend:

> *She waits, or to the Scaffold, or the Cell,*
> *When the last ling'ring Friend has bid farewel.*
> *Ev'n now she shades thy Evening Walk with Bays,*
> *(No Hireling she, no Prostitute to Praise).* . . .   (33–6)

'Ev'n now' suggests that this very poem is bestowing immortal 'Bays' on Harley, and Pope's insistence on the Muse's purity is a metaphorical assertion of his own honesty—as a poet he has willingly chosen to praise. For while Harley is saluted by all his aristocratic titles, 'the Muse' nevertheless claims to be his friend, as Parnell was (13) and as the Earl had treated Swift: 'Fond to forget the Statesman in the Friend' (8). Harley's response to the poem showed that he too saw its central theme as friendship, and its purpose to 'preserve an Old Friend in Memory'. With elegant reluctance he agreed to its publication on the ground that he was treated in it as a friend: 'I look back, indeed, to those Evenings I have usefully & pleasantly spent with Mr Pope, Mr Parnel, Dean Swift, the Doctor, &c. I should be glad the World knew you admitted me to your Friendship . . .' (*Corr.* II 91).

This final phrase is similar to what Pope often said of his epistles both in verse and in prose—he hoped they would commemorate his friendships with the addressees. In a letter to Dr Arbuthnot in 1734, he uses a similar figure: '. . . we have here little News or Company, and I am glad of it because it has given me the time to finish the Poem I told you of, which I hope may be the best Memorial I can leave, both of my Friendship to you, & of my own Character being such as you need not be ashamd of that Friendship' (*Corr.* III 431). Five of the seven epistles which are collected in the *Works* of 1735 as 'Epistles. . . . To Several Persons'—those to Harley, Addison, Jervas, Miss Blount and Arbuthnot —allude to this theme, which Pope seems to have felt deeply. One of his

---

[1] Rachel Trickett, *The Honest Muse*, Oxford 1967, 195.

earliest epistles, *To Mr Jervas* (greeted as 'my friend'), celebrated their
mutual devotion to the sister arts, and expressed the hope (admittedly
this is later subjected to very melancholy doubts) that their 'fate and
fame' would last together. In fact, Pope seems to have always been in
two minds about this. Although he had dedicated the *Dunciad* to Swift
in order to give fame to their friendship, he still had a strong sense of
fame's inadequacy to compensate for isolation during life and separation by death from those he loved: 'At all adventures, yours and my
name shall stand linked as friends to posterity, both in verse and prose,
and (as Tully calls it) in *consuetudine Studiorum*. Would to God our
persons could but as well, and as surely, be inseparable!'[1]

[1] To Swift, 23 March 1728: *Corr.* II 480.

Selected Bibliography and List of Abbreviations

ABBREVIATIONS OF PERIODICALS AND COLLECTIONS CITED

Augustan Milieu The *Augustan Milieu: Essays presented to Louis A. Landa.* Ed H. K. Miller, E. Rothstein and G. S. Rousseau. Oxford 1970.

Criticism and Aesthetics *Studies in Criticism and Aesthetics, 1660–1800. Essays in Honor of Samuel Holt Monk.* Ed H. Anderson and J. S. Shea. Minneapolis, 1967.

EA *Essential Articles for the Study of Alexander Pope.* Ed. Maynard Mack. Hamden, Conn. and London 1964;

EA2 2nd edn revised and enlarged, Hamden and London 1968.

E-CEL *Eighteenth-Century English Literature: Modern Essays in Criticism.* Ed James L. Clifford. New York 1959.

E-CS *Eighteenth-Century Studies.*

E in C *Essays in Criticism.*

JAAC *Journal of Aesthetics and Art Criticism.*

JEGP *Journal of English and Germanic Philology.*

JWCI *Journal of the Warburg and Courtauld Institutes.*

McKillop Festschrift *Restoration and Eighteenth-Century Literature. Essays in Honor of Alan Dugald McKillop.* Ed Carroll Camden. Chicago 1963.

MLQ *Modern Language Quarterly.*

MP *Modern Philology.*

N & Q *Notes and Queries.*

New CBEL *The New Cambridge Bibliography of English Literature* Ed George Watson. Cambridge 1969—.

PBA *Proceedings of the British Academy.*

PMLA   Publications of the Modern Language Association of America.
Pope and his Contemporaries   Pope and his Contemporaries; Essays presented to George Sherburn. Ed James L. Clifford and Louis A. Landa. Oxford 1949.
PQ   Philological Quarterly.
RES   Review of English Studies.
SEL   Studies in English Literature.
SP   Studies in Philology.
TSLL   Texas Studies in Literature and Language.

For abbreviations of other titles see following section. Place of publication is London unless otherwise stated.

I. PRIMARY TEXTS AND REFERENCE-ABBREVIATIONS

The Pope entry in *New CBEL* (II, coll 500–27), compiled by Vinton A. Dearing, includes a valuable check-list of Pope's works in order of publication.
Twickenham   The Twickenham Edition of the Poems of Alexander Pope, general ed John Butt, 11 vol, London and New Haven 1939–69:

I   *Pastoral Poetry and An Essay on Criticism.* Ed E. Audra and Aubrey Williams, 1961.
II   *The Rape of the Lock and Other Poems.* Ed Geoffrey Tillotson, 3rd edn 1962.
IIIi   *An Essay on Man.* Ed Maynard Mack, 1950.
IIIii   *Epistles to Several Persons (Moral Essays).* Ed F. W. Bateson, 2nd edn 1961.
IV   *Imitations of Horace, with An Epistle to Dr. Arbuthnot and the Epilogue to the Satires.* Ed John Butt, 2nd edn 1953.
V   *The Dunciad.* Ed James Sutherland, 3rd edn 1963.
VI   *Minor Poems.* Ed Norman Ault and John Butt, 1954.
VII, VIII   *The Iliad of Homer;* IX, X   *The Odyssey of Homer.* Ed Maynard Mack, with Norman Callan, Robert Fagles, William Frost and Douglas M. Knight, 1967.
XI   *Index.* Ed Maynard Mack, 1969.

This is the definitive edition of Pope's poetical works. It has been conveniently condensed as: *The Poems of Alexander Pope. A One-volume edition of the Twickenham Text with selected Annotations,* ed John Butt, 1963.

E-C *The Works of Alexander Pope.* Ed Whitwell Elwin and W. J. Courthope, 10 vol 1871-89.

Corr. The Correspondence of Alexander Pope. Ed George Sherburn, 5 vol Oxford 1956.

Spence Joseph Spence, *Observations, Anecdotes, and Characters of Books and Men.* Ed James M. Osborn, 2 vol Oxford 1966.

Other notable editions are those by William Warburton, *The Works of Alexander Pope,* 9 vol 1751; Joseph Warton 9 vol 1797; and William Lisle Bowles 10 vol 1806: also

The Poetical Works of Alexander Pope. Ed Herbert Davis. Oxford Standard Authors 1966.

The Prose Works of Alexander Pope. Ed Norman Ault. Vol I *The Earlier Works, 1711–1720,* Oxford 1936. To be completed by Maynard Mack.

The Art of Sinking in Poetry: Martinus Scriblerus' Peri Bathous. Ed Edna Leake Steeves. New York 1952.

Memoirs of the Extraordinary Life, Works, and Discoveries of Martinus Scriblerus. Ed Charles Kerby-Miller, New Haven 1950.

The Literary Criticism of Alexander Pope. Ed Bertrand A. Goldgar. Lincoln, Nebraska 1965.

George Sherburn, 'Letters of Alexander Pope's, chiefly to Sir William Trumbull', RESn.s. IX, 1958, 388–406. Fourteen new letters; for other additions to *Corr.* see *New CBEL* II, col 509.

Letters of Alexander Pope. Ed John Butt. 1960. A selection.

2. BIBLIOGRAPHIES AND CONCORDANCE

R. H. Griffith, *Alexander Pope: A Bibliography.* Vol I *Pope's own Writings,* 2 pts, Austin, Texas 1922–7. No more published.

Cecilia L. Lopez, *Alexander Pope: an Annotated Bibliography, 1945–1967,* Gainesville, Fla. 1970. Critical and scholarly studies.

James E. Tobin, *Alexander Pope: a List of Critical Studies Published from 1895 to 1944*, New York 1945.

Edwin Abbott, *A Concordance to the Works of Pope*, 1875. Based on Warburton's edition.

3. STUDIES MAINLY BIOGRAPHICAL

Bonamy Dobrée, *Alexander Pope*, 1951.

Marjorie Hope Nicolson and G. S. Rousseau, 'A medical case history of Alexander Pope', in *'This Long Disease, My Life': Alexander Pope and the Sciences*, Princeton 1968.

George Sherburn, *The Early Career of Alexander Pope*, Oxford 1934.

—'Pope on the Threshold of his Career', *Harvard Library Bulletin* XIII, 1959, 29–46.

—' "Timon's Villa" and Cannons', *Huntington Library Bulletin* VIII, 1935, 131–52.

W. K. Wimsatt, *The Portraits of Alexander Pope*, New Haven and London 1965.

4. CRITICAL STUDIES

[With the exception of book-length studies, the following list is intended to supplement, and not to duplicate, Professor Rousseau's 'On Reading Pope'.]

John M. Aden, *Something like Horace: Studies in the Art and Allusion of Pope's Horatian Satires*, Nashville, Tenn. 1969.

Alexander Pope: A Critical Anthology. Ed F. W. Bateson and N. A. Joukovsky. Harmondsworth 1971.

Norman Ault, *New Light on Pope*, 1949.

Benjamin, Boyce, *The Character-Sketches in Pope's Poems*, Durham, NC 1962.

R. L. Brett, *Reason and Imagination: A Study of Form and Meaning in Four Poems*, 1960. Ch iii, 'Pope's *Essay on Man*'.

Cleanth Brooks, 'The Case of Miss Arabella Fermor: a Re-examination', *Sewanee Review* LI, 1943, 505–24; rptd in his *The Well-Wrought Urn: Studies in the Structure of Poetry*, New York 1947, London 1949; and in *E A*.

Reuben A. Brower, *Alexander Pope: the Poetry of Allusion*, Oxford 1959.

John Butt, *Pope, Dickens, and Others: Essays and Addresses*, Edinburgh 1969; includes 'The Imitation of Horace in English Poetry', 'Science and Man in Eighteenth-Century Poetry', 'Pope and the Opposition to Walpole's Government'.

Norman Callan, 'Alexander Pope', in *The Pelican History of English Literature*, ed Boris Ford, Vol IV *From Dryden to Johnson*, Harmondsworth 1957; and in rev edn, *A Guide to English Literature*, Vol IV, 1962.

John Chalker, *The English Georgic: A Study in the Development of a Form*, 1969. Ch iii, on *Windsor Forest*.

J. S. Cunningham, *Pope: 'The Rape of the Lock'*, Studies in English Literature, 1961.

Peter Dixon, *The World of Pope's Satires: An Introduction to the 'Epistles' and 'Imitations of Horace'*, 1968.

Thomas R. Edwards, *This Dark Estate: A Reading of Pope*, Berkeley 1963.

William Empson, *Seven Types of Ambiguity*, 3rd edn 1953; especially 70–4, 125–8, 149–51.

—'Wit in the *Essay on Criticism*', *Hudson Review* II, 1950, 559–577; rptd in his *The Structure of Complex Words*, 1951; and in *E A*.

Howard H. Erskine-Hill, 'The Medal against Time: a Study of Pope's Epistle *To Mr. Addison*', *JW C I* XXVIII, 1965, 274–98.

—'The "New World" of Pope's *Dunciad*', *Renaissance and Modern Studies* ed J. Kinsley and R. S. Smith, VI, 1962, 49–67; rptd in *E A*.

—*Pope: 'The Dunciad'*, Studies in English Literature, 1972.

Lillian Feder, 'Sermon or Satire: Pope's definition of his Art', in *Criticism and Aesthetics*, 140–55.

Arthur Fenner, 'The Unity of Pope's *Essay on Criticism*', *P Q* XXXIX, 1960, 435–46; rptd in *E A*.

Paul Fussell, *The Rhetorical World of Augustan Humanism: Ethics and Imagery from Swift to Burke*, Oxford 1965.

S. L. Goldberg, 'Alexander Pope', *Melbourne Critical Review* VII, 1964, 49–65; rptd as 'Alexander Pope: the Creative Poet' in *Critics on Pope*, ed Judith O'Neill, 1968.

Malcolm Goldstein, *Pope and the Augustan Stage*, Stanford 1958.

Donald J. Greene, ' "Dramatic Texture" in Pope', in *From Sensibility to Romanticism: Essays presented to Frederick A. Pottle*, ed F. W. Hilles and Harold Bloom (New York 1965) 31–53.

Elizabeth Gurr, *Pope* (Writers and Critics) Edinburgh 1971.

G. S. Haber, 'A. Pope—imployed in Grottofying', *TSLL* X, 1968, 385–403.

J. P. Hardy, *Reinterpretations: Essays on Poems by Milton, Pope and Johnson*, 1971. Chs on *The Rape of the Lock* and *Epistle to Arbuthnot*.

E. N. Hooker, 'Pope on Wit: the *Essay on Criticism*', in R. F. Jones et al, *The Seventeenth Century*, Stanford 1951, 225–46; rptd in *E-CEL* and *EA*.

Arthur R. Huseboe, 'Pope's Critical Views of the London Stage', *Restoration and Eighteenth-Century Theatre Research* II, 1964, 25–37.

Ian Jack, *Augustan Satire: Intention and Idiom in English Poetry, 1660–1750*, Oxford 1952. Chs v–vii.

Alvin B. Kernan, *The Plot of Satire*, New Haven and London 1965. Ch. viii on *The Dunciad*. Original version in *SEL* II, 1962, 255–66; rptd in *EA*.

G. Wilson Knight, *Laureate of Peace: On the Genius of Alexander Pope*, London and New York 1954; reissued as *The Poetry of Pope, Laureate of Peace*, New York 1965.

Murray Krieger, ' "Eloisa to Abelard": the Escape from Body or the Embrace of Body', *E-CS* III, 1969, 28–47.

F. R. Leavis, *Revaluation: Tradition and Development in English Poetry*, 1936. Ch iii, 'Pope,' rptd in *EA*.

Roger Lonsdale, 'Alexander Pope', in *History of Literature in the English Language*, general ed Christopher Ricks, Vol IV, *Dryden to Johnson*, ed Roger Lonsdale, 1971.

Maynard Mack, *The Garden and the City: Retirement and Politics in the Later Poetry of Pope, 1731–1743*, Toronto and London 1969.

—'The Muse of Satire', *Yale Review*, XLI, 1951–2, 80–92; rptd in *Studies in the Literature of the Augustan Age*, ed R.C.Boys, Ann Arbor, Michigan 1952, and in *Satire: Modern Essays in Criticism*, ed Ronald Paulson, New Jersey 1971.

—'On Reading Pope', *College English* VII, 1946, 263–73; rptd *College English* XXII, 1960–1, 99–107.

Kathleen Mahaffey, 'Timon's Villa: Walpole's Houghton', *TSLL* IX, 1967, 193–222.

Thomas E. Maresca, *Pope's Horatian Poems*, Columbus, Ohio 1966.

Marjorie Hope Nicolson and G. S. Rousseau, *'This Long Disease, My Life': Alexander Pope and the Sciences*, Princeton 1968.

Rebecca Price Parkin, *The Poetic Workmanship of Alexander Pope*, Minneapolis 1955.

Martin Price, *To the Palace of Wisdom: Studies in Order and Energy from Dryden to Blake*, New York 1964. Ch v, 'Pope, Art and Morality'.

Paul Ramsey, 'The Watch of Judgement: Relativism and *An Essay on Criticism*', in *Criticism and Aesthetics*, 128–39.

Hugo M. Reichard, 'The Independence of Pope as a Political Satirist', *JEGP* LIV, 1955, 309–17.

R. W. Rogers, *The Major Satires of Alexander Pope*, Urbana, Ill. 1955.

Robert K. Root, *The Poetical Career of Alexander Pope*, Princeton 1938.

Manuel Schonhorn, 'The Audacious Contemporaneity of Pope's *Epistle to Augustus*', *SEL* VII, 1968, 431–43.

George Sherburn, *'The Dunciad, Book IV'*, in *Studies in English . . . University of Texas, 1944*, Austin, Texas 1945, 174–90; reptd in *EA*.

—'Pope and "The Great Shew of Nature"', in R. F. Jones et al, *The Seventeenth Century*, Stanford 1951, 306–15.

Patricia Meyer Spacks, *An Argument of Images: The Poetry of Alexander Pope*, Cambridge, Mass. 1971.

Geoffrey Tillotson, *On the Poetry of Pope*, 2nd edn, Oxford 1950.

—*Pope and Human Nature*, Oxford 1958.

—'Pope's "Epistle to Harley": an Introduction and Analysis', in *Pope and his Contemporaries*, 58–77.

Donald T. Torchiana, 'Brutus: Pope's last Hero', *JEGP* LXI, 1962, 853–67; rptd in *EA 2*.

Rachel Trickett, *The Honest Muse: A Study in Augustan Verse*, Oxford 1967.

Austin Warren, *Alexander Pope as Critic and Humanist*, Princeton 1929.

Earl R. Wasserman, *Pope's 'Epistle to Bathurst': A Critical Reading, with an Edition of the Manuscripts*, Baltimore 1960.

—*The Subtler Language: Critical Readings of Neoclassic and Romantic Poems*, Baltimore 1959. Ch iv on *Windsor Forest*.

Howard D. Weinbrot, *The Formal Strain: Studies in Augustan Imitation and Satire*, Chicago and London 1969.

Douglas H. White, *Pope and the Context of Controversy: the Manipulation of Ideas in 'An Essay on Man'*, Chicago and London 1970.

Aubrey L. Williams, 'Pope and Horace: *The Second Epistle of the Second Book*', in *McKillop Festschrift*, 309–21.

—*Pope's 'Dunciad': A Study of its Meaning*, 1955.

W. K. Wimsatt, 'One Relation of Rhyme to Reason: Alexander Pope', *MLQ* V, 1944, 323–38; rptd in *EA*, in *Studies in the Literature of the Augustan Age*, ed R. C. Boys, Ann Arbor 1952 and in *Alexander Pope*, ed F. W. Bateson and N. A. Joukovsky.

—'Rhetoric and Poems: Alexander Pope', *English Institute Essays 1948*, New York 1949. Both above rptd in his *The Verbal Icon: Studies in the Meaning of Poetry*, Kentucky 1954, London 1970.

5. BACKGROUND STUDIES

i. The Intellectual Background

The Augustan Age: Approaches to its Literature, Life, and Thought. Ed Ian Watt. Greenwich, Conn. 1968.

Gerald R. Cragg, *Reason and Authority in the Eighteenth Century*, Cambridge 1964.

D. G. James, *The Life of Reason: Hobbes, Locke, Bolingbroke*, 1949.

R. F. Jones, 'The Background of the Attack on Science in the Age of Pope', in *Pope and his Contemporaries*, 96–113; rptd in *E-CEL*.

A. O. Lovejoy, *Essays in the History of Ideas*, Baltimore 1948. Includes ' "Nature" as aesthetic Norm', and ' "Pride" in Eighteenth-century Thought'.

—*The Great Chain of Being: a Study of the History of an Idea*, Cambridge, Mass. 1936.

Michael Macklem, *The Anatomy of the World: Relations between Natural and Moral Law from Donne to Pope*, Minneapolis 1958.

Marjorie Hope Nicolson, *Newton Demands the Muse*, Princeton 1946.

Maren-Sofie Røstvig, *The Happy Man: Studies in the Metamorphoses of a Classical Ideal*; Vol I *1600–1700*, 2nd edn, Oslo 1962; Vol II *1700–1760*, Oslo 1958.

Leslie Stephen, *History of English Thought in the Eighteenth Century*, 3rd edn, 2 vol 1902.

Norman Sykes, *Church and State in England in the XVIIIth Century*, 1934.

Basil Willey, *The Eighteenth-Century Background: Studies on the Idea of Nature*, 1940.

ii. *The Social Scene*

C. H. C. and M. I. Baker, *The Life and Circumstances of James Brydges, First Duke of Chandos*, Oxford 1949.

M. Dorothy George, *London Life in the Eighteenth Century*, 3rd edn 1951.

H. J. Habakkuk, 'England', in *The European Nobility in the Eighteenth Century*, ed A. Goodwin, 1953.

—'English Landownership, 1680–1740', *Economic History Review*, X, 1939–40, 2–17.

William S. Holdsworth, *A History of English Law*, Vols X–XII, 1938.

A. R. Humphreys, *The Augustan World: Life and Letters in Eighteenth-Century England*, 1954.

Johnson's England: an Account of the Life and Manners of his Age. Ed A. S. Turberville, 2 vol Oxford 1933.

Dorothy Marshall, *English People in the Eighteenth Century*, 1956.

G. E. Mingay, *English Landed Society in the Eighteenth Century*, 1963.

J. H. Plumb, *England in the Eighteenth Century*, Harmondsworth 1950.

George Rudé, *Hanoverian London, 1714–1808*, 1971.

Leslie Stephen, *English Literature and Society in the Eighteenth Century*, 1904.

Sidney J. and Beatrice Webb, *English Local Government from the Revolution to the Municipal Corporation Act*, 8 vol 1906–29.

iii. *The Visual Arts*

B. Sprague Allen, *Tides in English Taste (1619–1800)*, 2 vol Cambridge, Mass. 1937.

I. W. U. Chase, *Horace Walpole, Gardenist*, Princeton 1943.

Miles Hadfield, *A History of British Gardening*, 1969 (rev edn of *Gardening in Britain*, 1960).

Jean H. Hagstrum, *The Sister Arts: The Tradition of Literary Pictorialism and English Poetry from Dryden to Gray*, Chicago 1958.

John Dixon Hunt, 'Emblem and Expressionism in the Eighteenth-Century Landscape Garden', *E - C S* IV, 1970–71, 294–317.

Christopher Hussey, *English Gardens and Landscapes, 1700–1750*, 1967.

Margaret Jourdain, *The Work of William Kent*, 1948.

James Lees-Milne, *Earls of Creation: Five Great Patrons of Eighteenth-Century Art*, 1962.

Edward Malins, *English Landscaping and Literature, 1660–1840*, 1966.

John Summerson, *Architecture in Britain, 1530–1830*, 4th edn 1963.

E. K. Waterhouse, *Painting in Britain, 1530–1790*, 1953.

M. I. Webb, *Michael Rysbrack, Sculptor*, 1954.

Laurence Whistler, *The Imagination of Vanbrugh and his Fellow-Artists*, 1954.

iv. *The Political Scene*

Britain after the Glorious Revolution, 1689–1717. Ed Geoffrey Holmes. 1969.

G. N. Clark, *The Later Stuarts, 1660–1714*, 2nd edn Oxford 1955.

V. H. H. Green, *The Hanoverians, 1714–1815*, 1948.

Archibald S. Foord, *His Majesty's Opposition, 1714–1830*, Oxford 1964.

Geoffrey Holmes, *British Politics in the Age of Anne*, 1967.

Isaac Kramnick, *Bolingbroke and his Circle: the Politics of Nostalgia in the Age of Walpole*, Cambridge, Mass. and London 1968.

J. H. Plumb, *The Growth of Political Stability in England, 1675–1725*, 1967.
—*Sir Robert Walpole*; Vol I *The Making of a Statesman*, 1965; Vol II *The King's Minister*, 1960. (To be completed.)

Charles B. Realey, *The Early Opposition to Sir Robert Walpole, 1720–1727*, Lawrence, Kansas 1931.

Robert Walcott, *English Politics in the Early Eighteenth Century*, Oxford 1956.

Basil Williams, *The Whig Supremacy, 1714–1760*, 2nd edn rev C. H. Stuart, Oxford 1962.

v. *Economics and Finance*

T. S. Ashton, *An Economic History of England: the Eighteenth Century*, 1955.

John Carswell, *The South Sea Bubble*, 1960.

J. H. Clapham, *The Bank of England: a History*, 2 vol 1944; Vol I *1694-1797*.

P. G. M. Dickson, *The Financial Revolution in England: a Study in the Development of Public Credit, 1688-1756*, 1967.

W. R. Scott, *The Constitution and Finance of English, Scottish and Irish Joint-Stock Companies to 1720*, 3 vol Cambridge 1910-12.

vi. *Literary Criticism*

J. W. H. Atkins, *English Literary Criticism: 17th and 18th Centuries*, 1951.

Jules Brodie, *Boileau and Longinus*, Geneva 1958.

A. F. B. Clark, *Boileau and the French Classical Critics in England (1660-1830)*, Paris 1925.

Critical Essays of the Seventeenth Century. Ed Joel E. Spingarn. 3 vol Oxford 1908-9.

Critical Essays of the Eighteenth Century, 1700-1725. Ed W.H. Durham. New Haven and London 1915.

Eighteenth-Century Critical Essays. Ed Scott Elledge. 2 vol Ithaca 1961.

Emerson R. Marks, *The Poetics of Reason: English Neoclassical Criticism*, New York 1968.

Samuel H. Monk, *The Sublime: a Study of Critical Theories in Eighteenth-Century England*, new edn, Ann Arbor 1960.

Neo-Classical Criticism, 1660-1800. Ed Irène Simon, 1971.

Miriam K. Starkman, *Swift's Satire on Learning in 'A Tale of a Tub'*, Princeton 1950.

George Watson, *The Literary Critics*, Harmondsworth 1962.

René Wellek, *Concepts of Criticism*, ed Stephen G. Nichols. New Haven and London 1963.

—*The Rise of English Literary History*, Chapel Hill 1941.

William K. Wimsatt and Cleanth Brooks, *Literary Criticism: a Short History*, New York and London 1957.

Index

Compiled by Mrs Brenda Hall, MA

TUCKER FREE LIBRARY

P.O. BOX 688 HENNIKER, NH 03242

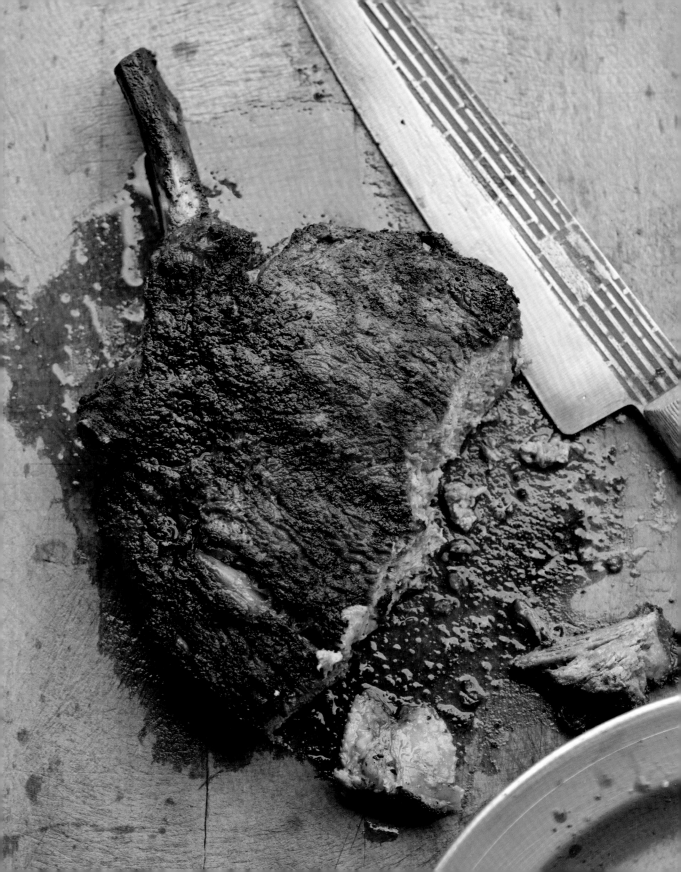

FIRE & SMOKE

A PITMASTER'S SECRETS

CHRIS LILLY

CLARKSON POTTER/PUBLISHERS
NEW YORK

Published in the United States by Clarkson Potter/
Publishers, an imprint of the Crown Publishing
Group, a division of Random House LLC, a
Penguin Random House Company, New York.
www.crownpublishing.com
www.clarksonpotter.com

CLARKSON POTTER is a trademark and POTTER
with colophon is a registered trademark of
Random House LLC.

Library of Congress Cataloging-in-Publication Data

Lilly, Chris.
Fire and smoke / Chris Lilly.—First edition.
Includes index.
1. Barbecuing. 2. Cooking (Smoked foods). I. Title.
TX840.B3L55 2014
641.7'6—dc23   2013026050

ISBN 978-0-7704-3438-0
eBook ISBN 978-0-7704-3440-3

Printed in China

BOOK & COVER DESIGN by Laura Palese
COVER PHOTOGRAPHS by Ben Fink

10 9 8 7 6 5 4 3 2 1

First Edition

TO THOSE WHO STARTED MY FIRE, cut my wood, and stirred my coals, ONLY TO KEEP MY FLAME BURNING BRIGHT. And to those who make it a joy to load up the pits day after day: MY PARENTS, BROTHER AND SISTERS, WIFE AND CHILDREN, MOTHER-IN-LAW AND FATHER-IN-LAW.

CONTENTS

INTRODUCTION

THERE'S NOTHING LIKE COOKING WITH
FIRE & SMOKE.

You can braise and roast and sauté all you want, but you can't get the same smoky, crusty char and deep flavor on foods without the intense heat of an open flame or smoldering wood. As a partner and pitmaster of Big Bob Gibson Bar-B-Q in Decatur, Alabama, I've been tending fires for years, gaining all the expertise I can in how to coax major flavor and succulent tenderness out of all shapes and sizes of meats. Most of my professional work is big—whole pork butts (shoulders), mounds of beef brisket, hundreds of whole chickens at a time—and while I can go head-to-head with other pitmasters in competition or catering, I have to figure out something else to do when I cook at home! The same recipe that works for the Memphis in May World Champion Barbecue Cooking Contest needs a good bit of reworking for me to make it for a backyard cookout for a few friends.

Now, I know I can't keep going here without addressing that same question that comes up all the time: What is the difference between barbecuing and grilling? If you've read any of the outdoor cookbooks on the market, you will know that barbecue is cooking over low indirect heat and grilling is utilizing high direct heat. There are clear differences between the two, but have we ever adequately explored the charcoal-gray area in between? As I started tweaking recipes here and there, working on the equipment I keep at home, I realized something: You can get some pretty great results when you mix barbecuing and grilling techniques for the same recipe. For example, a whole butterflied turkey sizzled over direct flame to yield a beautiful crisp charred skin, but then transferred to indirect heat to maximize the juiciness of the meat—is this barbecuing or grilling?

Or when cooking Charcoal-Seared Trout Fillet with brown butter (page 166), the cast iron skillet rests in a bed of coals while the fish sizzles to perfection. How do you classify this dish? Split Chicken Halves with Fresh Herb Marinade (page 158) breaks all the rules by cooking at a high temperature over indirect heat. We can argue all day about which method should be used in different circumstances, but it's actually the food that determines it. More often than not, and especially when cooking at home, it's best to use a combination of both barbecuing and grilling to get the greatest flavor.

Fire & Smoke will teach you how to get the most out of your outdoor cooking equipment and master the art of cooking with flames. Start with the recipes here that I've designed for grills and smokers, but then move on to adapt your own indoor recipes to the outdoors, thus reimagining dishes usually untouched by smoke and char. You'll be amazed at how fun and delicious it is to take unexpected foods to the grill or smoker. Yes, you can cook a dish of red-skinned potatoes in your oven, but wouldn't they be better simmering in the slow-cooked juices dripping from a barbecue beef brisket (page 130)? Charcoal-grilled avocado, tomatoes, and onions add an explosion of flavor to homemade guacamole (page 57). Once the Indonesian Sweet & Sour Shrimp Pizza (page 100) recipe shocks your dreary taste buds, the outdoor grill will replace the oven as the favorite family cooker. I even take some of my favorite family desserts to the grill! You've never tasted a cobbler (pages 221 and 223) so good.

There's a whole world of barbecue to explore, so let's get on outside, invite some folks over, and fire up the grill or smoker. And with that, I'd like to propose a toast. To good friends and great Q!

FIRE IN THE GRILL

The question I'm most often asked is "What is the best cooker to purchase for my own backyard?" This is impossible to answer on the spot, because without knowing a person's cooking style, I can't match them with the perfect cooker. This choice goes much deeper than what looks the best on your patio. Of course it makes sense to recommend a grill for people who are only interested in a quick cook over high heat and a smoker for those who fixate on cooking large cuts of meat low and slow—but there are many other things to consider. Do you like to cook with charcoal? Do you prefer wood? Is flavor or convenience more important to you? How often do you open your grill when cooking? Do you baste, turn, or flip? Are you more of a hands-off cook with the motto "If you're lookin', you ain't cookin'!"? Exactly how much smoke flavor do you like? How big is your family? Do you entertain guests often at your home? What do you cook most often? Do you like to cook multiple things at once at different temperatures? There are more questions than cooker types, but with each answer you get closer to reaching a perfect harmony of fire and flavor.

The only absolute in outdoor cooking is that there is no absolute right or wrong way to barbecue, and no perfect techniques when it comes to grilling. Your preferences and style may be completely different from mine, but you will never hear me say that my way is the only way. For example, basting is one way to add flavor while keeping the meat from drying out during the cooking process. Another way to achieve the same things is to keep the lid shut to trap the natural moisture from the meat. Both techniques work, but you may like one method over the other. It makes little difference whether you are cooking on a $20,000 combination smoker/grill or in a hole in the ground; both can come to the same delicious conclusion.

I like a cooker that provides flexibility. I'm a huge fan of the flavor charcoal imparts to food, and therefore opt for a cooker that uses charcoal as the main fuel source. My favorite cookers have the versatility of cooking with high or low temperatures, and direct or indirect heat. For example, I can cook slabs of ribs over low indirect heat, and then transfer them to direct fire to quickly caramelize the sauce. The ideal alternative is to have both a grill and a smoker.

In this chapter, I walk through eighteen types of grills, smokers, and combo cookers that are currently on the market. For practical purposes I limited this list to backyard models under $10,000. The goal here is twofold. After reading this chapter, you should easily be able to determine which kind of cooker best fits your cooking style. Also, every recipe notes whether it involves cooking with direct heat, indirect heat, or a combination of both, and the information here is a great reference for how to set up your grill for perfect performance.

KETTLE GRILL

Created in 1952, the kettle grill has become the most commercially successful charcoal grill design to date. George Stephen became frustrated with his open brazier grill (see Outdoor Flattop Grill, page 14) because he couldn't control the temperatures and it had no protection from the weather. As an employee of Weber Brothers Metal Works, his solution was to cut a metal buoy in half, making a dome-shaped grill that became the original Weber Kettle Grill.

This grill is simple and inexpensive, with no frills. The main reason for its success is that it works! Its hemispherical design consists of a charcoal grate and a cooking grate contained in one round open chamber. The size of the grill is perfect when cooking for a family or a small get-together. Grill at high temperatures with the lid off, or cover with the lid to hold a lower temperature steady. Because the charcoal is close to the cooking grate, the kettle is ideal for grilling and searing meat. Using a two-zone charcoal setup (see Pitmaster Tip), slow-cooking with indirect heat is also an option.

Pitmaster Tip: The easiest way to cook low and slow on a small backyard grill is to build a two-zone charcoal fire. Situate the hot coals on only one side of the grill, leaving the other side empty. This creates two cooking areas: one for direct grilling and the other for indirect cooking. If you want to add moisture to the cooking chamber to keep the meat from drying out, you can put a pan of water in the empty side of the grill.

FUEL: Charcoal and wood chips

CONVENIENCE: The temperature is controlled by airflow, not by a thermostat. Because of the limited space in the cooking chamber, the kettle grill has two distinct advantages. First, it can preheat fully in 10 minutes after hot coals are added. Second, it recoups lost heat rapidly, making it a great match for someone prone to opening and closing the lid often.

IDEAL FOR: This cooker is a great introductory tool for anyone who thinks they might have an interest in outdoor cooking. Everyone should own a kettle and learn barbecue basics before laying down the big money for an outdoor cooker with more capacity and features.

INDIRECT COOKING: Although cooking low and slow with indirect heat can be accomplished on the kettle cooker, it is more difficult to maintain a steady temperature than with other types of outdoor cookers.

DIRECT HEAT: Direct grilling is the ideal setup for the kettle grill.

COST: $100–$1,400

BARREL GRILL

The most popular model of barrel grill is a 55-gallon drum that's been cut in half lengthwise and hinged to form a lid. Charcoal goes into the lower portion of the drum, and the cooking

Pitmaster Tip: The more control you have over the airflow in a cooker, the better you can maintain cooker temperature. Cracks, crevices, and subpar spot-welding mean uncontrolled airflow. This leads to long days of fighting cooker temperatures while barbecuing. High-temperature caulk and gaskets found at your local auto and hardware stores (respectively) can remedy problems and give you a stress-free day at the outdoor cooker.

grate runs across the top edge of the barrel half. This old-school piece of equipment can be found in backyards and barbecue shacks all over the country. The barrel grill can be used in all sorts of ways, but it's really only as versatile as the person using it. You can do everything from cooking burgers for the entire neighborhood to creating different temperature zones with a tapered pile of charcoal.

Pitmaster Tip: There are many cookers on the market that make it easy to maintain a steady cooking temperature for long periods of time. This chapter highlights many of these, including gravity-fed charcoal cookers, pellet cookers, and all types of thermostatic controlled smokers. But more basic charcoal cookers require more hands-on monitoring of temperature and multiple refuelings to complete big-meat barbecues. In this case, always keep a lit charcoal chimney on standby to add hot coals to your cooker as needed. Placing unlit charcoal on top of lit coals will temporarily smother your fire and cause the temperature in your cooker to drop until the fire catches up.

More recently, innovators have turned the trusty barrel grill on its end, which changes the cooking performance dramatically. The disadvantage is that it cuts the direct grill space in half, but the advantages far outweigh the reduction in high-heat grilling area. First, because the firebox and grill grates are adjustable, it makes for a much more functional smoker. Second, there is more vertical room above the firebox, which allows you to cook on multiple levels.

FUEL: Charcoal and wood chunks or chips

CONVENIENCE: In both barrel orientations (horizontal or vertical), the temperature is controlled by airflow, not by a thermostat. Barrels can preheat fully less than 20 minutes after hot coals are added. Note that adding more charcoal to either cooker is a chore because you have to remove the food and cooking grates to refuel.

IDEAL FOR: I like using either barrel type for direct grilling for small parties of a dozen people. The horizontal barrel is a great match for someone who shifts, turns, and bastes food often, because it gives you easy access to a large cooking grate and the ability to create different temperature zones with charcoal. The vertical barrel is suited for someone who prefers to cook without peeking.

INDIRECT COOKING: Although cooking low and slow with indirect heat can be accomplished on the horizontal barrel cooker, it is more difficult to maintain a steady temperature than with the vertical barrel. Choose a barrel with airtight seams and thicker-gauge metal for better indirect temperature control.

DIRECT HEAT: Direct grilling is the ideal setup for both barrel types.

COST: $75–$450

GAS GRILL

Most gas grills consist of a metal frame, with side tables, that supports the cooking chamber and encloses the fuel tank. Gas grills typically use propane (LP) or natural gas (NG) as the fuel source. Gas burners in the bottom of the cooking chamber provide direct heat to the cooking surface or heat grilling elements, such as lava rock or a heat shield that holds and/or disperses heat. Temperature is controlled by knobs on the front of the grill that limit the amount of gas that goes to each burner. Gas grills are available in sizes ranging from a very small, four-burner capacity, to large catering units that are able to feed hundreds.

Many modern gas grills include options and accessories to make the grill more versatile. These include push-button igniters, infrared radiant burners (which provide high heat evenly across the burner), and a horizontal rotisserie.

There are two main complaints about gas grills. Many, including me, believe that the flavor of food cooked with gas cannot compare to the flavor of food cooked over charcoal and wood for the char and smoke flavor achieved. To combat this, some models offer a small metal smoker box (see Pitmaster Tip) to attempt to introduce some smoke flavor. The second problem is how hard it is to cook at low indirect heat. It's difficult to maintain low temperatures (below 250°F) on gas grills. The best way to do it is to turn one burner to low and keep the remaining burners off. This creates an area away from the coals for low indirect heat.

Pitmaster Tip: If you use a gas grill, you sacrifice the added flavor that comes from cooking over burning coals. Metal smoker boxes are a viable way to add real smoke flavor. Fill the box with soaked wood chips and put it beside a hot burner. The burner heats the metal box and causes the wood chips to smolder, creating smoke to flavor the food. Make your own box by putting wood chips soaked in water into a double-layer foil pouch with small slits cut in the top. Put the pouch under the cooking grate beside the hot flames. This is a quick and easy way to achieve the same effect.

FUEL: Gas, typically propane (LP) or natural gas (NG)

CONVENIENCE: The temperature is controlled by knobs on the front of the grill that limit the amount of gas to each burner. Most gas grills have push-button or automatic ignition.

IDEAL FOR: Using a gas grill is the quickest way to turn over large quantities of foods grilled over direct heat. This cooker type is ideal for someone who values a grill that provides maximum convenience.

INDIRECT COOKING: Not ideal for cooking with low indirect heat. It's difficult to maintain steady low temperatures with gas grills.

DIRECT HEAT: Direct grilling is the optimum setup for the gas grill.

COST: $100–$10,000+

OUTDOOR FLATTOP GRILL

The commercial outdoor flattop grill is composed of a large rectangular trough, which holds charcoal, topped with a cooking grate. The height of the grate can be adjusted and covers the entire area over the charcoal trough to maximize the space for direct cooking. This type of flattop grill is built for volume

Grilling oysters on an
**OUTDOOR
FLATTOP GRILL.**

and is commonly used by caterers. This is my cooker of choice when grilling bacon for 500 BLT sandwiches or when chargrilling 1,000 oysters.

The brazier grill is one of the most basic and inexpensive flattop charcoal grills. It's made up of a wire grate suspended over a charcoal pan. It doesn't have a lid or vents to control temperature, so the heat is adjusted by moving the cooking grid up or down over the charcoal pan.

Another type of outdoor flattop grill is the yakitori grill. These grills are used in Japanese cuisine to cook all types of skewered food over high-temperature direct heat. Yakitori grills are very narrow so the food cooks while the skewer hangs over the edge of the grill, keeping the skewer from burning and making rotating them much easier. Yakitori grills can range from very short, about 1 foot in length, to over 10 feet long.

All outdoor flattops are direct-heat grills only and are not built for low-heat indirect cooking. Because of the high heat and the closeness of the grate and charcoal, they are ideal for cooking vegetables and thin meats such as burgers, steaks, chops, and hot dogs.

FUEL: Charcoal, but some gas models are available

CONVENIENCE: Because the charcoal is exposed to so much open air, it burns without regulation. Temperature is controlled by how much charcoal is added to the trough, not by controlling airflow. This grill is easy to use when working with meats and vegetables that have short cooking times. Also, high volume and quick food turnover are benefits of larger models.

IDEAL FOR: I love to use large flattop grills when catering for a large number of people. Because the cooking grate extends over the entire charcoal trough, it has a huge capacity for direct grilling. Line up those skewers, burgers, and pork chops, and invite the neighborhood over!

INDIRECT COOKING: n/a

DIRECT HEAT: Direct grilling is the ideal setup for all flattop grills. The commercial outdoor flattop grill is perfectly designed for high-volume grilling.

COST: $35–$5,000

HIBACHI

The hibachi originated in Japan and is used as a small portable charcoal grill for all types of high-heat direct-fire cooking, including kebabs and satays. This grill consists of a heavy metal oval or rectangular firebox. Temperature is controlled by built-in air dampers on the bottom of the firebox. Because there is no lid on most authentic hibachis, the increased airflow results in very high temperatures. Because of its small size, it's not convenient for cooking lots of food, although most meats that are traditionally cooked on this grill type are cut thin and cook in minutes. The hibachi's simplicity and portability are its main advantages.

FUEL: Charcoal

CONVENIENCE: The hibachi is the simplest of all charcoal grills, as it is without hinged or moving parts. The portability of this grill is also a bonus.

IDEAL FOR: I like to think of a hibachi as a first-date grill. Surprise someone with a gourmet grilled dinner on a rock outcrop just off the nature trail. A quick charcoal sear of some thinly cut skewered meat and veggies, and you'll be sure to get a second date.

INDIRECT COOKING: n/a

DIRECT HEAT: Direct grilling is the ideal setup for the hibachi grill.

COST: $30–$100

TANDOOR

The tandoor is a cylindrical clay pot used for cooking and baking. The oldest examples of a tandoor were found in settlements in ancient India at a mound site in what is now Pakistan and dating back to 3000 BC. Traditionally the tandoor was fueled with wood and charcoal situated in the bottom of the pot. Although this is still prevalent, some modern-day tandoors are fueled by electricity or gas.

Tandoori cooking includes grilling skewers of meat, fish, and vegetables and baking bread. Skewers are placed through the top hole of the pot with the tip leaning against the lip, and the end of the skewer is anchored directly in the live fire (see page 70). To bake breads, rounds of dough are stuck to the porous clay sides of the tandoor. The combination of radiant heat from the clay and convection heat within the pot is perfect for baking. The capacity of a tandoor varies depending on the size of the pot. An average-size tandoor can hold 4 to 7 breads or 6 to 12 large skewers.

FUEL: Charcoal or wood

CONVENIENCE: The temperature is controlled by airflow, not by a thermostat. Because of the high insulation factor, these cookers typically preheat quickly. The tandoor has no moving parts and is easy to refuel.

IDEAL FOR: I like any cooking method that is rooted in history. With their excellent insulation, tandoors stay hot throughout cooking. If you love high heat and the flavor of foods cooked with a wood-burning oven, the tandoor might be for you.

INDIRECT COOKING: n/a

DIRECT HEAT: The tandoor is ideal for cooking with direct heat from the live fire in the bottom of the pot. Because of the combination of direct heat, radiant heat from the clay walls, and convection heat, the tandoor is capable of reaching temperatures up to 900°F, although its ideal temperature cooking range is between 350° and 600°F.

COST: $200–$2,000

KAMADO "CERAMIC" GRILLS

Today's ceramic grills are a modern-day evolution of the *kamado*. "Kamado" is a Japanese word for a traditional earthenware cooker. Although all of today's ceramic kamado-style grills resemble a giant egg, they come in a variety of colors and construction quality. The shells of these cookers are made from all types of refractory materials, ceramic, insulated steel, terra-cotta, or cement. Inside the shell is a firebox topped with several cooking grates at various levels. Ceramic plates are usually available to deflect heat and allow for indirect cooking as well as direct fire grilling. Air dampers on the bottom and top of the kamado regulate the temperature of the grill through airflow.

There are several reasons that today's kamado grills are extremely popular. The first reason is versatility. Whether you are cooking with direct or indirect heat, low temperatures or extremely high searing temperatures, these cookers can handle it. Second, they are the most efficient charcoal grill on the market. Because of the high insulation factor, these cookers can operate on a very low quantity of charcoal. Finally, because of the restricted airflow, ceramic grills tend to trap the natural humidity from whatever you are cooking. This guarantees

you'll have the high humidity necessary for yielding juicy meats cooked low and slow.

FUEL: Charcoal and wood chunks or chips

CONVENIENCE: The temperature is controlled by airflow, not by a thermostat. Because of the high insulation factor, these cookers typically preheat quickly and cook for long periods of time without requiring additional charcoal.

IDEAL FOR: I personally have three ceramic-type cookers. Each cooker is the perfect size for a get-together with a few couples, including kids. I like them because of the cooking versatility and charcoal efficiency, but when the parties get large, juggling three hot cookers gets a little tricky.

INDIRECT COOKING: Using a plate to diffuse the direct heat, the versatile kamado can cook with indirect heat. Reducing the airflow will allow low temperatures necessary for barbecuing.

DIRECT HEAT: The kamado is ideal for cooking with direct heat and capable of reaching searing temperatures exceeding 700°F.

COST: $400–$5,000

COMBO GRILL/SMOKER

Combo cookers come in all shapes and sizes, but the concept is the same: a cooker that can be set up as a grill (direct heat) or a smoker (indirect heat). There are models on the market already set up for this type of combination cooking, but you can also alter other grills. For example, a barrel grill can be converted into a combo cooker by adding an offset firebox to the side. Through creative uses of heat deflector shields, grease drainage, and ash pans, it is also possible for a vertical cooker to provide both direct and indirect heat. The advantage of combo cookers is versatility. Direct or indirect heat, high temperatures or low temperatures—the user is not limited by equipment cooking restrictions.

FUEL: Charcoal and/or wood

CONVENIENCE: The temperature is controlled by airflow, not by a thermostat.

IDEAL FOR: I have a problem, I've been told. My answer is always that my profession requires a multitude of grills and smokers to be showcased in my backyard. While I view it as necessary, others might call it a grill parking lot! When there is minimal patio space (or a significant other who restricts you to one outdoor cooker), a combo grill/smoker that's versatile with both direct and indirect heat should be your choice.

INDIRECT COOKING: Ideal for cooking over indirect heat from low to medium-high temperatures.

DIRECT HEAT: The combo cooker is equally proficient cooking with direct heat, from low to high temperatures.

COST: $200–$10,000+

PELLET COOKER

The pellet cooker uses compressed hardwood pellets as the fuel for heat. These hardwood pellets are poured into a hopper on the side of the cooker, and an electric auger rotates to feed the pellets to a burner in the center of the cooking chamber. A thermostat controls the speed of the auger, which in turn regulates the cooking temperature. Models are available that look similar to standard backyard gas grills, with plenty of space to cook large-cut meats such as beef brisket or pork butt (shoulder). Some pellet cookers have the look of a vertical smoker with stacked racks that substantially increase cooking capacity. Although pellet cookers are set up to cook with indirect heat, they can get up to temperatures exceeding 500°F, making high-temperature indirect grilling viable.

FUEL: Wood pellets are available in many different wood varieties. Choosing a different variety—for example, changing from hickory to apple—is the only way to control how much smoke flavor is imparted to your food.

CONVENIENCE: The pellet cooker is effortless compared to most other smoker types. The temperature is controlled by a thermostat, though the preheating process will take longer than with a comparable size of grill.

IDEAL FOR: If you have an aversion to barbecuing with gas, love the idea of cooking with real wood, and insist upon convenient temperature control, then you should join the cultish masses who call themselves "Pellet Heads."

Pouring
fuel into a
**PELLET
COOKER.**

INDIRECT COOKING: Perfect for cooking over indirect heat from low to high temperatures.

DIRECT HEAT: n/a

COST: $400–$10,000+

OFFSET FIREBOX COOKER

This style of cooker was made popular in Texas and is still the most popular model of cooker in this great state. Also called a "Texas-style cooker" or a "stick burner," it's composed of a side firebox and a horizontal cylindrical cooking chamber. The firebox is usually set lower than the cooking chamber so that the heat and smoke can easily move across the cooking grate. In some models, tuning plates or tubes run from the firebox through the bottom of the cooking chamber, creating adjustable temperature zones. Regardless, the temperature of the cooking chamber closest to the fire is usually hotter than

the section farthest away. Many barbecue veterans use different temperature zones to their advantage, increasing this cooker's versatility.

All offset firebox cookers are not created equal. Some models have double-walled insulated fireboxes and/or are constructed of thicker-gauge metal, which greatly affects performance.

FUEL: Wood and/or charcoal

CONVENIENCE: The temperature is controlled by airflow, not by a thermostat. The length of the firebox will dictate the time it takes to preheat the cooker. Because the firebox is separate, you can add more fuel to the fire without losing heat by opening the cooking chamber. Noninsulated models will require more attention and refueling during long cooks.

IDEAL FOR: The offset firebox cooker does not limit me because I like to cook with both charcoal and wood chunks. For those who like a little more smoke flavor, wood sticks can be substituted for other fuel. If complete control of wood smoke flavor is important to you and you don't mind tending the fire, this cooker is a must-have.

INDIRECT COOKING: Ideal for cooking over indirect heat from low to medium-high temperatures.

DIRECT HEAT: n/a

COST: $200–$10,000+

BULLET SMOKER

The bullet-shaped smoker is a very simple construction, with no bells and whistles. This vertical smoker consists of a charcoal grate, a round water pan, and one or two cooking grates, all wrapped in a cylindrical metal shell. The water pan serves two purposes. First, it provides extra moisture to the cooking chamber. Second, it acts

COOKING WITH WOOD

To be consistent, I included directions for charcoal cooking in all the recipes in this book. I didn't want to burden you with monotonous instructions on cooking with gas, pellets, and wood over and over in every recipe. The fact is, if you understand what indirect and direct cooking are, you can master any of these recipes on any type of outdoor cooker. It can be as easy as setting a thermostat on a pellet or gas smoker. On a gas grill you turn one burner on low while leaving the other burners off, creating a two-zone fire for direct and indirect heat. The only cooking fuel that definitely needs more discussion is wood.

The variety of woods that can be used for barbecuing is almost endless. The easiest way to categorize wood is by a mild (alder, seasoned fruitwood), medium (maple, fruitwood, seasoned hickory, seasoned oak), or heavy smoke flavor (mesquite, pimento, green hickory, or green oak). This will vary depending on how much bark you have and the age of the cut wood. Keep in mind that different woods will not only alter the flavor of your meats, but they'll also change the potency of dry rubs and sauces. If you cook two chickens with the same dry rub, but cook one over fruit wood and one over mesquite, you'll end up with two very different birds, because different spices in your dry rub will come to the forefront. Woods that impart a mild to medium smoke flavor, such as fruitwoods, tend to highlight the sweeter spices (such as cinnamon or ginger), while woods that give off a stronger smoke flavor such as mesquite will dull the sharper spices and bring out the earthy flavors (such as cumin or oregano). Sometimes it takes a mixture of woods to bring a dry rub or sauce to its full flavor potential.

Not only is the variety of wood critical, but age and bark thickness are also important factors. Fresh-cut wood is referred to as "green," and the greener the wood, the stronger and often more bitter the smoke's flavor. After three months, cut wood can be referred to as seasoned or aged. Dry wood burns fast and has less flavor. The longer wood sits after cutting, the dryer it gets. When burned, seasoned wood emits a less pungent aroma. Wood with thin or no bark produces a milder smoke flavor in meat than wood with heavy bark.

Newcomers to BBQ should not start with an all-wood fire, and instead use a combination of charcoal and wood. Many make the mistake of oversmoking their meat using all wood, giving the resulting BBQ an acrid taste. Think of wood as a seasoning rather than a fuel source. When adding wood chips to a charcoal fire, sprinkle them into the hot coals just before putting the food on the grill. Chips burn quickly, so putting them on early, while the grill is preheating, is useless because they burn up before go-time. If you're cooking large cuts over indirect heat, it is wise to step up to chunks rather than chips. Adding bigger pieces of wood allows you to keep the cooker lid shut, thus trapping the heat, moisture, and smoke. There is no need for adding wood chips every fifteen minutes. Use this rule of thumb: the longer the cook-time, the larger the wood.

This leads us to the question, "Do you soak wood chips and chunks before barbecuing?" Everything you hear and read supports the idea that water penetrates the wood and wet wood smolders on the hot fire, as opposed to burning up quickly. This is preposterous. Don't waste your time and energy. At best the water will wet the outside of the wood and only slow the combustion time slightly. The only time I would ever consider soaking wood chips is when quick grilling over direct heat with the food very close to the fire. The wet wood will buy you an extra minute before igniting into flame.

Next, you have to consider fire and airflow. Too much airflow will cause the wood to burn uncontrollably, resulting in high temperatures and escaping humidity. Picture a whirlwind of ash, wood particulates, and creosote swirling through the cooking chamber and then billowing out of the smokestack in a cloud of white smoke. The total opposite would be closing the smokestack and vents to a point where the wood is only smoldering, but the heavy smoke is trapped in the cooking chamber ensuring oversmoked meat. With optimum airflow, the fire in an all wood smoker can be maintained at a steady low temperature and the smoke escapes the stack in light blue wisps. This is the signal of a clean burn that yields ideal smoke flavor. Keep in mind that if the all-wood cooker has a water belly or added water pans, steam billowing out of the smokestack is no reason to be concerned.

Another method of cooking with all wood, used by only the most experienced pitmasters, is utilizing a separate burn pit. The most popular burn pits are comprised of a vertical barrel with an open top, a wide grate about a foot off the ground, and a shovel hole on the bottom side. Wood is piled into the top of the barrel and lit on fire. As the wood burns, hot coals fall through the wide grates. These coals are then shoveled into another pit or smoker where the meat slowly cooks. Cooking with all wood coals prevents oversmoking and temperature is controlled by how much coal is shoveled. This is both highly effective and time-consuming.

Although there are many barbecue restaurants that boast huge stacks of wood (including Big Bob Gibson Bar-B-Q) and stick-burners are often accepting awards in competitions all over the country, there is a learning curve when it comes to cooking with all wood. Take your time to learn about it, experiment with it, and find the fire for you.

as a heat shield between the fire and the cooking surface, thus providing indirect heat. Just like cooking low and slow barbecue, sometimes simple is the best way to go.

The bullet smoker shell is divided into three parts: firebox section, cooking grate section, and lid. I've seen ingenious people stack two or three grate sections over one firebox to double or even triple capacity while having to regulate only one fire.

FUEL: Charcoal and wood chunks or chips

CONVENIENCE: The temperature is controlled by airflow, not by a thermostat. Because of the limited space in the cooking chamber, the bullet grill has a couple of advantages. First, it can preheat fully in 30 minutes after hot coals are added. This is much quicker than other smokers

that use a water pan. Second, it retains heat and moisture well.

IDEAL FOR: The kettle is to grilling as the bullet is to smoking. This is a must-have for anyone who catches the smoking bug. Its reasonable price and consistent performance make it #1 on my list of economy smokers. The biggest drawback is limited space, since it's only just big enough to cook one medium whole turkey.

INDIRECT COOKING: Ideal for high-humidity cooking with low- to medium-temperature indirect heat.

DIRECT HEAT: I guess it would be possible to set up this cooker for direct cooking by removing the water pan, but the distance between the fire and the cooking grate would be too much to get the results you're looking for. Also, working the bottom cooking grate would be awkward. The bullet smoker is not really suited to direct-heat cooking.

COST: $100–$500

ELECTRIC SMOKER

Most electric smokers consist of a single chamber that holds an electric burner on the bottom, a box or plate containing wood chips, and cooking grates. When turned on, the electric burner raises the temperature in the cooking chamber while heating the metal holding the wood chips, which begin to smolder and emit smoke. Tabletop models can be as small as a large skillet, but bigger models can reach up to 6 feet high with multiple shelves for smoking large quantities of meat. I've seen these cookers everywhere, from backyards to the kitchen of the Culinary Institute of America.

Electric smokers come in all different levels of quality, so it is very hard to lump them all into the same short description. For example, double-walled and/or insulated smokers will perform better than single-walled units. Some electric smokers come with a thermostat and digital readouts that provide information such as cooker and meat temperature. A "cook and hold" option on some models allows you to cook the meat to a set internal temperature, and then automatically drop the cooker temperature to hold the meat warm until service.

FUEL: Electricity

CONVENIENCE: A dial on the cooker controls how hot the burner plate gets, which in turn affects the temperature of the cooking chamber. On some models, the temperature is controlled by a thermostat. The preheating process will take longer than it would with a comparably sized charcoal or gas grill.

IDEAL FOR: Think of this cooker as an indoor oven with an added opportunity to impart light to medium smoke flavor to foods. If you are interested in a very-easy-to-use smoker, this is a good choice.

INDIRECT COOKING: Perfect for cooking over indirect heat from low to medium temperatures. Many electric smokers max out at temperatures reaching 250°–300°F.

DIRECT HEAT: n/a

COST: $50–$1,800

GAS SMOKER

Gas smokers come in all shapes, sizes, and price ranges, but they all work the same way. A burner on the bottom of the cooker fired by natural gas (NG) or propane (LP) heats the cooking chamber. The burner and the cooking chamber are partially separated to diffuse the heat, creating an environment for indirect cooking. The temperature is controlled by turning the gas valve, thereby restricting or increasing the amount of gas flow to the burner.

The gas smoker is a barbecue purist's bane, because the primary fuel source is not wood or charcoal. Some would argue that food from this cooking apparatus is not real barbecue and that the flavor of food cooked with gas cannot compare to the flavor achieved from cooking with charcoal and wood. To combat this argument, some models offer a small metal smoker box that holds wood chips for added smoke flavor.

Other ingenious companies have coupled the ease of cooking with gas with the authentic use of real wood. These thermostatic-controlled units will flare the gas ignition on sticks of wood until the cooker temperature reaches the desired setting. The gas ignition will cut off while the wood burns, providing heat and smoke to the cooker. When the temperature goes below the desired setting, the gas flame will once again torch the wood. Some of these models also use a convection fan system to distribute the heat evenly throughout the cooking chamber.

FUEL: Gas, typically propane (LP) or natural gas (NG)

CONVENIENCE: The temperature is controlled by turning the gas valve, thereby restricting or increasing the amount of gas flow to the burner. On some models the temperature is controlled by a thermostat.

IDEAL FOR: A gas smoker that offers the opportunity to add charcoal and wood sticks for added flavor is appealing. Couple this with the ease of a dial-set temperature control, and fans of a traditional gas grill will make an easy transition to this cooking cousin!

INDIRECT COOKING: Cooking with indirect heat from low to medium-high temperatures is a gas smoker's specialty.

DIRECT HEAT: n/a

COST: $100–$10,000+

ROTISSERIE

There are two different types of rotisserie barbecue cookers: rotating shelves and spits. In both cases, rotisseries are used to cook whole or large cuts of meat evenly by rotating the meat horizontally over the fire or fuel source. The constant turning allows the meat to self-baste and cook in its own juices. Rotisseries can either be enclosed inside the shell of a grill or visible in open air, turning over a hot fire.

Many of today's barbecue rotisseries consist of rotating shelves enclosed in a cooking chamber. The shell of the chamber holds in heat while the movement of the rotisserie stirs the air to ensure an even cooking temperature. Fuel sources vary with modern rotisseries.

A spit is a long metal rod used to skewer and hold food while it slowly turns over fire or a burner. The spit is traditionally used to cook large cuts of meat or whole animals such as pigs, goats, or lamb and can be both open-air and enclosed. The open spit arguably offers the best atmosphere for an outdoor party, as the spit becomes the centerpiece of conversation while barbecue anticipation steadily builds. Closed spits are sometimes offered as accessories on all types of enclosed gas, pellet, and charcoal grills.

Although most of today's rotisseries utilize an electric motor to turn the food, old-school rotisseries have a handle to rotate the spit or shaft manually. Whichever style is used, it is very important to skewer the meat or whole animal through the center to get the proper balance so that the motor doesn't jam or the "spit boy" give out.

FUEL: Wood, charcoal, gas, or wood pellets

CONVENIENCE: The temperature is controlled by airflow on some rotisseries, while on others it is controlled by a thermostat. Enclosed rotisseries offer more temperature control than the open-air spit, which demands constant attention during the entire cooking process.

IDEAL FOR: This cooker has the ultimate "wow" factor for my outdoor parties. Whether it is the giant enclosed Ferris wheel action of a modern rotisserie or a whole pig roasting on an open spit, it is the centerpiece attraction. I like the advantages of self-basting and the guarantee of even cooking temperatures.

INDIRECT COOKING: While open spits are not designed for indirect cooking, many of the large-capacity enclosed barbecue rotisseries are set up for indirect cooking only.

DIRECT HEAT: Open spits and small grill rotisseries function best over direct heat, as the rendered fat and juices fall into the fire, resulting in flavorful moisture that keeps the meat from drying out.

COST: $25–$200 grill rotisserie accessory
$150–$3,000 open spit
$125–$10,000+ enclosed rotisserie

Pork butts on a
ROTISSERIE.

CINDER-BLOCK PIT

Back in the early 1920s, the cinder-block pit was the preference of my wife's great-grandfather Big Bob Gibson. These pits are assembled in many different ways but commonly consist of a rectangular box built of stacked cinder blocks. A metal cooking grate spans the center of the concrete blocks to form a raised cooking platform. Oftentimes the lid of a cinder-block pit consists of sheets of tin or stacked cardboard, while the floor is either dirt or bricks. A fire is built under the cooking grate via an access hole in the side wall of the blocks. For a less smoky flavor, wood can be burned in a separate "burn pit," and the hot coals can be shoveled through the access hole. These pits were the first models of the old-fashioned brick pits that are still popular in today's barbecue restaurants.

FUEL: Wood

CONVENIENCE: The temperature is controlled by airflow, not by a thermostat. This pit is probably the least convenient of all the cookers listed, because it takes continuous work to maintain a steady cooking temperature, but it is often the first choice of experienced pitmasters.

IDEAL FOR: If you need to read this chapter to determine what cooker best fits your style, then the cinder-block pit is not your ideal choice. This is the pitmaster's pit. You will know when you're ready.

INDIRECT COOKING: Cinder-block pits are easily converted into indirect smokers by building a fire on one side of the rectangular cooking chamber and putting the meat on the far side of the cooking grate.

DIRECT HEAT: Because the entire floor of most cinder-block pits can hold a hot fire, the entire cooking grate can handle direct grilling. Because of the extra distance between the floor of the pit and the cooking grate, direct cooking at low to medium temperatures is an option.

COST: $100–$10,000+

WATER BELLY SMOKER

Think of a water belly smoker as a vertical, two-chambered barbecue cooker. Between the two chambers is a pan filled with liquid. This pan serves two purposes. First, it separates the firebox from the cooking chamber, creating an atmosphere of indirect heat. Second, it creates extremely high humidity during the cooking process, helping to ensure moist and juicy food. This high humidity is extremely important when cooking large cuts of meat for long periods of time. Dry heat equals dry meat.

During the long hours of cooking items like whole hog, pork butt (shoulder), or beef brisket, the liquid in the pan will evaporate. You'll need to replenish the pan during cooking manually, or some models have a water flow regulator, where you attach a water hose to the cooker and it will automatically add water during cooking.

FUEL: Charcoal and/or wood

CONVENIENCE: The temperature is controlled by airflow, not by a thermostat. The water belly cooker takes longer to get up to temperature because of the liquid belly. It retains heat and moisture well because of the hot liquid.

IDEAL FOR: Wrapping the meat in foil for barbecuing is referred to as "the Texas crutch," the idea being to capture moisture and tenderize the meat by steaming. But you'll need none of that with a water belly smoker, because it gets so humid inside the cooker. If you like your Q tender and juicy, the water belly cooker is a steaming-hot choice.

INDIRECT COOKING: Ideal for high-humidity cooking with low- to medium-temperature indirect heat.

DIRECT HEAT: n/a

COST: $1,000–$10,000+

GRAVITY-FED CHARCOAL SMOKER

The gravity-fed charcoal smoker is a type of vertical smoker with a unique charcoal chute that runs upward beside the cooking chamber. Charcoal is poured through the top of the chute and is fed by gravity to the firebox located underneath the cooking chamber. Light the charcoal in the firebox and, as it burns, more unlit charcoal falls from the chute, fueling the fire. Wood can be added to the firebox for added smokiness. The heat and smoke are then transferred vertically to the multi-racked cooking chamber.

The continuous burn-and-feed process results in an extended cook time without having to refuel. A well-insulated gravity-fed smoker can get up to 1 hour of cook time, at 225°F, per pound of charcoal added.

FUEL: Charcoal and wood

CONVENIENCE: The temperature is controlled by airflow, not by a thermostat. Because of the high insulation factor and the gravity-fed chute, these cookers typically preheat quickly and cook for long periods of time without requiring time to refuel.

IDEAL FOR: I'm a fan of these smokers. They're perfect for the avid and more experienced barbecuer who loves charcoal cooking. Staying up all night long tending the fire is a bit overrated! I'll take the extra sleep that this cooker will allow.

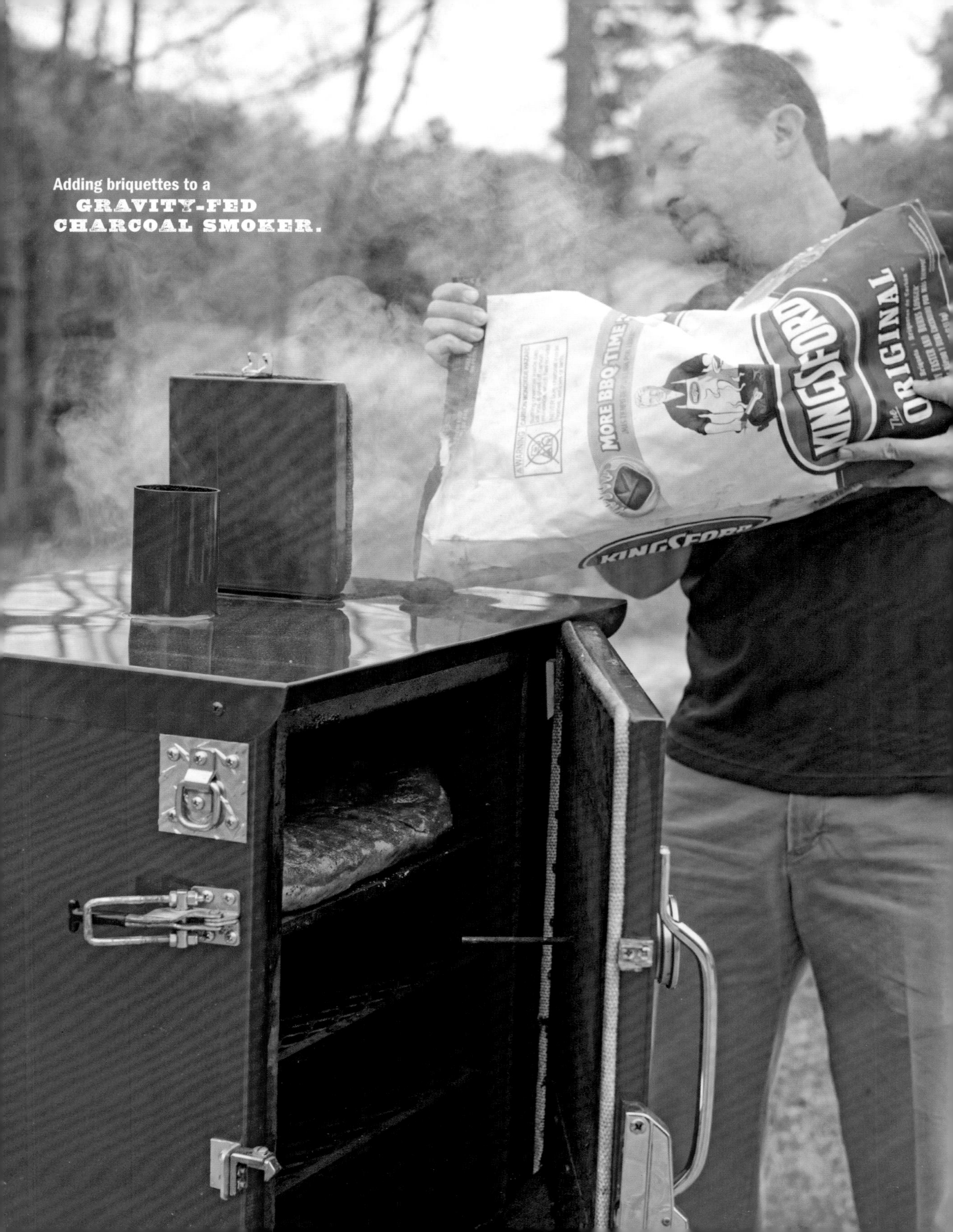

Adding briquettes to a
**GRAVITY-FED
CHARCOAL SMOKER.**

INDIRECT COOKING: Indirect cooking is the ideal for gravity-fed smokers. They can maintain a consistent temperature between 175° and 450°F during the cook cycle.

DIRECT HEAT: n/a

COST: $1,350–$4,000

CUBAN ROASTING BOX

Although many would argue that the Cuban roasting box is not grilling or barbecuing, it has become very popular for cooking large cuts of meat, including whole pigs or goats. These rectangular boxes are usually built with an outside shell made of plywood, the inside being lined with metal. La Caja China is the most popular brand on the market and is my preference for this type of cooker. Seasoned meat is put in the box and a metal lid with a recessed cavity filled with charcoal is placed on top of the box, sealing it tight. The charcoal-filled lid creates an environment of high heat and humidity within the cooking chamber.

The Cuban roasting box has both advantages and disadvantages. First, it halves the cook time of large-cut meats and whole animals because it utilizes both high heat and steam. Also, because the cooking chamber is sealed, it creates very high humidity, ensuring moist and juicy meat. Yet, for that same reason, there is no way to get charcoal or wood flavor to the meat. The flavor of the meat is limited to the seasonings placed in the box before beginning the cooking process.

FUEL: Charcoal

CONVENIENCE: The Cuban roasting box is one of the most convenient methods of cooking large cuts of meat because the charcoal pan is very accessible. Cooking is based more on time than on regulating exact temperatures.

IDEAL FOR: Once the food is prepped and put inside this hotbox, there is no fire maintenance or tending to the food. If little work, tender meat, and no smoke flavor appeal to you, then say yes to this cooker.

INDIRECT COOKING: Indirect roasting would be the way to describe cooking in the Cuban roasting box.

DIRECT HEAT: n/a

COST: $180–$1,500

There is no right or wrong choice when purchasing a grill or smoker. It is a personal selection that reflects your cooking interests and style. There is absolutely no relationship between how much money you pay for your cooker and how good your barbecue is. Give me a weekend and a wager, and I'll convince you of that! It is how often you use it that determines barbecue perfection. I've often said, "The greatness of a pitmaster is directly proportional to the size of his or her ash pile." So fire up the grill, pour yourself a cocktail, and relax where cooking was meant to be enjoyed—outdoors!

GRILLED COCKTAILS

BRANCH OUT FROM THE SAME EXPECTED MIXED DRINKS & SURPRISE YOUR GUESTS . . .

Many years back I was standing at my backyard grill, as I so often do, enjoying the sights, sounds, and smells of my lunch sizzling over a bed of hot coals. My grill often gets messy as I shuffle food back and forth on the grill grates, combining flavors and ingredients directly over the flame. I suddenly noticed a perfectly charred lemon slice glistening above the fire. This tasty fruit seemed to be begging to be squeezed over the plump pork chop smoking away on the grill. And yet, without really thinking about it, I plopped the juicy nugget into the highball I was sipping on. It only took one taste to realize the new and refreshing possibilities of grilled cocktails.

Caramelized lemons, smoked ice, sugared bacon, brisket bourbon, grilled olive skewers, smoked tequila—these are just a few ways you can utilize the grill to add more flavor to signature cocktails. Grilled drinks are easy when you're already standing at the outdoor cooker, searing steaks or tuna. Branch out from the same expected mixed drinks and surprise your guests with drinks like Barbecue Bloody Mary, Grilled Mango Mojito, or Grilled Apple Cider.

Barbecue Bloody Mary 36	**Spicy Martini** 41	**Grilled Apple Cider** 45
Grilled Mango Mojito 39	**Grilled Peach Sangria** 42	**Smoked Sweet Tea Margarita** 46
Whiskey Sour 40	**Grilled Lemonade** 44	**Homemade Hot Chocolate** 49

BARBECUE

BLOODY MARY

1 tablespoon **sugar**

1 **lemon**, halved

3 cups **tomato juice**

⅔ cup **barbecue beef brisket drippings** (see page 130)

¾ cup **vodka**

2½ tablespoons **Worcestershire sauce**

¾ teaspoon **prepared horseradish**

¾ teaspoon **Louisiana-style hot sauce** (or Sriracha sauce)

1½ teaspoons **smoked celery salt** (see Pitmaster Tip)

½ teaspoon freshly ground **black pepper**

1 teaspoon **kosher salt**

GARNISH (OPTIONAL)

Grilled lemon and jalapeño skewers

Grilled Sweet & Spicy Pickles (page 213)

With so many possible ingredients and variations, the traditional Bloody Mary offers many opportunities for infusion with the flavor of the grill. Smoked tomato juice, grilled celery sticks, grilled lemons, and smoked horseradish are only a few options. But one thing is certain: Nothing can start the day off better than spending time outdoors with a tall Bloody Mary and a smoking grill.

When I began experimenting with how to make the perfect Barbecue Bloody Mary, I mixed some concoctions together that would strip the rust off the old backyard grill. I kept at it, though, and started again with a table full of fresh ingredients. A weeklong string of very happy mornings ensued. By then I had forgotten what my goal was, but my ingredients were gone and this was the last recipe that I made. Delicious!

SERVES 4		SUGGESTED WOOD:		COOKING TIME:
COOKING METHOD: **Direct heat**		**Maple, pecan, oak** (see page 22)		**2 minutes**

1 Build a charcoal fire for direct grilling and preheat it to 450°F.

2 While the grill is heating, put the sugar on a plate and twist the face of each lemon half into the sugar.

3 Place the lemon halves facedown over direct heat and grill until the sugar caramelizes, about 2 minutes. Remove from the grill and set aside.

4 In a small pitcher, combine the tomato juice, beef brisket jus, vodka, Worcestershire, horseradish, hot sauce, ½ teaspoon of the smoked celery salt, and the pepper. Squeeze the juice from one lemon half into the pitcher, stir well, and refrigerate until chilled.

5 Run the remaining lemon half around the rim of 4 glasses. Combine the remaining 1 teaspoon celery salt and the kosher salt on a small plate. Twist the rims of the glasses into the salt. Fill the glasses with chilled Bloody Mary, garnish as desired, and serve.

Pitmaster Tip:

Smoked salt is a great way to add tasty smoke flavor to food and drinks when outdoor cooking is not an option. While you can purchase smoked salts, making your own at home saves money. Some of my favorites include several varieties of smoked sea salt, kosher salt, celery salt, garlic salt, and onion salt. By matching salt varieties with different woods you can create endless signature smoked salts.

TRY THESE COMBINATIONS OF SALT AND WOOD TYPE:

Sea salt +	mesquite, hickory
Kosher salt +	cherry, peach, apple
Celery salt +	pecan
Garlic salt +	hickory
Onion salt +	oak

Build a two-zone fire in a charcoal grill by situating the coals on only one side of the grill, leaving the other side empty. Preheat the grill to 200°F.

Spread the salt evenly over the bottom of a disposable aluminum pan. When the grill reaches 200°F, drop two handfuls of wood chips onto the hot coals, put the pan of salt over indirect heat, away from the coals, and close the grill lid. Close the damper to about ¼ inch to hold the low temperature and smoke for 1 hour. If the smoke disappears from the top dampers, add another handful of chips.

GRILLED MANGO MOJITO
WITH CARAMELIZED CANE SKEWER

After a decade of cooking at the South Beach Wine & Food Festival, I developed a fondness for sipping a cool refreshing mojito on the sands of Miami's South Beach once the work was done. Though it's such a simple drink, no two mojitos are exactly alike. Flavors range from the original lime to peach, mango, raspberry, mixed berry, and endless combinations. My festival friends and I embarked on a mojito tasting, which turned into a game to find out where to get the best one. Turned out that in this game everybody won! One of my favorites is an authentic lime mojito made at a Haitian restaurant called Tap Tap. Add in an order of malanga fritters, and I'm ready for the beach!

1 **mango**, peeled and cut into large chunks

2 **limes**, cut into ¼-inch-thick slices

¼ cup **cane syrup**

¾ cup **sugar**

4 **sugarcane skewers**

32 **mint leaves**

8 ounces **light rum**

5 cups **ginger ale**

GARNISH

Mint leaves

Grilled **lime wheel**

Caramelized **cane skewer**

SERVES 4	SUGGESTED WOOD:	COOKING TIME:
COOKING METHOD: Direct heat	Fruitwoods, maple (see page 22)	2 minutes

1   Build a charcoal fire for direct grilling and preheat it to 450°F.

2   In a small bowl, combine the mango, lime slices, and cane syrup. Put the sugar on a plate. Using a slotted spoon, remove the fruit from the syrup, put it on the plate of sugar, and turn to coat all sides. Roll the sugarcane skewers through the sugar. Immediately put the fruit and cane skewers over direct heat and grill until the sugar caramelizes, about 1 minute on each side. Remove the skewers and fruit from the grill and set aside.

3   In each of 4 tall glasses, put 8 mint leaves, ¼ cup grilled mango, and 1 lime slice cut in half. Muddle the mint and grilled fruit. Add 2 ounces of rum to each glass, fill each glass with ice, and top them off with ginger ale (about 1¼ cups). Shake or stir and serve, garnished with fresh mint leaves, a grilled lime wheel, and a caramelized cane skewer, if desired.

WHISKEY SOUR

WITH GRILLED LEMONS & SMOKED ICE

½ cup packed **dark brown sugar**

2 tablespoons **granulated sugar**

2 **lemons,** halved

1 tray **smoked ice**
　(see Pitmaster Tip)

4 shots **whiskey**

Pitmaster Tip: Though it may sound a little kooky, smoked ice is easy to make and is always great to have in your kitchen to add instant smoked flavor to cocktails and other recipes. Build a two-zone charcoal fire by situating the coals on only one side of the grill, leaving the other side empty. Preheat the grill to 225°F and then add your desired type of wood chips. Fill a small ovenproof saucepan with water and set it over indirect heat with the grill lid closed for 45 minutes. Remove the pan from the grill and let the water cool to room temperature. Pour the water into ice cube trays and place them in the freezer.

Although the whiskey sour is a very simple drink, the flavor is complex enough to satisfy as a before- or after-dinner drink. Of course, it's also nice to drink while eating food, since its tartness goes nicely with the mild flavors of chicken or fish.

The whiskey sour has changed over the years from a refreshing beverage made with fresh lemons and sugar to a candylike concoction made from bottled sweet and sour mix. I first went old-school with this recipe, bringing back the fresh lemons while adding brown sugar simple syrup. Then I grilled those lemons and added smoked ice to amp up this old barroom standby.

SERVES 4		
COOKING METHOD: **Direct and indirect heat**	SUGGESTED WOOD: **Fruitwoods, maple** (see page 22)	COOKING TIME: **7 minutes**

1　Build a two-zone fire in a charcoal grill by situating the coals on only one side of the grill, leaving the other side empty. Preheat the grill to 400°F.

2　In a small ovenproof saucepan, combine the brown sugar and ⅓ cup water. Put the uncovered pan over indirect heat, away from the coals, and close the grill lid. Cook the liquid until the sugar is dissolved and a simple syrup is formed, about 5 minutes. Remove the pan from the grill and set aside to let cool.

3　Put the granulated sugar on a plate and twist the face of each lemon half in the sugar. Put the lemon halves facedown over direct heat and grill until the sugar caramelizes, about 2 minutes. Remove from the grill and set aside.

4　Put 2 cubes of smoked ice in each of 4 glasses (adjust the number of cubes for desired smokiness). Add 1½ tablespoons of the simple syrup to each glass. Squeeze a grilled lemon half into each glass. Add 1 shot of whiskey to each glass, stir well, and serve.

SPICY MARTINI

WITH GRILLED OLIVE & PICKLED JALAPEÑO SKEWER

There have been endless variations on this classic mid-nineteenth-century bar drink. Vodka or gin, dry or wet, dirty or straight, olive or lemon; the options seem endless. Before you decide on a favorite, let's make your decision a little more complicated but much more tasty! Adding a grilled element to this drink improves both the flavor and the presentation of this iconic cocktail.

12 **green olives**

12 pickled **jalapeño slices**

4 (3-inch) **wooden skewers**

12 ounces **Absolut Peppar vodka**

4 ounces **dry vermouth**

SERVES 4

COOKING METHOD:
Direct heat

SUGGESTED WOOD:
Pecan, oak,
hickory
(see page 22)

COOKING TIME:
2 minutes

1 Build a charcoal fire for direct grilling and preheat it to 450°F.

2 Thread 3 green olives and 3 pickled jalapeño slices, alternating them, onto each skewer. Put the skewers over direct heat and grill until the olives char slightly, about 1 minute on each side. Remove from the grill and set aside.

3 Fill a cocktail shaker with ice and add 3 ounces of vodka and 1 ounce of vermouth. Shake vigorously and strain into a chilled martini glass. Repeat with the remaining vodka and vermouth. Garnish each glass with an olive-jalapeño skewer and serve.

GRILLED
PEACH SANGRIA

½ cup **sugar**

2 **peaches**, peeled and cut into quarters

1 **lemon**, sliced

1 **orange**, sliced

½ cup **peach brandy** or **schnapps**

½ cup frozen **lemonade concentrate**

½ cup **Triple Sec**

⅓ cup **orange juice**

1 (750 ml) bottle **dry red wine**

2 cups **club soda**

Pitmaster Tip: When making sangria, reach past the most expensive bottle of wine and grab an inexpensive table wine. For the benefit of the recipe, I was forced to experiment with several bottles of wine of varying prices and ratings. My conclusion is that the quality of the wine is less important than that of the fruit.

Sangria is typically a mix of red wine, spirits, fresh fruits, and club soda or lemonade served over ice. The wine turns this beverage the deep red color that inspired its name, which is derived from the Spanish word for "blood." Sangria's appeal is all about experimenting with the base ingredients, and you can even sub in white wine for red to make a white sangria. This drink is great at parties, backyard barbecues, and picnics on the beach—anywhere you need a pitcher of refreshing drinks.

Any drink with mixed fruit is the perfect opportunity to bring your grill into play, adding a caramelized and smoky element to the flavor. I always like to add a coat of sugar to the fruit before it hits the grill to highlight the sweetness of the pulp and to promote caramelization.

SERVES 8 TO 10	SUGGESTED WOOD:	COOKING TIME:
COOKING METHOD: Direct heat	Fruitwoods, maple (see page 22)	2 minutes

1 Build a charcoal fire for direct grilling and preheat it to 450°F.

2 In a medium bowl, combine the sugar, peaches, lemons, and oranges.

3 Immediately put the fruit on the grill over direct heat and grill until the sugar caramelizes, about 1 minute on each side. Remove the fruit from the grill and set aside.

4 In a blender, combine the peach brandy, frozen lemonade, Triple Sec, orange juice, and grilled peaches. Blend until smooth. Pour the mixture into a large pitcher, add the red wine, and stir well. Add the grilled lemon and orange slices and refrigerate until served.

5 To serve, add the club soda to the pitcher and mix well. Serve over ice.

G R I L L E D
LEMONADE

½ cup **honey**

1¼ cups **sugar**

2 **rosemary sprigs**

6 pounds **lemons**, halved

1 cup **bourbon**

GARNISH (OPTIONAL)

Grilled **lemon** wheels

This is about the only recipe in the book that I can't claim. I decided to include it because making it has become a tradition when we are grilling on the road. The second reason is because it's just that dang good! All praise for this delicious cocktail goes to Marcus Wang, a former employee at the Kingsford charcoal R&D facility. For years he kept our thirsts quenched and our cooking site smelling like caramelized lemons. Now it's Drew McGowan who carries on the tradition by never showing up near my grill without a bulging bag of citrus fruit.

SERVES 12		
COOKING METHOD: Direct heat	**SUGGESTED WOOD:** Rosemary sprigs	**COOKING TIME:** 12 to 14 minutes

1 Build a two-zone fire in a charcoal grill by situating the coals on only one side of the grill, leaving the other side empty. Preheat the grill to 400°F.

2 In a disposable aluminum pan, combine ½ cup water, the honey, ½ cup of the sugar, and the rosemary. Put the pan away from the coals, over indirect heat, and close the grill lid. Cook for 10 minutes. Remove the pan from the grill and set aside to let the simple syrup cool.

3 Put the remaining ¾ cup sugar on a plate. Twist the face of each lemon half into the sugar. Put the fruit on the grill, directly over the hot coals. Grill until the sugar caramelizes, 2 to 4 minutes. Remove from the grill and set aside to let cool.

4 When the lemons are cool to the touch, squeeze the juice from the lemons into a medium pitcher (they should yield 3 cups of juice). Pour in the simple syrup, discarding the rosemary sprigs. Add the bourbon and 6 cups cold water. Stir well and refrigerate until chilled.

5 To serve, pour over ice. Garnish each glass with a grilled lemon wheel, if desired.

GRILLED
APPLE CIDER

From the second you stir together the cinnamon, allspice, and sugar, you will crave apple cider. What makes this recipe truly unique is the thick coat of cider rub that the apples get just before hitting the grill. These spices and the sugar caramelize and take on a smoky flavor, adding a richness that you just can't get indoors. This is not the ordinary watered-down version of apple cider sold at the local grocery store. This homemade version gets thicker and richer as the pot of apples boils down on the grill. The more you reduce the liquid, the more powerful a wallop the cider will pack.

1¼ cups **sugar**

¼ cup ground **cinnamon**

¼ cup ground **allspice**

5-pound mix of **Fuji, Golden Delicious, and McIntosh apples**, peeled and sliced (about 10 medium to large apples)

Spiced rum (optional)

MAKES 3 PINTS; SERVES 6	SUGGESTED WOOD: Fruitwoods (see page 22)	COOKING TIME: 2 hours 20 minutes
COOKING METHOD: Direct and indirect heat		CHILLING TIME: 2 hours

1 Build a two-zone fire in a charcoal grill by situating the coals on only one side of the grill, leaving the other side empty. Preheat the grill to 450°F.

2 In a medium bowl, combine ½ cup of the sugar, the cinnamon, and allspice. Add the apple slices and toss well, making sure the rub sticks to the apple slices. Immediately put the sugared apple slices over direct heat and grill until the sugar caramelizes, about 1 minute on each side.

3 Transfer the apples to a medium stockpot. Add 12 cups of water and the remaining ¾ cup sugar to the pot. Put the pot over direct heat, bring to a boil, and cook until the liquid reduces by half, about 1 hour. Put a lid on the pot, move the pot over indirect heat, close the grill lid, and simmer until the apple slices turn to pulp, about 1 hour 15 minutes. Remove the pot from the grill and set aside to let cool.

4 Pour the juice from the pot through a strainer into a small pitcher. Squeeze the remaining pulp through four layers of cheesecloth into the pitcher. Discard the leftover pulp. Refrigerate for at least 2 hours.

5 Serve chilled. If desired, add 2 ounces spiced rum to each cup.

SMOKED
SWEET TEA
MARGARITA

1¼ cups **sugar**

2 tablespoons **molasses**

2 black **tea bags**

2 **lemons**, sliced

1 **orange**, sliced

1¼ cups **gold tequila**

½ cup **bourbon**

1 (12-ounce) can frozen **lemonade**

3 tablespoons fresh **lime juice**

GLASS RIM (OPTIONAL)

Crushed **lemon drop candy**

Molasses

In Alabama we love our sweet tea. I've never really understood the crazy confused looks I get from waitresses when I order it away from the South. The powdered packs of pink, blue, and white are a poor substitute for the smooth sweetness of dissolved sugar in fresh brewed tea. Better yet is a combination of both sugar and molasses in tea for a richer flavor. When I'm on the road, I miss many things about home. Sometimes all it takes is a tall cold glass of sweet tea to pacify my Southern withdrawals and get my mind right.

A Smoked Sweet Tea Margarita is a tasty drink for anyone relaxing at a campfire or beside the outdoor cooker. The smoked flavor of the fire-brewed tea matches well with the refreshing fruit flavors of a traditional margarita. Fire up the grill and enjoy.

SERVES 8			
COOKING METHOD: Direct and indirect heat		SUGGESTED WOOD: Fruitwoods, alder (see page 22)	COOKING TIME: 30 minutes

1 Build a two-zone fire in a charcoal grill by situating the coals on only one side of the grill, leaving the other side empty. Preheat the grill to 350°F.

2 In a heatproof saucepan, combine 8 cups water, ¾ cup of the sugar, and the molasses. Put the pan on the grill over indirect heat and close the grill lid. Cook until the temperature of the mixture reaches 170°F or higher, 20 to 30 minutes. Remove the pan from the grill, put the tea bags into the hot sugar water, and let them steep for 10 to 15 minutes. Discard the tea bags and set the tea aside.

3 Meanwhile, in a small bowl, combine the remaining ½ cup sugar, the lemon slices, and orange slices and toss to coat. Immediately put the fruit on the grill over direct heat (you can grill the fruit while the water is on the grill over indirect heat) and grill until the sugar caramelizes, about 2 minutes on each side. Remove the fruit from the grill and set aside.

4 In a medium pitcher, combine the tequila, bourbon, frozen lemonade, and lime juice. Add the sweet tea mixture and the grilled fruit, reserving several of the grilled lemon slices to garnish the glasses. Mix well and chill.

5 To rim the glasses, if desired, put the lemon drop candy in a resealable plastic bag and smash them with a hammer. Pour them onto a small plate. Pour a little molasses onto another small plate. Twist the rim of each glass into the molasses and then into the lemon drop candy.

6 Serve over ice and garnished with grilled lemon.

Variation
SMOKED SWEET TEA MARGARITA POPS

Let the grilled fruit cool and then remove the rind. Put the fruit in a pitcher and muddle it. Add the tequila, bourbon, frozen lemonade, and lime juice. Set aside 1½ cups of the smoked sweet tea for another use, and pour the remaining tea into the pitcher. Stir well. Fill an ice-pop mold with the tea mixture. Freeze until solid.

HOMEMADE HOT CHOCOLATE

WITH CHARCOAL-ROASTED MARSHMALLOWS

There's really no such thing as barbecue season unless you mean the twelve months immediately following the New Year. For me and many who love the outdoors, barbecuing is never limited to sunny days and warm weather. You just need to make a couple of adjustments to your setup so that the experience is pleasurable no matter what the temperature. First, all chairs should be situated closer to the grill or firebox for cold-weather cooking. Second, and most important, the drink selection should be based on the weather conditions.

Homemade hot chocolate with charcoal-roasted marshmallows is a must for families who like to hang out at the grill during the cold months of winter. And while a grill fork might not be the best tool for flipping steaks, it is perfect for roasting marshmallows. Top that off with my favorite blend of rich hot chocolate, and barbecue season just got longer!

2½ cups **whole milk**

1 cup **heavy cream**

2 pinches of **salt**

2 tablespoons **unsweetened cocoa powder**

½ cup **dark chocolate chips**

½ cup **milk chocolate chips**

6 large **marshmallows**

SERVES 4 TO 6

COOKING METHOD: Direct heat

SUGGESTED WOOD: Hickory, oak (see page 22)

COOKING TIME: 10 minutes

1 Build a charcoal fire for direct grilling and preheat it to 450°F.

2 While the grill is preheating, combine the milk, heavy cream, and salt in a small saucepan.

3 Put the pan over direct heat and cook until the liquid begins to steam. Whisk in the cocoa. When the liquid starts to boil, remove the pan from the heat and add the chocolate chips.

4 While the chocolate melts, place the marshmallows, two at a time, on the end of a grill fork. Roast the marshmallows over the charcoal fire until they turn toasty brown, about 2 minutes. Put one marshmallow into each of 6 empty mugs.

5 Whisk the hot milk mixture vigorously until the melted chocolate blends. Immediately pour the hot chocolate over the charcoal-roasted marshmallows and serve.

Variation

PEPPERMINT-VANILLA SPIKED HOT CHOCOLATE

Combine 6 cups hot chocolate with 4 ounces vanilla vodka and 4 ounces peppermint schnapps. Serve hot, with charcoal-roasted marshmallows.

Serves 6

APPETIZERS

WHILE THE LARGE CUTS OF MEAT ARE COOKING SLOWLY, YOU CAN PUT TOGETHER A FEW QUICK-FIRED APPETIZERS ON THE GRILL.

It's astounding to think back on the places I've traveled and the amazing chefs I've met, all in the name of Southern barbecue. Traveling outside of the region I call home has given me a different outlook on food and has provided new inspiration on the grill. While my last book was a total immersion in American barbecue, the recipes in this new book stay true to my roots while exploring unique flavors from around the world. Just in this one section you will notice inspiration from Japan, Greece, Mexico, Italy, Indonesia, and China.

While the large cuts of meat are cooking slowly, filling the afternoon air with succulent aromas, you can put together a few quick-fired appetizers on the grill. There is a favorite recipe for everyone here, from Chargrilled Oysters with Wilted Turnip Greens, Curry Chicken Satays with Coconut-Ginger Marinade, and Grilled Guacamole. Settle in and get ready for a full day of grilling!

SMOKED ARTICHOKES
WITH SPICY MAYONNAISE

2 artichokes

Spicy Mayonnaise (page 231)

Let's all try to show artichokes a little more love! Artichokes are not overlooked because they aren't tasty but because we don't know what to do with them. People tend to ignore this alien-looking veggie and select artichoke hearts confined in a cylindrical steel coffin. We don't know how to cook artichokes whole, and eating them is the pinnacle of confusion. Fear no more, the tasty solution for creating a delicious, healthy artichoke appetizer is below. Next time you are in the vegetable aisle, grab a produce bag and load up.

SERVES 6 TO 8	SUGGESTED WOOD:	COOKING TIME:
COOKING METHOD: Steaming and indirect heat	Oak, hickory (see page 22)	2 hours 40 minutes CHILLING TIME: Overnight

1 Wash the artichokes and cut the stems off at the base; reserve the stems. Using kitchen shears, cut the thorny tips from all of the leaves. Put the artichoke on a cutting board and, using a sharp knife, cut off the top 1 inch of the artichoke.

2 Put 2 quarts of water in a large stockpot and put it over high heat on the stovetop. Bring to a boil and add a steaming basket just above the waterline. Put the artichokes and stems in the basket, reduce the heat to low, and cover the pot. Cook until the artichoke leaves release with a slight tug, about 1 hour 45 minutes. Remove the artichokes and stems from the pot, let cool slightly, and wrap them in plastic wrap. Refrigerate overnight.

3 Build a charcoal fire for indirect cooking by situating the coals on only one side of the grill, leaving the other side empty. Preheat the grill to 225°F.

4 Remove the artichokes and stems from the plastic wrap and put them on the grill over indirect heat, away from the coals. Shut the grill lid, and cook until the artichokes have heated through, about 45 minutes. Remove them from the grill and slice the stems lengthwise into wedges. Serve the artichokes and stems hot, with the spicy mayonnaise on the side for dipping.

HOW TO EAT AN ARTICHOKE

I debated about including this section in the book until I thought about how mad someone would be after spending 2 days on a recipe only to end up with confusion and a growling stomach. Artichokes are easy to eat, but going at it the wrong way may mean a mouthful of tough plant fibers. That'll ruin it for you.

After cooking the artichoke, follow these simple guidelines:

1. With a soft tug, remove the leaves one at a time. Dip the white fleshy end of the leaf into the spicy mayonnaise. Put the end of the leaf in your mouth and scrape the soft delicious pulp off the more fibrous portion of the leaf with your teeth. Discard the leaf.

2. When all of the leaves are pulled, what is left is the artichoke heart covered in an inedible fur. Using a spoon, scrape out the fur from the heart and discard. Cut the artichoke heart into slices, dip them into the spicy mayonnaise, and eat.

PROSCIUTTO-WRAPPED DATES
WITH GOAT CHEESE, SPICED PECANS & SUN-DRIED TOMATOES

If you have never had a grilled date, you are missing out! Most grilled dates are wrapped with bacon and cooked until hot and crisp. The fat and salt of the bacon match well with the caramelized fruit, creating a tag team of flavor guaranteed to be a hit. My version is stuffed with a tasty combination of goat cheese, spiced toasted pecans, and sun-dried tomatoes. A wrap of prosciutto tidies up these little bundles and makes this the pinnacle of all grilled date recipes.

½ tablespoon **unsalted butter**

24 **pecan halves**

¼ teaspoon **salt**

⅛ teaspoon **cayenne pepper**

12 **Medjool dates**

2 ounces **goat cheese**

3 **sun-dried tomatoes**, cut into quarters

6 ounces sliced **prosciutto**

SERVES 6	SUGGESTED WOOD:	COOKING TIME:
COOKING METHOD: **Direct heat**	**Hickory, pecan, apple** (see page 22)	**7 minutes**

1 Build a charcoal fire for direct grilling and preheat it to 400°F.

2 Put the butter in a small skillet and put it over direct heat. Add the pecans, salt, and cayenne and stir. Heat until the pecans are lightly toasted, about 3 minutes. Set aside and let cool.

3 Split the dates open on one side to remove the pits. Stuff about a generous ½ teaspoon of the goat cheese into each date. Put one sun-dried tomato quarter on top of the cheese, and then put 2 pecan halves into each. Close the dates and try to form them into their original shape. Wrap each date in a thin slice of prosciutto and secure it with a 4-inch skewer.

4 Put the prosciutto-wrapped dates on the grill over direct heat. Grill until the prosciutto starts to brown, about 2 minutes on each side. Serve hot.

COAL-FIRED
PICO DE GALLO

6 **plum tomatoes**

1 **medium white onion**, cut into
½-inch-thick slices

2 **jalapeño peppers**, halved and
seeded

1 **banana pepper**, halved and
seeded

⅓ cup chopped fresh **cilantro**

2 **garlic cloves**, crushed

Juice of ½ **lime**

¾ teaspoon **salt**

½ teaspoon **sugar**

Flavor is not the only reason cooking outdoors is the first choice for my family. The atmosphere and casual attitude around the grill slow the pace of the day, making simple moments in life more enjoyable. The sights, sounds, and smells of the grill foster a relaxed joy, creating a mental, physical, and spiritual oasis in my backyard. Bit by bit, I've moved dishes typically confined to the indoor kitchen to the outdoors.

Grilled pico de gallo is a shining example of successful recipe relocation. The vegetables pick up a nice smoke and char as they sizzle over the open flame, which not only makes the salsa taste richer but also gives a great color. Because some of the vegetable juices are rendered to the fire Gods, just the right amount of the liquid remains to make a hearty pico and not runny soup.

MAKES 2 CUPS	SUGGESTED WOOD:	COOKING TIME:
	Maple, mesquite,	5 minutes
COOKING METHOD:	oak (see page 22)	STANDING TIME:
Direct heat		30 minutes

1 Build a charcoal fire for direct grilling and preheat it to 450°F.

2 Put the tomatoes, onion slices, and peppers over direct heat and cook, turning once, until they char and start to soften, about 5 minutes.

3 Remove the vegetables from the grill and chop them.

4 In a small bowl, combine the vegetables, cilantro, garlic, lime juice, salt, and sugar. Let the pico de gallo sit for 30 minutes for the flavors to meld together.

5 Serve at room temperature or chilled.

GRILLED GUACAMOLE

Guacamole originated with the Aztecs in Mexico as a sauce made from ground avocado and salt. Traditionally the avocados were mashed in a *molcajete* (a type of mortar and pestle) and then seasoned to taste. Over the years, ingredients such as tomatoes, onions, cilantro, and lime juice have become standard. But now, I want to introduce one more element of flavor: fire.

Don't ever forget the versatility of this green buttery mash of goodness. Because the flesh of the avocado is not sweet but creamy and fatty, it pairs well with both sweet and savory dishes. Guacamole, with its flavor, texture, and nutritional value, makes a great spread, dip, or sauce, but also delivers a flavorful punch to soups, salads, sandwiches, and sushi rolls or works as a stand-alone side dish.

3 **Roma tomatoes**

4 ripe **Hass avocados**, cut into ½-inch-thick slices

½ **red onion**, cut into ½-inch-thick slices

1 **jalapeño pepper**, halved and seeded

1 tablespoon fresh **lime juice**

1 **garlic clove**, minced

1 tablespoon chopped fresh **cilantro**

¾ teaspoon **kosher salt**

½ teaspoon ground **cumin**

⅛ teaspoon **cayenne pepper**

MAKES 2 CUPS

COOKING METHOD: Direct heat

SUGGESTED WOOD: Alder, maple (see page 22)

COOKING TIME: 5 minutes

Pitmaster Tip: The flesh of avocados is prone to enzymatic browning after the skin is removed, which means it turns brown quickly after exposure to air. To prevent this, squeeze a little lemon or lime juice on the avocados after they are peeled.

1 Build a charcoal fire for direct grilling and preheat it to 450°F.

2 Put the tomatoes, avocadoes, red onion, and jalapeño over direct heat and cook, turning once, until they char and start to soften, about 5 minutes.

3 Remove the vegetables from the grill and chop.

4 In a small bowl, combine the vegetables, lime juice, garlic, cilantro, salt, cumin, and cayenne and mix vigorously.

5 Serve at room temperature or chilled.

FLANK STEAK & SHIITAKE ROLL YAKITORI

MARINADE

¾ cup **soy sauce**

¾ cup **mirin** (sweetened rice wine)

Juice of ½ **lime**

½ cup **sugar**

1 **garlic clove**, minced

¾ teaspoon grated fresh **ginger**

1 tablespoon chopped fresh **cilantro**

⅛ teaspoon **red pepper flakes**

SKEWERS

28 **shiitake mushroom caps**

1 pound **flank steak**, cut across the grain into ¼-inch-thick slices

1 bunch **scallions**, tops only, cut into 1-inch pieces

14 (6-inch) **wooden skewers**, soaked in water

Salt and freshly ground **black pepper**

Yakitori is a Japanese term for skewered food, usually chicken, that is grilled over hot coals. Yakitori grills are narrow direct-fire grills set up to efficiently cook these small skewers. The width of the grill focuses direct heat on the meat while the skewer ends hang over the edge, protecting them from the fire. This also makes it safer to rotate the skewers on the hot grill.

My version here involves steak and a great Asian-style marinade. Flank steak is cut into thin strips and weaved around marinated shiitake mushrooms and scallion tops. With soy, mirin, garlic, ginger, and lime, the marinade is immensely flavorful yet simple to prepare.

MAKES 14 APPETIZER SKEWERS	SUGGESTED WOOD:	MARINATING TIME:
	Hickory, oak, mesquite (see page 22)	20 minutes
COOKING METHOD: Direct heat		COOKING TIME: 14 minutes

1 For the marinade: In a medium saucepan, combine ¼ cup water, the soy sauce, mirin, lime juice, sugar, garlic, ginger, cilantro, and red pepper flakes. Bring to a simmer over medium-high heat and cook until the marinade has reduced to 1¾ cups, about 10 minutes.

2 For the skewers: Cut the mushroom caps in half and put them in a medium bowl. Pour the hot marinade over the mushrooms, and let sit for 20 minutes.

3 Build a charcoal fire for direct grilling and preheat to 450°F.

4 Pierce a flank steak strip at one end with a skewer. Thread a mushroom cap half onto the skewer, followed by a scallion pierced crosswise. Weave the flank steak around the mushroom and scallion and pierce it. Repeat with more mushrooms and scallion pieces, weaving the flank steak around them until the steak strip ends. You should have about 4 mushroom halves, 4 onions, and one flank steak strip on each skewer. Lightly season the skewers with salt and pepper.

5 Dip each skewer into the leftover marinade and immediately place them on the grill over direct heat. Grill until the steak browns, about 2 minutes on each side. Transfer the skewers to a platter and serve hot.

Pitmaster Tip: Even after soaking, wooden skewers can smolder and burn because the water will evaporate when grilling over direct heat. To prevent this from happening, hang the exposed stick over the lip of the grill. This will also keep your hands away from the high heat when turning. Another method is to use aluminum foil strips placed on the grill grate as a buffer between the fire and the exposed skewers.

CURRY CHICKEN SATAYS
WITH COCONUT-GINGER MARINADE

A satay is a very popular snack or appetizer in Indonesia and Thailand. Often considered street food, a satay consists of a cube or strip of meat, seafood, or poultry skewered on a stick and grilled. Satays are usually marinated prior to grilling or they're dipped into a flavorful spicy peanut sauce right off the grill.

After experimenting through the years with some of my favorite Indonesian and Thai ingredients, I came up with this recipe, which highlights some of my favorite flavors. Satays are meant to be quick, simple, and flavorful. This recipe is exactly that, combining a dry rub and a marinade for a quick, delicious appetizer.

MAKES 18 APPETIZER SKEWERS

COOKING METHOD:
Direct heat

SUGGESTED WOOD:
Maple, apricot, pimento
(see page 22)

MARINATING TIME:
2 hours
30 minutes

COOKING TIME:
6 minutes

DRY RUB
2 tablespoons **curry powder**

1 tablespoon ground **coriander**

1 tablespoon **granulated sugar**

1 tablespoon **salt**

2 pounds boneless, skinless **chicken breasts**, cut into ¾-inch-wide strips

18 (8-inch) **wooden skewers**, soaked in water

MARINADE
1 cup **coconut milk**

¼ cup **peanut oil**

Juice of 3 **limes**

⅔ cup chopped fresh **lemongrass**

6 **garlic cloves**, crushed

1 tablespoon grated fresh **ginger**

2 tablespoons **dark brown sugar**

1 For the dry rub: In a medium bowl, combine the curry powder, coriander, granulated sugar, and salt. Toss the chicken strips in the dry rub. Thread each chicken strip individually, lengthwise, onto each skewer. Put the skewers into a shallow dish large enough to hold all of them in a single layer. Cover and refrigerate for 30 minutes.

2 For the marinade: In a food processor or blender, combine the coconut milk, oil, lime juice, lemongrass, garlic, ginger, and brown sugar and puree until smooth. Pour the liquid over the chicken, cover, and refrigerate for 2 hours longer.

3 Build a charcoal fire for direct grilling and preheat it to 450°F.

4 Remove the skewers from the marinade and immediately place them over direct heat. Grill until the juices run clear, 2 to 3 minutes on each side. Serve the skewers hot.

GRILLED CHICKEN
LETTUCE
WRAPS

¾ cup chopped **water chestnuts**

½ cup chopped **mushrooms**

¼ cup thinly sliced **scallions**

1 **garlic clove**, minced

1 tablespoon **dark brown sugar**

4 teaspoons **soy sauce**

1 tablespoon **sesame oil**

½ teaspoon **rice vinegar**

DRY RUB AND CHICKEN

1 tablespoon **curry powder**

1½ teaspoons **salt**

1½ teaspoons **granulated sugar**

¼ teaspoon **garlic powder**

⅛ teaspoon **lemon pepper**

⅛ teaspoon ground **ginger**

1¼ pounds boneless, skinless
chicken thighs (4 to 6 thighs)

Based on a popular Chinese dish, these light, healthy, and low-carb lettuce wraps are a great starter for any meal, though they also can be featured as an entrée. I like to serve them family-style, or as an "assemble your own" starter by the grill. The recipe is really versatile, so try substituting any kind of meat for the chicken or replace the meat with mushrooms or eggplant if you want a vegetarian delicacy dish. One important tip is that these lettuce wraps need to be paired with plenty of napkins, because they are juicy and a little messy.

SERVES 4	**SUGGESTED WOOD:**	
COOKING METHOD:	Pecan, oak, hickory	**COOKING TIME:**
Direct heat	(see page 22)	19 minutes

1 Build a charcoal fire for direct grilling and preheat it to 400°F.

2 In a medium bowl, combine the water chestnuts, mushrooms, scallions, garlic, brown sugar, soy sauce, sesame oil, and rice vinegar and mix well. Pull out a 24-inch piece of foil and fold it in half to make a 12 × 12-inch square. Pour the mixture onto the foil. Fold the foil over the vegetables and crimp the edges to form a flat pouch. Cut a few vents in the top.

3 For the dry rub: In a small bowl, combine the curry powder, salt, granulated sugar, garlic powder, lemon pepper, and ginger. Dredge the chicken in the rub, coating it generously.

4 Put the chicken on the grill over direct heat and cook until the juices run clear or the internal temperature of the thighs reaches 160°F, 7 to 8 minutes per side. At the same time, put the foil pouch over direct heat and cook until the vegetables soften, about 15 minutes.

5 Meanwhile, for the baste: In a small bowl, combine the honey, soy sauce, and chili paste.

6 Remove the chicken from the grill and brush half of the baste mixture on the chicken; reserve the remaining baste as a sauce. Return the chicken to the grill over direct heat until the sauce caramelizes, about 3 minutes. Remove the chicken from the grill, cut it into ¼-inch-wide strips, and put it in a serving bowl.

7 Open the foil pouch and pour the vegetables into the bowl with the chicken, discarding any excess liquid in the pouch. Pour the remaining honey-chili sauce into the bowl and mix well.

8 To serve, fill each lettuce leaf with the grilled chicken and vegetable mixture and put it on a serving plate, or serve the lettuce on the side of the bowl of chicken and vegetables for guests to fill as they desire.

BASTE

5 tablespoons **honey**

2 tablespoons **soy sauce**

1 tablespoon **chili paste**

8 iceberg **lettuce leaves**

CHARGRILLED OYSTERS
WITH WILTED TURNIP GREENS

WILTED GREENS

1 pound **turnip greens**, stems trimmed

2 slices thick-cut **bacon**, chopped

4 tablespoons (½ stick) **unsalted butter**

⅓ cup chopped **yellow onion**

2 **garlic cloves**, minced

¾ teaspoon ground **white pepper**

1½ tablespoons **distilled white vinegar**

Salt and freshly ground **black pepper**

COMPOUND BUTTER

8 tablespoons (1 stick) **unsalted butter**, at room temperature

1 tablespoon **garlic puree** (see Pitmaster Tip, page 66)

½ teaspoon freshly ground **black pepper**

½ teaspoon dried **oregano**

¼ teaspoon **kosher salt**

⅛ teaspoon ground **white pepper**

¾ cup shredded **Parmesan cheese**

¾ cup shredded **Romano cheese**

36 fresh live **oysters**

Pepper sauce (such as Unca Duke's Geaux Jus), for serving

This dish is a hybrid recipe of separate things I made for two different events. Originally, I served a version back in 2003 at the James Beard Foundation in New York City. Chargrilled oysters were the highlight appetizer of the reception, which was followed by a five-course white-tablecloth dinner for a prestigious charity. Then, in 2012, at the South Beach Wine & Food Festival, I was asked to offer a late-night appetizer for guests at a Champagne party called Q After Dark, which was attended by 1,000 people. The obvious answer was to pair Champagne with chargrilled oysters—delicious! But we took it up a level, adding a compound butter and a cheese mixture on top of some wilted greens. It sounded like a great idea, and it did taste great—but saying is easier than doing! Shucking 1,000 fresh Gulf oysters was a chore, to say the least. So, while I do not recommend inviting 1,000 of your closest friends over while you attempt this recipe for the first time in your backyard, it is most certainly a delicious and impressive treat for a mere handful of your closest family and friends. Shuck away!

SERVES 6 TO 12	SUGGESTED WOOD:	
COOKING METHOD: **Direct heat**	Hickory, pecan, mesquite, oak (see page 22)	COOKING TIME: **20 minutes**

1 For the wilted greens: Stack the turnip leaves, roll them into a tight log, and cut the log every ¼ inch.

2 Bring a small pot of water to a boil. Add the cut turnip leaves and boil for 2 minutes. Drain the leaves into a colander, pressing firmly to squeeze out all the water.

3 In a large skillet, cook the bacon over medium-high heat until it starts to brown slightly, about 2 minutes. Add the butter and onion and cook, stirring, until the onion starts to become translucent, about 2 minutes. Reduce the heat and add the garlic, white pepper, vinegar, and turnip leaves. Stir well and cook for 3 minutes. Season with salt and black pepper to taste. Remove the pan from the heat.

RECIPE CONTINUES

Pitmaster Tip: Making a puree of garlic makes it easy to evenly distribute the flavor throughout sauces, marinades, and compound butter without accidently offending your guests with potent chunks of garlic. Because garlic gets very sticky when you cut it, it doesn't puree by itself in a food processor. Here's how to do it: Put the cloves from one head of garlic and 4 teaspoons olive oil in a food processor and puree until you get a perfect paste; there should be about ¼ cup.

4 For the compound butter: In a small bowl, combine the butter, garlic puree, black pepper, oregano, salt, and white pepper.

5 In a separate bowl, combine the Parmesan and Romano.

6 Build a charcoal fire for direct grilling and preheat the grill to 500°F.

7 Check to see if the oysters are alive by making sure the shells are tightly closed. Scrub the oysters with a stiff brush under running water. Pry the oyster shells apart with an oyster knife. Discard the top shell, loosen the oyster meat with the tip of the oyster knife, and leave the oysters in the bottom shells.

8 Top each oyster with 1½ teaspoons of wilted greens, 1 teaspoon of the compound butter, and 1 tablespoon of the cheese mixture.

9 Put the oysters over direct heat and grill until the juices bubble and the cheese browns, about 3 minutes. Remove the oysters from the grill, sprinkle with the pepper sauce, and serve.

GRILLED SARDINE & ARTICHOKE BRUSCHETTA

WITH TOMATO SALAD

Don't turn up your nose at this one! Sardines are a food you think you don't like. Believe me because I was one of the doubters until friends encouraged me to experiment with cooking them on a charcoal grill. These little fish are inexpensive, sustainable, and chock-full of omega-3s. They contain virtually no mercury and are loaded with vitamins. Besides being healthy, they make a powerfully tasty appetizer.

The secret to this dish is the contrasting textures: crispy toasted bread and soft, salty sardine. Add a delicious tomato salad with oil and vinegar dressing, and you have a real treat.

SERVES 12

COOKING METHOD:
Direct heat

SUGGESTED WOOD:
No extra smoke advised

COOKING TIME:
8 minutes

1 Build a charcoal fire for direct grilling and preheat it to 450°F.

2 For the tomato salad: In a medium bowl, combine the tomatoes, onion, and basil.

3 In a small bowl, whisk together the olive oil and vinegars. Add to the tomatoes and toss lightly. Season with salt and pepper to taste and toss again. Refrigerate until ready to use.

4 For the bruschetta: Brush one side of the multigrain slices with olive oil.

5 Scale and clean the sardines. Do not remove the heads, as they will help the fish stay together while grilling. Coat the sardines and artichoke hearts with olive oil and season with salt and pepper. Grill the sardines over direct heat until the skin crisps slightly, about 3 minutes per side.

RECIPE CONTINUES

TOMATO SALAD

3 **plum tomatoes**, chopped

1 **yellow tomato**, chopped

⅓ cup thinly sliced **red onion**

3 tablespoons chopped fresh **basil**

3 tablespoons **extra-virgin olive oil**

3 teaspoons **balsamic vinegar**

1½ teaspoons **cider vinegar**

Salt and freshly ground **black pepper**

BRUSCHETTA

1 small loaf **multigrain bread**, cut into 1-inch slices

Extra-virgin olive oil, for coating

12 whole fresh **sardines**

12 whole **artichoke hearts**

Salt and freshly ground **black pepper**

2 **garlic cloves**, halved

6 Grill the artichokes over direct heat until lightly charred, 3 to 4 minutes per side. Grill the bread slices over direct heat until crisp and lightly charred, about 1 minute on each side.

7 Lightly rub the oiled side of each piece of crisp bread with a cut garlic clove. Cut the artichokes into ¼-inch-thick slices and put a sliced artichoke on top of each piece of bread. Cut the sardines into fillets and layer the fish on top of the artichokes. Spoon a generous amount of tomato salad over the sardines and serve.

Pitmaster Tip: When grilling breads, always remember to keep the grill lid open. Excess smoke trapped in the cooking chamber is absorbed more quickly by breads than meats. Plenty of great chargrilled flavors will transfer into breads on an open grill with no extra wood chips added.

MARINADES

Marinades serve two different functions: They are a flavor enhancer and, to a lesser degree, a tenderizer. The first takes place as the marinade penetrates the surface of the food through "absorption," while the similar term "adsorption" refers to the process of how a marinade adheres to and flavors the surface of the food. Acid in marinades helps it seep into the meat. While marinades affect the texture of the outer layer of the meat, they do nothing to flavor or tenderize the inside portion of thicker cuts. If high-acid marinades are left on too long, they can "cook" the surface of the meat, causing it to dry out.

Marinades work faster on meats such as chicken and fish because the muscle structure is not as dense as it is with pork or beef. For denser meats, marinades work better if the meat is cut up or sliced thinly to increase the surface area, and you'll need to give them more time.

When creating a marinade, I like to break it down into 5 components:

ACID: This important ingredient in a marinade ensures a greater flavor transfer to the meat and adds an irresistible tartness. Examples include vinegar, fruit juices, Worcestershire sauce, and wine.

OIL: Oil has less to do with flavor and more to do with adding a barrier of protection between the hot fire and the meat's surface.

SALT: Along with the obvious benefit of flavor, salt can also help with the marinade absorption into the meat through osmosis.

SUGAR: This is an important addition, because it acts as a flavor-balancing agent against the salt and acid components. Sugar will also foster the browning reaction of proteins, adding flavor and visual appeal.

FLAVOR: What herbs and spices appeal to you? This is where a stock marinade becomes your signature marinade.

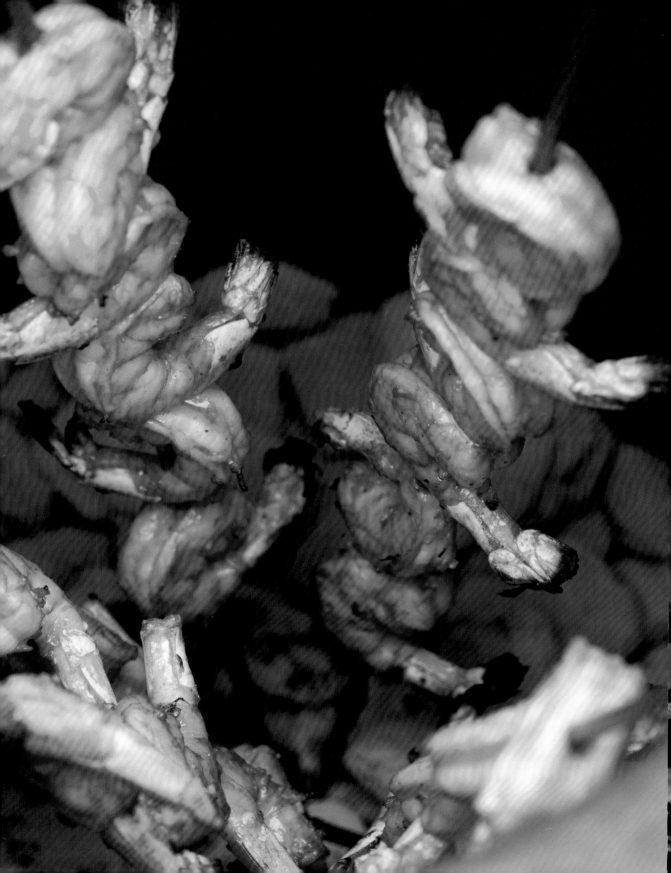

YUZU SHRIMP SKEWERS

A yuzu is a sour Japanese citrus fruit. The rind is used for flavor and as an aromatic in all types of drinks and dishes. Although the fruit is very difficult to find in the United States, yuzu powder, paste, and juice are available at ethnic grocers or through online ordering. The juice has a pleasant aroma, and the flavor is a cross between a tangerine and a lemon.

My first experiment with yuzu was working on Indonesian Sweet & Sour Shrimp Pizza (page 100) for an event at Seghesio Vineyard in Sonoma County, California. I quickly became a fan of yuzu juice because you get the great sour flavor without the harsh tartness of limes or lemons. After trying this recipe, I think you will look for excuses to add this shrimp to pizza, salads, and sandwiches, but it's hard to beat right off the stick!

The photo shows the shrimp cooking in a tandoor; see page 17 for more information on that type of cooker.

SERVES 6 TO 8

COOKING METHOD: Direct heat

SUGGESTED WOOD: Alder, maple (see page 22)

MARINATING TIME: 20 minutes

COOKING TIME: 4 minutes

MARINADE

5½ tablespoons **yuzu juice**

¼ cup **honey**

2½ tablespoons **soy sauce**

4 teaspoons **sesame oil**

4 teaspoons **chili-garlic sauce** (Sriracha)

2 teaspoons **salt**

1 teaspoon **curry powder**

1 teaspoon grated fresh **ginger**

1 teaspoon minced **garlic**

2 pounds large **shrimp** (31–35 count), peeled, tail left on

16 (6-inch) **wooden skewers**, soaked in water

1 For the marinade: In a small bowl, whisk together the yuzu juice, honey, soy sauce, sesame oil, chili-garlic sauce, salt, curry powder, ginger, and garlic. Put the shrimp in a shallow dish or a resealable plastic bag and pour the marinade over the shrimp, turning to coat. Cover or seal and marinate in the refrigerator for 20 minutes.

2 Build a charcoal fire for direct grilling and preheat it to 450°F.

3 Remove the shrimp from the marinade and thread 4 or 5 shrimp onto each skewer, piercing each shrimp twice (just above the tail shell and then through the meatiest part). Put the skewers on the grill over direct heat and cook until the shrimp firms and turns opaque, about 2 minutes on each side. Serve hot.

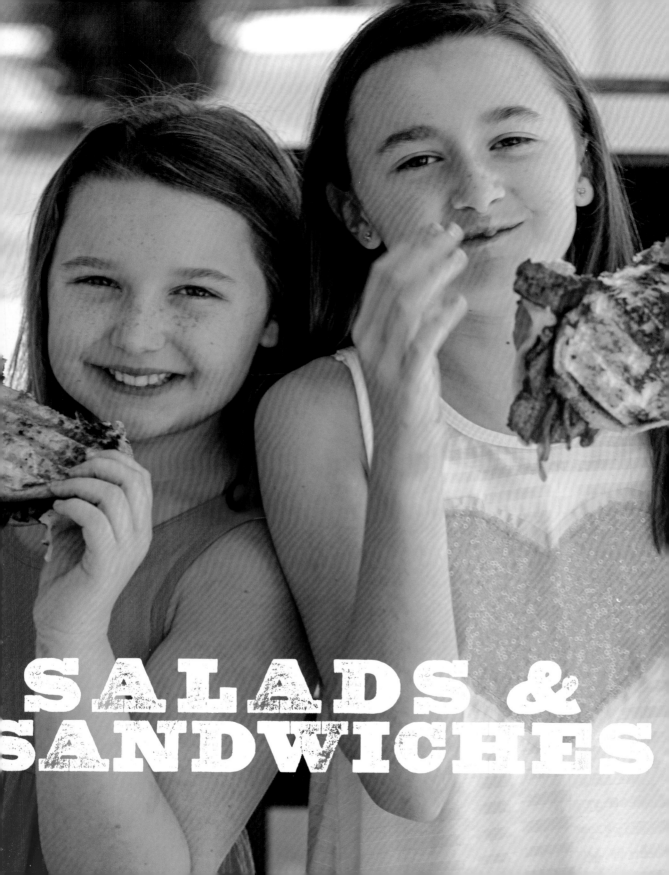

SALADS & SANDWICHES

BARBECUE: IT'S NOT JUST FOR BREAKFAST ANYMORE.

I subscribe to the motto of the Kansas City Barbecue society: "Barbecue: It's not just for breakfast anymore." This chapter is for all those who need an extra nudge in the right direction to accept outdoor cooking as a versatile all-day activity. Grilled Sweet Potato Steaks & Sausage is a dish that can be served for breakfast or brunch, or as a side dish for any of the sandwiches in this chapter. Low and slow recipes such as Smoked Pork Tenderloin & Spinach Salad and the quick-to-prepare Grilled Watermelon & Tomato Salad, where the watermelon takes a turn over the hot charcoal, make excellent lunches or light dinners. Sound crazy? It just might be. But it also might be the best thing you've ever put in your mouth! And sandwiches cooked up over the flames—like the Grilled Brick Panini with Smoked Gouda, Sweet Bacon & Caramelized Onions—takes them to a whole new level of satisfying.

GRILLED WATERMELON & TOMATO SALAD

1 small **watermelon**

Salt

½ cup **extra-virgin olive oil**

1¾ pounds **tomatoes**, cut into ¾-inch cubes

1 small **red onion**, halved and thinly sliced

½ cup **red wine vinegar**

1 tablespoon **sugar**

¼ cup thinly sliced fresh **basil**

Freshly ground **black pepper**

½ cup crumbled **feta cheese**

One of my favorite things to do when I travel is eat at restaurants I've never been to before. The culinary industry is really a very small world, so I rely on the opinions of my friends who are chefs to let me know where to find the tasty hot spots. I don't consciously go looking for recipe ideas, but when I taste something that excites me, I can't wait to get back to the grill!

However, locally, my favorite place to eat is with friends. Sometimes people will tell me they are intimidated when I'm a guest at their dinner table. That should never be a concern, because I'm just grateful for the invitation, the meal, and good company.

This recipe came about after I ate a simple watermelon and tomato salad at the house of Mark and Margaret Hooper. It was absolutely delicious, but I couldn't help wondering how it'd be after putting the watermelon to the grill. So, surprise, Mark and Margaret! Maybe including this story in my book will get me more dinner invitations.

SERVES 10 TO 14	SUGGESTED WOOD:	COOKING TIME:
	Alder, fruitwoods	6 minutes
COOKING METHOD:	(see page 22)	
Direct heat		CHILLING TIME:
		1 hour

1 Build a charcoal fire for direct grilling and preheat it to 450°F.

2 Cut the watermelon into rounds 1¼ inches thick. Generously salt both sides of each and put them on a wire rack set over a rimmed baking pan for 15 minutes.

3 Rinse the salt from the watermelon rounds and pat them dry with paper towels. Brush the watermelon pieces with ¼ cup of the oil. Put the watermelon on the grill over direct heat and cook until grill marks appear, about 3 minutes on each side. Remove the watermelon from the grill, trim and discard the rind, and cut it into 1-inch cubes, picking out as many seeds as you can.

4 In a medium bowl, combine the watermelon, tomatoes, onion, the remaining ¼ cup olive oil, the vinegar, sugar, and basil. Season with salt and pepper to taste, cover the bowl, and refrigerate for 1 hour.

5 Sprinkle the feta cheese over the top before serving.

GRILLED SWEET POTATO STEAKS & SAUSAGE

4 large **sweet potatoes**

¾ pound **smoked sausages**

Salt and freshly ground **black pepper**

I was at the restaurant one day and received a call from NASCAR asking me to do a breakfast-brunch catering on the racetrack infield before the Daytona 500. I knew right away I had to keep the menu simple because of the travel logistics, but at the same time it had to explode with flavor.

Adding my favorite sausage to an iron skillet sweet potato dish was the solution, and I knew it would be a fan favorite at the track because the sweet and salty combination of these potatoes and sausage is "good morning" magic!

This recipe is delicious and simple and can be cooked entirely on the backyard grill. Grilling potato steaks adds charred flavor and firms the outer crust while ensuring a soft and creamy center. With the maple-pecan butter, these sweet potato steaks are a great addition to any breakfast, lunch, or dinner tailgate at the race.

SERVES 8			
COOKING METHOD: Direct and indirect heat	**SUGGESTED WOOD:** Maple, hickory, oak (see page 22)	**COOKING TIME:** 1 hour 35 minutes	**COOLING TIME:** 30 minutes

1 Build a two-zone fire in a charcoal grill by situating the coals on only one side of the grill, leaving the other side empty. Preheat the grill to 400°F.

2 Wash the sweet potatoes and wrap individually in foil. Put the wrapped sweet potatoes over indirect heat, away from the coals. Close the grill lid and cook until they are soft, about 1 hour 15 minutes.

3 Remove the sweet potatoes from the grill, unwrap, and stop the cooking process by dipping them into a bowl of ice water for 4 minutes. Remove the sweet potatoes from the ice water and set aside to cool for at least 30 minutes before cutting.

4 While the potatoes cool, put the smoked sausages on the grill over indirect heat. Close the lid and cook until the internal temperature reaches 165°F, about 15 minutes. Transfer the sausages to a cutting board and let them rest for 10 minutes. Slice the sausages on an angle into ¼-inch pieces and set aside.

5 For the maple pecan butter: In a small saucepan, melt the butter over direct heat. Add the maple syrup, pecans, cinnamon, cayenne, and salt. Heat the mixture until a layer of bubbles forms over the surface, less than 1 minute. Remove the pan from the heat; set aside and keep warm.

6 Cut the sweet potatoes crosswise into ½-inch-thick medallions. Lightly season each sweet potato "steak" with salt and pepper. Grill each steak over direct heat until lightly charred, about 3 minutes per side. Transfer the potatoes to a cast iron skillet, arranging them in an overlapping fashion. Arrange the sausage slices on top of the potatoes in the same way, and drizzle the top with the warm maple-pecan butter. Serve hot.

MAPLE-PECAN BUTTER

4 tablespoons (½ stick) **unsalted butter**

¼ cup **maple syrup**

3 tablespoons chopped **pecans**

⅛ teaspoon ground **cinnamon**

⅛ teaspoon **cayenne pepper**

⅛ teaspoon **salt**

SMOKED PORK TENDERLOIN & SPINACH SALAD

DRESSING

¼ cup **vegetable oil**

1 tablespoon **balsamic vinegar**

1 tablespoon **distilled white vinegar**

¼ teaspoon **hot sauce**

4 teaspoons **granulated sugar**

¼ teaspoon **salt**

⅛ teaspoon freshly ground **black pepper**

LIQUID SEASONING

3 tablespoons **soy sauce**

2 tablespoons **extra-virgin olive oil**

1 tablespoon fresh **lemon juice**

4 teaspoons **dark brown sugar**

¼ teaspoon **garlic powder**

¼ teaspoon freshly ground **black pepper**

In 2009, I had the pleasure and honor of being named a Celebrated Chef by the National Pork Board. Imagine being selected to travel the country with great chefs like Michael Paley, John Sundstrom, Tyler Wiard, and Kevin Storm, feasting at some of America's premier restaurants. It was a true celebration of swine, as we learned about breeds, production, health, and nutrition. From rooter to tooter, all was explained. The year of the hog was so informative, I now feel like the guy at Disney World under the sign that says, "ASK ME." I can talk about pigs all day!

During our travels we were asked to each create an original recipe to teach to the attendees at our media luncheons. To be fair, we drew straws to see who would create a recipe for each portion of the meal. Of course, I drew salads. To this day, I think it was a "Give the BBQ man lettuce" conspiracy! In the end, I was happy with my assignment because I ended up with this, a new favorite recipe.

MAKES 4 MAIN-DISH OR 6 SIDE SALADS

COOKING METHOD:
Direct and indirect heat

SUGGESTED WOOD:
Hickory, oak, cherry (see page 22)

COOKING TIME:
45 minutes

1 Build a charcoal fire for indirect cooking by situating the coals on only one side of the grill, leaving the other side empty. Preheat the grill to 275°F.

2 For the dressing: In a medium bowl, whisk together the vegetable oil, vinegars, hot sauce, granulated sugar, salt, and pepper. Set aside.

RECIPE CONTINUES

DRY RUB

1 tablespoon **dark brown sugar**

2 teaspoons **salt**

1½ teaspoons **paprika**

¼ teaspoon ground **cumin**

¼ teaspoon **garlic powder**

¼ teaspoon freshly ground **black pepper**

Pinch of ground **cinnamon**

Pinch of ground **ginger**

1 pound **pork tenderloin**

5 slices **bacon**

½ **red onion**, cut into ½-inch-thick slices (1½ cups)

5 ounces **spinach leaves** (about 6 cups)

2 **clementines**, peeled and separated, or canned Mandarin **orange**s

3 For the liquid seasoning: In a small bowl, combine 2 table-spoons water, the soy sauce, olive oil, lemon juice, brown sugar, garlic powder, and pepper. Set aside.

4 For the dry rub: In a small bowl, combine the brown sugar, salt, paprika, cumin, garlic powder, pepper, cinnamon, and ginger. Season the pork tenderloin liberally with the dry rub.

5 In a 10-inch cast iron skillet, on the stovetop, cook the bacon over medium-high heat until it is crisp and browned, about 5 minutes. Transfer the bacon to a paper towel–lined plate. Add the seasoned pork tenderloin to the skillet and sear for about 30 seconds on each side. Remove the skillet from the heat and pour the liquid seasoning over the pork.

6 Put the skillet over indirect heat on the outdoor grill, close the lid, and cook, turning once, until the internal temperature of the pork reaches 145°F in the center of its thickest portion, about 30 minutes. Transfer the pork to a cutting board and let it rest.

7 Put the skillet, with the cooking juices, on the stovetop over medium-high heat. Add the red onion and cook, stirring, until softened but still slightly crisp, about 4 minutes. Transfer the onions to a bowl.

8 Rinse the skillet under running water to cool it and wipe it dry. Fill the skillet to the top rim with spinach leaves. Top the spinach with the onions, clementines, and bacon. Slice the tenderloin into medallions and arrange them on top of the salad. Drizzle the top with the dressing and serve in the cast iron skillet family-style.

THE PERFECT BURGER

Believe it or not, the best burgers have less to do with toppings and more to do with the ground beef. There are endless ways to dress up a burger patty, but without the best meat you will never achieve burger greatness. One thing to look for at the grocery store is fat content. I look for about a 75/25 or 70/30 lean meat to fat ratio. Fat gives you flavor and moisture, so you need the perfect blend of greasy goodness with lean beef in your patty. There are several options for ground beef at the grocery store: ground beef, ground chuck, ground round, ground sirloin, and others. For the average burger patty, these grinds will work fine as long as you pay close attention to the ratio of fat to meat.

The Perfect Burger, though, requires extra attention for composing the patty. I chose three distinctly different cuts of meat to grind together in order to get the most moist and flavorful patty. Please don't get upset with me when you start deboning the oxtail. I said the Perfect Burger, not Simplest Burger. You can replicate this at home with a meat grinder or ask your friendly butcher to do you a big favor.

SERVES 6	SUGGESTED WOOD:	COOKING TIME:
COOKING METHOD: Direct heat	Hickory, oak, mesquite (see page 22)	8 minutes

1 For the burger mixture: Grind the beef brisket, short rib, and oxtail meats together (see burger grinding tips, page 82). Form 6 patties about ⅓ pound each and 1¼ inch thick. Refrigerate until needed.

2 Build a charcoal fire for direct grilling and preheat it to 400°F.

3 For the burger baste: In a small bowl, combine the soy sauce, garlic powder, onion powder, ginger, paprika, and sugar. Set aside.

RECIPE CONTINUES

BURGER MIXTURE

1 pound **beef brisket point**

½ pound boneless **beef short rib meat**

½ pound boneless **oxtail meat** (meat from 2 oxtails)

BURGER BASTE

¾ cup **La Choy soy sauce** (see Pitmaster's Tip, page 82)

1 teaspoon **garlic powder**

1 teaspoon **onion powder**

1 teaspoon ground **ginger**

1 teaspoon **paprika**

1 teaspoon **sugar**

BACON

2 tablespoons **sugar**

1½ teaspoons **chili powder**

⅛ teaspoon ground **cumin**

⅛ teaspoon **cayenne pepper**

⅛ teaspoon **salt**

9 slices thick-cut **bacon**

Steer Gear Rub (page 243)

6 slices sharp **cheddar cheese**

Butter, for the buns

6 quality **hamburger buns**, split

Condiments: **ketchup, mustard, mayonnaise, tomato slices, dill pickle slices, lettuce, onion slices**

4 For the bacon: In a small bowl, combine the sugar, chili powder, cumin, cayenne, and salt. Season the bacon liberally with the rub.

5 Season the burger patties with the Steer Gear Rub.

6 Put the bacon over direct heat and cook until the bacon is charred and browned, about 1 minute on each side. Put the burgers over direct heat and cook, basting every couple of minutes, until the juices run clear, about 3½ minutes on each side. In the last minute of cooking, put a slice of cheese on each burger.

7 Lightly butter the cut sides of the burger buns and put them over direct heat with the grill lid open. Cook until lightly browned and toasted, about 30 seconds.

8 Serve the burgers on the toasted buns with your favorite condiments.

BURGER GRINDING TIPS

1. Trim all the connective tissue from the meat. A meat grinder will not make gristle and tough tissue disappear.

2. Cut the meat into cubes or strips no larger than 1 to 2 inches thick.

3. Both the meat and the grinder should be cold when grinding. The warmer the meat gets, the softer it becomes, and the harder it is to chop. Grinding meat in a walk-in cooler is the absolute best option. Otherwise, after cutting the meat into cubes or strips, return it to the refrigerator until ready to grind. And put the meat grinder in the freezer for about 1 hour before starting.

4. When grinding, use a relatively high speed to accelerate the process. This will ensure your grinder and the meat remain cold.

5. Start with a coarse grinding plate. If you want a smaller grind, change to a medium-size plate, and run the ground meat through a second time. Stay away from small or fine grinding plates.

GRILLED BRICK PANINI

WITH SMOKED GOUDA, SWEET BACON & CARAMELIZED ONIONS

CARAMELIZED ONIONS

2 tablespoons **unsalted butter**

2 teaspoons **soy sauce**

½ large **onion**, thinly sliced (1¼ cups)

Salt and freshly ground **black pepper**

BACON

2 tablespoons sugar

1½ teaspoons **chili powder**

⅛ teaspoon ground **cumin**

⅛ teaspoon **cayenne pepper**

⅛ teaspoon **salt**

8 slices thick-cut **bacon**

Butter, for the bread

8 (1¼-thick) slices **Italian bread**

8 ounces smoked **Gouda cheese**, sliced

3 **bricks**, wrapped in foil

You can very easily transform your grill into a makeshift panini press by using a foil-wrapped brick. The hot brick seals in moisture, compresses the sandwich, and accentuates grill marks while cooking from both sides. In this recipe, I actually use the grill in two ways: first, grilling the bacon, which is seasoned with a sweet rub; and second, grilling the sandwich itself. After tasting this recipe you will add a brick to your list of must-have grill tools.

SERVES 4	SUGGESTED WOOD:	COOKING TIME:
COOKING METHOD:	No extra smoke advised	6 minutes
Direct heat		

1   Build a charcoal fire for direct grilling and preheat it to 450°F.

2   For the caramelized onions: In a skillet, melt the butter over direct heat. Add the soy sauce and onions; season with salt and pepper to taste. Cook, stirring, until the onions have caramelized, about 5 minutes.

3   At the same time, for the bacon: In a small bowl, combine the sugar, chili powder, cumin, cayenne, and salt. Season the bacon liberally on both sides with the sweet rub. Put the bacon over direct heat and cook until charred and browned, about 1 minute on each side.

4   Remove the onions and bacon from the grill and set aside.

5   Put the foil-wrapped bricks on the grill grate and lower the lid on the grill.

6   Lightly butter one side of each of the bread slices. Divide the sliced cheese among 4 slices of the bread, placing the slices on the unbuttered side. Top each with 2 slices of bacon. Divide the caramelized onions among the 4 sandwiches and top with the 4 remaining slices of bread, buttered side out.

7 Put the sandwiches over direct heat and top each with a foil-wrapped brick. Cook for 30 seconds, flip the sandwiches, and replace the bricks. Cook for 30 seconds more, remove the sandwiches from the grill, and serve hot.

ITALIAN SMOKED PORK SANDWICH

PORK

⅓ cup chopped fresh **parsley**

4 **garlic cloves**

Leaves from 1 sprig **rosemary**

2 tablespoons **kosher salt**

½ teaspoon cracked **black pepper**

¼ teaspoon **fennel seeds**

2 teaspoons **extra-virgin olive oil**

1 (4-pound) **boneless pork shoulder** (pork butt)

2 cups **chicken stock**

GREENS

2 teaspoons **salt**

1 pound **turnip greens**

¼ cup **extra-virgin olive oil**

¼ medium **onion**, chopped (½ cup)

2 **garlic cloves**, chopped

½ teaspoon **red pepper flakes**

Salt and freshly ground **black pepper**

10 **Italian rolls** or **crusty hoagie rolls**, split and toasted

20 slices **provolone cheese**

The Italian roast pork sandwich is a South Philadelphia tradition. Restaurants like Tony Luke's made it famous. My fondness for this sandwich was not born in Philadelphia, since I haven't had the opportunity to eat there, but rather in New York City at a restaurant called Shorty's. I realize I'm going to catch grief for including a sandwich from the City of Brotherly Love in my cookbook when I've never actually eaten it there, especially when my inspiration came from the Big Apple. I'm coming clean here, because it's just such a good sandwich! In my version, the pork is removed from the oven roasting pan and transferred to an outdoor cooker, where smoke comes into play. Additionally, seasoned turnip greens are substituted for broccoli rabe, the vegetable of choice on the traditional sandwich. When word of this recipe gets out, lines will form at bookstores everywhere, except maybe in South Philly.

MAKES 10 SANDWICHES	SUGGESTED WOOD:	COOKING TIME:
COOKING METHOD: Direct and Indirect heat	Hickory, oak, pecan (see page 22)	12 hours

1 Build a charcoal fire for indirect cooking by situating the coals on only one side of the grill, leaving the other side empty. Preheat the grill to 225°F.

2 For the pork: In a food processor, combine the parsley, garlic, rosemary, salt, pepper, fennel seeds, and olive oil. Process until a coarse paste is formed. Spread the paste all over the pork. Roll the pork into a log and secure it with butcher's twine. Set a wire rack in a 9 × 13-inch baking pan, and put the pork on the rack.

Pour ¾ cup water into the bottom of the pan. Fold a piece of heavy-duty foil to make a 18-inch square. Tent the foil over the pork log, leaving 1 inch of headspace between the foil and the pork, securing the foil to the sides of the pan. With a sharp knife, cut a 1 × 4-inch rectangular hole in the foil directly over the pork. Make sure the foil remains tented.

3 Put the pan over indirect heat and cook until the internal temperature of the pork reaches 180°F, about 12 hours.

4 Transfer the pork to a cutting board and let it rest for 15 minutes before slicing.

5 Return the pan to direct heat and add the chicken stock. Cook, stirring and scraping up any browned bits from the bottom of the pan. Slice the pork and put it into the stock. Keep warm.

6 For the greens: Fill a 1-gallon stockpot with 3 quarts water and the salt. Put the pot over high heat on the stovetop and bring the water to a rolling boil. Cook the turnip greens until the leaves are limp, about 3 minutes. Reserving ⅔ cup of the cooking liquid, drain the greens.

7 In a large skillet, heat the olive oil over medium-high heat. Add the onion and garlic and cook, stirring, until the onions become translucent, about 3 minutes. Reduce the heat to medium-low and add the reserved cooking liquid, cooked turnip greens, and red pepper flakes. Simmer until the greens soften, about 5 minutes. Season the greens with salt and pepper to taste and keep warm.

8 To serve, put 2 slices of provolone on each of the toasted rolls. Fill the rolls liberally with pork and top with turnip greens.

SMOKED PORK SHOULDER TACOS

PORK

4 teaspoons **salt**

1 tablespoon **granulated sugar**

1½ teaspoons **dark brown sugar**

1¼ teaspoons **paprika**

1 teaspoon **ancho chile powder**

½ teaspoon **garlic powder**

¼ teaspoon ground **cumin**

¼ teaspoon freshly ground **black pepper**

1 (6- to 8-pound) bone-in **pork shoulder** (pork butt)

ASSEMBLY

20 (8-inch) **flour tortillas**

Black Bean Barbecue Sauce (page 233)

Coal-Fired Pico de Gallo (page 56)

Serrano Pepper Coleslaw (page 194)

I'm always in for a party where everyone puts together their own pizza, burger, or tortilla. Guests can use their creativity and follow their tastes to make their perfect dish. This interactive approach to a dinner party adds a certain comfort and relaxation that all get-togethers with family and friends should have.

Usually less is more when it comes to good food, but this tortilla is an exception. Each part of it is packed with flavor, and so, together, they push the limits.

SERVES 8 TO 10

COOKING METHOD:
Direct heat and indirect heat

SUGGESTED WOOD:
Hickory, oak (see page 22)

COOKING TIME:
9 to 11 hours

1　Build a two-zone fire in a charcoal grill by situating the coals on only one side of the grill, leaving the other side empty. Preheat the grill to 235°F.

2　For the pork: In a small bowl, combine the salt, sugars, paprika, ancho chile powder, garlic powder, cumin, and pepper. Coat the pork evenly with the rub, patting it gently until the mixture adheres to the meat.

3　Put the pork butt over indirect heat, away from the coals, close the lid, and cook until the internal temperature of the pork reaches 195°F, 9 to 11 hours. Transfer the meat to a cutting board and let it rest for 15 minutes.

4　Put the tortillas over direct heat. Grill until grill marks form, 20 to 30 seconds on each side.

5　Debone and chop the pork. Put ⅓ cup of meat onto each flour tortilla and top with a generous helping of the barbecue sauce, pico de gallo, and coleslaw.

BEER-BASTED PULLED PORK SLIDERS

DRY RUB

1 tablespoon **dark brown sugar**

2 tablespoons **granulated sugar**

1 tablespoon **paprika**

4 teaspoons **kosher salt**

3½ teaspoons **garlic salt**

¾ teaspoon **chili powder**

¼ teaspoon dried **oregano**

¼ teaspoon **cayenne pepper**

¼ teaspoon ground **cumin**

¼ teaspoon freshly ground **black pepper**

As stated in the first chapter, there are many different cooking styles, and how a person likes to cook determines what type of cooker is best for them. This recipe is for all those who just can't keep the cooker lid closed. When opening and closing the cooker, valuable heat and moisture leak from the cooking chamber. Someway, somehow, you have to add it back or risk serving dry meat. But this old-school sop mop baste ensures great results by returning moisture to the cooker, along with added flavor and fat (butter) to protect the bark, the flavorful outside shell of the meat, from drying out.

SERVES 12	SUGGESTED WOOD:	COOKING TIME:
COOKING METHOD:	Hickory,	9 hours
Indirect heat	oak, pecan	
	(see page 22)	

1   Build a charcoal fire for indirect cooking by situating the coals on only one side of the grill, leaving the other side empty. Add a small disposable aluminum pan to the empty side of the grill and fill it halfway with water. Preheat the grill to 160°F.

2   For the dry rub: In a small bowl, combine the sugars, paprika, salt, garlic salt, chili powder, oregano, cayenne, cumin, and black pepper.

3   Coat the pork evenly with dry rub, patting gently until the mixture adheres to the meat.

4 Put the pork on the grill over the water pan, close the lid, and cook over indirect heat until the internal temperature of the pork reaches 160°F, about 5 hours.

5 Meanwhile, for the baste: In a medium saucepan, combine the beer, vinegars, butter, Worcestershire sauce, soy sauce, lemon juice, chili powder, salt, sugar, black pepper, dry mustard, paprika, and cumin. Put the pan over medium-low heat on the stovetop and heat until the butter melts. Keep warm.

6 Continue cooking the pork, basting every hour, until the internal temperature of the pork reaches 195°F, about 4 hours longer.

7 Transfer the pork to a cutting board and let it rest for about 15 minutes. Pull the cooked meat from the bone and serve it mounded high on slider buns topped with your favorite barbecue sauce.

1 (7-pound) **pork butt** (pork shoulder)

BASTE

1 (12-ounce) bottle **dark beer**

1¼ cups **cider vinegar**

1¼ cups **distilled white vinegar**

2 sticks (½ pound) **unsalted butter**

½ cup **Worcestershire sauce**

¼ cup **soy sauce**

1½ tablespoons fresh **lemon juice**

3 tablespoons **chili powder**

2 tablespoons **salt**

1 tablespoon **sugar**

2 teaspoons freshly ground **black pepper**

2 teaspoons **dry mustard**

2 teaspoons **paprika**

1 teaspoon ground **cumin**

24 slider **buns**

Favorite bottled **barbecue sauce**

GRILLED PIZZA

THIS CHAPTER COVERS ALL YOU NEED TO KNOW TO CREATE THE TASTIEST GRILLED PIZZAS.

One of the best outdoor parties I've ever attended had the guests creating their own signature pizzas to be cooked on the grill. There was lots of dough, several sauces to choose from, and a multitude of toppings that guests could use to craft the pies to their taste. Everyone had a blast.

This chapter covers all you need to know to create the tastiest grilled pizzas. The grill setup isn't complicated, and I share my recipe for the foundation of perfect pizza: the crust. Many pizza dough recipes don't transfer well from oven cooking to the grill, so I've worked on my recipe to get the crispiest results possible. Then, I share my favorite recipes, which include delicious homemade sauces. I would argue that if the same sauce is used, it's the same pizza, regardless of whether pepperoni or sausage graces its top. To truly get a different pizza, try out new and distinct sauces. Toppings are the next step and are unlimited in types and combinations. The recipes that follow suggest my favorite combinations, but I encourage you to get your creative pizza juices flowing and improvise. The last thing that you should consider in developing the perfect pizza pie is the garnish. Although many overlook these finishing touches, which are placed on a pizza before serving, they can be the difference between subpar and sensational wedges.

GRILLED PIZZA DOUGH

4½ cups unbleached **all-purpose flour**, plus more for rolling

2 teaspoons **kosher salt**

1½ teaspoons **active dry yeast**

1¾ cups very **cold water**

3 tablespoons **olive oil**, plus more for greasing the baking sheets

1 tablespoon **maple syrup**

Cooking spray

Cornmeal, for the pizza peel

It's amazing that minute changes in the ratios of flour, water, and yeast can make a dramatic difference in the texture of a pizza crust. Perfecting the ratio comes down to personal preference, so this recipe is totally about pleasing me! I like a thin to medium crust that is crispy, similar to a New York–style crust. If you prefer a thicker pizza crust, add an extra ½ teaspoon of active dry yeast to this recipe.

Another thing that's important is how you handle the dough after you make it. This can be the difference between a dense, chewy crust and a light, crispy slice of heaven. It's a two-day investment to make this recipe, but if you follow these instructions closely, I guarantee that your pizza crust will be pleasing to me—or your money back!

MAKES 4 (8-INCH) CRUSTS OR 3 (12-INCH) CRUSTS	SUGGESTED WOOD: Maple, alder, fruitwoods (see page 22)	RISING TIME: 2 days
COOKING METHOD: Direct heat on a pizza stone		COOKING TIME: 8 to 12 minutes

1 In a large bowl, combine the flour, salt, and yeast. If you are mixing by hand, stir in the water, olive oil, and maple syrup with a large cold metal spoon. Stir vigorously until a smooth, sticky dough ball forms, about 5 minutes. If using a stand mixer fitted with a dough hook, add the water, oil, and maple syrup and mix until the dough pulls away from the sides of the bowl, about 5 minutes. Turn the dough out onto a floured work surface. Cut the dough into 3 or 4 equal pieces (3 for 12-inch crusts; 4 for 8-inch crusts).

2 Put a piece of parchment paper on a large baking sheet and lightly grease it with oil. Separate the dough balls on the parchment paper and mist them with cooking spray. Cover with plastic wrap and refrigerate overnight.

RECIPE CONTINUES

3 Take the baking sheet out of the refrigerator. Lightly flour your hands and punch the dough balls down, letting the trapped air escape. Flip each piece of dough over and then fold the edges of the dough to the center of the dough circle. Shape it back into a ball and put each ball back on the parchment paper, seam sides down. Lightly mist the dough with cooking spray, cover with plastic wrap, and refrigerate overnight.

4 On day three, the dough is ready to make pizza; it will keep in the refrigerator for 2 more days. Two hours before making pizza, remove the dough from the refrigerator.

5 Build a charcoal fire for direct grilling. Put a pizza stone on the cooking grate directly over the charcoal. Preheat the grill to 500° to 600°F.

6 Generously sprinkle cornmeal on a pizza peel or the back of a baking sheet. Put a piece of dough onto a floured work surface and, using a floured rolling pin, roll it out until it is 8 to 12 inches in diameter. Transfer the dough to the peel or baking sheet, making sure there is plenty of cornmeal for it to slide freely. Spread your desired pizza sauce (about ½ cup for a 12-inch pizza or ⅓ cup for an 8-inch pizza) over the dough and top with assorted toppings and cheese.

7 Slide the pizza off of the peel onto the preheated stone. Close the grill lid and cook for 8 to 10 minutes for 8-inch pizzas or up to 12 minutes for 12-inch pizzas. Monitor the crust frequently and remove the pizzas when the crust starts to brown and crisp. Garnish as desired, cut, and serve.

BARBECUE PINEAPPLE & CHICKEN PIZZA

One thing about writing a cookbook is that it is necessary to try a recipe over and over again until it is perfect. This was exactly the case with pizza crusts. It's amazing that the few base ingredients of flour, water, and yeast can be altered slightly with drastically different results. Somewhere in my experimentation between too dense and too chewy, my son Andrew requested I make him this pizza. It turned out to be a great afternoon perfecting the crunch and eating pizza. Sometimes the experience of sharing food can be just as great as enjoying the taste, if not better. How could I not include this one?

Sauce: Barbecue Pizza Sauce (page 103)

Toppings: Grilled chicken and grilled pineapple

Cheese: Shredded mozzarella and Parmesan cheese

Garnish: Chopped fresh basil and red pepper flakes

GRILLED CHICKEN & CONECUH SAUSAGE PIZZA

WITH ALABAMA WHITE BARBECUE PIZZA SAUCE

The fun thing about making your own signature pizza is that you can tailor it to regional flavors. I like the idea of using local products from home in recipes so that when I travel I can truly give others a taste of Alabama. Nothing says Alabama like white barbecue sauce and Conecuh sausage. White barbecue sauce has been a staple on chicken at Big Bob Gibson Bar-B-Q since 1925. Conecuh is a company in Evergreen, Alabama, that has been smoking sausage since 1947. The tangy, peppery sauce and deep smokiness of the sausage is a killer combination.

Sauce: Alabama White Barbecue Pizza Sauce (recipe follows)

Toppings: Grilled or BBQ chicken (leftover Curry Chicken Satays, page 61, or Barbecue Chicken Thighs, page 156), grilled Conecuh sausage, and grilled red bell peppers (recipe follows)

Cheese: Shredded mozzarella

Garnish: Chopped fresh basil

ALABAMA WHITE BARBECUE PIZZA SAUCE

1 tablespoon **unsalted butter**

3 tablespoons chopped **onion**

¾ teaspoon minced **garlic**

¼ cup **distilled white vinegar**

2 tablespoons **sugar**

3 tablespoons finely grated **Parmesan cheese**

¾ cup **mayonnaise**

½ teaspoon fresh **lemon juice**

¾ teaspoon chopped fresh **basil**

¾ teaspoon chopped fresh **oregano**

¾ teaspoon chopped fresh flat-leaf **parsley**

¾ teaspoon coarsely ground **black pepper**

½ teaspoon **salt**

⅛ teaspoon **cayenne pepper**

MAKES: 1¼ cups (enough to cover 2 large pizzas or 3 medium pizzas)
COOKING METHOD: Stovetop
COOKING TIME: 2 minutes

In a small saucepan, melt the butter over medium heat. Add the onion and cook, stirring, until it starts to soften, about 2 minutes. Remove the pan from the heat and stir in the vinegar and sugar until the sugar dissolves. Pour the mixture into a small bowl. Add the Parmesan and mix well. Stir in the mayonnaise, lemon juice, basil, oregano, parsley, black pepper, salt, and cayenne. The sauce can be used immediately or stored in an airtight container in the refrigerator for up to 5 days.

GRILLED RED BELL PEPPERS

2 **red bell peppers**

2 tablespoons **extra-virgin olive oil**

2 teaspoons **salt**

2 teaspoons freshly ground **black pepper**

1 Build a charcoal fire for direct grilling and preheat it to 450°F.

2 Halve the peppers lengthwise and remove the stem, core, and seeds. Lightly coat the peppers with olive oil and season with salt and pepper. Grill over direct heat until grill marks are visible, about 2 minutes on each side. Remove the peppers from the grill and set aside to let cool. Thinly slice the peppers and use immediately or refrigerate in an airtight container for up to 5 days.

INDONESIAN SWEET & SOUR SHRIMP PIZZA

Whenever chefs get together it usually turns into a verbal jam session on who cooked what, for whom, and how they cooked it. But the more interesting conversations are when ideas are discussed. Recently, I was enjoying the company of a couple of chefs, Ken Hess and Stephen Gustard, and I threw out the idea of making pizzas with ingredients from far-flung places. Indonesia came up, and everyone began talking passionately about things like Thai basil and coconut milk. In 15 short minutes, this recipe was completed on paper—and boy is it exceptional!

Sambal oelek is the most common type of sambal, found in the international aisle of grocery stores. In its simplest form, it is a spicy Southeast Asian sauce made from ground chile and salt. This condiment oftentimes includes vinegar, sugar, garlic, fish sauce, shallots, and lime juice. "Oelek" refers to the mortar and pestle used to grind the chiles into paste.

Sauce: Indonesian Sweet & Sour Pizza Sauce (recipe follows)

Toppings: Yuzu Shrimp (page 71) and Grilled Red Bell Peppers (page 99)

Cheese: Shredded mozzarella and provolone

Garnish: Pickled Red Onions (recipe follows) and chopped fresh Thai basil or regular basil

INDONESIAN SWEET & SOUR PIZZA SAUCE

1 tablespoon **extra-virgin olive oil**

½ **garlic clove**, minced

½ teaspoon minced fresh **ginger**

½ **shallot**, minced

4½ tablespoons **tomato paste**

5 tablespoons **rice vinegar**

5 tablespoons **sugar**

¼ cup **sambal oelek**

¼ cup **coconut milk**

2 tablespoons **fish sauce**

1 sprig fresh **Thai basil** or regular **basil**

⅛ teaspoon dried **marjoram**

⅛ teaspoon dried **oregano**

⅛ teaspoon freshly ground **black pepper**

MAKES: 1¼ cups
(enough to cover 2 large pizzas
or 3 medium pizzas)
COOKING METHOD: Stovetop
COOKING TIME: 6 minutes

In a medium saucepan, heat the olive oil over medium heat. Add the garlic, ginger, and shallot and cook, stirring, until the shallot starts to soften, about 2 minutes. Add the tomato paste, rice vinegar, sugar, sambal oelek, coconut milk, fish sauce, basil, marjoram, oregano, and pepper. Bring the mixture to a simmer and cook until the sauce thickens slightly, about 5 minutes. Use immediately or refrigerate in an airtight container for up to 5 days.

PICKLED RED ONIONS

½ cup **rice vinegar**

½ cup **sugar**

1 teaspoon **salt**

1 **red onion**, very thinly sliced

In a small saucepan, combine the vinegar, sugar, and salt. Bring the mixture to a boil over medium-high heat and add the red onion. Bring the mixture back to a boil, remove the pan from the heat, and let sit for 3 minutes. Drain the onions, discarding the liquid, and use immediately or refrigerate in an airtight container for up to 2 weeks.

GRILLED STEAK & TOMATO PIZZA

Simple is usually best when it comes to making pizza. The famous American "kitchen sink" pizza takes away from the stars of traditional pies, which are the crust and a flavorful sauce highlighted by just a few fresh toppings. Just like one of my go-to choices, the simple margherita pizza, this grilled steak and tomato pizza, comprising only a few simple ingredients, is a standout.

Sauce: Barbecue Pizza Sauce (recipe follows)

Toppings: Grilled beef filet thinly sliced, sliced tomatoes

Cheese: Shredded mozzarella

Garnish: Crumbled feta cheese and chopped fresh oregano

BARBECUE PIZZA SAUCE

1 (6-ounce) can **tomato paste**

3 tablespoons **Big Bob Gibson Championship Red Sauce** or your favorite store-bought BBQ sauce

¼ cup grated **Parmesan cheese**

1 teaspoon minced **garlic**

¾ teaspoon **onion powder**

¼ teaspoon dried **basil**

¼ teaspoon dried **oregano**

¼ teaspoon dried **marjoram**

¼ teaspoon **salt**

¼ teaspoon freshly ground **black pepper**

⅛ teaspoon **red pepper flakes**

⅛ teaspoon **cayenne pepper**

MAKES: 1 cup
(enough to cover 2 large pizzas or 3 medium pizzas)
COOKING METHOD: Stovetop
COOKING TIME: 5 minutes

In a medium saucepan, combine ¼ cup water, the tomato paste, barbecue sauce, Parmesan, garlic, onion powder, basil, oregano, marjoram, salt, black pepper, red pepper flakes, and cayenne. Bring to a simmer over medium heat and cook until the mixture starts to thicken, about 8 minutes. Use immediately or refrigerate in an airtight container for up to 5 days.

BELLIES & BACON

TRY SPENDING A WEEK WITH A SLAB OF IN-HOUSE CURED BACON & TELL ME THERE IS NO PIG LOVE!

Of everything in this book, it's the bellies and bacon section that excites me the most. The main reason for that is because we are dealing with big meats. My specialty has always been taking the largest cuts of meat and, through the process of low and slow cooking with real wood smoke, turning them into tender and tasty delights. Second, this section dives into great techniques utilizing brines and cures. There is a certain attachment—call it love—that you develop while spending the necessary time seasoning, cooking, and basting large barbecued meats. Try spending a week with a slab of in-house cured bacon and tell me there is no pig love! Finally, with a large cut of meat and a long cook time, there is much more room for being creative with seasoning. There are so many opportunities to layer flavors for unique and delicious results.

With some pork bellies weighing in at more than 16 pounds, they can be a little intimidating to work with, not to mention the refrigerator space needed to pull off a seven-day cure. Typically, I like to cure whole slabs of bacon or cook a belly in its entirety in order to optimize my time. I do have large walk-in coolers at my restaurant, and they make it a little easier. Once the meat is cooked, I'll go ahead and slice the bacon and portion the belly to use immediately or to store in the refrigerator until needed. If this is not an option for you, purchase fresh pork bellies in 4-pound slabs. This will lessen the intimidation factor and ensure the smaller cut can fit nicely in your refrigerator.

SMOKED
PORK BELLY

WITH SHOCK TOP HONEY MUSTARD GLAZE

DRY RUB

¼ cup **sugar**

1 tablespoon **chili powder**

1 tablespoon **kosher salt**

¼ teaspoon ground **cumin**

¼ teaspoon **cayenne pepper**

1 (4-pound) skin-on **fresh pork belly**

Shock Top Honey Mustard Glaze (page 237)

I'll start with the simplest pork belly. In fact, the glaze for this recipe will take more time to prepare than the belly itself. The flavoring for this pork comes from the dry rub application, the wood smoke, and, finally, the intense glaze. This three-step process is straightforward, but the real key to success is shifting from indirect to direct heat, and then back to indirect. A two-zone fire for both direct and indirect cooking is imperative for pork belly perfection.

SERVES 8		
COOKING METHOD: Direct and indirect heat	**SUGGESTED WOOD:** Hickory, oak, apricot (see page 22)	**COOKING TIME:** 5 hours 10 minutes

1 Build a two-zone fire in a charcoal grill by situating the coals on only one side of the grill, leaving the other side empty. Preheat the grill to 225°F.

2 For the dry rub: In a small bowl, combine the sugar, chili powder, salt, cumin, and cayenne.

3 Apply the dry rub liberally to all sides of the pork belly, except for the skin. Put the seasoned belly, skin side down, over indirect heat, away from the coals, and close the grill lid. Cook until the internal temperature of the pork belly reaches 205°F, about 5 hours. Transfer the belly to a cutting board and let it sit for 10 minutes. Slice off the pork skin and cut the belly into 2½-inch squares.

4 Add more coals to the grill and increase the temperature to 450° to 500°F. Put a cast iron skillet over direct heat and let it get very hot.

5 Put the pork belly squares into the hot skillet, fat side down (where the skin was removed). Sear until browned and crispy, about 1 minute. Remove the skillet from the grill and the pork belly from the skillet.

6 Coat the pork belly squares generously with the glaze. Put the belly on the grill, seared side up, over indirect heat, close the lid, and cook until the glaze caramelizes, about 10 minutes. Transfer the bellies to a cutting board and let them rest for 10 minutes.

7 Serve the bellies whole or slice them into ½-inch-thick pieces to make delicious sandwiches

SMOKED PORK BELLY CONFIT

One unctuous bite of pork belly can alter consciousness into a realm filled with lewd desires or into a valley of peaceful clarity. How you are affected is a personal matter, but you will be moved, and your life will be changed forever. As the late great Jerry Garcia once said, "What a long strange trip it's been." Close your eyes and enjoy.

Confit is a French word used to describe the process of slowly cooking and preserving meat in its own fat. One advantage to this type of cooking is the impossibility of drying out the meat. You are guaranteed the most moist and juicy bites possible. Another plus is that you can keep the meat refrigerated for up to 6 months, which might come in handy, especially for those who can't eat a whole 16-pound pork belly in one sitting. Just think of what would result if you mixed the low and slow cooking art of American barbecue with the methods of confit cooking. Imagine no further.

1 (4-pound) skin-on **fresh pork belly**

Peach Tea Brine (page 242)

DRY RUB

¼ cup **sugar**

1 tablespoon **chili powder**

½ teaspoon **kosher salt**

¼ teaspoon ground **cumin**

¼ teaspoon **cayenne pepper**

2 pounds lard

Shock Top Honey Mustard Glaze (page 237) or your favorite store-bought barbecue sauce

---

SERVES 8

COOKING METHOD:
Direct and indirect heat

SUGGESTED WOOD:
Hickory, oak, maple (see page 22)

BRINING TIME:
10 hours

COOKING TIME:
5 hours 10 minutes

CHILLING TIME:
5 hours 30 minutes

---

1 Put the pork belly in a medium nonreactive pan. Pour the brine over the pork until it is submerged. Cover the pan and refrigerate for 10 hours.

2 Build a charcoal fire for indirect cooking by situating the coals on only one side of the grill, leaving the other side empty. Preheat the grill to 225°F.

3 For the dry rub: In a small bowl, combine the sugar, chili powder, salt, cumin, and cayenne. Remove the pork belly from the brine and apply the dry rub liberally to all sides of the pork belly except for the skin. Put the seasoned belly, skin side down, over indirect heat, away from the coals, and close the grill lid.

RECIPE CONTINUES

Cook until the internal temperature of the pork belly reaches 155°F, about 1 hour 30 minutes. Transfer the belly to a medium ovenproof pan with the skin up. Select a pan that is as close to the size of the pork belly as possible.

4 In a small saucepan, melt the lard over medium heat on the stovetop. Pour the lard over the pork, completely submerging it. Put the pan back onto the grill over indirect heat and continue to cook until the internal temperature of the pork belly reaches 205° to 210°F, about 3 hours 30 minutes. Set the pan of pork aside to cool for 30 minutes.

5 Cover the cooled pan entirely with plastic wrap. Put an empty pan on top of the plastic wrap, and then put something heavy like bricks into the empty pan to compress the pork belly fat and make it more uniform. Refrigerate until the lard totally solidifies, at least 5 hours.

6 Build a two-zone fire in a charcoal grill by situating the coals on only one side of the grill, leaving the other side empty. Preheat the grill to 450°F. Put a cast iron skillet over direct heat until it gets very hot.

7 Remove the pan from the refrigerator and cut the belly from the cold fat. Put the belly on a cutting board, scrape off the remaining lard, and slice off the pork skin. Cut the belly into 2½-inch squares. Put the pork into the hot skillet, fat side down (where the skin was removed). Sear until the fat is browned and crispy, about 1½ minutes. Shift the cast iron skillet to indirect heat, away from the coals, close the grill lid, and cook until the internal temperature of the belly reaches 140°F, 8 to 10 minutes. Remove the skillet from the grill and the pork belly from the skillet.

8 Brush each square with the glaze. Put the pork, seared side up, over indirect heat, close the grill lid, and cook until the glaze caramelizes, about 5 minutes. Remove from the grill and serve the bellies whole or slice them into ½-inch-thick pieces to make delicious sandwiches.

HICKORY-SMOKED MAPLE & BLACK PEPPER BACON

When making bacon, you can get carried away with all of the seasoning options you have to choose from. To date, this is my favorite homemade bacon recipe, but I would certainly encourage you to do a little experimenting of your own.

There are several ways to morph this recipe into your own signature version. First, try replacing the granulated sugar in the cure with brown sugar. Remove the black pepper or maple syrup altogether from the recipe. Substituting dark molasses for the cane syrup is an option. Using applewood instead of hickory will yield a less intense smoke flavor. Whatever direction you choose, you will enjoy the process of making your own in-house cured bacon.

BACON CURE

3 tablespoons **kosher salt**

1 tablespoon **sugar**

¾ teaspoon **tinted cure mix** (pink salt)

1 (4-pound) fresh **pork belly**, skin removed

¼ cup coarsely ground or cracked **black pepper**

⅓ cup **maple syrup**

SERVES 8	SUGGESTED WOOD: Hickory (see page 22)	COOKING TIME: 2 hours 15 minutes
COOKING METHOD: Indirect heat	CURING TIME: 7 days	CHILLING TIME: 5 hours

1 For the bacon cure: In a medium bowl, combine the salt, sugar, and cure mix.

2 Cover the entire pork belly evenly with the cure, patting it with your hand so the cure will adhere. Evenly cover the belly with the pepper and use the heel of your hand to press it firmly into the belly.

RECIPE CONTINUES

3 Put the pork in a medium ovenproof pan. Select a pan that is as close to the size of the pork belly as possible. Coat both sides of the pork evenly with the maple syrup, letting the pan catch the excess. Cover the pan with plastic wrap and refrigerate for 7 days to let the belly cure. Every 2 days, remove the pan from the refrigerator, recoat both sides of the belly with the syrup in the bottom of the pan, flip the belly, and return it to the refrigerator.

4 After 7 days, remove the pork from the refrigerator. Gently rinse the cure from the pork, being careful not to wash off all of the black pepper. Put the cured pork into a clean pan and refrigerate it, uncovered, for 5 hours to let it air-dry.

5 Build a charcoal fire for indirect cooking by situating the coals on only one side of the grill, leaving the other side empty. Preheat the grill to 200°F.

6 Put the cured belly over indirect heat, away from the coals, close the grill lid, and cook until the internal temperature of the pork reaches 155°F, 2 hours to 2 hours 15 minutes. Remove the bacon slab from the grill and let rest for 10 minutes. Wrap it in plastic wrap and refrigerate it for 5 hours.

7 Remove the slab bacon from the refrigerator and slice it into bacon strips of desired thickness.

STEAKS

FAT IS FLAVOR.

The secret to cooking a great steak is knowing what to get in the grocery store. I can give you the best steak recipes in the world, but if you select the wrong steaks, you'll make both of us look bad. It is less important to read labels and more important to read the beef. Oftentimes, the wording on the labels misleads you into thinking you are getting a better grade of meat, so make sure that you look at the steak itself before tossing it into your shopping cart.

When selecting a steak, look for an even, bright red color. Bright is not shiny! Stay away from wet-looking beef, especially if there is noticeable liquid pooling in the Styrofoam tray. If the steaks are vacuum-packed, you should be less concerned about liquid pooling in the protective plastic.

Fat is flavor. When I say fat, I'm not talking about the globs of fat around the outside of the meat. That stuff should be trimmed down to ⅛ inch. The good fat is an even distribution of intramuscular white striations, or marbling. This fat is the most important criterion for grading beef. In the grocery store, you will most likely see USDA Select and Choice grades, with Prime being held for high-end restaurants and meat purveyors. Because the meat quality varies even within each USDA grade, it is beneficial if you can do your own beef grading so you can pick out the absolute best available.

Don't be afraid to make conversation with the butcher. He can be your best friend when it comes to selecting beef—and a good friend will trim the extra fat from the exterior of the steak before weighing it! Be sure to ask how long the meat has aged in the shrink-wrap since harvest. In my opinion 20 to 30 days is best. If handled correctly, and you trust your butcher, I wouldn't hesitate to go a week longer. Dry-aged beef is achieved uncovered in a refrigerator that has carefully controlled temperature, humidity, and air current. The result is a very tender piece of meat with a more pronounced earthy-mushroomy flavor. Ask your friendly butcher if dry-aged beef is an option.

COWBOY RIBEYE

WITH COFFEE CHOP DRY RUB

4 (16-ounce) bone-in **ribeye steaks**
Coffee Chop Dry Rub (page 243)

Pitmaster Tip: When it comes to extra-thick steaks, oftentimes the outside of the meat gets perfectly charred while the inside remains underdone. Cooking any longer over an open flame will burn the exterior. This is why it's important to build a two-zone fire when cooking steaks. When they are perfect on the outside, shift them away from the coals and shut the grill lid. This little maneuver will protect the exterior while allowing the inside of the meat to cook to perfection.

We all know the old saying "You never get a second chance to make a first impression." It's true that, right or wrong, we often judge people in the first few minutes of greeting them. We do the same thing at home around the grill. Your backyard grillmaster prowess is sized up by guests before the first charred morsel goes into their mouth. The sights, sounds, and smells of your grill make an instant first impression, and there's no better sensory explosion than an ultra-thick cowboy-style ribeye with a coffee-laced dry rub.

A cowboy ribeye is created by cutting between the bones of a ribeye roast. It differs from a standard ribeye because the bone is left on the steak and not trimmed off. An average bone-in ribeye is 1¼ inches thick and weighs 16 ounces. Though sometimes served to appease the heartiest appetite, it's more often considered steak for two. Still not impressed? Ask your butcher for a "double-cut" bone-in ribeye. This steak is double the meat on one bone and hits the grill at 2½ inches thick while weighing a whopping 2 pounds!

SERVES 4 TO 8		SUGGESTED WOOD:		
COOKING METHOD:		Hickory, oak, mesquite (see page 22)		COOKING TIME:
Direct and indirect heat				7 to 10 minutes

1   Build a two-zone fire in a charcoal grill by situating the coals on only one side of the grill, leaving the other side empty. Preheat the grill to 500°F.

2   Season the steaks liberally with the rub. Put the steaks over direct heat and grill for 4½ minutes on each side for rare doneness. For medium-rare, move the beef over indirect heat, away from the coals, close the grill lid, and cook for 2 more minutes. For medium, flip the steak, close the grill lid, and cook for 2 more minutes.

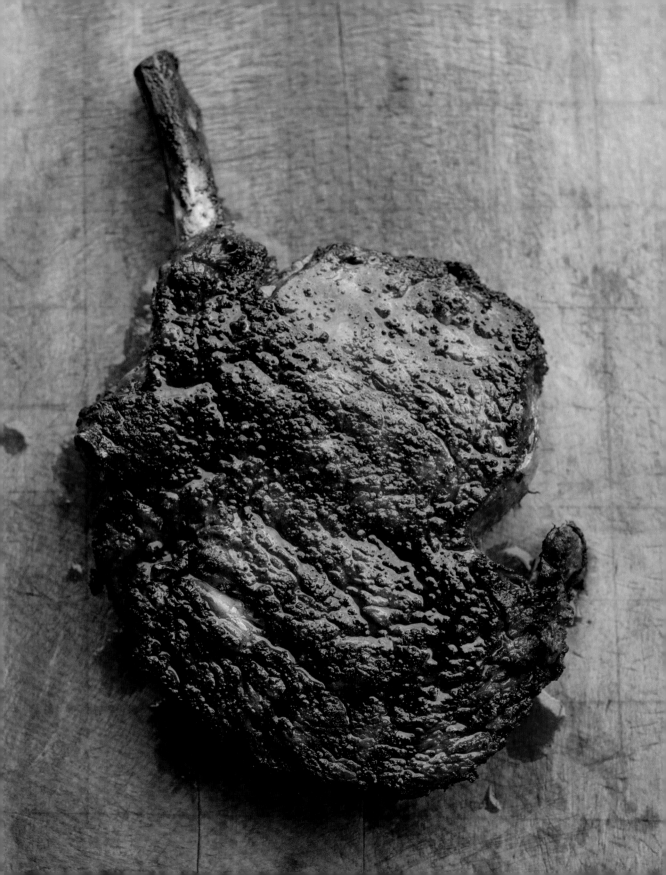

PAN-SEARED NEW YORK STRIP
WITH BOURBON CREAM SAUCE

Some of my favorite wine country memories are of time spent at the house of Pete and Kathy Seghesio outside of Healdsburg, California. Most often their parties start with a wine and charcuterie tasting in their tower overlook, and as the night progresses, the gathering ultimately finds its way to the kitchen, where they have an indoor wood-fired oven.

Don't make the mistake of thinking that wood-fired ovens are only good for pizza. Fact is, anything you can cook in a standard, less flavorful oven can be cooked in a wood-fired one. This is about the only indoor substitute for the outdoor grill. It was at the Seghesios' that I had my first steak cooked in a wood-fired oven. I found a way to re-create that amazing flavor on my grill back home, and trust me, it's worth a try.

SERVES 4	SUGGESTED WOOD:	
	Hickory, oak, mesquite (see page 22)	
COOKING METHOD:		COOKING TIME:
Direct heat		8 to 9 minutes

1 Build a charcoal fire for direct grilling. Put a cast iron skillet on the cooking grate, close the grill lid, and preheat it to 500°F.

2 Coat the steaks with the olive oil. Season them generously with salt and pepper.

3 Put the steaks in the skillet, close the grill lid, and cook for 4 minutes on each side for medium rare, or 4½ minutes on each side for medium. Remove the skillet from the grill and set it on a heatproof surface. Transfer the steaks to a cutting board and let them rest for 10 minutes.

4 Pour the bourbon into the hot skillet. Stir in the cream, soy sauce, and garlic.

5 Serve the steak whole or cut each into ¼-inch slices. Drizzle generously with the bourbon cream sauce.

4 (1-inch-thick) **New York strip steaks**

¼ cup **extra-virgin olive oil**

Kosher salt and coarsely ground **black pepper**

¾ cup **bourbon**

¾ cup **heavy cream**

1 teaspoon **soy sauce**

1½ teaspoons minced **garlic**

Pitmaster Tip: Seasoning steak is a little like mixing a bourbon drink. You don't dilute 30-year-old top-shelf bourbon with a bunch of mixers. You drink it straight or, at the most, with a touch of water or an ice cube. Treat nice steaks the same way, using only coarse salt and some freshly cracked black pepper. An average grocery store steak needs a little more help and a few more ingredients to maximize its flavor. Remember, the better the steak, the fewer the seasonings.

PEPPERED FILET MIGNON

WITH ROASTED GARLIC HERB BUTTER

STEAKS

4 teaspoons **extra-virgin olive oil**

4 teaspoons **soy sauce**

½ teaspoon **cider vinegar**

3 tablespoons coarsely ground **black pepper**

4 teaspoons **kosher salt**

4 teaspoons **dark brown sugar**

6 (1½-inch-thick) **filet mignon steaks**

I get excited when *Food & Wine* magazine calls wanting a recipe. To be included in this prestigious magazine is an honor that many great chefs never achieve. So when you get the call, you better make sure the recipe is flawless. The requirements they gave me: an easy steak recipe with intense flavor. I guess my favorite steak is a bone-in ribeye, but there's something about an aged beef filet sizzling in a bath of roasted garlic and black pepper that's just sexy and delicious. It took an entire week and a whole beef tenderloin to fine-tune this recipe into something worthy of gracing the pages of *Food & Wine*, but all you'll need is a few thick steaks and a couple of hours to deliver an awesome meal to your guests.

SERVES 6	SUGGESTED WOOD: Hickory, oak, mesquite (see page 22)	CHILLING TIME: 30 minutes
COOKING METHOD: Direct and indirect heat	MARINATING TIME: 1 to 2 hours	COOKING TIME: 55 minutes

1 For the steaks: In a small bowl, stir together the oil, soy sauce, vinegar, pepper, salt, and brown sugar to form a paste. Apply 1 tablespoon of the paste to each steak and coat evenly on all sides. Wrap each steak tightly in plastic wrap and let the steaks marinate for 1 to 2 hours in the refrigerator.

2 Build a two-zone fire in a charcoal grill by situating the coals on only one side of the grill, leaving the other side empty. Preheat the grill to 250°F.

RECIPE CONTINUES

ROASTED GARLIC HERB BUTTER

4 **garlic cloves**, unpeeled

¼ teaspoon chopped fresh **thyme**

¼ teaspoon chopped fresh **rosemary**

¼ teaspoon chopped fresh **oregano**

1 tablespoon **extra-virgin olive oil**

4 tablespoons (½ stick) **salted butter**, at room temperature

3 For the garlic herb butter: Pull out a length of foil and double it to form a square. Put the garlic cloves, thyme, rosemary, and oregano on the foil. Drizzle the oil over the ingredients and close the foil in a tight packet. Put the packet over indirect heat and cook until fragrant, 45 minutes.

4 Remove the pouch from the grill, open the foil, and let cool slightly. Squeeze the garlic cloves from their skins into a small bowl and add the herbs to the bowl. Mash the garlic and cooked herbs together into a paste. Stir in the butter and mix well. Spoon the mixture onto a sheet of plastic wrap and roll it into a small log. Refrigerate until firm, about 30 minutes. The butter will keep in the refrigerator for 2 weeks.

5 Remove the steaks from the refrigerator. Increase the grill temperature to 500°F. Unwrap the steaks, put them over direct heat, and grill for 3½ minutes on each side for rare doneness. For medium-rare, move the beef over indirect heat, away from the coals, close the grill lid, and cook for 2 more minutes. For medium, flip the steak, close the grill lid, and cook for 2 more minutes.

6 Remove the steaks from the grill. Cut the herb butter into 6 pats and put a pat on each steak. Let the steak rest for 5 to 10 minutes before serving.

GRILLED CAP OF RIBEYE

Picture a thick, juicy ribeye steak cooked to perfection and lying in a pool of juices waiting to be cut. Where do you start? The circular eye, almost filet like, is beckoning the knife in its direction. But no, that's not what my heart and stomach desire. It is the tender and juicy tail of steak wrapped around the eye of ribeye that will undoubtedly be the most luscious tasting meat on the plate. If there is a tiny morsel of steak left on this plate, it will not be that tail, that delicious "cap." In my opinion, the cap of ribeye is absolutely the best-tasting meat on the ribeye.

If you go to the grocery store and ask for a cap of ribeye (also called spinalis), you will have to repeat yourself several times before they tell you no. The only way to get it is to carve it out of a whole ribeye roast yourself (see pictures, pages 125–127). The good news is that now everyone can enjoy this beef delicacy and not have to worry about spinalis thieves.

¾ cup **La Choy soy sauce** (see Pitmaster Tip, page 82)

1 teaspoon **garlic powder**

1 teaspoon **onion powder**

1 teaspoon ground **ginger**

1 teaspoon **paprika**

1 teaspoon **sugar**

4 (8-ounce) **spinalis steaks**

3 tablespoons **Steer Gear Rub** (page 243)

SERVES 4	SUGGESTED WOOD:	MARINATING TIME:
COOKING METHOD: Direct heat	Hickory, oak, mesquite (see page 22)	10 minutes COOKING TIME: 7 to 10 minutes

1 Build a two-zone fire in a charcoal grill by situating the coals on only one side of the grill, leaving the other side empty. Preheat the grill to 500°F.

2 In a small bowl, combine the soy sauce, garlic powder, onion powder, ginger, paprika, and sugar. Put the steaks in a single layer in a medium nonreactive pan. Pour the marinade over the steaks and let them stand for 10 minutes.

3 Remove the steaks from the marinade and season them liberally with the rub. Put the steaks on the grill over direct heat and cook for 3½ minutes on each side for rare doneness, 4 minutes on each side for medium-rare, or 4½ minutes on each side for medium. Remove the steaks from the grill and let them rest for 5 minutes before serving.

EYE OF

RIBEYE

If you remove the spinalis from the whole ribeye, the majority of steaks left will be eye of ribeye. These steaks can be cut thick or thin and cooked a variety of different ways. I always cook a ¾- to 1-inch steak for about 4 minutes on each side for medium rare, or 4½ minutes on each side for medium at 500°F directly over a hot bed of coals. Although these steaks look like a filet, they have more fat and can carry a deeper steak flavor. Don't expect filet-type tenderness, but the eye of ribeye is extremely versatile. Because of its richness, this cut matches well with all traditional steak preparations. Here are some tasty ideas.

BLACK PEPPER MAPLE BACON—WRAPPED EYE OF RIBEYE

1 Season with Steer Gear Rub (page 243).

2 Wrap in Hickory-Smoked Maple & Black Pepper Bacon (page 111) before cooking.

EYE OF RIBEYE WITH CHIMICHURRI SAUCE

1 Season with salt and freshly ground black pepper.

2 Top with Chimichurri Sauce (page 240).

EYE OF RIBEYE WITH BARBECUE HOLLANDAISE SAUCE

1 Season with Steer Gear Rub (page 243).

2 Top with Barbecue Hollandaise Sauce (page 232).

EYE OF RIBEYE WITH ROASTED GARLIC HERB BUTTER

1 Season with salt and freshly ground black pepper.

2 Top with Roasted Garlic Herb Butter (from Peppered Filet Mignon, page 120).

BLUE CHEESE EYE OF RIBEYE

1 Season with salt and freshly ground black pepper.

2 Top with blue cheese and olive oil.

BUTCHERING A WHOLE RIBEYE

No matter what type of steak you are purchasing, cutting whole muscles at home is more economical, and it gives you more control over cut types and thickness. Search your local grocery store for a ribeye steak and you will find one choice and one thickness. By purchasing a whole ribeye instead of those precut, you have more control and variety.

Remove the steak from the wrap and put it on a cutting board. Cut out a couple of thick bone-in steaks (for Cowboy Ribeye, page 116) by slicing between the large bones. Remove the spinalis from the remaining roast by cutting along the fat line between the cap and the circular eye of ribeye. Cut the spinalis (for Grilled Cap of Ribeye, page 123) and the eye of ribeye into individual steaks.

By acting as your own butcher, you can produce traditional ribeyes, bone-in cowboy cuts, eye of ribeyes, spinalis steaks, and even ribeye skewers in whatever thickness you desire. These aged steaks can be used immediately or frozen until needed.

BONE-IN
RIBEYE
STEAK

EYE OF
RIBEYE
STEAKS

AP OF
RIBEYE
TEAKS

BEEF
RIBS

MAINS

THIS IS WHERE THE PROTEIN HITS THE GRILL

If you don't have stains on your apron, you're doing something wrong. In this chapter we explore how to do things right, from turkey to trout, pork ribs to beef ribs, and chops to chicken. This is where the protein hits the grill with some of my favorite direct-fire recipes, such as Charcoal-Seared Trout Fillet and Chipotle Grilled Tri-Tip. There's also Apple Cider Ribs and Seasoned Mustard Drumsticks that stay away from direct flame and are cooked over indirect heat. Then, I mix things up with Peach Tea Smoked Rack of Pork and Charcoal-Grilled Turkey—recipes that take a turn over both direct and indirect sides of the grill.

Flavor is my main focus in this chapter, and I optimize it both with seasonings and sauces, as well as with cooking temperatures and exposure to charcoal and wood. Marinades and dry rubs are very important when cooking outdoors, too, but they matter little if you're cooking at an incorrect temperature or on the wrong spot on the cooking grate. The recipes in this chapter will help you explore different cooking methods and learn them well so that you can master your grill.

BARBECUE
BEEF BRISKET
FLAT

DRY RUB

½ tablespoon **sugar**

½ tablespoon **paprika**

½ tablespoon **salt**

½ tablespoon freshly ground **black pepper**

¾ teaspoon **garlic powder**

½ teaspoon **onion powder**

¼ teaspoon dried **oregano**

⅛ teaspoon ground **coriander**

1 (5- to 6-pound) **beef brisket flat**

1 tablespoon **beef base**

1 cup low-sodium **beef stock**

Pitmaster Tip: The only reason I ever wrap a beef brisket during the cooking process is to capture the beef drippings as they seep from the slab of meat. This delicious liquid is great to drizzle back over the sliced meat or to freeze and save for sauces, gumbo, or brisket hash. If you have reserved drippings saved from another brisket, try cooking this brisket recipe without wrapping for a more intense smoked flavor and a deeper beef taste. Use the reserved drippings to baste the meat after slicing.

Many times a whole beef brisket is just too big for the average family, since a 12-pound brisket will yield about 5 pounds of usable meat. Next time a craving for beef brisket hits, try downsizing to a beef brisket flat, which is much leaner than the fatty point of the whole cut and has a better yield. You can expect that about 60 percent of the flat will become usable meat. Though you will likely have some leftovers, you won't be eating beef for the rest of the week.

The flat has a very intense beef flavor, and you end up with an intense beef jus to match. The important thing to remember about any brisket is to slice it across the grain. And make sure to drizzle the drippings back over the slices before serving.

SERVES 10 TO 12	SUGGESTED WOOD:	COOKING TIME:
COOKING METHOD: Indirect heat	Hickory, oak (see page 22)	5 to 6 hours

1 Build a charcoal fire for indirect cooking by situating the coals on only one side of the grill, leaving the other side empty. Preheat the grill to 225°F.

2 For the dry rub: In a small bowl, combine the sugar, paprika, salt, pepper, garlic powder, onion powder, oregano, and coriander.

3 Rub the entire brisket with the beef base. Coat the brisket evenly with the dry rub.

4 Put the brisket over indirect heat, away from the coals, close the lid, and cook until the internal temperature of the brisket reaches 160° to 170°F, about 4 hours.

5 Transfer the brisket to a shallow baking pan or disposable aluminum pan. Pour the stock over the brisket and cover the pan with foil. Put the baking pan over indirect heat and cook until the internal temperature of the brisket reaches 185°F, 1 to 2 hours.

6 Remove the baking pan from the grill and let the meat rest for 20 to 30 minutes. Slice the brisket across the grain and serve.

BARBECUE
BEEF SHORT RIBS ADOBO

Adobo is considered to be the national dish of the Philippines, typically made with pork or chicken. The meat is braised until tender in a mixture of ingredients such as vinegar, soy sauce, garlic, and herbs.

This beef short rib recipe borrows the greatest elements of traditional adobo and mixes them with the techniques of true Southern barbecue. The secret to this delicious sauce is putting the beef base on the rib before cooking. Beef base is a paste made from concentrated beef stock. You can find it in the grocery store with the soups and broths.

12 **beef short ribs**, cut into individual ribs or cut across the bones (3 pounds)

2½ tablespoons **beef base**

1½ cups **coconut milk**

1½ cups low-sodium **beef stock**

¾ cup **rice vinegar**

¾ cup **soy sauce**

12 **garlic cloves**

1½ teaspoons freshly ground **black pepper**

SERVES 6			
COOKING METHOD: Indirect heat	SUGGESTED WOOD: Hickory, oak (see page 22)	COOKING TIME: 3 hours 15 minutes	

1 Build a charcoal fire for indirect cooking by situating the coals on only one side of the grill, leaving the other side empty. Preheat the grill to 250°F.

2 Rub the ribs with the beef base. Put them bone side down over indirect heat, away from the coals, close the lid, and cook until the internal temperature reaches 155° to 160°F, about 1 hour.

3 Meanwhile, in a small saucepan, combine the coconut milk, stock, vinegar, soy sauce, garlic, and pepper. Heat on the stovetop over low heat, but do not boil.

4 Transfer the ribs to an 8 × 10-inch baking pan, meat side down. Pour the coconut milk mixture over the ribs. Cover tightly with foil and place the pan over indirect heat, away from the coals. Close the grill lid and cook until the meat is fork-tender and the internal temperature reaches 210°F, about 2 hours.

5 Set the beef ribs aside to rest. Pour the liquid from the baking pan into a small saucepan; discard the garlic. Set the saucepan over medium heat on the stovetop, bring the liquid to a boil, and cook until it reduces by half, about 15 minutes.

6 Pour the sauce over the ribs and serve.

Pitmaster Tip: Even if a cutting board is washed well and stored properly, it can transfer sour, off flavors to your foods. Why would you spend hours barbecuing only to compromise the end result? A great way to prevent this is to prep your cutting board by wiping it down with juices rendered from your barbecue meats. If no pooled juices are available, I like to mix 2 parts water and 1 part white soy sauce to season my cutting board before slicing meats and grilled vegetables.

SMOKED MONTREAL BEEF TENDERLOIN

WITH BIG HOSS' MUSHROOM COGNAC CREAM SAUCE

1 tablespoon **black peppercorns**

1 tablespoon **coriander seeds**

½ tablespoon **fennel seeds**

1 teaspoon **cumin seeds**

1½ teaspoons dried **rosemary**

1½ teaspoons dried **thyme**

2 tablespoons **kosher salt**

1 tablespoon granulated **garlic**

½ tablespoon **red pepper flakes**

2 teaspoons **paprika**

1 (12-pound) **beef tenderloin**

Big Hoss' Cognac Mushroom Cream Sauce (page 238)

The flavorful blend of spices called Montreal Steak Seasoning is hugely popular today on steaks and chops that are cooked over direct flames. Though made popular in Canada, the blend was originally created in Eastern Europe for use as a pickling spice for smoked meats. Although the makeup of this blend changes from brand to brand, most all of them include black peppercorns, garlic, coriander, red pepper flakes, and salt.

When making dry rubs and seasoning blends, it's best to start with fresh spices. I mean, if the collection in your cabinets has been sitting there for more than ten years, how old are the ground spice bottles in your favorite grocery store? The only way to ensure freshness is to grind them yourself. When I spring for a whole beef tenderloin, you better believe I'm breaking out the mortar and pestle.

SERVES 20		
COOKING METHOD: Direct and indirect heat	SUGGESTED WOOD: Hickory, oak (see page 22)	COOKING TIME: 44 minutes

1 Build a two-zone fire in a charcoal grill by situating the coals on only one side of the grill, leaving the other side empty. Preheat the grill to 550°F.

2 Put the black peppercorns, coriander seeds, fennel seeds, cumin seeds, rosemary leaves, and thyme in a spice grinder and pulse until coarsely ground; or use a mortar and pestle. There should not be any whole seeds or peppercorns left. Pour the mixture into a small bowl. Add the kosher salt, granulated garlic, red pepper flakes, and paprika and stir well.

3 With a sharp knife, remove the fat and silver skin from the outside of the beef tenderloin. Take the tail, or thinner end, of

the tenderloin and fold it back under itself to ensure an even thickness to the roast. Secure the tail with a piece of butcher's twine. Generously coat the tenderloin with the seasoning.

4   Put the tenderloin over direct heat and grill until browned, about 2 minutes on each side. Transfer the tenderloin to indirect heat, away from the coals, close the lid, and cook until the internal temperature reaches 130°F for medium-rare or 135°F for medium, 35 to 40 minutes. Transfer the tenderloin to a cutting board and let rest for 10 minutes before slicing.

5   Serve topped with the Cognac cream sauce.

Pitmaster Tip: Have you ever thought you should toast whole spices and seeds before grinding them to make a dry rub? Well, the amazing aromatics may smell delightful, but don't be tempted to do it! I've found that toasting beforehand releases the flavors too early, leaving the barbecue with a dulled spice profile. Let the fire toast the spices and seeds while on the meat to capture the entire flavor the seasoning has to offer.

CHIPOTLE GRILLED TRI-TIP

When cooking a beef tri-tip, think of it as a very thick sirloin steak and treat it as such. This is the perfect example of why a two-zone fire is important. You should start the tri-tip out directly over the hot flame. When the beef is charred to perfection, it's still raw inside. You then transfer it to the indirect side of the grill and cover with the lid, which ensures the meat can finish cooking without turning the shell into a crispy meteorite.

Since all sirloin, tri-tip included, has less fat content than a ribeye and is much more toothy than a filet, I would recommend using a high-impact seasoning as I did in this recipe. That's right, not all beef has rich, buttery fat to hold flavor and keep the cut fork-tender. Using chipotle (which are smoked jalapeños) as a base for a marinade provides just enough punch to turn even the lowly tri-tip into a star.

1 (7.5-ounce) can **chipotle peppers in adobo**

Grated zest and juice of 2 **limes**

⅓ cup **extra-virgin olive oil**

5 **garlic cloves**, minced

¼ cup chopped fresh **cilantro**

2 tablespoons **kosher salt**

1 tablespoon coarsely ground **black pepper**

1 teaspoon ground **cumin**

2 teaspoons **paprika**

2 teaspoons **chili powder**

1 (2½-pound) **beef tri-tip**

SERVES 6 TO 8

COOKING METHOD:
Direct and indirect heat

SUGGESTED WOOD:
Hickory, oak
(see page 22)

MARINATING TIME:
8 hours

COOKING TIME:
40 minutes

1 Finely chop the chipotles and put them and the adobe sauce in a gallon-size resealable plastic bag. Add the lime zest and juice, oil, garlic, cilantro, salt, pepper, cumin, paprika, and chili powder. Add the tri-tip, toss to coat, seal the bag, and marinate in the refrigerator for 8 hours.

2 Build a two-zone fire in a charcoal grill by situating the coals on only one side of the grill, leaving the other side empty. Preheat the grill to 500°F.

3 Put the tri-tip over direct heat and grill until it is browned and charred, 4 to 5 minutes per side. Transfer it to indirect heat, away from the coals, close the lid, and cook until the internal temperature reaches 130°F for medium-rare or 135°F for medium, 25 to 30 minutes. Transfer the tri-tip to a cutting board and let rest for 10 minutes.

4 Slice the meat across the grain and serve.

SOUTHERN MAN'S
BEEF RIBS

DRY RUB

1½ tablespoons **kosher salt**

2½ teaspoons **paprika**

2 teaspoons freshly ground **black pepper**

2 teaspoons **garlic powder**

1½ teaspoons **Worcestershire powder**

1½ teaspoons **Accent** (optional; see Pitmaster Tip)

1 teaspoon **cayenne pepper**

¾ teaspoon ground **coriander**

¾ teaspoon **celery salt**

½ teaspoon **onion powder**

¼ teaspoon **turmeric**

¼ teaspoon ground **nutmeg**

6 pounds **beef back ribs**

1½ cups **cola**, at room temperature and flat

The popularity of barbecue competitions has exploded. These cook-offs are regularly featured on television and used by local organizations as fund-raisers and a way to promote tourism. With this increased attention, corporate America has joined in with support and monetary backing, which has added more fuel to the competitive fire. Now there are countless organizations and sanctioning bodies that put on these events and offer barbecue judge certification classes. Because of the increased number of contests, barbecuers have a multitude of choices of where to compete on any given weekend. Competitive barbecue season, which was once popular only during the summer months, now lasts all year long.

Gradually, competition barbecue has morphed into something that is far different from what I grew up with. It has turned into a face-off to see who can pack the most complex flavors into their meat by using multiple dry rubs, sauces, liquid seasoning wraps, and bastes. The judges may eat only one or two bites of your entry, so you have to grab their attention immediately.

With that said, there is a current movement to take barbecue back to what it used to be while still enjoying the competition and camaraderie around the grill. These back-to-basic competitions can restrict the use of pans, foil, digital thermometers, and certain flavor enhancers. (For example, Accent, a brand name for monosodium glutamate [MSG], is restricted in some contests; see Pitmaster Tip, opposite.) The winning recipes are usually the ones where the meat is the star and simplicity is rewarded. This is a recipe I used successfully at just such an event, the Meatopia contest at the Eat Real Festival in Oakland, California. We won Best Beef Ribs and overall Grand Champion with this simple yet tasty dish. Meats, smoke, dry rub, and cola: very simple and very Southern.

SERVES 6

COOKING METHOD:
Indirect heat

SUGGESTED WOOD:
Hickory, oak
(see page 22)

COOKING TIME:
4 to 5 hours

1 Build a charcoal fire for indirect cooking by situating the coals on only one side of the grill, leaving the other side empty. Preheat the grill to 250°F.

2 For the dry rub: In a small bowl, combine the salt, paprika, black pepper, garlic powder, Worcestershire powder, Accent (if using), cayenne, coriander, celery salt, onion powder, turmeric, and nutmeg.

3 Season the beef ribs generously with the rub. Pour the cola into an empty spray bottle.

4 Put the beef ribs bone side down over indirect heat, away from the coals, close the lid, and cook for 2 hours. Open the grill and mist the beef ribs with the cola. Close the lid and continue cooking, misting the ribs with cola every 45 minutes, until the ribs are tender or the internal temperature reaches 205°F, 2 to 3 more hours. Because of varying thicknesses of beef ribs, it is impossible to determine an exact cook time. Transfer the ribs to a cutting board and let them rest for 5 to 10 minutes.

5 Cut the ribs into smaller pieces and serve.

Pitmaster Tip: I included an optional ingredient in this recipe called Accent, which is a common brand name of monosodium glutamate (MSG) found in the spice section of the grocery store. MSG is a crystalline powder resembling salt that has no flavor of its own but is used to intensify the flavor of savory foods. It's found naturally in foods such as seaweed, some vegetables, and sugar beets. MSG has been used for over a century to season foods and is generally recognized as safe by the FDA, but some people are sensitive to it.

SMOKED LAMB RIBS

WITH ROSEMARY & FIG BARBECUE SAUCE

SEASONING PASTE

¾ teaspoon dried **thyme**

¾ teaspoon dried **rosemary**

¾ teaspoon dried **oregano**

2 tablespoons **extra-virgin olive oil**

1½ teaspoons **soy sauce**

3½ teaspoons **salt**

3 teaspoons **paprika**

2 teaspoons freshly ground **black pepper**

2 teaspoons **garlic powder**

¾ teaspoon ground **ginger**

3 (2½-pound) slabs lamb ribs

Rosemary & Fig Barbecue Sauce (page 228)

As an active competitor in various cooking competitions, I had a tough time figuring out just how much I was willing to disclose in my cookbook. If I were to release the exact recipe with which I've won awards, I'd be opening the door for me to compete against my own food the next time around. But I got over that pretty quickly, since I firmly believe that as soon as you become complacent with competition recipes, you will not win. My goal for each competition is to come up with something unique anyway.

And, so, here is the exact lamb rib recipe I used to win Best Lamb Ribs and overall Grand Championship at the Meatopia Bare Bones BBQ Contest at the Eat Real Festival in Oakland, California, in 2012. The seasoning paste and sauce do nothing to mask the great flavor of lamb; they only help to enhance and celebrate this bold meat. I'm giving you gold with this one!

SERVES 4 TO 6	SUGGESTED WOOD:	COOKING TIME:
COOKING METHOD: Indirect heat	Hickory, oak, cherry (see page 22)	3 hours 40 minutes

1 Build a charcoal fire for indirect cooking by situating the coals on only one side of the grill, leaving the other side empty. Preheat the grill to 250°F.

2 For the seasoning paste: Lightly chop the thyme, rosemary, and oregano. Put the herbs into a small bowl and add the oil, soy sauce, salt, paprika, black pepper, garlic powder, and ginger. Mix well until a paste forms.

3 Apply the paste evenly to each lamb slab.

4 Put the lamb ribs over indirect heat, away from the coals, close the grill lid, and cook the ribs until they are dark brown and tender, about 3 hours 30 minutes. Remove the ribs from the grill and generously coat them with the barbecue sauce. Return the ribs to indirect heat, close the grill lid, and cook until the sauce caramelizes, about 10 minutes. Transfer the ribs to a cutting board and let them rest for 5 minutes.

5 Cut the ribs between the bones and serve.

MARINATED PORK CHOPS

Everyone loves a good pork chop. Part of the attraction to this well-known cut of meat lies in its versatility. It can be served as a breakfast food, matching nicely with grits or eggs, and then it's also at home on a sandwich or beside a pile of homemade mashed potatoes. You can even dress it up to be the star of a white-tablecloth dinner. This grilled pork chop recipe was originally developed to be served with Grilled Pickled Peaches (page 214). Try glazing the pork chops with the peach syrup during the last 3 minutes of cooking.

MARINADE

½ cup **soy sauce**

¼ cup **peanut oil**

¼ cup fresh **lemon juice**

1 **garlic clove**, minced

1 tablespoon **dark brown sugar**

2 teaspoons **chili powder**

½ teaspoon freshly ground **black pepper**

4 (6- to 8-ounce) bone-in **pork chops** or boneless loin chops (¾ inch thick)

SERVES 4	SUGGESTED WOOD:	MARINATING TIME:
COOKING METHOD: Direct heat	**Hickory, fruitwoods, maple** (see page 22)	**2 to 4 hours** COOKING TIME: **14 minutes**

1 For the marinade: In a small bowl, whisk together the soy sauce, oil, lemon juice, garlic, brown sugar, chili powder, and pepper.

2 Put the pork chops in a resealable plastic bag and pour in the marinade. Marinate the pork chops in the refrigerator for 2 to 4 hours.

3 Build a charcoal fire for direct grilling and preheat it to 450°F.

4 Grill the pork chops over direct heat until the internal temperature reaches 145° to 150°F, 6 to 7 minutes on each side. Remove the chops from the grill and let them rest for 5 minutes before serving.

APPLE CIDER RIBS

DRY RUB

¼ cup **dark brown sugar**

4 teaspoons **garlic salt**

4 teaspoons **chili powder**

2 teaspoons **salt**

1 teaspoon freshly ground **black pepper**

½ teaspoon **celery salt**

¼ teaspoon **cayenne pepper**

¼ teaspoon ground **cinnamon**

¼ teaspoon ground **white pepper**

2 (2½-pound) slabs **loin back ribs** (baby back)

Cooking pork ribs, in my opinion, is a three-step process. The first thing you do is apply the dry rub to the rib. This is the most important step and allows for an infinite amount of flavor possibilities. Next, after cooking the ribs for a little while, put the ribs in a foil packet with a liquid seasoning that helps tenderize the ribs and add still more flavor. Then, finally, finish them with a glaze, a sweet sauce that caramelizes on the rib—in this case, just a store-bought barbecue sauce. None of these steps is mandatory, and you can use them in any combination that suits your fancy.

SERVES 4 TO 6	SUGGESTED WOOD:	COOKING TIME:
COOKING METHOD: **Indirect heat**	**Hickory, apple, peach** (see page 22)	**3 hours 30 minutes**

1 Build a charcoal fire for indirect cooking by situating the coals on only one side of the grill, leaving the other side empty. Put a small disposable aluminum pan in the empty side of the grill and fill it halfway with water. Preheat the grill to 250°F.

2 For the dry rub: In a small bowl, combine the brown sugar, garlic salt, chili powder, salt, black pepper, celery salt, cayenne, cinnamon, and white pepper. Measure out 1 tablespoon of the rub and set it aside for the liquid seasoning mixture.

3 Remove the membrane from the back of the ribs. Generously apply the dry rub onto the front and back of the ribs. Gently pat to ensure that the rub adheres.

4 Put the ribs meat side up over indirect heat, away from the coals, and cook until the meat is well browned, about 2 hours 15 minutes. Transfer each rack of ribs to a large piece of doubled foil. The foil should be large enough to completely wrap the rack.

5 For the liquid seasoning: In a small bowl, combine the cider, apple jelly, honey, brown sugar, and reserved 1 tablespoon dry rub. Divide the liquid between the two rib racks and tightly wrap and seal each rack in the foil. Put the wrapped ribs over indirect heat and cook until they are tender, about 1 hour.

6 Remove the ribs from the grill, unwrap, and discard the foil. Brush the barbecue sauce on both sides of the ribs. Return the ribs to the grill and cook over indirect heat until the sauce caramelizes, about 15 minutes. Transfer the ribs to a cutting board and let rest for 10 minutes.

7 Slice the ribs between the bones and serve.

LIQUID SEASONING

½ cup **apple cider**

¼ cup **apple jelly**

¼ cup **honey**

¼ cup packed **dark brown sugar**

1 cup favorite store-bought **barbecue sauce**

Pitmaster Tip: Wrapping ribs in foil during the cooking process has advantages and disadvantages. On the positive side, the foil lets the meat stay in contact with the cooking liquid for a longer period of time, which helps tenderize the slab and prevents the ribs from drying out. Also, wrapping provides the opportunity to layer more flavors into the ribs through a tasty liquid seasoning. The disadvantage is that the wrapping prevents some of the smoke flavor from reaching the ribs and steam prevents a crusty bark from forming. Wrapping ribs in foil is a double-edged sword and only personal preference will determine if this method is best for you.

ST. LOUIS CUT
SPARE RIBS
WITH SWEET CHERRY & BLACKBERRY BARBECUE SAUCE

DRY RUB

2 tablespoons **dark brown sugar**

2 tablespoons **paprika**

1 tablespoon **garlic salt**

1½ teaspoons **onion salt**

1½ teaspoons **chili powder**

¾ teaspoon freshly ground **black pepper**

½ teaspoon **cayenne pepper**

¼ teaspoon dried **oregano**

¼ teaspoon ground **cumin**

2 (3-pound) slabs **St. Louis cut spare ribs**

LIQUID SEASONING

⅔ cup pitted **cherries**

⅔ cup **blackberries**

½ cup **apple juice**

¼ cup **honey**

¼ cup packed **dark brown sugar**

1 cup **Big Bob Gibson Championship Red Sauce** or your favorite store-bought barbecue sauce

This is the best example I can give you of how to totally change the flavor of a rib through a three-step cooking process. Compare this recipe to the Apple Cider Ribs. Though we have the same elements—dry rub, liquid seasoning, and finishing glaze—they're each altered to dramatically affect the flavor. Once you master the three-step technique, use your imagination to create your own signature recipe.

SERVES 4 TO 6	SUGGESTED WOOD:	COOKING TIME:
	Hickory,	3 hours
COOKING METHOD:	apple, cherry	45 minutes
Indirect heat	(see page 22)	

1 Build a charcoal fire for indirect cooking by situating the coals on only one side of the grill, leaving the other side empty. Preheat the grill to 250°F.

2 For the dry rub: In a small bowl, combine the brown sugar, paprika, garlic salt, onion salt, chili powder, black pepper, cayenne, oregano, and cumin. Measure out 2 tablespoons of the rub and set aside for the liquid seasoning.

3 Remove the membrane from the back of the ribs. Generously apply the dry rub onto the front and back of the ribs. Gently pat to ensure that the rub adheres.

4 Put the slabs meat side up over indirect heat, away from the coals, close the lid, and cook until the ribs are well browned, about 2 hours 30 minutes.

5 Meanwhile, for the liquid seasoning: In a blender or food processor, puree the cherries and blackberries. Add the apple juice and puree until smooth. Strain the mixture, discarding the seeds and pulp. Add the honey, brown sugar, and the reserved 2 tablespoons dry rub to the liquid. Reserve 1 cup of the liquid seasoning.

6 Transfer each slab to a large piece of doubled foil. The foil should be large enough to completely wrap each slab. Set aside half of the liquid seasoning. Divide the remaining liquid seasoning between the two slabs and tightly wrap and seal each slab in the foil. Put the wrapped slabs back over indirect heat, close the lid, and cook until the ribs are tender, about 1 hour.

7 In a small bowl, combine the barbecue sauce with the reserved liquid seasoning.

8 Remove the ribs from the grill, unwrap, and discard the liquid and foil. Brush the barbecue sauce mixture on both sides of the ribs. Return the ribs to indirect heat and cook until the sauce caramelizes, about 15 minutes. Transfer the ribs to a cutting board and let rest for 10 minutes.

9 Slice the ribs between the bones and serve.

THE PERFECT PIG

There is much fat to cut through before you get to the perfect pig. Every pork producer and independent hog farmer claims to have the best pork on the planet, so much so that the information is confusing to the consumer. *Free-range, organic, all-natural,* and *heritage* are some of the many terms used to convince you to buy a specific brand.

The two most important things to consider when choosing pork are color and marbling. The color is determined by the acid level in the meat and is an indicator of water retention and stress level during harvesting. Light pink pork has very little water retention and yields dry meat when cooked. Select pork that is reddish-pink instead of pinkish-red for optimum moisture and flavor. Blood-red meat is the result of improperly harvested or mishandled meat and turns mushy after cooking. Marbling is the amount of intramuscular fat in the meat. Choose pork where the fat marbling is evident for more flavor and moisture. It is a little known fact that pork, just like beef, is graded, and color and marbling make up the grading system.

The great thing about today's pork production is the choices we have. Better research, breeding, and improved production facilities have given us better-quality commodity pork with far less fat and yet higher moisture retention.

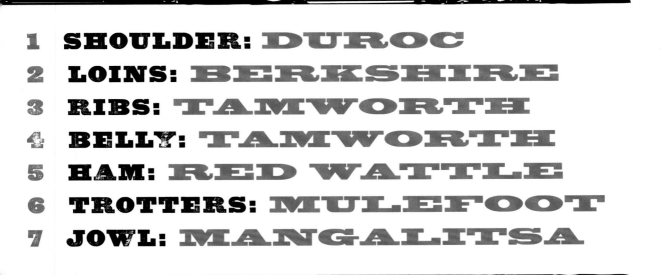

1 **SHOULDER: DUROC**
2 **LOINS: BERKSHIRE**
3 **RIBS: TAMWORTH**
4 **BELLY: TAMWORTH**
5 **HAM: RED WATTLE**
6 **TROTTERS: MULEFOOT**
7 **JOWL: MANGALITSA**

What excites me the most is that in recent years, small heritage pig farms have started up across the country. Heritage-breed pigs are from bloodlines going back hundreds of years to when pigs were raised on open-pasture farms all over the world. The difference in genes along with the lifestyle, feed, and pasture terrain led to a variety of different characteristics including deep pork flavor, creamy fat, and rich marbling. The reemergence of niche farms specializing in individual breeds gives us a selection of pork that we've never had before, not to mention how it saves the purebred bloodlines from disappearing forever.

When I say that I spend my time traveling, teaching, and preaching the art of barbecue, more often than not I have pork on my mind. I've had the pleasure of working with some of the foremost experts in the field along with the National Pork Board. More important, I've cooked, tasted, and shared rib bones with some of the best chefs in the country. Pork is always a topic of conversation, and the "Perfect Pig" is the most vehemently debated discussion. What is the Perfect Pig? Take a butcher's-cut diagram of a whole pig and choose which pig breed you would choose to eat for each cut. This sounds simple, but make sure the pig farmer you ask isn't holding a cleaver when you offer debate! Behold my "Perfect Pig."

PEACH TEA SMOKED RACK OF PORK

DRY RUB

3 tablespoons **turbinado sugar**

1 tablespoon **kosher salt**

1 tablespoon **paprika**

1 tablespoon **garlic powder**

1 teaspoon **celery salt**

1 teaspoon **onion salt**

1 teaspoon freshly ground **black pepper**

1 teaspoon **curry powder**

1 teaspoon **chili powder**

¼ teaspoon **lemon pepper**

¼ teaspoon ground **cinnamon**

⅛ teaspoon **cayenne pepper**

⅛ teaspoon ground **allspice**

1 (8-pound) **rack of pork** or **bone-in pork loin roast**

Peach Tea Brine (page 242)

Cooking at the Big Apple Barbecue Block Party is an annual event for Big Bob Gibson Bar-B-Q. This weekend-long event that takes place in New York City's Madison Square Park is filled with long hours of work and very little sleep as we cook about two tons of pork butts (shoulders) for the endless lines of people. While working, you wonder what could ever make you volunteer for such torturous long hours. Then you realize it's the reception and appreciation of the New Yorkers that make it all worthwhile.

A few years ago at this event a friend of mine, Shane McBride, executive chef at Balthazar, dropped by for a visit with a whole Berkshire rack of pork. Anyone who knows a little about pork knows how special a gift that is. Toward the end of the long weekend of cooking it was time to put the rack of pork on, but there was nothing left to season it with. All I could find was a round of salt, a little bit of dry rub, and a couple bottles of Snapple Peach Tea. After a moment's thought, a Snapple quick brine injection was the answer. Five hours later, after my first taste, I knew I was on to something.

A whole bone-in pork loin or rack of pork weighs around 24 pounds untrimmed. For this recipe I used an 8-pound bone-in pork loin roast, one-third of the whole loin. A competent butcher will cut you the ideal size roast for your friends and family. Using the injection ratio of ½ cup of brine per 2 pounds of pork, you can easily adjust the recipe up or down. Most large hardware stores with grilling sections carry the inexpensive handheld meat injector necessary for this recipe.

SERVES 10 TO 12	SUGGESTED WOOD:	COOKING TIME:
COOKING METHOD: Indirect heat	Hickory, peach, apple (see page 22)	3 hours

1 Build a charcoal fire for indirect cooking by situating the coals on only one side of the grill, leaving the other side empty. Preheat the grill to 250°F.

RECIPE CONTINUES

2 For the dry rub: In a small bowl, combine the turbinado sugar, salt, paprika, garlic powder, celery salt, onion salt, black pepper, curry powder, chili powder, lemon pepper, cinnamon, cayenne, and allspice.

3 Put the rack of pork, bone side down, on a large baking sheet. Inject the pork with 2 cups of the brine (½ cup for every 2 pounds of pork). Distribute the brine evenly throughout the roast by injecting in a 1-inch square pattern. Apply the dry rub to the meat in an even coating, patting so the rub adheres. (An alternative method to injecting is to submerge the pork in the peach tea brine and refrigerate for 12 hours. Afterward, apply the dry rub.)

4 Put the pork directly on the cooking grate over indirect heat, away from the coals, close the grill lid, and cook until the internal temperature reaches 145°F, about 3 hours. Transfer the pork to a cutting board and let it rest for 10 minutes. Slice the pork between each rib bone with a heavy knife or cleaver, and serve.

S P I R A L
SLICED HAM
WITH SPICY APRICOT GLAZE

Don't let the idea of cooking a ham intimidate you. Most hams that are sold in grocery stores are cured, smoked, and cooked, but reheating a cooked ham can end up a little disappointing, because in the end that's all you get: a reheated ham.

This simple recipe is a great way to turn a grocery store ham into something unique. The spiral cut allows the spicy apricot mixture to seep into the cracks, getting flavor down to the bone. And don't skip the final 10 minutes of cooking, because that's when the heat caramelizes the glaze quickly, turning it into a delicious crust.

SERVES 8	SUGGESTED WOOD:	COOKING TIME:
COOKING METHOD:	Fruitwoods, hickory	3 hours 10 minutes
Indirect heat	(see page 22)	

1 Build a charcoal fire for indirect cooking by situating the coals on only one side of the grill, leaving the other side empty. Preheat the grill to 300°F.

2 For the glaze: In a medium bowl, combine the preserves, honey, mustard, Worcestershire sauce, soy sauce, sugar, paprika, black pepper, cayenne, garlic powder, cinnamon, sage, and cloves.

3 Put the ham, flat side down, in the center of a large doubled sheet of foil. Pour ½ cup of the glaze on top of the ham and spread it evenly over the entire ham. Wrap the foil tight over the ham and seal it.

4 Put the wrapped ham over indirect heat, away from the coals, close the lid, and cook until the internal temperature reaches 140°F, about 3 hours.

5 Remove the ham from the grill, unwrap and discard the foil, and put the ham in the center of a baking pan. Pour the remaining glaze over the top of the ham and spread it evenly. Return the ham to indirect heat, close the lid, and cook until the glaze firms, about 10 minutes. Remove the ham from the grill and serve.

SPICY APRICOT GLAZE

½ cup **apricot preserves**

¼ cup **honey**

1 tablespoon **Dijon mustard**

1½ teaspoons **Worcestershire sauce**

½ teaspoon **soy sauce**

2 tablespoons **dark brown sugar**

½ teaspoon **paprika**

¼ teaspoon freshly ground **black pepper**

¼ teaspoon **cayenne pepper**

¼ teaspoon **garlic powder**

⅛ teaspoon ground **cinnamon**

⅛ teaspoon dried rubbed **sage**

Pinch of ground **cloves**

1 (8-pound) bone-in spiral-sliced **cured ham**

SEASONED MUSTARD DRUMSTICKS

WITH PEACH MOLASSES GLAZE

This recipe is one of my favorite backyard family dishes because it is both adult- and kid-friendly. Adults appreciate the depth the seasoned mustard gives to this grilled dish, while children love how fun it is to eat a chicken leg, not to mention the sweet fruity flavor of the glaze.

Mustard is the star of this recipe. I use two mustards in different applications. First, yellow mustard coats the chicken, so that the dry rub will adhere to each drumstick. Yellow mustard also helps to ensure you'll get a nice golden-brown color on the chicken skin without an overpowering flavor. Next, Dijon mustard goes into the glaze as a nice accent to the sweetness of the preserves and the saltiness of the soy sauce.

SERVES 6	SUGGESTED WOOD:	
COOKING METHOD: Indirect heat	Hickory, peach, apple (see page 22)	COOKING TIME: 48 minutes

DRY RUB

4 teaspoons **dark brown sugar**

2 teaspoons **kosher salt**

2 teaspoons **garlic salt**

2 teaspoons freshly ground **black pepper**

1¼ teaspoons **paprika**

12 **chicken drumsticks**

½ cup **yellow mustard**

PEACH MOLASSES GLAZE

1 cup **peach preserves**

4 teaspoons **molasses**

1 tablespoon **soy sauce**

1 tablespoon **Dijon mustard**

1 Build a charcoal fire for indirect cooking by situating the coals on only one side of the grill. Preheat the grill to 300°F.

2 In a small bowl, combine the dry rub ingredients. Paint each drumstick with a light coat of the yellow mustard and season with the dry rub mix (about 1 teaspoon per drumstick).

3 Put the drumsticks over indirect heat, away from the coals, close the grill lid, and cook until the internal temperature reaches 175° to 180°F, about 40 minutes.

4 Meanwhile, for the glaze: In a blender or food processor, combine the peach preserves, molasses, soy sauce, and Dijon mustard and puree. Pour the glaze into a shallow bowl.

5 Dip each drumstick into the glaze, completely coating it, and return it to the grill over indirect heat. Cover the grill and cook until the sauce caramelizes, about 8 minutes. Transfer the drumsticks to a platter and serve.

BARBECUE CHICKEN THIGHS

DRY RUB

2 tablespoons **turbinado sugar**

2 tablespoons **salt**

2 teaspoons **garlic powder**

2 teaspoons **paprika**

1 teaspoon freshly ground **black pepper**

1 teaspoon **onion powder**

¼ teaspoon **cayenne pepper**

⅛ teaspoon ground **cinnamon**

⅛ teaspoon ground **allspice**

8 bone-in, skin-on **chicken thighs**

8 tablespoons (1 stick) **unsalted butter**

8 tablespoons (1 stick) **margarine**

¼ cup **Worcestershire sauce**

1 tablespoon fresh **lemon juice**

1 **garlic clove**, minced

There is a reason why judges at most any barbecue competition in the country will see an abundance of thighs whenever it is time to score the chicken category. Competitors know that this dark meat will give them an advantage in moisture and tenderness when compared to other cuts. This recipe starts with a bath of butter, Worcestershire, and fresh garlic, followed by smoking over indirect heat, and finishes with a sweet fruity glaze that caramelizes over the hot flames.

SERVES 6 TO 8	**SUGGESTED WOOD:**	**COOKING TIME:**
COOKING METHOD: Indirect heat	Hickory, apple, maple, oak (see page 22)	1 hour 5 minutes

1 Build a charcoal fire for indirect cooking by situating the coals on only one side of the grill, leaving the other side empty. Preheat the grill to 300°F.

2 For the dry rub: In a small bowl, combine the turbinado sugar, salt, garlic powder, paprika, black pepper, onion powder, cayenne, cinnamon, and allspice. Measure out 4 teaspoons and set aside.

3 Season the chicken thighs on all sides with the remaining rub. Place the chicken thighs, skin side up, in a 9 × 13-inch baking pan.

4 In a small saucepan, melt the butter and margarine on a stovetop. Add the Worcestershire sauce, lemon juice, garlic, and reserved 4 teaspoons dry rub. Carefully pour the mixture over and around the chicken so the dry rub doesn't wash off the skin.

5 Put the baking pan over indirect heat, away from the coals, close the grill lid, and cook until the internal temperature reaches 180°F, about 1 hour.

6 Meanwhile, for the sauce: In a small saucepan, combine the granulated sugar, apple juice, vinegar, and cherry juice. Cook over medium heat until the sugar dissolves, about 2 minutes. Add the agave nectar, jelly, barbecue sauce, Worcestershire sauce, and salt. Bring to a simmer and cook until the sauce has reduced to about 2 cups, about 15 minutes.

7 Remove the chicken thighs from the baking pan and liberally coat them with the warm sauce. Put the chicken thighs directly on the grill grate over indirect heat, away from the coals, close the lid, and cook until the sauce caramelizes, about 5 minutes.

8 Transfer the chicken to a platter and serve.

SAUCE

¾ cup **granulated sugar**

¼ cup **apple juice**

¼ cup **distilled white vinegar**

2 tablespoons **black cherry juice**

½ cup **agave nectar**

3 tablespoons **red pepper jelly**

¾ cup store-bought **barbecue sauce**

1 tablespoon **Worcestershire sauce**

½ teaspoon **salt**

SPLIT CHICKEN HALVES

WITH FRESH HERB MARINADE

MARINADE

6 tablespoons **extra-virgin olive oil**

¼ cup **peanut oil**

2 tablespoons fresh **lemon juice**

2 tablespoons **Dijon mustard**

4 teaspoons **Worcestershire sauce**

4 teaspoons **dark brown sugar**

1 **garlic clove**, minced

¼ cup chopped fresh **parsley**

2 tablespoons chopped fresh **basil**

2 tablespoons chopped fresh **oregano**

2 teaspoons **salt**

½ teaspoon freshly ground **black pepper**

2 split **chicken halves** (3 to 3½ pounds)

This recipe strays from what most people consider barbecued chicken. Instead of a sauce, it features a tasty marinade of fresh herbs and bright lemon juice. By cooking the chicken in a pan instead of directly on the grill grate, the meat gets extra protection from drying out. Finally, the cooking temperature is substantially higher than the barbecue norm of 225°F to 275°F. The elevation in temperature ensures that the chicken skin will cook up crispy, and not be gummy and inedible. For all these differences, there's no less smokiness in the meat, since closing the grill lid lets it take on a complementary and mellow smoke flavor.

SERVES 4	SUGGESTED WOOD:	MARINATING TIME:
	Hickory, apricot, apple, oak (see page 22)	8 to 12 hours
COOKING METHOD: Indirect heat		COOKING TIME: 2 hours

1 For the marinade: In a small bowl, whisk together the olive oil, peanut oil, lemon juice, mustard, Worcestershire sauce, brown sugar, garlic, parsley, basil, oregano, salt, and pepper. Put the chicken halves in a resealable plastic bag and pour in the marinade. Seal the bag and marinate in the refrigerator for 8 to 12 hours.

2 Build a charcoal fire for indirect cooking by situating the coals on only one side of the grill, leaving the other side empty. Preheat the grill to 300°F.

3 Remove the chicken from the marinade and put it, skin side up, in a 9 × 13-inch baking pan. Pour the remaining marinade over the chicken. Put the pan over indirect heat, away from the coals, close the grill lid, and cook until the internal temperature reaches 175°F, about 2 hours. Baste with the pan drippings before serving.

CHARCOAL-GRILLED
TURKEY
WITH FRESH HERB BUTTER

1 (12-pound) whole **turkey**

Extra-virgin olive oil, for coating

Kosher salt and coarsely ground **black pepper**

HERB BUTTER

2 sticks (½ pound) **unsalted butter**

⅓ cup chopped **flat-leaf parsley**

⅓ cup chopped **scallion greens**

2 tablespoons chopped fresh **sage**

2 tablespoons chopped fresh **thyme**

2 tablespoons chopped fresh **basil**

1 tablespoon fresh **lemon juice**

1 tablespoon **Dijon mustard**

1½ teaspoons **garlic salt**

1½ teaspoons **celery salt**

1 teaspoon freshly ground **black pepper**

If you are looking for a traditional Thanksgiving turkey, you will not find it here. My last book, *Big Bob Gibson's BBQ Book,* has that kind of recipe. But if you want a unique turkey, fire up that grill and invite the in-laws over, because this bountiful bird is like nothing you have seen or tasted. Butterflying ensures a more evenly cooked turkey than with a normal preparation, and it helps you get the seasoning in contact with more meat. There is no need to resort to the usual tricks to add flavor with an injection, a brine, or rubbing seasoning under the skin.

SERVES 10	SUGGESTED WOOD:	COOKING TIME:
COOKING METHOD:	Hickory, pecan, oak, maple (see page 22)	2 hours 40 minutes
Direct and indirect heat		

1 Build a charcoal fire for indirect cooking by situating the coals on only one side of the grill, leaving the other side empty. Preheat the grill to 450 to 500°F.

2 Put the whole turkey, breast side down, on a cutting board. Remove the neck and giblets and set them aside for when you make the turkey stock. Using a sharp knife or a pair of kitchen shears, cut the turkey down each side of the backbone, removing it completely. Open the turkey and press it flat on the cutting board. Using a sharp knife, loosen the breastbone from between the turkey breasts and remove it with your fingers. (It is a dark-colored bone that is often called a keel bone because of its shape.) Now the turkey can be opened completely flat. Apply a light coating of olive oil to the turkey skin and liberally season it with salt and pepper.

3 For the herb butter: In a medium saucepan, melt the butter over low heat. Add the parsley, scallions, sage, thyme, basil, lemon juice, mustard, garlic salt, celery salt, and pepper. Keep warm.

4 Put the butterflied turkey, skin side down, over direct heat and baste with the herb butter. Grill the turkey until the skin starts to turn golden brown and begins to crisp, 5 to 7 minutes. Transfer the turkey, skin side up, to a 10 × 10-inch roasting pan. Put it over indirect heat, away from the coals, and baste the turkey with the herb butter. Cover the grill and close the air dampers, reducing the temperature to 350°F. Cook, basting every hour with the remaining herb butter, until the internal temperature of a thigh reaches 180°F (the breast meat should reach 160° to 165°F), about 2 hours 30 minutes. Remove the turkey from the grill, cover it with foil, and let it rest for 15 minutes before carving.

5 Meanwhile, for the stock: In a medium saucepan, combine 3½ cups water, 1¾ teaspoons salt, and the reserved turkey neck and giblets and bring to a boil on the stovetop over medium heat. Reduce the heat to low, cover, and simmer until the stock has reduced by one-third, about 40 minutes.

6 For the gravy: Scrape the drippings and liquid from the bottom of the roasting pan into a small bowl. Skim the fat from the top of the liquid and discard. Pour the liquid (you should have about ¾ cup) into a small saucepan. In a small bowl, whisk 2 tablespoons water into the cornstarch until smooth. Add the cornstarch slurry and 2 cups of the turkey stock to the saucepan. Cook over medium heat, stirring occasionally, until the gravy thickens. Reduce the heat and keep warm over low heat.

7 Carve the turkey and serve it drizzled with the gravy, or with the gravy on the side.

STOCK AND GRAVY

1¾ teaspoons **salt**

Turkey neck and giblets (discard the liver)

4 teaspoons **cornstarch**

ASIAN
SMOKED
DUCK

BRINE

2 cups **soy sauce**

½ cup **honey**

1 cup packed **dark brown sugar**

½ cup **granulated sugar**

2 (3-inch) pieces fresh **ginger,** coarsely crushed

2 (3-inch) pieces fresh **lemongrass,** chopped

1 bunch **scallions,** chopped

1 head **garlic,** split in half horizontally

3 whole **star anise**

½ cup chopped fresh **cilantro**

¼ cup **kosher salt**

2 tablespoons **fish sauce**

1 (5- to 7-pound) whole **duck**

Kosher salt and freshly ground **black pepper**

Let me start out by saying this is not a Peking duck recipe, but it was inspired by the same Asian flavors. *Subtlety* is the key word here, because instead of the heavy-handed oyster sauce and hoisin, the duck is made with a lighter brine and has a delicate smoke flavor.

While the brine and seasonings are important for the flavor and juiciness of the duck, equally important is the cooking technique. Piercing the skin with a fork and cooking at a lower temperature helps render the fat, and the final stage of cooking—at the high heat of 500°F—ensures a thin crisp skin.

SERVES 4 TO 6	**SUGGESTED WOOD:** Apple, apricot, cherry (see page 22)	**BRINING TIME:** 8 hours
COOKING METHOD: Indirect heat	**COOLING TIME:** 40 minutes	**COOKING TIME:** 3 hours 5 minutes

1 For the brine: In a large pot set over medium heat, combine 4 quarts water with the soy sauce, honey, brown and granulated sugars, ginger, lemongrass, scallions, garlic, star anise, cilantro, salt, and fish sauce. Bring to a simmer and cook until the liquid has reduced by one-fourth, about 20 minutes. Remove the pot from the heat and refrigerate until cool, about 40 minutes. The brine can be made up to 2 days in advance.

2 Remove the neck and giblets from the duck and discard. Prick the skin of the duck all over with a fork, put the duck in a nonreactive pot, and pour in the cooled brine. Refrigerate for at least 8 hours.

3 Build a two-zone fire in a charcoal grill by situating the coals on only one side of the grill, leaving the other side empty. Put a disposable aluminum drip pan on the empty side of the grill under where the duck will cook. Close the lid and preheat the grill to 375°F.

4 Remove the duck from the brine and lightly season it with salt and pepper. Put the duck over indirect heat, away from the coals, close the grill lid, and cook until the internal temperature of the legs and breast reaches 165°F, 2 hours to 2 hours 30 minutes.

5 Remove the duck from the grill and increase the grill temperature to 500°F. Put the duck back over indirect heat, close the lid, and cook until the skin crisps, about 15 minutes. Transfer the duck to a cutting board and let it rest for 10 minutes.

6 Slice the duck meat from the bone and serve.

PEPPERED AHI TUNA
WITH CANTALOUPE & PINEAPPLE SALSA

The Hawaiian name for yellowfin tuna is *ahi*. You'll find it marked both ways in grocery stores. It is excellent for grilling directly over hot charcoal, giving it a quick sear and keeping the center rare.

I created this recipe for a get-together at the American Royal Barbecue Contest in Kansas City. We were trying out the new Competition Briquets from Kingsford, and my good friend and Kingsford employee Drew McGowan wanted to bring the grills up to a very high searing temperature. Ahi tuna was the perfect match for the occasion.

A trick I often use for fish is to turn a simple dry rub blend into a oil-based seasoning paste, since the added oil helps keep the fish from drying out. The sweet cantaloupe and pineapple in the salsa nicely offset the high ratio of black pepper on the tuna.

SERVES 6	SUGGESTED WOOD:	MARINATING TIME:
	Alder, maple	30 minutes
COOKING METHOD:	(see page 22)	
Direct heat		COOKING TIME:
		3 to 6 minutes

1 For the salsa: In a medium bowl, combine the cantaloupe, onion, pineapple, cilantro, lime juice, and jalapeño. Season with salt to taste. The salsa can be served at room temperature or refrigerated until ready to use or up to 3 days in advance.

2 For the pepper paste: In a small bowl, combine the olive oil, soy sauce, vinegar, pepper, salt, brown sugar, and garlic salt. Coat the tuna steaks evenly with the pepper paste. Wrap each steak in plastic wrap and refrigerate for 30 minutes.

3 Build a charcoal fire for direct grilling and open all dampers for maximum heat. Preheat the grill to 500° to 600°F.

4 Lightly coat the grill grates with oil. Remove the tuna steaks from the plastic wrap and place them over direct heat. Grill on each side for 3 minutes or less, depending on how rare you like them. The tuna should be firm with pink in the middle.

5 To serve, slice the tuna into ¼-inch-wide strips and top with a generous amount of salsa, or put the fish slices on a bed of salsa.

SALSA

1½ cups chopped **cantaloupe**

½ cup chopped **red onion**

½ cup chopped **pineapple**

¼ cup chopped fresh **cilantro**

2½ tablespoons fresh **lime juice**

2 teaspoons minced **jalapeño pepper**

Salt

PEPPER PASTE

2 tablespoons **extra-virgin olive oil**

2 tablespoons **soy sauce**

¾ teaspoon **cider vinegar**

¼ cup coarsely ground **black pepper**

2 tablespoons **kosher salt**

2 tablespoons **dark brown sugar**

¼ teaspoon **garlic salt**

6 (¾- to 1-inch-thick) **ahi tuna steaks**

Olive oil, for the grill grates

CHARCOAL-SEARED
TROUT FILLET

WITH SUN-DRIED TOMATO BROWN BUTTER

9 tablespoons **unsalted butter**

4 (6- to 7-ounce) **trout fillets**

Kosher salt and freshly ground **black pepper**

¼ cup **sun-dried tomatoes**, thinly sliced

2 tablespoons **capers**

2 tablespoons chopped fresh **parsley**

½ cup **dry white wine**

Juice of ½ **lemon**

By this point, you've probably picked up on my love for cooking in a cast iron skillet. What's so great about it is that it catches the juices rendering from the meat so that you don't lose them to the fire. And cast iron is so strong that it can easily handle high grill heat over coals, and even in the coals. That's right, when ripping-hot pan temperatures are needed to sear fish, scallops, or any other meat, there is no better way than to nestle the cast iron directly into a pile of white-hot charcoal.

SERVES 4 COOKING METHOD: Direct heat	SUGGESTED WOOD: Alder, oak, maple, hickory (see page 22)	COOKING TIME: 5 minutes

1 Build a charcoal fire for direct grilling. Put a cast iron skillet directly in the hot coals.

2 In a medium saucepan, melt 3 tablespoons of the butter. Dredge the trout fillets through the melted butter and season each with salt and pepper.

3 Put the trout fillets, flesh side down, in the hot skillet and cook for 1½ minutes. Flip the fillets and cook, skin side down, until the fish starts to flake with pressure, about 1½ minutes. Remove the pan from the coals and set it on a heatproof surface. Transfer the trout to a plate.

4 Wait 1 minute for the pan to cool slightly. Add the remaining 6 tablespoons butter and cook until the butter starts to brown, about 30 seconds. Add the sun-dried tomatoes, capers, and parsley to the pan and cook, stirring, for 30 seconds. Pour in the white wine and lemon juice and stir for 1 minute, scraping up any bits from the bottom of the pan. Simmer until the sauce has reduced by half. Season with salt and pepper, if desired.

5 Drizzle the sauce over the trout fillets and serve.

GRILLED LOBSTER TAILS
WITH BLACKENED BUTTER

BLACKENED BUTTER

8 tablespoons (1 stick) **unsalted butter**, at room temperature

½ teaspoon fresh **lemon juice**

½ teaspoon **Worcestershire sauce**

¼ teaspoon **hot sauce**

2 tablespoons **Creole Spice Rub** (page 246)

4 (8- to 10-ounce) jumbo **Maine lobster tails**

1 **lemon**

Pitmaster Tip: If jumbo Maine lobster tails are not available, or if you prefer smaller portions, smaller lobster tails or rock lobster can be used. Adjust the cook time to 2½ minutes in boiling water and 2 minutes on each side over hot coals.

You don't have to get too fancy with complicated recipes when cooking lobster. The key to successfully grilling lobster is a combination of parboiling followed by a quick hit on the grill. This ensures tender, juicy meat instead of the rubbery lobster you get from only grilling it. And lobsters that skip the grill altogether lack the depth of flavor from charring and browned butter.

Typically when I make blackened butter, I'll double the recipe so that I have it around to use on foods such as chicken wings, pork chops, shrimp skewers, or traditional New Orleans barbecue shrimp. Put the extra softened blackened butter in a small piece of plastic wrap and roll it into a log. Refrigerate it until firm, and then remove the plastic wrap. Dynamic flavor is just a pat away.

SERVES 4	SUGGESTED WOOD:	COOKING TIME:
COOKING METHOD:	Alder, maple, apple (see page 22)	20 minutes
Direct heat		

1 For the blackened butter: In a small bowl, combine the butter, lemon juice, Worcestershire sauce, hot sauce, and spice rub. Set aside.

2 Build a charcoal fire for direct grilling and preheat it to 450°F.

3 Bring a large pot of salted water to a boil on a stovetop. Boil the lobster tails for 4 minutes. Transfer the lobster to a cutting board. Using kitchen shears or a sharp knife, cut down the center of the soft underbelly of each tail. Slice the meat down to the tail shell without puncturing the shell. Rub about 2 teaspoons of blackened butter into the knife cut of each lobster tail.

4 Put the lobster tail, meat side down, on the grill over direct heat and cook until slightly charred, about 3 minutes. Flip the lobster and spoon about 1 tablespoon blackened butter into each knife slit. Cook until the lobster is cooked through and the tail starts to curl, about 3 minutes.

5 Transfer the tails to a serving platter and squeeze the lemon over them before serving.

WHOLE SMOKED
MAHI-MAHI

One of my most memorable South Beach visits was in 2007, when I was invited to cook at the Bubble Q event. On that trip, a great friend of mine, Adam Perry Lang, chef, restaurateur, and author, invited me to join him on a deep-sea fishing trip off the coast of the Florida Keys. We enjoyed the adrenaline rush of fighting sailfish and king mackerel, and our catch for the day included three beautiful mahi-mahi.

On our way back, we planned a fresh fish barbecue. My barbecue trailer was tucked away in an alley beside our hotel and could handle slow-smoking the fish. Our guest list included everyone we knew in Miami and all of the lucky people who happened down that alley. Our only worry was being shut down by the festival because we weren't an official South Beach event. But staring at the huge buffet of food, we realized we had plenty of bribes to offer!

This recipe is all about protecting the flesh of the fish. Leaving the skin on one side traps the juices and keeps the hot fire from drying out the flesh. The mayonnaise takes care of the exposed flesh by providing a buffer of fat between the fish and the flame.

1 (15-pound) whole **mahi-mahi**, head on, scaled, and gutted

3 tablespoons **mayonnaise**

Fish & Seafood Rub (page 248)

1 **lemon**, for squeezing

SERVES 12	SUGGESTED WOOD:	COOKING TIME:
COOKING METHOD: Indirect heat	Alder, oak, maple (see page 22)	35 minutes

1 Build a charcoal fire for indirect cooking by situating the fire on only one side of the grill, leaving the other side empty. Preheat the grill to 250°F.

2 Slit the skin of the fish just behind the gills from the backbone to the belly, on one side only. On the same side, make a slit down the backbone and across the tail. With a pair of pliers, grip the skin just behind the gills and forcefully pull it off the fish. The fish should be skinned on one side only.

3 Coat the flesh with the mayonnaise. Apply a generous coat of the dry rub and put the fish, skin side down, over indirect heat, away from the coals. Close the grill lid and cook until the internal temperature reaches 130°F, about 35 minutes.

4 Squeeze the lemon over the fish and serve hot.

BACON-CRUSTED CEDAR PLANK SALMON

WITH MAPLE-GINGER GLAZE

MARINADE

¾ cup **soy sauce**

¾ cup **vegetable oil**

3 tablespoons **rice vinegar**

1½ teaspoons **sesame oil**

2 tablespoons grated fresh **ginger**

3 **garlic cloves**, minced

1 (2- to 3-pound) skin-on center-cut **salmon fillet** (about 1½ inches thick)

6 slices thick-cut **bacon** (or 8 strips regular cut)

¼ cup **panko breadcrumbs**

½ cup **maple syrup**

Don't let the name of this recipe mislead you into thinking that it's difficult. In fact, the only thing complex about it is the deeply layered flavors of salmon, ginger, soy, bacon, and maple syrup. Well, I guess it is difficult . . . difficult to mess up!

There is a reason that cooking salmon on cedar planks is very popular. It works! The flat plank protects the fish by providing a buffer between it and the hot fire. Second, the hot wood imparts just the right amount of a subtle, lightly bitter smokiness that doesn't overwhelm the fish like some traditional smoking woods do.

SERVES 6	SUGGESTED WOOD: No added wood	MARINATING TIME: 20 minutes
COOKING METHOD: Direct and indirect heat	SUPPLIES: 6 × 12-inch cedar plank (or larger)	COOKING TIME: 20 minutes

1 Build a two-zone fire in a charcoal grill by situating the coals on only one side of the grill, leaving the other side empty. Preheat the grill to 450 to 500°F. Soak the cedar plank in a pan of water for 15 minutes.

2 For the marinade: In a small bowl, combine the soy sauce, vegetable oil, vinegar, sesame oil, ginger, and garlic. Measure out ¼ cup of the marinade and set aside for the glaze.

3 Put the salmon in a 1-gallon resealable plastic bag, pour the marinade over the salmon, seal the bag, and marinate in the refrigerator for 20 minutes.

4 Put a large skillet over direct heat. Add the bacon and cook until it is blondish-brown but not crispy, about 5 minutes. Transfer the bacon and bacon grease to a food processor. Add the panko and process until fine crumbles are formed. Transfer the bacon crumbles to a baking sheet. Arrange them tightly on an area that's the same size as the salmon fillet.

5 Remove the salmon from the marinade and press the flesh side of the salmon into the bacon crumbles. Lay the salmon on the cedar plank, skin side down. Put the cedar plank on the grill grate over indirect heat or high enough over the fire so that the flames aren't touching the board. Close the lid and cook until the salmon and bacon crust browns, about 8 minutes.

6 Meanwhile, in a small bowl, combine the reserved ¼ cup marinade and the maple syrup to make a glaze.

7 Open the grill lid and spoon the glaze over the salmon fillet. Close the lid and cook until the internal temperature reaches 130°F, about 7 minutes. Remove the cedar plank from the grill and let the salmon rest on the plank for 3 minutes before serving.

BARBECUE PAELLA

WITH CHICKEN, SHRIMP & CHORIZO SAUSAGE

1½ teaspoons **saffron threads**

10 boneless, skinless **chicken thighs**

¼ cup **Veggie Seasoning** (page 249)

¼ cup **extra-virgin olive oil**

1 pound **chorizo**, chopped

1 medium **white onion**, chopped

1 **red bell pepper**, thinly sliced

1 bunch **scallions**, white parts chopped and green parts sliced

1 **jalapeño pepper**, minced

6 **garlic cloves**, minced

2 cups **medium-grain rice**

¼ cup **dry white wine**

2 cups **chicken stock**

1 pound extra-jumbo **shrimp** (16/20 count), peeled and deveined

1 cup frozen **green peas**, thawed

A popular rice dish, paella originated in a region of Spain called Valencia. The word *paella* has its roots in Latin from the word for *plate* or *pan*. This dish can made with a multitude of different ingredients, including chicken, pork, shellfish, fish, eel, sausage, beans, peas, peppers, or artichokes. Many believe that there are only three essential ingredients: rice, olive oil, and saffron (which turns the rice a vibrant golden color).

Paella is perfect for the outdoor grill because you need to start off hot and gradually reduce the temperature. The first step to making paella is browning the meat. Next, the rice needs to simmer as the other ingredients are added. The last and most wonderful part of the paella process is serving it out of the pan while it rests on the open grill.

SERVES 12 TO 14	SUGGESTED WOOD:	COOKING TIME:
COOKING METHOD: Direct heat	Hickory, oak, pimento (see page 22)	50 minutes

1   Build a charcoal fire for direct grilling and preheat it to 400°F.

2   Put a small saucepan on the grate directly over the fire. Add the saffron threads and toast them until you can smell the saffron aroma, about 1½ minutes. Add 2 cups water, bring to a simmer, and cook for 5 minutes. Remove the pan from the grill and set aside.

3   Season the chicken thighs evenly with the veggie seasoning.

4   Put a paella pan or an 18-inch cast iron skillet over direct heat. Add the olive oil. When the oil is hot, put the chicken into the pan and sear until nicely browned, 3 minutes on each side. Transfer the chicken to a plate and set aside.

5   Put the chorizo into the hot pan and cook until browned, about 3 minutes. Add the onion, bell pepper, scallion whites, jalapeño, and garlic and cook, stirring, until the vegetables brown slightly and soften, about 2 minutes. Add the rice and stir to coat in oil. Toast the rice for 2 minutes. Pour in the white wine and stir,

scraping any browned bits off the bottom of the pan. Pour in the saffron water, return the chicken to the pan, and cover with the chicken stock.

6 Reduce the temperature to 350°F, close the grill lid, and cook for 10 minutes. Open the grill and stir in the shrimp and peas. Close the lid and cook until the rice is done and the chicken reaches an internal temperature of 175°F, 15 to 20 minutes.

7 Remove the paella from the grill and serve it directly from the pan.

BARBECUE LEFTOVERS

MY PASSION FOR COOKING BIG-PROTEIN BARBECUE HAS OVERLOADED MY REFRIGERATOR WITH LEFTOVERS.

After nine chapters, I think we have known each other long enough where I'm comfortable giving you my testimony. I have a recurring problem. My passion for cooking big-protein barbecue has overloaded my refrigerator with leftovers. When I cook whole pork butts (shoulders), chickens, and beef brisket, mounds of meat stack up like cordwood. The recipes in this chapter are the only way I know to face my addiction head-on and finally have a place to put a gallon of milk. Luckily for me, my daughter is tired of eating dry cereal in the morning and is happy to try something like Barbecue Beef Brisket Benedict and Southwest Smoked Brisket Hash instead. And Grilled Greek Salad Pita with Barbecue Chicken Salad and Overstuffed Pulled Pork Potato make warm-up meat even tastier the second time around. With a little help, we can get through this together. Let me know if you need any leftovers.

BARBECUE BEEF BRISKET BENEDICT

9 tablespoons **soy sauce**

6 tablespoons **extra-virgin olive oil**

3 tablespoons fresh **lemon juice**

2 tablespoons **dark brown sugar**

¾ teaspoon **garlic powder**

¾ teaspoon freshly ground **black pepper**

1 **white onion**, halved and thinly sliced

6 **eggs**

3 **English muffins**, split

1 pound leftover **beef brisket** (from Barbecue Beef Brisket Flat, page 130), reheated with drippings (see Pitmaster Tip, page 130)

Barbecue Hollandaise Sauce (page 232)

Make the best of your barbecue leftovers with a breakfast classic. A grilled English muffin half is covered with beef brisket and caramelized grilled onions, and then topped with a poached egg, and a barbecue Hollandaise sauce, and drizzled with brisket jus.

This recipe is so good it was an easy choice when deciding what to serve the attendees of the 2012 South Beach Wine & Food Festival Q Event. Keep in mind that making Barbecue Beef Brisket Benedict for a family of five is much easier than poaching eggs and making Hollandaise sauce for 1,000 people! In one night, I lost my appetite for eggs for the rest of the year and just about lost my sous chef, Ken Hess, forever! After the party, we asked chef Wylie Dufresne if he would have executed things differently and his answer was, "Absolutely. I would have said no!"

SERVES 6			
COOKING METHOD: Direct heat		**SUGGESTED WOOD:** Hickory, oak (see page 22)	**MARINATING TIME:** 30 minutes **COOKING TIME:** 15 minutes

1 In a small bowl, whisk together 6 tablespoons water, the soy sauce, olive oil, lemon juice, brown sugar, garlic powder, and pepper. Pour the marinade into a resealable plastic bag and add the onion. Let marinate for 30 minutes.

2 Build a charcoal fire for direct grilling and preheat it to 450°F.

3 Drain the onion and put the slices in a grill basket. Put the basket over direct heat and grill, stirring often, until the onions brown and start to soften, about 5 minutes. Remove the onions from the grill and set aside.

4 Bring a large saucepan filled with 4 inches of water to a boil on the stovetop over medium-high heat. Reduce the heat to medium-low to keep a slight simmer; the water temperature should be 160° to 180°F. Crack 3 eggs into 3 separate ramekins or small

bowls. Gently stir the simmering water with a spoon. Carefully pour each egg into the water making sure there is space between them so that they don't join together. To maintain the shape of the eggs, swirl the water in a circular motion. Cook until the whites are set and the yolks begin to thicken, 3 to 5 minutes. Remove with a slotted spoon. Repeat with the remaining 3 eggs.

5 Put the English muffin halves over direct heat and toast until browned, about 2 minutes. Transfer each muffin half to a serving plate, using 1 muffin half per plate. Top each muffin half with leftover beef brisket, the grilled onions, and a poached egg. Drizzle with the Hollandaise sauce and brisket drippings.

SOUTHWEST SMOKED
BRISKET HASH
WITH GREEN CHILE SALSA

3 cups cubed (½-inch) **potatoes**

3 tablespoons **lard** or **vegetable oil**

¼ **yellow onion**, chopped (½ cup)

½ **red bell pepper**, chopped (½ cup)

1½ tablespoons **paprika**

1½ teaspoons **salt**

1 teaspoon **garlic powder**

1 teaspoon **chili powder**

1 teaspoon freshly ground **black pepper**

2 cups chopped leftover **beef brisket** (from Barbecue Beef Brisket Flat, page 130) plus 2 cups brisket drippings

6 **eggs**

Green Chile Salsa (page 239)

I'm very fortunate to be able to travel to some of the most amazing venues in the country all in the name of barbecue. If you are a sports fan, doing what I do has some fantastic perks, such as trips to the Super Bowl, ESPN studios, Cowboys Stadium, Yankee Stadium, and ballparks all over the country. I've appeared on television with Joe Thiesmann, Ozzie Smith, Mitch "Wild Thing" Williams, Mike Golic, and Robert Smith. Cooking on the popular show *College Football Live* and ESPN *Game Day* has been a highlight of my culinary career. I'd have to say, though, that one of the most interesting jobs I've had is catering at NASCAR races.

I'll have to admit that I was never a big NASCAR fan, but all that changed when they hired me to cook on the infield at several racetracks across the country. My job is to provide the ultimate breakfast/brunch barbecue experience for guests at the NASCAR Garage Charity and at corporate events prior to the race. To think that my barbecue breakfast could indirectly determine who wins the race is pretty cool! Therefore I have to step up my game.

This dish hits the mark every time. It is a stick-to-your-ribs meal that can successfully carry you through the big race or just start your day off right. The green chile salsa is really spicy and livens up the eggs and potatoes. The beef brisket jus is the key to this recipe, so make sure you use a very flavorful beef stock when you make the brisket. No worries—the time it takes you to make this recipe in the morning can be made up in the car on the way to work. Remember, it's race day!

SERVES 6	COOKING METHOD: Stovetop	COOKING TIME: 45 minutes

1 In a large pot, combine the cubed potatoes with water to cover. Bring to a boil over high heat and cook until the potatoes soften slightly, about 8 minutes. Drain the potatoes and set aside.

2 In a large skillet, melt the lard over medium-high heat. Add the potatoes and cook, stirring occasionally, until golden brown, about 10 minutes. Add the onion, bell pepper, paprika, salt, garlic powder, chili powder, and black pepper. Cook, stirring, until the vegetables are soft, about 5 minutes. Add the chopped brisket

and brisket jus. Reduce the heat to medium and cook until the drippings reduce by half, about 15 minutes.

3 Meanwhile, heat a separate large oiled skillet over medium heat. Fry the eggs until the yolks are set but still runny, 3 to 4 minutes.

4 Serve the brisket hash hot topped with a fried egg and the salsa.

BARBECUE GUMBO

GUMBO

1¼ cups (2½ sticks) **unsalted butter**

⅔ cup **all-purpose flour**

1 large **yellow onion**, chopped (about 2½ cups)

1 **green bell pepper**, chopped (about 1½ cups)

2 **celery ribs**, chopped (1 cup)

2 tablespoons **Creole Spice Rub** (page 246)

1 tablespoon **Worcestershire sauce**

1 **garlic clove**, minced

4 cups **chicken broth**

1½ cups **beef brisket drippings** (from Barbecue Beef Brisket Flat, page 130) or beef broth

1¼ cups canned **crushed tomatoes**

1 cup chopped **barbecue chicken** (such as Barbecue Chicken thighs, page 156)

1 cup chopped **beef brisket** (from Barbecue Beef Brisket Flat, page 130)

1 pound **andouille sausage**, cut into ¼-inch cubes

2 **bay leaves**

1 teaspoon fresh **lemon juice**

¼ cup chopped fresh **parsley**

2 teaspoons **salt**, or to taste

This recipe was born from my deep love of Louisiana Creole cooking. I've traveled the Southern Coast and sampled some of the finest gumbo in the world, and the rich depth of a thick bowl of this seafood concoction is mesmerizing. My version here forgoes the tradition of stirring the okra into the stew in favor of using the okra to make a crispy topper, like croutons on a salad. One taste of this and, sonamagun, we'll have big fun on the bayou!

SERVES 16 TO 20	COOKING METHOD: Stovetop and oven	COOKING TIME: 1 hour 35 minutes

1   For the gumbo: In a large cast iron skillet, melt 1 stick (8 tablespoons) of the butter over medium-low heat. Gradually add the flour and cook, stirring the mixture constantly to prevent lumps from forming, until the roux is the color of peanut butter, 30 to 40 minutes. Remove the pan from the heat and set aside.

2   In a separate large skillet, melt the remaining 1½ sticks (12 tablespoons) butter. Add the onion, bell pepper, and celery, and cook, stirring, until the vegetables start to brown, about 10 minutes. Add the Creole spice rub, Worcestershire sauce, and garlic and cook until the mixture starts sticking to the bottom of the pan, about 5 minutes.

3   Transfer the cooked vegetables to a large pot and add the roux. Add the chicken broth, beef drippings (or broth), tomatoes, chicken, beef brisket, sausage, and bay leaves. Bring to a boil, reduce the heat to low, and simmer for 30 minutes.

4   Add the lemon juice, parsley, and salt to the pot and simmer for 10 more minutes.

RECIPE CONTINUES

OKRA TOPPING

Vegetable oil

2 pounds fresh **okra**, cut into
½-inch-thick slices

½ cup **cornmeal**

2 teaspoons **salt**

1 teaspoon freshly ground **black
pepper**

16 to 20 cups cooked **white rice**,
for serving

5 Meanwhile, for the okra topping: Pour vegetable oil into a large rimmed baking sheet, making sure that it covers the bottom. Put the pan in the oven and preheat the oven to 450°F.

6 In a medium bowl, combine the okra, cornmeal, salt, and pepper. Pour the okra into the preheated baking pan and gently stir to coat the okra in hot oil; spread the okra into a single layer. Return the pan to the oven and cook, stirring every 5 minutes, until the okra turns crisp and brown, about 25 minutes.

7 Serve the hot gumbo over a bowl of rice and top with the crispy okra.

BARBECUE CHICKEN SALAD

Why does it always seem that there is more leftover chicken than any other type of meat? Either I need to work on my recipes or maybe it's just a little harder to translate a head count into chicken pieces. Regardless, a refrigerator packed with leftovers guarantees a delicious meal the next day.

This salad is one of my go-to recipes for day-after-grilling fare. Whether served on crackers before a party, on a bed of lettuce for a light lunch, or as a sandwich during the game, this chicken salad has a punch of barbecue flavor that the traditional mayonnaise-based salad can't deliver.

MAKES 3 CUPS; ENOUGH FOR 8 SANDWICHES | **COOKING METHOD:** None | **PREP TIME:** 3 minutes

2½ cups chopped leftover **barbecue chicken** (such as Curry Chicken Satays, page 61)

⅓ cup chopped **dried cranberries**

1 small **celery ribs**, chopped (⅓ cup)

¼ cup chopped **pecans**

4 teaspoons **sweet pickle relish**

¾ cup **mayonnaise**

¼ cup favorite store-bought **barbecue sauce** (I use Big Bob Gibson Championship Red Sauce)

2 teaspoons **Worcestershire sauce**

¼ teaspoon **salt**

¼ teaspoon freshly ground **black pepper**

1 In a small bowl, combine the barbecue chicken, cranberries, celery, pecans, and pickle relish. Mix well and set aside.

2 In a separate bowl, combine the mayonnaise, barbecue sauce, Worcestershire sauce, salt, and pepper. Stir the dressing into the chicken mixture. Serve immediately or refrigerate in an airtight container for up to 4 days.

GRILLED
GREEK SALAD PITA
WITH BARBECUE CHICKEN

The olive-loving gene skipped a generation in my family. My mother has always kept a jar of olives handy in the refrigerator for the frequent occasion when a dish demanded a briny zing, but I never liked them much. Granted, it's possible I can attribute my dislike to an ill-fated search for sweet green grapes. I'm sure my older brother and sister put me up to it, adding to my childhood trauma.

I created this recipe as a nod to one of my mother's loves and as a test to see how well my taste buds have developed. I can honestly say that thanks to this recipe, I truly love olives! Whether you have enough chicken to fill pitas to the brim or only enough for a salad topper, this recipe will work great.

SERVES 6 TO 8	COOKING METHOD: Direct heat	COOKING TIME: 6 minutes

1 For the dressing: In a small bowl, whisk together the olive oil, lemon juice, olives, oregano, and pepper. Set aside.

2 Build a charcoal fire for direct grilling and preheat it to 450°F.

3 Put the pita bread over direct heat and cook until grill marks are visible, 1 minute on each side. Transfer to a plate.

4 For the salad: Put the cucumbers, onions, and whole tomato over direct heat and cook, turning once, until they brown and start to soften, about 4 minutes. Transfer the vegetables to a cutting board and chop them.

5 Put the chopped vegetables in a medium bowl and pour the dressing over them. Let stand for 5 minutes before adding the lettuce and feta cheese.

6 Fill each pita pocket with leftover chicken and the salad.

GREEK DRESSING

2 tablespoons **extra-virgin olive oil**

4½ teaspoons fresh **lemon juice**

1½ tablespoons finely chopped **Kalamata olives**

½ teaspoon dried **oregano**

⅛ teaspoon freshly ground **black pepper**

4 **pita breads**, halved crosswise to make 8 half-moon pockets

SALAD

1 **cucumber**, cut into ½-inch-thick slices

½ **red onion**, cut into ½-inch-thick slices

1 **tomato**

2 cups **romaine lettuce**, cut into 1-inch shreds

¼ cup crumbled **feta cheese**

1 pound leftover **barbecue chicken** (such as Split Chicken Halves, page 158) reheated (see Pitmaster Tip, page 188)

OVERSTUFFED PULLED PORK POTATO

4 (20-ounce) extra-large **baking potatoes**

8 tablespoons (1 stick) **salted butter**

½ cup **sour cream**

6 ounces **cheddar cheese**, finely shredded (1½ cups)

4 **scallions**, chopped

4 slices **bacon**, cooked and crumbled

1 pound leftover **pulled barbecue pork** (such as Beer Basted Pulled Pork, page 90), reheated (see Pitmaster Tip)

Pitmaster Tip: Let's talk about the best way to reheat leftover barbecue. I prefer to refrigerate barbecue in as large pieces as possible. You will have much better results retaining moisture when refrigerating and reheating a whole pork butt than a pan of chopped pork.

To reheat, put the meat in a baking dish and cover with foil. Reheat in a 300°F oven until the internal temperature of the meat reaches 145°F, about 1 hour. If the meat is chopped or sliced, it is best to vacuum-seal the leftovers and reheat in a pot of simmering water for 30 minutes. Whichever method you choose, always remember to cover the meat to trap the juices.

This recipe has been a house favorite at Big Bob Gibson Bar-B-Q for two decades. It features our famous pulled pork butt (shoulder)—served in Decatur, Alabama, since 1925—which has won seven World Titles at the Memphis in May World Championship Barbecue Cooking Contest. Add in a plate-size, overloaded potato and this is a meal that only the heartiest appetites can tackle. I can assure you we have plenty of those, because on a good day 500 of these will be loaded down and hoisted through our order window. Many times we have just as many people working the potato bar as we have on the cutting boards!

SERVES 4	COOKING METHOD: Indirect heat	COOKING TIME: 1 hour 40 minutes

1 Build a charcoal fire for indirect cooking by situating the coals on only one side of the grill, leaving the other side empty. Preheat the grill to 450°F.

2 Wash the potatoes and wrap each of them in foil. Place the potatoes over indirect heat, away from the coals, close the grill lid, and cook until the potatoes soften, about 1 hour 30 minutes.

3 Transfer the potatoes to a cutting board. Cut a slit in the top of each potato and divide the butter, sour cream, cheese, scallions, and crumbled bacon among them. Top each potato with the leftover barbecue pork and serve.

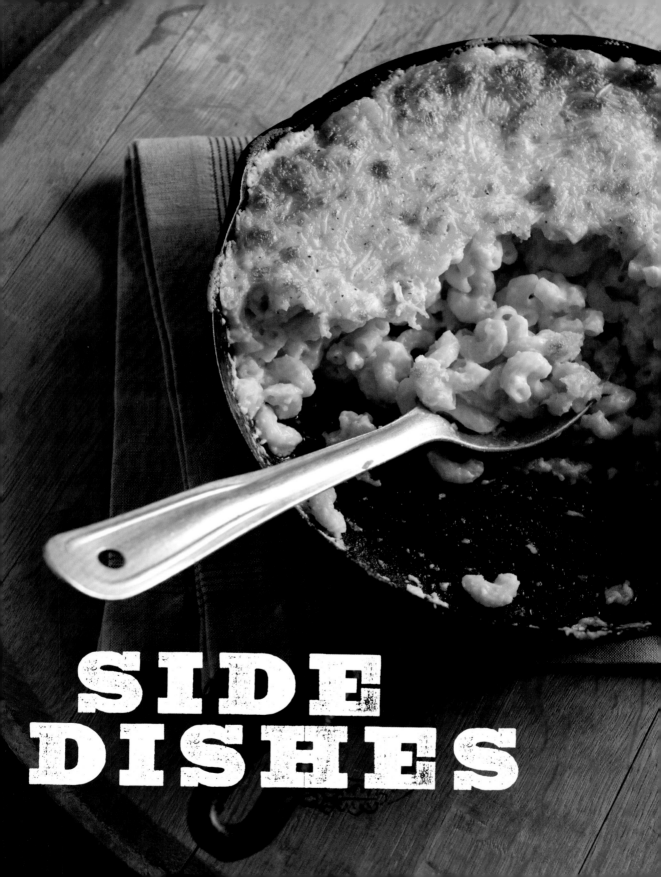

SIDE DISHES

YOUR COOKOUT JUST GOT A LOT MORE INTERESTING.

You know, the great thing about cooking barbecue is that you generally have plenty of downtime while the meat slowly simmers on the grill. With all of this extra time, there is no excuse not to create side dishes that are just as impressive as the main course. Ask anyone from the South—there is nothing better than a home-cooked "meat and three veggies," unless it's a meat and three veggies off the grill.

With a little strategy, grilled side dishes can be prepared at the same time and next to the main course on the outdoor cooker. By utilizing a two-zone fire, it is possible to do both direct and indirect cooking at the same time. On smokers with multiple racks, it is advantageous to cook side dishes below large-cut meats to catch the drippings, which really amps up both flavor and moisture.

This chapter is all about my favorite side dishes that go well with the main course. Along with each recipe will be recommended pairings with meat entrées, such as Drip-Pan Potatoes paired with Asian Smoked Duck (page 162), or Grilled Pickled Peaches paired with Marinated Pork Chops (page 141). The suggestions not only match complementary flavors, but they also optimize grill space and shorten cooking time. Your cookout just got a lot more interesting.

SPICY ASIAN COLESLAW
WITH GRILLED HOG JOWL

½ cup **canola oil**

2 tablespoons **soy sauce**

½ tablespoon **Dijon mustard**

¾ teaspoon **honey**

½ teaspoon plus ⅛ teaspoon **sesame oil**

¼ teaspoon fresh **lemon juice**

½ **jalapeño pepper**, seeded

½ tablespoon chopped fresh **ginger**

½ teaspoon chopped **garlic**

½ tablespoon **sambal oelek** (see page 100)

½ head **green cabbage**, shredded (5 cups)

1 **carrot**, shredded

1 **red bell pepper**, thinly sliced

Salt and freshly ground **black pepper**

HOG JOWL

½ cup **sugar**

2 tablespoons **chili powder**

½ teaspoon ground **cumin**

½ teaspoon **cayenne pepper**

½ teaspoon **salt**

½ pound **smoked hog jowl**

Let's keep the slaw party rolling with a unique fusion of foods that I love. This recipe combines the spicy and nutty flavors of an Asian dressing with the rich flavors of the Southern soul food I grew up with. The crisp vegetables and charred chewiness of the jowl are perfect complementary textures. Separately, the slaw and jowl are very good dishes, but together they are an extraordinary pair.

SERVES 6 TO 8

COOKING METHOD:
Direct heat

SUGGESTED WOOD:
Hickory, oak, mesquite
(see page 22)

CHILLING TIME:
30 minutes

COOKING TIME:
4 minutes

SERVE WITH:
Asian Smoked Duck (page 162) or Charcoal-Grilled Turkey (page 160)

1 In a food processer, combine the canola oil, soy sauce, mustard, honey, sesame oil, lemon juice, jalapeño, ginger, garlic, and sambal oelek and puree until smooth. Set aside.

2 In a large bowl, combine the cabbage, carrot, and bell pepper. Add the dressing and toss well. Season to taste with salt and pepper. Refrigerate for 30 minutes.

3 For the hog jowl: Build a charcoal fire for direct grilling and preheat it to 450°F.

4 In a medium bowl, combine the sugar, chili powder, cumin, cayenne, and salt. Slice the smoked hog jowl into ¼-inch-thick strips (similar to thick-cut bacon). Season liberally on both sides with the spice mixture.

5 Put the hog jowl over direct heat and grill until it is charred and browned, 1 to 2 minutes on each side. Transfer the jowl to a cutting board and cut it crosswise into matchsticks.

6 Serve the coleslaw topped with grilled hog jowl.

SERRANO PEPPER COLESLAW

½ head **green cabbage**, shredded

½ **red onion**, halved and thinly sliced

1 **carrot**, grated (½ cup)

3 **serrano peppers**, seeded and thinly sliced

½ cup **distilled white vinegar**

2 tablespoons **vegetable oil**

½ cup **sugar**

1½ teaspoons **salt**

1 teaspoon **dry mustard**

½ teaspoon ground **cumin**

This recipe is a good coleslaw choice if you are looking for a sweet side dish with a peppery bite. More often than not, when I make this recipe, I make a big batch—half for eating right away and half to use later as a topping for tacos or sandwiches. It's awesome on fish tacos and pulled pork sandwiches.

SERVES 6 TO 8

COOKING METHOD: None

SERVE WITH: Smoked Pork Shoulder Tacos (page 88) or Beer-Basted Pulled Pork Sliders (page 90)

In a large bowl, combine the cabbage, onion, carrot, peppers, vinegar, oil, sugar, salt, dry mustard, and cumin. Serve chilled or refrigerate in an airtight container for up to 5 days.

CREAMY CREOLE COLESLAW

Coleslaw is the most popular side dish for Southern barbecues. I think one reason has to be because it is quick and easy to make. Also, with a few heads of cabbage and some common ingredients, you can feed an army.

Everyone needs several types of coleslaw in their recipe arsenal. The decision on what slaw to make should be determined by what main dish is being served. This recipe is my go-to when I need a less-sweet creamy slaw. I use this recipe for dishes like taco salad, grilled pork pies, and grilled or fried catfish.

SERVES 6 TO 8

COOKING METHOD:
None

SERVE WITH:
Grilled Brick Panini (page 84) or Barbecue Chicken Thighs (page 156)

½ head **green cabbage**, shredded (5 cups)

1 **tomato**, chopped

½ **red onion**, finely chopped (1 cup)

½ **red bell pepper**, chopped (½ cup)

2 tablespoons finely chopped **celery**

1 tablespoon **sugar**

¾ cup **mayonnaise**

2½ tablespoons **sweet pickle relish**

2 tablespoons **Creole mustard**

4 teaspoons **cider vinegar**

½ teaspoon **salt**

⅛ teaspoon **hot sauce**

1   In a large bowl, combine the cabbage, tomato, onion, bell pepper, celery, and sugar and toss until the sugar dissolves.

2   In a separate bowl, combine the mayonnaise, relish, mustard, vinegar, salt, and hot sauce. Pour the dressing over the cabbage mixture and toss well. Serve chilled or refrigerate in an airtight container for up to 4 days.

DRIP-PAN POTATOES

The unique thing about this recipe is that the flavor of this dish changes based on what meat is paired with it, because the meat slowly cooks on a grate over the pan of potatoes. The flavorful drippings from the meat baste the potatoes and pool in the bottom of the pan. You can make the recipe with many large cuts of meat, including whole chicken, duck, beef brisket, beef ribs, pork butt (shoulder), and pork belly.

Stacking food in an outdoor cooker not only maximizes flavor but also saves cooking space and time, and it works with all kinds of vegetables. The cooking time is flexible and varies with the cooking time and temperature of the meat.

2 pounds **new potatoes**

4 tablespoons (½ stick) **unsalted butter**

¼ cup **extra-virgin olive oil**

2 teaspoons chopped fresh **rosemary**

2 teaspoons chopped fresh **thyme**

2 teaspoons **Veggie Seasoning** (page 249)

SERVES 6

COOKING METHOD:
Indirect heat

SUGGESTED WOOD:
Hickory, oak, maple
(see page 22)

COOKING TIME:
1 hour 30 minutes
to 2 hours
30 minutes

SERVE WITH:
Southern Man's
Beef Ribs
(page 136) or
Asian Smoked
Duck (page 162)

---

1 Build a charcoal fire for indirect cooking by situating the coals on only one side of the grill, leaving the other side empty.

2 Put the potatoes in a large baking pan in a single layer. (When selecting the pan size, take into consideration the shape of the meat that will be cooking above the pan.) In a small saucepan, melt the butter, then add the olive oil. Drizzle the butter and olive oil mixture over the potatoes; sprinkle the rosemary, thyme, and veggie seasoning evenly over the potatoes; and toss together.

3 Put the potato pan on the grill over indirect heat, directly under the rack that holds the large cut of meat. Close the grill lid and continue cooking the meat. While the juices are rendered from the meat, they will season the potatoes as they cook. The temperature at which you are cooking the meat will determine how long it takes for the potatoes to get done: 2 hours 30 minutes at 225°F, 2 hours at 250°F, or 1 hour 30 minutes at 300°F.

4 Remove the potatoes from the grill and serve in the baking pan family-style along with your meat of choice.

SMOKED CHEESE GRITS

1½ teaspoons **salt**

½ teaspoon freshly ground **black pepper**

½ teaspoon **garlic powder**

1½ cups **quick (5-minute) grits** (not instant)

1½ sticks (6 ounces) **unsalted butter**

8 ounces extra-sharp **cheddar cheese**, shredded (2 cups)

4 ounces **Muenster cheese**, shredded (1 cup)

⅓ cup **whole milk**

¾ teaspoon **Worcestershire sauce**

¾ teaspoon **hot sauce**

3 **eggs**, lightly beaten

What I like most about grits is not their Southern roots, but their versatility. There are not many dishes that can start your day as a side to a couple slices of thick-cut bacon, and then fill your belly for lunch, along with greens and cornbread, or provide a delicious bed for grilled shrimp on the dinner plate. So why are grits so underappreciated in America? Beats me. Maybe my version, which infuses the grits themselves with great smoky flavors, will help change some minds.

SERVES 8

COOKING METHOD:
Indirect heat

COOKING TIME:
1 hour

SERVE WITH:
Yuzu Shrimp Skewers (page 71) or Marinated Pork Chops (page 141)

1 Build a charcoal fire for indirect cooking by situating the coals on only one side of the grill, leaving the other side empty. Preheat the grill to 350°F.

2 In a large saucepan, combine 5 cups water, the salt, pepper, and garlic powder and bring the water to a boil over medium-high heat on the stovetop. Add the grits, cover the pan, reduce the heat to low, and simmer, stirring occasionally, until the grits thicken slightly, about 7 minutes. Remove the pan from the heat and stir in the butter, cheeses, milk, Worcestershire, and hot sauce. Let the grits cool until they are no longer hot to the touch, and then add the eggs.

3 Pour the mixture into a 10-inch cast iron skillet. Put the skillet on the grill over indirect heat, close the lid, and cook until the grits firm up and the top browns, about 50 minutes.

4 Remove the pan from the grill and serve hot.

STUFFED RED PEPPERS

WITH POTATO MASH

This recipe takes the idea of twice-baked potatoes to new heights. First, the potato shell is replaced by a hollowed bell pepper. Second, and most important, the element of fire lends a smoky flavor that the indoor oven can't achieve.

Although these will be some of the creamiest, richest mashed potatoes you have ever eaten, they will be at their best with a little gravy. Call it a Southern thing, but gravy makes everything better.

SERVES 6

COOKING METHOD:
Direct and indirect heat

COOKING TIME:
1 hour 50 minutes

SERVE WITH:
Barbecue Beef Short Ribs Adobo (page 131) or Barbecue Beef Brisket Flat (page 130)

4 extra-large **potatoes**

3 **red bell peppers**

1¾ cups **sour cream**

¼ cup **whole milk**

4 tablespoons (½ stick) **unsalted butter**

1 ounce **Gouda cheese**, shredded (¼ cup)

1 ounce **Muenster cheese**, shredded (¼ cup)

2 **scallions**, sliced, white and green parts kept separate

1½ teaspoons **salt**

¾ teaspoon freshly ground **black pepper**

1 Build a two-zone fire in a charcoal grill by situating the coals on only one side of the grill, leaving the other side empty. Preheat the grill to 400°F.

2 Scrub the potatoes and wrap them individually in foil. Put the potatoes over indirect heat, away from the coals, close the grill lid, and cook until soft, about 1 hour 30 minutes.

3 While the potatoes cook, cut the bell peppers in half vertically, beside or through the stem. Discard the ribs and seeds.

4 Remove the potatoes from the grill and let them cool for 10 minutes. Unwrap them and scoop the potato flesh out of the skins into a bowl. To the bowl, add the sour cream, milk, butter, cheeses, scallion whites, salt, and pepper. Mash and mix well.

5 Fill the peppers with the potato mixture. Put the stuffed peppers over indirect heat, close the grill lid, and cook for 15 minutes. Move the peppers to direct heat and cook until the peppers start to blister, about 5 minutes.

6 Transfer the peppers to a serving plate, garnish with the scallion greens, and serve immediately.

IRON SKILLET MACARONI & CHEESE

TOPPING

5 ounces **sharp cheddar cheese**, shredded (1¼ cups)

3 ounces **Muenster cheese**, shredded (¾ cup)

⅔ cup **mayonnaise**

1 teaspoon **Frank's Red Hot hot sauce**

¼ teaspoon **salt**

⅛ teaspoon freshly ground **black pepper**

1 (16-ounce) package **elbow macaroni**

8 tablespoons (1 stick) **unsalted butter**

8 ounces **Muenster cheese**, shredded (2 cups)

4 ounces **sharp cheddar cheese**, shredded (1 cup)

8 ounces sliced **Velveeta**

2 cups **half-and-half**

¼ teaspoon **salt**

After the continual disappointment of eating noodles swimming in cheeselike sauce served in restaurants all over the country, I set out to make the perfect "grown-up" mac and cheese. This task is a little easier said than done. The mandatory elements of the perfect mac and cheese, to me, are sharp, creamy, and toasty—but it sure is hard to translate these descriptors into a successful ingredient list and cooking technique! I can honestly say that noodles and cheese claimed a week of my life—2 weeks if you count the extra week of feeling miserable after sampling bowl after bowl of this not-so-healthy delight! My success was summed up on Food Network's *Best in Smoke* by Judge and Chef Tim Love when he said, "That is some *@&% #&$%* mac and cheese!"

SERVES 6 TO 8 COOKING METHOD: Indirect heat	SUGGESTED WOOD: No extra smoke advised COOKING TIME: 36 minutes	SERVE WITH: Apple Cider Ribs (page 142) or Split Chicken Halves (page 158)

1 Build a charcoal fire for indirect cooking by situating the coals on only one side of the grill, leaving the other side empty. Preheat the grill to 350°F.

2 For the topping: In a small bowl, combine the cheddar, Muenster, mayonnaise, hot sauce, salt, and pepper. Set aside.

3 Bring a medium pot of lightly salted water to a boil. Add the macaroni and cook until al dente, 6 to 7 minutes. Drain the macaroni and immediately return the noodles to the pot. Add the butter and stir until melted. Add the Muenster, cheddar, and Velveeta cheeses and stir until melted. Add the half-and-half and salt. Pour the macaroni mixture into a 10-inch cast iron skillet. Sprinkle the topping mixture evenly on top.

4 Put the skillet over indirect heat, away from the coals, close the grill lid, and cook until the topping is golden brown, about 30 minutes. Remove the skillet from the grill and serve hot.

GRILLED
RATATOUILLE

One of the questions most asked of me is, "Can you do more than just meat on the grill?" Outdoor cooking is not always about meat. As in this recipe, sometimes it's the vegetables that are the star of the grill. I like this recipe because it can be served as a side dish or as a main course. Grilled ratatouille is the perfect example of how you can cook anything outdoors that you would cook in an indoor kitchen, but with more flavor.

SERVES 10 TO 12

COOKING METHOD:
Direct and indirect heat

SUGGESTED WOOD:
Fruitwoods, hickory
(see page 22)

COOKING TIME:
1 hour

SERVE WITH:
Cowboy Ribeye
(page 116)
or Peach Tea
Smoked Rack of
Pork (page 148)

1 pound **Italian sausage**

3 **yellow squash**, cut lengthwise into ½-inch-wide slabs

2 **zucchini**, cut lengthwise into ½-inch-wide slabs

½ **eggplant**, cut lengthwise into ½-inch-wide slabs

2 **yellow bell peppers**, quartered

2 large **green bell peppers**, quartered

2 medium **onions**, cut into ½-inch-thick slices

Extra-virgin olive oil

Salt and freshly ground **black pepper**

1 cup **tomato juice**

1 (15-ounce) can **cannellini beans**, drained

4 **garlic cloves**, crushed

2 **thyme sprigs**

1 **rosemary sprig**

1 **bay leaf**

3 **plum tomatoes**, chopped

1 Build a two-zone fire in a charcoal grill by situating the coals on only one side of the grill, leaving the other side empty. Preheat the grill to 450°F.

2 Put the sausage over direct heat and grill until it's well browned, about 4 minutes on each side. Remove the sausage from the grill and set aside.

3 Lightly drizzle the vegetables with olive oil and season with salt and pepper. Grill the vegetables over direct heat until they soften and brown, about 2 minutes on each side. Remove the vegetables from the grill and chop them into ½-inch chunks. Put the vegetables into a 9 × 13-inch baking pan.

4 Cut the sausage into ¼-inch diced pieces and add to the baking pan. Add the tomato juice, cannellini beans, garlic, thyme, rosemary, bay leaf, and tomatoes.

5 Reduce the grill temperature to 300°F. Put the baking pan over indirect heat, away from the coals, close the grill lid, and cook until the juices begin to bubble and steam, about 35 minutes. Remove the baking pan from the grill and pour the vegetables into a colander set over a bowl to catch the juices. Pour the juices back into the baking pan, put the pan over direct heat, and simmer until reduced by half, about 12 minutes. Return the vegetables to the baking pan and stir well. Season with salt and pepper and serve.

GRILLED
ASPARAGUS
WITH PARMESAN-HERB BUTTER

4 tablespoons (½ stick) **unsalted butter**, at room temperature

1½ teaspoons **Dijon mustard**

¼ teaspoon fresh **lime juice**

¼ teaspoon **hot sauce**

2 teaspoons grated **Parmesan cheese**

½ teaspoon **garlic salt**

¼ teaspoon dried **thyme**

¼ teaspoon dried **parsley**

⅛ teaspoon freshly ground **black pepper**

1½ pounds **asparagus**, trimmed

There is no better example than this recipe of how outdoor cooking can add more flavor to a dish while cutting fat and calories. I challenge you to sauté asparagus indoors in a skillet and end up with something more delicious than the same vegetable infused with the flavor of hot coals. The charred taste that the open fire imparts as the melting butter hits the flame can't be matched.

SERVES 4 TO 6

COOKING METHOD:
Direct heat

SUGGESTED WOOD:
Maple, alder
(see page 22)

COOKING TIME:
6 minutes

SERVE WITH:
Pan-Seared
New York Strip
(page 119) or
Whole Smoked
Mahi-Mahi
(page 171)

1   Build a charcoal fire for direct grilling and preheat it to 450°F.

2   In a small bowl, combine the butter, mustard, lime juice, hot sauce, Parmesan, garlic salt, thyme, parsley, and pepper. Smear the butter evenly onto the asparagus.

3   Put the asparagus over direct heat and cook until it starts to soften and the exterior gets slightly charred and crispy, about 3 minutes on each side.

4   Transfer to a serving plate and serve hot.

Pitmaster Tip: I always keep compound butter in my refrigerator to accentuate the flavor of all types of recipes. The butter used in this dish is amazing, but don't stop there. Use your imagination and combine different herbs and seasonings to make your own recipe. Once made, put the butter on a piece of plastic wrap and roll it into a log. It will keep in the refrigerator for 2 weeks.

GRILLED OKRA

When you think of the perfect burger or sandwich, you probably picture a large stack of French fries or a mound of potato chips alongside it. So it seems that the most popular sandwich accompaniments are always crispy, salty, and not so healthy.

Well, there's a new sheriff in Burger Town! Grilled okra is now the star of the sandwich plates I make at home. The hot charcoal fire crisps the outer shell of the okra, while the well-balanced and salty Veggie Seasoning seasons it perfectly. It's a healthier complement to sandwiches, and can also be a tasty finger food on game day.

1 pound fresh **okra**
Extra-virgin olive oil, for brushing
Veggie Seasoning (page 249)

Pitmaster Tip: One of the most useful tools for the grill is a perforated grill pan or basket. When grilling small or chopped potatoes or vegetables, it keeps the veggies from falling through the grill grates and into the fire, while allowing the smoke and flame to have direct contact with the food. Charred vegetables are good; charcoal vegetables are not!

SERVES 6	SUGGESTED WOOD:	SERVE WITH:
	Maple, alder (see page 22)	The Perfect Burger (page 81) or Italian Smoked Pork Sandwich (page 86)
COOKING METHOD: Direct heat	COOKING TIME: 8 minutes	

1   Build a charcoal fire for direct grilling and preheat it to 400°F.

2   Lightly brush each piece of okra with olive oil. Coat all sides of the okra evenly with a generous amount of the rub. Put the okra on a perforated grill pan over direct heat and cook until it browns and is slightly charred, about 8 minutes, turning once.

3   Transfer the okra to a plate and serve hot.

GRILLED MEXICAN CORN

This recipe is a personal favorite and one of the easiest side dishes in this book. A traditional Mexican street food, it is made by coating sweet corn with mayonnaise, chili powder, and Cotija cheese. I decided to decrease the fat and amp up the flavor by cutting the mayonnaise with yogurt and lime juice, and by using a seasoning blend of chili powder, cumin, and cayenne pepper. Serve this delicious dish next to most any protein, or put it on a stick to make it a more portable tailgate food.

¾ cup **plain yogurt**

¾ cup **mayonnaise**

5 tablespoons fresh **lime juice**

4 ounces **Cotija cheese**, finely grated (1 cup)

4 teaspoons **chili powder**

2 teaspoons **cayenne pepper**

2 teaspoons ground **cumin**

1 teaspoon **salt**

8 ears **corn**, husks removed

SERVES 8

COOKING METHOD:
Direct heat

SUGGESTED WOOD:
Oak, mesquite
(see page 22)

COOKING TIME:
7 minutes

SERVE WITH:
Seasoned
Mustard
Drumsticks
(page 153) or
Spiral Sliced Ham
(page 151)

Pitmaster Tip: Don't worry about cooking too much Grilled Mexican Corn. Expect people to come back for seconds. If by chance you do have leftovers, don't throw away the extra ears. Carve the corn kernels off the cob and make Grilled Corn Pudding (page 210). The added dry rub and cheese only make the pudding better.

1 Build a charcoal fire for direct grilling and preheat it to 450°F.

2 In a small bowl, combine the yogurt, mayonnaise, and lime juice. In a separate small bowl, combine the cheese, chili powder, cayenne, cumin, and salt.

3 Grill the corn directly over direct heat, turning every 2 minutes, until the kernels start to soften, 6 to 7 minutes. Remove the corn from the grill and apply a light coat of the yogurt mixture to each ear.

4 Sprinkle each ear liberally with the cheese mixture and serve.

GRILLED CORN PUDDING

4 ears **corn**, husks removed

1½ sticks (6 ounces) **unsalted butter**, plus more for the dish

1 cup **heavy cream**

7 large **eggs**, beaten

¼ cup **all-purpose flour**

6 tablespoons **granulated sugar**

2 teaspoons **baking powder**

2 tablespoons **dark brown sugar**

¼ teaspoon ground **cinnamon**

Corn pudding is a somewhat obscure Southern dish that's hard to comprehend until you taste it. With a mixture of both sweet and savory flavors, it's quite versatile, as it makes a delicious stand-alone side dish, a great bed for a savory smoked entrée, or a surprisingly tasty dessert.

One of the tastiest corn puddings I've eaten was introduced to me by Ken Hess after we hired him to work at Big Bob Gibson Bar-B-Q. I'm guessing that his inspiration for this dish was born during his time cooking at The Greenbrier resort in West Virginia and not while a student at the Culinary Institute of America in New York. Thanks to a little leftover Grilled Mexican Corn, I realized an added grilled element could only improve this down-home dish. Now, this is corn pudding!

SERVES 12

COOKING METHOD:
Direct and
indirect heat

SUGGESTED WOOD:
No added wood

COOKING TIME:
36 minutes

SERVE WITH:
Charcoal-Seared
Trout Fillet
(page 166) or
St. Louis Cut
Spare Ribs
(page 144)

1 Build a two-zone fire in a charcoal grill by situating the coals on only one side of the grill, leaving the other side empty. Preheat the grill to 450°F.

2 Grill the corn over direct heat, turning every 2 minutes, until the kernels char and start to soften, about 6 minutes. Transfer the corn to a cutting board and let cool. Close the grill lid and reduce the grill temperature to 350°F.

3 In a medium saucepan, melt the butter on the stovetop over low heat. Stir in the cream, remove the pan from the heat, and let cool slightly. Add the beaten eggs.

4 In a small bowl, combine the flour, granulated sugar, and baking powder. Slowly whisk the flour mixture into the butter mixture until a loose batter forms. Using a sharp knife, cut the corn kernels from the cobs and add them to the batter.

5 In a separate bowl, combine the brown sugar and cinnamon.

6 Grease a 9 × 13-inch baking dish with butter. Pour the batter into the dish and put it over indirect heat, away from the coals. Close the grill lid and cook until the pudding firms slightly, about 15 minutes. Sprinkle the cinnamon sugar on the top of the pudding, close the grill lid, and cook until the top of the corn pudding turns golden brown, about 15 minutes.

7 Remove the dish from the grill and serve hot.

GRILLED

SWEET & SPICY PICKLES

What are grilled pickles? They do sound odd, but trust me, they're delicious! You take cucumbers and onion, grill them until they have a good amount of smoke and char, and then make homemade quick pickles with them. They're really beautiful and make excellent gifts. When people come to dinner, I like to set the pickles out in the center of the table as a sort of centerpiece—they're so much better than flowers because you can eat them!

1¼ cups **distilled white vinegar**

1 cup **sugar**

2 tablespoons **salt**

10 small **cucumbers** (4 to 5 inches long), quartered lengthwise

1 medium **onion**, halved and cut into ½-inch-thick slices

6 **dill sprigs**

3 **garlic cloves**, minced

3¾ teaspoons **red pepper flakes**

MAKES 3 PINTS

COOKING METHOD:
Direct heat

SUGGESTED WOOD:
Alder, maple, oak
(see page 22)

COOKING TIME:
14 minutes

SERVE WITH:
Barbecue Chicken
Salad (page 185)
or Grilled Brick
Panini (page 84)

1   In a medium saucepan, combine 1¼ cups water, the vinegar, sugar, and salt. Cook over medium-high heat until the sugar dissolves, about 4 minutes. Remove the pan from the heat, cover, and set aside.

2   Build a charcoal fire for direct grilling and preheat it to 500°F.

3   Grill the cucumbers over the hot coals until they char and slightly soften, about 2 minutes on each triangular side. Grill the onion slices until they char and slightly soften, about 2 minutes on each side. Divide the cucumbers and onions among 3 hot sterilized pint jars. Add 2 sprigs of the dill, one-third of the garlic, and 1¼ teaspoons red pepper flakes to each jar. Pour the pickling liquid evenly into each jar and tighten the sterilized lid. Let cool to room temperature before refrigerating. Serve chilled.

4   The pickles will keep refrigerated for 4 weeks.

GRILLED PICKLED PEACHES

2 teaspoons **pickling spices**

½ cup fresh **orange juice**

½ cup **maple syrup**

¼ cup **cider vinegar**

½ cup **sugar**

4 **peaches**, sliced

I accidently created this recipe when trying to come up with a glaze for pork chops. Originally, I pureed the peaches in a food processor and combined them with the glaze. The results were outstanding, but the peaches were so ripe and juicy I wasn't happy destroying them. That's when I decided I could achieve the same glaze flavor by creating a side dish instead. The sweet pickling syrup can do double duty, too, because you can use it as a glaze for grilled pork chops. Fire up the grill and save the peaches!

SERVES 4

COOKING METHOD:
Direct heat

COOKING TIME:
10 minutes

SERVE WITH:
Marinated Pork Chops (page 141) or Peach Tea Smoked Rack of Pork (page 148)

1 Build a charcoal fire for direct grilling and preheat it to 400°F.

2 Put the pickling spices in the center of a square of cheesecloth. Gather the edges of the cheesecloth and tie them together to form a small bag.

3 In a medium saucepan, combine the orange juice, maple syrup, vinegar, sugar, and the spice pouch. Bring the mixture to a boil over medium-high heat on the stovetop, then reduce the heat to medium-low. Add the peaches and simmer until they soften slightly, about 4 minutes.

4 Remove the peaches from the syrup and put them on the grill over direct heat. Grill the peaches until the syrup caramelizes and grill marks appear, about 2 minutes on each side.

5 Transfer the peaches to a serving plate and drizzle with the hot syrup. Serve hot.

GRILLED DESSERTS

FRUITS ARE THE PERFECT CHOICE FOR A GRILLED DESSERT.

Whenever desserts on the grill are mentioned I think of two things: fruit and a cast iron skillet. Fruits are the perfect choice for a grilled dessert because their natural sugars caramelize deliciously on the grill. The cast iron does a nice job cooking cakes and cobblers by evenly transferring heat no matter where the hot flame hits the pan. Be careful when cooking cakes and cobblers on a closed grill because it is easy to oversmoke them: The crumb quickly soaks up the smokiness. I also like how nice it is to serve a dessert family-style, right out of the skillet, and the desserts will stay warm for a while since cast iron retains the heat. It also means no more excuses to my wife about why her baking pans are stained black.

Another favorite of mine for the grill is hand pies. I call them grilled pies, though others might call them fruit empanadas. But one thing is for sure: These stuffed pastries are best when cooked over hot coals. The secret to a great grilled pie is the crust. Too much moisture and the dough will stick to the grate, but we certainly don't want a stiff, dry crust either. Once the crust is mastered, it's on to the fruit of choice. They're versatile, portable, and delicious.

OLD-FASHIONED GRILLED PEACH PIES

DOUGH

2½ cups **all-purpose flour**

½ teaspoon **salt**

2 sticks (½ pound) cold **unsalted butter**, cut into cubes

⅓ cup plus 1 tablespoon **ice cold water**

SUGAR RUB

¼ cup **granulated sugar**

½ teaspoon ground **cinnamon**

⅛ teaspoon **cayenne pepper**

Pinch of ground **nutmeg**

In the South, eyes light up at the mention of fried pies. Traditionally they're made by filling pie dough with a sweet fruit filling and frying them in a pan with butter until they're crispy and golden brown. But by grilling the peaches before making the filling, and then cooking the pies over hot charcoal, you can make this Southern dessert staple superior.

SERVES 8		SUGGESTED WOOD:		CHILLING TIME:
COOKING METHOD:		No added wood		Overnight
Direct heat				COOKING TIME:
				10 minutes

1   For the dough: In a small bowl, combine the flour and salt. Cut in the butter (using two knives slicing in opposite directions and breaking the butter up in the flour mixture) until the mixture resembles coarse crumbs. Slowly add the ice water, mixing constantly, until a ball of dough is formed. Put the dough ball in a medium bowl, cover with plastic wrap, and refrigerate overnight.

2   Unwrap the dough and put it on a floured work surface. Using a floured rolling pin, roll it out until it is ⅛ inch thick. Cut the dough into rounds 5 to 6 inches in diameter. Reroll any scraps to cut out a total of 8 rounds. Pick up and flip the dough rounds to make sure they don't stick.

3   Build a charcoal fire for direct grilling and preheat it to 400°F.

4   For the sugar rub: In a medium bowl, combine the sugar, cinnamon, cayenne, and nutmeg. Set aside.

RECIPE CONTINUES

FILLING

2 pounds ripe **peaches** (3 large or
    4 medium)

1 tablespoon **salted butter**

6 tablespoons **light brown sugar**

3 tablespoons **all-purpose flour**

1 tablespoon fresh **orange juice**

Oil, for the grill grates

5 For the filling: Peel the peaches, remove the pits, and cut each peach into 8 wedges. Toss the peach wedges with the sugar rub. Immediately put the peaches on a grill pan over direct heat and grill until they caramelize, about 2 minutes per side. Transfer the peaches to a cutting board and cut them into ½-inch pieces. Transfer the peaches to a medium bowl, add the butter, and let sit until the butter melts. Add the brown sugar and flour. Stir in the orange juice.

6 Put 2 heaping tablespoons of the filling onto the center of each round of dough. Lightly moisten the edges of the dough with water. Fold the dough in half to create a half-moon. Gently press the pie edges together and crimp them with a fork to seal.

7 Lightly brush the grill grates with oil. Grill the pies over direct heat until the dough turns a crispy golden brown, about 3 minutes on each side. Serve hot.

IRON SKILLET APPLE COBBLER

Employee family meals at Big Bob Gibson Bar-B-Q are not organized or scheduled; they just seem to happen. If someone is tired of barbecue and decides to cook, they sometimes graciously cook extra so everyone scheduled to work that day can enjoy a sample. This gives the staff a "barbecue break" and allows for cooking creativity. A typical day in the kitchen finds Jim at the oven with steaming pans of country cooking. Debbie bakes up a cake or cookies to celebrate a birthday or special occasion. Every so often, Jane will even put a cobbler in the oven. The simple everyday things, like eating with friends and family, give me inspiration and fresh ideas. Jane's cobbler is clearly the inspiration here, as I couldn't help but take the idea and put it on the grill.

2 cups plus 2½ tablespoons **granulated sugar**

1½ tablespoons **light brown sugar**

¼ teaspoon ground **cinnamon**

Pinch of ground **nutmeg**

2 pounds **Rome** or **Granny Smith apples**, peeled, cored, and cut into wedges (5 cups)

2 sticks (½ pound) **salted butter**, plus more for the skillet

2 cups **whole milk**

½ teaspoon **vanilla extract**

2 cups **self-rising flour**

SERVES 8 TO 10

COOKING METHOD:
Indirect heat

SUGGESTED WOOD:
No added wood

COOKING TIME:
1 hour

1 Build a charcoal fire for indirect cooking by situating the coals on only one side of the grill, leaving the other side empty. Preheat the grill to 350°F.

2 Butter a 10-inch cast iron skillet. In a medium bowl, combine 2½ tablespoons of the granulated sugar, the brown sugar, cinnamon, and nutmeg. Add the apple slices, toss to coat evenly, and pour into the skillet.

3 In a large saucepan, melt the 2 sticks butter on the stovetop over low heat. Remove the pan from the heat and add the milk, vanilla, flour, and remaining 2 cups sugar. Stir the mixture together but do not blend. Pour the mixture over the apples. Place the skillet over indirect heat, away from the coals, close the grill lid, and cook until the cobbler is golden brown on top, about 1 hour.

4 Serve hot right out of the skillet.

IRON SKILLET
BLACKBERRY COBBLER

I love cobbler because it's so versatile—and every iteration is delicious. Big, ripe blackberries picked in the height of summer are my favorite fruit for this dish. But don't stop with blackberries, because the combinations of fruit are endless. Try adding peaches or apricots, or make a mixed berry cobbler by including raspberries, blueberries, and/or strawberries. While you experiment, I'll stick with this one!

2 sticks (½ pound) **salted butter**, plus more for the skillet

2 cups **whole milk**

½ teaspoon **vanilla extract**

2 cups **self-rising flour**

2 cups **sugar**

5 cups **blackberries**

SERVES 8 TO 10

COOKING METHOD:
Indirect heat

SUGGESTED WOOD:
No added wood

COOKING TIME:
1 hour

1 Build a charcoal fire for indirect cooking by situating the coals on only one side of the grill, leaving the other side empty. Preheat the grill to 350°F.

2 In a large saucepan, melt the 2 sticks butter over low heat. Remove the pan from the heat and add the milk, vanilla, flour, and sugar. Stir together but do not blend.

3 Butter a 10-inch cast iron skillet. Put the blackberries in the bottom of the skillet and pour the batter over them. Put the skillet over indirect heat, away from the coals, close the grill lid, and cook until the cobbler is golden brown on top, about 1 hour.

4 Serve hot right from the skillet.

GRILLED
PINEAPPLE UPSIDE-DOWN CAKE

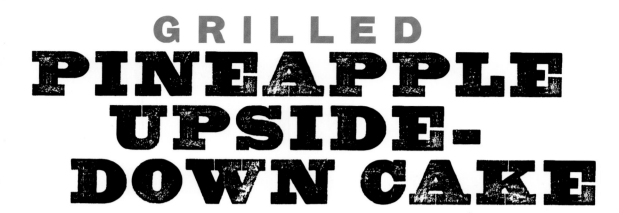

1 (20-ounce) can juice-packed **pineapple slices**, drained, juice reserved

4 tablespoons (½ stick) **unsalted butter**

¼ cup chopped **pecans**

¾ cup packed **dark brown sugar**

¾ cup **all-purpose flour**

¾ teaspoon **baking powder**

Pinch of ground **cinnamon**

Pinch of **salt**

2 large **eggs**, separated

¾ cup **granulated sugar**

¾ teaspoon **vanilla extract**

There are very few dessert presentations prettier or more delicious looking than a pineapple upside-down cake. It's one of those dishes that you just hate to cut! Years ago, knife in hand, I stood in a mesmerized stupor looking at a freshly baked pineapple upside-down cake, and I thought, "Something is missing." The pineapples didn't have grill marks and lacked the charred notes and caramelization of flame-kissed fruit. Instantly I knew how to take this dessert staple to the next level by combining what I know with what I love.

SERVES 8 TO 10		
COOKING METHOD: Direct and indirect heat	SUGGESTED WOOD: No added wood	COOKING TIME: 47 minutes

1 Build a two-zone fire in a charcoal grill by situating the coals on only one side of the grill, leaving the other side empty. Preheat the grill to 400°F.

2 Put 8 pineapple slices over direct heat and cook until grill marks are visible, about 1 minute on each side. Remove the pineapple and set aside. Close the grill lid and reduce the temperature to 350°F.

3 In a 10-inch cast iron skillet on the stovetop, melt the butter. Put the grilled pineapple slices in a single layer on the bottom of the skillet. Sprinkle the chopped pecans over the pineapple slices, followed by the brown sugar.

4 In a medium bowl, whisk together the flour, baking powder, cinnamon, and salt.

5 Using an electric mixer, beat the egg whites until they form stiff peaks.

6 In a separate medium bowl, beat the egg yolks, then beat in ½ cup of the reserved pineapple juice, the granulated sugar, and vanilla. Gradually add the flour mixture. Using a rubber spatula, fold in the egg whites.

7 Pour the batter into the skillet over the pineapple. Put the skillet over indirect heat, away from the coals, close the grill lid, and cook until the cake is golden brown on top and a wooden pick inserted in the center of the cake comes out clean, about 45 minutes. Remove the skillet from the grill and let cool for 10 minutes.

8 Use a knife to loosen the edges of the cake. Turn the cake out on a serving plate and serve hot.

SAUCES & DRY RUBS

THEY'RE VERSATILE & FUN TO MIX AND MATCH

How could a barbecue and grilling book be complete without sauces and dry rubs? Any of these all-purpose beauties can be made ahead of time and used for all-weekend barbecues or last-minute meal ideas. Whether your intention is to feed a family, impress the neighbors, or win a World Barbecue Championship, the recipes in this chapter are invaluable.

Most all of the goodies in this chapter are used in at least one recipe in this book. Feel free to use them in combination with one another, like I do in some of the recipes. They're versatile and fun to mix and match. That said, unless you're an experienced barbecue cook, you shouldn't freely alter the ingredients in the sauces and rubs. Once you get an understanding of how the seasonings work with one another and with the meat they're paired with, then you can start fiddling.

ROSEMARY & FIG
BARBECUE SAUCE

1½ cups **port**

¾ cup **black cherry juice**

4 **Black Mission figs**

1 **rosemary sprig**

1 cup **distilled white vinegar**

¾ cup plus 2 tablespoons **Heinz ketchup**

1 teaspoon **honey**

¾ cup **dark brown sugar**

1 tablespoon **chili powder**

1¾ teaspoons **kosher salt**

1¼ teaspoons freshly ground **black pepper**

½ teaspoon **cayenne pepper**

This recipe might just be my favorite sauce creation in the book. The uniqueness of the ingredients is outstanding, and it's great as a sauce or glaze for pork, lamb, or chicken. The inspiration for this recipe came from a good friend, Scotty Bragwell. He is an avid outdoor cook who especially loves things that cook all day, low and slow. One evening he brought a pork butt and homemade barbecue sauce to a dinner party. Without trying to sound egotistical, it was a very bold move considering he knew I was going to be there. Needless to say, I was impressed, especially with the simplistic goodness and depth of his traditional barbecue sauce. He enthusiastically shared the recipe when I told him I would like to put it in my new book. I can't wait to see his face when he finds out I added port wine, black cherry juice, figs, and rosemary to his secret sauce. Gotcha, Scotty!

MAKES 2¼ CUPS	COOKING METHOD: Stovetop	COOKING TIME: 35 minutes

1 In a medium saucepan, combine the port, black cherry juice, figs, and rosemary. In a separate medium saucepan, combine the vinegar, ketchup, honey, brown sugar, chili powder, salt, black pepper, and cayenne. Bring each pan to a boil over high heat. Reduce the heat to medium and simmer both mixtures, stirring occasionally, until each is reduced by half, about 30 minutes.

2 Remove the pans from the heat. Remove the figs and rosemary from the port mixture and discard. Pour the port mixture into the vinegar mixture. Use immediately or store in an airtight container in the refrigerator for up to 2 weeks.

BIG BOB GIBSON WHITE SAUCE #2

1¼ cups **Duke's mayonnaise**

¾ cup **distilled white vinegar**

1 teaspoon fresh **lemon juice**

1 tablespoon coarsely ground **black pepper**

1 teaspoon **sugar**

1 teaspoon **salt**

There are as many white barbecue sauce recipes as there are brands of mayonnaise. Although I'm not quite sure where mayonnaise originated, I do know where barbecue white sauce came from. Big Bob Gibson was baptizing his whole split chickens in this tangy, peppery sauce back in 1925 in Decatur, Alabama. The many white sauce recipes gracing restaurant tabletops and grocery store shelves across the country are tweaked versions of his original sauce. It's time to add one more version to the mix, and it happens to be a favorite of mine.

MAKES 2 CUPS

In a medium bowl, combine the mayonnaise, vinegar, lemon juice, pepper, sugar, and salt. Use immediately or store in an airtight container in the refrigerator for up to 2 weeks.

SPICY MAYONNAISE

1 cup **mayonnaise**

4 teaspoons **ketchup**

1 teaspoon fresh **lemon juice**

1 teaspoon **maple syrup**

½ teaspoon **Worcestershire sauce**

½ teaspoon prepared **horseradish**

½ teaspoon **cayenne pepper**

½ teaspoon **salt**

¼ teaspoon freshly ground **black pepper**

¼ teaspoon **garlic powder**

¼ teaspoon **chili powder**

¼ teaspoon dried **dill**

This recipe is not only a tasty condiment for sandwiches but also a delicious dipping sauce for vegetables. It's good on everything from beef brisket sandwiches to fish tacos. But my favorite way to enjoy spicy mayonnaise is as a dipping sauce for Smoked Artichokes (page 52).

MAKES 1 CUP

In a small bowl, combine the mayonnaise, ketchup, lemon juice, maple syrup, Worcestershire sauce, horseradish, cayenne, salt, black pepper, garlic powder, chili powder, and dried dill. Use immediately or store in an airtight container in the refrigerator for up to 2 weeks.

BARBECUE HOLLANDAISE SAUCE

2 **egg yolks**

¾ teaspoon **distilled white vinegar**

11 tablespoons **unsalted butter,** melted

⅛ teaspoon **salt**

Pinch of **cayenne pepper**

2 tablespoons of your favorite store-bought **barbecue sauce**

If Hollandaise is one of the five mother sauces of French cuisine, then what the heck is it doing in a barbecue book? I'm a nondiscriminatory pitmaster. If there is an ingredient or sauce available that will make my barbecue taste better, you will find me grinding star anise or whipping eggs until my arm falls off.

The simple adjustment of changing white wine to vinegar and adding cayenne pepper and barbecue sauce to the traditional Hollandaise recipe makes this sauce a better match for barbecue dishes. It's fantastic on Barbecue Beef Brisket Benedict (page 178) or your favorite steak.

MAKES 1½ CUPS	COOKING METHOD: Stovetop	COOKING TIME: 10 minutes

1   In a stainless steel bowl, combine the egg yolks, vinegar, and ¾ teaspoon water. Vigorously whisk the mixture until it has thickened and doubled in volume. Put the bowl over a saucepan of barely simmering water (just below a boil); the bottom of the stainless bowl should not touch the water. Whisk constantly, making sure the eggs don't get too hot or they will scramble. While whisking constantly, very slowly drizzle the melted butter into the mixture and cook, whisking, until the mixture thickens and doubles in volume, 8 to 10 minutes.

2   Remove the bowl from the heat, stir in the salt, cayenne, and barbecue sauce and serve immediately. Unfortunately, the sauce won't keep, so it should be used right away.

BLACK BEAN BARBECUE SAUCE

The unique flavor and versatility of this recipe make it one of my favorites in the book. I've served this recipe on catering jobs from the Florida coast to California. Grilled chicken breakfast burritos with scrambled eggs, cheddar cheese, and this sauce were a hit at the NASCAR garage at the Daytona 500. Pulled pork tacos with shredded cheese, grilled guacamole, pico de gallo, and this sauce got rave reviews at Seghesio Vineyards in Healdsburg, California. I keep a bottle handy in my refrigerator for topping nachos, burgers, or morning eggs.

MAKES 3 CUPS	COOKING METHOD: Stovetop	COOKING TIME: 20 minutes

3 tablespoons **distilled white vinegar**

2 tablespoons **molasses**

1 (14-ounce) can **stewed tomatoes**

1 cup **black beans**, canned or fresh cooked

½ cup packed **dark brown sugar**

2 **serrano peppers**, seeded

1 **garlic clove**

1 tablespoon chopped fresh **chives**

1¼ teaspoons **red chile paste**

1 teaspoon **salt**

½ teaspoon freshly ground **black pepper**

1   In a blender or food processor, combine the vinegar, molasses, tomatoes, beans, brown sugar, serrano peppers, garlic, chives, red chile paste, salt, and black pepper. Blend until the sauce is smooth.

2   Pour the mixture into a saucepan and bring to a low boil over high heat. Reduce the heat to medium and simmer, stirring often, until it has reduced by one-fourth, about 20 minutes.

3   Use warm or store in an airtight container in the refrigerator for up to 1½ weeks. Reheat before serving.

ESPRESSO

BBQ SAUCE

If white sauce is at one extreme of barbecue sauces, this one is the polar opposite. It has a powerful depth of flavor and should appeal to people who fancy dark chocolate or dark beer. The rich intensity of this sauce works equally well with chicken, pork, and beef, or as an ingredient in mole sauce. It can even be used as a braising liquid, though it will become even more intense and rich.

MAKES 2 CUPS	COOKING METHOD: Stovetop	COOKING TIME: 35 minutes

In a medium saucepan, combine the ketchup, vinegar, espresso, corn syrup, Worcestershire sauce, molasses, soy sauce, brown sugar, cocoa powder, chili powder, onion powder, dry mustard, garlic powder, cayenne, black pepper, and salt. Bring to a boil over high heat, reduce the heat to medium, and simmer, stirring occasionally, until the sauce is reduced by half, about 30 minutes. Use immediately or store in an airtight container in the refrigerator for up to 2 weeks.

1 cup **ketchup**

⅓ cup **cider vinegar**

6 tablespoons **strong brewed espresso**

6 tablespoons **dark corn syrup**

¼ cup **Worcestershire sauce**

1 tablespoon **molasses**

1 teaspoon **soy sauce**

¾ cup packed **dark brown sugar**

2 teaspoons **dark unsweetened cocoa powder**

1¼ teaspoons **chili powder**

½ teaspoon **onion powder**

½ teaspoon **dry mustard**

½ teaspoon **garlic powder**

¼ teaspoon **cayenne pepper**

¼ teaspoon freshly ground **black pepper**

¼ teaspoon **salt**

15-MINUTE BARBECUE SAUCE

½ cup **distilled white vinegar**

⅓ cup **cider vinegar**

⅓ cup **Worcestershire sauce**

1 tablespoon **Hog Shake** (page 249)

1 cup **ketchup**

¼ cup **tomato paste**

¼ cup **maple syrup**

2 tablespoons **cherry jalapeño jelly**

1 tablespoon **honey**

1 tablespoon **molasses**

¼ teaspoon **Sriracha hot sauce**

1¼ cups packed **dark brown sugar**

In 2012, I competed along with my right-hand man, Ken "Big Hoss" Hess, on Food Network's *Best in Smoke*. Our stint on this reality cooking show was filled with quick-fire challenges, mystery ingredient baskets, races to the refrigerated truck for meats, catering at Yankee Stadium and on Broadway, and long hours of outdoor cooking. I felt like I had run a marathon and triathlon back-to-back after this grueling weeklong competition.

I made it to the finale, and everything fell into place when I was given whole bone-in pork butt to cook for the judges. I was also given two other meats that make common appearances on my grill: flank steak and pork tenderloin. I was set up for victory but knew the producers would throw one more curveball. We'd been teased with a 15-minute barbecue sauce challenge with limited pantry ingredients, so I was expecting that. This recipe was going through my mind when the last challenge was revealed: tofu.

I've cooked just about everything on my outdoor cooker but tofu is not one of them. I don't think you can even buy tofu in Alabama! You know, second place is not too bad against stiff competition, but I will always wonder what would have happened if they had let us make sauce instead.

Cherry jalapeño jelly is a delicious thing that you can get at www.TexasPepperJelly.com, or you can mix cherry jelly and jalapeño jelly together.

MAKES 3½ CUPS	COOKING METHOD: Stovetop	COOKING TIME: 10 minutes CHILLING TIME: 30 minutes

1 In a nonreactive medium saucepan, combine the vinegars, Worcestershire sauce, and Hog Shake. Bring to a boil over high heat and cook until reduced by half, about 10 minutes.

2 Remove the pan from the heat and stir in the ketchup, tomato paste, maple syrup, jelly, honey, molasses, hot sauce, and brown sugar. Pour the sauce into an airtight container and refrigerate for 30 minutes before using. The sauce will keep in an airtight container in the refrigerator for up to 2 weeks.

SHOCK TOP
HONEY MUSTARD GLAZE

This recipe was originally intended to be a pork belly glaze. I wanted a sauce that would balance the high fat of the belly with a bold acidic sweetness. It was an absolute success. I was so impressed with this sauce that I've since used it on chicken wings and as a turkey breast glaze. Perhaps my favorite use is as a condiment on grilled sweet bacon BLT sandwiches that I served in Oakland, California, at the Eat Real Festival.

MAKES 1 QUART

1 In a nonreactive bowl, combine the beer, vinegars, mustard seeds, salt, pepper, allspice, cinnamon, cloves, and nutmeg. Cover and let the mixture sit at room temperature until the mustard seeds soften, 1 to 2 days.

2 Pour the mixture into a food processor and puree either briefly to a coarse-grain mustard or for longer until you get a smooth mustard. Stir in the honey. Use immediately or store in an airtight container in the refrigerator for up to 6 months.

¾ cup **Shock Top beer**

¼ cup **balsamic vinegar**

¼ cup **distilled white vinegar**

¾ cup **black mustard seeds**

1½ teaspoons **kosher salt**

½ teaspoon freshly ground **black pepper**

⅛ teaspoon ground **allspice**

⅛ teaspoon ground **cinnamon**

⅛ teaspoon ground **cloves**

⅛ teaspoon ground **nutmeg**

2¾ cups **honey**

BIG HOSS' COGNAC MUSHROOM CREAM SAUCE

1 tablespoon **unsalted butter**

1 cup **cremini mushrooms,** quartered

¼ cup **shallots**, minced (about 1½ **shallots**)

1 **garlic clove**, minced

½ cup **Cognac**

¼ cup **beef brisket drippings** (from Barbecue Beef Brisket Flat, page 130) or beef broth

2 cups **heavy cream**

½ teaspoon **kosher salt**

¼ teaspoon freshly ground **black pepper**

⅛ teaspoon **cayenne pepper**

Big Hoss, otherwise known as Ken Hess, showed up on the doorstep of Big Bob Gibson Bar-B-Q in 2009. His culinary background is as diverse as barbecue itself, so we decided that a Big Hoss in the kitchen could not be a bad thing. He graduated from Oklahoma State with a degree in Hotel and Restaurant Management and then went on to culinary school at the CIA in Hyde Park, New York. I first met him at The Greenbrier resort in West Virginia, where he did his apprenticeship and was the Catering Chef and Barbecue Pitmaster.

I've always found Big Hoss helpful in discussing recipe ideas, making sure I don't fall into a culinary rut with predictable ingredients, and most of all, as a second set of taste buds. I've grown to value his opinion and trust him to execute my recipes flawlessly.

I wish I could tell you how we spent days collaborating on this wonderful recipe, but I can't. This is a Big Hoss original. It's a beautiful thing drizzled over Smoked Montreal Beef Tenderloin (page 132) or on a charcoal-grilled steak.

MAKES 2 CUPS	COOKING METHOD: Stovetop	COOKING TIME: 17 minutes

In a medium skillet, melt the butter over medium heat. Add the mushrooms and cook, stirring, until they soften slightly, 3 to 4 minutes. Add the shallots and garlic and cook until the shallots are translucent, about 1 minute. Remove the skillet from the heat and add the Cognac. Immediately return the pan to the heat and ignite the Cognac, using a long barbecue lighter, at the edge of the pan. Cook until the flames die and the liquid is almost gone, about 2 minutes. Add the brisket drippings (or broth) and simmer for 4 minutes. Add the cream and simmer until the mixture thickens, about 10 minutes. Add the salt, black pepper, and cayenne. Serve immediately or store in an airtight container in the refrigerator for up to 4 days. Reheat before serving.

GREEN CHILE SALSA

Warning, this green chile salsa ranges from hot to spicy hot depending on what variety of pepper you select! Unlike many hot sauces on the market, this condiment wasn't made by a chili head in an Arizona laboratory. Flavor takes precedence over spice in this recipe, and you can adjust the heat by adding or removing a pepper or two. Use this recipe anywhere you would enjoy salsa, but don't miss trying it with Southwest Smoked Brisket Hash (page 180).

20 fresh **tomatillos**, husk removed

4 **Anaheim peppers**, stems removed

9 **jalapeño peppers**, stems removed

2 tablespoons fresh **lemon juice**

4 **garlic cloves**

2 teaspoons **salt**

MAKES 1 QUART	COOKING METHOD:	COOKING TIME:
	Stovetop	20 minutes

1   In a medium pot, combine the tomatillos and all of the peppers with water to cover. Bring to a boil over high heat, reduce the heat to medium, and simmer until tender, about 20 minutes.

2   Drain the vegetables and transfer them to a blender or food processor. Add the lemon juice, garlic, and salt. Puree until the salsa is the consistency you desire. Serve immediately or store in an airtight container in the refrigerator for up to 1 week.

CHIMICHURRI SAUCE

WITH GRILLED JALAPEÑOS

2 jalapeño peppers

3½ tablespoons **red wine vinegar**

1 tablespoon fresh **lemon juice**

1½ cups chopped fresh **parsley**

6 **garlic cloves**

2 tablespoons finely chopped **red onion**

2 tablespoons chopped fresh **oregano**

1 teaspoon **salt**

¾ teaspoon freshly ground **black pepper**

¼ teaspoon **red pepper flakes**

⅔ cup **extra-virgin olive oil**

Chimichurri is an Argentinian sauce used to top grilled meat. I've found that its acidic flavor works well with beef, fish, and chicken, and is also great as a dip for grilled vegetables or as a sandwich condiment. It can even be used as a high-impact quick marinade.

The ingredients in a typical chimichurri are garlic, parsley, olive oil, oregano, and vinegar. Everything else is optional, so creativity is endless. I added grilled jalapeños, red onions, and a combination of black and crushed red peppers to get the taste I was looking for.

MAKES 2½ CUPS	COOKING METHOD: Direct heat	COOKING TIME: 4 minutes

1 Build a charcoal fire for direct grilling and preheat it to 500°F.

2 Put the peppers over direct heat and grill until they are charred, 1 to 2 minutes on each side. Remove the peppers from the grill and immediately wrap them in plastic wrap.

3 In a food processor, combine the vinegar, lemon juice, parsley, garlic, red onion, oregano, salt, black pepper, and red pepper flakes. Remove the jalapeños from the plastic wrap, peel off the charred skin, remove the seeds and core, and add the peppers to the food processor. Blend until the ingredients are coarsely chopped. With the processor running, add the olive oil and blend until smooth. Serve immediately or store in an airtight container in the refrigerator for up to 1 week.

PEACH TEA BRINE

1 (32-ounce) bottle **Snapple Peach Tea**

½ cup plus 3 tablespoons **salt**

¼ cup **sugar**

4 **garlic cloves**, crushed

4 sprigs fresh **thyme**

2 **rosemary sprigs**

2 **bay leaves**

2 teaspoons freshly ground **black pepper**

It's obvious that where someone grows up has direct influence on where they stand on the regional barbecue debate. Barbecue, politics, and religion are the three things most likely to incite a riot in Alabama—well, those and college football. Where I come from, pork is king, and I've always subconsciously let that influence my grilling habits.

This brine has thrown me into a huge rut I can't seem to climb out of. Whether I'm working with pork tenderloin, loin, bellies, or ham, it's my favorite option for flavor. I use it as a brine on smaller meats but switch to injecting this solution into large meats or when in a time crunch. There's nothing overpowering here, only a pleasing herbal flavor that complements barbecue pork.

MAKES 3½ CUPS	COOKING TIME:	COOLING AND CHILLING TIME:
COOKING METHOD: **Stovetop**	**15 minutes**	**1 hour**

1 In a medium saucepan, combine the tea, salt, sugar, garlic, thyme, rosemary, bay leaves, and pepper. Bring the liquid to a boil over high heat, reduce the heat to low, and simmer for 10 minutes to reduce the liquid slightly. Remove the pan from the heat and let cool for 30 minutes.

2 Strain the liquid and chill for 30 minutes before using. Or store in an airtight container in the refrigerator for up to 1 month.

COFFEE CHOP
DRY RUB

This is simply the best coffee rub I've ever tasted. I call it a chop rub because it's good on a thick-cut pork chop as on a juicy steak. I never use a crossover seasoning blend for two different meats without tweaking the ratios, but there is no need to with this rub. If you like coffee and meat, this is a happy day!

MAKES ½ CUP

In a small bowl, combine the salt, coffee, brown sugar, chili powder, black pepper, onion powder, garlic powder, cayenne, coriander, and turmeric. The rub will keep in an airtight container at room temperature for 6 months.

7 teaspoons **salt**

4½ teaspoons **ground coffee**

4 teaspoons **dark brown sugar**

4 teaspoons **chili powder**

1½ teaspoons freshly ground **black pepper**

1 teaspoon **onion powder**

1 teaspoon **garlic powder**

½ teaspoon **cayenne pepper**

Pinch of ground **coriander**

Pinch of ground **turmeric**

STEER GEAR
RUB

My job has afforded me the pleasure of traveling the country and cooking in some of the most amazing places; but with pleasure comes pain, since the logistics of cooking in another city with someone else's grill usually takes more time to work through than the trip itself. When beef is on the menu, I have to take my steer gear, and this rub is an essential part of it.

The salt-to-sugar ratio for beef differs from anything I use on pork. Notice the salt-to-sugar ratio in this rub compared to the 50/50 ratio of a pork rub. The meats are different and have to be treated as such. Steer gear rub is tasty on any beef, but I especially like it on steak.

MAKES ⅔ CUP

In a small bowl, combine the kosher salt, paprika, black pepper, garlic powder, Accent (if using), coriander, sugar, onion salt, celery salt, turmeric, cayenne, and nutmeg. The rub will keep in an airtight container at room temperature for 6 months.

8½ teaspoons **kosher salt**

4½ teaspoons **paprika**

4 teaspoons freshly ground **black pepper**

1 tablespoon **garlic powder**

1 tablespoon **Accent** (optional; see Pitmaster Tip, page 137)

1½ teaspoons ground **coriander**

1½ teaspoons **sugar**

1 teaspoon **onion salt**

1 teaspoon **celery salt**

1 teaspoon **turmeric**

1 teaspoon **cayenne pepper**

½ teaspoon ground **nutmeg**

SWEET CRISP BACON RUB

I promised myself I would not release this rub mix publicly. The problem is, after serving it so many times all over the country, it has generated more of a mad-food publicity love fest than any other recipe I've done! I guess it can't hurt that bacon is involved. So, do I lie to myself or to all the people I've thanked for the compliments and asked to wait for my next book? Either way, I think I'm out of the woods now.

MAKES ⅔ CUP

½ cup **sugar**
2 tablespoons **chili powder**
½ teaspoon ground **cumin**
½ teaspoon **cayenne pepper**
½ teaspoon **salt**

In a small bowl, combine the sugar, chili powder, cumin, cayenne, and salt. The rub will keep in an airtight container at room temperature for 6 months.

CREOLE SPICE RUB

2 teaspoons **salt**

1½ teaspoons **garlic powder**

1½ teaspoons **paprika**

1 teaspoon **onion powder**

1 teaspoon dried **thyme**

1 teaspoon dried **oregano**

1 teaspoon freshly ground **black pepper**

¾ teaspoon **cayenne pepper**

½ teaspoon ground **cumin**

½ teaspoon **dry mustard**

Pitmaster Tip: Turn your Creole Spice Rub into an awesome blackened butter grill baste by adding a few extra ingredients. Combine ¼ cup of the rub with 1 cup melted butter, ½ teaspoon fresh lemon juice, ½ teaspoon hot sauce, and ½ teaspoon Worcestershire sauce. It's great for basting seafood, steaks, and vegetables or wherever a little spicy flavor is needed.

I'm a big fan of Paul Prudhomme–style rub blends. His seasonings pack in the flavors of Southern Louisiana and make me yearn for a journey to NOLA. For me, this rub is a seven-hour road trip in a bottle. It is my New Orleans aphrodisiac that sustains me until my next visit.

MAKES ¼ CUP

In a small bowl, combine the salt, garlic powder, paprika, onion powder, thyme, oregano, black pepper, cayenne, cumin, and dry mustard. The rub will keep in an airtight container at room temperature for 6 months.

FISH & SEAFOOD RUB

3½ teaspoons **garlic powder**

1 tablespoon **paprika**

1 tablespoon turbinado **sugar**

1 tablespoon **kosher salt**

2 teaspoons **celery salt**

1½ teaspoons dried **thyme**

1½ teaspoons **onion powder**

1 teaspoon **lemon pepper**

1 teaspoon dried **oregano**

1½ teaspoons **curry powder**

1½ teaspoons freshly ground **black pepper**

¼ teaspoon **cayenne pepper**

Pitmaster Tip: There is no such thing as the perfect all-purpose seasoning. Different types of meats and vegetables can never be treated the same. Beef, pork, lamb, poultry, seafood, and vegetables all demand different seasoning ratios for optimum flavor. Take some time and mix the seasoning blends found in this chapter. Pour them into individual airtight containers and label them clearly. This will save you time and stress when it's your turn to cook. Your family will thank you!

I would need to give the nod to Forrest Gump if I wanted to list all of the uses for this beautifully balanced rub blend. I originally started using it to season fish fillets on the grill, but quickly found it to be a go-to blend for all types of fish and seafood. Try this seasoning on a thick grouper fillet and baste it with butter while it sizzles over the open flame. Whether your seafood of choice lands in a hot pan or on a grill grate, you can't go wrong with this rub. If it's shrimp you like, there's shrimp kebabs, shrimp Creole, shrimp gumbo, pineapple shrimp, lemon shrimp, coconut shrimp, pepper shrimp, shrimp soup, shrimp stew . . .

MAKES ½ CUP

In a small bowl, combine the garlic powder, paprika, turbinado sugar, kosher salt, celery salt, thyme, onion powder, lemon pepper, oregano, curry powder, black pepper, and cayenne. The rub will keep in an airtight container at room temperature for 6 months.

HOG SHAKE

It is true: We will sell no swine before its time! Go-time will never arrive unless a little love is sprinkled on the pork, before it hits the grill. Hog shake is a versatile dry rub specifically formulated for pork that is delicious from the jowl to the trotter, and everywhere in between. This seasoning blend maximizes the natural flavor of pork, while enhancing color and bark caramelization. Give your hog a shake!

MAKES ½ CUP

In a small bowl, combine the sugars, paprika, chili powder, garlic salt, kosher salt, black pepper, celery salt, cayenne, curry powder, cinnamon, sage, and coriander. The rub will keep in an airtight container at room temperature for 6 months.

3 tablespoons **dark brown sugar**

1 tablespoon **granulated sugar**

1 tablespoon **paprika**

1 tablespoon **chili powder**

4 teaspoons **garlic salt**

1 teaspoon **kosher salt**

¾ teaspoon freshly ground **black pepper**

½ teaspoon **celery salt**

½ teaspoon **cayenne pepper**

¼ teaspoon **curry powder**

¼ teaspoon ground **cinnamon**

¼ teaspoon dried **sage**

Pinch of ground **coriander**

VEGGIE SEASONING

In my opinion, a vegetable seasoning blend should most closely resemble a poultry dry rub, and the salt content should exceed the sugar. The sugar, if any is used at all, should only be there for balance. This recipe contains many of my favorite seasonings for both chicken and vegetables. If you are trying to cut down on your salt intake, try using this blend as a substitute for table salt; it's hard to overseason with this blend.

MAKES ½ CUP

In a small bowl, combine the sugar, salt, garlic salt, paprika, black pepper, onion salt, celery salt, white pepper, ginger, thyme, coriander, and curry powder. The rub will keep in an airtight container at room temperature for 6 months.

3 tablespoons **granulated sugar**

4 teaspoons **kosher salt**

4 teaspoons **garlic salt**

4 teaspoons **paprika**

1 tablespoon freshly ground **black pepper**

2 teaspoons **onion salt**

1 teaspoon **celery salt**

½ teaspoon ground **white pepper**

½ teaspoon ground **ginger**

½ teaspoon dried **thyme**

¼ teaspoon dried **coriander**

¼ teaspoon **curry powder**

ACKNOWL

AFTER SPENDING ENDLESS HOURS OF BRAINSTORMING, MIXING SPICES, SEASONING, SEARING, SMOKING, AND OF COURSE, TWO-FINGER TYPING,

it's easy to reference this writing as "my book." There is a certain reality check when making a list of all the people who contributed to *Fire & Smoke*. Wow! This is not my book after all, but the work of so many people who have supported me and traded tongs and stories over a hot fire. All I'm able to offer you is a huge thanks and some good recipes that will always remind me of your dedication and friendship.

First and foremost, I thank my wife, Amy, who put up with the late nights and stacks of greasy pans, and who could creatively fit a leftover duck into an already full refrigerator! Thank you for sharing my fire, my passion, and my leftovers. Let's do it again!

Next I want to thank my children, Jacob, Andrew, and Caroline. My inspiration and enjoyment comes from spending time with you, especially around the grill. Thank you for sharing your lives with me.

Everyone in the barbecue industry knows how lucky I am to work so closely with Don and Carolyn McLemore. To me, the term "barbecue" describes not only slow-cooked deliciousness, but also food enjoyed and memories made with friends and family. Thank you for introducing me to my life's passion and giving me the freedom to explore and create.

To my road crew, especially my brother Owen, who travels at a moment's notice to help me try

these recipes coast to coast. We've had some great memories from Daytona to Dallas and beyond. Have BBQ, will travel!

My right-hand man, Ken "Big Hoss" Hess, is always there, period. He's the best and biggest batter board in the business! I can always count on him to knock me out of my culinary ruts and offer fresh ideas for the grill. You make life easier and barbecue tastier!

To Kingsford Charcoal, enormous thanks for our relationship and continued contributions to the entire barbecue industry. Many of the recipes in this book were born from our inspired collaboration. I'm not only proud to use the product, but equally proud to be associated with the people of Kingsford and the current PR team. After all, barbecue is more than the food; it's the people you share your grill with.

I'm proud to call Drew and Laura McGowan friends. They not only give me a pat on the back, but also a kick in the butt when needed. I trusted you to take a first look at my manuscript, and it's a much better book because of it.

I couldn't have done this without the unfailing support and guidance of my publisher, Clarkson Potter. Thank you, Ashley Phillips, for working with me so closely to hone this wood-slinging barbecue man into an author. I appreciate your

expert guidance and, most of all, your patience. To Rica Allannic, who has been with me through two books, I know my book will be a success with you looking over my shoulder. Thank you for your shared talent and experience. Much of the appeal of this book lies not with pictures of me; it is the art direction of Jane Treuhaft and designer Laura Palese who transformed my scribbling into something so visually appealing. And to Pam Krauss, thank you for the continued support and the invitation to join the Clarkson Potter team so many years ago. I would like to think that I'm the reason you're back!

There is a group of people who shared with me one of the most demanding and intense weeks of my life—for the second time! Ben Fink is an artist who used his camera as a brush and my book as his canvas. I'm proud to have your work in these pages. Thanks to Jeffery Kavanaugh for assisting Ben with the photos and helping with the magic. I was ecstatic that *Southern Living* let Pam Lolley spend another week of her life in Decatur. Her eye for aesthetic beauty and food fashion made a difference. Thank you for offering to join the team, Chris Grove. Awesome job on the grill!

Angela Miller is my literary agent, and without her gentle push, this book would not have happened. Thank you for helping me put my concept down on paper and sharing it with my friends at Clarkson Potter.

Huge thanks to all of the pitmasters and barbecue fanatics who I can truly call friends—and who have never been bashful about giving away advice and secrets. I can't mention one without mentioning all, and I can't mention everyone without writing another chapter. This book is filled with the knowledge we have shared for over decades of all-night cookouts.

The National Pork Board is filled with people willing to share expert information. I've been lucky enough to work with this organization as one of their Celebrated Chefs and my knowledge and recipes have gotten better because of it.

There are many people and companies I can rely on with one phone call. Writing a book will have you wearing out your Rolodex ("Contacts" for you kids). Bob Fite gathered a wide assortment of cookers in his backyard for an all-day photo shoot. I hope those grilled oysters (page 64) were payment enough! Bobbie Damalino, with Restaurant Equipment and Supply in Decatur, graciously allowed me to stock up on plates and props for the photo shoot. Chuck Baker, of Barrel House Barbecue in Lynchburg, Tennessee, gave me the parts and pieces to put together an awesome cinder-block pit (page 28). Snake River Farms contributed lots of high-quality beef that you should enjoy as you look through these pages and that I enjoyed right off the grill! Thanks, Kim Glineski, for answering my call. The list of friends who contributed cookers, ingredients, and expertise to these pages is endless. I couldn't have done it without you.

Finally, a debt of gratitude goes to the entire staff of Big Bob Gibson Bar-B-Q. The hard work and dedication of my work family, under the leadership of Steve Bullard and Jane Davis, provided me the extra time I needed to write a book. Thank you for manning the fires and keeping our customers happy. I couldn't ask for a better team.

INDEX